Shipping Derivatives and Risk Management

Shipping Derivatives and Risk Management

Amir H. Alizadeh & Nikos K. Nomikos

Faculty of Finance, Cass Business School, City University, London

First published 2009 by
PALGRAVE MACMILLAN

Palgrave Macmillan in the UK is an imprint of Macmillan Publishers Limited, registered in England, company number 785998, of Houndmills, Basingstoke, Hampshire RG21 6XS.

Palgrave Macmillan in the US is a division of St Martin's Press LLC, 175 Fifth Avenue, New York, NY 10010.

Palgrave Macmillan is the global academic imprint of the above companies and has companies and representatives throughout the world.

Palgrave® and Macmillan® are registered trademarks in the United States, the United Kingdom, Europe and other countries

ISBN-13: 978–0–230–21591–7   hardback
ISBN-10: 0–230–21591–2   hardback

This book is printed on paper suitable for recycling and made from fully managed and sustained forest sources. Logging, pulping and manufacturing processes are expected to conform to the environmental regulations of the country of origin.

A catalogue record for this book is available from the British Library.

Library of Congress Cataloging-in-Publication Data
Alizadeh, Amir H., 1966-
   Shipping derivatives and risk management / Amir H. Alizadeh, Nikos
   K. Nomikos.
      p. cm.
   Includes bibliographical references and index.
   ISBN-13: 978–0–230–21591–7   (alk. paper)
   ISBN-10: 0–230–21591–2   (alk. paper)
   1. Shipping.   2. Risk management.
   I. Nomikos, Nikos K., 1970-   II. Title.

   HE571.A45 2009
   388'.044–dc22
2008041040
10   9   8   7   6   5   4   3   2   1
18   17   16   15   14   13   12   11   10   09

Transferred to Digital Printing in 2010

Contents

About the Authors   xv

Preface and Acknowledgements   xvi

Foreword   xviii

Figures   xix

Tables   xxv

Chapter 1:   Introduction to Risk Management and Derivatives   1

1.1 Introduction   1
1.2 Types of risks facing shipping companies   3
1.3 The risk-management process   6
    1.3.1 Why should firms manage risks?   7
1.4 Introduction to derivatives: contracts and
    applications   8
    1.4.1 Forward contracts   9
    1.4.2 Futures contracts   10
    1.4.3 Swaps   12
    1.4.4 Options   12
1.5 Applications and uses of financial derivatives   13
    1.5.1 Risk management   13
    1.5.2 Speculators   14
    1.5.3 Arbitrageurs   14
    1.5.4 The price discovery role of derivatives markets 15
    1.5.5 Hedging and basis risk   16
    1.5.6 Theoretical models of futures prices: the
        cost-of-carry model   18
1.6 The organisation of this book   20
Appendix 1.A: derivation of minimum variance
hedge ratio   23

Chapter 2:   Introduction to Shipping Markets   24

2.1 Introduction   24
2.2 The world shipping industry   24
2.3 Market segmentation in the shipping industry   28
    2.3.1 The container shipping market   30
    2.3.2 The dry-bulk market   31
    2.3.3 The tanker market   34

2.4 Shipping freight contracts   35
    2.4.1 Voyage charter contracts   37
    2.4.2 Contracts of affreightment   39
    2.4.3 Trip-charter contracts   40
    2.4.4 Time-charter contracts   41
    2.4.5 Bare-boat or demise charter contracts   41
2.5 Definition and structure of costs in shipping   42
    2.5.1 Capital costs   42
    2.5.2 Operating costs   43
    2.5.3 Voyage costs   43
    2.5.4 Cargo-handling costs   44
2.6 Spot freight-fate formation   44
2.7 Time-charter rate formation   48
    2.7.1 Time-charter equivalent of spot rates (TCE)   51
2.8 Seasonal behaviour of freight rates   52
2.9 The market for ships   55
    2.9.1 Factors determining ship prices   55
    2.9.2 The newbuilding market   56
    2.9.3 The second-hand market   58
    2.9.4 The scrap or demolition market   60
2.10 Summary and conclusions   63

Chapter 3: Statistical Tools for Risk Analysis and Modelling   65

3.1 Introduction   65
3.2 Data sources and data-collection methods   65
3.3 Descriptive statistics and moments of a variable   67
    3.3.1 Measures of central tendency (location)   67
    3.3.2 Measures of dispersion   69
    3.3.3 The range   69
    3.3.4 Variance and standard deviation   70
    3.3.5 Coefficient of skewness   73
    3.3.6 Coefficient of kurtosis   74
    3.3.7 Coefficient of variation   75
    3.3.8 Covariance and correlation   77
    3.3.9 Comparison of risk across different vessel
        size and contracts   78
3.4 Time-varying volatility models   80
    3.4.1 Rolling-window or moving-average variance   82
    3.4.2 Exponentially weighted average variance
        (EWAV)   83
    3.4.3 Realised volatility models   84

3.5 ARCH and GARCH models   85
   3.5.1 The theory of ARCH models   85
     3.5.1.1 GARCH models   86
   3.5.2 Asymmetric GARCH models   88
   3.5.3 GJR threshold GARCH model   90
   3.5.4 Exponential GARCH model   90
   3.5.5 Markov regime-switching GARCH models   94
   3.5.6 The term structure of forward-curve and
     freight-rate volatility   97
   3.5.7 Stochastic volatility models   99
   3.5.8 Multivariate GARCH models   100
3.6 Forecasting volatility   102
   3.6.1 Historical volatility forecast   102
   3.6.2 Exponentially weighted average volatility
     (RiskMetrics)   103
   3.6.3 GARCH models   103
3.7 Summary and conclusions   106

Chapter 4: Freight Market Information   **107**

4.1 Introduction   107
4.2 Baltic Exchange freight-market information   108
   4.2.1 Baltic Capesize Index (BCI)   108
   4.2.2 Baltic Panamax Index (BPI)   110
   4.2.3 Baltic Supramax Index (BSI)   111
   4.2.4 Baltic Handysize Index (BHSI)   111
   4.2.5 Baltic Dry Index (BDI)   112
   4.2.6 Baltic Clean Tanker Index (BCTI)   113
   4.2.7 Baltic Dirty Tanker Index (BDTI)   115
   4.2.8 Other indices   117
4.3 Calculation of the Baltic Indices and the role of
   the panellists   118
   4.3.1 Route selection and route changes   120
   4.3.2 Calculation of the Baltic Indices   120
4.4 The freight-futures market – historical developments   121
4.5 Summary and conclusions   123

Chapter 5: Forward Freight Agreements   **125**

5.1 Introduction   125
5.2 What is a forward freight agreement (FFA)?   125
   5.2.1 Volume by sector and trade   127

5.3 How are forward freight agreements traded?   131
    5.3.1 Trading FFAs in the OTC market   133
    5.3.2 Contract documentation in the OTC market   134
        5.3.2.1 The FFABA contract   135
        5.3.2.2 ISDA® Master Agreement and Schedule   137
    5.3.3 Credit risk and clearing   137
        5.3.3.1 How clearing houses operate   138
        5.3.3.2 Margining and marking to market   141
        5.3.3.3 A marking-to-market example   143
    5.3.4 Trading via a 'hybrid' exchange   145
5.4 Hedging using forward freight agreements   147
    5.4.1 Hedging trip-charter freight-rate risk   148
    5.4.2 Hedging using voyage FFAs   149
    5.4.3 Time-charter hedge   152
    5.4.4 Tanker hedge   157
    5.4.5 Hedge-ratio calculation for tanker FFAs   157
5.5 Issues to consider when using FFAs for hedging   158
    5.5.1 Settlement risk   158
    5.5.2 Basis risk   160
5.6 Uses of forward freight agreements   164
5.7 Price discovery and forward curves   166
    5.7.1 Baltic Forward Assessments (BFA)   169
5.8 Summary and conclusions   173
Appendix 5.A: FFABA 2007© Forward Freight
Agreement contract   174

Chapter 6: Technical Analysis and Freight Trading Strategies   **181**

6.1 Introduction   181
6.2 Technical analysis   181
    6.2.1 Chart analysis   182
6.3 Technical trading rules   186
6.4 Moving averages (MA)   186
    6.4.1 Moving average crossover trading rule   186
    6.4.2 Stochastic oscillators   189
6.5 Filter rules   192
    6.5.1 Moving average envelopes   193
    6.5.2 Bollinger Bands   194
6.6 The momentum trading model   197
6.7 Spread trading in FFA markets   199
    6.7.1 Tanker spread trading   201
    6.7.2 Dry-bulk spread trading   203

6.8   Time-charter and implied forward rates   207
      6.8.1 The relative value trading rule   211
6.9   Technical trading rules and shipping investment 211
6.10 Summary and conclusions   215

Chapter 7: Options on Freight Rates   217

7.1   Introduction   217
7.2   A primer on options   217
7.3   Properties of option prices   222
      7.3.1 Boundary conditions for European call prices   222
      7.3.2 Boundary conditions for European put prices   224
      7.3.3 Put-call parity   224
      7.3.4 Factors affecting the value of call and put
            options   225
7.4   Practicalities of trading options in the freight
      market   226
7.5   Risk-management strategies using options   227
      7.5.1 An example of hedging using options   231
      7.5.2 Hedging using a collar   232
            7.5.2.1 Constructing a zero-cost collar in the
                    dry-bulk market   234
7.6   Option-trading strategies   236
      7.6.1 Bull spreads   236
      7.6.2 Bear spreads   240
      7.6.3 Ratio spreads   241
      7.6.4 Box spread   243
      7.6.5 Straddle combinations   244
      7.6.6 Strangle combinations   245
      7.6.7 Strips and straps   247
      7.6.8 Butterfly spreads   248
7.7   Summary and conclusions   249
Appendix 7.A: FFABA 2007© Freight Options
Contract   250

Chapter 8: Pricing and Risk Management of Option Positions   258

8.1   Introduction   258
8.2   Pricing freight options   258
      8.2.1 Which approach is better for pricing
            freight options?   259
      8.2.2 The Black-Scholes-Merton (BSM) model (1973)   261
      8.2.3 The Black Model (1976)   263

8.2.4 The Turnbull and Wakeman Approximation
(1991)   264
8.2.5 Lévy (1997) and Haug et al. (2003) Discrete
Asian Approximation   265
8.2.6 Curran's Approximation   266
8.2.7 Applications for freight markets   267
8.2.8 An option-pricing example   269
8.3   Asian options with volatility term structure   271
8.4   Implied volatility   273
8.5   Pricing Asian options using Monte Carlo
simulation   276
8.6   Risk management of option positions   281
8.7   Hedging a short-call position: an example   282
8.8   Option-price sensitivities: 'Greeks'   283
8.9   Delta (Δ)   284
8.9.1   Delta hedging   286
8.9.2   Delta hedging of Asian options   290
8.10 Gamma (Γ)   292
8.10.1 Gamma-neutral strategies   294
8.11 Theta (Θ)   295
8.11.1 The relationship between theta, delta and
gamma   297
8.12 Vega (Λ)   298
8.13 Rho (P)   299
8.13.1 Interpretation of Greek parameters:
reading the Greeks   300
8.14 Dynamic hedging in practice   300
8.14.1 Greeks and trading strategies   302
8.15 Summary and conclusions   302

Chapter 9:   Value-at-Risk in Shipping and Freight Risk Management   303

9.1 Introduction   303
9.2 Simple VaR estimation   305
9.2.1 VaR of multi-asset portfolios   310
9.3 VaR estimation methodologies   312
9.3.1 Parametric VaR estimation   312
9.3.1.1 The sample variance and covariance
method   313
9.3.1.2 The exponential weighted average
variance and RiskMetrics method   313

9.3.1.3 GARCH Models and VaR estimation 313
9.3.1.4 Monte Carlo simulation and VaR
estimation 314
9.3.1.5 Recent advances in parametric VaR
models 317
9.3.2 Nonparametric VaR estimation methods 319
9.3.2.1 Historical simulation 319
9.3.2.2 The bootstrap method of estimating
VaR 321
9.3.2.3 The quantile regression method 322
9.4 VaR for non-linear instruments 322
9.4.1 Mapping VaR for options 323
9.4.2 Delta approximation 325
9.4.3 Delta-gamma approximation 325
9.5 Principal component analysis and VaR estimation 328
9.6 Backtesting and stresstesting of VaR models 333
9.7 Summary and conclusions 335
Appendix 9.A: Principal component analysis 336

Chapter 10: **Bunker Risk Analysis and Risk Management** **338**

10.1 Introduction 338
10.2 The world bunker market 339
10.3 Bunker-price risk in shipping operations 341
10.4 Hedging bunker risk using OTC instruments 343
10.5 Hedging bunker prices using forward contracts 343
10.5.1 Long hedge using forward bunker contract 343
10.5.2 Short hedge using forward bunker contract 344
10.6 Bunker swap contracts 346
10.6.1 Plain vanilla bunker swap 347
10.7 Exotic bunker swaps 350
10.7.1 Differential swap 350
10.7.2 Extendable swap 351
10.7.3 Forward bunker swap 352
10.7.4 Participation swap 353
10.7.5 Double-up swap 354
10.7.6 Variable volume swap or swing 354
10.8 Hedging bunker price using options 354
10.8.1 Bunker caps and floors 355
10.8.2 Collars or cylinder options 356
10.9 Summary and conclusions 362

Chapter 11: Financial and Interest Rate Risk in Shipping   **363**

11.1 Introduction   363
11.2 Reference rates and international
     financial markets   364
11.3 Term loans   366
    11.3.1 A fixed-rate loan example   367
    11.3.2 Floating-rate loans examples   369
11.4 Hedging interest-rate risk   371
11.5 Forward-rate agreements   371
11.6 Interest-rate futures   374
    11.6.1 Eurodollar futures contracts   374
11.7 Interest-rate swaps   375
    11.7.1 Pricing and unwinding of
           interest-rate swaps   378
11.8 Interest-rate options   381
    11.8.1 Interest-rate caplets and floorlets   381
        11.8.1.1 An example of a caplet
                 option hedge   382
    11.8.2 Interest-rate caps and floors   384
    11.8.3 Interest-rate collars   388
        11.8.3.1 An example of a zero-cost
                 collar   389
11.9 Pricing caps and floors using Black's model   391
11.10 Forward swaps and swaptions   395
11.11 Hedging using currency swaps   396
    11.11.1 Pricing currency swaps   397
11.12 Summary and conclusions   398

Chapter 12: Credit Risk Measurement and Management in Shipping   **399**

12.1 Introduction   399
12.2 What is credit risk?   399
12.3 What is the source of credit risk in shipping?   400
    12.3.1 Qualitative vs. quantitative credit-risk
           analysis   401
12.4 Credit ratings and rating agencies   402
    12.4.1 Shipping high-yield bond issues   404
12.5 Estimating probability of default   407
    12.5.1 Extracting default probabilities from
           traded bonds   407
    12.5.2 Historical default probabilities   409

12.5.3 Estimating default probabilities using
Merton's model 411
12.6 Credit-risk management and credit derivatives 414
12.6.1 Collateralisation 415
12.6.2 Downgrade triggers 415
12.6.3 Contract design and netting 416
12.6.4 Diversification 416
12.6.5 Credit derivatives 417
12.6.5.1 Credit default swap (CDS) 418
12.6.5.2 Total return swap (TRS) 420
12.6.5.3 Credit spread options (CSO) 422
12.7 Summary and conclusions 424

Chapter 13: Ship Price Risk and Risk Management 425

13.1 Introduction 425
13.2 Ship-price formation 426
13.3 Comparison of ship-price risk across sectors 428
13.3.1 Dynamics of volatility of ship prices 430
13.4 Ship-price risk management 432
13.4.1 Portfolio theory and diversification 432
13.4.2 Derivatives on ship values 439
13.4.3 Forward Ship Value Agreements (FoSVA) 439
13.4.4 Forward curves for ship prices 444
13.4.5 Baltic Demolition Index (BDA) 446
13.5 Summary and conclusions 450

Chapter 14: Real Options and Optionalities in Shipping 451

14.1 Introduction 451
14.2 Financial versus real options 451
14.3 Conventional NPV versus real option valuation 452
14.3.1 Valuation of a shipping project 454
14.4 Real options in shipping 455
14.4.1 Option to abandon/exit 455
14.4.2 Option to expand 457
14.4.3 Option to contract 459
14.4.4 Option to switch 460
14.4.5 Option to lay-up 461
14.4.6 Option to delay (wait) 462
14.5 Other options in shipping 463
14.5.1 Option to extend a period time-charter
contract 463

14.5.2 Option on newbuilding orders   465
14.5.3 Purchase option on a time-charter contract   467
14.5.4 Option on writing-off part of a debt   470
14.6 Pricing real options using simulation   472
14.6.1 Sensitivity analysis and interval estimates   474
14.7 Summary and conclusions   475
Appendix 14.A: The binomial option pricing
model (BOPM)   477

References   **481**

Index   490

About the Authors

AMIR ALIZADEH is Reader in Shipping Economics and Finance at Cass Business School, City University, London, UK. His research interests include modelling commodity and shipping freight markets, derivatives and risk management, and forecasting. He has published in several academic journals in the area of transportation, risk management, finance and economics, and has worked as an advisor and a consultant.

NIKOS NOMIKOS is Reader in Shipping Risk Management and Director of the MSc degree in Shipping, Trade and Finance at Cass Business School, City University, London, UK. He commenced his career at the Baltic Exchange as Senior Market Analyst. Since November 2001, he has been with the Faculty of Finance at Cass Business School, where he specialises in the area of freight derivatives and risk management. He has published numerous papers in academic journals and his research has been presented at conferences worldwide. He also acts as a consultant on issues of risk management for a number of companies in the shipping and financial sectors.

Preface and Acknowledgements

The idea of writing a book on derivatives and shipping risk management was initially triggered during the development of a new elective module at Cass Business School in summer 2002 which was delivered for the first time in 2003. However, it was not until 2005 when we completed a series of professional courses, in collaboration with the Baltic Exchange, that the structure of the book was shaped and topics were selected to reflect the need of the industry and academia in the field of shipping risk management.

The shipping derivatives market has evolved very rapidly over the past few years and has become more sophisticated as participants from other sectors, including utility and trading companies, financial institutions, hedge funds, and clearing houses, became involved. To that extent, the volume of trade in FFAs increased at an almost exponential rate over the period 2000 to 2008 to an estimated $150 billion per year by mid-2008. Part of this growth can be attributed to the increase in the awareness of the participants in the shipping industry about market volatility as well as a change in the way they viewed and managed such risks. As liquidity in the market increased, new products such as options and swaps were also developed and new trading techniques and strategies were adapted. One major breakthrough was the involvement of clearing houses in offering clearing facilities to shipping derivatives contracts on both freight and bunker, which helped the growth in trading these products by eliminating counter-party risk.

The aim of this self-sufficient book is to guide the reader through newly developed topics in the area of risk management in shipping finance and operations with a particular emphasis on derivatives products developed in recent years. In this respect, we begin with an introduction to risk and risk management and expand to economics of the freight market and the market for ships as background analysis. Next, we present the statistical methods used in risk measurement and modelling as an essential prerequisite to more technical chapters on shipping risk management and derivatives products. A significant part of this book is devoted to the development and evolution of the freight derivatives market including FFAs and freight options as well as issues regarding trading, pricing and clearing these products. Several chapters are also dedicated to examining the other sources of risk in shipping investment and operations including: financial risk due to changes in the interest rates and exchange rates based on which the vessel is financed; bunker price risk as part of voyage costs in operations; credit risk or counter-parties' default risk in shipping contracts, transactions and deals; and finally ship price risk, which is considered to have a substantial impact on the profitability and survival of any shipping business. As with any other line of business, the issue of monitoring risk is also an important one in shipping; therefore, a chapter is devoted to discussing and illustrating the statistical methods and techniques used in risk monitoring. Finally, we explore the topic of real options and assess the benefits in evaluating strategic and managerial flexibilities (optionalities) embedded in shipping investment and operations. Such options and optionalities are used extensively in the shipping industry; however, in many cases they are granted for free, or for a nominal fee, without being properly valued.

Acknowledgements

In no particular order, we would like to thank the Baltic Exchange for providing the data and their support in establishing and running professional courses in Shipping Risk Management and Advanced Freight Modelling and Trading, which helped to put the topics covered in this book together. We would also like to thank participants on those courses for their helpful comments and feedback. Our thanks must also go to our MSc students who attended our elective course on Shipping Risk Management at Cass Business School and provided us with a testing ground for many of the examples and ideas presented in the book. We would also like to thank Lene Marie Refvik, Knut Moystad and Erland Engelsatd of Imarex for their supportive remarks and the permission to use their valuable FFA data for some of the empirical analysis in this book, and Dr Martin Stopford, Managing Director of Clarkson Research Studies, for providing us with plentiful shipping, economic and trade data through their website and Shipping Intelligence Network (SIN) database. Finally our thanks are also due to Panos Pouliassis for his valuable assistance in putting together the material for chapters 9 and 11, Gladys Parish who very patiently proofread the manuscript, and Rick Bouwman for his editorial assistance.

Amir Alizadeh and Nikos Nomikos
December 2008

Foreword

Jeremy Penn, Chief Executive, the Baltic Exchange

The publication of this book is timely – at the time of writing we are in the midst of very troubled times for the dry-bulk shipping markets. Falling demand for dry commodities, an oversupply of ships and a freeze in credit have seen daily hire rates for bulk carriers drop from all-time highs to near all-time lows within the space of a few months.

From freight rates to bunker prices, credit risk to asset values, the financial risks faced by shipping market participants are significant. The management of freight-rate volatility in particular continues to cause headaches in boardrooms around the world, whether it is the shipping company unsure of future earnings or the charterer worried about the huge financial implications of future freight bills.

For companies responsible for moving millions of tonnes of cargo every year, freight has become a multi-million dollar financial risk which needs to be managed.

Over the past five years we have seen a huge growth in freight derivative trading volumes, a shift from 'over-the-counter' trades to cleared trades and a wide range of financial players entering the sector. While we are moving into a period of market uncertainty, the financial risks faced by the shipping sector remain high.

The Baltic Exchange already works closely with the authors of this book, running a series of training courses for those seeking a sound academic underpinning to their understanding of risk management in the shipping markets. No-one is better qualified than Amir Alizadeh and Nikos Nomikos to provide, as they have, a complete presentation of freight risk and freight derivatives from a practical standpoint, but with sound academic and statistical underpinning. A thorough understanding of the issues raised in this book is vital to anyone involved in the shipping markets and I commend it to you.

Figures

Figure 1.1	Long and short forward payoffs	10
Figure 1.2	Backwardation and contango forward curves	16
Figure 1.3	The impact of hedging on the expected cash flows	17
Figure 2.1	Pattern of international seaborne trade in major commodities	25
Figure 2.2	The growth of the world shipping fleet since 1948	26
Figure 2.3	World cargo-carrying shipping fleet	27
Figure 2.4	Historical growth of the world container fleet by size category	31
Figure 2.5	Historical growth of the world dry-bulk fleet by size category	32
Figure 2.6	Historical growth of the world tanker fleet by size category	34
Figure 2.7	Shipowners' cost allocations under different charter contracts	44
Figure 2.8	Market-clearing supply-demand framework in shipping freight-rate determination	45
Figure 2.9	Historical spot freight rates for four Capesize routes	47
Figure 2.10	Historical spot freight rates for tankers of different sizes	47
Figure 2.11	Historical six-month, one-year and three-year time-charter rates for Capesize dry-bulk carriers	50
Figure 2.12	Historical values of six-month, one-year and three-year time-charter rates for Panamax dry-bulk carriers	51
Figure 2.13	Seasonal behaviour of tanker freight rates	53
Figure 2.14	Comparison of seasonal changes in freight rates for Capesize dry-bulk carriers	53
Figure 2.15	Comparison of seasonal changes in freight rates for Panamax dry-bulk carriers	54
Figure 2.16	Comparison of seasonal changes in freight rates for Handysize dry-bulk carriers	54
Figure 2.17	Newbuilding prices for dry-bulk carriers of different sizes	57
Figure 2.18	Historical newbuilding prices for tankers of different sizes	58
Figure 2.19	Historical second-hand prices for five-year-old dry-bulk carriers of different sizes	59

Figure 2.20   Historical second-hand prices for five-year-old tankers
              of different sizes   59
Figure 2.21   Historical scrap prices for dry-bulk carriers of
              different sizes   61
Figure 2.22   Historical scrap prices for tankers of different sizes   61
Figure 2.23   Historical newbuilding, five-year-old second-hand,
              and scrap prices for VLCC tankers   62
Figure 2.24   Historical newbuilding, five-year-old second-hand,
              and scrap prices for Panamax dry-bulk carriers   63
Figure 3.1   Plot of daily VLCC freight rates for TD3 Baltic route   69
Figure 3.2   Plot of daily VLCC freight rates for TD3 Baltic route   70
Figure 3.3   Distributions with positive, negative and zero
              coefficient of skewness   74
Figure 3.4   Distributions with different coefficients of kurtosis   75
Figure 3.5   Distribution of returns of asset with different risk
              profiles   76
Figure 3.6   Comparison of the risk-return relationship of different
              assets   77
Figure 3.7   Estimates of time-varying volatility of spot freight
              rates for tankers of different sizes   83
Figure 3.8   Plots of volatility of spot freight rates for tankers of
              different sizes estimated using GARCH models   88
Figure 3.9   Impact of shocks with different sign and size on
              volatility   89
Figure 3.10   Estimated VLCC TD3 and Capesize C4 volatilities using
              GARCH, TGARCH and EGARCH models   93
Figure 3.11   GARCH, TGARCH and EGARCH news-impact curves for
              VLCC TD3 and Capesize C4 rates   94
Figure 3.12   Plot of MRS GARCH volatility and regime probability
              estimates against GARCH and EGARCH volatility
              estimated for TD3   97
Figure 3.13   The relationship between slope of forward curve and
              FFA volatility   98
Figure 3.14   Plot of GARCH versus stochastic volatility estimates
              for TD3   100
Figure 3.15   Historical and forecast of volatility of TD3 tanker
              route using GARCH and RiskMetrics models   105
Figure 4.1   Baltic Dry-Indices: September 2000 to January 2008   114
Figure 4.2   Baltic Tanker Indices: September 2000 to January
              2008   117
Figure 4.3   BIFFEX trading volume (1994–2002)   123
Figure 5.1   Spot, first, second and third-quarter FFA rates for
              BPI 4TC   127

Figure 5.2	Spot, first, second and third-quarter FFA rates for BCI 4TC	128
Figure 5.3	Estimated volume of trade in the dry FFA market	129
Figure 5.4	Dry FFA trade volume for the period July 2007 to April 2008	130
Figure 5.5	Composition of dry FFA trade volume, 2006	130
Figure 5.6	Composition of wet FFA trade volume, 2006	132
Figure 5.7	Trading structure of the FFA market	132
Figure 5.8	The FFA clearing system	140
Figure 5.9	A BCI C4 margining example	145
Figure 5.10	IMAREX dry-route margin curves	146
Figure 5.11	Payoff from the short BPI 2A FFA contract	150
Figure 5.12	Baltic Handysize (BHSI) and Supramax (BSI) indices and their ratio	162
Figure 5.13	TD3 forward curves for the period March 2003 to December 2007	168
Figure 6.1	Linear trend lines with upper and lower bands for Panamax 4TC Q2 (second nearest quarter) FFA prices	183
Figure 6.2	Head and shoulders pattern in Q2 Panamax 4TC FFA rates	184
Figure 6.3	Triangle pattern in second-quarter Panamax 4TC FFA rates	184
Figure 6.4	Support and resistance bands for Panamax 4TC first-quarter FFA prices	185
Figure 6.5	Plot of Panamax 4TC Q2 FFA prices and moving average series	187
Figure 6.6	MA crossover trading rule on Panamax Q2 second-quarter 4TC FFAs	190
Figure 6.7	40-Day stochastic oscillator and its MA10 on Q2 Panamax 4TC FFA	191
Figure 6.8	Plot of MA10 and 5 per cent envelope for Panamax 4TC Q2 FFA	193
Figure 6.9	Plot of moving average (MA10) and Bollinger Bands for second-quarter Panamax 4TC FFA	196
Figure 6.10	Trading relative strength index (RSI) for Q2 Panamax 4TC FFA	199
Figure 6.11	Historical second-month TD3 and TD5 tanker FFAs	201
Figure 6.12	Historical Capesize-Panamax average 4TC Calendar FFAs and 1-2 Capesize-Panamax FFA ratio	204
Figure 6.13	1-2 Capesize-Panamax calendar 4TC FFA ratio and cumulative profit of technical trading rules	207
Figure 6.14	Relative value index based on premium or discount of 6m TC on 12m TC	212

Figure 6.15   MA trading rule on log P/E ratio and its cumulative
              returns in the Panamax sector   215
Figure 7.1   Long-call and put-option payoffs   220
Figure 7.2   Short-call and put-option payoffs   221
Figure 7.3   Value of a long call at different times to maturity   224
Figure 7.4   Hedging positions using long calls and puts   228
Figure 7.5   Writing covered and protective positions   230
Figure 7.6   An owner's zero-cost collar   235
Figure 7.7   Payoff from bull spread using call options   238
Figure 7.8   Payoff from bull spread using put options   239
Figure 7.9   Payoff from bear spread using put options   240
Figure 7.10   Payoff of a 2:1 call spread   241
Figure 7.11   Payoff of a 1:2 call spread   242
Figure 7.12   Payoff of a box spread combination   243
Figure 7.13   A long straddle combination   244
Figure 7.14   A short straddle combination   246
Figure 7.15   A long strangle combination   246
Figure 7.16   Payoff of a strap strategy   247
Figure 7.17   A long butterfly spread   248
Figure 8.1   Empirical volatility smiles for equities
              and commodities   274
Figure 8.2   Selected sample paths of BPI 4TC Monte
              Carlo simulation   279
Figure 8.3   Payoff of a short-call option position   282
Figure 8.4   Call-option delta calculation   285
Figure 8.5   Variation of call and put option delta
              with respect to the value of the underlying   285
Figure 8.6   Variation of call-option delta with respect to
              remaining time to expiration   286
Figure 8.7   Performance of the FFA delta hedge for a range
              of FFA rates   288
Figure 8.8   Hedging error from the dynamic, static and naked
              hedging strategies   290
Figure 8.9   Average price-call deltas for different average
              price pevels   291
Figure 8.10   Average price deltas for different times to maturity   292
Figure 8.11   Hedging error induced by option-price curvature   293
Figure 8.12   Relationship between call-option gamma and delta   294
Figure 8.13   Variation of call-option gamma with respect to time
              to maturity   294
Figure 8.14   Variation of call and put options theta   296
Figure 8.15   Variation of call-option theta with respect to time
              to maturity for ITM, OTM and ATM options   297

Figure 8.16   Relationship between gamma and theta with respect
              to changes in the underlying   298
Figure 8.17   Variability of vega with respect to underlying price   299
Figure 9.1   The relationship between VaR, confidence level
              and holding period   306
Figure 9.2   Probability distribution of TD3 FFA value after
              ten days   308
Figure 9.3   Mean reversion and VaR estimation   315
Figure 9.4   Calculating VaR from the simulated distribution   316
Figure 9.5   Historical vs. normal distribution of four-month TD3
              FFA returns   320
Figure 9.6   Distribution of changes: long- and short-call positions   324
Figure 9.7   Plot of differences in the option VaR-estimation
              methods   329
Figure 9.8   Eigenvectors from principal components analysis on
              freight rates   332
Figure 10.1   Weekly spot bunker prices in five major ports   340
Figure 10.2   Plain vanilla swap contract between shipowner and
              swap counter-party   347
Figure 10.3   Comparison of one-year fixed for floating swap price   348
Figure 10.4   Bunker price to be paid by a caplet holder   358
Figure 10.5   Zero-cost collar payoff to the shipowner and purchase
              prices after hedge against different bunker prices
              at expiry   360
Figure 10.6   Zero-cost collar payoff to the bunker supplier and
              bunkers selling price against different bunker prices
              at expiry   361
Figure 11.1   Evolution of LIBOR rates   366
Figure 11.2   Sensitivity of cash flows to changes in interest rates   371
Figure 11.3   Swap structure for the shipowner   376
Figure 11.4   Interest rate to be paid or received by a caplet and
              a floorlet holder   385
Figure 11.5   Collar-hedge payoff to the shipowner and effective
              interest rates after hedge against different LIBOR
              rates at expiry   392
Figure 11.6   The timing of interest-rate option payoff   394
Figure 11.7   Structure of the currency swap   397
Figure 12.1   Historical yield spread of shipping bonds with
              different ratings   405
Figure 12.2   Dynamic behaviour of credit premium of the shipping
              bond index   406
Figure 12.3   Theoretical credit premium of bonds with different
              rating and maturity   407

Figure 12.4 Distribution of asset value at maturity of debt and
probability of default   413
Figure 12.5 The global trend in credit derivatives market   418
Figure 12.6 Cash flow of a credit swap deal   419
Figure 12.7 Cash flow of a simple total return swap   421
Figure 12.8 Cash flows of a total return swap on two reference
portfolios   422
Figure 12.9 Payoffs of long-call and long-put positions on
credit spread options   423
Figure 13.1 Plot of dynamics of price volatility of tankers
of different sizes   431
Figure 13.2 Plot of dynamics of price volatility of dry-bulk
carriers of different sizes   431
Figure 13.3 Risk reduction through portfolio diversification   434
Figure 13.4 Risk-and-return graph of a two-asset portfolio with
different weights   435
Figure 13.5 Plot of Baltic Exchange Sale and Purchase Assessment
(BSPA) Indices for different types of ships   441
Figure 13.6 Baltic Ship Value Assessments and 1st, 2nd, 3rd
Calendar 4TC FFA rates for Capesize dry-bulk carriers   444
Figure 13.7 Baltic Ship Value Assessments and 1st, 2nd, 3rd
Calendar 4TC FFA rates for Panamax dry-bulk carriers   444
Figure 13.8 Forward freight curves and implied forward ship
values for different types of dry-bulk carriers in
May 2008   447
Figure 13.9 Baltic Exchange Demolition Assessment Indices for
different types of ships and delivery locations   448
Figure 14.1 'Drivers' of NPV and real option valuation
techniques   453
Figure 14.2 Evolution of freight revenue, voyage costs and
operating expenses, and decision to lay-up a vessel   462
Figure 14.3 Evolution of HTD ratio of the term loan   471
Figure 14.4 Simulated paths for NPV of a project with an
expansion option   473
Figure 14.5 Probability distributions of possible project
values at maturity   474
Figure 14.6 Distribution and sensitivity of the exit option value
calculated using binomial tree when input factors are
simulated   476
Figure 14.7 Convergence of binomial to Black-Scholes option prices 480

Tables

Table 1.1	Differences between forward and futures contracts	11
Table 2.1	Fleet size and its growth in different sectors of world shipping from January 1996 to May 2008	27
Table 2.2	Different classes of vessels within each shipping sector	30
Table 2.3	Different types of dry-bulk carriers, cargoes they carry and typical trading routes	33
Table 2.4	Tankers of different sizes, cargoes they carry and typical trading routes	36
Table 2.5	Examples of reported fixtures under different types of shipping contracts	38
Table 3.1	Approximation of returns, variances and standard deviations to annualised values	72
Table 3.2	Mean and standard deviation of spot, six-month, one-year and three-year time-charter rates for Panamax dry-bulk carriers	72
Table 3.3	Comparison of descriptive statistics across different sizes of vessels and contract duration in the dry and wet markets	79
Table 3.4	Estimates of parameters of GARCH (1,1) models for tanker spot freight rates	88
Table 3.5	Estimates of parameters of TGARCH and EGARCH models for VLCC TD3 and Capesize C4 weekly spot rates	92
Table 3.6	Estimates of GARCH, EGARCH and Markov regime-switching GARCH models for VLCC TD3 freight rates	96
Table 4.1	Baltic Capesize Index (BCI) route definitions	109
Table 4.2	Baltic Panamax Index route definitions	110
Table 4.3	Baltic Supramax Index (BSI) route definitions	112
Table 4.4	Baltic Handysize Index (BHSI) route definitions	113
Table 4.5	Baltic Clean Tanker Index (BCTI) route definitions	114
Table 4.6	Baltic International Tanker Routes (BITR) Asia definitions	115
Table 4.7	Baltic Dirty Tanker Index (BDTI) route definitions	116
Table 4.8	Baltic Dirty Tanker Index (BDTI) route definitions	118
Table 4.9	Baltic LPG and palm oil route definitions	118
Table 4.10	BPI Index calculation on 2 January 2007	121

Table 5.1	Tanker FFA volume for 2006 and 2007	131
Table 5.2	List of contracts cleared by different clearing houses	139
Table 5.3	A marking-to-market example	144
Table 5.4	An example of hedging freight rates using forward freight agreements	149
Table 5.5	Voyage hedging example payoffs – positions are settled at maturity	151
Table 5.6	Voyage hedging example payoffs – entering offsetting trades for Q3 and Q4	152
Table 5.7	Panamax 4TC FFA quotes on 10 October 2005	152
Table 5.8	Hedging spot Panamax earnings using FFAs	154
Table 5.9	Hedging period time-charter Panamax earnings using FFAs	156
Table 5.10	Average percentage differences between FFA settlement rates and freight rates during the settlement month	159
Table 5.11	Outcome of the BSI/BHSI hedge for Q4 2006 and Q1 2007 using a hedge ratio of 0.7	163
Table 5.12	Directional accuracy of tanker forward curves	169
Table 5.13	Reporting periods for dry Baltic Forward Assessments	172
Table 5.14	Reporting periods for wet Baltic Forward Assessments	173
Table 6.1	Risk-return comparisons of static buy-and-hold and MA trading strategies	188
Table 6.2	Comparison of return and risk of static buy-and-hold and stochastic oscillator trading strategies	192
Table 6.3	Comparison of return and risk of buy-and-hold against MA envelope trading rules on Q2 Panamax 4TC FFA	194
Table 6.4	Comparison of return and risk of buy-and-hold against Bollinger Band trading rules on Q2 Panamax 4TC FFA	196
Table 6.5	Return and risk of RSI trading with different lower and upper bands for Q2 Panamax 4TC FFA	198
Table 6.6	The TD5-TD3 spread narrows from 49 to 34	203
Table 6.7	Capesize-Panamax calendar 4TC ratio widens from 0.818 to 1.001	205
Table 6.8	Comparison of performance of different trading rules on 1-2 ratio of Capesize-Panamax FFA contracts	206
Table 6.9	Forecasting performance of implied forward time-charter rates against alternative econometric models	209
Table 6.10	Profitability of technical chartering strategies based on the period January 2002 to May 2007	213
Table 6.11	Results of empirical simulation of trading strategies	214
Table 7.1	Imarex option quotes for TD3 route on 23 August 2005	218

Table 7.2	Moneyness conditions for call-and-put options	222
Table 7.3	An example of hedging freight rates using freight-rate options	233
Table 7.4	Imarex option quotes for TD3 route on 23 August 2005	237
Table 8.1	Comparison of option premia for TD3 (in WS points)	269
Table 8.2	Imarex TD3 implied volatilities on 24 September 2007	274
Table 8.3	Calculation of call-option payoffs for 10 randomly sample paths	280
Table 8.4	Option-price sensitivities with respect to different inputs	283
Table 8.5	Option-price sensitivities for the Black-Scholes (1973) model	284
Table 8.6	Simulation of dynamic delta hedging	289
Table 9.1	Individual VaRs and correlation matrix	311
Table 9.2	VaR calculation using Monte Carlo simulation	318
Table 9.3	Using principal components analysis to calculate VaR	331
Table 10.1	Descriptive statistics of bunker prices in major bunkering ports	340
Table 10.2	Long hedge using a forward bunker contract	345
Table 10.3	Short hedge using a forward bunker contract	346
Table 10.4	Cash flows between counter-parties in a 12-month bunker swap contract	348
Table 10.5	Bunker forward curve and spot interest rate yield curve	349
Table 10.6	Terms of an extendable fixed-for-floating swap	352
Table 10.7	Settlement and cash flows of the forward bunker swap contract	353
Table 10.8	Hedging against bunker-price fluctuations using a cap	357
Table 10.9	Payoff of the zero-cost collar and overall cost of bunkers for shipowner	359
Table 11.1	Fixed-rate term loans repayment examples	368
Table 11.2	Floating-rate term loans examples	370
Table 11.3	Hedging interest-rate risk using FRAs	373
Table 11.4	Eurodollars futures prices	375
Table 11.5	Cash flows for the shipowner in a five-year interest-rate swap contract	377
Table 11.6	Interest-rate swaps	377
Table 11.7	Hedging against interest-rate fluctuations using a caplet	383
Table 11.8	Hedging against interest-rate fluctuations using a cap	387
Table 11.9	The payoff of the collar hedge and overall borrowing cost	390
Table 11.10	Hedging against interest-rate fluctuations using a collar	393

Table 11.11	Cash flows for the shipowner in a four-year currency swap contract	397
Table 12.1	Important variables in qualitative and quantitative credit-risk analyses	402
Table 12.2	Fitch, Standard & Poor's and Moody's rating scales	403
Table 12.3	Shipping high-yield bond offerings by year of issue (1992–2002)	405
Table 12.4	2003 average ultimate recovery rates	409
Table 12.5	Historical cumulative probability of default	409
Table 12.6	Year-on-year historical probabilities of default	410
Table 12.7	Sample CDS quotes for different companies in different sectors on 23 January 2008	420
Table 13.1	Comparison of ship-price risk across dry-bulk carriers of different sizes	429
Table 13.2	Risk and return of a two-asset portfolio with different weights	434
Table 13.3	Correlation matrix and distribution of returns on tankers of different sizes	435
Table 13.4	Correlation matrix and distribution of returns on dry-bulk carriers of different sizes	437
Table 13.5	Comparison of risk and return of different portfolios of ships	438
Table 13.6	BSPA Standard-type ship specifications	440
Table 13.7	Results of hedging resale value for a VLCC using FoSVAs	442
Table 13.8	Average ship prices, 4TC FFA rates, and their correlations for Capesize and Panamax dry-bulk carriers	445
Table 13.9	Results of hedging scrap price of a vessel using BDA forward contracts	449
Table 14.1	Financial options versus real options	452
Table 14.2	NPV calculation of shipping acquisition	454

1
Introduction to Risk Management and Derivatives

1.1 Introduction

Few will argue that these are not interesting times for the shipping industry. Freight rates have risen to unprecedented levels and have increased by almost 300 per cent over the period from 2003 to mid-2008. This increase in freight rates was followed by a corresponding drop of 95 per cent over the last quarter of 2008. A number of factors have contributed to this high volatility in the market, which also seems to have changed the way the industry views and manages its risks. In addition to freight-rate volatility, we have also seen the emergence, maturing and corresponding growth in the derivatives market for freight. Traditionally, this was a market where players in the physical freight market could hedge their risks, although this is now changing rapidly with the increasing participation of investment banks, hedge funds and other traders that may not be involved in the underlying physical market. Overall, this has resulted in the commoditisation of the freight market. Nowadays, freight rates can be bought and sold like any other commodity, despite the fact that freight rates essentially represent the cost of providing the service of seaborne transportation and hence are not classified as a tangible commodity.

This has created a shipping environment where market participants are more aware of the risks they face and also try to explore avenues to hedge or manage those risks. It is therefore within this dynamic framework that this book fits; its aim is to discuss and analyse all types of risk which market practitioners face in the shipping industry and also to present state-of-the-art approaches regarding both their measurement and their management. Our analysis is not only confined to freight-rate risk, although more than half of the book is devoted to freight-rate risk management and trading. We also discuss other types of risk which are equally important for a shipping venture and to which practitioners are exposed in the market; these include ship price risk, bunker risk, credit risk and interest-rate risk. In all cases, we present: how these factors affect the cash flows of traders in the market; practical examples of how the risks can be hedged; and the various instruments participants can use in order to manage those risks. Our approach is practical but we also provide the necessary theoretical underpinnings to ensure the validity and robustness of the examples presented.

The motivation for most of the topics presented here comes from the industry via both discussions and interaction with practitioners – through our lectures and consultancy activities – and from an academic interest in the structure of freight markets and their risk management. More specifically, the following issues are addressed:

- Freight-rate risk management using forward contracts is discussed and we show how these contracts can be used in a variety of hedging situations. We also consider important issues that practitioners face in the market, such as basis and settlement risk, and discuss how these risks can be mitigated.
- Trading strategies for freight using technical and statistical analysis are presented. We implement a variety of trades, including spread trades, and assess the effectiveness of different strategies.
- Freight options also form part of this book. Options have gained in popularity over recent years and participants are becoming aware of the usefulness of options in the freight market. We discuss how to price freight options and present the relevant pricing methodologies used in the market. We also present pricing examples and compare option prices generated from different theoretical models.
- We explore the issue of how to manage short positions in freight options using the option price sensitivities.
- With the growth in trades in the forward and freight-options market, participants need to be aware and monitor their exposures closely. 'Value-at-risk' therefore, has become an integral part of the risk management process of major shipping companies and is also analysed here through presenting examples and applications from the freight derivatives market.
- A range of other risks which participants in the shipping markets face, such as bunker price risk, interest rate and foreign exchange risk, credit risk and asset (i.e., ship price) risk, are also analysed. In each case we present a detailed analysis of how the risk in question can affect the profitability of a shipping company and why its management is important in shipping operations. We also present examples of how these risks can actually be managed.
- Finally, a feature of shipping markets' operations is that in many cases there is a number of options that are embedded in shipping contracts. Most of these options are implicit in the contracts and may even be granted for free without being priced properly. With the growth in the paper market for freight, such options can now be traded separately and their value can be monetised using traditional options analysis. Therefore, we also discuss these issues in the real options section of the book.

In this chapter, as the introduction to the book, we begin with the process of risk management using derivative contracts. In Section 1.2, we discuss the types of risks which shipping companies face. Section 1.3 describes the steps that shipping companies have to undertake in the risk management process. The basic types of derivative contracts and how they can be used in the price-risk management process are discussed in sections 1.4 and 1.5 respectively. Finally, Section 1.6 presents the organisation and structure of the book.

1.2 Types of risks facing shipping companies

In general, business-risk management is concerned with the possible decline in the value of a shipping company due to an event, or a change, in any of the factors that affect its value. Fundamentally, the value of a company depends on the expected net cash flows from its operations. Therefore, any factor that may have a negative impact on the expected net cash flows is identified as a risk. Harrington and Niehaus (2003) classify business risks in three categories: price risk, credit risk and pure risk

Price risk

Price risk refers to uncertainty over the magnitude of cash flows, due to possible changes in output and input prices. *Output price risk* refers to the risk of changes in the prices that a firm can demand for its goods and services. *Input price risk* refers to the risk of changes in the prices that a firm must pay for labour, raw materials etc. These risks are mainly external to the individual company and companies do not have any direct control of the price determination of those external factors. For a shipping company, for instance, we can identify the following sources of price risk:

Freight-rate risk

Freight-rate risk refers to the variability in the earnings of a shipping company due to changes in freight rates. This is perhaps the most important source of risk for a shipping company, since volatility in the freight market has a direct impact on the profitability of the company.

Operating-costs risk

In addition to freight-rate volatility, volatility on the costs side is also a factor affecting the profit margins of shipping companies. Perhaps the most important cost components for a shipping company is the cost of fuel oil, called bunkers, used by the vessel in performing a voyage. Bunker costs, on average, account for more than 50 per cent of the total voyage costs and, as a result, sharp and unanticipated changes in bunker prices have a major impact on the operating profitability of shipping companies and ship operators. This is because bunker prices are naturally related to world oil prices, which have been shown to exhibit substantial variability both in the short and long term. Therefore, it is of utmost importance for shipping companies and ship operators to control their exposure to bunker-market fluctuations, in order to secure their operating profit.

Interest-rate risk

Interest-rate risk arises from exposure to changes in interest rates. Due to the capital-intensive nature of shipping, and the fact that most vessel acquisitions are financed through term loans priced on a floating rate basis, unanticipated changes in interest rates may create cash flow and liquidity problems for companies which may no longer be able to service their debt obligations. Consequently, interest-rate risk measurement and mitigation is an indispensable aspect of shipping risk management. Shipping companies may also be exposed to currency risk if, for instance, they need to convert freight income, denominated in US dollars, to another currency; or in cases when they borrow in a currency other than US dollars and then use US dollar-denominated freight income to pay off of the debt.

Asset-price risk

Asset-price risk arises from fluctuations in the price of the assets of the company. For a shipping company, the major asset is of course the value of its ships. Volatility of ship prices is an important factor for shipowners, not only because it affects the balance sheet value of the company, but also because a reduction in the value of a ship may affect the creditworthiness of a shipowner and its ability to service debt obligations, because ships are used as collateral in ship-finance transactions. For this reason, ship-finance banks, shipowners and ship operators tend to monitor ship-price volatility and incorporate such information in their lending and investment decisions.

Credit risk

Credit risk, also known as 'counter-party risk', is the uncertainty surrounding whether a counter-party to a transaction will perform its financial obligations in full and on time. Examples of credit risk include the failure of a debtor to repay a loan, or the failure to receive a payment for a product or service which a firm has provided. Credit risk in shipping arises because most of the deals, trades and contracts are negotiated directly between the counter-parties, which means that the two parties agree to do business with each other and rely on each other's ability to honour the agreement. The agreement could be a charter contract between a shipowner and a charterer, a new building contract between an investor and a shipyard, a freight-derivatives transaction between two investors, or even a bunker transaction between a shipowner and a bunker supplier. In any case, parties to contracts can be exposed to each other's ability to perform the contract. The issue of credit risk in shipping and the techniques and instruments used in its management are discussed extensively in Chapter 12.

Pure risk

This is defined as the risk of reduction in the value of business assets due to physical damage, accidents and losses; it also covers the risk of loss due to physical risks, technical failure and human error in the operation of the assets of a company, as well as the risk of legal liability for damages as a result of actions of the company. For a shipping company, for instance, pure risk can include the risk of a collision, accidents or liability from oil or chemical spillage.

The distinguishing factors between price risk and pure risk are that, in general, the potential liability for a company as a result of a pure risk (such as an accident, collision, oil pollution liability etc.) can be very large in relation to the size of the business and may even threaten the firm's viability.[1] In addition, the underlying causes of factors associated with pure risks are often specific to a particular firm and depend on a firm's actions. As a result, companies can reduce the frequency and severity of losses through actions that alter the underlying causes. For instance, by chartering a well-maintained double-hull tanker vessel, the likelihood of an oil spill and the potential severity of such loss will be significantly reduced. In contrast, companies have very little control on the underlying factors that drive price risk. For instance, the economic factors that cause interest rates, and, hence, the cost of borrowing, to increase are beyond the control of an individual shipowner.

Pure risks are usually managed by purchasing insurance contracts. Due to the firm-specific nature of pure risks, which implies that events causing large losses to a given firm will have very little impact on losses experienced by other firms, insurance companies which underwrite these risks can reduce their exposure through diversification. On the other hand, insurance contracts are not used for managing financial losses arising from price risk since, in general, price risk affects a large number of firms at the same time and, hence, an insurance contract in that case would be extremely expensive. Instead, price risk is usually managed through derivative contracts, such as forwards, swaps and options, which enable price risk to be shifted to participants who may have an opposite exposure to the particular risk. For instance, an increase in the level of freight rates will have a positive impact on the cash flows of a shipowner but will have a negative impact on the cash flow of a charterer; consequently both parties can then manage their risk by taking opposite positions in a freight derivative contract.

A brief summary of derivatives contracts is provided in Section 1.4 and discussed more thoroughly in the relevant chapters of the book dealing with

---

[1] It should be mentioned that there are also cases when the losses from financial transaction may be very large in relation to the company's resources. This is, for instance, the case with losses from derivatives transactions which can be disproportionately large in relation to the value of a corporation.

the different price risks to which shipping companies are exposed. Pure risks are an integral part of shipping operations but are beyond the scope of this book and, hence, are not analysed further. For more on the management of those risks using the insurance markets, the interested reader may consult Harrington and Niehaus (2003) and Christoffersen (2003).

1.3   The risk-management process

Regardless of the type of risk being considered, the risk-management process involves several key steps, as identified by Harrington and Niehaus (2003). These are the following:

1. Identification of all significant risks affecting the value of the company (risk identification);
2. Evaluation of the potential frequency and severity of losses due to those risks (risk evaluation);
3. Development and implementation of appropriate methods for the management of the risks (risk management);
4. Monitoring the performance and suitability of the risk management methods and strategies on an ongoing basis (risk monitoring)

1.   Risk identification

The first step in the risk-management process is risk identification; in other words, the identification of loss exposures. There are various ways to implement this step. One approach, for instance, is to analyse the financial statements of a company and identify from those the factors that mostly affect the value of the company. Regardless of the method used, risk identification requires an overall understanding of the business and the specific economic, legal and regulatory factors which affect the business.

2.   Risk evaluation

This typically involves managers quantifying the exposure of the company to each risk factor, and usually involves measuring the expected losses and the standard deviation of losses over a period of time. This step generates the right incentive for a company to hedge, but also helps managers to assess the costs and benefits of loss control. Another important parameter here is the sensitivity of each company to the different risk factors. This varies from company to company but also depends on the operational strategy of each company in the market. For instance, an increase in bunker prices will, in general, have a negative impact on the cash flow positions of shipping companies. However, this impact will be less for a company that has chartered out her fleet on long term basis, compared to a company that operates in the spot market and will therefore need to increase freight rates in order to maintain its profit margin.

3. Risk management

After the risks have been identified and the sensitivity of a company to those risks has been adequately quantified, the next step is to select the instruments which are best suited to the management of those risks. As mentioned above, this also depends on the type of risk that is to be hedged. For instance, due to their nature, pure risks are usually managed using appropriately drafted insurance policies. Price risks, on the other hand, are managed using derivative contracts such as futures, options and swaps.

4. Risk monitoring

Finally, the last step in the risk-management process is monitoring the performance and suitability of the risk-management methods and strategies on an ongoing basis. As market dynamics change continuously, the exposure of the company to the different sources of risk may change accordingly. Some risks may become more significant than others. The company needs to be aware of how its exposure to the different sources of risks changes and what parameters it needs to consider in order to implement risk-management strategies. Even in cases where price risk is hedged, using a derivative contract, there is a possibility that due to shifts in market fundamentals the hedge may no longer be necessary; therefore, risk monitoring is required even for positions that are fully hedged.

1.3.1 Why should firms manage risks?

Before discussing the instruments that companies can use in order to manage price risk, it is also interesting to present some of the reasons companies decide to manage their risks in the first place. A number of reasons have been proposed (see for instance, Christoffersen, 2003 and Harrington and Niehaus, 2003), some of which are based on the theory of corporate finance and the optimal capital structure of an organisation – but not all of them may be applicable to a shipping company. However, we can identify four reasons as being quite important and also as justifying the use of risk-management strategies. These are:

Bankruptcy costs: the direct and indirect costs of bankruptcy are an important factor affecting the value of corporations. These include the administration costs associated with bankruptcy and also costs such as loss of customers, loss of key employees, and restrictions imposed on the operations and management of the company. These costs are directly related to the probability of default and are discussed in Brealey et al. (2007). Since risk management reduces the variability of expected earnings, it also reduces the probability of an organisation approaching bankruptcy and, hence, it can increase the value of a firm.

Capital structure and the cost of capital: a major source of corporate default is the inability of a company to service its debt. Other things being equal, the higher the debt-to-equity ratio for a company, the riskier the firm. Risk management can therefore be seen as allowing the firm to have a higher debt-to-equity ratio, which may be beneficial due to increased interest tax shields.

Benefits for public listed companies; there is empirical evidence that risk management reduces the variability of share prices in the mining and energy sectors in relation to changes in the price of the underlying commodity. Studies have also found that companies that follow active risk-management strategies tend to outperform comparative companies that do not manage their risks. A summary of these findings is presented in Christoffersen (2003).

Taxes: risk management can help reduce tax liability by reducing the volatility of expected earnings. The argument is that lowering the volatility of future pre-tax income will result in lower variability of the expected tax position and, hence, higher expected after-tax income.

However, not every company chooses to manage their risks and risk-management approaches, and strategies differ from one company to another. This partly reflects the fact that risk-management goals differ across companies. In particular, some firms use cash flow volatility as a benchmark, while established public listed companies use the market value of the company as the risk-management objective. Christoffersen (2003) also mentions that it is generally the case that larger firms tend to manage risks more actively than smaller companies, which may be due to the fact that smaller firms have only limited access to derivatives markets and may also lack the expertise to trade in these markets, despite the fact that being smaller they are generally considered as being riskier.

1.4　Introduction to derivatives: contracts and applications

As discussed, price risk is managed using derivative contracts. In this section, therefore, we present a brief introduction to the different derivative contracts that can be used for risk management. A derivative is a contract for a transaction whose value depends or derives from the values of other more basic underlying variables. The underlying asset is the financial asset, commodity, reference rate or index from which a derivative contract derives its value. Generally these instruments specify the terms of a transaction that will take place in the future. Examples include forward, futures, swaps, and options. The two major classifications of derivatives are 'exchange traded' and 'over the counter' (OTC)

In an exchange-traded market, individuals trade standardised contracts whose terms have been defined by the an exchange. The first organised exchange was the Chicago Board of Trade, established in 1848 as a market to bring farmers and merchants together. Initially, its main task was to standard-ise the quantities and qualities of the grains that were traded but within a few years the first contract for future delivery of wheat (also known as a 'to-arrive contract') was traded (Hull, 2006). Nowadays such futures exchanges exist all over the world.

Traditionally, exchanges have used an 'open-outcry' system, where traders meet on the floor of the exchange and use shouting and a complicated set of hand signals to indicate the trades they would like to carry out. In recent years however, they have moved from open-outcry to electronic trading. The latter involves traders entering their trades into a computer system which then automatically matches buyers and sellers in the market. As will be discussed in more detail later, contracts traded at organised exchanges have no credit risk.

In an over-the-counter (OTC) market, contracts are bought and sold through a computer- and telephone-linked network of dealers, who do not physically meet in the marketplace. The key feature of this market is that the terms of the contract are not specified by an exchange but are tailored to meet the specific needs of the clients. As such, the participants have the flexibility to negotiate any mutually attractive deal in terms of expiry date, reference price, amount, underlying commodity etc. However, there is usu-ally some credit risk involved in these transactions, usually the risk that a counter-party may default on any particular deal.

1.4.1 Forward contracts

A forward contract is an agreement entered into today between two parties, A and B, according to which, Party B has the obligation of delivering at some fixed future date a given quantity of a clearly specified underlying asset, and Party A the obligation of paying at that date a fixed amount that is agreed today (at 'date 0'), and that is called the forward price at date 0 of the asset at date T, denoted as $F(0, T)$. The underlying asset can be a financial asset (such as interest-rate payments) or a commodity (gold or oil) although in many cases cash settlement is also possible where the amount exchanged is the cash value of the commodity or asset; this is, for instance, so in the case of many financial assets, commodities and freight. Bearing in mind that the buyer of the forward contract can immediately sell the underlying asset at the maturity of the forward contract, the profit and loss (P&L) of Party A (who is the buyer of the forward and is also called 'long forward') and Party B (who is the seller, called 'short forward'), are shown in Figure 1.1.

We can see that the profit of the long position is the same as the loss of the short position, which means that the contract is a zero-sum game. In practice, Party A (long forward) represents an economic agent who wants to hedge against a possible rise in the price of the underlying asset between date 0 and T and locks, at date 0, to a purchase price equal to $F(0, T)$. Party B, on the other hand, is worried about a drop in the level of either the selling price or the value of his position. The price thus agreed today between the two

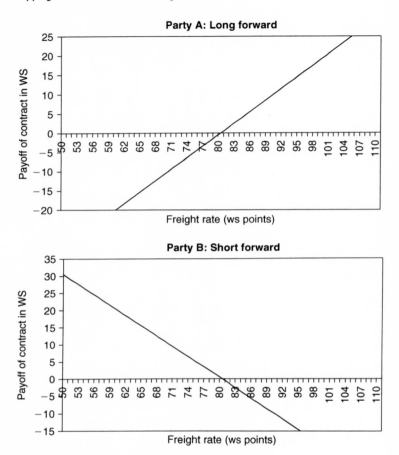

Figure 1.1   Long and short forward payoffs

counter-parties represents their expectations today at time 0 of how much the underlying asset *S* will be worth at date *T*, together with the risk premium that they are willing to pay or receive (see Geman, 2005).

1.4.2   Futures contracts

Futures contracts are very similar to forward contracts in terms of both their definition and functioning in that they are a contract for the delivery of a specified quantity of an underlying asset at some future date, at a price agreed today. There are, however, some key differences between forwards and futures:

- Futures are traded in organised exchanges. whereas forwards are traded over-the-counter, usually through a broker.

Table 1.1   Differences between forward and futures contracts

	Futures	Forwards
Trading	Exchange-traded	OTC
Credit risk	Guaranteed by clearing house	Counter-party risk (OTC clearing also possible)
Deposit/Collateral	Initial margin deposit	Usually not required
P&L	P&L realised daily through marking-to-market	P&L realised at the settlement of the contract
Contract terms	Highly standardised	Tailor-made
Closing position	Usually by closing contracts on the exchange; offset or reversing trade	Negotiated between the counter-parties or via offsetting trades

- Since futures are exchange-traded contracts, they are guaranteed by a clearing house which effectively acts as a central counter-party for each trade and guarantees the performance of the underlying contracts. Forward contracts, in contrast, are traded on a principal-to-principal basis and, as such, the counter-parties have to assume each other's credit risk, that is, the risk of a loss because of the default of the other party in the contract. It should be noted that it is also possible to have clearing for OTC contracts, where a contract that has been traded outside an exchange can then be cleared through a clearing house. This is, for instance, the case for freight derivatives, as we will see in Chapter 5. The issue of credit risk in general is discussed in more detail in Chapter 12.
- Traders need to deposit an initial margin with the clearing house and then the P&L from the position is realised on a daily basis through a process known as 'marking to market'. On the other hand, for a forward contract there is, usually, no requirement for margin deposit and the P&L from the position is realised at the contact's maturity.
- Futures contracts are standardised in terms of their specifications, such as the underlying asset, contract quantity, maturity etc. Forward contracts, on the other hand, are tailor-made to suit the requirements of each party to the contract.
- Finally, because futures contracts are traded in exchanges, most of the positions are terminated prior to the settlement of the contract simply by closing out the position. However, since forward contracts tend to be bespoke contracts between the counter-parties, these positions are usually carried to maturity, although early termination may be negotiated between the counter-parties.

Table 1.1 Summarises the key differences between forward and futures contracts.

1.4.3   Swaps

A swap is an agreement between two or more parties to exchange a sequence of cash flows over a period of time, at specified intervals. For example, Party A might agree to pay a fixed rate of interest on a notional principal of US$1 million each year, for five years, to Party B. In return, Party B will pay a floating rate of interest on US$1 million every year for the next five years. This particular swap is called a 'fixed-for-floating interest-rate swap'.

Swaps are mostly negotiated OTC and are very similar to forward contracts. In fact, as we will see in Chapter 11 when we discuss the valuation of interest-rate swaps, a swap contract is equivalent to a portfolio of forward contracts. There are four basic kinds of swaps: 'interest-rate swaps', where payments based on two different interest rates on a notional principal are exchanged, similar to the example presented above; 'currency swaps', which involve exchange of interest payments denominated in two different currencies; 'asset swaps', which involve the exchange of fixed for floating returns based on the returns of an underlying asset that could be a stock, stock index, stock portfolio, or a commodity ; and a 'credit swap', a contract that is designed to transfer credit risk from one counter-party to another. Swaps can also be classified as 'plain vanilla' or 'flavoured'. For instance, the fixed-for-floating swap described above is a plain vanilla swap; with flavoured swaps, the terms of the contracts can be customised to meet the particular needs of the swap counter-parties. Interest-rate and currency swaps are discussed in Chapter 11 while credit-default swaps are discussed in Chapter 12.

1.4.4   Options

Options are financial contracts which give their holder flexibility; that is the right – but not the obligation – to either buy or sell an asset at a specified price, if market conditions are favourable. There are two major classes of options: 'call options' and 'put options'. The owner of a call option has the right, but not the obligation, to purchase the underlying good at a specific price and this right lasts until a specific date. The owner of a put option has the right, but not the obligation, to sell the underlying good at a specific price and this right lasts until a specific date. In other words, the owner of a call option can call the underlying good away from someone else. Likewise, the owner of a put option can put the good to someone else by making the opposite party buy the good. (Kolb and Overdahl, 2007). Obviously this right is very valuable and, hence, to acquire these rights option buyers must pay the price, called a premium, to the option seller.

In an option, all rights lie with the owner of the option. In purchasing an option, the buyer makes payments and receives rights to buy or sell the underlying good on specific terms. In selling an option, the seller receives the option premium and promises to sell or purchase the underlying good on specific terms – at the discretion of the option owner. Therefore, we can see that the owner of the option has all the rights, and the option seller has all the obligations, which he undertakes in exchange for the receipt of the option premium. Freight options are discussed more extensively in chapters 7 and 8.

1.5 Applications and uses of financial derivatives

Derivatives markets have attained their popularity for a number of reasons. In this section, we briefly discuss some of the main benefits they provide to market participants. These are: risk management; speculation; arbitrage; and price discovery.

1.5.1 Risk management

Derivatives products were originally designed to meet the needs of hedgers. Organised trading in commodity futures markets dates back to the mid-1860s with the opening of the Chicago Board of Trade. The market at the time was designed to assist farmers who wanted to lock in advance a fixed price for their harvest. Market participants are confronted with price risk which arises mainly from supply and demand imbalances in the market. Derivatives markets provide a way in which these risks may be transferred to other individuals who are willing to bear them. The activity of trading futures contracts with the objective of reducing or controlling future spot-price risk is called hedging. Hedging essentially involves taking a position in the derivatives market which can offset any gains or losses made in the physical market by locking into a fixed price, or buying a price floor or price ceiling. For a futures contract, for instance, hedging involves taking a position in the futures market that is opposite to the position one already has in the spot market. For a futures contract to reduce spot-price risk effectively, any gains or losses in the value of the spot position, due to changes in the spot prices, will have to be countered by offsetting changes in the value of the futures position.

Hedges are either short or long. A short or 'selling' hedge involves selling futures contracts as a protection against a perceived decline in spot prices. For instance, a shipowner, fearing that freight rates will fall, will be a seller of freight forwards. A long or 'buying' hedge, on the other hand, involves buying futures as a protection against a price increase. For instance, a charterer will be a buyer of freight forwards contracts; this will enable him to protect his future freight requirements in case the physical market rises, thus forcing him to pay higher freight rates. In general, using derivative products for risk management gives participants the opportunity to participate in risky activities which they would not otherwise undertake. In addition, trading away price risk using derivatives results in a more efficient allocation of resources compared to physical methods of price-risk management.

1.5.2   Speculators

Depending on their expectations about future market conditions, speculators buy and sell derivative contracts to make a profit. Derivative markets are essentially markets for transferring risk from those having excess risk which they want to hedge (hedgers) to those that are willing to bear this risk in return for higher profits. Therefore, speculators fulfil the role of accepting the risk that hedgers want to hedge in the market. Although derivatives markets were initially designed for the purposes of risk management, nowadays it seems that the majority of trades in established derivatives markets are for speculation purposes. In fact, derivatives are ideally suited for this purpose. First, derivatives markets tend to be more liquid than the underlying spot markets; second, transaction costs in derivatives markets tend to be lower than in the underlying market; third, derivatives enable traders to speculate easily on a falling market, such as by buying put options or selling forwards, which is more difficult or costly to do in the physical market; fourth, derivatives also provide leveraged positions for speculating. For instance, buying or selling a futures contract requires depositing an initial margin which is usually a fraction of the value of the contract. Therefore, with the same amount of money, one can buy a given position in the underlying contract, and get a multiple of that position in the derivatives market which results in higher profits if the market moves to their favour (and also higher losses if the market moves against them). Finally, derivative contracts enable participants to achieve customised risk-return trade-offs which cannot be accomplished by trading the underlying market alone such as, for instance, through spread trades and volatility strategies.

1.5.3   Arbitrageurs

Arbitrageurs represent a small – but important – group of participants in futures and options markets. An arbitrage is a riskless profit realised by simultaneously entering into several transactions in two or more contracts.

In derivatives markets, arbitrage exploits price discrepancies between a derivative contract and its underlying asset. For instance, arbitrage opportunities may exist if the futures price gets out of line with its underlying spot price, or when the price on an option exceeds certain boundary conditions. Arbitrage opportunities are difficult to uncover and they do not last for long. For instance, if an instrument is underpriced, then the buying activity will force its price back in line with the fundamentals. In fact, the existence of arbitrageurs in the market ensures that major disparities between the prices of assets cannot exist in the first place. As Kolb and Overdahl (2007) put it: 'the existence of arbitrage opportunities is equivalent to money being left on the street without being claimed.' For that reason, the fair theoretical prices of derivative contract are usually derived on the assumption that arbitrage opportunities do not exist: this is called the 'no-arbitrage principle'.

The theoretical textbook definition of an arbitrage portfolio is that it is a portfolio which requires a null initial investment and generates a guaranteed (that is, risk-free) positive return. In practice, traders searching for arbitrage opportunities are looking for 'quasi-riskless' arbitrage strategies in which there is a mispricing in the asset based on their expected or fair theoretical values. Such strategies are known as statistical arbitrage and entail the risk that the actual returns may differ from the expected returns of the asset due, for instance, to model error. Irrespective of the type of arbitrage used, the existence of arbitrageurs is beneficial to the market because it increases market efficiency and ensures that prices are always in line with their fair theoretical values.

1.5.4 The price discovery role of derivatives markets

Derivatives markets provide a mechanism through which the supply and demand for an asset are brought into alignment, both in the present and over time. According to Edwards and Ma (1992), derivative prices reflect the current expectations of the market regarding the level of spot prices which may prevail in the future. Therefore, through derivatives trading, information about the expectations of market participants regarding the future supply-and-demand balance for a commodity is assimilated to produce the price of the derivatives instrument for a later date. As a result, derivatives trading and contracts contribute to a more transparent market.

By reflecting expectations about future spot prices, derivative prices trigger production and consumption decisions that reallocate the temporal supply and demand for a commodity in a way that promotes an efficient allocation of economic resources. In particular, expected future shortages of a commodity could be alleviated by increased future production, while current shortages are alleviated by the deferral of current consumption to a later period, when spot prices will be lower. Overall, the price discovery function helps market players plan their investment and consumption by providing information about future commodity prices. In addition, due to their liquidity and price transparency, derivative prices are also used for determining the underlying spot prices in many commodity markets where the underlying market may not be transparent or visible. This is, for instance, the case in the oil and agricultural markets.

In summary, the existence and functioning of derivatives markets determines and makes visible both current and expected spot prices. This availability of information contributes to market transparency, reduces search costs and provides signals which guide production and consumption decisions, and result in a more efficient allocation of economic resources. Moreover, the benefits of price discovery accrue not only to the futures markets' participants, but also to anyone else with an interest in the future value of the underlying asset.

1.5.5 Hedging and basis risk

Understanding basis is fundamental to using futures for hedging. The basis in a hedging situation is defined as: spot price of the asset to be hedged, S_t, minus the price of forward contract used for hedging, $F(t, T)$:

$$\text{Basis} = S_t - F(t, T)$$

Depending on the sign of the basis, the market is also characterised as being in 'backwardation' or 'contango'. For instance, if the basis is positive (that is, the spot is higher than the forward) we say that this contract is backwardated. On the other hand, if the basis is negative then the market is in contango. The terms backwardation and contango are also used to describe the entire shape of the forward curve as well. For instance a rising forward curve, where forward prices increase as time to maturity increases, is said to be in contango; and a falling forward curve is said to be in backwardation, as shown in Figure 1.2. We can see that the market is in contango when the futures price is above the spot price and the two converge as maturity approaches. Similarly, the market is in backwardation when the futures price is below the spot price and the two converge as the maturity approaches. For simplicity, we assume that the spot price remains constant. In practise, S and hence F will fluctuate as we approach T but with $F > S$ if the market is in contango and $F < S$ if the market is in backwardation.

If the asset to be hedged and the asset underlying the futures contract are the same then the basis should be zero at the expiration of the futures contract. Prior to expiration the basis may be positive or negative. If futures and spot prices always change by the same amount (that is, spot and futures prices are perfectly correlated) the basis will not change. In this case the magnitude of changes in spot and futures positions is identical and, in a hedged portfolio, any gain (loss) in the physical position will be offset by a corresponding

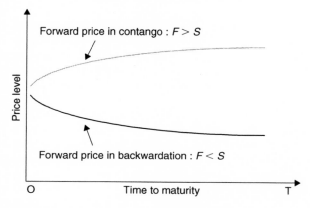

Figure 1.2   Backwardation and contango forward curves

loss (gain) in the forward position. Such a hedge is called a perfect or text-book hedge but, unfortunately, it is the exception rather than the rule since in practice hedging always entails some degree of risk. The most important risk perhaps comes from variations in the level of the basis. This 'basis risk' can cause futures prices to deviate from cash prices and, as a consequence, the hedger's position will not be covered completely and effectively using futures contracts. Such a variation in basis may arise if the asset whose price is to be hedged is not exactly the same as the asset underlying the futures contract; when the hedger is uncertain of the exact date on which the underlying asset will be bought or sold; or when the hedge may also require the futures contract to be closed out before its delivery month.

Basis risk, therefore, primarily arises because of an imperfect correlation between spot prices and futures prices since an effective hedge requires a high correlation between price changes in the spot and the futures markets, as can be seen in Figure 1.3, which illustrates the distribution of expected cash flows of the individual firm under different hedging strategies. Hedging narrows the variability of the expected cash flows around the mean of the distribution and the greater the correlation between the forward and the spot price the more effective the hedge. In a perfect hedge the hedged portfolio will have no variability. It should also be mentioned that risk reduction is not necessarily the same as value maximisation. Hedging adds value only to the extent that the expected value shifts to the right in Figure 1.3. In fact, if hedging is not free, meaning that the firm must expand resources to undertake hedging activity by paying, for instance, the premia to buy options, then hedging will add value only if the rightward shift is sufficiently large to compensate for the cost of hedging.

In general, in order to accommodate basis risk, practitioners adjust the size of the futures position relative to their exposure in the underlying market.

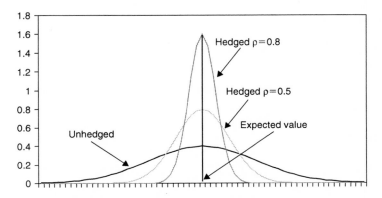

Figure 1.3   The impact of hedging on the expected cash flows

We call this ratio of futures to spot holdings the 'hedge ratio'; in most cases, the hedge ratio is set equal to one. However, this strategy is effective only if the spot and futures prices are perfectly correlated and have exactly the same volatility. In practice, the hedger should choose a hedge ratio that minimises the risk of the hedged position. This ratio is called the 'minimum variance hedge ratio' (MVHR) and is estimated as the ratio of the covariance between spot and future price changes (returns) over the unconditional variance of spot price returns, as follows (see the Appendix, p. 23, for the derivation of the MVHR)

$$\gamma^* = \frac{\text{Cov}(\Delta S_t, \Delta F_t)}{\text{Var}(\Delta S_t)} \qquad (1.1)$$

The MVHR is the hedge ratio that minimises the risk of a given position in the physical market (Ederington, 1979). Applications of this methodology in the freight futures (BIFFEX) market by Nomikos (1999) and Nomikos and Kavussanos (2000a; 2000b) have shown that hedgers can achieve greater risk reduction by using the MVHR compared to a hedge ratio of 1.0. One can also measure the hedging effectiveness which is defined as the proportion of the risk in the unhedged position that is eliminated through hedging using the MVHR. Mathematically:

$$1 - \frac{\text{Var}(\Delta S_t - \gamma^* \Delta F_t)}{\text{Var}(\Delta S_t)} \qquad (1.2)$$

The larger the reduction in the unhedged variance, the higher the degree of hedging effectiveness. When γ^* in equation (1.2) is the hedge ratio of equation (1.1) then this measure of hedging effectiveness is the same as the R^2 of regression of spot on futures returns as shown in the appendix. Finally, an extension of that approach is to estimate time-varying hedge ratios (TVHR). This procedure involves re-estimating the MVHR at frequent intervals, and re-adjusting the position in the forward market accordingly, as shown by Kroner and Sultan (1993) and applied in the freight futures market by Kavussanos and Nomikos (2000a; 2000b) using Multivariate GARCH models. The application of these models in the freight market is discussed in Chapter 3.

1.5.6   Theoretical models of futures prices: the cost-of-carry model

Spot and futures prices for storable commodities are related through the 'cost-of-carry' relationship, which states that the price today, at time t, of a futures contract for delivery at time T in the future, equals the price of the underlying asset today plus all the costs associated with purchasing and holding the underlying asset from time t to T. These costs include the financing costs associated with purchasing the commodity, the storage costs (such as warehouse and insurance costs), transportation costs and so on. In addition, one also has to consider the return that investors get from holding inventories of the underlying commodity, called the 'convenience yield'. This measures the returns that accrue to the holders of the underlying commodity but not to the holders of a long futures position. Mathematically:

$$F(t, T) = S_t\, e^{(r+c-y)(T-t)} \tag{1.3}$$

Where $F(t, T)$ is the price of the futures contract today for delivery at time T

S_t is the spot price today

r is the interest rate representing the cost of financing

c represents the carrying costs, in percentage terms, necessary to carry the commodity forward from period t to the delivery date of the futures contract, at time T.

y is the convenience yield which measures the return that investors get for holding physical inventories of the underlying commodity.

Essentially, equation (1.3) represents a no-arbitrage condition since any deviation from this relationship will be restored in the market through what is known as 'cash and carry' or 'reverse cash and carry' arbitrage (see for instance Kolb and Overdahl, 2007; Geman, 2005). Therefore, the existence of arbitrage opportunities is the underlying factor that links spot and futures prices for commodities which can be stored and carried forward over time. These include metals, oil and oil products, agricultural commodities, and even financial securities such as stock indices; in the last case the cost of carry is modified so that c in equation (1.3) is zero and y reflects the dividend yield of the stock index. In the shipping markets, the cost-of-carry model can be used for the valuation of bunker forwards as well as for the valuation of theoretical forward ship prices, as will be discussed in Chapter 13.

However, the concept of carrying charges does not apply to commodities which are non-storable, such as electricity and, most importantly, shipping freight. Forward contracts on shipping freight, called 'forward freight agreements' (FFAs) and discussed extensively in chapters 4 and 5, trade the expected value of the service of seaborne transportation, which is not practical to store or carry forward in time. As a result, FFA rates and the underlying spot rates are not linked through arbitrage, but are driven by the expectations of market agents, regarding the spot prices that will prevail at the expiry of the contract. Mathematically:

$$F(t, T) = \mathrm{E}(S_T | \Omega_t) \tag{1.4}$$

where $\mathrm{E}(.|.)$ is the mathematical conditional expectations operator at time t_t and Ω_t is the information set available to market participants at the same time conditional on which the expectation is computed. Equation (1.4) states that the price today of a futures contract for delivery at time T equals the spot price that the market agents expect to prevail at maturity. In forming their expectations, they consider all relevant information available to them at time t_0. This pricing relationship is also called the 'unbiasedness hypothesis' since it implies that forward prices are unbiased predictors of the realised spot prices and, on average, the forecast error from the forward contracts will be zero. The issue of unbiasedness for the freight market is discussed in more detail in Chapter 5. It should be noted however, that equation (1.4) does not represent a no-arbitrage condition and is usually tested statistically using historical spot and forward prices. In addition, deviations from this relationship may be attributed to the existence of a risk premium in the market representing the additional compensation which speculators in the market may require for bearing the excess risk of hedgers.

1.6 The organisation of this book

This book is divided into 14 chapters, including the present one, in three sections each devoted to a different area of shipping risk management. The first section (chapters 1 to 3) introduces the practice of risk management and the structure and statistical properties of the freight market. The second section (chapters 4 to 9) covers the area of freight-rate risk management and trading. Finally, the third part (chapters 10 to 14) covers other types of shipping risk, such as bunkers, and financial, credit and ship-price risk.

The structure and organisation of shipping markets is discussed in Chapter 2. Here we present the organisation of the market as well as the different types of trades, contracts, and vessel types that are prevalent in the shipping industry. We also discuss the fundamentals of the supply and demand for shipping services and explain how the unique structure of the market gives rise to some very interesting statistical properties of freight rates such as asymmetric volatility, mean reversion in freight rates and volatility term structure.

The statistical properties of freight rates are the topic of Chapter 3. Here we present descriptive statistics and perform risk-return comparisons for ship prices and freight rates across different vessel sizes and different sectors in the market. Such a comparison gives an insight into the statistical properties of the market and also on the factors that should be considered in the development of risk-management strategies. Finally, in the same chapter we present different methodologies for the estimation of volatility and compare the results from different models across a range of freight rates.

In Chapter 4 we provide an overview of the freight-market information that is used for the pricing and the settlement of freight derivative contracts. Trading of derivative contracts relies on the availability of continuous, measurable and fully transparent price information on the underlying asset. The emphasis is on the indices produced by the Baltic Exchange as this is the leading provider of freight-market information and most of the derivative transactions in the dry and wet markets are settled on the basis of those indices. In the same chapter we also provide a brief historical overview of the development of the first derivatives market for freight – the freight futures contract – which eventually paved the way for the development of forward freight agreement (FFA) contracts.

The FFA market is discussed in Chapter 5. Here we describe the structure and functioning of the FFA market, the practicalities of trading in the market, the types of contract used in the trades, applications and uses of FFAs for risk management and speculation, as well as how to deal with issues such as settlement risk and basis risk. We also discuss the statistical properties of the forward curves and the price discovery role of the market.

With the continuing growth of the FFA market, we have also seen an increase in the sophistication of trades used by market traders. One of the techniques used by market practitioners in order to identify trading opportunities in the FFA market is technical analysis. This is the topic of Chapter 6 which presents and discusses a number of technical analysis methods and trading rules applied to shipping-freight and FFA markets, as well as to the market for ships. In addition, we provide examples of how technical trading rules can be applied to the physical market in the form of establishing chartering strategies.

The freight options market is discussed in Chapter 7. Freight options are traded as OTC instruments, in the same fashion as FFAs, and they are becoming increasingly popular with market practitioners. In this chapter we consider the properties of freight options and present the profit patterns from buying or selling call and put options; we also discuss the practicalities of trading freight options. We then examine risk-management applications of freight options by considering the use of caps, floors and collars. Finally, we also consider trading strategies using freight options.

Chapter 8 examines two important issues in the area of freight options – the issue of options pricing and how to hedge a short options position. Determining the fair option premium to charge when selling a freight option is quite important. This should reflect, among other things, the risks that option sellers face in the market and should provide a fair level of compensation for those risks. Due to the fact that freight options are average price options, their pricing presents additional complications, which are discussed in the chapter. We also present approximations for the pricing of freight options as well as pricing examples, using Monte Carlo simulation. Finally, we discuss the hedging techniques that option sellers can use in order to reduce the risk of their short positions.

Chapter 9 demonstrates 'Value-at-Risk' (VaR) applications for freight markets. VaR is a tool used by traders for monitoring their risk exposure. We present a variety of VaR methodologies for FFA portfolios as well as different approaches used to test the validity of these models, such as back-testing techniques and stresstesting. In addition, we also show how to calculate the VaR for options positions, as well as how to decompose the risk factors for a large portfolio using Principal Component Analysis.

Bunker-risk management is discussed in Chapter 10. We illustrate and assess the fluctuations of bunker prices and highlight the importance of bunker-price risk to shipping operations. We also discuss the different derivatives instruments available to shipowners, operators and bunker suppliers to control their exposure to risk involved in bunker prices; we analyse the pros and cons of different contracts used in bunker-risk management and provide examples of how they can be used effectively.

Due to the capital-intensive nature of shipping, shipping companies are exposed to volatility and fluctuations in the level of interest rates. Therefore, Chapter 11 examines the issue of financial risk. We review interest-rate risk-hedging strategies, using a variety of hedging instruments, such as forward-rate agreements, interest-rate futures, interest-rate swaps and interest-rate options. The pricing of these instruments is also discussed. Finally, the chapter covers the hedging and pricing function of currency swaps.

Chapter 12 examines credit risk. This arises because most of the deals in shipping are negotiated privately between market participants on a principal-to-principal basis. Therefore, parties to contracts can be exposed to each other's ability to perform the contract or credit risk. In this chapter, we define credit risk and discuss different methods of measuring it. We also present different methods of managing credit risk, with particular emphasis on the newly developed credit-risk-management products known as credit derivatives.

Chapter 13 examines ship-price risk. We discuss how ship prices are determined and highlight the factors influencing them. We then examine the volatility of ship prices and compare them across different sizes and types of ships. Next, we review the risks involved in investing in ships and holding them in portfolios, as well as how portfolio risk can be optimised, providing examples from the tanker and the dry-bulk markets. Finally, we present and discuss recently reported ship-price indices as well as derivatives developed to trade ship values. In this context, we show how such derivative contracts can be structured and used for ship-price risk management as well as for trading purposes, and extend the discussion to how such derivatives can be priced.

Finally, Chapter 14 deals with real options in shipping. Real options analysis is used to value flexibility in shipping projects. Since there are a number of strategic and managerial flexibilities embedded in shipping investment and operation projects – such as, for instance, the option to lay up, or to switch markets – we focus on the use of real options analysis in evaluating such optionalities in shipping. We also discuss several options that are embedded in shipping contracts, such as the option to extend a time-charter contract, the option to place a follow-up newbuilding order, and a purchase option on a time-charter contract. The issue of identifying and then pricing these options is a major theme of this chapter.

Appendix 1.A: derivation of minimum variance hedge ratio

Ederington (1979) applies the principles of portfolio theory to show that the hedge ratio which minimises the risk of a given spot position is given by the ratio of the unconditional covariance between spot and futures price changes over the unconditional variance of futures price changes. To illustrate this, consider the case of a shipowner who wants to secure his freight rate income using FFAs. The change on the shipowner's portfolio of spot and forward positions, ΔP_t, is given by

$$\Delta P_t = \Delta S_t - \gamma \Delta F_t \qquad (1.5)$$

where, $\Delta S_t = S_t - S_{t-1}$ is the change in the spot position between $t - 1$ and t; $\Delta F_t = F_t - F_{t-1}$ is the change in the futures position between $t - 1$ and t; and γ is the hedge ratio. Using the formula for the portfolio variance of two risky assets, the variance of the returns of the hedged portfolio is given by

$$Var(\Delta P_t) = Var(\Delta S_t) - 2\gamma Cov(\Delta S_t, \Delta F_t) + \gamma^2 Var(\Delta F_t) \qquad (1.6)$$

where $Var(\Delta S_t)$, $Var(\Delta F_t)$ and $Cov(\Delta S_t, \Delta F_t)$ are, respectively, the unconditional variance of the spot and futures price changes and their unconditional covariance. The hedger must choose the value of γ that minimises the variance of his portfolio returns i.e. min $[Var(\Delta P_t)]$. Taking the partial derivative of equation (1.6) with respect to γ, setting it equal to zero and solving for γ, yields the minimum variance hedge ratio (MVHR), γ^*

$$\gamma^* = \frac{Cov(\Delta S_t, \Delta F_t)}{Var(\Delta F_t)} \qquad (1.7)$$

which is equivalent to the slope coefficient, γ^*, in the following regression

$$\Delta S_t = \gamma_0 + \gamma^* \Delta F_t + u_t; \ u_t \sim iid(0, \sigma^2) \qquad (1.8)$$

In this model, the degree of variance reduction in the hedged portfolio achieved through hedging is given by the R^2 of the regression, since this represents the proportion of risk in the spot market which is eliminated through hedging; the higher the R^2 the greater the effectiveness of the minimum variance hedge.

2
Introduction to Shipping Markets

2.1 Introduction

The shipping industry has been developed to facilitate international trade through connecting sources of supply and demand for commodities including raw materials, manufactured goods, and finished products, as well as transportation of passengers, cars and even livestock, between ports and countries. The growth in seaborne trade in the last century has led to the expansion of the shipping industry and its related businesses and markets such as shipbuilding, ship-broking, insurance, together with shipping finance and investment. In addition, the growth in international trade has also been the reason behind the design of larger and more specialised ships to carry specific commodities in order to achieve economies of scale in sea transportation. Furthermore, the shipping market has been shaped and structured in such a way as to accommodate the needs of charterers by defining different types of contracts varying in their duration, method of payment and cost allocations.

The aim of this chapter is to provide a review of the shipping market and its segmentation into different sectors and sub-sectors, as well as fleet composition and trading patterns of main shipping sectors. We also discuss the different types of shipping contracts and the costs involved in shipping operations as well as the formation of freight rates under different types of contracts. Furthermore, we explore the seasonal behaviour of shipping freight rates and discuss differences in seasonal freight movements across different types of ships and freight contract duration. Finally, we review the market for newbuilding, second-hand and scrap vessels, and discuss the main factors in ship price determination.

2.2 The world shipping industry

It is estimated that shipping contributes more than 75 per cent of the volume of world trade in commodities and manufactured products, and this

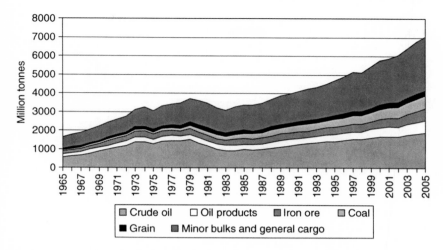

Figure 2.1 Pattern of international seaborne trade in major commodities
Source: Clarkson's SIN.

is increasing as faster, larger and more efficient ships are designed, built and employed. The total volume of world seaborne trade has increased over the last 50 years due to several reasons. Firstly, discovery of new sources of raw materials around the globe, as well as development of new sources of demand as economies grow, have changed the international trade pattern and increased the volume of sea transportation. Second, advances in ship design and shipbuilding which led to the construction of larger vessels for cost-effective transportation and, consequently, growth in international seaborne trade. Third, liberalisation in international trade which allowed companies not only to outsource their raw material and labour force, but also to spread their operations to more cost-effective locations, and to transport their finished products to the end-users' market, has also been an important factor in the growth in sea transportation. Finally, overall world economic growth, improvement in economic conditions and changes in people's lifestyles have also contributed to the increase in demand for manufactured products and goods which, in turn, requires transportation of raw materials.

For the purpose of shipping operations, market analysis and research, the international seaborne trade can be broadly classified into: liquid bulk; dry bulk; general cargo; and unitised transportation or container trade. There are also several other types of cargoes, such as natural gas, refrigerated cargoes, automobiles, forest products and livestock, which require special types of ships for transportation. Figure 2.1 illustrates the evolution of the international seaborne trade in major dry and liquid-bulk commodities, as well as

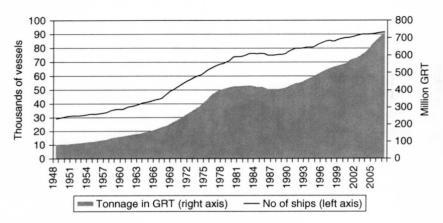

Figure 2.2   The growth of the world shipping fleet since 1948
Source: Lloyd's Register of Shipping, *World Fleet Statistics*.

general cargo and containers, over the period 1965 to 2005. It can be seen that the volume of international seaborne trade has increased from 1750 million tonnes in 1965 to more than 7000 million tonnes in 2005, representing an average annual growth rate of 3.5 per cent.

The growth in international trade in the last century led to the huge expansion of the shipping fleet to match the requirements of seaborne trade. Figure 2.2 presents the growth of the world shipping fleet since the second world war. It can be seen that the size of the merchant fleet has grown from nearly 80 million gross registered tonnes (grt) to 720 million grt, and the number of ships has increased from 29,300 to 91,500 vessels.[1] The evolution of the size of the cargo carrying fleet, measured in deadweight tonnes (dwt), is presented in Figure 2.3.[2] Out of the total of 1020 million dwt, dry-bulk carriers constitute 40 per cent of the fleet, while tankers make up about 38 per cent of the total fleet. The rest are container ships – around 14 per cent – and other types of ships such as chemical carriers, RoRo (roll-on roll-off) ships, general cargo or multipurpose vessels, LPG carriers and reefer ships, which make up the remaining 8 per cent.

Table 2.1 presents the world fleet statistics, as of May 2008, and the growth rate in different shipping sectors over the period 1996 to 2008. It can be seen that the sizes of the dry-bulk and tanker fleets have increased by 5.15 per cent and 3.37 per cent per year respectively, whereas the container fleet has increased at rate of 18.74 per cent per year. The growth

---

[1] The statistics are for ships of 1000 grt (gross registered ton) and over. Source: Lloyd's Register of Shipping, *World Fleet Statistics*.
[2] The statistics are for ships of 10,000 dwt (deadweight ton) and above.

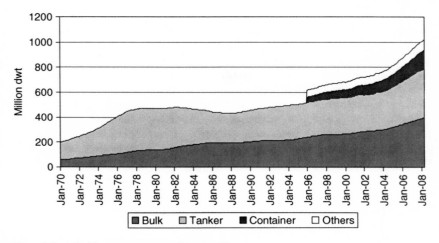

Figure 2.3 World cargo-carrying shipping fleet
Container and other fleet statistics are only available from 1996.
Source: Clarkson's Shipping Intelligence Network (SIN).

Table 2.1 Fleet size and its growth in different sectors of world shipping from January 1996 to May 2008

	Dry-bulk	Tanker	Container	MPP	Chemical	Others
Fleet size (ships)	6779	4651	4477	2735	1104	3390
Fleet Size dwt	398.84	389.7	149.54	24.78	27.58	29.52
% of total dwt	39.1%	38.2%	14.7%	2.4%	2.7%	2.9%
Average growth	5.15%	3.37%	18.74%	1.94%	14.43%	1.35%

Notes:
- Statistics are for vessels above 10,000 dwt.
- 'MPP' stands for multi-purpose ships involved in general cargo trade.
- 'Others' includes RoRo ships, reefer ships and LPG carriers.
- Average growth in fleet size is calculated as average annual per cent increase in dwt over the period January 1996 to May 2008.

rate in other sectors seems to be between 2 per cent to 14 per cent per year. All other sectors appear to show a steady growth over this period. In the case of the tanker fleet, the excessive expansion during the 1970s was followed by a relatively large decline in the 1980s due to the collapse of seaborne trade in petroleum and petroleum products. The largest growth from 1970 to the present was in the container fleet. This was mainly because of the containerisation of trade in manufactured goods and the increase in the number of large container carriers (such as the Panamax and

Post-Panamax classes) in recent years, due to the expansion of trade between the Far East, Europe and North America. In addition, the containerisation of some commodities, previously carried by general cargo or reefer ships, has also contributed to the growth of the container fleet. This trend may continue for some time because currently – as of May 2008 – there are about 500 Post-Panamax container ships on order. The growth rate in the dry-bulk carrier fleet has also increased in recent years as the order book for these types of ships has increased substantially over the past five years. Currently, there are about 700 Capesize, 900 Panamax, and more than 1000 Handy class (Handysize, Handymax and Supramax) vessels on order for deliveries extending to 2012 and 2013. The tanker fleet is also enjoying a large expansion phase due to the large number of orders placed over the last few years.

2.3   Market segmentation in the shipping industry

Generally speaking, in international shipping the charterer's (shipper's) decision to hire a certain type of vessel for ocean transportation of a certain commodity depends on three main factors: i) the type of the commodity transported; ii) the commodity parcel size; and iii) the route and loading and discharging port facilities. Since it is the type of commodity that determines which type of ship the charterer requires, any change in the trade pattern for that commodity will be reflected in the demand and freight rate for that type of vessel. For example, industrial growth in the Far East, especially in South Korea and China, in the past two decades has increased the demand for Panamax and Capesize vessels for transportation of raw materials to those countries. Another example is the fall in demand for Capesize vessels in the Atlantic, due to the decline in Europe's grain imports from the United States after the 1980s, as a result of the increase in the EU's grain production.

The second factor that charterers consider in the transportation of commodities is the conventional shipment size of cargo, generally known as 'commodity parcel size'. This is defined as the average shipment size of a commodity for sea transportation, considering the economies of scale and associated transportation and storage costs for that commodity. The commodity parcel size also depends on the economics of the industrial process or consumption of such commodities, in the form of raw materials, for manufacturing and production of other goods and finished products. The economies of scale in sea transportation have reduced the transportation costs for certain commodities, such as iron ore, crude oil and coal, to such an extent that it is more economical to hire very large vessels for transportation of these commodities. Therefore, parcel sizes for those commodities are quite large (for instance, for crude petroleum the parcel size ranges from 80,000 to 450,000 tons and for iron ore from 80,000 to 300,000 tons). On the other hand, commodities such as petroleum products and agricultural products are carried in smaller shipments. For these products the parcel sizes range from 12,000 to 60,000 tons, again depending on the type of cargo as well as the routes over which commodities are transported. This is mainly because of the perishable nature of agricultural products and the fact that they need specialised storage facilities (such as special silos). Therefore, traders prefer smaller shipments to facilitate the storage of these products and to market them in time. In addition, the higher storage and inventory costs of agricultural commodities and oil products compared to lower-value goods (such as iron ore, coal and crude oil), suggest that it is more economical to transport these commodities in smaller consignments.

Finally, when deciding which size vessel to hire, the shipper must consider factors such as loading and discharging port facilities, draught restrictions, and cargo-handling equipment. The draught factor is important because large ships with deep draughts cannot approach ports with shallow harbours and the costs of lightening them at the anchorage should be compared against the capacity loss when using smaller vessels. In addition, shippers tend to hire geared vessels when cargo-handling facilities in loading or discharging ports are limited or not adequate.

Therefore, in general, shippers and charterers try to minimise the associated transportation costs through hiring an optimally sized vessel, considering all the above factors. These costs and size optimisations suggest that there is a close relationship between certain types of commodities and vessel sizes; that is, different classes of vessels are employed in transportation of different types of commodities and in specific routes. As a result, each shipping sector has been broadly divided into different sub-sectors. For example, vessels employed in the liner sector have been classified into Feeder (100 to 500 twenty-foot equivalent units or TEU[3]), Feedermax (500 to 1000 TEU), Handysize (1000 to 2000 TEU), Sub-Panamax (2000 to 3000 TEU), Panamax (3000 to 4000 TEU), and Post-Panamax (more than 4000 TEU). The dry-bulk sector comprises five main sub-sectors according to the cargo-carrying capacity of vessels. These are Handysize (20,000 to 35,000 dwt), Handymax (35,000 to 45,000 dwt), Supramax (45,000 to 55,000 dwt), Panamax (60,000 to 75,000 dwt) and Capesize (more than 80,000 dwt) markets. The tanker sector is also differentiated into five main sub-sectors: that is, Handysize (20,000 to 45,000 dwt), Panamax (50,000 to 80,000 dwt), Aframax (80,000 to 120,000 dwt), Suezmax (130,000 to 160,000 dwt) and Very Large Crude Carriers (VLCC) (more than 160,000 dwt, normally 250,000 to 320,000 dwt). Table 2.2 presents the size classification of vessels in different shipping sectors along with their cargo-carrying capacity and an indication of the speed at which they may sail.

---

[3] TEU is a unit of measurement equivalent to one twenty-foot shipping container. This measurement is used to quantify the container capacity of a ship or it may be the unit on which freight is payable.

Table 2.2   Different classes of vessels within each shipping sector

The liner and container shipping market		
Vessel type	**Ship size (TEU)**	**Approximate speed (knots)**
Feeder	100–499	15–20
Feedermax	500–999	15–20
Handy	1000–1999	15–20
Sub-Panamax	2000–2999	20–25
Panamax	3000–3999	20–30
Post-Panamax	>4000	20–30

The dry-bulk shipping market		
Vessel type	**Ship size (dwt)**	**Approximate speed (knots)**
Handysize	20,000–35,000	12–16
Handymax	35,000–45,000	12–16
Supramax	45,000–55,000	12–15
Panamax	60,000–75,000	12–15
Capesize	80,000–300,000	12–14

The tanker shipping market		
Vessel type	**Ship size (dwt)**	**Approximate speed (knots)**
Handysize	20,000–45,000	14–16
Panamax	50,000–70,000	14–16
Aframax	70,000–120,000	13–15
Suezmax	130,000–160,000	12–14
VLCC-ULCC	160,000–500,000	12–14

2.3.1   The container shipping market

Container shipping has been the fastest growing sector of the global shipping market. At the end of 2007 the fully cellular container fleet capacity was 144 million dwt or 10.7 million TEU, with 4364 vessels. Historical growth and the composition of the container fleet according to size is presented in Figure 2.4. The total container fleet consists of 0.136 million TEU (mTEU) of Feeder ships, 0.58 mTEU of Feedermax, 1.64 mTEU of Handysize, 1.67 mTEU of Sub-Panamax, 2.94 mTEU of Panamax and 3.77 mTEU of Post-Panamax vessels.

The total world trade in container shipments reached an estimated level of 1244 million tonnes in 2007 which means an average growth rate of

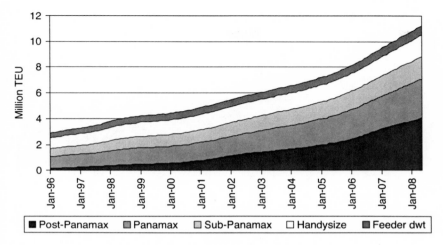

Figure 2.4 Historical growth of the world container fleet by size category
Source: Clarkson's SIN.

9.9 per cent per year since 1986 when the trade was only 173 million tonnes. The world container trade can be classified into mainline trade routes, which include transpacific trade, Far East-to-Europe trade, and transatlantic trade. There are several other routes, known as north-south trade, in which container trade volume has increased significantly in recent years. These include: the Far East to the Middle East, Australia and South America; North America to South America and Australia; and Europe to the Middle East and South America. There are also regional trading routes between smaller ports, for example, in the Far East, northern Europe, and Central America.

2.3.2 The dry-bulk market

The world dry-bulk fleet constitutes about 40 per cent of the total world shipping fleet in terms of capacity, with more than 6600 ships providing 392.4 million dwt in 2007.[4] Historical growth and the composition of the dry bulk fleet in terms of vessel size is presented in Figure 2.5. The composition of the fleet has also changed over time and at the end of 2007, the world dry-bulk fleet consisted of 2841 Handysize vessels with total capacity of 75.82 mdwt, 1591 Handymax vessels with a total capacity of 76.52 mdwt, 1471 Panamax vessels with a total capacity of 107.6 mdwt, and 763 Capesize vessels with a total capacity of 130.35 mdwt.

In 2006, the estimated total world seaborne trade in dry-cargo commodities reached 5000 million metric tonnes (mmt), of which 3000 mmt were

---

[4] According to Clarkson's *Shipping Review and Outlook*.

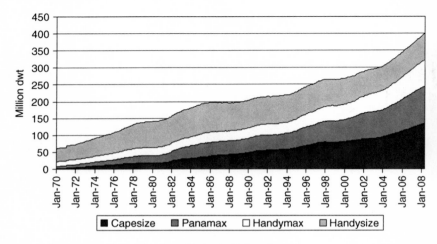

Figure 2.5   Historical growth of world dry-bulk fleet by size category
Source: Clarkson's SIN.

dry bulk; that is, 788 mmt of iron ore, 778 mmt of coal, 295 mmt of grain, 116 mmt of bauxite, alumina and phosphate rock, and 1,029 mmt of minor dry-bulk commodities. Table 2.3 summarises the three broad categories of vessels in the dry-bulk sector as well as major commodities and routes which are served by these vessels. For instance, Handysize vessels are mainly engaged in the transportation of grain commodities from North and South America, and Australia, to Europe and Asia; and of minor dry-bulk commodities such as bauxite and alumina, fertilisers, rice, sugar, steel and scrap around the world. Due to their small size, shallow draught, and cargo-handling gears, these vessels are quite flexible in terms of the trading routes and ports they can serve. Handymax vessels are also engaged in similar trades as Handysize ships. A new class of dry-bulk carrier which has emerged recently is the Supramax class, which is also used for transportation of minor bulk and grain commodities. These ships are slightly bigger than Handymax ships but smaller than Panamax vessels. Panamax vessels, which are known as the 'workhorse' of the dry-bulk shipping industry, are used in many trades including coal, grain and – to some extent – in iron ore transportation, from North America and Australia to the Far East and western Europe. These vessels are not equipped with cargo-handling gear and have a deeper draft; therefore, they mainly serve major routes, but are not as flexible as Handymax and Supramax dry-bulk carriers. The majority of the Capesize fleet is engaged in transportation of iron ore from South America and Australia to the Far East, western Europe and North America, and also in coal transportation from Australia, South Africa and North America to the Far East and western Europe. Due to their

Table 2.3 Different types of dry-bulk carriers, cargoes they carry and typical trading routes

Class of bulk carriers	Commodities (percentage of total shipments)				
	Iron ore	Coal	Grain	Bauxite and alumina	Phosphate rock
Capesize	70%	45%	7%	–	–
Panamax	22%	40%	43%	45%	20%
Handy class	8%	15%	50%	55%	80%
			Major routes		
Capesize (80k + dwt)	• Brazil to western Europe and the Far East; Western Australia to western Europe and the Far East	• Eastern Australia to the Far East, Japan and western Europe • South Africa to western Europe and the Far East	• Argentina and River Plate to the Near East, and eastern Europe		
Panamax (60k–80k dwt)	• Brazil to western Europe and the Far East • Australia to western Europe and Japan	• North America to Japan and western Europe • Eastern Australia to the Far East, Japan and western Europe	• North America to the Far East, western Europe and the Near East		
Handy class (25k–50k dwt)	• India to Japan and Korea • Canada to the USA and Japan • Liberia and Mauritania to western Europe	• South Africa to the Far East and Europe	• Australia to the Far East, Japan and the Middle East; • North America to Africa and western Europe	• Caribbean to North America and western Europe • West Africa to western Europe and the Far East • Australia to the Far East and western Europe	• Morocco to western Europe • Russia to western Europe • US to the Far East and western Europe

Source: Fearnleys, *World Bulk Trade* and *Lloyd's Shipping Economist*.

deep draught and the limited number of commodities they transport, the operation of these vessels in terms of trading routes and the ports they can approach is restricted.

A number of studies in the literature have argued that the risk-and-return characteristics of ships operating in different sub-sectors vary across vessel sizes. For example, Kavussanos (1996; 1997) shows that freight-rate volatilities and second-hand ship price volatilities are higher for larger vessels compared to smaller ones, and relates such differences to the operational (in)flexibility and trading restrictions of larger vessels. Such strong contrast in risk, return and operational profitability among different size dry-bulk carriers stems from differences in their supply, demand, freight rate and price determination factors which reflect their trading and operational flexibility. This, in turn, implies a high degree of disaggregation in this shipping sector.

2.3.3   The tanker market

According to Clarkson's fleet statistics, the world tanker fleet constitutes about 38 per cent of the total world shipping fleet in terms of cargo-carrying capacity. The number of tankers in the wet-bulk sector exceeded 4500 ships of a combined 385 million dwt at the end of 2007, when the estimated total world seaborne trade in oil and petroleum products reached 2757 mmt, out of which 1986 mmt were crude oil and 771 mmt were petroleum products.

The two larger-size tankers, namely VLCC and Suezmax vessels, are involved in crude-oil transportation. Aframax vessels are also involved in the transportation of crude oil; however, they are also occasionally involved

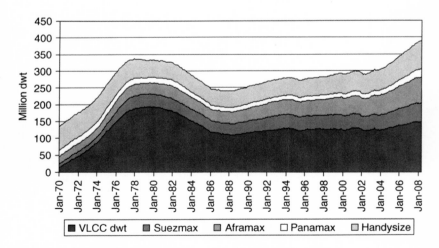

Figure 2.6   Historical growth of world tanker fleet by size category
Source: Clarkson's SIN.

in the transportation of oil products. Handysize tankers are mainly involved in the transportation of clean and dirty oil products, although they can be employed in short-haul crude-oil transportation at times. The employment of Handysize tankers in oil-product transportation is mainly due to the small parcel size of petroleum products, which rarely exceed 60,000 tons.

Due to the limited number of petroleum export and import regions around the world, as well as draught and capacity restrictions in ports, oil terminals and canals, the operation of larger tankers is restricted to only a few routes. For instance, the three major routes for VLCCs are from the Persian Gulf to; i) the Far East; ii) North America; and iii) northwestern Europe via the Cape, in addition to trades from West Africa, to North America and to the Far East. Suezmax tankers mainly operate between the Persian Gulf and northwestern Europe through the Suez Canal, as well as from West Africa, to the US Gulf states and to the US East Coast. The major routes for Aframax tankers are: from West Africa and the North Sea to the US East Coast; from North Africa and the Black Sea to the Mediterranean and northern Europe; and from the Persian Gulf to the Far East. Handysize tankers are mainly employed in regional dirty- and clean-product transportation (the US Gulf states and the US East Coast, the Persian Gulf, western Europe and the Far East), as well as some long-haul routes such as the Persian Gulf to the Far East and Europe, and Europe to North America. Table 2.4 summarises the four size categories of vessels in the tanker market and the associated cargo types and routes in which these vessels trade. Similar to the dry-bulk sector, the size of vessel in this sector is also an important determinant of the operational flexibility of tankers in terms of the routes and ports they serve as well as the cargoes that carry. Therefore, one would expect smaller-sized tankers to be more flexible compared to larger ones, in terms of their commercial operation.

2.4   Shipping freight contracts

Under a shipping freight contract, the shipowner agrees to provide a service to the charterer or shipper for a specified amount of money per day for ship hire, or per ton of cargo transported between two ports, known as the freight rate. This service is provided under certain contractual agreements and documentation, known as the 'charter party'. Depending on the type and duration of the service required by charterers, different types of charter contracts have been developed and used in international shipping. These can be classified into five main types:

- Voyage charter contracts
- Contracts of affreightment (CoA)
- Trip-charter contracts

Table 2.4 Tankers of different sizes, cargoes they carry and typical trading routes

Class of tanker	Commodities (percentage of total shipments)		
	Crude oil	Dirty products	Clean products
VLCC	60%	0%	0%
Suezmax	30%	5%	0%
Aframax	10%	35%	20%
Handysize	0%	60%	80%

Major routes

Class of tanker	Crude oil	Dirty products	Clean products
VLCC (160,000 + dwt)	• Middle East to US East Coast, western Europe and the Far East • West Africa to the US and the Far East		
Suezmax (130–160k dwt)	• Middle East to the US East Coast, western Europe and the Mediterranean via the Suez Canal • Middle East to the Far East • North Sea to US East Coast • West Africa to the US and Europe	• Middle East to the US East Coast, western Europe and the Far East	
Aframax (80–120k dwt)	• North Sea to the US • West & North Africa to the US and Europe • Singapore and Malaysia to Japan • Venezuela to US Gulf states	• Middle East to US East Coast, western Europe and the Far East • US Gulf states to different destinations • Other minor routes around the world	• Middle East to US East Coast, western Europe and the Far East • US Gulf to different destinations • Mediterranean and western Europe • Other routes around the world
Handysize (20–40k dwt)		• Middle East to US East Coast, western Europe and the Far East • US Gulf states to different destinations • Mediterranean and western Europe • Other routes around the world	• Middle East to US East Coast, western Europe and the Far East • US Gulf states to different destinations • Mediterranean and western Europe • Other routes around the world

- Time-charter contracts
- Bareboat or demise charter contracts.

Charter contracts are normally negotiated between shipowners and charterers through brokers and, once the terms are agreed, the charter party is drafted and signed by the two parties. Under each type of contract, duration of the service is specified, the type and the amount of cargo to be carried is agreed, methods of payment are standardised, and costs and expenses are allocated to the agents involved. Single-voyage, trip-charter and time-charter are the most common types of contracts used in the dry-bulk market. Single-voyage and trip-charter contracts, although different in their method of payment and cost allocations, can be classified as short-term or spot-charter shipping contracts because they both cover only a single voyage. On the other hand, time-charter contracts are long-term (period) contracts and cover more than one voyage. In the following sections we provide a brief description of each type of contract.

2.4.1 Voyage charter contracts

Under a voyage charter contract, the shipowner agrees to transport a specified amount of cargo from a designated loading port to a designated discharging port (destination) in return for a sum of money, known as 'freight'. These contracts are also known as 'spot contracts' in the shipping industry. The freight paid by the charterers (cargo owners) is normally expressed in US dollars per metric tonne (US$/mt) of cargo or as a lump-sum.[5] Once the cargo has been discharged safely, the contract is fulfilled and the shipowner's responsibility is over. Under a voyage charter contract, the shipowner is responsible for all expenses incurred during the voyage. These expenses are categorised into four main types: voyage costs; operating costs; capital costs; and cargo-handling costs (see Section 2.5 for definitions of these costs). In some cases, depending on the contract, the charterer pays the cargo-handling costs.

---

[5] In contrast to the dry market, tanker voyage rates are negotiated and reported on the Worldscale basis. The Worldscale Association in London calculates the cost of performing a round-trip voyage between any two ports for tanker cargoes in the world. The freight cost is calculated for a standard 75,000 mt dwt Aframax vessel after making certain assumptions regarding voyage costs (such as port charges, canal charges and bunker costs) applicable for each voyage. The resulting freight rate, which is quoted as US$/mt, is known as Worldscale 100 or as the Worldscale flat rate and is effectively the break-even rate for the particular voyage. The negotiated rate for any trip will then be a percentage of that rate. For instance, assume that for route TD3 the flat rate is US$13.5/mt. If the negotiated rate is WS 50 then the agreed rate is 50 per cent of 13.5 i.e. US$6.75/mt. The reference WS 100 rates for each voyage are usually updated once a year to reflect changes in the cost of performing a voyage.

Table 2.5   Examples of reported fixtures under different types of shipping contracts

Contract type	Fixture report
Voyage charter	*Mobile to Iskenderun – Florita, 60,000t ± 10%, US$10.85, fio, 30,000t/12,000t, end Aug. (Maran Coal)*
Trip charter	*Dynamic (29,332 dwt, Panamanian, 13k on 28t + 2t, built 1979) delivery Recalada Aug 21-25, trip redelivery South Brazil, US$7,500 daily. (Dantas)*
Period charter	*Darya Radhe (73,705 dwt, Hong Kong, 13.5k on 30t, built 1999) delivery Jorf Lasfar end Aug-early Sept, for three to five months trading, US$12,000 daily. (Kingston Maritime)*

Source: Lloyd's List, Friday, 18 August 2000.

For example, the first row of Table 2.5 reports an actual fixture of a single voyage charter contract. In this fixture, 'Maran Coal' (the shipper) has employed *Florita* (a Panamax bulk carrier) to transport a cargo of coal of 60,000 ± 10% mt, from Mobile in the US Gulf to Iskenderun in Turkey at the end of August 2000, at US$10.85/mt.

The time period, or the window of dates by which the ship is allowed to report to the loading port, which is known as the 'lay/can',[6] is defined in the charter-party. Under the agreement, the ship must report and be ready for loading the cargo at the loading port within the lay/can period. There are also other terms in the charter-party that define different conditions under which the cargo has to be transported,[7] including time allowed for loading and discharging and any differentials which should be considered in the calculation

---

[6] Lay/can or Laydays/Cancellation times are the earliest and latest dates a ship can tender her Notice of Readiness. If a ship tenders the Notice of Readiness after the cancelling date, the cargo owner has the right to cancel the charter contract. If the ship arrives and tenders her Notice of Readiness before the laydays commence, the cargo owner does not have to accept the Notice of Readiness until the commencement of the laydays.

[7] An example of a basic general charter-party is the BIMCO 'Gencon'. The principal sections in the BIMCO 'Gencon' can be subdivided into six major sections. Section 1 includes details of the ship and the contracting parties, such as the name of the ship, the shipowner, charterer and broker as well as the ship's size, position, cargo capacity and the brokerage fee. Section 2 includes the description of the cargo, and the name and the address of the shipper. In section 3 the terms on which the cargo must be carried are given. These include the dates on which the vessel should be available at the loading port, the loading area (port), the discharging port(s), laytime, demurrage and payments of loading and discharging. Section 4 includes the terms of payment; that is, the freight rate, method of payment, currency, etc. Section 5 sets penalties for any non-performance or defaults and section 6 includes administrative clauses such as appointments of agents, issuing bills of lading and matters on arbitration in case of any disputes.

of demurrage and dispatch.[8] For instance, in the above example the loading rate is specified as 30,000 mt per day and the discharge rate is 12,000 mt per day, which means two days' loading and five days' discharging time for 60,000 mt of coal. However, more details on loading and discharging terms, called 'laytime', along with additional clauses on payments and actions to be considered in the event of a default, are specified in the charter party. Finally, the term 'fio' (free in and out) means that all the expenses of the loading and unloading of the cargo are borne by the shippers and and free of charge to the ship.

2.4.2 Contracts of affreightment

Contracts of affreightment (CoA) are those shipping contracts under which the shipowner agrees to transport specified amounts of cargo from the loading port or area to the discharging port or region. This type of contract is normally used when the amount of cargo is large and cannot be transported in a single shipment. For example, in the case of industrial commodities such as coal and iron ore, steel mills purchase large amounts of iron ore or coal (say, 1 or 2 million tonnes), in order to secure their supply of raw materials for a long period while minimising their storage space and inventory. Therefore, shipments of coal or iron ore from the supply area to the steel mill should take place over a period of time on a regular basis. Thus, a CoA at a fixed rate can be used by the shipper to secure the sea transportation of the commodity over a period of time. The method and terms of payment in CoAs is similar to voyage-charter contracts; that is, freight rate is in US$/mt and the shipowner is responsible for all the costs. However, the frequency of payment, which is specified on the charter party, might vary from contract to contract.

As an example, consider a shipping company which enters into a CoA with a charterer. Under this contract the shipowner agrees to transport 600,000 tonnes of coal from Australia to Japan for a Japanese power company under a CoA over six months. Terms such as delivery frequency, amount, loading and discharging ports, and freight rate, are specified in the contract. Therefore, the shipping company can use its own fleet or even charter ships which are available at the loading area to lift the cargo when appropriate, and enjoy the flexibility of scheduling its vessels to optimise the operation. This type of contract gives the charterer the advantage of having a fixed transportation cost as well as defined contract terms for the whole cargo, over a certain

---

[8] The terms demurrage and dispatch are used for the calculation of the delays in loading and discharging due to unexpected events such as weather disruptions, stevedores' strikes, cargo availability and cargo gear failures. Demurrage is the difference the charterer has to pay the shipowner for delays exceeding the contract duration. Dispatch, which is normally considered to be half the amount of demurrage, is paid by the shipowner to the charterer to compensate for early termination of the contract due to faster-than-planned discharge of cargo.

period, thus guaranteeing the availability of ships for transportation of cargo and optimising the inventory costs.

2.4.3 Trip-charter contracts

A trip-charter contract is a shipping contract under which the charterer agrees to hire the vessel from the shipowner for the duration of a specified trip. Normally the charterer takes charge of the vessel from the point of delivery to the point of redelivery (after transportation of cargo) and pays the freight on a dollar-per-day basis (US$/day). Under this type of contract, the shipowner has the operational control of the vessel, while the charterer is responsible for the voyage costs during the trip. The delivery point is normally the loading port and the redelivery point is the discharging point; however, cases in which the charterer hires the vessel from the discharging port or region for a round trip are also common. It is also quite common to terminate the trip-charter contract as soon as the voyage ends; that is, when the discharging is completed.

The advantage of the trip-charter contract over the voyage charter for the shipowner is that the payments are on a US$/day basis; therefore he is compensated for any delay during the voyage. Single-voyage contracts, by contrast, are charged on a US$/mt basis and delays are settled through lay-time and demurrage. In the latter case, any delay during the voyage, apart from loading and discharging delays, may reduce the daily earnings of the vessel. Moreover, since the shipowner is not responsible for voyage costs, any changes in bunker prices or voyage costs will not affect his operating profit. On the other hand, charterers may benefit from voyage cost cuts which can arise through their arrangements for bunkers and port charges. It is very common for companies operating large shipping fleets to hire their seasonal or periodical shortage of tonnage from the trip-charter market. This gives them the opportunity to operate the vessel for a single voyage in the same way that they would operate a vessel under a long-term time-charter contract.

The trip-charter market and the single-voyage charter market move very closely together and show similar fluctuations over time. This is because under both shipping contracts the ship is hired for a single voyage. Also, because both the charterer and the shipowner are fully aware of prevailing market conditions and transportation costs in that particular voyage, and try to maximise their utility function by minimising costs and maximising profit, any difference between the two types of contracts is arbitraged away and eliminated instantaneously. As a result, both charter contracts cost the same for the charterer and yield the same profit to the shipowner.

An example of a trip-charter fixture is given in the second row of Table 2.5. In this example *Dynamic*, a 29,332 dwt bulk carrier with Panamanian flag, is hired for a trip by 'Dantas'. Since the charterer is responsible for voyage costs (fuel, port charges, etc.) under a trip-charter contract, the vessel's speed (13 knots) and consumption (28 tons) figures are disclosed. In addition, the geographical location (Recalada), the window date (21–25 August) at which the charterer takes the delivery, the area for redelivery of the vessel (South Brazil), and the agreed charter rate per day (US$7500/day) are all specified.

2.4.4 Time-charter contracts

Under a time-charter contract, the charterer agrees to hire the vessel from the shipowner for a specified period of time (any period from a round trip to several years) and under certain conditions defined in the charter party. These conditions include: the vessel's performance specifications (speed, consumption, etc.); the condition and location of the vessel during delivery and redelivery; fuel on board; and trading areas, as well as several other terms. In this type of shipping contract, freight rates are agreed upon and paid on a US$/day basis, usually every 15 days or every month. Under a time-charter contract the charterer takes the commercial control of the vessel, and benefits from operational flexibility as well as security in transportation costs. This means that the charterer can use the vessel for several voyages on different routes as permitted by the contract, without worrying about delays and laytime penalties. Time-charter contracts also give the shipowner the benefit of reliance on a secure stream of revenue, which would not be the case if the ship were operated in the spot market. Under time-charter contracts, the charterer is responsible for the costs incurred during the voyage and the shipowner is responsible for all other costs.

In time-charter contracts, the terms of the charter party will define the owner's obligations for maintaining the vessel in a seaworthy condition for the use of the charterer. Any period in which the vessel becomes off-hire (not operational) will be excluded from the time-charter period and the owner has to reimburse the freight rate for that period. As the charterer is responsible for the voyage costs during the contract period, all the inventory, fuel and diesel oil on board at the beginning and end of the contract are estimated and differences are settled between the two parties.

The third row in Table 2.5 shows an example of a time-charter fixture. In this contract, *Darya Radhe*, a dry-bulk carrier, is hired by Kingston Maritime for a period of three to five months at US$12,000 per day. The vessel's specifications disclosed are: the speed (13.5 knots), the consumption at that speed (30 tons per day), the year that the ship was built (1999) and the deadweight capacity of the vessel. The time-charter fixture report is similar to the trip-charter fixture report, with some additional information such as the geographical location at which the ship is delivered to the charterer (Jorf Lasfar) as well as the approximate delivery date (end of August–early September 2000).

2.4.5 Bare-boat or demise charter contracts

In cases where the charterer wants to have full commercial as well as operational control of the vessel, but does not want to own the vessel, a bareboat charter contract is arranged. This type of contract allows the charterer to manage and run the vessel on a day-to-day basis and pay all the costs, including voyage, operation and cargo handling, but not the capital costs, which remain the owner's responsibility. Bare-boat charter contracts were very popular during the 1960s and 1970s, particularly with the oil majors. More recently, in the 1990s and 2000s, bareboat charters have become quite common in the container sector.

The major incentive for charterers to enter into such contracts is that they can have full control over the vessel without having the value of the vessel on their balance sheet. This is because excessive fluctuations in the price of the vessel can distort the figures in the balance sheet and in annual financial reports. On the other hand, the owners are investors who finance the vessel and do not want to get involved in the operation. The duration of this type of charter contract is normally long and may cover the whole economic life of the vessel. Freight rates are normally paid on a US$/day basis every month. Essentially, a bareboat charter is comparable to a financial lease agreement.

2.5 Definition and structure of costs in shipping

Owning and running a ship involves different costs, which can be divided into four categories: namely, capital costs; operation costs; voyage costs; and cargo-handling costs. These costs depend on various factors such as size, age, speed, type, and the financial structure of the purchased vessel. For example, larger vessels have higher voyage costs because they consume more fuel than smaller vessels, and likewise older vessels may consume more fuel than newer vessels.

2.5.1 Capital costs

Capital costs are those costs that cover interest and capital repayments and depend on the terms of finance of the purchase as well as the level of interest rates. There are different methods available to shipowners to finance their fleet, ranging from full equity to bank loans (asset-backed mortgages), bonds, public offerings and private placements. The availability of these funds to shipowners and shipping companies depends on their operational and financial capabilities, reputation and fleet size, among other factors. For example, highly reputable shipowners with a large fleet that can be used as collateral may enjoy better financing terms than a shipowner with relatively lower levels of credit and collateral.

A vessel's capital costs depend on the current and prevailing market conditions at the time of purchase as well as the terms of finance. For example, when freight rates are high and the shipowner has a secure long-term time-charter contract, providers of funds may relax their terms of finance, compared to periods when the market is tight and the purchaser does not have a secure contract. Furthermore, the amount of equity invested by the shipowner to purchase the vessel is inversely related to the capital cost of the vessel; that is, the lower the debt-to-equity ratio, the lower the capital costs. Finally, the relationship between shipowner and the financier and the creditworthiness of the shipowner are important factors in determining the terms of the loan and capital costs. Capital costs may vary over time due to changes in interest rates, based on which the vessel is financed (see Chapter 11 for more details on ship finance).

2.5.2 Operating costs

Operating costs or fixed costs are those incurred in the day-to-day running of the ship, whether the vessel is active or idle, and are generally the responsibility of the shipowner. The only exception is with bare-boat charters, under which the charterer has full commercial and operational control over the day-to-day operation of the vessel and, therefore, is responsible for operational costs. These costs include: crew wages, stores and provisions, maintenance and insurance and depend on the type, size and age of the vessel; management costs; and the company's strategy in manning and maintaining the vessel. The age of the ship is also an important factor because older vessels require more provision for repairs and maintenance and a larger crew. The manning costs depend on the company's policy, the flag under which the ship is registered and the classification society which is used to monitor the vessel's seaworthiness and class certificates. Although, efforts have been made to improve and maintain standards across different registries and classification societies, there are still discrepancies in manning scales, competency of crew, level of salaries and required maintenance levels of vessels. For example, requirements for manning vessels under certain flags of convenience may not be as strict as for those vessels sailing under more restricted registries. Therefore, similar ships, when operated under different flags, may have different operating costs. Finally, maintenance costs depend largely on owners' strategies; some owners prefer a well-maintained vessel or fleet, which involves a high level of maintenance spending, while others may prefer a low level of maintenance and expenditure.[9] In contrast to voyage costs, operating costs do not fluctuate over time, but they grow at a constant rate, which is normally in line with inflation.

2.5.3 Voyage costs

These are costs incurred during a particular voyage in which the ship is involved, and mainly include fuel costs, port charges, pilotage and canal dues. These costs depend on the specific voyage undertaken as well as the

---

[9] The choice of the maintenance level, among other factors, depends on the age of the vessel and the owner's maintenance policy. For example, owners who operate preventive maintenance policies may incur lower costs, while owners with no preventive maintenance policies may incur higher costs (see Stopford, 1997).

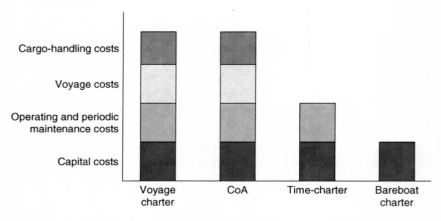

Figure 2.7   Shipowners' cost allocations under different charter contracts

type and size of the vessel. For example, fuel costs are normally higher for longer voyages compared to short ones and older vessels compared to new ones. Port charges and canal dues also depend on the size and type of vessel. For example, Suez Canal and Panama Canal tolls are based on the Net Suez Tonnage and Net Panama Tonnage[10] of the vessel, respectively.

2.5.4   Cargo-handling costs

These are costs involved in the loading, stowage, lightering and discharging of the cargo. Again these costs depend on the type, size and age of the vessel and, for spot voyages or CoAs, normally are the shipowner's responsibility unless it is specified otherwise in the contract. Figure 2.7 graphically summarises the allocation of costs under different shipping contracts. We can see, for instance, that in voyage-charter contracts, the shipowner is responsible for the voyage costs, whereas in time-charter contracts, the charterer is responsible for the voyage costs.

2.6   Spot freight-rate formation

As in any other market, the shipping freight market is also characterised by supply and demand schedules (functions), each of which depends on several factors that interact constantly so that the equilibrium freight rate can be determined. Therefore, in order to see how shipping freight rates are formed one has to study the supply and demand for freight services, their shapes, and the way they behave and interact.

---

[10] These are measurements for the calculation of canal tolls and are based on the Net Registered Tonnage of the vessel.

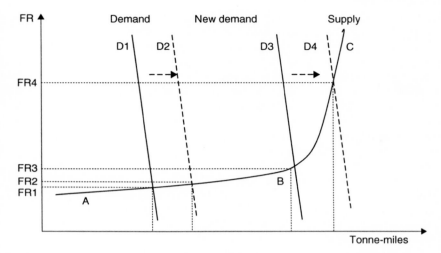

Figure 2.8 Market-clearing supply-demand framework in shipping freight-rate determination

Starting with the demand for shipping services, it has been well documented that this is a derived demand which depends on several factors, such as world economic activity, international seaborne trade, seasonal and cyclical changes for different commodities transported by sea, and the distance between sources of production, and consumption of commodities. On the other hand, the supply of shipping services is the amount (tonne-miles) of transportation service offered by shipowners based on the optimisation of their fleet revenue. The supply of shipping services at any point in time depends on the stock of fleet available for trading, shipbuilding production, scrapping rates and losses, fleet productivity, and the level of freight rates in the market. Therefore, freight rates at any point in time reflect the balance between supply and demand for shipping services which, in turn, depend on factors such as world economic activity, the stock of fleet, political events and international commodity trade (see Stopford 1997).

It has also been shown in the shipping economics literature that, while demand for ocean shipping is inelastic, the supply of shipping services is convex in shape due to the limitation of supply at any given point in time. This convexity in the shape of the supply curve implies that the supply for shipping services is highly elastic at low freight-rate levels (points A to B in Figure 2.8) and becomes inelastic when freight rates are at very high levels (points B to C in Figure 2.8). The reason for such bimodality of the elasticity of the shipping supply curve is the availability of excess capacity during periods when the market is in recession; that is, when vessels cannot find employment, are laid up, slow steam or even carry part cargo, and freight rates are at very low levels. Under such market conditions, any changes in demand due to external factors such as seasonal changes in trade or random shocks (events) can be absorbed by the extra available capacity and, therefore, the impact on freight rates would be relatively small. For instance, in Figure 2.8, assuming the demand curve is D_1 and given the supply function, the equilibrium freight rate is at FR_1. An increase in demand would shift the demand curve to, say, D_2 and, assuming that in the short term the supply curve for shipping services does not move, the new equilibrium freight rate will be determined through the new intersection between the demand and supply curves. This means that the freight rate will increase to a new level, FR_2, which represents a relatively small increase compared to the increase in demand.

As market conditions improve, vessels are employed until the point where the stock of fleet is fully utilised and any increase in supply is only possible by increasing productivity through increasing speed and shortening port stays and ballast legs. Under such conditions, the supply curve becomes almost vertical and inelastic. Consequently, any changes in demand due to external factors such as seasonal changes in trade, random events and the like would result in a relatively large change in freight-rate levels. For instance, in Figure 2.8, when freight rate is at FR_3, supply and demand schedules are very tight, and the fleet is fully utilised. In this case if, due to some external factors, demand for shipping services increases and the demand curve shifts from D_3 to D_4, then assuming supply in the short term is constant, the new equilibrium freight rate shoots up from FR_3 to FR_4, which is a relatively large increase. Therefore, it can be argued that market conditions, availability of fleet and level of freight rates are important factors influencing the magnitude of price changes and volatility in the market.

Figure 2.9 presents historical movements of voyage or spot freight rates, in US\$/mt, for Capesize vessels in four major routes: namely, iron ore from Tubarão, Brazil, to Japan and from Western Australia to Rotterdam, and coal from Queensland to Japan and from Richards Bay, South Africa, to Rotterdam. It can be seen that, while there are co-movements between the series in the long run, short-run movements are quite different across these voyage charter rate series. The existence of co-movements between the series in the long run can be explained by the fact that these rates are driven by the same common factor; that is, the aggregate demand for international commodity transport and general supply conditions for Capesize vessels and their services. Differences between the behaviour of voyage freight rates for Capesize ships in the short term are due to some distinct factors related to trade in a specific route, port conditions and the availability of tonnage over a short period in that specific route.

Similarly, historical voyage freight rates for differently sized tankers in Worldscale are plotted in Figure 2.10. It can be seen that, generally, freight rates are higher for smaller vessels compared to larger ones, in both Worldscale and US\$/mt terms. This is because of the economies of scale in hiring

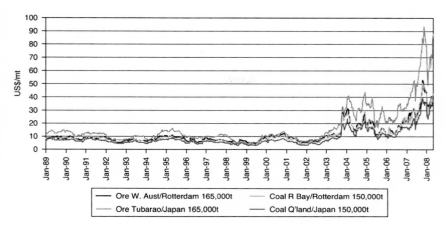

Figure 2.9 Historical spot freight rates for four Capesize routes
Source: Clarkson's SIN.

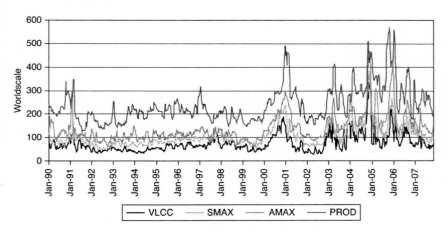

Figure 2.10 Historical spot freight rates for tankers of different sizes
Source: Clarkson's SIN.

and using larger vessels, which reduces the US$/mt cost of transportation. It is also clear that there are co-movements between the spot rates in the long run while, in the short run, freight rates for tankers with different sizes behave quite differently. The co-movement of the series in the long run is because rates are driven by the aggregate demand for international oil transport as well as supply of tanker shipping services. Differences between the behaviour of freight rates in the short term emanate from the specific factors affecting the trade in those routes that differently sized tankers serve over short periods.

2.7   Time-charter rate formation

While voyage or spot freight rates are determined through the interaction between current supply and demand schedules and conditions for shipping services, time-charter or period rates are believed to be determined through the market agents' expectations about future spot rates. The theory which relates the spot rates to time-charter rates is known as the expectations hypothesis and the term-structure relationship. This theory was developed in the bond and interest-rate markets and was first adapted and used to explain the relationship between spot and period charter rate in shipping by Zannetos (1966) and later on by Glen et al. (1981), Hale and Vanags (1989) and Kavussanos and Alizadeh (2002b), among others. The 'term-structure relationship' is based on the no-arbitrage argument, which states that the agents (shipowner or charterers) should be indifferent in entering into a long-term charter contract or a series of spot/voyage contracts over the life of the long-term contract. In other words, it is assumed that the freight market is efficient and agents should not be able to make excess profit by choosing to operate under either type of contract consistently.

To illustrate the term-structure relationship in the shipping freight market and the formation of time-charter rates, consider the following example. At any point of time, a shipowner has the option to operate under a n period TC^n contract or a series of spot contracts, each with a duration of m periods ($m < n$ and $k = n/m$) and a rate of FR. Obviously, the shipowner may know what is the freight rate for the first voyage, but has to form some form of expectation about the future evolution of spot rates over the life of the TC^n contract. Let us assume these are $E_t FR_{t+i}$, where E_t is the expectation operator at time t, and also that the shipowner has to pay VC_t as voyage cost for the first voyage and expected $E_t VC_{t+i}$ for subsequent voyages. Then the shipowner should be able to compare the TC earnings given the expected earnings from the spot-market operation. Therefore, assuming that shipping freight markets are efficient, there should not be any difference between the discounted present value of earnings from an n period TC^n contract and the discounted present value of earnings from a series of spot voyages, each with a duration of m periods. This can be written mathematically as:

$$\sum_{i=1}^{k} \frac{TC_t^n}{(1+r)^i} = \sum_{i=1}^{k} \frac{(E_t FR_{t+im}^m - E_t VC_{t+im}^m)}{(1+r)^i} \quad k = n/m \quad (2.1)$$

where, r is the discount rate, $E_t FR_{t+im}^m$ is the expected spot charter rate at time t of a contract which lasts over m periods from $t + im$ to $t + (i+1)m$, and $k = n/m$ is a positive integer indicating the number of spot-charter contracts in the life of a time-charter contract. $E_t VC_{t+im}^m$ is the expected voyage costs. The difference between expected spot rates, $E_t FR_{t+im}^m$ and expected voyage costs, $E_t VC_{t+im}^m$, reflects the expected earnings in the spot operation on a daily basis, or the expected time-charter equivalent of spot rates. Equation (2.1) can be used to derive the n period TC rate at time t, in terms of expected spot or voyage charter rates, expected voyage costs, and discount rate as

$$TC_t^n = \sum_{i=1}^{k} \frac{(E_t FR_{t+im}^m - E_t VC_{t+im}^m)}{(1+r)^i} \bigg/ \sum_{i=1}^{k} \frac{1}{(1+r)^i} \quad k = n/m \qquad (2.2)$$

However, one important difference between the spot and TC operations is the security of the period contract compared to the spot operation, because under a TC contract the shipowner is guaranteed to receive TC rates whatever happens to the market over the life of the period contract.[11] In contrast, under the spot operations the earnings of the shipowner may vary depending on the future condition of the spot market. Therefore, there is a risk element which should be considered in the spot and TC rates relationship. The risk element can be interpreted as the price that the shipowner is willing to pay to pass the uncertainty of the spot market to the charterer. This is also known as the risk premium, ϕ, which is in fact a discount in the TC rate, which the shipowner is prepared to forego in the TC market compared to the spot-market earnings, to obtain a secure long term TC contract. Therefore, we can write

$$TC_t^n = \left(\sum_{i=1}^{k} \frac{(E_t FR_{t+im}^m - E_t VC_{t+im}^m)}{(1+r)^i} \bigg/ \sum_{i=1}^{k} \frac{1}{(1+r)^i} \right) - \phi_t \quad k = n/m \qquad (2.3)$$

A number of arguments have been put forward in the literature as to why the risk premium term enters into the relationship. First, shipowners operating in the spot market are generally exposed to higher price risk in comparison to those operating in the time-charter market because spot rates show higher fluctuations compared to time-charter rates. Secondly, for a shipowner operating in the spot market, there is always some degree of unemployment risk when it is not possible to fix a voyage contract for a period of time. Thirdly, there are cases when the owner has to relocate the vessel from one port to the other for a new spot charter contract; this involves substantial time and costs. Finally, if voyage spot rates (rather than trip-charter rates) are compared to time-charter rates, shipowners are also exposed to voyage (mainly bunker) cost fluctuations. Thus, shipowners operating in the time-charter market are essentially accepting lower rates in return for a secure stream of income. On the other hand, charterers are willing to enter into a time-charter contracts if

---

[11] One element of risk here is credit risk; in other words the risk that the charterer may not honour the contract if there is a significant drop in freight rates in the market. However, we do not consider this type of risk here. Credit risk is discussed extensively in Chapter 12.

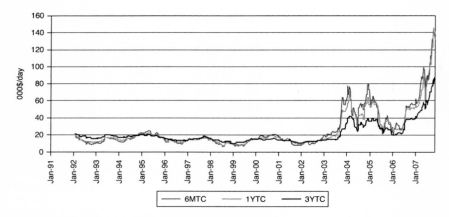

Figure 2.11   Historical six-month, one-year and three-year time-charter rates for Capesize dry-bulk carriers
Source: Clarkson's SIN.

the discount forgone by the shipowners is enough to cover the risk associated in operating in the spot market.

Furthermore, the views and requirements of the banks and lenders in shipping finance is another important factor in the shipowner's decision to operate in the spot or the time-charter market. Financiers have a different view of clients (shipowners) who are committed to long-term shipping contracts when financing a ship purchase or newbuilding, since this ensures a relatively secure stream of income for the shipowner and reduces the probability of repayment default. Thus, shipowners may be prepared to forego a certain amount of earnings when fixing their vessel on a long-term contract, as opposed to short-term ones, in order to fulfill the lender's requirements for the loan. This argument can be quite important during periods of market uncertainty, suggesting that the premium might be time-varying (see Kavussanos and Alizadeh, 2002b).

Figures 2.11 and 2.12 plot six-month, one-year, and three-year time-charter rates for Capesize and Panamax dry-bulk carriers respectively over the period 1992 to 2008. In general, time-charter rates seem to show fewer short-term fluctuations compared to spot rates. This is expected, as long-term charter contracts have been argued to be a weighted average of expected spot rates over the life span of the long-term contract (see, for example Zannetos, 1966; Glen et al, 1981). Therefore, fluctuations in period rates are expected to be smoothed through the aggregation of expected spot rates, which is thought to be the underlying assumption in the formation of period rates. Moreover, period time-charter contracts are normally used by industrial and trading firms for the transportation of industrial commodities, such as iron ore and minerals, which more or less follow regular trading patterns over the year. In contrast to time-charter contracts, voyage charter contracts are generally

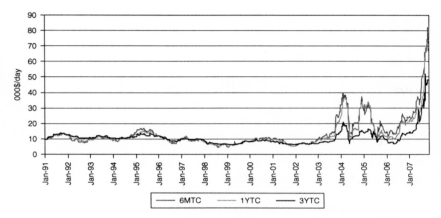

Figure 2.12 Historical values of six-month, one-year and three-year time-charter rates for Panamax dry-bulk carriers
Source: Clarkson's SIN.

used for transportation of commodities with irregular and cyclical patterns, such as grain (see Stopford, 1997). It is also well known that industrial charterers use time-charter contracts in order to meet most of their long-term transportation requirements and use spot contracts for their extra needs, which might be seasonal or cyclical. This type of chartering strategy affects the supply, demand and behaviour of prices of shipping contracts of different duration. It seems that the longer the duration of the contract, the smoother the rates.

Furthermore, the plot of time-charter rates of dry-bulk carriers indicates a large increase in the levels and volatility of these rates over the past few years. More precisely, while until mid-2003 time-charter rates for Capesize vessels fluctuated roughly between US$10,000/day to US$25,000/day, and for Panamax vessels between US$6000/day and US$18,000/day, after mid-2003, fluctuations in time-charter rates for these ships have increased and rates have reached levels of US$140,000/day for Capesize and US$75,000/day for Panamax ships. The main reason time-charter rates for dry-bulk carriers were pushed to such unprecedented levels was the increase in demand and shortage of supply in recent years, along with some periods of congestion in certain ports, which reduced fleet productivity and supply for shipping services.

2.7.1 Time-charter equivalent of spot rates (TCE)

It was mentioned earlier that methods of payment, freight calculations and cost allocations vary depending on the type of charter contract. This is because, in contrast to time-charter contracts, under a spot contract the shipowner is responsible for voyage costs and, as a result, these will be included in spot freight rates, while time-charter contracts are exclusive of voyage costs. In other words, time-charter rates reflect the net freight earnings through shipping operations. Therefore, shipowners tend to calculate time-charter equivalent of spot rates (TCE) whenever there is a need to compare available offers in the spot market, as well as to compare earnings between spot and time-charter operations.

In order to calculate the TCE of a spot fixture in a particular voyage (route) for the vessel, first the spot rate (US$/mt) is used to calculate the total freight payment, by multiplying it by the amount of cargo. The total voyage costs for that particular voyage (port charges, canal dues and bunker costs) are then deducted from the total freight payment and the result is divided by the number of days for a round trip, in that route, based on the vessel's particulars. The resulting figure, which is now expressed on a US$/day basis, is known as time-charter equivalents of spot rates.

2.8   Seasonal behaviour of freight rates

It was argued earlier that the demand for shipping services is a derived demand which depends on the economics of the commodities transported, world economic activity and the related macroeconomic variables of major economies. Some of these macroeconomic variables have been shown to be highly seasonal.[12] The same is also true for trade figures in several commodities; for instance, there are seasonal elements in the grain and petroleum trade. This means that the seasonal nature of trade in certain commodities can be transmitted to shipping freight rates and prices. For instance, Figure 2.13 presents the Baltic Dirty and Clean Tanker indices (described later in Chapter 4), over the period from August 1998 to February 2008, along with bars which highlight the cold-winter season, that is, October to January every year. It can be seen that freight rates show a significant increase in the form of sharp spikes over these months, especially after 2002.

Such seasonal behaviour in freight rates has been documented by Denning et al. (1994) who found that there are elements of seasonality in the Baltic Freight Index (BFI),[13] and by Kavussanos and Alizadeh (2001; 2002a) on the seasonal behaviour of dry-bulk and tanker freight rates, respectively; see as well Alizadeh and Nomikos (2002) for a review of studies on the seasonality in shipping freight rates. The latter studies model seasonal behaviour of freight rates and compares them: a) across differently sized vessels; b) across freight contracts with different maturities; and c) under different market conditions. The results of their study on seasonal behaviour of freight rates for

---

[12] A time series, measured more than once a year (at monthly, quarterly or semi-annual intervals, for example), is said to contain a seasonal components when there are systematic patterns in the series at the measured points (seasons) within the year.
[13] BFI was a weighted average index of spot and trip-charter rates in 11 routes representing freight rates in the dry-bulk sector of the shipping industry. It has now been replaced by the Baltic Dry Index (BDI); shipping indices are discussed in Chapter 4.

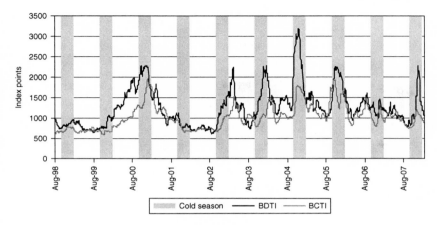

Figure 2.13   Seasonal behaviour of tanker freight rates
Source: Baltic Exchange.

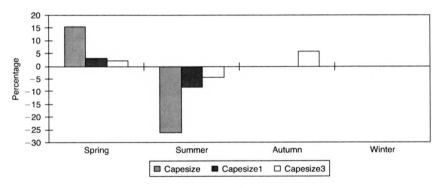

Figure 2.14   Comparison of seasonal changes in freight rates for Capesize dry-bulk carriers
Note: Capesize, Capesize1 and Capesize3 represent the spot, one-year and three-year TC rates, respectively.

three differently sized dry-bulk carriers are summarised in graphical form in Figures 2.14, 2.15 and 2.16. Each bar indicates the average percentage increase or decrease in the freight rate over that particular season. There are several points which can be observed here.

First, freight rates for all dry-bulk carriers increase significantly in the first quarter and decrease significantly in summer months. This may be due to two reasons; the reduction in the level of industrial production and trade in mid-summer, or a switch by spot operators to time-charter operation after the end of the Japanese and harvest-led spring upsurge, which causes an oversupply

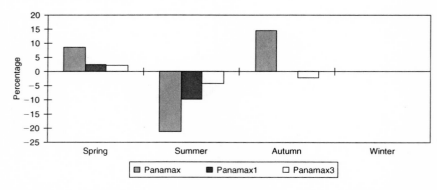

Figure 2.15 Comparison of seasonal changes in freight rates for Panamax dry-bulk carriers
Note: Panamax, Panamax1 and Panamax3 represent the spot, one-year and three-year TC rates, respectively.

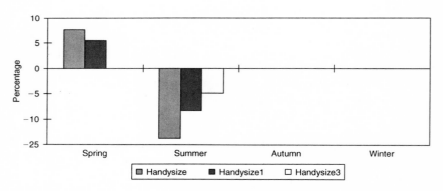

Figure 2.16 Comparison of seasonal changes in freight rates for Handysize dry-bulk carriers
Note: Handysize, Handysize1 and Handysize3 represent the spot, one-year and three-year TC rates, respectively.

in the time-charter market. Also, since time-charter rates are linked to the current and expected spot rates, a drop in the spot market is transmitted to the time-charter market accordingly. There is no seasonal change in the third and the fourth quarter of the year; the only exception is an increase in Panamax spot rates in the autumn.

Second, for all vessel types, the seasonal spring increase and summer drop in freight rates decline as the duration of contracts increases. For instance, the impact of seasonal fluctuations is more pronounced for the spot rates and declines as we move to the one-year and three-year time-charters, across all types of vessels. This is because one-year time-charter rates, say, are formed as the expected future spot rates over the year (see Section 2.7). Therefore, one would expect that one-year time-charter rates would have already incorporated expected future seasonal variations and are smoother than spot rates. On the other hand, spot rates reflect the current market conditions, and any seasonal change in demand for shipping has a direct impact on spot or short-term rates.

Third, the magnitude of seasonal change is related to the size of ships; that is, freight rates for larger vessels show relatively greater seasonal change compared to smaller ones. The weaker seasonal increase or decline in average freight rates for smaller-sized vessels may be attributed to their flexibility, which enables them to switch between trades and routes more easily compared to the larger ships.

Finally, seasonal changes in freight rates for all dry-bulk carriers are more pronounced during a freight-market expansion and less distinct when the market is in recession. This is in line with the shape of the supply and demand curve for freight services in freight rate determination as shown in Figure 2.8. More precisely, when the market is in the expansion phase, supply is inelastic and any seasonal change in demand can result in a sharp change in freight rates. When the market is in recession, and there is spare capacity and tonnage, the supply function for freight services is elastic, and any seasonal change in demand for freight services can be absorbed by excess supply, which results in a moderate change in freight rates.

2.9   The market for ships

The market for ships consists of three different sub-markets, namely: the newbuilding market; the second-hand market; and the scrap market. Almost all ship sales and purchases (S&P) are carried out through specialist S&P brokers, with the exception of newbuildings, which may be ordered by investors to shipyards directly. The sale and purchase of ships is a lengthy process, which can take anything between a few weeks and several months to complete. This process involves different stages of placing the ship in the market, the negotiation of price and conditions of contract, preparing the memorandum of agreement, inspections and final closing of the deal, after which the ship is delivered to the buyer.

2.9.1   Factors determining ship prices

The factors affecting the price of a vessel can be classified as vessel-specific and market-specific. Vessel-specific factors are those related to the particulars and condition of the vessel. These are size, type, age and general condition, as well as quality of design, build, equipment and engine. In general, we expect larger vessel to be more expensive than smaller ones, older vessels to be less expensive than newer vessels, and certain types of specialist vessels (LNG carriers, RoRo vessels, cruise liners) to be more expensive than conventional box-shaped bulk carriers. In addition, the general condition and state of the vessel is important because well-maintained vessels tend to be more employable compared to those that are not maintained properly. The age of the vessel is another important factor in the determination of the second-hand price, and generally older ships are less expensive than modern ones. This is not only because ships are subject to depreciation and, as time passes, lose part of their value,[14] but the advances in shipbuilding technology over time mean that more modern ships are built with better specifications in terms of fuel consumption and efficiency as well as operating efficiency.[15]

The market condition is also an important factor in the determination of vessel prices. It is generally believed and documented in the shipping-economics literature that ships are capital assets which generate income and they are priced according to their expected profitability (see Chapter 13 for more details) using an asset-pricing model. This means that ship prices depend on their current and expected operational earnings over their economic life. What determines current and expected earnings for a ship is the general state of the freight market. Therefore, current and expected freight-rate levels and market conditions are among the most important factors in ship-price formation.

2.9.2   The newbuilding market

As the name suggests, the newbuilding market is the market for newly built ships or ships which are ordered by shipping companies, shipowners and investors to be delivered after the construction period, which takes between several months and a few years. The perfect-market condition also holds for this market as not only do international shipowners take several quotations from various shipyards before placing orders, but there are also no barriers to shipyards marketing their products internationally and competing with other shipyards. Newbuilding prices are also determined through supply and demand factors for new ships and are generally negotiated and settled between investors and shipyards. In general, newbuilding prices depend on the market condition and other determinants such as steel prices, the level of freight rates, the backlog of the shipyard (or the shipbuilding industry in general), terms of contract, and so on. For example, in a good market, when freight rates are high and shipyards' order-books are full, newbuilding

---

[14] Ships are considered to be capital assets with limited life of normally 20 to 40 years, depending on the type, size and quality of build. Therefore, they are depreciated at a relatively high rate.

[15] Modern, efficient ships not only consume less fuel for propulsion in comparison to older ships, but they are designed to operate with a smaller crew, which also reduces operating costs. Generally, modern ships benefit from better design and material quality which requires less maintenance and is also supposed to elongate their economic life.

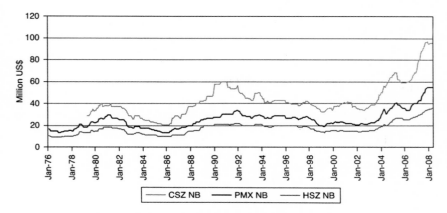

Figure 2.17 Newbuilding prices for dry-bulk carriers of different sizes
Source: Clarkson's SIN.

prices may rise considerably, whereas when the freight market is depressed and shipbuilding activity is low, newbuilding prices may fall rapidly. This is because shipyards are willing to accept orders at very low prices in order to survive and avoid downsizing or even closure.

Figure 2.17 plots monthly newbuilding prices for three sizes of dry-bulk carriers over the period January 1976 to December 1997 – except Capesize prices, which are available from April 1979. It can be seen that newbuilding prices vary by vessel size but show similar behaviour over time. In fact, it can be argued that these series follow similar patterns and move together in the long run, that is, price levels follow a similar cyclical pattern. For example, price levels for all sizes of vessel show peaks between 1980 and 1982, and 1989 and 1992, while there are troughs in price levels between 1976 and 1979, 1983 and 1988 and 1992 and 1997. The cyclical behaviour of newbuilding prices is believed to be the combined result of fluctuations in world economic activity (international seaborne trade) and the investment (ordering) behaviour of shipowners (see, for example Tinbergen, 1934; Vergottis, 1988; Stopford, 1997). More precisely, when investors expect the freight market to rise, they place new orders to take advantage of the positive market prospects. Therefore, there is excess demand for new vessels, order books grow and prices rise. By the time the new vessels are delivered: i) there might be an excess tonnage in the market due to excessive orders; ii) the freight market may collapse due to excess supply, both from reduction in scrapping old vessels and the arrival of new deliveries; or iii) demand for shipping services may collapse due to a drop in world economic activity. This effect is then transmitted back to the shipbuilding market through the investment decisions of agents, reducing the demand for newbuilding and

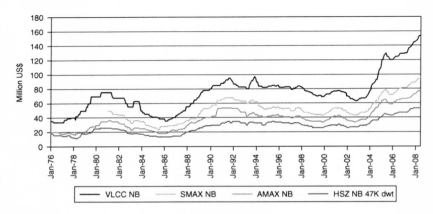

Figure 2.18   Historical newbuilding prices for tankers of different sizes
Source: Clarkson's SIN

depressing prices for new ships. Shipbuilding cycles, which are caused by the mismatch between investors' expectations and global economic activity, have been repeatedly observed in the shipping industry. Similar conclusions emerge when we consider newbuilding prices for tanker vessels in Figure 2.18.

2.9.3   The second-hand market

The second-hand market, better known as the 'sale and purchase' (S&P) market, is the market for vessels that are ready for trade and aged anything between a year and 20 years or more. In terms of liquidity, about 1000 vessels are bought and sold in the S&P market every year, of which about 30 per cent are dry-bulk carriers and 30 per cent tanker ships, that is, about one of each vessel every day. The S&P market is known as one of the most competitive markets in the world because it is an open market, and buyers and sellers are under no obligation to follow any sort of price restrictions. Therefore, prices are determined through supply and demand conditions that in turn depend on current and expected world economic activity, current and expected freight market conditions, current and expected bunker prices, as well as expected ship prices. In other words, second-hand prices directly depend on the profitability of the market.[16]

Figure 2.19 presents monthly prices for three different sizes of five-year-old dry-bulk carriers over the period January 1976 to April 2008, while Figure 2.20 presents monthly prices for different sizes of five-year-old second-hand tankers. A visual inspection reveals that dry-bulk second-hand prices move together in the long run. This is the case as the price series are thought

---

[16] See, for example, Beenstock (1985), Beenstock and Vergottis (1989) and Strandenes (1984).

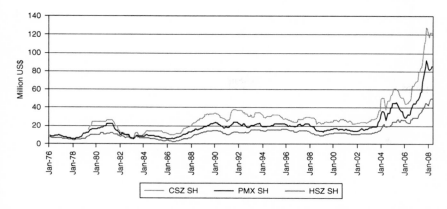

Figure 2.19 Historical second-hand prices of five-year-old dry-bulk carriers of different sizes
Source: Clarkson's SIN.

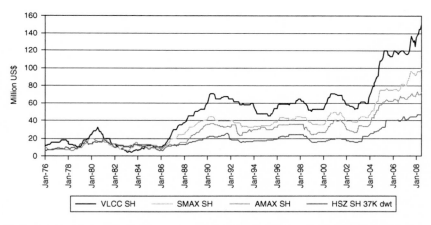

Figure 2.20 Historical second-hand prices of five-year-old tankers of different sizes
Source: Clarkson's SIN.

to be linked through a common stochastic trend, that is, world economic activity and the volume of international seaborne trade (see Glen, 1997). However, short-run dynamics of second-hand prices do not seem to be identical. These differences are due to variations in the demand for differently sized vessels and the profitability of the freight market for each size because current and expected freight rate levels are argued to be the major determinants of second-hand prices.

Another interesting point which can be observed from the evolution of the price series is that when the market is in recession (that is, when prices are at their lowest levels), the three price series converge and the difference between prices reduces compared to when the market is good. For example, during the 1982 to 1986 recession, prices for Handysize, Panamax and Capesize vessels seemed to converge. The price difference between a second-hand Capesize and second-hand Handysize during this period was less than US$8m. On the other hand, when the market is in expansion phase, second-hand prices diverge as larger vessels become relatively more expensive than smaller ones. For example, between 1988 and 1994, the difference between second-hand prices for Capesize and Handysize vessels was between of US$15m and US$20m. Since it is the operational profitability that determines second-hand prices, the divergence and convergence of prices can be explained by the relative profitability of these vessels under different market conditions. For example, larger vessels generate more revenue and operating profit during expansion periods as they can be used for carrying larger amounts of cargo; however, they bear the higher risk of unemployment during recessions due to their operational inflexibility. In contrast to larger vessels, smaller bulk carriers are not as profitable during periods of market expansion, but they are more flexible and can switch between trades during recessions. Therefore, smaller vessels are more likely to be employed in tight markets in comparison to larger vessels, and generate reasonable profit even in bad times.

2.9.4   The scrap or demolition market

The third market for ships is where ships not economical to operate are sold for demolition or scrapping. Ship-breakers buy scrap vessels from shipowners for their scrap metal on a US$/ldt (light displacement tons)[17] basis, and dismantle them to reuse the steel and other parts and equipment. The age at which ships are sold for scrap varies over time and largely depends on the condition of the freight market as well as the second-hand, the newbuilding and the scrap markets. For example, when freight rates are low and the expectations for future market improvements are not so positive, owners of relatively inefficient vessels, which may have been laid up due to unemployment, may be forced to sell their vessels for scrap to avoid further losses. Consequently the increase in supply of scrap vessels causes the scrap price to fall. On the other hand, when freight rates are relatively high and there is a shortage in the supply of shipping services, even older, less efficient vessels could be profitable; therefore, there may not be any pressure to scrap such vessels. As a result, there will be a shortage of supply in the scrap market, which causes the scrap price to rise.

Figures 2.21 and 2.22 plot the monthly scrap prices, in millions of $US, for different sizes of dry-bulk and tanker vessels respectively over the period

---

[17] Light displacement tons (ldt) stands for the actual weight of the ship in tons, without any cargo, bunkers and fresh water on board.

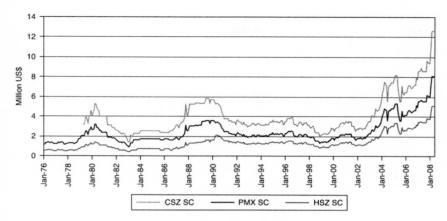

Figure 2.21 Historical scrap prices for dry-bulk carriers of different sizes
Source: Clarkson's SIN.

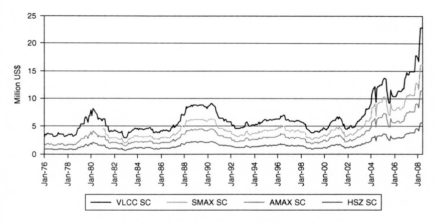

Figure 2.22 Historical scrap prices for tankers of different sizes
Source: Clarkson's SIN.

January 1976 to February 2008. It can be seen that, in general, scrap prices in both sectors tend to follow the trend in shipping freight markets. Scrap values of larger vessels are higher than those of smaller vessels in both sectors because of their greater steel content and light displacement weight. In addition, scrap prices for all types of ships seem to have reached record highs in recent years, due to bullish freight-market conditions, increases in world scrap steel prices, and the limited number of vessels available for scrapping. Furthermore, it seems that scrap prices for larger vessels show relatively greater variation compared to those of smaller ships. This is evident from

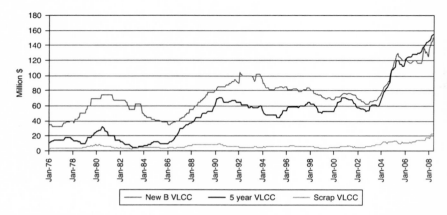

Figure 2.23   Historical newbuilding, five-year-old second-hand, and scrap prices for VLCC tankers
Source: Clarkson's SIN.

the range within which scrap prices fluctuate. For instance, while historical scrap values of Capesize vessels vary between US$1.5m and US$12m, historical scrap prices for Handysize dry-bulk carriers vary between US$0.3m and US$5m. A similar pattern can be observed for scrap prices for tankers.

Figure 2.23 plots the historical newbuilding, second-hand and scrap prices for VLCC tankers. It can be seen that newbuilding and scrap prices set an upper and a lower barrier for VLCC prices, respectively, and second-hand prices for five-year-old VLCCs fluctuate within this band over time. However, an interesting point to note is that when the shipping market was in recession (1982 to 1986), second-hand prices were closer to scrap prices, and when the market was at its peak (1988 to 1990, and 2002 to 2006) second-hand prices were close to newbuilding prices. Furthermore, when the tanker market is exceptionally profitable, and the order book for newbuildings is full, the second-hand price can exceed the newbuilding price, as was the case in the period 2006 to 2008. This is mainly because investors are prepared to pay a premium for immediate delivery in the second-hand market in order to avoid waiting a relatively long time for newbuilding delivery. In recent years, given record order-book levels and delivery times of four to five years (up to 2012 and 2013 for orders placed in 2008), buying a second-hand ship was preferred to placing a newbuilding order. This is because, given the freight-rate levels, investors can benefit now from high freight revenue and recoup part of their investment rather than waiting for newbuilding delivery in the future. A similar pattern can be observed in the market for Panamax dry-bulk carriers, presented in Figure 2.24, where second-hand prices in 2007 and 2008 reached US$80m to US$90m, while newbuilding prices hovered around US$50m.

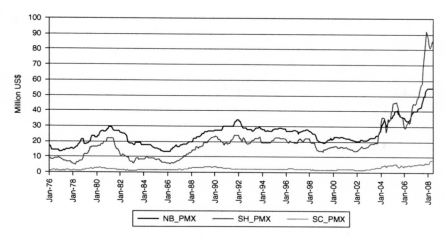

Figure 2.24 Historical newbuilding, five-year-old second-hand, and scrap prices for Panamax dry-bulk carriers
Source: Clarkson's SIN.

The higher sensitivity of second-hand prices to market conditions implies that second-hand prices are more volatile than newbuilding and scrap prices. However, scrap or demolition prices for ships generally depend on world scrap steel prices and ship-breaking activities. This means that the volatility of scrap prices for ships is linked to the volatility and changes in the market for scrap steel, in addition to the changes in the freight market. The statistical properties of ship prices are discussed more extensively in Chapters 3 and 13.

2.10   Summary and conclusions

The shipping industry is an integral part of the international trading system and its function is to facilitate international trade through connecting sources of supply and demand for commodities. The aim of this chapter was to provide an overall review of this industry as well as the causes and results of segmentation of the industry into many sub-sectors. In particular, we discussed the changes and growth in each sub-market and presented the trade patterns for each type of ship. We also introduced different types of freight contracts used in ocean transportation and explored the formation of freight rates under voyage and time-charter agreements. It was mentioned that while voyage-charter contracts are determined through the interaction between the supply and demand for shipping services, period or time-charter rates are formed on the basis of expected future voyage-charter rates and voyage costs. In addition, in the formation of time-charter rates agents tend to consider market risk and incorporate such uncertainty in their decision-making process. As a result, time-charter earnings are in general lower than voyage-charter earnings because they incorporate a negative time-varying risk premium.

The seasonal movements in shipping freight rates and differences in seasonality across different types of contracts and vessel size were also high-lighted. Furthermore, we explored the market for ships and factors which affect ship prices. It was argued that the market for ships is divided into the newbuilding, second-hand and scrap markets, and it was shown that prices in each sub-market are determined through both vessel-specific and market-specific factors. In addition, while ship prices in each market are linked to the general condition of the freight markets and the profitability of shipping operation, there are other factors, such as delivery time and scrap-steel prices, that can influence the price level in each sub-market.

3
Statistical Tools for Risk Analysis and Modelling

3.1 Introduction

Shipping is an integral part of the transportation and logistics network and has always been considered as one of the most volatile industries, where agents are exposed to substantial financial and business risks. These risks emanate from fluctuations in freight rates, bunker prices, the price of the vessels, and even from fluctuations in the level of interest rates and exchange rates. All these factors affect the cash flows of shipping investment and operations and, as such, have a profound impact on the profitability of shipping companies as well as their business viability. Therefore, having a good understanding of risk and its dynamics is important in the setting up and implementation of effective risk-management techniques, efficient portfolio construction and asset allocation, derivatives pricing and trading, as well as value-at-risk (VaR) estimation and risk monitoring.

In this chapter, we present different statistical tools that are used for analysis of risk and modelling the dynamics of volatility of variables in shipping markets. In particular, we present descriptive statistics which are used to explain the distributional properties of variables such as freight rates and ship prices. Such analysis is important in risk modelling and measurement and, as such, is an integral part of the risk-management process. We further discuss and explore recently developed models which are used to capture the dynamics of volatility of shipping variables. These techniques include: 'exponentially weighted average variance' (EWAV) estimates; 'autoregressive conditional heteroscedasticity' (ARCH) and 'generalised ARCH' (GARCH) models; 'regime-switching GARCH' and 'stochastic volatility' models; as well as 'multivariate GARCH' models. Finally, we present the application of different dynamic volatility models in forecasting freight rate volatilities.

3.2 Data sources and data-collection methods

Any statistical analysis requires the collection and processing of data, examination and testing of variables in univariate or multivariate form and, finally, interpretation of the results. Therefore, the availability of reliable and consistent data is important for any statistical analysis and modelling exercise, as well as for forecasting, for investment decision-making and risk management. For example, knowing the price of a tanker at different points in time will provide information on whether the price, as it stands today, is relatively high or low compared to the past prices for this type of ship. In addition, comparison of ship prices over time will provide a measure of relativity in terms of how the price of the tanker fares amongst a number of alternative shipping investments, as well as grounds for the decision on how much of this type of vessel to hold in a portfolio of assets (fleet).

The first step in statistical analysis is to collect and process either new data, referred to as 'primary data', or an existing data set, referred to as 'secondary data', in relation to the question of interest, or the underlying variable. Primary data may be collected directly from the source through recording values of variables (prices, rates, etc.), statistical experiments, or survey methods (such as questionnaires). The distinguishing feature of primary data is that it is collected for a specific project and for the first time. As a result, primary data may take a long time to collect and might be expensive. Secondary data, in contrast, is the data which is obtained from sources other than the original source. Several organisations have specialised in collecting and processing primary data, and then disseminating them to the public, individuals, businesses, financial institutions, governmental departments and research institutes. For instance, data vendors such as Datastream, Bloomberg, Reuters, and many others provide a wide range of information and data on economic variables and indicators, financial price data, trade statistics, and company reports and accounts. In shipping markets, the Baltic Exchange, Clarkson's Shipping Intelligence Network, Lloyd's Maritime Information Unit, and other firms such as Fearnleys and Drewry provide data and statistics related to the international shipping and maritime industry.

Over the past few decades a number of firms in the shipping industry, particularly ship-brokers, have started collecting shipping-related information and news to set up databases and produce up-to-date periodic market reports and industry analysis. Among these are the Baltic Exchange, Clarkson Research Studies (CRS), the International Maritime Exchange (Imarex), Simpson, Spence and Young Consultancy and Research Ltd (SSY), Lloyds Maritime Information Unit (LMIU), the Institute of Shipping Economics and Logistics (ISL) in Bremen (Germany), and Fearnleys (Norway). Lloyds Shipping Economist (LSE) and Lloyd's Ship Manager (LSM) use the LMIU database, which contains information on almost every fixture, sale and purchase, new order and delivery, demolition and loss, and vessel movements in both wet- and dry-bulk markets. Clarkson's Shipping Intelligence Network (SIN) also provides a vast amount of shipping-related information and publishes reports on a weekly, monthly and semi-annual basis.

Having collected the relevant data on the problem under investigation, it is also important to recognise whether the data is a 'population' or a 'sample'. Population can be defined as the total collection of data for the problem at hand, which encompasses every observation or measurement of a variable or variables. In practice, it is usually very difficult and time-consuming to collect the information or data about the total population. Therefore, we normally collect information about a subset of population, known as the sample.[1] For example, a sample of Panamax ship prices refers to prices for this type of vessel over a particular period or a sample of Capesize time-charter rates refers to a series of observations on time-charter prices for Capesize vessels over a particular period of time.

3.3 Descriptive statistics and moments of a variable

In statistical analysis, we use single numbers known as descriptive statistics to summarise and report the information about the distributional properties of a set of data or a variable. These statistics, which relate to measures of location, dispersion and shape of the distribution, are also called 'moments of the variable' and can be calculated directly from the original data set. The first four moments of a variable which are used to characterise its distribution are: the mean; variance; coefficient of skewness; and coefficient of kurtosis. The following sections are devoted to discussion of how each of these moments can be calculated and be interpreted.

3.3.1 Measures of central tendency (location)

Central tendency of any variable is the information or indication as to where the variable is most likely to be or which value the variable is most likely to take. There are different methods of measuring central tendency of a variable, but the most important ones are: the mean (arithmetic average), the mode and the median.

The arithmetic mean

This is the simple arithmetic average of all the observations in a sample or a population and reflects the average value of the variable. Arithmetic mean is the most widely used measure of central tendency, but it can be affected by extreme values in the data set because observations are given equal weight

---

[1] In order to draw correct inferences from a sample about the population, the sample should be a fair representative of the population and its characteristics. There are various ways to select a sample out of population data such as random sampling, systematic sampling, stratified sampling, etc. However, the important point is that the fundamental principle that the sample has to be a fair representative of the population should be maintained. This is important if we want the results of the analysis to be unbiased and be extendable to the whole population.

when calculating the simple average. Depending on whether we are dealing with a population or a sample data set, we use the following formulae and notation in calculating and reporting the mean.

Sample mean	Population mean
$$\bar{x} = \frac{\sum_{i=1}^{n} x_i}{n}$$	$$\mu = \frac{\sum_{i=1}^{N} x_i}{N}$$

Where x_i is the value of the variable for observation number i, μ is the population mean, $\bar{x}$ is the mean of the sample, N is the number of observations in the population, and n is the number of observations in the sample.

The median

The median of a variable, which is arranged in order of magnitude, is either the middle value, when there is an odd number of observations, or the arithmetic mean of the two middle values, when there is an even number of observations. The median is a good measure of location for skewed data, since it will be close to the observation most repeated in the sample or population, and it cannot be affected by extreme values. However, the median does not consider all the values of observations in the data set, since only the central observation is used. The median is commonly used for analysis of qualitative (non-numerical) data.

Mode

The mode of a data set, sample or population, is the value which is repeated or observed with the greatest frequency; that is, it is the most common observation or value in the data set. Its advantages and disadvantages are the same as those of the median; however, at times, it may be difficult to interpret since there may be more than one mode in a data set.

To illustrate the measures of central tendency of a variable, consider the daily VLCC tanker freight rates for cargoes from the Persian Gulf to Japan (TD3) over the period January 1998 to April 2008, presented in Figure 3.1.[2] It can be seen that over the sample period, the maximum VLCC freight in Worldscale rate is 342.97 WS on 10 November 2004, and the minimum rates is 28.0 WS on 22 April 2002. However, the average freight rate over the sample period is 89.34 WS, while the mode is 102.5 WS and median is 75.34 WS.[3]

---

[2] This is route TD3 of the Baltic Dirty Tanker Index produced by the Baltic Exchange; the market information produced by the Baltic Exchange is presented in Chapter 4.

[3] These statistics can easily be calculated in Microsoft Excel using '=Average()', '=Mode()', and '=Median()' functions, where the brackets contain the range of the series.

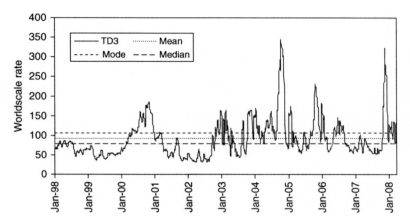

Figure 3.1 Plot of daily VLCC freight rates for TD3 Baltic route
Source: Baltic Exchange.

3.3.2 Measures of dispersion

Apart from knowing what a typical value is for a variable, it is also useful to know the variability or the dispersion of the variable around this typical or average value. Dispersion of a variable can be measured in many ways, including the 'range', the 'inter-quartile range', and the 'percentile range', as well as the 'variance' and the 'standard deviation', which are the most commonly used methods of measuring and reporting the dispersion and 'volatility' of a variable.

3.3.3 The range

A very basic and crude measure of dispersion of a variable is the 'range' over which the variable fluctuates. This is essentially the difference between the largest and the smallest values of a population or a sample. The range is an indication of the boundaries within which the variable may fluctuate. However, the range can be affected by extreme values and events, so to avoid this we use the 'inter-quartile range'. This is defined as the difference between the first and the third quartile of the data. The first quartile, Q_1, is the observation that reflects the lowest 25 per cent of the data and the third quartile, Q_3, is the observation that reflects the lowest 75 per cent of the data (Note: Q_2 is the median). Therefore, the inter-quartile range can be calculated as the difference between Q_3 and Q_1 (inter-quartile range $= Q_3 - Q_1$), and hence, it represents the middle 50 per cent of the data. The advantage of the inter-quartile range is that it avoids extreme values and observations, but its disadvantage is that it does not use all the information in the data set. An alternative method of measuring range is to use the difference between the top and the bottom ($\alpha/2$) per cent of the ordered values of a variable,

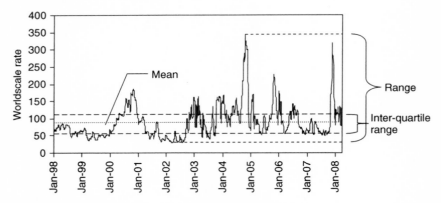

Figure 3.2   Plot of daily VLCC freight rates for TD3 Baltic route

which is called an '1-α per cent percentile range'. For instance, 90 per cent percentile range defines the range between the lowest and highest 5 per cent of observations in a data set, and 95 per cent percentile range defines the range between the lowest and highest 2.5 per cent observations in a data set.

To illustrate how range and inter-quartile range can be calculated, consider the TD3 rates used earlier. The simple range is 314.97 WS, which is the difference between the maximum freight rate of 342.97 WS and the minimum of 28.0 WS. This means that over the sample period, TD3 rates fluctuated within a large range of 314.94 WS points, indicating the high volatility in this route. The inter-quartile range for this route, calculated as the difference between the first and third quartile, is 54.24 WS [110.10 minus 55.86] which still indicates a high fluctuation range in TD3 rates. It can be noted that the inter-quartile range is much lower than the range due to the exclusion of top and bottom 25 per cent of values in the sample, as shown in Figure 3.2.

3.3.4   Variance and standard deviation

Most commonly, the dispersion of a variable is measured by the 'variance'. The variance is the average of the squared deviations of the observations from their arithmetic mean. Mathematically we can calculate the variance of a sample and a population, using the following formulae.

Sample variance	Population variance
$$s^2 = \frac{\sum\limits_{i=1}^{n}(x_i - \bar{x})^2}{n-1}$$	$$\sigma^2 = \frac{\sum\limits_{i=1}^{N}(x_i - \mu)^2}{N}$$

It is important to note that, in the case of population, the sum of squared deviations is divided by the total number of observations (N), whereas, in the case of a sample, the sum of squared deviations is divided by the number of observations in the sample minus one. This is done to avoid statistical issues in estimating sample variance for small samples,[4] however, as sample size increases the difference in sample and population variance decreases; that is, sample variance becomes a more accurate estimate of population variance. The variance can be used to express the dispersion of the observations around the mean by a single value; however, because in calculating this statistic, the deviations of observations from the mean are squared, the variance does not have a meaningful unit of measurement. An alternative is to report the square root of the variance which is known as the 'standard deviation'. The standard deviation is the most commonly used measure of dispersion and it has the convenient property of having the same unit of measurement as the original data. It is calculated simply as the square root of the variance; i.e. $\sigma^2 = \sqrt{\sigma^2}$ for population and, $s = \sqrt{s^2}$ for sample.

There are two important issues to note when calculating and reporting variance and standard deviation of variables. First, the general convention is to calculate and report the variance or standard deviation of the percentage changes in variables, rather than their levels. The percentage change in a variable can be calculated as periodic percentage change in price (returns) r_t, or continuously compounded returns using natural logarithm as

Periodic percentage return	Continuously compounded return
$r_t = \dfrac{P_t - P_{t-1}}{P_{t-1}} = \dfrac{P_t}{P_{t-1}} - 1$	$r_t = \ln\left(\dfrac{P_t}{P_{t-1}}\right) = \ln(P_t) - \ln(P_{t-1})$

Note that P_t and P_{t-1} are prices at time t and t − 1, respectively, and ln is the natural logarithm.

The second important point is that it is a common practice to report the standard deviation of a variable (price, rate or index) in annualised form, even if the periodicity of the data which is used to calculate standard deviation is not annual (daily, weekly, monthly, etc.). Therefore, in practice, we first calculate the variance and standard deviation of percentage changes in the variable using daily, weekly or any other periodicity, and then convert the variance or standard deviation to annualised values. For instance, if daily data is used to calculate average daily return r_{daily} based on 250 trading days a year, annualised average return can be approximated by multiplying the

---

[4] To calculate the variance of a sample we divide the sum of squared deviations by n − 1 to allow for the loss of degrees of freedom. This is because we need to first estimate the mean before estimating the variance; therefore, we lose one degree of freedom in this process.

Table 3.1   Approximation of returns, variances and standard deviations to annualised values

Frequency	Mean	Variance	Standard deviation
Daily	$r_{yearly} \approx r_{daily} \times 250$	$s^2_{yearly} \approx s^2_{daily} \times 250$	$s_{yearly} \approx s_{daily} \times \sqrt{250}$
Weekly	$r_{yearly} \approx r_{weekly} \times 52$	$s^2_{yearly} \approx s^2_{weekly} \times 52$	$s_{yearly} \approx s_{weekly} \times \sqrt{52}$
Monthly	$r_{yearly} \approx r_{monthly} \times 12$	$s^2_{yearly} \approx s^2_{monthly} \times 12$	$s_{yearly} \approx s_{monthly} \times \sqrt{12}$
Quarterly	$r_{yearly} \approx r_{quar} \times 4$	$s^2_{yearly} \approx s^2_{quar} \times 4$	$s_{yearly} \approx s_{quar} \times \sqrt{4}$

Note: It is assumed that the number of daily observations (e.g. trading days) in a year is 250. This figure may vary depending on the number of trading days in a year for different markets and prices.

Table 3.2   Mean and standard deviation of spot, six-month, one-year and three-year time-charter rates for Panamax dry-bulk carriers

	Spot	6m TC	1y TC	3y TC
Weekly mean	0.0017	0.0015	0.0015	0.0010
Weekly standard deviation	0.0512	0.0531	0.0465	0.0436
Annualised mean	0.089	0.080	0.077	0.052
Annualised standard deviation	0.370	0.383	0.335	0.315
Monthly mean	0.0071	0.0056	0.0057	0.0037
Monthly standard deviation	0.1044	0.1137	0.1075	0.0803
Annualised mean	0.086	0.067	0.069	0.044
Annualised standard deviation	0.362	0.394	0.372	0.278

Note: Spot rates are for a 55,000 mt Panamax cargo of heavy soya sorghum (HSS) from the US Gulf to Japan.
Source: Clarkson's SIN

average daily return by 250, as presented in Table 3.1. Similarly, the sample standard deviation calculated from daily observations, s_{daily}, can be used to approximate the annual standard deviation of returns by multiplying daily standard deviation by the square root of number of days in a year (e.g. 250), as presented in Table 3.1.

To see an example of how variances and standard deviations can be annu-alised, let us look at the Panamax voyage (spot), six-month, one-year and three-year time-charter (TC) rates over the period January 1989 to February 2008. The weekly and monthly mean and standard deviations of these rates are presented in Table 3.2, along with annualised statistics as approximations from the weekly and the monthly data. The volatility of the spot route, measured as the annualised standard deviation of weekly percentage change in freight rate, is 37 per cent. Similarly, volatilities of six-month, one-year and three-year time-charter rates are 38.3 per cent, 33.5 per cent and 31.5 per cent, respectively. Comparison of annualised standard deviations, obtained from weekly and monthly data, indicates that the approximations of annualised returns and standard deviations are generally quite close, with minor discrepancies, due to sampling and approximation.

In addition, we can observe an important property of volatility of shipping freight contracts, which is the decline in volatility of freight rates as the duration of contract increases. This is known as the 'volatility term structure' and can be attributed to the fact that spot and short-term shipping contracts are more sensitive to current market events compared to long-term charter contracts, which essentially should reflect the expected market conditions during the life of the contract. A similar pattern can be observed in the forward freight agreement (FFA) market, where contracts with long time to maturity show lower volatility compared to those with short term to maturity (see Chapter 5 for the volatility term structure of FFA contracts).

3.3.5 Coefficient of skewness

Another useful descriptive statistic is the 'coefficient of skewness' or the third moment of the variable around its mean which contains information on the shape of the distribution of the variable. The coefficient of skewness indicates whether the distribution of the variable is symmetric around its mean value or is skewed to either left or right, and can be estimated using the following formulae, depending on whether we are dealing with a sample or a population.

Sample skewness	Population skewness
$\hat{\alpha}_3 = \dfrac{\sum_{i=1}^{n}(x_i - \overline{x})^3 \Big/ (n-1)}{s^3}$	$\alpha_3 = \dfrac{\sum_{i=1}^{N}(x_i - \mu)^3 \Big/ N}{\sigma^3}$

The estimated coefficient of skewness shows how symmetric is the distribution of a variable. For instance, if the estimated sample skewness is positive, $\hat{\alpha}_3 > 0$, then the distribution is positively skewed; that is, the right tail of the distribution is longer and fatter compared to the left tail (Figure 3.3(a)). On the other hand, if the estimated sample skewness is negative, $\hat{\alpha}_3 < 0$, the distribution is negatively skewed; that is, the left tail of the distribution is longer and fatter compared to the right tail (Figure 3.3(b)). Finally, if the estimated sample skewness is zero, $\hat{\alpha}_3 = 0$, the distribution is symmetric around its mean; that is, the left and the right tails of the distribution are identical (Figure 3.3(c)). Also, as can be seen from the three distributions presented in Figure 3.3, when the distribution of a variable is negatively skewed, the mean is less than the median and the mode whereas when the distribution of a variable is positively skewed, the mean is greater than the median and the mode. When the distribution is symmetric, then mean, median and mode are equal.

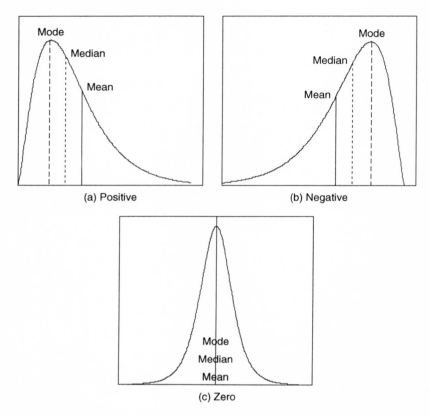

Figure 3.3   Distributions with positive, negative and zero coefficient of skewness

3.3.6   Coefficient of kurtosis

Coefficient of kurtosis, also known as the fourth moment of a variable around its mean, refers to the peakness of the distribution of the variable. The coefficient of kurtosis, α_4, of a variable can be estimated using the following formulae, depending on whether we are dealing with a sample or population data.

Sample kurtosis	Population kurtosis
$\hat{\alpha}_4 = \dfrac{\sum\limits_{i=1}^{n} (x_i - \overline{x})^4 \Big/ (n-1)}{s^4}$	$\alpha_4 = \dfrac{\sum\limits_{i=1}^{N} (x_i - \mu)^4 \Big/ N}{\sigma^4}$

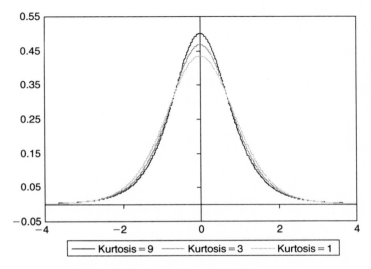

Figure 3.4 Distributions with different coefficients of kurtosis

The peakness of the distribution of a variable is usually compared with the peakness of a normal distribution. A normal distribution, which is extensively used in statistics and finance, has a symmetrical bell shape with a coefficient of kurtosis of three. Therefore, if the estimated sample kurtosis is less than 3, $\hat{\alpha}_4 < 3$, then the sample distribution is relatively flatter than a normal distribution and it is called 'platykurtic'. On the other hand, if the estimated sample kurtosis is greater than 3, $\hat{\alpha}_4 > 3$, then the sample distribution has a relatively greater peakness than a normal distribution and it is called 'leptokurtic'. Finally, if the estimated sample kurtosis is 3, $\hat{\alpha}_4 = 3$, the distribution has a peakness similar to a normal distribution and it is called 'mesokurtic'. The three types of distribution are plotted in Figure 3.4.

3.3.7 Coefficient of variation

The coefficients of dispersion discussed so far give partial information about the distribution of a data set or a variable, and sometimes it may be difficult to compare the dispersion of variables in isolation. Thus, it might be useful to measure the relative spread or dispersion that considers both the amount of dispersion and the location of the mean of the variable. This can be achieved by calculating the 'coefficient of variation', which is defined as the ratio of standard deviation to the mean of a distribution, $CV = s/\bar{x}$. The higher the coefficient of variation the more dispersed the data is around the mean. The inverse of the coefficient of variation, that is, the

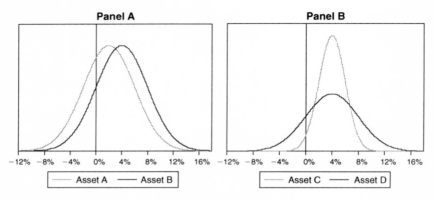

Figure 3.5   Distribution of returns of asset with different risk profiles

return-to-risk ratio, is known as the 'Sharpe ratio' and is used in financial economics and investment analysis to compare the risk-return profile of different
assets.[5]

To illustrate, consider two assets, A and B, with different expected or mean
returns of 2 per cent and 4 per cent respectively, and similar standard deviations or risk of 4 per cent. Distributions of returns of the two assets are
plotted in panel (a) of Figure 3.5. A rational and profit-maximising investor
will choose Asset B over Asset A since, with a similar risk level, asset B
offers a higher expected return. Moreover, a comparison of Sharpe ratios
also indicates that Asset B is a better investment, with a Sharpe ratio of
1 (4 per cent/4 per cent) compared to Asset A with a Sharpe ratio of 0.5
(2 per cent/ 4 per cent). Now consider the two assets, C and D, for which the
return distributions are plotted in panel (b) of Figure 3.5. Asset C offers 4 per
cent expected or mean return with 2 per cent standard deviation, whereas
Asset D offers 4 per cent expected or mean return with 4 per cent standard
deviation. Again, a rational investor will choose Asset C over Asset D, since it
offers a similar expected return with lower uncertainty or risk. Comparison of
Sharpe ratios also indicates that Asset C is a better investment, with a Sharpe
ratio of 2 (4 per cent/2 per cent) compared to Asset A with a Sharpe ratio of
1 (4 per cent/4 per cent).

---

[5] In the financial economics literature, the Sharpe ratio is defined as the ratio of the
excess return on an asset over the risk free rate (r_f) divided by the standard deviation
of the asset returns, σ_i, that is, $SR = (\bar{r}_i - r_f)/\sigma_i$. However, when comparing Sharpe
ratios of assets the results are not affected by whether we use excess returns or simple
returns.

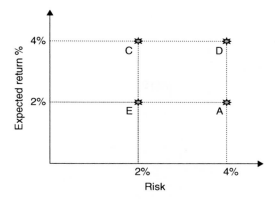

Figure 3.6 Comparison of the risk-return relationship of different assets

We can look at the risk-and-return profiles of assets in a different way. For instance, the risk-return profile of four assets, A, C, D and E are plotted in Figure 3.6. It is not difficult to see that, of these, Asset C offers the highest return-to-risk ratio, while Asset A has the lowest ratio. Therefore, in general, a rational investor prefers assets with lowest risk and highest expected return. However, it might be more difficult to choose between Asset E and Asset D, since they seem to have the same return-to-risk ratios. In such cases, the important factors which determine the choice of asset are the investor's risk appetite or the trader's risk limit. If the trader has high risk limits, he may choose to invest in D, but if there are constraints on the amount of risk that the trader can take, then he may choose to invest in Asset E.

3.3.8 Covariance and correlation

Another important statistical concept is the 'correlation' between two variables, which measures the degree and strength of co-movement between two variables. In order to measure the correlation between two variables, we first calculate the 'covariance' of two variables (say, x_i and y_i) as

Sample covariance	Population covariance
$$s_{x,y} = \frac{\sum\limits_{i=1}^{n}(x_i - \overline{x})(y_i - \overline{y})}{n-1}$$	$$\sigma_{x,y} = \frac{\sum\limits_{i=1}^{N}(x_i - \mu_x)(y_i - \mu_y)}{N}$$

where $s_{x,y}$ and $\sigma_{x,y}$ represent sample and population covariance, and n and N are the number of observations in the sample and population, respectively. We can then calculate the correlation coefficient, ρ_{xy}, by dividing the covariance between x_i and y_i by the product of the standard deviations of x_i and y_i. Therefore:

Sample correlation	Population correlation
$\hat{\rho}_{x,y} = \dfrac{Cov(x_i, y_i)}{s_x \cdot s_y} = \dfrac{s_{x,y}}{s_x \cdot s_y}$	$\rho_{x,y} = \dfrac{Cov(x_i, y_i)}{\sigma_x \cdot \sigma_y} = \dfrac{\sigma_{x,y}}{\sigma_x \cdot \sigma_y}$

The correlation coefficient is a measure of the degree of co-movement of variables and is used in: asset allocation; portfolio selection and diversification; hedging and selecting hedging instruments, especially when futures contracts are involved; and trading strategies, especially in pair or long-short trading in futures markets. Depending on whether the levels or changes in variables are used, long- or short-run correlation can be calculated, respectively. Long-run correlation reflects the long-term co-movement and the relationship between variables, while short-run correlation reveals information on the co-movements between the two variables in the short term. In general, short-run correlation between variables is less than long-run correlation, as variables tend to follow a common trend in the long run, but they may deviate more often in the short term, due to noise or changes in market conditions.

3.3.9 Comparison of risk across different vessel size and contracts

Having discussed the descriptive statistics, we now present estimated values of those statistics for freight rates for different ship sizes and freight-contract duration in both the tanker and dry-bulk sectors. The estimated statistics are presented in Table 3.3 for the following sample periods: 10 January 1992 to 16 November 2007 for VLCC and Aframax; 23 December 1994 to 16 November 2007 for Suezmax tankers; 26 April 1991 to 16 November 2007 for Handymax and Panamax; and 7 February 1992 to 16 November 2007 for Capesize dry-bulk carriers.

The results in Table 3.3 reveal several interesting points about the distributional properties of freight rates across different markets and contracts of different durations. First, we can notice that there is a direct relationship between vessel size and average freight rates, as well as vessel size and the standard deviation (volatility) of freight rates in the spot, one-year and three-year time-charter contracts. For example, in the dry-bulk market, average spot earnings for Capesize, Panamax and Handymax are US\$26,727/day, US\$17,832/day, and US\$16,275/day, while annualised standard deviations are 62.8 per cent, 51.4 per cent, and 24.6 per cent respectively. Similar patterns emerge for one-year and three-year time-charter contracts in the dry-bulk and tanker markets. The greater volatility for larger ships compared to smaller ones can be attributed to their operational inflexibility in the sense that larger ships are employed in the transportation of a limited number of

Table 3.3 Comparison of descriptive statistics across different sizes of vessels and contract duration in the dry and wet markets

Panel A: The tanker market

	VLCC			Suezmax			Aframax		
	Spot	1y-TC	3y-TC	Spot	1y-TC	3y-TC	Spot	1y-TC	3y-TC
Mean US$/day	36,765	33,307	32,543	31,886	25,913	23,875	24,766	18,588	18,018
Mean return %	0.054	0.010	−0.002	0.013	0.062	0.030	0.025	0.008	−0.010
Standard dev. %	1.011	0.271	0.141	1.016	0.232	0.176	0.843	0.163	0.157
Skewness	0.421	1.964	1.025	0.738	4.435	3.764	0.433	0.586	−0.239
Kurtosis	7.278	19.467	16.521	6.560	66.378	55.878	7.025	11.877	23.628
CV	18.746	26.589	−82.102	76.989	3.734	5.781	34.331	21.013	−16.213

Panel B: The dry-bulk market

	Capesize			Panamax			Handymax		
	Spot	1yTC	3yTC	Spot	1yTC	3yTC	Spot	1yTC	3yTC
Mean US$/day	26,727	24,413	21,040	17,832	13,023	10,982	16,275	12,800	11,189
Mean return %	0.141	0.123	0.088	0.103	0.113	0.112	0.087	0.113	0.087
Standard dev. %	0.628	0.330	0.250	0.514	0.400	0.367	0.246	0.213	0.147
Skew	0.609	0.720	0.868	0.281	0.188	0.222	0.044	1.568	−0.420
Kurtosis	7.411	12.782	21.211	5.686	8.630	26.794	8.437	31.168	23.507
CV	4.448	2.675	2.835	4.994	3.531	3.285	2.834	1.880	1.688

Note: Sample period: weekly data from 10 January 1992 to 16 November 2007 for VLCC and Aframax; 23 December 1994 to 16 November 2007 for Suezmax; 26 April 1991 to 16 November 2007 for Handymax and Panamax; 7 February 1992 to 16 November 2007 for Capesize.
Source of data: Clarkson's SIN.

commodities in relatively fewer routes whereas, in general, smaller ships are more versatile and involved in the transportation of a variety of commodities in almost every sea route around the world. This means that, when the markets are depressed there is greater employment opportunity for smaller ships compared to larger ones. As a result, their profitability is not as sensitive as larger ships to global economic activity, seaborne trade and shipping market conditions.

There also seems to be a negative relationship between the average daily earnings and the duration of contract. For instance, average daily earnings for VLCCs decline from US$36,765 in the spot market to US$33,307 for one-year TC and US$32,543 for 3-year TC. Similarly, for Capesize vessels, average daily earnings decline from US$26,727 in the spot market to US$24,413 for a one-year time charter and US$21,040 for three-year time charter. Kavussanos and Alizadeh (2002b) attribute the lower charter rates of long-term contracts, compared to short-term contracts, to the higher risk associated with short-term compared to long-term freight contracts. They argue that shipowners, in general, are prepared to accept lower hire rates for longer-term contracts relative to short-term contracts and that such a discount (negative risk premium) is time-varying depending on market conditions. Furthermore, it can be seen that changes in freight rates, across all sizes and contract duration, are positively skewed, with the exception of the three-year time charter of Handysize dry-bulk carriers. The coefficient of kurtosis indicates that freight-rate changes are leptokurtic and the excess kurtosis increases as the duration of contract increases.

3.4   Time-varying volatility models

So far, we have estimated variance and standard deviation of changes in a variable as measures of the dispersion of the variable or its volatility. While these methods give us an indication of the fluctuations of the variable over the sample period, they can be somehow inaccurate since volatility may change over time. This is especially true in commodity and freight markets, where prices and freight rates are determined through the interaction between supply and demand schedules with particular characteristics such as limitation of supply and inelastic demand. As was seen in Chapter 2, in shipping freight markets, there are periods when there is oversupply of tonnage and any changes in demand or shock to the market can be absorbed without any significant impact on freight rates. These periods are when the freight rate volatility is relatively low. On the other hand, there are periods where supply and demand are very tight, perhaps due to shortage of tonnage and excessive demand, and any change in demand due to seasonal, cyclical or random shocks results in a sharp change in freight rates and high volatility. Therefore, it is important to recognise these dynamics in freight-rate volatility, which is known as 'volatility clustering', and to consider such changes when estimating volatility.

The phenomenon of volatility clustering was first noticed by Mandlebrot (1963) in the stock market, where he noticed that large (small) price changes tend to be followed by large (small) price changes. Mandlebrot's observation inspired a series of studies in investigating and modelling the behaviour of variance of financial and economic time series. For instance, Klein (1977) estimates a time-varying variance model using a rolling sample method to capture the dynamics of volatility of stocks, whereas Engle (1982) introduces autoregressive conditional heteroscedasticity (ARCH) models for modelling the time-varying volatility of time-series variables. Following Engle's (1982) seminal paper, there have been numerous studies in modelling the time-varying volatility of stock and commodity prices, interest rates and other financial assets. For example, Bollerslev (1986) proposes the Generalised ARCH (GARCH) model; Engle et al. (1987) introduce the ARCH in mean model; Bollerslev et al. (1988) develop the multivariate GARCH model; Geweke (1986) and Pantula (1986) introduce nonlinear ARCH models; Nelson (1991) extends ARCH models to allow for asymmetric effects of shocks on volatility (exponential ARCH), among many others.

A number of studies also investigated the time-varying volatility of shipping freight rates and ship prices, and concluded that freight-rate volatility is time-varying. For instance, Kavussanos (1996) examines time-varying volatilities of dry-bulk freight rates across vessel sizes as well as their aggregate spot and time-charter rates using ARCH and GARCH models. He finds that the pattern and magnitude of time-varying volatilities in the dry-bulk freight markets are different across vessel sizes. In particular, freight rates for larger vessels tend to be more volatile than smaller ones. In another study on time-varying volatilities of ship prices, Kavussanos (1997) examines the dynamics of volatilities of second-hand prices for differently sized dry-bulk carriers. He concludes that, in general, price volatilities in the dry-bulk sector respond together and symmetrically to external shocks; however, there are differences, which are due to market segmentation and the fact that these vessels are employed in different routes and trades. Also, he notes that price volatilities are also positively related to the size of vessel; that is, prices for larger vessels show higher volatilities compared to those for smaller ones. This is attributed to the fact that larger vessels are less flexible than smaller ones in terms of trading routes and commodities that they carry. As a result, responses of profitability and prices for larger vessels to any unexpected changes in the market are more drastic compared to smaller vessels.

The following sections are devoted to discussing how different statistical and econometric techniques can be used to capture and model the dynamics of volatility of freight rates. In particular, we focus on three approaches for modelling time-varying volatility of shipping freight rates, namely: simple rolling variance, exponentially weighted average variance, and the family of ARCH and GARCH models, which have become an integral part of risk-modelling practices and risk-management systems.

3.4.1   Rolling-window or moving-average variance

The simplest, but not very accurate approach to capture the time-variation of volatility is to use a rolling window of observations to estimate the variance or standard deviation of a variable. To implement this method, a small window of observations, k (for example, $k = 52$ weeks for weekly data or $k = 90$ days for daily data) is chosen at the beginning of the sample, and the variance is estimated over the chosen window as σ_1^2. Then the sample is rolled by one observation; that is, one observation is dropped from the beginning and one is added to the end, to keep the number of observations in the window constant (k), and the variance is estimated for the new set of observations in the widow as σ_2^2. Repeating the procedure by rolling the window of observations forward, and recording the estimated variances until the end of the sample, a sequence of rolling variances can be produced. The rolling variance estimates vary over the sample period and reflect changes in the volatility of the underlying variable over time.

To illustrate how the dynamics of volatility can be captured through using the rolling variance estimation method, we consider weekly spot tanker freight rates for four different routes.[6] We estimate a 52-week rolling variance and turn them to a series of annualised standard deviations over the period January 1990 to November 2007. Panel A of Figure 3.7 plots the estimated rolling standard deviations for VLCC, Suezmax, Aframax and Handysize tankers over the sample period. It can be observed that tanker freight-rate volatilities show significant time variation, which are clearly different across different sectors.

Tracking time-varying volatilities of tanker spot rates, it seems that after the relatively turbulent markets of the early 1990s, volatility of tanker freight rates was more or less stable, with some changes in the range of 40 per cent to 70 per cent until the early 2000s. However, from early 2002, there seems to be a significant increase in volatility of freight rates for VLCC and Suezmax tankers. In the VLCC market, freight-rate volatility reached the high level of 200 per cent in 2003. Volatility of Aframax and Handysize tankers, on the other hand, seems to have been relatively lower and more stable compared to larger tankers.

---

[6] Spot tanker freight rates are; VLCC rates for TD3 route (Ras Tanura to Chiba), Suezmax TD5 (Bonny to Philadelphia), Aframax TD7 (Ras Tanura to Singapore), and clean product routes for 30,000 mt of products from Ras Tanura to Chiba. The exact definitions of those routes are presented in Chapter 4.

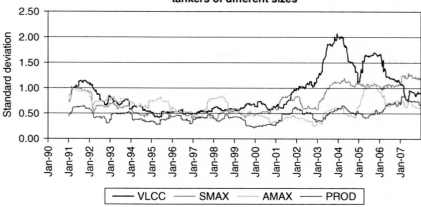

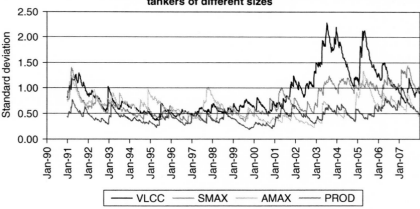

Figure 3.7 Estimates of time-varying volatility of spot freight rates for tankers of different sizes

3.4.2 Exponentially weighted average variance (EWAV)

Although using rolling variance estimates can capture the time-variation of volatility, this approach is criticised because it assigns equal weights to observations in the window over which the variance is estimated. This is argued to be inappropriate because distant past observations and events (shocks) are believed to have lesser impact on volatility compared to recent past observations and events. One way to address this issue is to use exponentially declining weights, as in the following formula, to estimate an exponentially weighted rolling variance

$$\sigma_t^2 \approx (1 - \lambda) \sum_{i=1}^{n} \lambda^{i-1}(r_{t-i} - \bar{r})^2 \tag{3.1}$$

where λ is the weighting coefficient, $0 < \lambda < 1$. In this setting, the value of λ determines the persistence or memory of the time-varying variance; that is high (low) values of λ yield high (low) persistence in volatility. This is also known as the RiskMetrics method of estimating volatility and can be shown to be equivalent to

$$\sigma_t^2 \approx \lambda \sigma_{t-1}^2 + (1 - \lambda)r_{t-1}^2 \tag{3.2}$$

It has been shown that values of λ between 0.90 and 0.98 are sufficient to capture the dynamics of volatility of many assets when daily or weekly observations are used.

Once again, to show how exponentially weighted variance can be applied, we use weekly spot tanker freight rates over the period January 1990 to November 2007. Exponentially weighted time-varying volatilities of VLCC, Suezmax, Aframax and Handysize tankers over the sample period are plotted in Panel B of Figure 3.7. It is not surprising to see that tanker freight-rate volatilities show somewhat similar dynamics to those observed in Panel A, when a simple rolling variance method was used to estimate time-varying volatility of tanker freight rates. However, this time there seems to be a degree of persistence in volatilities after a shock, as volatility increases sharply and declines slowly.

3.4.3   Realised volatility models

'Realised volatility models' are based on high-frequency data volatility, which assume that volatility is *observed* as movement in the price. In this approach an unbiased estimator of such a measure is the squared returns process. There-fore, assuming the intraday returns series, $r_{i,t}$, can be constructed by dividing each day into N equidistant intraday periods, then the realised volatility of day t for a portfolio of assets can be estimated as:

$$\sigma_t^2 = \sum_{i=1}^{N} r_{i,t}^2 + 2\sum_{i=1}^{N} \sum_{j=i+1}^{N} r_{j,t}r_{j-1,t} \tag{3.3}$$

Under the assumption that returns are independent with a zero mean, σ_t^2 is an unbiased estimator of the true variance (Andersen and Bollerslev; 1998).

3.5 ARCH and GARCH models

In his pioneering study, Engle (1982) introduced a formal approach for modelling the variance of a time series by conditioning it on the square of lagged disturbances – error terms or shocks – of the series in an autoregressive form known as the 'autoregressive conditional heteroscedasticity' (ARCH) model. Since the introduction of the original ARCH model numerous forms of time-varying risk models have been developed and applied in different areas of empirical finance, including asset pricing, modelling of financial time-series and risk management. Bera and Higgins (1992), Bollerslev et al. (1992) and Engle (1993) provide detailed reviews of applications and extensions of ARCH-type models. The following sections provide a review of ARCH and GARCH methodologies in modelling volatility of shipping freight rates.

3.5.1 The theory of ARCH models

The classical linear regression model requires the residuals of the model, ε_t, to be independent and normally distributed with mean zero and constant variance.

$$r_t = \alpha_0 + \alpha_1 x_{1,t} + \cdots + \alpha_p x_{p,t} + \varepsilon_t, \quad \varepsilon_t \sim \text{IN}(0, \sigma^2) \tag{3.4}$$

where, r_t represents changes or returns on a variable, $x_{1,t}$ to $x_{p,t}$ are explanatory variables of the regression, and ε_t is the estimated residual series (shocks), and α_0, α_1, to α_p, are parameters of interest to be estimated. Under classical linear regression model assumptions, the 'ordinary least squares' (OLS) estimation method yields the 'best linear unbiased estimators' (BLUE)[7] of the regression parameters. In this respect, perhaps the most important underlying assumption is the condition of homoscedasticity of the residuals, σ^2, which requires the variance of residuals to be constant. However, if σ^2 is time dependent, that is to say that residuals show time-varying heteroscedasticity, then the OLS estimators may not be BLUE. This is due to the lack of efficiency of parameter estimates caused by the time-varying variance of residuals, σ_t^2, as in equation (3.5).

$$r_t = \alpha_0 + \alpha_1 x_{1,t} + \cdots + \alpha_p x_{p,t} + \varepsilon_t, \quad \varepsilon_t \sim \text{IN}(0, \sigma_t^2) \tag{3.5}$$

Engle (1982) proposes that the conditional variance of the dependent variable in the regression equation (3.5), which is equivalent to the variance of the

---

[7] In statistics, we want the estimated parameter of our regression models to have desirable statistical properties; that is, the estimator should be unbiased, efficient and consistent. Essentially these properties determine the statistical reliability of the parameter estimates of a regression. See, for instance, Gujarati (2005) for an explanation of the properties of estimators.

error terms, can be specified and estimated using a similar autoregressive equation, as follows:

$$\sigma_t^2 = \beta_0 + \sum_{i=1}^{m} \beta_i \varepsilon_{t-i}^2 \qquad (3.6)$$

where β_0 and β_i, $i = 1,\ldots,$ m, are parameters of lagged squared error terms in the variance model. Notice that if the parameters of lagged squared error terms are not statistically significant, there is no correlation between the lagged squared residuals, which means that the variance is constant and there are no autoregressive conditional heteroscedasticity (ARCH) effects in the error terms. In addition, for the conditional variance to be positive and stationary at all times, the conditions are $\beta_0 > 0$ and $0 < \sum \beta_i < 1$ should be satisfied.

3.5.1.1   GARCH models

Bollerslev (1986) argues that the ARCH models can be over-parameterised and proposes a parsimonious model for the conditional variance, known as the 'generalised autoregressive conditional heteroscedasticity' (GARCH) model. In this setting, the variance is conditioned on both its own lagged values as well as lagged squared error terms as

$$\sigma_t^2 = \beta_0 + \sum_{i=1}^{p} \beta_{1,i} \varepsilon_{t-i}^2 + \sum_{j=1}^{q} \beta_{2,j} \sigma_{t-j}^2 \qquad (3.7)$$

where the variables are the same as before and $\beta_{1,i}$, $\beta_{2,j}$ are the parameters of interest. The significance of lagged variance parameters, $\beta_{2,j}$, in equation (3.7) indicates the dependence of the current value of the conditional variance on its lagged values. On the other hand, if the parameters of lagged squared errors and variance are not statistically significant, then the variance in equation (3.7) is constant. Also, the non-negativity constraints requires $\beta_0 \geq 0$, and $\beta_{1,i}$, $\beta_{2,j} > 0$, in order for the variance to be positive definite. In addition, the sum $\sum \beta_{1,i} + \sum \beta_{2,j}$ must be less than one for the unconditional variance [that is, $\sigma_0^2 = \beta_0 / (1 - \sum \beta_{1,i} - \sum \beta_{2,j})$] to be defined. The latter condition is necessary for the variance to be stationary and non-explosive.

The number of the lagged error (p) and variance (q) terms in the variance equation is called the order of ARCH or GARCH model, denoted as ARCH (p) or GARCH (p,q). Although many different versions of GARCH models have been proposed in the literature and used for empirical research, the most common type of GARCH model used to model the variance of economic and financial time series is GARCH(1,1) since it captures the dynamics of the variance quite adequately.

Parameters of GARCH models can be estimated using several different methods, including the 'maximum likelihood' (ML) and the 'generalised method of moments' (GMM). (See Hamilton, 1994, for more details on estimation of GARCH models.) However, the ML estimation method has been used extensively in estimation of ARCH models in empirical studies due to its simplicity and power. The ML method utilises the defined log-likelihood function of the regression model and uses mathematical optimisation techniques to maximise the log-likelihood function with respect to the parameters of the model.[8]

To illustrate how GARCH models can be used in estimating time-varying volatilities of shipping freight rates, once again consider the weekly tanker spot rates for VLCC, Suezmax, Aframax and Handysize product tankers. We construct time series of percentage changes (returns) of spot rates, and use the following autoregressive (AR) model for the mean and, the GARCH(1,1) specification to capture the dynamics of variance of spot freight rates.

$$r_t = \alpha_0 + \sum_{i=1}^{k} \alpha_i r_{t-i} + \varepsilon_t, \quad \varepsilon_t \sim \text{IN}(0, \sigma_t^2)$$

$$\sigma_t^2 = \beta_0 + \beta_1 \varepsilon_{t-1}^2 + \beta_2 \sigma_{t-1}^2 \tag{3.8}$$

Estimation results of GARCH models for spot rates for differently sized tankers are presented in Table 3.4. All estimated parameters are statistically significant according to the t-statistics and it seems that there is greater persistence in volatility of freight rates for larger vessels compared to smaller ones. The degree of persistence of time-varying volatilities, reported as $\beta_1 + \beta_2$, indicate that volatility of VLCC and Suezmax freight rates show higher persistence (VLCC, 0.9934 and Suezmax, 0.9978) compared to volatility of freight rates for smaller tankers (Aframax, 0.8886 and Handysize, 0.9286). Furthermore, unconditional annualised volatilities reported as 96.23 per cent, 91.78 per cent, 66.38 per cent and 46.74 per cent for VLCC, Suezmax, Aframax and Handysize tankers respectively are also in line with the theory explained earlier that volatility and size are positively related. Finally, Figure 3.8 plots the time-varying volatility of spot tanker rates estimated using GARCH models. These are quite similar to those estimated by EWA variance plotted in Panel B of Figure 3.7.

---

[8] Another important assumption regarding the maximisation of the log likelihood function is that of normality. There are occasions where the normality assumption regarding the residuals in GARCH models does not hold, therefore specifying a normal log likelihood function for estimation purposes would be inappropriate. This issue has been pointed out and explored by many authors. For example, Bollerslev (1987) proposes a student-t distribution in order to capture fat-tails in the conditional density. Similarly, Nelson (1991) uses the normalised generalised error distribution (GED) in order to define the density function and estimate the log-likelihood function of his EGARCH model. Finally, Bollerslev and Wooldridge (1992) propose the quasi-maximum likelihood estimation procedure. This procedure adjusts the standard errors, which are not consistent in the presence of non-normality

Table 3.4   Estimates of parameters of GARCH (1,1) models for tanker spot freight rates

$$\sigma_t^2 = \beta_0 + \beta_1 \varepsilon_{t-1}^2 + \beta_2 \sigma_{t-1}^2$$

	VLCC TD3	SMAX TD5	AMAX TD7	Clean Product
β_0	0.0001	0.0000	0.0009	0.0003
	[2.667]	[1.695]	[5.299]	[4.285]
β_1	0.0487	0.0258	0.1400	0.0585
	[5.495]	[4.875]	[5.767]	[4.861]
β_2	0.9448	0.9721	0.7486	0.8701
	[94.876]	[146.41]	[20.099]	[35.133]
$\beta_1 + \beta_2$	0.9934	0.9978	0.8886	0.9286
Uncond. vol	96.23%	91.78%	66.38%	46.74%

Note: Figures in squared brackets are t-statistics of estimated parameters.
Sample period: weekly data from January 1990 to November 2007.
Source of data: Clarksons, SIN.

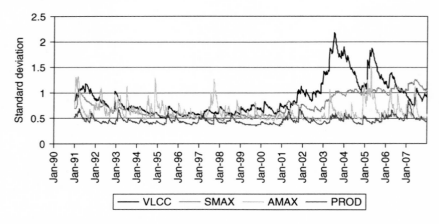

Figure 3.8   Plots of volatility of spot freight rates for tankers of different sizes estimated using GARCH models

3.5.2   Asymmetric GARCH models

In the financial economics literature, it has been shown that different news (shocks, error terms or innovations)[9] might have different impacts on the

---

[9] News, shocks, or innovations are the terms used to express error terms or residuals of the mean regression model. These are essentially the part of the variation in the dependent variable (r_t) which cannot be explained by explanatory variables, and considered to be due to the random movement in the dependent variable caused by arrival of news to the market between time $t - 1$ and t.

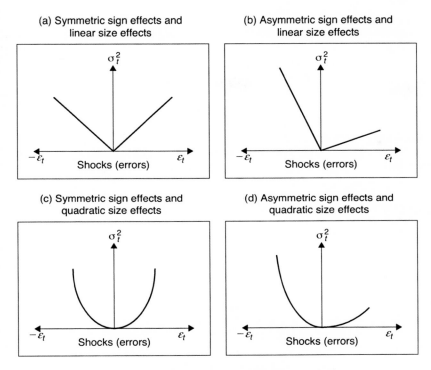

Figure 3.9   Impact of shocks with different sign and size on volatility

behaviour of the volatilities of time series. In other words, the impact of positive shocks on the volatility can be different from the impact of negative shocks with the same magnitude. This phenomenon, which is known as the leverage effect, is quite important when modelling the variance (the second moment) of financial time series. GARCH models allow lagged residuals to have a symmetric effect on the time-varying variance; therefore, in the presence of the leverage effect, GARCH models might be mis-specified and lead to biased estimates of volatilities, as well as to inaccurate forecast intervals.[10]

The asymmetric impact of shocks with different sign and magnitude on volatility can be graphically presented using the 'news-impact curve'. This is a graph of volatility against error terms or shocks. Figure 3.9 presents schematic

---

[10] Engle and Ng (1993) develop a set of tests to detect any form of misspecification in GARCH models due to the asymmetric behaviour of volatility to shocks. These tests are based on regressing the standardised residuals ($es = \hat{e}_t/\sigma_t$) on a series of dummies which are constructed using the sign and relative size of shocks (ε_t) in the mean equation and are called sign and size bias tests.

diagrams of different types of news-impact curves depending on the effect that positive and negative shocks may have on price volatility. For instance, panel (a) illustrates that positive and negative shocks have equal impact on volatility regardless of their size. Panel (b) shows that negative shocks have greater impact on volatility than positive shocks and that the impact is linearly proportional to the size of the shock. Panels (c) and (d) illustrate the cases where larger shocks have proportionately greater impact on volatility compared to smaller shocks. In addition, while the impact of negative and positive shocks is symmetric in Panel (c), negative shocks have greater impact on volatility compared to positive shocks in Panel (d). In other words, there is a symmetric size effect on volatility in Panels (a) and (b), but there is asymmetric size effect on volatility in Panels (c) and (d). On the other hand, there is symmetric sign effect in Panels (a) and (c), but there is asymmetric sign effect in Panels (b) and (d).

3.5.3 GJR threshold GARCH model

Glosten et al. (1993) propose an extension of the GARCH model to capture the possible asymmetric impact of shocks with different signs on volatility. They suggest augmenting the GARCH variance specification with a new term, which is a dummy variable taking the value of one when the shock is negative ($d_t = 1|\varepsilon_t < 0$), and zero if the shock is positive ($d_t = 0|\varepsilon_t \geq 0$). Therefore,

$$\sigma_t^2 = \beta_0 + \sum_{i=1}^{P} \beta_{1,i}\varepsilon_{t-i}^2 + \sum_{i=1}^{q} \beta_{2,i}\sigma_{t-i}^2 + \beta_3 d_{t-1}\varepsilon_{t-1}^2 \qquad (3.9)$$

In the above threshold GARCH (TGARCH) specification, when the shock is positive the coefficient of lagged error term is β_1, and when the shock is negative the coefficient of lagged error term is $\beta_1 + \beta_3$. Therefore, the statistical significance of β_3 is regarded as evidence for asymmetric effect of shocks with different signs on volatility. If coefficient β_3 is positive and significant, then negative shocks tend to have greater impact on volatility compared to positive shocks with the same magnitude. On the other hand, if β_3 is negative and significant, positive shocks tend to have greater impact on volatility compared to negative shocks.

3.5.4 Exponential GARCH model

Nelson (1991) argues that ARCH and GARCH models suffer from three major drawbacks. Firstly, ARCH and GARCH models fail to take into account the asymmetric effect of the shocks on conditional volatility. In fact, conventional GARCH models allow shocks, positive or negative, to have a symmetric effect on the conditional variance. Second, GARCH models do not take into account the asymmetric effect of shocks with different magnitude on conditional volatility. It has been argued in the literature that the relative impact of small shocks might be smaller than the relative impact of large shocks on the conditional volatility. Finally, GARCH models imply non-negativity restrictions on the parameters that sometimes lead to estimation problems. Hence, Nelson (1991) proposes an exponential GARCH (EGARCH) specification as a remedy for these shortcomings in GARCH models. This approach is based on the nonlinear form of ARCH models, suggested by Geweke (1986) and Milhoj (1987) in order to relax the assumption of non-negativity of the parameters, and uses an extra term to capture any size-asymmetric effects in the following form

$$\sigma_t^2 = \exp\left(\beta_0 + \sum_{i=1}^{p}\beta_{1,i}\left(\frac{\varepsilon_{t-i}}{\sigma_{t-i}}\right) + \sum_{j=1}^{q}\beta_{2,j}\log(\sigma_{t-j}^2) + \sum_{i=1}^{p}\beta_{3,i}\left|\frac{\varepsilon_{t-i}}{\sigma_{t-i}} - E\left(\frac{\varepsilon_{t-i}}{\sigma_{t-i}}\right)\right|\right)$$

(3.10)

The conditional variance, as specified in equation (3.10), is known as 'Nelson's exponential GARCH model' and allows the conditional variance parameters, $\beta_0, \beta_{1,i}, \beta_{2,i}$, and $\beta_{3,i}$, to take any real value. The functional form of the innovations, used in the model, allows the variance to respond differently to positive and negative shocks. More specifically, the asymmetric effects of shocks on the conditional variance in an EGARCH specification are as follows. If the coefficient of standardised residual, $\beta_{1,i}$, is negative and significant, then negative (positive) shocks tend to increase (decrease) the conditional variance. The asymmetric effect of shocks with different sizes is captured by construction because the model is specified in exponential form. Therefore, as long as the coefficient of the term which represents the difference between the size of the shock at time t and the expected value of the shock, $|(\varepsilon_t/\sigma_t) - E(\varepsilon_t/\sigma_t)|$, is statistically significant, there is a size asymmetry. Therefore, if the estimate of $\beta_{3,i}$ is positive and statistically significant, it indicates that larger-than-average shocks tend to increase the volatility relatively more compared to smaller-than-average shocks. Another notable difference between the EGARCH model and the GARCH or TGARCH models is that the impact of size of error on volatility is exponential rather than quadratic by construction.

We use two asymmetric GARCH models to estimate time-varying volatility of weekly freight rates for VLCC TD3 and Capesize C4 routes (see Chapter 4 for the definition of the routes). The estimated coefficients of TGARCH(1,1) and EGARCH(1,1) models for the two routes are presented in Table 3.5. The coefficient representing the asymmetric effect of shocks on variance in the TGARCH model is β_3. This coefficient is positive and statistically significant in both models for TD3 and C4, which means that negative shocks tend to have greater impact on volatility compared to positive shocks with the same

Table 3.5   Estimates of parameters of TGARCH and EGARCH models for VLCC TD3 and Capesize C4 weekly spot rates

$$\text{TGARCH}(1,1)\ \sigma_t^2 = \beta_0 + \beta_1 \varepsilon_{t-1}^2 + \beta_2 \sigma_{t-1}^2 + \beta_3 d_{t-1}\varepsilon_{t-1}^2$$

$$\text{EGARCH}(1,1)\ \sigma_t^2 = \exp\left(\beta_0 + \beta_1 \left(\frac{\varepsilon_{t-1}}{\sigma_{t-1}} \right) + \beta_2 \log(\sigma_{t-1}^2) + \beta_3 \left| \frac{\varepsilon_{t-1}}{\sigma_{t-1}} - E\left(\frac{\varepsilon_{t-1}}{\sigma_{t-1}} \right) \right| \right)$$

	VLCC TD3		Capesize C4	
	TGARCH(1,1)	EGARCH(1,1)	TGARCH(1,1)	EGARCH(1,1)
β_0	0.0004	−0.0911	0.00001	−0.1158
	[3.810]	[−5.076]	[2.401]	[−5.940]
β_1	0.0592	−0.0170	0.0107	−0.0266
	[3.291]	[−1.074]	[2.652]	[−3.452]
β_2	0.8828	0.9953	0.9644	0.9896
	[51.031]	[406.32]	[186.56]	[366.82]
β_3	0.0816	0.0963	0.0516	0.0830
	[2.970]	[6.388]	[5.711]	[8.718]

Figures in squared brackets are t-statistics of estimated parameters.
Sample period: weekly data from January 1990 to November 2007.

magnitude. This finding is also confirmed by the estimated β_1 coefficients in EGARCH models, since they are negative, but only statistically significant in the model for the Capesize C4 route. The fact that the coefficient measuring sign asymmetry in EGARCH models is negative implies that negative shocks tend to increase freight-rate volatility while positive shocks tend to reduce freight-rate volatility. However, it should be noted that the sign and size effects should be considered jointly in the EGARCH model and not in isolation since the combined effect of both size and sign effect means that negative and positive shocks both tend to increase volatility, but with different magnitude, as seen in Figure 3.11. Therefore, estimated coefficients of TGARCH and EGARCH models suggest that there are leverage effects in volatility of VLCC TD3 and Capsize C4 spot rates.

   Estimated GARCH, TGARCH and EGARCH volatilities of VLCC TD3 and Capesize C4 spot rates are presented in Panel A and B of Figure 3.10, respectively. It is clear that the three estimated volatilities for TD3 and C4 are very close, with minor differences due to the structure of the models and the incorporation of asymmetric terms. Moreover, the news impact curves of different volatility models for TD3 and C4 freight-rate series are presented in Panel A and Panel B of Figure 3.11, respectively. A close look at these graphs reveals that while GARCH volatilities are symmetric in terms of the impact of shocks with different signs, the TGARCH and EGARCH models

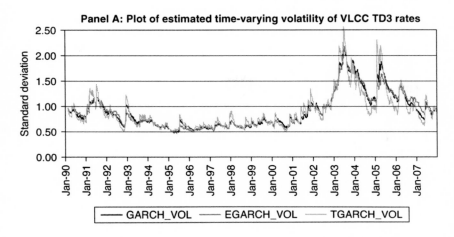

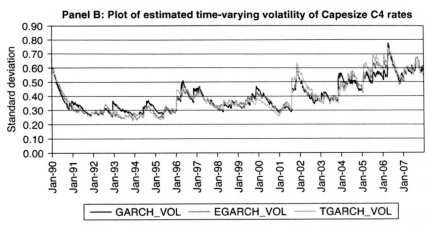

Figure 3.10 Estimated VLCC TD3 and Capesize C4 volatilities using GARCH, TGARCH and EGARCH models

reveal an asymmetric response of volatility to shocks with different signs; that is, negative news increases volatility more that positive news with the same magnitude. This is a surprising finding because, given the supply-and-demand fundamentals of the freight market which were analysed in Chapter 2, we expect higher volatility in the market when freight rates are high and supply-and-demand conditions are very tight. In this case, the fleet is utilised at full capacity and there is very little that can be done to increase the stock of fleet in the short run. As a result, because the market operates at the steep part of the supply curve, volatility in the market will be higher, since even

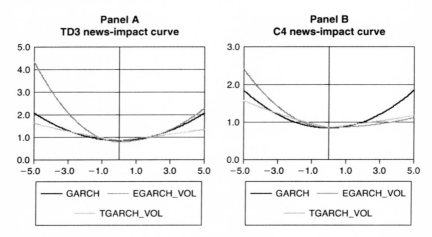

Figure 3.11   GARCH, TGARCH and EGARCH news-impact curves for VLCC TD3 and Capesize C4 rates

a small change in the supply or demand for shipping services will have a comparatively larger impact on the level of freight rates.

3.5.5   Markov regime-switching GARCH models

It is sometimes argued that due to the shape of the supply and the demand functions for shipping services, the freight market can be characterised as a bimodal market. This was shown in Chapter 2 where supply and demand curves for shipping services and the equilibrium price determination frame-work were discussed. There it was shown that when there is an oversupply of tonnage, which means that freight rates are low, shocks to the market can be absorbed by spare tonnage and, therefore, the market is in a low-volatility state. At the other end, when supply and demand for shipping services are very tight, freight rates are high, and the market is very sen-sitive to shocks. As a result, the market can be in a highly volatile state. In addition, the behaviour and dynamics of freight-rate volatility might be different under different market conditions. This suggests that changes in freight-market conditions should be recognised and incorporated in volatil-ity models to enhance the performance of models in capturing the dynamics of volatility. An approach to estimating time-varying volatility, which allows for changes in the state of the market to be incorporated in the model, is proposed by Hamilton and Susmel (1994), and implemented to model economic and financial variables by Gray (1996), Deuker (1997), Alizadeh and Nomikos (2004), and Alizadeh et al. (2008), among others. These are known as 'regime-switching volatility models', which allow the mean and the variance specification to switch between two (or more) different processes, dictated by the state of the market.

In order to allow volatility of freight rates to be dependent on market conditions, we can extend the simple GARCH model to a two-state Markov regime-switching GARCH as

$$r_t = \alpha_{0,st} + \alpha_{1,st}x_{1,t} + \cdots + \alpha_{P,st}x_{1,t} + \varepsilon_{t,st}, \ \varepsilon_{t,st} \, \text{iid}(0,\sigma^2_{st,t})$$

$$\sigma^2_t = \beta_{0,st} + \beta_{1,st}\sigma^2_{t-1,st} + \beta_{2,st}\varepsilon^2_{t-1,st} \tag{3.11}$$

where, $s_t = 1$ and 2, indicates the state in which the market is in.[11] The link between the two states of the market in equation (3.11) is provided through a first-order Markov process with the following transition probabilities:

$$\text{transition probability matrix} = \begin{pmatrix} p_{11} & 1-p_{11} \\ 1-p_{22} & p_{22} \end{pmatrix}$$

$$p_{21} = \Pr(s_t = 1 | s_{t-1} = 2), \quad p_{22} = 1 - p_{21} = \Pr(s_t = 2 | s_{t-1} = 2)$$

$$p_{12} = \Pr(s_t = 2 | s_{t-1} = 1), \quad p_{11} = 1 - p_{12} = \Pr(s_t = 1 | s_{t-1} = 1)$$

where in the above transition probability matrix, p_{12} represents the probability that state 1 will be followed by state 2, and p_{21} is the probability that state 2 will be followed by state 1. Transition probabilities p_{11} and p_{22} are the probabilities that there will be no change in the state of the market in the following period. These transition probabilities can be assumed to remain constant between successive periods and can be estimated along with the other parameters of the model. Alternatively, one can model the transition probabilities along with the mean and variance equations. Finally, the probability of the market being in regime 1 is P_1 and that of being in regime 2 is P_2, which can be calculated as

$$P(s_t = 1) = P_1 = \frac{1-p_{22}}{2-p_{11}-p_{22}} \text{ and } P(s_t = 2) = P_2 = \frac{1-p_{11}}{2-p_{11}-p_{22}}$$

Once the model and the log-likelihood functions for different regimes are specified, regime probabilities (P_1 and P_2) are used to link the log-likelihood

---

[11] In the model presented here we assumed two regimes or states. In practice, determination of the number of states/regimes for a model is a difficult task and it not only depends on the theoretical framework in which is market operates, but is also a matter of empirical analysis. However, increasing the number of regimes usually leads to over-parameterisation and difficulty in estimation, as regime-switching models are highly non-linear.

Table 3.6   Estimates of GARCH, EGARCH and Markov regime-switching GARCH models for VLCC TD3 freight rates

TGARCH(1,1) $\sigma_t^2 = \beta_0 + \beta_1 \varepsilon_{t-1}^2 + \beta_2 \sigma_{t-1}^2 + \beta_3 d_{t-1} \varepsilon_{t-1}^2$

EGARCH(1,1) $\sigma_t^2 = \exp\left(\beta_0 + \sum_{i=1}^{p} \beta_{1,i} \left(\frac{\varepsilon_{t-i}}{\sigma_{t-i}} \right) + \sum_{j=1}^{q} \beta_{2,j} \log(\sigma_{t-j}^2) + \sum_{i=1}^{p} \beta_{3,i} \left| \frac{\varepsilon_{t-i}}{\sigma_{t-i}} - E\left(\frac{\varepsilon_{t-i}}{\sigma_{t-i}} \right) \right| \right)$

MRS GARCH(1,1) $\sigma_t^2 = \beta_{0,st} + \beta_{1,st} \sigma_{t-1,st}^2 + \beta_{2,st} \varepsilon_{t-1,st}^2$ st = 1, 2

	VLCC TD3			
	GARCH(1,1)	EGARCH(1,1)	MRS GARCH(1,1) St = 1	MRS GARCH(1,1) St = 2
β_0	0.0004 [3.810]	−0.0911 [−5.076]	0.0666 [11.106]	0.0541 [4.435]
β_1	0.0592 [3.291]	0.0963 [6.388]	0.4648 [8.652]	0.0000 [0.000]
β_2	0.8828 [51.031]	0.9953 [406.320]	0.4850 [4.997]	0.987 [37.353]
β_3	0.0816 [2.970]	−0.0170 [−1.074]		
P_{12}, P_{21}			0.0032 [1.034]	0.0048 [1.835]

Note: Figures in squared brackets are t-statistics of estimated parameters.
Sample period: weekly data from January 1990 to November 2007.

functions and parameters of interest can be estimated using an estimation method such as 'maximum likelihood'. Regime-switching GARCH models are generally difficult to estimate due to their highly non-linear nature and the fact that estimates of past volatility have to be aggregated across two different states.

To illustrate how the Markov regime-switching GARCH model can be applied to estimate time-varying volatility of shipping freight rates, we again use VLCC TD3 rates and estimate the MRS-GARCH(1,1) model of equation (3.11) over the period January 1990 to November 2007. Estimation results of the MRS model are presented in Table 3.6 along with those from GARCH and EGARCH models. The estimated coefficients of MRS GARCH suggest that in regime 1 (st = 1), which is a low-volatility state, the variance shows less persistence (0.950), while in the high-volatility state of regime 2 (st = 2), volatility persistence is higher (0.987). In addition, the low values of estimated transition probabilities (p_{12} and p_{21}) indicate that there is also high

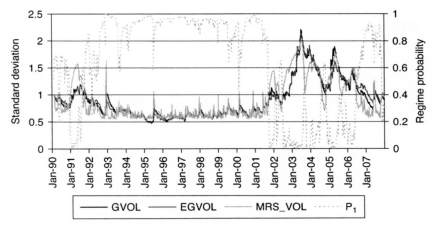

Figure 3.12 Plot of MRS GARCH volatility and regime probability estimates against GARCH and EGARCH volatility estimated for TD3

Note: GVOL, EGVOL, and MRS_VOL represent GARCH, exponential GARCH, and Markov regime-switching volatility estimates respectively; P_1 is the probability of the market being in a low-volatility state.

persistence in each regime; that is, when the market is in one state, there is a low probability of moving to a different regime.

Furthermore, the plot of estimated volatilies against regime probabilities, shown in Figure 3.12, clearly shows the association of regime probabilities with low- and high-volatility periods. For instance, the model captures the low-volatility period of 1993 to 2001, when the probability of being in the low-variance regime, P_1, is close to one. On the other hand, the model indicates that from 2003 to 2006 the market was in a high-volatility state because the probability of being in a low-variance regime, P_1, is close to zero over this period. It also seems that TD3 rates return to a low-variance regime in the second half of 2006 and 2007. Moreover, the dynamics of the Markov regime-switching GARCH model for VLCC TD3 is very similar to those of GARCH and EGARCH models, with the latter models showing greater volatility persistence compared to the regime-switching GARCH.

3.5.6 The term structure of forward-curve and freight-rate volatility

An alternative way of incorporating market conditions into volatility models is to use a proxy variable for market conditions, such as leading market indicators, world economic growth, or any other similar variable. One interesting variable which can be used as a market indicator is the slope of the freight forward curve (FFA curve) or the term structure of freight rates. Alizadeh and Nomikos (2007b) investigate the relationship between the slope of the

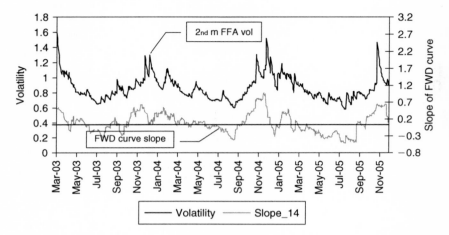

Figure 3.13   The relationship between slope of forward curve and FFA volatility

tanker freight forward curve (FFA curve) and the volatility of FFAs using an augmented ARMA-TGARCH model (TGARCH-X) of the following form

$$r_t = \alpha_0 + \sum_{i=1}^{m} \alpha_{1,i} r_{t-i} + \sum_{i=1}^{n} \alpha_{2,i} \varepsilon_{t-i} + \varepsilon_t$$

$$\sigma_t^2 = \beta_0 + \beta_1 \varepsilon_{t-1}^2 + \beta_2 \sigma_{t-1}^2 + \beta_3 d_{t-1} \varepsilon_{t-1}^2 + \gamma SL_{t-1} \qquad (3.12)$$

where SL_t is the slope of the forward curve measured as the difference between the natural logarithm of the current-month and fourth-month TD3 FFA rates. Using daily tanker FFA data over the period January 2003 to December 2005, they show that there is a positive relationship between the slope of FFA forward curves and the volatility of nearby FFA contracts. This can be explained by the fact that when the market is in backwardation, that is, when current and nearby forward prices are above forward contracts with longer maturities, it is an indication that supply for shipping services is falling behind demand. Therefore, any changes in demand would result in a sharp change in freight rates and an increase in freight-market volatility. On the other hand, when the forward freight curve is in contango, that is, current and nearby forward prices are below long-term forward contracts, it can be an indication that supply exceeds demand for shipping services. Consequently, any shock to the market can be absorbed by the slack capacity and the freight and forward rate volatility thus remains low. Figure 3.13 presents the estimated TGARCH-X volatility of second-month VLCC TD3 FFAs and the slope of the FFA curve, where it seems that there is a strong visual correlation between the two series;

that is, when the forward curve is in backwardation, volatility increases and when the forward curve is in contango, volatility is relatively low.

Furthermore, Alizadeh and Nomikos (2007c) use an augmented EGARCH model (EGARCH-X) to examine the relationship between the shape of the term structure and the volatility of freight rates. Using a freight data set covering the period January 1992 to September 2007, they find evidence that supports the argument that volatility of freight rates is related to the shape of the term structure of freight rates. More precisely, they argue that there is a nonlinear relationship between volatility of freight earnings and the slope of the forward curve in the form of a cubic function, implying that the rate of increase in volatility increases (decreases) as the degree of forward curve market backwardation (contango) increases.

3.5.7 Stochastic volatility models

A recent development in modelling volatility uses the concept that volatility of asset prices can behave stochastically. This led to the introduction of the family of 'stochastic volatility models' where the variance is decomposed into a deterministic part and a stochastic part. For instance, Taylor (1986) proposes a logarithmic 'autoregressive stochastic volatility' (ARSV) of the following form[12]

$$r_t = \gamma^* \varepsilon_t \sigma_t$$

$$\log \sigma_t^2 = \phi \log \sigma_{t-1}^2 + v_t \qquad (3.13)$$

where, once again r_t is the return at time t, σ_t^2 is the stochastic variance, γ^* is a scale parameter which removes the necessity of including a constant term in the log-variance equation, and ε_t is a normally distributed disturbance term in the mean equation with zero mean. v_t is also an independent

---

[12] Several different versions of stochastic volatility models have been proposed. One model which has been used and discussed extensively in the literature for derivatives pricing is Heston's (1993) stochastic volatility model with the following specification.

$$dS = \mu S\, dt + \sigma S\, dz$$

$$dV = \alpha(\overline{V} - V)dt + \xi \sqrt{V}\, dw$$

where S is the asset price, dt is a infinitesimal fraction of time, $V = \sigma^2$, dw and dz are two random variables which may be correlated, $\overline{V}$ is the long-term variance, ξ is a coefficient which determines the fluctuation in the variance (the standard deviation of the variance). It can be seen that the mean is a geometric Brownian motion (GBM) process with a time-varying variance, which itself is explained through a mean reverting process. The absolute volatility of the variance is $\xi \sqrt{V}$. Also note that different processes can be used to explain the mean, for instance mean-reversion (MR) or mean-reversion jump diffusion (MRJD) processes.

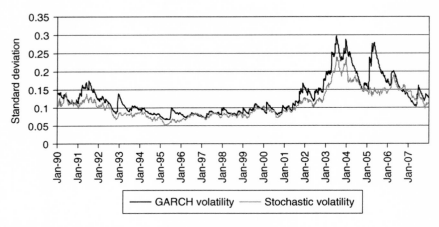

Figure 3.14 Plot of GARCH versus stochastic volatility estimates for TD3

and normally distributed random disturbance term with mean zero and constant variance, σ_v^2. The variance of the log-volatility process, σ_v^2, measures the uncertainty about future volatility and as it gets closer to zero, volatility of r_t becomes smoother and at the limit, with $\phi = 1$ and $\sigma_v^2 = 0$, the returns will have constant variance.

The empirical application of stochastic volatility models has been limited mainly due to the difficulties involved in their estimation. The major problem is that the likelihood function is hard to evaluate, despite the recent introduction of several new estimation methods in the literature (see Broto and Ruiz, 2004, for a detailed survey and discussion of stochastic volatility estimation methods). To illustrate how the stochastic volatility model can be applied to estimate time-varying volatility of shipping freight rates, we use VLCC TD3 rates and estimate (equation 3.13) over the period January 1990 to November 2007. The result of the estimated stochastic volatility and GARCH models, plotted in Figure 3.14, indicate that the two volatility estimates are close to each other with some minor differences. It also appears that the stochastic volatility model exhibits a lower degree of persistence compared to the GARCH model.

3.5.8 Multivariate GARCH models

Another important extension to the family of GARCH models are multivariate GARCH models, which have been developed with several different specifications, to model the means and variances of two or more variables simultaneously. These types of models have been suggested by Bollerslev et al. (1988) who find that multivariate models perform better than univariate models in asset pricing and capturing volatility dynamics.

Koutmos and Tucker (1996) extend the multivariate GARCH model in order to estimate the interaction between the means and variances of the returns on spot and future stock indices through a 'bivariate exponential GARCH model'; they also report that the multivariate model outperforms univariate volatility models. Kavussanos and Nomikos (2000a; 2000b; 2000c) use multivariate GARCH models to estimate dynamic hedge ratios and examine the performance of such techniques in risk management in the BIFFEX freight futures markets. Finally, Alizadeh (2001) uses multivariate GARCH models to examine spillover effects amongst volatility of freight rates for three sizes of ships (Capesize, Panamax and Handysize) in the dry-bulk market.

A multivariate GARCH model can be set up by specifying a multivariate model for the mean (such as a 'multivariate vector auto regression' (VAR) or a 'vector error-correction model (VECM)) and a corresponding multivariate setting for the time-varying variance and covariance terms. However, as the number of variables or the dimension of the multivariate GARCH model increases, the number of parameters to be estimated increases as well, which consequently may lead to a significant loss of degrees of freedom. Another problem with the multivariate GARCH models is that very often they can be difficult to estimate. This is because of the problems with non-negativity of parameter estimates as well over-parameterisation due to the large dimensions of the model. Engle and Kroner (1995) propose a 'generalised multivariate GARCH', known as a 'BEKK[13]model', as a solution for the non-negativity problem associated with multivariate GARCH, in which the time-varying variance-covariance matrix is guaranteed to be positive definite.

$$r_t = \Pi' x_t + \varepsilon_t; \quad \varepsilon_t \sim MN(0, \Sigma_t)$$

$$\Sigma_t = CC' + \sum_{j=1}^{n} A_j \Sigma_{t-j} A_j' + \sum_{j=1}^{m} B_j \varepsilon_{t-j} \varepsilon'_{t-j} B_j' \qquad (3.14)$$

where r_t is an (n × 1) vector of dependent variables, x_t is an (k × 1) vector of independent variables, ε_t is an (n × 1) vector of regression residuals which follows a multivariate normal distribution, and Π' is an (n × k) matrix of parameters in the mean equation. In the variance equation, Σ_t is a symmetric variance-covariance matrix, C is a (n × n) lower triangular matrix of constant parameters, while A_j and B_j are (n × n) matrices of parameters for the lagged variance and squared residual terms, respectively. Although the specification in (3.14) ensures a positive definite variance covariance matrix, it requires estimation of a large number of parameters, which results in excessive loss of degrees of freedom, especially when the sample is not very large. One way to

---

[13] The BEKK model was originally proposed by Baba et al. (1987) from whom it takes its name.

overcome this problem is to restrict some or all of the off-diagonal elements in A_j and B_j matrices to be zero as follows:

$$
A_1 = \begin{pmatrix} a_{11} & 0 & \cdots & 0 \\ 0 & a_{22} & \cdots & 0 \\ \vdots & & \ddots & \vdots \\ 0 & 0 & \cdots & a_{nn} \end{pmatrix}, B_1 = \begin{pmatrix} b_{11} & 0 & \cdots & 0 \\ 0 & b_{22} & \cdots & 0 \\ \vdots & & \ddots & \vdots \\ 0 & 0 & \cdots & b_{nn} \end{pmatrix}
$$

This specification, which is known as the 'diagonal BEKK', reduces the number of parameters of the model significantly, but at the same time it restricts the specification of the time-varying covariance.

Alizadeh (2001) utilises a multivariate BEKK GARCH model to investigate freight-rate volatility transmissions between different sizes of dry-bulk vessels, both in the spot and time-charter markets. Results of volatility models reveal that there are unidirectional volatility spillover effects from larger- to smaller-sized vessels in the spot and period markets. It is argued that volatility transmissions could be due to substitution effects among different sizes of ships in the dry-bulk market as well as to the higher sensitivity of freight rate for larger vessels to unexpected news compared to small ones which may force operators of larger vessels to switch to and from the market for smaller vessels and subsequently disturb the supply-and-demand balance in those markets.

3.6 Forecasting volatility

An important use of time-varying variance models is to produce forecasts of future volatility, which could then be used in derivative pricing, value-at-risk (VaR) estimation, and asset allocation and trading strategies. As discussed earlier, there are a number of different ways to model the volatility dynamics of a time series. Each of these approaches could also be used to produce volatility forecasts. The following sections discuss how volatility forecasts are produced with EWAV and GARCH models.

3.6.1 Historical volatility forecast

If we assume that volatility is constant, then we can use an historical-moving-average estimate of volatility over a window of n period and roll this estimation window to re-estimate the volatility every period as

$$
\sigma_t^2 = \frac{\sum_{i=1}^{n} (r_{t-i} - \bar{r})^2}{n - 1} \tag{3.15}
$$

In this setting, the forecast of volatility for time $t + 1$, σ_{t+1}^2 will be the estimate of volatility at time t, σ_t^2; that is, $\sigma_{t+1}^2 = \sigma_t^2$. Since the estimate of volatility at time t is based on a rolling window of observations, the one-step-ahead forecast of volatility is time-varying but static. This method has the limitation that it uses the equally weighted average of squared deviations for estimating and forecasting volatility, and thus does not reflect fully the volatility dynamics, because volatility could be more dependent on recent past events/shocks than on distant past events.

3.6.2 Exponentially weighted average volatility (RiskMetrics)

One way to address the problems associated with equally weighted rolling variance in estimating and projecting volatility is to use exponentially declining weights as in equation (3.2), known as exponentially weighted average volatility (EWAV) or RiskMetrics method. It has been shown that $\lambda = 0.94$ is sufficient to capture the dynamics of volatility for daily data. Furthermore, it is not difficult to see that one period forecast of volatility using this setting will be

$$\sigma_{t+1}^2 \approx \lambda \sigma_t^2 + (1 - \lambda) r_t^2 \tag{3.16}$$

In other words, one can forecast the next period's variance using the current variance and current price change, r_t. Also, if we take the expectations of the next period's volatility, knowing that $E(r_t^2) = \sigma_t^2$, we can write

$$E(\sigma_{t+1}^2) \approx \lambda \sigma_t^2 + (1 - \lambda)\sigma_t^2 = \sigma_t^2 \tag{3.17}$$

Similarly, we can extend the projection to k period ahead as $E(r_{t+k}^2) = \sigma_t^2$, for $k = 1, 2, 3, \ldots$, which means that the forecast of volatility k-periods ahead is the volatility today.

3.6.3 GARCH models

GARCH models can also be used to produce multi-step volatility forecasts. For instance, consider the following GARCH(1,1) model:

$$\sigma_t^2 = \beta_0 + \beta_1 \varepsilon_{t-1}^2 + \beta_2 \sigma_{t-1}^2 \tag{3.18}$$

To produce one-step-ahead forecast of volatility, σ_{t+1}^2, using information at time t, we can lead equation (3.18) by one period:

$$\sigma_{t+1}^2 = \beta_0 + \beta_1 \varepsilon_t^2 + \beta_2 \sigma_t^2 \tag{3.19}$$

Therefore, the one-period-ahead forecast of volatility is the weighted average of current volatility and error term, where the weights are the estimated coefficients of the GARCH model. The procedure can be repeated each time to produce new one-step-ahead forecasts of volatility as new information arrives. This type of forecast is known as the 'static volatility forecasting' technique.

To produce forecasts more than one step ahead, one has to use forecasts of volatility over intermediate periods to obtain multi-period-ahead forecasts. For instance, to produce two-step-ahead forecasts, we first produce a one-step ahead forecast of volatility (σ_{t+1}^2) and returns (r_{t+1}^2) and then use these values as inputs in (3.19) to produce multi-step-ahead forecasts of volatility. This method is known as 'dynamic volatility forecasting' technique. In GARCH type models, as the forecast horizon increases, the volatility settles to a long-run value provided that the volatility is non-explosive (that is, stationary). To illustrate this, consider the GARCH model in equation (3.18). This model suggests that the long-term volatility is $V = \beta_0/(1 - \beta_1 - \beta_2)$. To prove this we rearrange the long-run volatility to $\beta_0 = (1 - \beta_1 - \beta_2)V$ and substitute it in the GARCH model, to get

$$\sigma_t^2 = (1 - \beta_1 - \beta_2)V + \beta_1 \varepsilon_{t-1}^2 + \beta_2 \sigma_{t-1}^2 \tag{3.20}$$

Furthermore, we can rearrange the above model to

$$\sigma_t^2 - V = \beta_1(\varepsilon_{t-1}^2 - V) + \beta_2(\sigma_{t-1}^2 - V) \tag{3.21}$$

which can then be solved forward to obtain

$$\sigma_{t+k}^2 - V = \beta_1(\varepsilon_{t+k-1}^2 - V) + \beta_2(\sigma_{t+k-1}^2 - V) \tag{3.22}$$

Also, given that expected value of $E(r_{t+k-1}^2) = \sigma_{t+k-1}^2$ we can write

$$E(\sigma_{t+k}^2 - V) = (\beta_1 + \beta_2)E(\sigma_{t+k-1}^2 - V)$$

or \hfill (3.23)

$$E(\sigma_{t+k}^2) = V + (\beta_1 + \beta_2)^k(\sigma_t^2 - V)$$

It can be seen that as long as $\beta_1 + \beta_2 < 1$, the second term on the right-hand-side approaches zero as k increases, and the volatility converges to V, the long-run volatility. Therefore, as long as $\beta_1 + \beta_2 < 1$, in the long run, the volatility settles to a level which is $V = \beta_0/(1 - \beta_1 - \beta_2)$.

In order to illustrate how a GARCH model can be used to forecast freight-rate volatility, we use weekly VLCC TD3 rates over the period January 1990 to November 2007. We estimate a GARCH model over the period January 1990 to November 2006 and use the last 52 observations (December 2006 to November 2007) to produce static (denoted as GARCH_FOR_S) and dynamic (denoted as GARCH_FOR_D) forecasts for volatility of TD3 freight rates. In addition, we use RiskMetrics exponentially weighted average variance of equation (3.17) (denoted as RM) and rolling variance methods of (3.15) (denoted as Roll_Vol_For) to produce one-step-ahead static forecasts. Forecasts produced by each model over the forecast period are plotted against

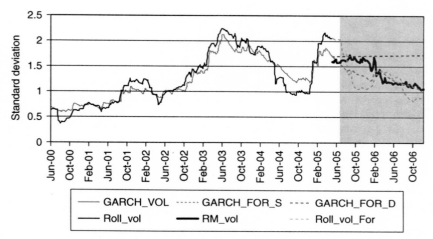

Figure 3.15 Historical and forecast of volatility of TD3 tanker route using GARCH and RiskMetrics models

Forecast period: December 2006 to November 2007.

actual rolling volatilities over the estimation period. Generated forecasts from different models seem to be quite different over the forecast period and several observations are worth noting here. First, the GARCH dynamic forecast seems to converge to the long-run volatility level with few fluctuations, as expected, while the GARCH static one-step-ahead forecast seems to fluctuate as the arrival of new information is incorporated in variance estimates in each period. This is also the same for forecasts produced by RiskMetrics and rolling-variance methods. RiskMetrics forecasts seem to be more in line with those of GARCH static forecasts, as expected, since these two methods are similar in the way they condition volatility on past volatility values. The difference is that in RiskMetrics the coefficient of lagged variance is fixed and predetermined, while in GARCH models this coefficient is estimated from past data.

Alizadeh and Nomikos (2007b) compare the forecasting performance of different GARCH models to establish whether using market information variables, such as the slope of the forward curve, can improve their forecasting accuracy. They compare volatility forecasts of different GARCH models against the realised squared returns in freight rates, and measure the amount of over-prediction and under-prediction of each model. Their out-of-sample test results suggest that including the slope of the forward curve in the model results in superior volatility forecasts in the Panamax, Handymax and VLCC markets, although this is not the case for the Capesize, Suezmax and Aframax markets.

3.7   Summary and conclusions

One of the most important steps in any risk-management process is risk measurement and quantification. In shipping, fluctuations of freight rates, bunker prices, ship prices, and even interest rates and exchange rates can have a severe impact on the operating profitability and business viability of the agents involved. Therefore, having a good understanding of risk and its dynamics is important, not only in setting up and implementing effective risk-management techniques, but also for portfolio construction and asset allocation, derivatives pricing and trading, value-at-risk estimation and risk monitoring.

In this chapter we discussed various statistical tools used for the analysis of the distributional properties of shipping variables, including freight rates, ship prices and their returns. In particular, we presented descriptive statistics used to explain the location and shape of the distribution. We further reviewed models designed to capture the dynamics of volatility of freight rates and asset prices, including exponentially weighted average variance (EWAV) estimates, generalised ARCH (GARCH)-type models, Markov regime-switching GARCH, stochastic volatility, and multivariate GARCH models. Finally, we presented and compared several applications of different dynamic volatility models in modelling and forecasting shipping freight rate risk.

4
Freight Market Information

4.1 Introduction

In all lines of business, exposure to unanticipated fluctuations, on both the revenue and the cost sides, is not desirable. The shipping industry is no different from other industries in this respect. Extreme fluctuations in freight rates and ship prices throughout the years have been affecting shipping companies' cash flows and, in some cases, forced some of those companies out of business. In markets dominated by uncertainty and risk, it is always prudent to employ methods which reduce or eliminate such uncertainties. The significance of risk management in the freight market has been recognised among the participants in the shipping industry for a long time, as indicated by the development of physical hedging methods, such as period time-charter contracts and contracts of affreightment (CoA); the use of these instruments for hedging freight rate risk has been discussed extensively by Gray (1990). However, it was not until the early 1980s when shipowners, charterers and other parties involved in shipping realised that risk-management techniques which had been applied successfully in commodity and financial markets (such as hedging using futures, forwards, swaps and options) could also be developed and applied for risk management in the shipping industry.

In order to trade derivatives on freight, a necessary condition is the availability of reliable price information on the underlying freight market, based on which derivatives can be priced and settled. This is an important requirement since trading any derivative contract relies on the availability of continuous, measurable and fully transparent price information on the underlying asset. Therefore, the aim of this chapter is to provide an overview of the freight-market information that is used for the pricing and the settlement of freight derivative contracts. The emphasis is on the indices produced by the Baltic Exchange as this is the leading provider of freight-market information and most of the derivative transactions in the dry and wet markets are settled on the basis of these indices, and also because the structure and composition of these indices gives us insights on how freight derivatives can be used for the purposes of hedging. The different types of freight-market information are discussed in the first part of the chapter. In the second part, we provide a brief historical overview on the development of the first derivatives market for freight – the BIFFEX market. We briefly discuss the characteristics of the contract as well as its deficiencies which eventually led to its demise and the ensuing development of the FFA market.

4.2   Baltic Exchange freight-market information

The first daily freight index was published by the Baltic Exchange in January 1985. The Baltic Freight Index (BFI) initially consisted of 13 voyage routes covering a variety of cargoes ranging from 14,000 metric tons (mt) of fertiliser up to 120,000 mt of coal, and was developed as a settlement mechanism for the then newly established Baltic International Freight Futures Exchange (BIFFEX) futures contract. It quickly won worldwide acceptance as the most reliable general indicator of movements in the dry-cargo freight market. Over the years, the constituent routes of that original index were refined to meet the ever-increasing and changing needs of the derivative markets. Trip-charter routes were added to the index and gradually, Handysize and Capesize routes were excluded from the index. As a result, in November 1999, the Baltic Panamax Index (BPI) superseded the BFI as the underlying asset of the BIFFEX contract.[1] In addition to the BPI, which reflects freight rates for Panamax vessels of 74,000 metric tons (mt) dead-weight (dwt) the Baltic Exchange also produces a wide range of other shipping indices covering different vessel sizes and different cargo types. These include the following: the Baltic Capesize Index (BCI) – for Capesize vessels of 175,000 mt dwt; the Baltic Supramax Index (BSI) – for Supramax size vessels of 52,000 mt dwt; and the Baltic Handysize Index (BHI) – for Handysize vessels of 28,000 mt dwt. In addition, there are indices covering the movement of tanker cargoes: the Baltic Clean Tanker Index (BCTI) and the Baltic Dirty Tanker Index (BDTI). These are discussed in the next sections.

4.2.1   Baltic Capesize Index (BCI)

The Baltic Capesize Index (BCI) reflects cargo movements of Capesize vessels. The current definitions of the BCI route, as of November 2008, are presented in Table 4.1. The Index consists of six voyage routes (Routes C2 to C7 and C12) and four trip-charter routes (Routes C8_03 to C11_03). The voyage routes are

---

[1] For a more detailed overview of the changes in the structure of the BFI as well as the statistical linkages between the different routes see as well Nomikos (1999), Nomikos and Alizadeh (2002) and Haigh et al. (2004). The 'History of the Baltic Indices' published by the Baltic Exchange (2007) also contains detailed information about all the changes that have been implemented to the various indices produced by the Baltic Exchange since their inception in 1985.

Table 4.1 Baltic Capesize Index (BCI) route definitions

Route	Cargo type and size	Route description	Weighting
C2	160,000 mt iron ore	Tubarão to Rotterdam	10%
C3	150,000 mt iron ore	Tubarão to Beilun–Baoshun	15%
C4	150,000 mt coal	Richards Bay to Rotterdam	5%
C5	150,000 mt iron ore	Western Australia to Beilun–Baoshun	15%
C7	150,000 mt coal	Bolivar to Rotterdam	5%
C8_03	172,000 mt dwt TC	Delivery Gibraltar–Hamburg for a Trans-Atlantic round voyage, redelivery Gibraltar – Hamburg range. Duration 30–45 days	10%
C9_03	172,000 mt dwt TC	Delivery ARA–Mediterranean for a trip to the Far East, redelivery China–Japan range. Duration 65 days	5%
C10_03	172,000 mt dwt TC	Delivery China–Japan for a Pacific round voyage, redelivery China–Japan range. Duration 30–40 days	20%
C11_03	172,000 mt dwt TC	Delivery China–Japan for a trip to ARA or the Mediterranean. Duration 65 days	5%
C12	150,000 mt coal	Gladstone to Rotterdam	10%

Notes: This table presents the definitions of the Baltic Capesize Index routes as of November 2008. TC stands for a trip-charter route; dwt stands for dead-weight tons; lt stands for long tons; ARA stands for Amsterdam–Rotterdam–Antwerp range.
Routes 8_03 to 11_03 are based on a standard 'Baltic Capesize' vessel of the following specifications: 172,000 metric tons (mt) dead-weight (dwt), not over 10 years of age with a cargo-carrying capacity of 190,000 cubic metres (cbm) of grain. Maximum length overall (LOA) 289m, maximum beam 45m and maximum draft of 17.75m; the vessel is capable of 14.5 knots when laden and 15 knots when in ballast on 56 mt of fuel oil per day, with no diesel consumption while at sea.
Source: Baltic Exchange.

quoted in terms of US$/mt of cargo transported and the trip-charter routes are measured in terms of US$/day for each day of hire.

The voyage routes reflect freight rates for iron ore and coal cargoes. The most important iron ore routes are C3 and C5, which reflect cargo movements from Tubarão in Brazil to Beilun and Baoshun in China and from Western Australia to China, respectively. For the coal routes, the most important ones are C4 and C7 which reflect freight rates for the transportation of coal from Richards Bay in South Africa and Bolivar in Colombia to Rotterdam, respectively. The four trip-charter routes cover the four major trading routes on which Capesizes operate, namely: Atlantic Trade (C8_03), Pacific Trade (C10_03), trips from the Continent to the Far East (C9_03) and trips back from the Far East to the Continent (C11_03). More specifically, Route C8_03 is the main trans-Atlantic route; the charterer takes delivery of the vessel in Europe, anywhere between Gibraltar and Hamburg; the vessel will then sail to either US Gulf, East Coast South America or the US East Coast for transportation of cargoes back to Europe, where the vessel will be re-delivered to her owner. Similarly, Route C9_03 is the trip out to the Far East. The vessel is delivered in Europe for a voyage to the Far East for re-delivery in the region between China and Japan. Route C10_03 is the Trans-Pacific route in which the vessel is delivered in the area between China and Japan for a voyage to load cargo in Australia and then return to the same region. Finally, route C11_03 is the return leg of Route C9_03 where the vessel is delivered in the Far East for a voyage to Europe. The freight rates for all these voyage routes are estimated on the basis that the trip is performed by a standard 'Baltic Capesize' vessel, the particulars of which are presented in Table 4.1.

4.2.2   Baltic Panamax Index (BPI)

The Baltic Panamax Index (BPI) reflects cargo movements of Panamax vessels of 74,000 mt dwt. The current definitions of the BPI are presented in Table 4.2. We can see that the index consists of four trip-charter routes whose geographical pattern is broadly similar to that of the Capesize routes in Table 4.1. For instance, Route P1A_03 is the main trans-Atlantic route; the charterer

Table 4.2   Baltic Panamax Index route definitions

Route	Description	Weighting
P1A_03	Delivery Skaw–Gibraltar range for a trans-Atlantic round voyage (including ECSA), redelivery Skaw–Gibraltar range. Duration 45–60 days	25%
P2A_03	Delivery Skaw–Gibraltar for a trip to the Far East, redelivery Taiwan–Japan range. Duration 60–65 days	25%
P3A_03	Delivery Japan–South Korea for a trans-Pacific round voyage, either via Australia or NOPAC, redelivery Japan–South Korea range. Duration 35–50 days	25%
P4_03	Delivery Japan–South Korea for a trip to continental Europe (via US West Coast–British Columbia range), redelivery Skaw–Gibraltar range. Duration 50–60 days	25%

Notes: This table presents the definitions of the Baltic Panamax Index routes as of November 2008. ECSA stands for East Coast South America; NOPAC stands for North Pacific.
Routes 1A_03, 2A_03, 3A_03 and 4_03 are based on a 'Baltic Panamax' vessel of 74,000 mt dwt vessel, not over seven years of age with a cargo-carrying capacity of 89,000 cbm grain. Maximum LOA 225 m and maximum draft 13.95 m; the vessel is capable of about 14 knots on 32 mt/day fuel oil when laden and 28 mt/day fuel oil when in ballast, with no diesel consumption while at sea.
Source: Baltic Exchange.

takes delivery of the vessel in the continent in the range between Cape Skaw (Denmark) and Gibraltar; the vessel will sail across to either the US Gulf, East Coast South America or the US East Coast for transportation of cargoes back to Europe, where the vessel will be re-delivered. Similarly, Route P2A_03 is the trip out to the Far East. The vessel is delivered in Europe to perform a voyage to the Far East for redelivery in the region between Taiwan and Japan. Route P3A_03 is the Trans-Pacific Panamax route where the vessel is delivered between Japan and South Korea for a voyage to load cargo in Australia or the north Pacific and then redeliver the cargo to the same region. Finally, route P4_03 is the return leg of Route P2A_03 where the Panamax vessel is delivered in the Far East for a voyage to Europe via the US West Coast. All these voyage routes are estimated on the basis that the trip is performed by a standard 'Baltic Panamax' vessel, the particulars of which are presented in Table 4.2.

4.2.3 Baltic Supramax Index (BSI)

Table 4.3 presents the Baltic Supramax Index (BSI) which reflects freight rates for a 52,000 mt dwt Supramax-type vessel.

We can see that the index consists of nine trip-charter routes but only the first six of those routes are used in the calculation of the Index. Again the composition of these routes is broadly similar to that of the BCI and BPI. For instance, routes S1A and S1B are trips from Europe (either the northern Continent, in the case of route S1A, or the northeast Mediterranean, in the case of S1B) for delivery anywhere in the region between Singapore and Japan; their combined weighting in the index is 25 per cent. Similarly, route S2 is the trans-Pacific route reflecting movements of cargoes from Australia to Japan, South Korea or China. Route S3 is the trip back from the Far East to Europe. Finally, routes S4A and S4B reflect cargo movements in the Atlantic basin; route S4A is for a trip from the US Gulf to Europe and route S4B is for a trip from Europe to the US Gulf. Overall, we can see that the weightings of these routes are 25 per cent for the trips from Europe to the Far East (Routes 1A and 1B), 25 per cent for the trans-Pacific route (S2), 25 per cent for the trip from the Far East back to Europe (S3) and 25 per cent for the Atlantic routes S4A and S4B.

4.2.4 Baltic Handysize Index (BHSI)

The definitions of the Baltic Handysize Index (BHSI) are presented in Table 4.4. The BHSI consists of six trip-charter routes based on a 28,000 mt dwt Baltic Handysize vessel.

Routes HS1 and HS2 are for trips across the Atlantic from Europe (Skaw–Passero range) to the east coasts of South and North America respectively, with a combined weight of 25 per cent. Similarly, routes HS3 and HS4 reflect cargo movements from South America and the US Gulf back to Europe. Turning next to the HS5 and HS6 they reflect cargo

Table 4.3   Baltic Supramax Index (BSI) route definitions

Route	Description	Weighting
S1A	Delivery Antwerp–Skaw for a trip to the Far East, redelivery Singapore–Japan range including China. Duration 60–65 days	12.5%
S1B	Delivery Canakkale for a trip to the Far East, redelivery Singapore–Japan range including China. Duration 50–55 days	12.5%
S2	Delivery Japan–South Korea for a Pacific round voyage, redelivery Japan–South Korea. Duration 35–40 days	25%
S3	Delivery Japan–South Korea for a trip to the Continent, redelivery Gibraltar–Skaw range. Duration 60–65 days	25%
S4A	Delivery US Gulf for a trip to the Continent, redelivery Skaw–Passero. Duration 30 days	12.5%
S4B	Delivery Skaw–Passero for a trip to US Gulf. Duration 30 days	12.5%
S5	Delivery West Africa for a trip, via East Coast South America, to the Far East, redelivery in Singapore–Japan range. Duration 60–65 days	
S6	Delivery Japan–South Korea for a trip to India via Australia. Duration 50–55 days	
S7	Delivery India or Sri Lanka for a trip to China, for a cargo of iron ore. Duration 20–30 days	

Notes: This table presents the definitions of the Baltic Supramax Index routes as of November 2008. All routes are based on a standard 'Tess 52' Supramax-type vessel with grabs as follows: 52,454 mt dwt self-trimming single-deck bulk carrier on 12.02 m salt-water draft; 189.99 m LOA, 32.26 m beam with five holds and five hatches and cargo-carrying capacity of 67,756 cbm grain or 65,600 cbm bale; the vessel is capable of 14 knots when laden and 14.5 knots when in ballast on 30 mt/day (380 cst) fuel oil and no consumption of diesel while at sea. The vessel has four cranes of 30 mt lifting capacity each, with 12 cum grabs. Maximum age – 10 years.
Source: Baltic Exchange.

movements in the Pacific basin. HS5 covers cargo movements from Australia to South East Asia; the vessel will be delivered in South East Asia for a round trip via Australia. Finally, HS6 covers cargo movements from the North Pacific to South East Asia. We can see therefore, that 50 per cent of the composition of the BHSI reflects cargo movement in the Atlantic basin (Routes HS1 to HS4) and 50 per cent reflects cargo movements in the Pacific basin (Routes HS5 and HS6).

4.2.5   Baltic Dry Index (BDI)

Finally, the BDI is a composite index calculated as the equally weighted average of the BCI, BPI, BHSI and BHI. The index is widely used by practitioners

Table 4.4 Baltic Handysize Index (BHSI) route definitions

Route	Description	Weighting
HS1	Delivery Skaw–Passero for a trip to East Coast South America (Recalada–Rio range). Duration 35–45 days	12.5%
HS2	Delivery Skaw–Passero for a trip to the East Coast of North America (Boston–Galveston range). Duration 35–45 days	12.5%
HS3	Delivery East Coast South America (Recelada–Rio range) for a trip to continental Europe (Skaw–Passero range). Duration 35–45 days	12.5%
HS4	Delivery US Gulf for a trip to continental Europe (Skaw–Passero range) via US Gulf or North Coast South America. Duration 35–45 days	12.5%
HS5	Delivery South East Asia for a trip to Singapore–Japan range including China via Australia. Duration 25–30 days	25%
HS6	Delivery Japan–South Korea for a trip, via North Pacific, to Singapore–Japan range including China. Duration 40–45 days	25%

Notes: This table presents the definitions of the Baltic Handysize Index (BHSI) routes as of November 2008.
Routes are based on a standard 'Baltic Handysize' vessel with the following specifications: 28,000 mt dwt self-trimming single deck bulk carrier on 9.78m salt-water draft, max LOA 169m and 27m beam with five holds and five hatches and cargo-carrying capacity of 37,523 cbm grain or 35,762 cbm bale. Capable of 14 knots average speed when laden or ballast with a consumption of 22 mt (380 cst) of fuel oil per day and no consumption of diesel while at sea. The vessel has four cranes of 30 mt lifting capacity each. Maximum age 15 years.
Source: Baltic Exchange.

as a general market indicator reflecting the movements in the dry-bulk market. It is in other words the 'barometer' of dry-bulk shipping. The BDI was first introduced on 1 November 1999 and replaced the Baltic Freight Index (BFI) which was the first shipping index published by the Baltic Exchange. More recently, in July 2008, Imarex launched derivative contracts on the BDI as well.

Figure 4.1 presents the graph of all the dry-bulk indices from September 2000 to January 2008.[2] Notice the gradual increase in the level of dry-freight rates which occurred after January 2003 and the increase in the market volatility from that period onwards.

4.2.6 Baltic Clean Tanker Index (BCTI)

Turning next to the tanker routes, Table 4.5 presents the definitions of the Baltic Clean Tanker Index routes (BCTI). These routes reflect voyages for

---

[2] In Figure 4.1, the BSI starts from July 2005 and the BHSI from September 2006 since these indices were introduced more recently than the BPI and BCI.

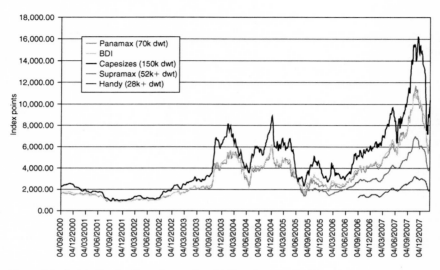

Figure 4.1 Baltic Dry Indices: September 2000 to January 2008
Source: Baltic Exchange.

Table 4.5 Baltic Clean Tanker Index (BCTI) route definitions

Route	Cargo	Route description	Indicative route
TC1	75,000 mt CPP/UNL naptha condensate	Middle East Gulf (MEG) to Japan	Ras Tanura to Yokohama
TC2	37,000 mt CPP/UNL	Europe to US Atlantic Coast (USAC)	Rotterdam to New York
TC3	38,000 mt CPP/UNL	Caribbean to USAC	Aruba to New York
TC5	55,000 mt CPP/UNL naptha condensate	MEG to Japan	Ras Tanura to Yokohama
TC6	30,000 mt CPP/UNL	Algeria/Euromed	Skikda to Lavera
TC8	65,000 mt CPP/UNL middle distillate	MEG to UK or continental Europe	Jubail to Rotterdam
TC9	22,000 mt CPP/UNL middle distillate	Baltic to UK or continental Europe	Ventspils to Le Havre

Notes: This table presents the definitions of the Baltic Clean Tanker Index (BCTI) routes as of November 2008. All routes are quoted in Worldscale points.
All vessels should have oil major approval.
CPP stands for clean products; UNL: unleaded gasoline; MEG: Middle East Gulf; USAC: US Atlantic Coast.
Routes TC2 and TC3 are also quoted as TC2_37 and TC3_38 reflecting the fact that they are based on voyages performed by 37,000 mt dwt and 38,000 mt dwt vessels respectively.
Source: Baltic Exchange.

Table 4.6 Baltic International Tanker Routes (BITR) Asia definitions

Route	Cargo	Route description	Indicative route
TC4	30,000 mt CPP/UNL	Singapore to Japan	Singapore to Chiba
TC7	30,000 mt CPP	Singapore to East Coast Australia	Singapore to Sydney
TC10	40,000 mt CPP/UNL	South Korea to NOPAC	South Korea to Vancouver–Rosarito range

Notes: This table presents the definitions of the Baltic International Tanker Routes (BITR) Asia as of November 2008. All routes are quoted in Worldscale points except route TC10 which is quoted in US$/mt. All vessels should have oil major approval.
NOPAC stands for North Pacific.
Source: Baltic Exchange.

clean-tanker cargoes and are quoted in Worldscale (WS) points. Clean products consist of the lighter distillates of the crude-oil refining process such as kerosene, gasoline, naptha and the like and are usually shipped in vessels with coated tanks. One of the most important routes is TC2 which is for the transportation of 37,000 mt of clean products or unleaded gasoline from Rotterdam to New York. Also important is Route TC5 for the transportation of 55,000 mt of naptha condensate from Ras Tanura to Yokohama.

Since 2007, some of the BCTI routes that reflect cargo movements in the Far East are estimated on the basis of assessments provided primarily by Far East-based shipbrokers and are published in the market at a time which is more suitable for trading in the Far East. These routes – which also form part of the BCTI – are known as Baltic International Tanker Routes (BITR) Asia, and their current definitions are presented in Table 4.6. Perhaps the most prominent route in this Group is route TC4 for the transportation of clean products from Singapore to Japan.

4.2.7 Baltic Dirty Tanker Index (BDTI)

Turning next to the tanker routes, Table 4.7 presents the definitions of the Baltic Dirty Tanker Index routes (BDTI). These routes reflect voyages for 'dirty' cargoes, mainly crude oil as well as lower distillates of the oil refining process such as fuel oil; these cargoes are transported in conventional tanker vessels although their low viscosity sometimes necessitates the use of steam-heating coils in the cargo tanks, as is the case, for instance, on routes TD8 and TD16. These rates are also quoted in Worldscale (WS) points. The vessel sizes range from VLCC (very large crude carrier) of 260,000 mt dwt, Suezmaxes (130,000 mt dwt), Aframaxes (80,000 mt dwt) and some smaller sizes. The most important routes in terms of physical trade are TD3, TD5 and TD7. TD3 is a VLCC route for the transportation of crude oil from the Middle East to the Far East. TD5 is a Suezmax route for the transportation of crude oil from

Table 4.7 Baltic Dirty Tanker Index (BDTI) route definitions

Route		Route description	Indicative route
TD1	280,000 mt	MEG to US Gulf	Ras Tanura to LOOP
TD2	260,000 mt	MEG to Singapore	Ras Tanura to Singapore
TD3	260,000 mt	MEG to Japan	Ras Tanura to Chiba
TD4	260,000 mt	West Africa to US Gulf	Bonny to LOOP
TD5	130,000 mt	West Africa to USAC	Bonny to Philadelphia
TD6	135,000 mt	Black Sea to Mediterranean	Novorossiysk to Augusta
TD7	80,000 mt	North Sea to Continent	Sullom Voe to Wilhelmshaven
TD8	80,000 mt (crude and/or DPP heat 135F)	Kuwait to Singapore	Mena al Ahmadi to Singapore
TD9	70,000 mt	Caribbean to US Gulf	Puerto la Cruz to Corpus Christi
TD10D	50,000 mt fuel oil (double hull)	Caribbean to USAC	Aruba to New York
TD11	80,000 mt	Cross Mediterranean	Banias to Lavera
TD12	55,000 mt fuel oil	ARA to US Gulf	Antwerp to Houston
TD14	80,000 mt NHC	SE Asia to East Coast Australia	Seria to Sydney
TD15	260,000 mt NHC	West Africa to China	Bonny to Ninqpo
TD16	30,000 mt fuel oil heat 135F	Black Sea to Mediterranean	Odessa to Augusta
TD17	100,000 mt	Baltic to UK or continental Europe	Primorsk to Wilhelmshaven
TD18	30,000 mt	Baltic to UK or continental Europe	Tallinn to Rotterdam

Notes: This table presents the definitions of the Baltic Dirty Tanker Index (BDTI) routes as of November 2008. All routes are quoted in Worldscale points. All cargoes are for the transportation of crude oil unless stated otherwise. All vessels should have oil major approval. LOOP stands for Louisiana Oil Port; NHC: no-heat crude; DPP: dirty products.
Source: Baltic Exchange.

the Bonny offshore facility in Nigeria to the US; finally, TD7 is an Aframax route for the transportation of crude oil from the Sullom Voe terminal in the North Sea to the Continent.

Figure 4.2 presents the graph of the BCTI and BDTI since their inception in 2000. These indices are constructed as the equally weighted average of the routes in Tables 4.5, 4.6 and 4.7. We can see that the tanker indices exhibit a clear seasonal pattern with a peak in freight rates occurring at around the fourth quarter of each year. This is due to the fact that demand for crude

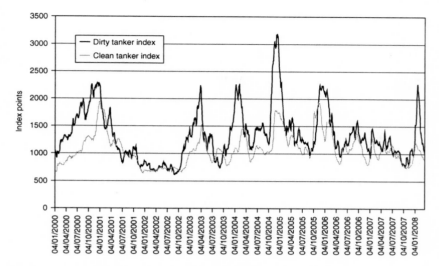

Figure 4.2 Baltic Tanker Indices: September 2000 to January 2008
Source: Baltic Exchange.

oil and its distillates is driven by the so-called 'heating' and 'driving' seasons in the US. Overall, seasonality is more prominent in the tanker market than in the dry, which is due to the fact that the dry market is primarily driven by the steel industry which exhibits less seasonality compared to the oil market.

In addition to freight rates in world-scale points for clean and dirty cargoes, the Baltic Exchange also produces time-charter equivalent (TCE) rates for VLCC, Suezmax, Aframax and MR product tankers. The definitions of these routes are presented in Table 4.8. These rates reflect the daily earnings (in US$/day) of standard-type vessels performing a range of voyages and are calculated as the net freight rate for each voyage (that is, the amount of freight income received minus broker's commissions) minus the voyage costs for performing the voyage – such as bunker costs and port charges – divided by the typical duration of each voyage, including time allowed for loading and unloading the cargo. These TCE rates are similar to the trip-charter rates in the dry market and therefore measure the profitability of the vessel performing a basket of voyages as opposed to the freight income received from a specific voyage (see Section 2.7.1 for details on how TCE rates are calculated).

4.2.8 Other indices

In addition to the dry- and wet-market information, the Baltic Exchange also provides information on the freight rates for liquefied petroleum gas (LPG) and palm oil cargoes. These route definitions are presented in Table 4.9.

Table 4.8   Baltic Dirty Tanker Index (BDTI) route definitions

Route	Vessel size	Indicative route
VLCC TCE	300,000 mt dwt double hull	Average earnings of TD1 and TD3
Suezmax TCE	160,000 mt dwt double hull	Average earnings of TD5 and TD6
Aframax TCE	105,000 mt dwt double hull	Average earnings of TD7, TD8, TD9, TD11, TD14, TD17
MR TCE	47,000 mt double hull	Average earnings of TC2 and TC3

Notes: This table presents the definitions of the Dirty Time-Charter Equivalent rates (TCE) as of November 2008. All routes are quoted in US$/day.
The VLCC-TCE rate is based on a 300,000 mt dwt, double-hull vessel with 155,000 mt dwt Suez Canal Net Tonnage. The vessel is capable of 14.5 knots on 80 mt/day of intermediate fuel oil (IFO) when in ballast and on 100 mt/day of IFO when laden.
The Suezmax-TCE is based on a 160,000 mt dwt, double-hull vessel. The vessel is capable of 14.5 knots on 50 mt/day of IFO when in ballast and on 60 mt/day of IFO when laden.
The Aframax-TCE is based on a 105,000 mt dwt, double-hull Aframax vessel. The vessel is capable of 14.5 knots on 48 mt/day IFO when in ballast and on 54 mt/day of IFO when laden.
Source: Baltic Exchange.

Table 4.9   Baltic LPG and palm oil route definitions

Route	Cargo	Route description
LPG	44,000 mt	Ras Tanura (MEG) to Chiba (Japan)
Palm oil	35/40,000 mt	Indonesian Straits (Belawan – Dumai – Kuantan range) to Rotterdam

Notes: This table presents the definitions of the Baltic LPG and palm oil as of November 2008.
Source: Baltic Exchange.

Finally, in addition to the indices produced by the Baltic Exchange, other providers of market information and independent shipbrokers produce their own assessment of freight rates for use as market indicators and for settlement of freight derivatives. For instance, a number of tanker trades for routes TC4 and TC5 are priced and settled on the basis of indices produced by Platts.

4.3   Calculation of the Baltic Indices and the role of the panellists

The Baltic Indices are calculated on a daily basis by the Baltic Exchange, from data supplied by a panel of independent international shipbrokers, and are reported in the market at 13:00 hrs London time (16:00 hrs for the tanker routes). Essentially this is an assessment market and the role of the panellists is to assess and report a professional judgement of the prevailing open-market level at their time of reporting on each publication day (which is every day on which the market in London is open) for routes defined by the Baltic Exchange. The use of reporting panellists' assessments is motivated by the fact that due to the nature of the shipping markets it is very difficult to have a verifiable market rate every day for every route published by the Baltic Exchange; for instance, even identical types of vessels may command different rates due to the fact that one vessel is better maintained than another. Therefore, there is no independently verifiable 'right' or 'wrong' rate and the rates which are reported on any trading day by the panellists, although they should represent a fair assessment of the current market levels at any particular time, are ultimately a matter of judgement.

In reaching their rate assessments, panellists are expected to take into account all relevant market information available to them, appropriately adjusted to accord with the route definitions. The exact route definitions are detailed in the *Manual for Panellists* produced by the Baltic Exchange, which provides a guide to freight reporting and index production; the manual is intended to assist in ensuring common practice amongst panellists when making their freight-rate assessments and also offers quality assurance about the market information products. [3] The panellists' manual contains guidance about the factors that panellists should consider in making their assessment. For instance, panellists will take note of recently concluded fixtures and current negotiations, as well as the supply of ships balanced against cargo demand. Because the Baltic route descriptions are very tightly defined, it is likely that deals which are actually concluded in the market differ from the definition of the reporting routes, in which case the panellists are expected to assess the relevance of any deviation from the route definitions. These may include differences in the specification of the ship or in the delivery and re-delivery periods (for trip-charter routes) or differences between loading and discharge terms or ports, as well as differences between cargo types and sizes (for voyage charters).

Special care also has to be exercised when reporting during derivative settlement periods, particularly during the last seven days of the month when some of the voyage routes are settled. There may be occasions when the physical market may be affected by principals seeking to influence panel returns and hence the settlement rate which will be applied to their FFA positions. As stipulated in section 6(e) of the *Manual for Panellists*, in such circumstances panellists need to exercise special care; for instance, panellists are entitled to take into consideration all relevant market information but are not bound to return a 'last fixed' rate if, in their opinion, other factors, such as tonnage offering below last done, or charterers bidding higher, suggest that the reported fixture no longer represents the market.

Overall, the assessments should provide fair and accurate representations of prevailing market conditions which, given the nature of the freight market, is a complicated task. The underlying freight market consists of frequently

---

[3] See Baltic Exchange (2008): www.balticexchange.com.

unrelated fixtures concluded between principals, each of which may involve different terms, and different market judgements. Similarly, the underlying physical activity for particular routes may be limited or non-existent at any particular time. In these circumstances, panellists exercise judgements which cannot be tested against current negotiations or fixtures.

4.3.1 Route selection and route changes

The freight market is constantly changing. For instance, previously import-ant trades can lapse into disuse and new trade routes and ship designs can become important. The composition of the Baltic routes has to reflect current trends and developments in the freight market and its updates are decided regularly by the Baltic Exchange and its appropriate committees, which con-sult with the industry, market users and derivative brokers to ensure that market information remains representative of market trends. In selecting the component routes, the Baltic Exchange is guided by the following three prin-ciples: i) *market coverage* – the component routes should be as representative as possible of the world's principal bulk-cargo trades; ii) *liquidity* – a steady and significant turnover of fixtures on index routes, or on routes related to them, is important, and; iii) *transparency* – a reasonable volume of accurately reported fixtures on the underlying routes should be available.

4.3.2 Calculation of the Baltic Indices

The Baltic Indices are calculated every market day by the Baltic Exchange from data supplied by a panel of independent shipbrokers. The freight rate which is reported in the market is the simple average of all the panellists' assessments received by the Baltic Exchange on that day.[4] The average freight rates are then multiplied by a constant number to convert individual freight rates (measured in US$/day or US$/mt) into an index number. To illustrate, how the conversion from US$/day or US$/mt to index points takes place, consider the following example based on actual market data. On 2 January 2007, the average panellists' return for route 1A_03 of the BPI was US$33,086/per day, as shown in Table 4.10. Then this average rate is multiplied by a constant number (called the 'multiplier' in column 3 of the table) to calculate the contribution of each route to the BPI, shown in column 4. The sum of the contributions of each route then gives the BPI for the day, which on 2 January 2007 was 4272 points.

The multiplier is a unique constant number for each route and reflects the importance of each component route for the calculation of the overall index. For instance, the multiplier for Route 1A_03 is calculated as follows: on 22 December 2006, the BPI had an index value of 4258. The composition

---

[4] This practice has been adopted since September 2002. Before that, the highest and lowest assessments for each route were excluded from the calculation of the average freight rate.

Table 4.10 BPI Index calculation on 2 January 2007

Route	Freight rate	Multiplier	Contribution (rate × multiplier)
BPI 1A_03	33,086	0.032280358	1068.03
BPI 2A_03	34,006	0.031407559	1068.05
BPI 3A_03	35,456	0.030123107	1068.04
BPI 4A_03	35,894	0.029755057	1068.03
			4272.00

of the BPI was changed on that day and the weight of route 1A_03 was thus increased to 25 per cent. This meant that the average rate returned by the panellists on that day had to be adjusted so that the contribution of route 1A_03 to the BPI would be 1064.42 points (25 per cent of 4258). The average rate returned by the panellists for route 1A_03 on that day was US$32,947/day. The weighting factor applied was therefore 1064.42/32,947 = 0.032280358 (some differences may be to rounding); the multipliers for the other routes were calculated in a similar fashion. On the next reporting day (on 2 January 2007, since there is no market activity during the Christmas period), the freight rates were multiplied by these multipliers to give the value of the index on that day. These multipliers then remained unchanged until there was a change in the composition of the index, that is, if the route weightings were changed or new routes were added or some existing routes were removed. By calculating the index numbers in this way there is a continuity in the level of the aggregate index when there are revisions in the composition of the index. Finally, the multiplier also reflects the effect of a US$1/day change in the freight rate on the BPI. For example, if the rate on route 1A increases by US$1/day then the BPI will increase by 0.0322 points. The multipliers for all the other indices are available from the *A History of the Baltic Indices* (Baltic Exchange, 2007a).

4.4 The freight-futures market – historical developments

The benefits of providing a futures market in freight rates had been recognised by shipping market practitioners as early as the 1960s (Gray, 1990). However, such a market was eventually established only in 1985. The reason was that the underlying asset of the market – the service of seaborne transportation – is not a physical commodity which can be delivered at the expiry of the futures contract; by its very definition, a futures contract is an agreement to deliver a specified quantity and grade of an identified commodity at a fixed time in the future. This obstacle was overcome with the introduction of the cash-settlement procedure for stock index futures contracts in 1982; when the underlying commodity is not suitable for actual physical delivery then an alternative is to deliver the cash value of the commodity at that time.

This innovation led to the development of the first exchange-traded freight-futures contract. Trading on the Baltic International Freight Futures Exchange (BIFFEX) contract commenced on 1 May 1985. The contract was traded at the London Commodity Exchange, that is now part of the Euronext.LIFFE exchange in London; the underlying asset of the contract was the Baltic Freight Index (BFI). The commodity which was delivered at the settlement date of the futures contract was the cash equivalent of the general level of the freight market at that time as represented by the level of the BFI. The settlement price was computed as the average value of the index over the last seven trading days of each contract month, and the monetary value of the settlement price was US$10 per index point.

The introduction of the BIFFEX contract gave, for the first time, the opportunity to shipping-market agents to control their freight-rate risk in the physical market through hedging. This was an entirely 'paper' financial transaction and no real ships or cargoes were involved. Additionally, through the price-discovery function, futures prices could also help reveal information about expected spot prices and hence provide valuable signals to market agents regarding the likely future direction of freight rates in the markets. Although the BIFFEX contract was quite innovative at the time, it quickly became apparent that the heterogeneous composition of the underlying index dramatically affected the performance of hedges in the market. This was due to the fact that futures prices did not capture accurately the fluctuations on the individual routes that comprised the BFI but, rather, followed the movements of the BFI itself. Effectively, therefore, hedging on BIFFEX was like a 'cross-hedge'.

Unlike other futures markets, in which futures contracts are used as a hedge against price fluctuations in the underlying asset, in the BIFFEX market futures contracts are employed as a cross-hedge against freight rate fluctuations on the individual shipping routes which constitute the BFI. As such, there is the risk that fluctuations on these routes may not be accurately tracked by the futures prices thus reducing the effectiveness of the contract as a hedging instrument. Cross-hedging freight-rate risk using an index-based futures contract is only successful when the freight rate and the futures price move together. However, when a large number of underlying routes constitute an index, the relationship between these routes and the index will not be very strong. Therefore, BIFFEX market participants, who used the contract to hedge their freight rate risk on specific shipping routes, made small gains in terms of risk reduction. In a series of studies, Kavussanos and Nomikos (2000a; 2000b) showed that the hedging effectiveness of the BIFFEX contract varied from 4 per cent to 19.2 per cent across the different shipping routes which constituted the underlying index. This was well below the risk reduction evidenced in other commodity and financial markets, which range from 70 per cent to 99 per cent.

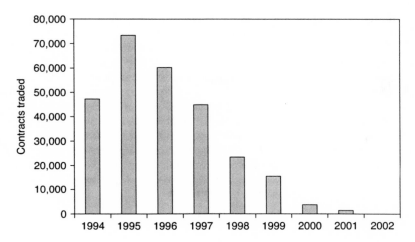

Figure 4.3 BIFFEX trading volume (1994–2002)
Note: Each contract trades the expected value of the BFI. The value of each contract is $10 per index point.
Source: Euronext.LIFFE.

The poor hedging performance of the contract is also thought to be the primary reason for the low trading activity evidenced in the market. Figure 4.3 presents the volume of trade for the BIFFEX contract for the period 1994–2002. From February 1996 to June 2000 the average daily trading volume in the market was only 146 contracts. The daily monetary value of these contracts roughly corresponded to the average freight cost of transporting 108,000 tons of grain from the US Gulf to Japan; market sources estimated that this level of futures trading activity corresponded to only 10 per cent of the total physical activity in the dry-bulk shipping market during the same period. As a result of the low trading activity in the market, the BIFFEX contract was eventually de-listed in April 2002.

The reduction in the trading activity of the BIFFEX contract after the mid-1990s was also due to the development of an over-the counter forward market for shipping freight called forward freight agreements (FFA), which are cash-settled against a single underlying shipping route or a basket of routes. Because of the fact that these contracts are traded against specific routes rather than a general index they also avoid the problem of basis risk, which was evidenced in the BIFFEX market. The mechanics of FFA contracts are described in Chapter 5.

4.5 Summary and conclusions

In this chapter we provided a description of market information produced by the Baltic Exchange and also explained how these assessments are calculated. Since their introduction in January 1985, the component freight routes and indices have been widely recognised by market practitioners as being reliable indicators of market conditions in the shipping industry. This availability of information is even more important in an industry such as shipping where a number of deals in the physical market are concluded on a private and confidential basis and, hence, price information is not openly disclosed to the market. Therefore, the availability of market information also provides price transparency in a market which has traditionally been very secretive. We also discussed the development of the first exchange-traded futures contract on freight, the BIFFEX contract, as well the deficiencies that led to its demise. Nowadays, the hedging tool used by market participants to hedge their freight rate exposure are FFAs. The practicalities of trading FFAs are described in the next chapter.

5
Forward Freight Agreements

5.1 Introduction

From the early 1990s a new market for trading the forward value of freight emerged, primarily as a response to the needs of market players who were aware of the deficiencies of the BIFFEX contract as a hedging instrument. These players wanted a hedging tool which would provide a more precise match to their exposure in the physical market and, hence, a more accurate hedging mechanism. Since the first recorded trade of a forward freight agreement (FFA) in 1992, the market has grown at almost an exponential rate and, according to market sources, in February 2008 the total value of trades in the market was worth US$125 billion, which represents a 150 per cent increase compared to 2007.[1] In this chapter, therefore, we describe the structure and functioning of the FFA market, the trading practices, documentation and type of contract used in the trades, applications and uses of FFAs for risk management and speculation, as well as how to deal with issues such as settlement risk and basis risk.

5.2 What is a forward freight agreement (FFA)?

A forward freight agreement (FFA) is an agreement between two counterparties to settle a freight rate or hire rate, for a specified quantity of cargo or type of vessel, for one or a basket of the major shipping routes in the dry-bulk or the tanker markets at a certain date in the future. The underlying asset of FFA contracts is a freight rate assessment for an underlying shipping route or basket of routes which is produced by the Baltic Exchange or by other providers of market information, such as Platts in the tanker sector. FFAs are settled in cash on the difference between the contract price and an appropriate settlement price.

---

[1] *Financial Times* (2008) 'Freight Futures Surge as Funds Seek Refuge', 24 February.

The calculation of the settlement price differs with the type of the contract being traded. For instance, the settlement rate for FFAs on individual routes from the BCI or BPI is calculated as the average of the route over the last seven trading days of a month. For FFAs on the average of the trip-charter (TC) routes of the BCI, BPI, BHMI and BSI, the settlement rate is calculated as the average of the month; finally, tanker FFAs are also settled as the average of the month. Although the calculation of an average settlement rate is used to ensure that settlement rates are not susceptible to large moves due to very high volatility or market manipulation on any specific trading day, the different averaging periods used in the calculation of the settlement rates reflect the market convention and stem from the use of FFAs as a risk-management tool. For instance, FFAs on individual routes are typically used to hedge specific voyages, so averaging over a shorter period of time and, therefore, having better correlation with the underlying physical route during settlement, is preferred.[2] On the other hand, market participants use basket routes, such as the average of the 4 TC routes of the BCI or BPI, in order to hedge their average monthly earnings; in this case, calculating the settlement rate as the monthly average is preferred, since it provides a better fit to the requirements of the traders in the physical market and more closely matches the monthly earnings of the vessel. More recently, FFAs for BCI C4 (Richards Bay–Rotterdam) and BCI C7 (Bolivar–Rotterdam) which are settled as monthly averages were also introduced, although they have not yet attracted a large trading volume.

Although trades are possible for every route published in the market, there seems to be a tendency for trades to concentrate on certain routes only. For instance, in the Capesize market most of the trades are on the BCI C4 and BCI C7 routes as well as on the average of the four trip-charters of the BCI (BCI 4TC), which is calculated as the equally weighted average of routes C8_03 to C11_03 of the BCI. In the Panamax market, the majority of the trades are on the BPI 4TC average, which is the equally weighted average of the four TC routes of the BPI; there is also liquidity on the BPI P2A (Far East trip out) and BPI P3A (Trans-Pacific round), particularly for shorter maturities. For the Supramax market, there is activity in the paper market on the weighted average of 6 TC routes, with the weights presented in Table 4.3. Finally, there is very little activity in the Handysize market, which may be due to the fact that the market for smaller ships is more fragmented than the market for Capesizes and Panamaxes and, hence, the routes used in the calculation of the Handysize index may not represent accurately the underlying physical market. The basket TC routes are used by practitioners to hedge their average monthly TC earnings. As we saw in the previous chapter, these TC routes cover the major trading patterns on which dry-bulk carriers operate (that

---

[2] This is analysed and discussed further in section 5.5.1 below.

Figure 5.1 Spot, first, second and third-quarter FFA rates for BPI 4TC
Source: Baltic Exchange.

is, Atlantic trades, Pacific trades, trip-out from Europe to the Far East and trip-back from the Far East to Europe) and, therefore, the average of these routes reflects the average earnings for those vessels. Turning next to the tanker market, on the dirty market most of the trades are on routes TD3, TD5 and TD7 and on the clean market, trades concentrate on routes TC2, TC4 and TC5, where TC4 and TC5 are usually settled on the basis of information provided by Platts (see Tables 4.5 to 4.7 for the definition of those routes).

Figure 5.1 and Figure 5.2 present the spot rates and the FFA rates for the first three quarters for the average of the four trip-charter routes for BPI and BCI, respectively. The graphs cover the period from March 2005 to January 2008. We can note that there is a strong degree of co-movement between the spot and FFA rates. We can also note that as we move from the spot to the forward rates, the forward rates appear to be less volatile than the spot rates, which is indicative of a volatility term structure pattern in the forward rates.

5.2.1 Volume by sector and trade

The FFA market has evidenced considerable growth over recent years. It is estimated that in February 2008, the market was worth US$125 billion, which represents a 150 per cent increase on 2007. Although this increase in value may partly be attributed to the exceptionally high levels of freight rates in 2007, it is nevertheless indicative of the growth in the paper market; this

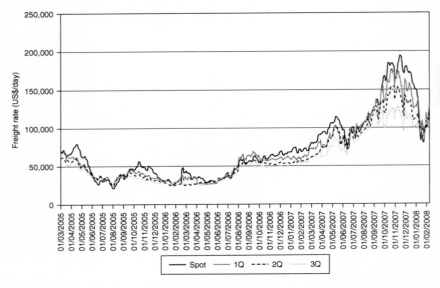

Figure 5.2   Spot, first, second and third-quarter FFA rates for BCI 4TC
Source: Baltic Exchange.

growth was a result of the surge in freight rates, particularly in the dry sector, which also resulted in an increase in the use of freight derivatives for
risk-management purposes. Another important driver behind the expansion
in the FFA market is market volatility, which has attracted trading interest
from players outside the shipping markets; therefore, over recent years there
has been an influx of new participants in this market, including investment
banks and hedge funds. Figure 5.3 presents the volume of trades in the FFA
market for the period 1997 to 2007; these figures are estimates provided by
the London-based FFA broker Freight Investor Services (FIS) and reflect the
estimated number of lots which have been traded in the dry market; the market convention is to measure the volume of trades in terms of lots where one
lot either represents 1000 mt of cargo carried or a one-day unit of trip-charter
hire. We can see from Figure 5.3 that the market has been growing constantly
over the past decade.

Since July 2007, information on the volume of trade has also been reported
by the Baltic Exchange. This information is provided to the Baltic Exchange
on a weekly basis by major international FFA brokers, clearing houses and
exchanges, and is then aggregated and reported to the market. In the dry
sector, trading volume, defined as lots traded, is estimated for the Capesize, Panamax and Supramax markets, and the trades are also classified as
to whether they are cleared or not; as in the previous case, a dry lot is
defined as either one trip-charter day or 1000 mt of voyage-based ocean

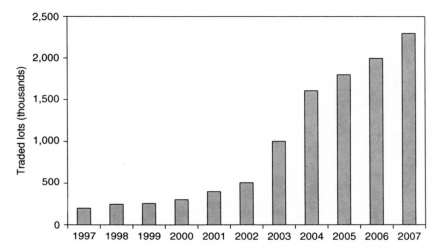

Figure 5.3 Estimated volume of trade in the dry FFA market
Note: Each lot corresponds to either 1000 mt of cargo or one day of TC hire.
Source: Freight Investor Services (FIS). Reported figures are market estimates.

transportation.[3] In each case a single transaction, although having a buyer and a seller, is counted only as one lot. Figure 5.4 presents the number of lots traded in the dry FFA market for the period June 2007 to April 2008 from data provided by the Baltic Exchange.

We can see that most of the trades concentrate on the Panamax market, which currently accounts for 55 per cent of the total trades. Capesizes account for approximately 29 per cent of the total traded volume and the remaining 16 per cent reflects trades in the Supramax market. We also note that, on average, 40 per cent of the trades are cleared through one of the clearing houses. It is also interesting to note that this pattern in the distribution of FFA trades among the differently sized vessels is not in line with the distribution of the world total fleet, where currently 40 per cent of world trade is conducted by Handysize and Supramax vessels, 40 per cent through Panamaxes and only 20 per cent through Capesizes.[4] The low volume in the Supramax and Handysize FFA sectors may be attributed to the fact that, for the smaller sizes, the underlying shipping market is more fragmented, with more smaller trades not represented by the Baltic Indices, as opposed to the Panamax and Capesize sectors.

---

[3] Defining traded volume in terms of lots may underestimate the significance of trades in the larger-sized vessels since, for instance, one day of trip-charter hire in the Capesize sector reflects twice as much volume of cargo transported than one Panamax FFA lot.
[4] Source: FIS.

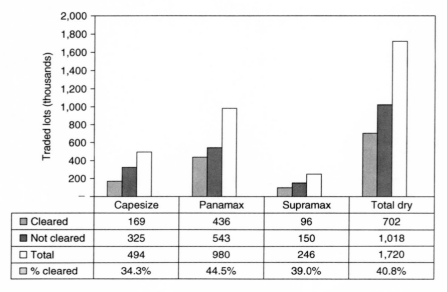

	Capesize	Panamax	Supramax	Total dry
☐ Cleared	169	436	96	702
■ Not cleared	325	543	150	1,018
☐ Total	494	980	246	1,720
☐ % cleared	34.3%	44.5%	39.0%	40.8%

Figure 5.4   Dry FFA trade volume for the period July 2007 to April 2008
Note: Reported figures are market estimates provided by major FFA brokers and exchanges. Each lot corresponds to either 1000 tons of cargo or one day of TC hire.
Source: Baltic Exchange.

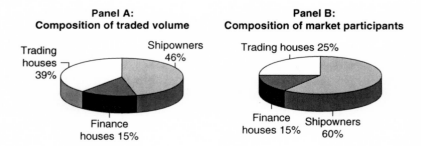

Figure 5.5   Estimated composition of dry FFA trade volume, 2006
Source: Market estimates for 2006 from FIS.

Finally, Figure 5.5 presents the percentage composition of traded volume by the type of market participants (Panel A) and the percentage composition of market participants (Panel B). We classify market participants as shipowners and operators, trading houses (which includes commodity and energy companies), as well as financial companies (which includes investment banks and hedge funds). We can see that, although owners account for 60 per cent of the market participants, they account only for 46 per cent of the trades,

Table 5.1   Tanker FFA volume for 2006 and 2007

2007	Trades	Volume in mt	Value of Trades (in US$'000s)
Not cleared	7,139	200,880,440	3,384,224
Cleared	6,212	173,990,000	3,345,291
Total	13,351	374,870,440	6,729,515
% of market cleared	46.5	46.4	49.7
2006	Trades	Volume in mt	Value of trades (in US$'000s)
Total	12,758	329,434,250	5,474,277

Source: Baltic Exchange (2006, 2007).

with trading houses accounting for 39 per cent, despite their smaller representation in the market. Finally, finance houses account for 15 per cent of the traded volume, although with the increasing participation of investment banks and hedge funds this percentage is expected to increase over time.

Turning next to the tanker market, Table 5.1 presents the volume information for the wet trades, provided by the Baltic Exchange. The information presented here refers to the number of trades, volume of trades in metric tonnes and the value of trades in thousands of US$ for 2006 and 2007. We can see that the total number of FFA trades is less than the corresponding total for the dry market, although the market has been growing steadily over the past few years. We can also note that a larger percentage of trades in the tanker market is cleared through one of the clearing houses (approximately 50 per cent) compared to the dry market.

Finally, Figure 5.6 presents the percentage composition of traded volume by type of market participant (Panel A) and the percentage composition of market participants (Panel B) for the wet market. Here we have four types of market participants: owners and operators who are natural sellers in the market; energy companies who are natural buyers; finally, trading houses and investment banks who take predominantly speculative positions and, hence, can be either buyers or sellers. In line with the dry market, we can see that although owners account for 45 per cent of market participants, they account for only 15 per cent of trades. Trading companies and investment houses, on the other hand, account for 40 per cent of counterparties in the wet market and trade more than 70 per cent of the volume. Overall, the 'traditional' players in the market (that is, energy companies and owners) account for only 30 per cent of the trades, a fact that suggests that most of the trades may be for speculative purposes.

5.3   How are forward freight agreements traded?

Forward freight agreements can be traded either over the-counter (OTC) or through a 'hybrid' exchange, as shown in Figure 5.7. Trading in the OTC

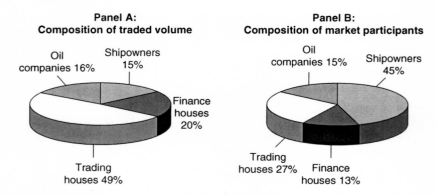

Figure 5.6   Estimated composition of wet FFA trade volume, 2006
Source: Market estimates for 2006 from Heidmar and Imarex.

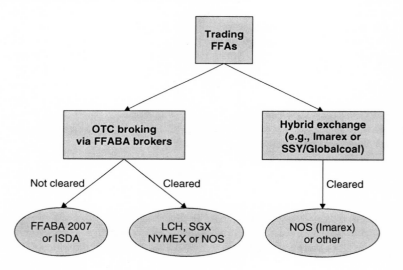

Figure 5.7   Trading structure of the FFA market

market takes place though specialist FFA brokers via 'traditional' telephone-based broking. Trades can be either on the basis of a principal-to-principal contract between the two counterparties, using one of the standard contract forms that are used in the market, such as FFABA 2007 or the ISDA® Master Agreement, or, alternatively, trades may be cleared through one of the clearing houses that provide services to the freight market, such as the London Clearing House (LCH.Clearnet), the Singapore Exchange (SGX) Asia Clear Service, the Norwegian Futures and Options Clearing House (NOS) or the New York Mercantile Exchange (NYMEX). In addition, FFAs can also be traded through a 'hybrid' exchange, the most popular of which is the International Maritime Exchange (Imarex); Imarex provides a trading screen where standardised contracts are traded which are then cleared straight through NOS. Each of these options will be discussed in more detail in the following sections.

5.3.1 Trading FFAs in the OTC market

In the over the-counter (OTC) market, the terms of the FFA contract are negotiated through a broker between the two counterparties (or 'principals' as they are known in the shipping industry) in a manner similar to a conventional negotiation in the physical market. The brokers are members of the Forward Freight Agreement Brokers Association (FFABA). FFABA was formed in 1997 by members of the Baltic Exchange and 'seeks to promote the trading of FFAs and the use of other over-the-counter and Exchange-traded derivative products for freight risk management'; in addition, it aims to develop and promote the use of standard contracts for the trading of freight derivatives.

The FFABA also publishes guidelines that outline the procedure which FFABA member brokers must follow during the contract negotiation process as well as the standard good practice that must be adhered to. All members of the FFABA need to have a thorough knowledge of and to comply with the provisions of those guidelines.[5] The trading procedure briefly comprises the following steps:

- First, the broker establishes trading interest and obtains a firm 'Bid' and 'Offer' from both counterparties. During the negotiating process, the principals must agree to all the terms of the deal. The main terms of the agreement cover: the agreed route; the day, month and year of settlement; the contract quantity (or duration for TC routes) and the contract rate at which differences will be settled. Brokers must not divulge the identity of their principals prior to agreement, unless there is specific authority from a principal concerned. There may also be cases where the approval of the counterparties is to be effected after the agreement of the other terms and conditions of the contract. This can be agreed between the counterparties and final acceptance should be done within as short a time as possible and within a specified time limit after the remaining contract terms have been agreed. In addition, a contract cannot be concluded without the express acceptance of both counterparties. During the negotiating process, brokers must maintain accurate written records and also record telephone conversations.

---

[5] See as well Baltic Exchange (2003) 'Guide to Market Practice for Members of the FFABA' which outlines the details and rules that must be followed by members of the FFABA.

- Second, a trade confirmation is then agreed verbally between the counter-parties. A trade recap is then issued detailing the main terms of the trade. The full contract is subsequently issued for signing, usually within two business days of the contract day; usually this is the responsibility of the seller's broker.
- Third, at the settlement day, which is typically the last trading day of the month, the settlement price is calculated – as the average over a certain period as specified in the contract terms – and a settlement statement is issued.
- Finally, settlement funds are paid no later than five London banking days after the settlement date.

The contract is a principal-to-principal contract, made directly between the two counter-parties and, as a result, the broker acts as an intermediary only and is not responsible for the non-performance of a contract by either of the principals. Consequently, the issue of credit risk and counter-party performance becomes quite important and, hence, market participants should exercise utmost care to ensure that their counter-party in the FFA transaction is a reputable company which will honour its obligations. The significance of this has been highlighted following a number of defaults in the FFA market which resulted in financial losses for participants in the market. Alternatively, companies may elect to trade cleared contracts and hence have their contract guaranteed by a clearing house (see Section 5.3.3 on the function of clearing houses). While FFAs are principal-to-principal contracts with each principal bearing the counter-party risk, brokers should not mislead the counterparties with respect to the status of either principal. Brokers are therefore expected to exercise reasonable care in respect of all pre-contract representations and not to withhold any material information. In addition, since the contract is traded in the OTC market, the terms of the contract may be tailor-made to fit the requirements of the counterparties. Finally, brokers receive commission which is agreed in advance with the principals, and is typically 25 basis points (0.25 per cent) from each party on the fixed (or expected) freight rate.

5.3.2   Contract documentation in the OTC market

As the FFA market developed in the late 1990s, the need to introduce a 'standard' form of contract for trading FFAs became apparent. Initially, the FFA route to contract documentation developed along two channels. The first came from the FFA broking community which looked at developing a new contract to trade FFAs; the second came from market users and traders who were already active in the commodity and financial derivatives markets and were thus looking at utilising the contracts used in those markets and adapting them to the FFA market. Overall, this led to the development of the two different, but related, types of contract documentation that are used by market practitioners today. These are: the FFABA contract and the ISDA® contract.

5.3.2.1 The FFABA contract

The FFABA developed its own version of standard contract to be used in FFA transactions. The first version of the FFABA contract contained the main terms of an FFA agreement (such as the agreed contract route, the contract duration, the settlement dates and so on). This version of the contract was known in the industry as the FFABA 2000 contract. As the market developed and the complexity and sophistication of trades increased, it became apparent that the FFABA 2000 contract had a number of deficiencies, primarily in respect to its provisions when it came to counter-party credit risk. More specifically, the FFABA 2000 contract did not provide any rights or provisions to terminate an FFA early if there is bankruptcy or insolvency of a counterparty in an FFA transaction; this is standard in many derivatives transactions but its absence from the FFA market meant that a close-out process was complicated and could also lead to increased exposure. In addition, the original contract did not allow for the netting of payments in the event that two counterparties had a number of contract positions which were due to be settled at the same point in time; the process of netting is beneficial for market participants because it makes the administration of settlement easier and also reduces the exposure in the event of insolvency or bankruptcy of one counter-party. More importantly, there was no provision in the FFABA 2000 contract to net off all contracts in the event that the other party in the agreement defaulted. As a result, parties trading in the FFABA 2000 contract could not view their exposure on a netted basis. Instead, each party had to view its exposure looking solely at its in-the-money positions, which magnified credit risk and resulted in lower credit-risk limits.

As trading volume in the market increased, it became apparent that the contract had to incorporate certain provisions which would suit the needs of the industry. This led to the development of the FFABA 2005 contract; this contract closely resembles the FFABA 2000 contract but, most importantly, incorporates the 1992 International Swaps and Derivatives Association (ISDA®) Master Agreement (Multicurrency–Cross Border).[6] This is the most common legal contract for derivatives transaction in the world today and

---

[6] The International Swaps and Derivatives Association (ISDA) represents participants in the OTC derivatives industry and is the largest global financial trade association, by number of member firms, as it currently has over 800 member institutions from 55 countries on six continents. The primary purpose of ISDA is to 'encourage the prudent and efficient development of the privately negotiated derivatives business by, among others, promoting practices conducive to the efficient conduct of the business, including the development and maintenance of derivatives documentation'; see www.isda.org.

has been extensively adopted by all major financial institutions that trade derivatives; in addition, its terms also provide adequate provisions for all the deficiencies that had been previously identified with the FFABA 2000 contract. Even though the ISDA® Master Agreement is a standard-form contract, in practice it is usually tailored to the individual needs of the parties or the trade and is negotiated and executed separately from the negotiation and execution of individual trades. In general, counterparties transact on a 'long-form' basis; that is, they incorporate the Master Agreement in the FFABA contract by reference and by making the necessary modifications and elections in the main body of the contract. The main motivation for that is to create a standard-form document that ensures market conformity and liquidity.

An updated version of the FFABA 2005 contract was introduced in 2007. This new version, known as FFABA 2007, also incorporates the ISDA Master Agreement 1992 and provides certain improvements to the earlier version of the FFABA contract, particularly relating to the calculation of the contract quantity and settlement sum as well as regarding the netting provisions and the early termination of the contract in the event of a default.[7] A sample specimen FFABA 2007 contract is presented in Appendix 5.A.

The main terms of the contract are as follows:

- Clause 1: The agreed contract route (for example, BCI C4).
- Clause 2: The contract rate at which differences will be settled (say, US$40/mt). This is effectively the FFA rate.
- Clause 3: The total contract quantity, and quantity by contract month. The distinction between total quantity and quantity by month is useful in cases when contracts are traded for the duration of more than one month or when the total quantity is spread across a range of months. Suppose for instance that we trade one Capesize cargo for one month; then, both the total quantity and quantity by contract month are 150,000 mt; if, on the other hand, we trade half in the first month and half in the second month then the total quantity will be 150,000 mt and the quantity by contract month is 75,000 mt.
- Clause 4: Contract months – these are the settlement months that will be traded (e.g., January 2008).
- Clause 5: Settlement dates – this is the last Baltic Index publication date of the contract month.
- Clause 6: Settlement rate. This clause specifies how the settlement rate will be calculated. In the example presented here, that could either be the average of the last seven days of the contract month or the average of

---

[7] A more detailed discussion of the differences between the FFABA 2005 and FFABA 2007 contracts is provided in Reed Smith Richards Butler (2008). For more on the incorporation of the ISDA Master Agreement in the FFABA 2005 contract see Shaw and Weller (2006) and Perrot (2006).

the month. The same clause also makes provisions for the calculation of the settlement rate if, for whatever reason, the Baltic Exchange does not publish the rates over the settlement period.

- Clause 7: Settlement sum. The settlement sum is the difference between the contract rate (in Clause 2) and the settlement rate (in Clause 6) multiplied by the quantity by contract month. If the settlement rate is higher than the contract rate, the seller (short) pays the buyer (long) the settlement sum; similarly, if the settlement rate is less than the contract rate, the buyer shall pay the seller the settlement sum.

- Clause 9: ISDA Master Agreement. This clause incorporates the ISDA® Master Agreement by reference; the subsections to this clause specify the exceptions to the Master Agreement that are relevant to the FFABA contract. For instance, Clause 9(a) specifies that netting of payments will cover all contracts between the two parties that settle on the same day and in the same currency. Similarly Clause 9(f) is an Automatic Early Termination Clause which allows the early termination of the contract in the event of a default.

5.3.2.2 ISDA® Master Agreement and Schedule

In addition to the FFABA contract, practitioners also use the ISDA® Master Agreement and Schedule to trade FFAs. These are likely to be companies from the energy and the commodities sector where the same contract is used for trading derivatives in those markets and, hence, it is logical to bring this tried-and-tested contact into the area of FFAs. In addition, since July 2004, freight has been included in the commodity derivatives definitions used by ISDA.

The ISDA prescribed-form agreement for swap transactions includes a Master Agreement which sets forth the terms of the ongoing legal and credit relationships between the parties. Any amendments to the Master Agreement are set forth in an attached schedule. From a legal perspective, the advantage of the ISDA form is that it has been used as the standard form of derivative contract for the great majority of traded commodities and as such has been subject to judicial review and found to be enforceable in a number of international jurisdictions. As a result, the legal risk of uncertainty surrounding the interpretation of the terms of the ISDA Master Agreement is greatly reduced.[8]

5.3.3 Credit risk and clearing

One of the major risks when it comes to trading FFAs is that of credit risk. Credit risk refers to the risk of loss caused by non-payment or bankruptcy of the counter-party in an OTC FFA transaction. Credit risk can be mitigated

---

[8] See Kennedy and Califano (n.d.).

using a variety of methods, some of which are more effective than others. For instance, using a contract specification such as FFABA 2007 or the ISDA Master Agreement provides participants with more rights and greater protection in the event of counter-party default, as was discussed in the previous section. In addition, bank guarantees or letters of credit provide reassurance that the bank will guarantee a payment up to a certain amount in the case that a counter-party defaults in an FFA transaction. Alternatively, traders can establish bilateral credit lines with the counterparties with whom they trade. Finally, another method that market participants can use is a 'credit sleeve'. This refers to the practice whereby two counterparties without a sufficient line of credit with each other get a third party to act as a middleman in a trade so that both counterparties trade with the middleman who takes a difference in the price between the two trades. Credit sleeves can be provided by investment banks as well as by trading companies active in the FFA market, and is an effective method for providing both liquidity and some degree of credit security to the counterparties.

Perhaps the most effective method for reducing credit risk in FFA trades is clearing. Although, traditionally, clearing houses have been closely associated with exchange-traded contacts, since the late 1990s we saw the emergence of clearing services for OTC contracts traded outside an organised exchange. Currently, OTC clearing services for freight are provided by LCH.Clearnet, SGX, NOS and NYMEX. The list of underlying routes, along with the contract specifications that are cleared by each clearing house, are presented in Table 5.2.

5.3.3.1   How clearing houses operate

Clearing houses are well-capitalised financial institutions that guarantee counter-party trade performance on both sides, and eliminate the restrictions of pre-approved counter-party limits, the need for bilateral credit arrangements, and the reliance on sleeving arrangements. The clearing house guarantees that cleared trades will be honoured and it serves this role by interposing itself between the buyer and the seller by adopting the position of a buyer to every seller and vice-versa. In order to clear through a clearing house, companies must be members of the clearing house – or clearing members as they are known; brokers or traders that are not clearing members and wish to have their contracts cleared must channel their contracts through one of these clearing members. For a company to become a clearing member, it has to satisfy the strict financial criteria determined by the clearing house. For instance, in the case of LCH.Clearnet, individual companies wishing to become clearing members must satisfy conditions for minimum capital requirements; they need to have in place the appropriate banking arrangements; companies also need to have staff of sufficient experience and knowledge of the products being cleared and appropriate systems able to cope with their clearing activities. In addition, the company must deposit

Table 5.2 List of contracts cleared by different clearing houses

Route	Settlement	Lot size	LCH.Clearnet	SGX	NOS	NYMEX
C3	7-day	1000 mt	X	X		
C4	7-day	1000 mt	X	X	X	
C5	7-day	1000 mt	X	X		
C7	7-day	1000 mt	X	X	X	
C4 M	Month	1000 mt	X		X	
C7 M	Month	1000 mt	X		X	
BCI 4TC	Month	1-day	X	X	X	
P2A	7-day	1-day	X	X	X	
P3A	7-day	1-day	X	X	X	
BPI 4TC	Month	1-day	X	X	X	
BSI 6TC	Month	1-day	X	X	X	
BHSI 6TC	Month	1-day	X		X	
TD3	Month	1000 mt	X	X	X	X
TD5	Month	1000 mt	X		X	X
TD7	Month	1000 mt	X		X	X
TD8	Month	1000 mt			X	
TD9	Month	1000 mt			X	X
TD10D	Month	1000 mt				X
TD11	Month	1000 mt			X	
TD17	Month	1000 mt			X	
TC1	Month	1000 mt				X
TC2	Month	1000 mt	X		X	X
TC4	Month	1000 mt	X	X	X	X
TC5	Month	1000 mt	X	X	X	X
TC6	Month	1000 mt			X	

Notes: Settlement denotes whether the settlement rate is calculated as the average of the last seven days or the average of the month of the underlying spot rate. Lot size is the minimum lot size that can be cleared. SGX also allows clearing half-days for the BCI 4TC, BPI 4TC and BSI 6TC routes.
For NOS, TC4 and TC5, routes are settled on the basis of price information provided by Platts.
For NYMEX, all rates are quoted in US$/mt instead of Worldscale points. Also, routes TC1, TC4 and TC5 are assessed on the basis of Platts reports.
Sources: LCH.Clearnet, SGX, Imarex/NOS and NYMEX as of March 2008. See as well the route descriptions in Chapter 4 for the exact definitions of the different routes.

a minimum of £100,000 to the default fund of the clearing house. Clearing members serve a number of functions. They approve and set up clearing accounts; they set up and monitor position and margin limits for their customers' accounts; they also manage the margin requirements and settlements for the accounts of their individual customers (the process of margining is described in the next section).

Figure 5.8 presents the structure of a clearing system for OTC FFAs. First, the principals wishing to have their contracts cleared must either have an account with one of the clearing member companies or be clearing members

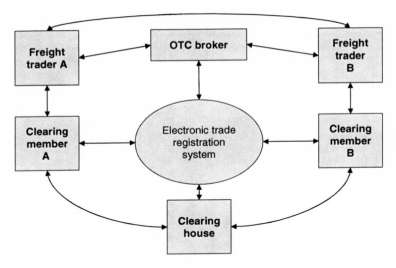

Figure 5.8   The FFA clearing system

themselves. In the example presented in Figure 5.8, there are two princi-pals in the market; freight trader A and freight trader B. Each has a clearing account with a clearing member; freight trader A with clearing member A and freight trader B with clearing member B, although it may also be possible that both use the same clearing member or that one or both of them are clearing members themselves. Both freight trading companies are very active traders in the FFA market; suppose, for instance, that they want to trade BCI 4TC for the first quarter of 2007 at a rate of US$100,000/day. They agree the details of the deal in the OTC market through an FFABA broker; alternatively, the prin-cipals can also trade directly between themselves, as indicated in Figure 5.8. After the terms of the deal have been agreed, the broker enters the details of the trade in the trade registration system of the clearing house. This is an elec-tronic system that notifies the clearing house of the trade between the two counterparties; the system accepts trades that have been effected by brokers for principals who have established clearing accounts with clearing members.

Following that, both clearing members accept the trade and assume counter-party responsibilities to their respective principals. This essentially means that counter-party risk now lies between freight trader A and clearing member A, as well as between freight trader B and clearing member B. The clearing house, on the other hand, will be the central counter-party to the two clearing members, A and B. Through the clearing arrangement, there is no need for the two principals to enter into a direct contract with each other, such as FFABA 2007 or ISDA. The terms of the specific trade are governed by the rules and regulations of the clearing house.

5.3.3.2 Margining and marking to market

While the clearing house has a balanced portfolio of long and short positions, the potential losses in case of a default are very large. As a result, clearing houses operate a system of margins as follows: every time a trader either buys or sells a contract, he needs to place a deposit on his account with his clearing member, either in the form of cash, letter of credit, bank guarantees, certificates of deposit or any other form of acceptable security as determined by the clearing house.[9] This deposit is called the 'initial margin' and represents the estimated potential losses on a position between the last mark-to-market value and the close-out position in the case of a default. Initial margins differ for each contract and are calculated using statistical analysis. In general, clearing houses calculate the level of initial margins using the SPAN© methodology, which stands for Standardised Portfolio Analysis of Risk. This is the leading margining system, which has been adopted by most options and futures exchanges around the world, and is based on a sophisticated set of algorithms that determine the level of margin according to an assessment of the one-day risk for a given position.[10] Generally, the level of margin depends on the volatility of the position, the liquidity in the market and also on the maturity of the position due to the volatility term structure of forward rates. In addition, the margin also depends on whether the individual trader has outright positions in contracts or whether he has spread positions where he takes a long and a short position in two different routes or in the same route but across two different maturities; in the later case, depending on the level of correlation between the two routes, there will be a commensurate decrease in the level of the initial margin. For instance, for a spread between Panamax and Capesize FFAs, there will be a reduction of 65 per cent on initial margins required by LCH.Clearnet. Finally, although the level of margins is generally set by the clearing house, individual clearing members may require higher margins from their clients.

After the initial margin has been deposited with the clearing member, then, at the end of each trading day, the trader's margin account is adjusted to reflect his profit or loss from his position. This practice is referred to as 'marking to market'. The trader is entitled to withdraw any balance in the margin account in excess of the initial margin and, similarly, any losses are deducted from the margin account. To ensure that the balance of the account never becomes negative, a 'maintenance margin', which is lower than the initial margin, is also set. This represents the minimum amount of funds required to be maintained in an account for each outstanding contract or

---

[9] Financial institutions and banks may also facilitate this process by providing what is known as 'margin financing services'.

[10] For an example on how margins are calculated for LCH.Clearnet positions see LCH.Clearnet (2008).

open position. If the balance in the margin account falls below the maintenance margin the trader receives a 'margin call' and is expected to top up his margin account back to the initial margin level the following day. The additional funds deposited are also known as the 'variation margin'. If the trader cannot meet the margin call, then he is in default of his obligations to the clearing member.

The process of marking to market limits the clearing member's exposure to loss from a trader's default and ensures all losses due to daily price fluctuations are accounted for and settled. This enables the clearing member to liquidate the positions if necessary without accumulating loss-generating positions over a long period of time. Essentially, the clearing member will lose on the default only if the loss on one day exceeds the amount of margin. In addition to the initial margin that the trader deposits with the clearing member, the clearing house will, in turn, demand margin deposit from the clearing members to cover all futures positions that they represent to the clearing house.

The process of daily marking to market and payment of variation margins removes a vast amount of credit risk. A principal who has made profits on a FFA position will receive the profits on a daily basis and need not be concerned with the counter-party's ability to pay their losses. This is different from the OTC FFA market, where the gains or losses from a position are exchanged at the settlement date of the contracts. This deferral between an economic event causing a gain or loss and its ultimate payment introduces a high degree of credit risk between counter-parties. Another significant benefit of clearing is the potential for multilateral netting. Although the FFABA 2007 contract incorporates netting provisions, it does not enable netting of positions across multiple counterparties. Processing these trades through a clearing house, however, permits multilateral netting and frees up credit lines across counterparties. As a result, a party's net position with a clearing member can be considerably less than the individual gross positions it has with different counterparties. More efficient netting enables traders to trade more, potentially increasing revenues for trading firms, exchanges, clearing houses, clearing members and brokers. Multilateral netting is at the core of central clearing and delivers the greatest benefit in terms of reduced credit risk, significantly beyond that available from bilateral netting. Evidence from other OTC markets has also shown that the availability of OTC clearing and multilateral netting has led to a significant increase in OTC trading volumes and the same pattern is also expected to prevail in the freight market. For instance, since the Nord Pool Scandinavian Power market introduced OTC clearing, OTC volume has increased about four times.[11]

At the same time, clearing has been viewed by some as expensive because of the requirement to post initial margin and the process of marking to market

---

[11] See Claughton and Undseth (2002).

to cover any potential losses. Another implication, particularly for freight markets, is that the nominal size of the contracts that are used for hedging purposes can be quite large. Take the example of a calendar 2009 contract for BCI 4TC which trades at US$100,000/day in May 2008. Although one has the possibility to trade and clear a minimum lot size of one day, when this contract is used by an owner to hedge his earnings for a calendar year, the notional freight income is US$36.5m (=US$100,000/day × 365 days) and the initial margin that one needs to post in order to clear the contract is approximately 15 per cent of that amount, or around US$5.5m. In addition, if this position is running a loss because the freight market is getting stronger, then there will be a cash outflow due to margin calls until the settlement of the contract; however, the owner will not be receiving any income from operating the vessel in the market until after he has chartered his vessel in the market in January 2009. Therefore, there is a mismatch between the cash flows from the cleared contract and the cash flows from the operation of the vessel in the physical market. Given the nature of the market and in particular the size of the contracts this is another important consideration when it comes to using cleared contracts.

5.3.3.3 A marking-to-market example

Suppose in mid-November 2007, a charterer bought a BCI C4 FFA for settlement at the end of the month, being concerned about the high volatility of freight rates and the possibility that rates in the market may increase even further up to the end of the month. The charterer buys the FFA at a rate of US$48.5/mt. The level of initial margin required by SGX for this trade is US$3645 per 1000 mt lot and the maintenance margin is US$2700. Upon establishing the position, the trader thus deposits on his account with the clearing member the initial margin of US$3645 per 1000 mt lot (that is, US$546,750 for an entire Capesize cargo of 150,000 mt). Table 5.3 presents the evolution of the marking-to-market procedure for a 1000 mt lot contract until its settlement at the end of the month. The following day, on 13 November 2007, the closing rate for the November C4 FFA contract is US$48.875/mt which is the Baltic Forward Assessment (BFA) for the November FFA on that day (BFAs are assessments of the forward rates produced by the Baltic Exchange and are discussed more extensively in Section 5.7.1). Effectively, the charterer has realised a profit of US$375 per 1000 mt lot (=(48.875 − 48.50) × 1000) which is credited into his margin account. Any excess amount that the trader has on his margin account which is above the initial margin level can be withdrawn from the trader; at the same time the party who went short on the FFA contract will have a loss of US$375 which will be debited from his account. The following day, on 14 November 2007, the BFA rate is US$48.908/mt which results in a further profit of US$33 which is added to the charterer's account.

Table 5.3   A marking-to-market example

Date	Day	BFA rate (US$/mt)	Daily P&L (US$)	Margin account (US$)	Variation margin (US$)
12/11/2007	1	48.500		3,645	
13/11/2007	2	48.875	375	4,020	
14/11/2007	3	48.908	33	4,053	
15/11/2007	4	49.083	175	4,228	
16/11/2007	5	49.292	209	4,437	
19/11/2007	6	48.792	−500	3,937	
20/11/2007	7	48.750	−42	3,895	
21/11/2007	8	48.542	−208	3,687	
22/11/2007	9	47.500	−1,042	2,645	1,000
23/11/2007	10	46.450	−1,050	2,595	1,050
26/11/2007	11	45.930	−520	3,125	
27/11/2007	12	45.780	−150	2,975	
28/11/2007	13	45.922	142	3,117	
29/11/2007	14	46.400	478	3,595	
30/11/2007	14	46.330	−70	3,525	

Source: BFA rates are provided by the Baltic Exchange. The initial and maintenance margins are US$3650 and US$2700 per 1000 mt lot, respectively (SGX).

The same process is repeated for all the remaining trading days. Notice as well that on 22 November, the forward market drops overnight by more than US$1/mt which results in a loss of US$1042. This is debited from his margin account and, as a result, the balance of the margin account drops below the maintenance margin level of US$2700. At this point the charterer receives a margin call and he thus has to deposit a variation margin on his account to bring it back to the initial margin level; the variation margin in this case is US$3645 − US$2645 = US$1000. Despite this, the following day the market drops even further to a rate of US$46.45/mt thus resulting in a further loss of US$1050 on the position, which is again debited from the margin account; as a result, the charterer receives another margin call and pays a variation margin of US$1050. This process continues until the settlement of the contract on 30 November. The settlement rate is US$46.33/mt which is calculated as the average of the underlying spot rate over the last seven trading days of November. Overall, the total profit or loss from this position is calculated as: final margin − initial margin − variation margin payments: that is, US$3525 − US$3645 − US$1000 − US$1050 = − US$2170. This is also the same as the P&L from the OTC market which would be (US$46.33 − US$48.50) × US$1000 = −US$2170. The difference is that in the OTC market the settlement amount will be paid in full at expiry while in the cleared market the P&L is realised on a daily basis; although the total amount in the end is the same in both cases, the fact that part of this amount is received earlier, before maturity, means that in terms of the time value of money there

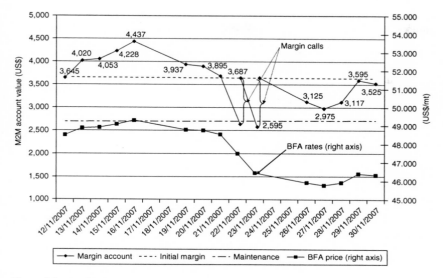

Figure 5.9 A BCI C4 margining example

will be some differences between the two approaches. The evolution of the marking-to-market process is presented in Figure 5.9.

5.3.4 Trading via a 'hybrid' exchange

This involves trading through an electronic screen, the most successful and popular of which is the International Maritime Exchange (Imarex). Imarex is a publicly listed company, based in Oslo, offering an authorised and regulated marketplace for trading and clearing of freight derivatives. It offers a screen-based trading system in which principals (that is, those trading directly for their own account) can trade freight derivatives electronically on screen in real time, or via an Imarex exchange broker. All principals trade anonymously, and all trades are automatically cleared through NOS in a process known as 'straight-through clearing'.

Imarex was established in 2000 and it was one of the first companies to offer a screen-based trading system for FFAs, in 2001; the major advantage of a screen-based system is that it offers price transparency, since traders can see the actual prices – firm bids and offers – in the market. In addition, it offers immediacy because trades can be executed simply by clicking on the screen, which facilitates and speeds up the trading process. In addition, Imarex was the first exchange to offer clearing services for trading FFAs, and all the trades that are concluded through the Imarex screen are automatically cleared through NOS. Finally, another advantage of the screen-based system is that it offers the ability to trade smaller lots; minimum lot sizes are 1000 mt

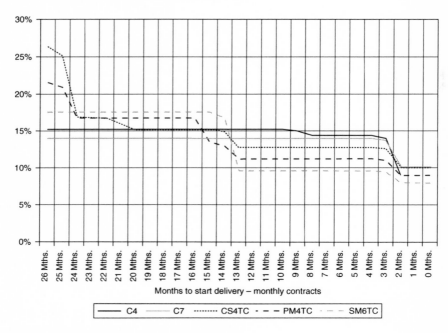

Figure 5.10   Imarex dry-route margin curves
Source: Imarex (revised 5 May 2008).

of cargo or one-day hire for voyage and trip-charter routes respectively which, in turn, enables market participants to trade smaller quantities. According to Imarex estimates, the average trading volume in Imarex is US$300,000 which is smaller than in the OTC market, thus also making the market accessible and more affordable to more participants from different sectors of the market.

Clearing services are provided through NOS. NOS ASA was founded in 1987 to become the clearing house for the Norwegian domestic financial derivatives market. The structure of NOS is similar to that of other clearing houses. Principals wishing to trade freight need either to be clearing members of have an account with one of the clearing members of NOS. The margin requirement is calculated as a percentage of the market value of the open position based on a version of the SPAN© system. The principal of margin calculation is that it should cover more than 99.8 per cent of all the expected price movements over the time that it takes to liquidate a defaulting member's portfolio.

Figure 5.10 presents the margin curves for selected dry routes; these reflect the percentage of the value of the contract that needs to be deposited as initial margin. We can see that this varies from route to route and also declines for longer maturities, which is consistent with the volatility term structure, that is, with the fact that longer-maturity contracts are less risky than shorter ones.

NOS operates a system of dynamic margining – the trader needs to maintain in his margin account a percentage of the value of the contract – which effectively means that if the value of his position increases, the amount of the required margin will increase as well, and vice-versa. This is in contrast to the marking-to-market system used by LCH.Clearnet and SGX, as described in section 5.3.3.3, where traders deposit a fixed monetary amount as initial margin. In addition to Imarex trades, NOS also offers OTC clearing services for trades between two NOS members that are concluded via an FFABA broker, which is similar to the services offered by LCH.Clearnet and SGX.

We can see therefore, that Imarex is like an exchange, in the sense that it provides a regulated marketplace in which to trade standardised contracts; principals can trade in the market either directly or through an Imarex broker and all trades are guaranteed through a clearing house. However, the market is not open to brokers outside Imarex. Therefore, FFA brokers cannot use the system to post prices or to facilitate trades for their clients. In that sense therefore, Imarex operates a 'hybrid' or 'almost-exchange' market system because the market is not open to all market participants, in particular to non-Imarex-based competitive FFABA brokers.

A similar 'hybrid' market structure has also been developed by Simpson, Spence and Young (SSY), a London-based ship- and FFA broker in collaboration with GlobalCoal, a coal-trading platform. The SSY/GlobalCoal trading platform offers a screen-based facility for trading dry and wet FFAs which can then be cleared through either LCH.Clearnet or NOS.

5.4 Hedging using forward freight agreements

Market agents are confronted with risks that arise from the ordinary conduct of their businesses. Derivative markets provide a way in which these risks may be transferred to other individuals who are willing to bear them, through hedging. Hedges are either short or long. A 'short' or 'selling' hedge involves selling FFAs as a protection against an unexpected decline in freight rates; for instance, shipowners or ship operators who want to protect their freight income are sellers of FFAs – since when freight rates fall, the reduction in freight income will be compensated through a gain in the forward position.

A 'long' or 'buying' hedge, on the other hand, involves buying futures as a protection against a price increase. For instance, charterers are buyers of FFAs; this enables them to protect their forward freight requirements in case the physical market rises, which would thus force them to pay higher freight rates. FFAs were initially traded for risk-management purposes by charterers and shipowners although, currently, they are primarily used for the purpose of speculating on the future direction of the freight markets – some examples of which are discussed in the next chapter. The following examples illustrate the use of FFAs for hedging purposes.

5.4.1 Hedging trip-charter freight-rate risk

FFAs are traded for individual trip-charter routes of the Panamax index. Consider the following example. In early July 2001, a shipowner has just fixed a Panamax vessel for a trip from Australia to the Atlantic which will leave the vessel open for business in the Continent around the middle of September. He feels the market is likely to soften in the coming months so, by the time he fixes his vessel at the end of August, freight rates may be lower compared to their current levels. He therefore decides to hedge the vessel forward for a trip-charter to the Far East by selling a BPI Route 2A (Europe–Far East trip-charter) FFA for settlement in August. The settlement rate will be the average rate of route 2A over the last seven trading days in August and the settlement price will be calculated on the basis of a voyage duration of 60 days (as per the definition of the BPI routes shown in Table 4.2).

The hedging example is presented in Table 5.4. On 2 July 2001, route 2A is at US\$11,158/day and Route 2A FFA is at US\$10,050/day. The FFA trades at a discount of 9.93 per cent (10,050/11,158 − 1) compared to the physical rate which reflects the market's view that freight rates may fall between July and end of August. As a result, the expected freight rate income, implied by the FFA rates, is US\$603,000 (=US\$10,050/day × 60 days). The shipowner considers this forward rate attractive and decides to 'lock' in this rate by selling a route 2A FFA for delivery in August 2001.

By the time he fixes the vessel, on 31 August 2001, the Panamax market has weakened and the hire rate has now fallen to US\$7483/day. The shipowner fixes his vessel at that rate and his total freight rate revenue for the duration of the voyage will be US\$7483/day × 60 days = US\$448,980, which represents a decrease of US\$154,020 (= US\$448,980 − US\$603,000) over his expected position in early July. At the same time, FFA rates have also fallen; the settlement price of the FFA contract is US\$7545/day. His FFA position therefore generates a profit of (US\$10,050 − US\$7545) × 60 = US\$150,300. Combining the 'loss' in the physical market with the gain in the futures market gives an overall loss of only US\$3720.[12] In addition, the owner would also have to pay broker's commission which will typically be 0.25 per cent of the total freight rate; that is, 0.25 per cent × US\$603,000 = US\$1507.50.

In an ideal hedging situation, known as a 'textbook hedge', the difference between the expected and the realised outcome should be zero. In this example the loss of US\$3720 is due to the fact that the rate at which the FFA is settled – which is the average over the last seven days in August – is different from the rate at which the ship is fixed in the market. We call this type of risk 'settlement risk' and its impact on the performance of hedges is analysed

---

[12] The term 'loss' here does not refer to an actual monetary loss but rather to the notional loss from fixing at a rate which is below the rate anticipated back in July. It is, in other words, the opportunity cost for not hedging.

Table 5.4   An example of hedging freight rates using forward freight agreements

Two-month hedge for the period 2 July 2001 to 31 August 2001	
Physical market	**FFA market**
2 July 2000	
Route 2A freight rate: US$11,158/day	Route 2A August 2001 FFA: US$10,050/day
Freight cost:	Expected freight:
US$669,480 (= US$11,158 × 60 days)	US$603,000 (= US$10,050 × 60 days)
Shipowner **sells** August 2001 FFA contract	
31 August 2001	
Route 2A freight rate: US$7483/day	August 2001 FFA settlement: US$7545/day
Actual freight cost: US$448,980	
Loss in the physical market	Gain from FFA transaction
US$448,980 − US$603,000 = US$154,020	(US$10,050 − US$7545) × 60 = US$150,300
Net result from hedging = − US$3720	

in Section 5.5.1. It should also be stressed that, in this example, we have implicitly assumed that the Panamax vessel which the owner operates is of an identical specification to the Baltic Panamax vessel used in the calculation of the Baltic Indices. Of course this is usually the exception rather than the rule and, in practice, one would have to assess the premium or the discount his vessel would normally expect to command in relation to the Baltic Panamax type; for instance, an older vessel, with higher fuel consumption and less cargo carrying capacity will be earning, say, US$2000/day less than the standard Panamax vessel. In this case, and using the same example as before, the owner would have been looking to protect a forward income that is US$2000/day less than the BPI level, which would introduce an element of basis risk in the performance of the hedge. Finally, Figure 5.11 presents the payoff of the forward position across different settlement rates. We can see, for instance, that if the settlement rate becomes US$12,000/day, then the FFA position would result in a loss of US$1950/day, which would be offset by the higher rate at which the vessel is fixed in the market. As a result, in either case, the combined FFA and physical position would result in a locked freight rate which is close to US$10,050/day.

5.4.2   Hedging using voyage FFAs

In this example we will consider the case of a shipowner who hedges a series of four voyages using voyage FFAs. The shipowner operates a Capesize bulk carrier, which is mainly employed in the coal trade between South Africa and continental Europe. In mid-October 2005, the owner wishes to hedge

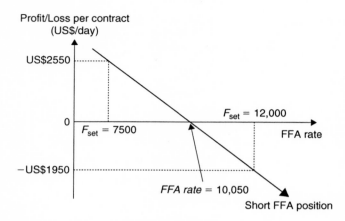

Figure 5.11   Payoff from the short BPI 2A FFA contract

against a decline in freight rates for coal due to a possible downturn in steel production and a forecasted decrease in power demand in Europe. BCI route 4 (150,000 mt of coal, Richards Bay to Rotterdam) currently stands at US$17/mt and Calendar 2006 FFAs on C4 currently trade at US$14/mt. Such a contract calls for four quarterly settlements at the end of January, April, July and October 2006; the settlement rate is calculated as the average of the last seven trading days in each of these months. Since a voyage from Richards Bay to Rotterdam and back takes longer than one month, this pattern of settlement also offers a good fit to the requirements of the shipowner in the physical market. Given the economic forecasts about the state of the freight market in 2006, the shipowner would like to 'lock in' a freight rate of US$14/mt for 2006; at the same time, in order to take advantage of any rise in the physical market, the shipowner will only hedge 50 per cent per voyage (that is, 75,000 mt).

His FFA broker identifies a European electricity utility with a large coal-import program, wishing to fix its coal shipping costs for 2006. They both agree at a rate of US$14/mt for a half C4 Cal06 contract; each party will have to pay broker's commission of $4 \times US\$14\,mt \times 75,000\,mt \times 0.25$ per cent $= US\$10,500$. We are going to consider two different variations of this hedging example. In the first case, the shipowner will carry each hedging position until expiry and will settle each of these contracts individually. In the second case, he will settle the first two quarters but, as the market reaches its low point during the summer months, he decides that he does not need the hedge any more and will offset the two remaining hedging positions in the market.

First Case – shipowner settles each FFA at its respective expiry

In this case, each contract is settled at its respective settlement date. Table 5.5 presents the outcome of this hedging strategy. For instance, consider the

Table 5.5 Voyage hedging example payoffs – positions are settled at maturity

	Settlement rate ($/mt)	Profit/loss from short Cal06 FFA at US$14/mt	Payoff from FFA (75,000 mt)
Q1 (January 06)	10.75	+US$3.25/mt	US$243,750
Q2 (April 06)	12.5	+US$1.5/mt	US$112,500
Q3 (July 06)	16.5	−US$2.5/mt	−US$187,500
Q4 (October 06)	22.5	−US$8.5/mt	−US$637,500

January settlement. The FFA settlement rate, calculated as the average of the BCI C4 freight rate over the last seven days in January, is US$10.75/mt and, hence, the shipowner receives (US$14 − US$10.75) × US$75,000 = US$243,750 from the FFA counter-party. Therefore, although the owner fixes his vessel in the market at a lower rate than he anticipated, he is partly compensated through the FFA contract payoff. Similarly, for Q2, the FFA contract is settled below the selling price and, hence, the owner receives a settlement sum of US$112,500. After the settlement of the second contract, the freight market recovers and as a result the July contract is settled at US$16.5/mt which results in a net outflow for the owner of US$187,500. The market gets even stronger for Q4, which results in a net loss of US$8.5/mt for that position. At the same time however, the owner fixes his vessel at a much higher freight rates in the physical market; combining the physical with the FFA position results in a net freight income of approximately US$14/mt for the hedged position.

Second Case – shipowner unwinds his hedge for Q3 and Q4

Suppose that it is now mid-June. The Q1 and Q2 contracts have already been settled and the spot rate for C4 trades at US$13/mt. Since dry-bulk freight rates are usually depressed in the summer months, it is believed that this is going to be the lowest level of the market for the year and that the market is going to recover after that. Consequently, the owner decides to lock in the profits for the next two settlements and he thus buys back one July and one October contract for 75,000 mt for US$13.25/mt and US$13/mt, respectively, as shown in Table 5.6. This way the owner secures a profit of US$0.75/mt (US$14/mt − US$13.25/mt) for Q3 and US$1/mt (US$14/mt − US$13/mt) for Q4, irrespective of the settlement rates for these FFA contracts. In order to initiate these hedges, the owner will have to pay additional broker's commission of 0.25 per cent on the total expected rate of US$13.25 × 75,000 + US$13 × 75,000 = US$4922.

By unwinding the hedges for Q3 and Q4, the owner locks in a given FFA profit but, at the same time, he is no longer hedged in the market and he is thus exposed to the possibility of the freight market going further down later

Table 5.6   Voyage hedging example payoffs – entering offsetting trades for Q3 and Q4

	Settlement rate	P&L from short Cal06 at US$14/mt	P&L from long Jul 06 at US$13.25/mt	P&L from long Oct 06 at US$13/mt	Total payoff in US$/mt	Payoff from FFA (75,000 mt)
Q1 (Jan 06)	10.75	+US$3.25/mt			+US$3.2/mt	US$243,750
Q2 (Apr 06)	12.5	+US$1.5/mt			+US$1.5/mt	US$112,500
Q3 (Jul 06)	16.5	−US$2.5/mt	+US$3.25/mt		+US$0.75/mt	US$56,250
Q4 (Oct 06)	22.5	−US$8.5/mt		+US$9.5/mt	+US$1.0/mt	US$75,000

Table 5.7   Panamax 4TC FFA quotes on 10 October 2005

Contract	FFA rate (US$/day)
Spot	22,762
Q4 05	23,825
Q1 06	21,750
Q2 06	20,750
Q3 and Q4 2006	17,775
Cal 06	19,550

Source: FIS

in the year. In the example presented here, unwinding the hedge turned out to be the best decision since it enabled the owner to take advantage of the increase in freight rates in the second half of 2006.

5.4.3   Time-charter hedge

Here we consider an example of the use of quarterly contracts to hedge Pana-max earnings for a period of six months. An owner operates a 65,000 mt dwt Panamax vessel built in 1997. Currently, on 10 October 2005, the vessel is under a six-month period time-charter for US$22,000/day which will expire in three months, around the middle of January. Under the terms of the charter the vessel will be re-delivered to her owner at around 10–15 January 2006 in the Far East.

The owner is worried about the possibility that the market may soften when the time comes to fix the vessel and thus decides to hedge the vessel's earnings for the first six months of 2006. Since he wants to hedge against the volatility in the Panamax sector, the most appropriate strategy is to sell the 4 TC average of the BPI for Q1 and Q2 2006. Freight Investor Services (FIS) quote FFA rates of US$21,750/day and US$20,750/day for Q1 and Q2 2006 respectively, as shown in Table 5.7. Effectively each of those contracts is a strip of three-monthly FFAs, covering the respective quarter, at the given rate. He thus sells Q1 2006 at US$21,750/day and Q2 2006 at US$20,750/day, which he holds until he can find suitable employment for his vessel.

In order to illustrate how this hedging strategy can be implemented, we are going to consider two different variations regarding the owner's choices in the physical market. In the first case, the owner will be operating the vessel in the spot market and as he fixes a voyage he will be gradually unwinding some of his FFA positions; in the second case, the owner will fix his vessel on a period time-charter basis for the first six months of 2006 so that he will have to unwind his entire FFA portfolio at once. We consider each case next.

First Case – shipowner operates his vessel in the spot market

In the first case, the owner operates the vessel in the spot market. He feels that the Pacific basin presents the most attractive employment opportunities, so he will be fixing the vessel for consecutive Trans-Pacific round voyages (that is, route 3A of the BPI) for the first six months of 2006. The first voyage is fixed at around the end of December 2005 for delivery to take place in the middle of January; the vessel will be chartered for a Trans-Pacific round voyage (route BPI 3A) for an estimated voyage duration of 47 days at around US$16,500/day. In this case, the vessel is fixed approximately 15 days before the date it is actually delivered to the charterer which reflects the laycan period for the vessel (see Chapter 2). For instance in the example presented here the laycan period could be 'laydays 13 January cancelling 15 January'. This means that the charterer is not obliged to accept delivery of the vessel until after the first of these dates (13 January) and has the option to cancel the charter agreement altogether if the vessel arrives after the end of the second of the dates (15 January). All the Baltic Panamax indices have a laycan period of 15–20 days ahead of the index which effectively means that today's spot rate reflects a delivery period which is at least 15 days forward. For hedging purposes, this effectively means that if an owner wants to hedge a voyage that will commence, say, in the middle of September, the appropriate contract maturity to use for hedging is that of August; this was the case, for instance, in the example presented in Section 5.4.1.

The owner has now secured employment for his vessel from the middle of January until the end of February (47 days) and, as a result, he no longer requires the hedging position for January and February. He thus unwinds the January 2006 and February 2006 contracts at a rate of US$16,014/day and US$16,276/day, respectively;[13] he can unwind his position either by agreeing with his FFA counter-party to terminate the contracts early or by entering into an offsetting long position for January 2006 and February 2006 with another counter-party. The outcome of this strategy is presented in Table 5.8. By selling the FFAs for January and February, the owner locks in a charter rate of US$21,750/day for each day in January and February, which

---

[13] These rates are the BPI 4TC Baltic Forward Assessment rates (see Section 5.7) at the time the hedge is lifted.

Table 5.8   Hedging spot Panamax earnings using FFAs

				Panel A: FFA market			
FFA maturity	**Number of days**	**FFA rate (US$/day)**	**Locked in monthly (US$)**	**Settlement**		**FFA P/L (US$)**	
				Date	**Rate (US$/day)**	**Daily**	**Monthly**
January	31	21,750	674,250	31 Dec 05	16,014	5,736	177,816
February	28	21,750	609,000	31 Dec 05	16,276	5,474	153,272
March	31	21,750	674,250	15 Feb 06	18,550	3,200	99,200
April	30	20,750	622,500	15 Feb 06	16,925	3,825	114,750
May	31	20,750	643,250	31 Mar 06	17,533	3,217	99,727
June	30	20,750	622,500	15 May 05	20,945	−195	−5,850
Total paper			**US$3,845,750**				**US$638,915**

	Panel B: Physical market		
Delivery	**Voyage duration (days)**	**Freight rate ($/day)**	**Trip earnings (US$)**
13 Jan 06	47	16,500	775,500
02 Mar 06	47	18,500	869,500
18 Apr 06	44	16,000	704,000
01 Jun 06	45	16,200	729,000
Total physical	183		**US$3,078,000**
Total paper and physical			**US$3,716,915**

implies monthly earnings of US$674,250 (=US$21,750/day × 31) for January and US$609,000 (=US$21,750/day × 28) for February. The hedging position is closed as soon as the owner has secured the next voyage for the vessel, at around the end of December 2005, and the FFA contracts for January and February are thus settled at US$16,014/day and US$16,276/day, respectively. For instance, for the January contract, this results in a profit of US$5736/day (=US$21,750 − US$16,014) or a total profit of US$177,816 (US$5,736 × 31) for the entire month of January. The vessel is then delivered to the charterer for the Trans-Pacific round voyage at US$16,500/day for a voyage duration of 47 days, resulting in trip earnings of US$775,500, as shown in Panel B of Table 5.8.[14]

The vessel will be delivered back to her owner in early March, so the owner needs to make provisions for fixing her next voyage. Around the middle of February the vessel is fixed for another Trans-Pacific round voyage of 47 days for US$18,500/day, for delivery in early March. Again, as soon as the owner has secured employment for the vessel for the next 47 days, he has to

---

[14] In the example presented here we ignore broker's commission on both the physical and FFA markets.

unwind his FFA positions for March and April. The short March and April FFA contracts are thus settled at a rate of US$18,550/day and at US$16,925/day, respectively, as shown in Table 5.8. Notice as well that by closing the April contract when fixing the second voyage, the owner no longer has cover against freight rate changes for the second part of April. This can be important because the vessel will be open again after 18 April so the owner will be exposed to freight rate volatility for the period 18–30 April. One way round this could be for the owner to close the April contract later, when fixing the third voyage; this of course would result in an uncovered or speculative short FFA position for the first part of April. Alternatively, the owner could settle half of his April contract (that is, 15 days) when he fixes the second voyage and the remaining 15 days when he fixes the third voyage; this would provide a more accurate hedge but such a strategy could be hindered by the fact that liquidity in trading half months in the market is more limited.

Overall, by fixing his vessel spot, the owner would realise earnings of US$3,078,000 for the first six months of 2006. Combining this with the total payoff from the FFA contracts, which is US$638,915, results in a total income from the physical and the paper market of US$3,716,915. Notice that when the owner entered the hedge back in October 2005, the aim was to lock in a total income of US$3,845,750 for the first six months of 2006. There is therefore a discrepancy of 3.4 per cent between the expected and the actual freight income, which is the hedging error from implementing this strategy.

Second Case – shipowner charters his vessel for a period time-charter of six months

In this case, the owner secures a period time-charter contract for the first six months of 2006. Therefore, around the end of December 2005 he fixes his vessel for a six-month time-charter, with a duration of 183 days, for US$15,500/day. At the same time, he offsets his FFA position by buying Q1 and Q2 2006 contracts at a rate of US$16,250/day and US$15,500/day, respectively. Table 5.9 presents the outcome of this strategy. We can see that the six-month time-charter provides earnings of US$2,836,500; combined with the profit from the FFA position, this results in overall earnings of US$3,809,250, which suggests a hedging error of 0.95 per cent compared to the expected locked-in value.

Overall, we can note that the hedging strategy worked reasonably well with a relatively small hedging error. The magnitude of the hedging error and, hence, the effectiveness of a hedging strategy, depends on a number of factors, some of which include:

- *Timing mismatch between paper and physical contracts*: paper contracts are settled at the end of each month, whereas fixtures in the physical market can be concluded any time in that period. Depending on the volatility of the underlying market this mismatch can have an important effect

Table 5.9   Hedging period time-charter Panamax earnings using FFAs

Panel A: FFA market							
FFA maturity	Number of days	FFA rate (US$/day)	Locked in monthly (US$)	Settlement		FFA P/L (US$)	
				Date	Rate (US$/day)	Daily	Monthly
January	31	21,750	674,250	31 Dec 05	16,250	5,500	170,500
February	28	21,750	609,000	31 Dec 05	16,250	5,500	154,000
March	31	21,750	674,250	31 Dec 05	16,250	5,500	170,500
April	30	20,750	622,500	31 Dec 05	15,500	5,250	157,500
May	31	20,750	643,250	31 Dec 05	15,500	5,250	162,750
June	30	20,750	622,500	31 Dec 05	15,500	5,250	157,500
Total paper			US$3,845,750				US$972,750

Panel B: Physical market			
Delivery	Voyage duration (days)	Freight rate (US$/day)	Trip earnings
13 Jan 06	183	15,500	US$2,836,500
Total paper and physical			US$3,809,250

on the performance of the hedge; this is analysed more extensively in Section 5.5.1.

- *Basis risk*: this arises due to the fact that the route underlying the FFA is different from the exposure in the market. For instance, in the example presented here, we use BPI 4TC FFAs to hedge exposure on route P3A. Although one could use an FFA on this route, the performance of the hedge could be affected by liquidity costs since FFAs on this route are less liquid than on the 4TC routes, particularly for longer maturities; basis risk is analysed more extensively in Section 5.5.2.
- *Size mismatch*: this could also cause basis risk when the vessel whose earnings we want to hedge is different from the reference vessel used in the calculation of the underlying rates. For instance, in this example we operate an eight-year-old 65,000 mt dwt Panamax vessel, whereas the Baltic assessments are calculated on the basis of a 74,000 mt dwt Baltic Panamax-type vessel, with a maximum age of seven years.
- *Relocation or non earning-day mismatch*: this could arise if, for instance, the vessel is off-hire for some days during the six-month period; in this case there will be a mismatch because the earnings period hedged is actually different from the period over which earnings are received from the operation of the vessel.
- *Liquidity risk*: If liquidity in the market is low, establishing a hedging position or unwinding a hedge will occur at a premium due to the

non-availability of counter-parties to trade in the market at the specified rate. This can particularly be the case if one trades on routes where there is little trading interest, and also in cases when one trades at the far end of the forward curve where liquidity in general tends to be low.

5.4.4 Tanker hedge

It is early April 2001, a TD7 (80,000 mt North Sea to continental Europe) is trading at Worldscale (WS) 125 for June. An energy-trading company is worried that freight rates will increase over the following 12 weeks, when the company expects to charter in a tanker for transportation of oil from North Sea to Wilhelmshaven in Germany, and decides to use FFAs to cover this risk. The company thus buys 80 TD7 June 2001 contracts at WS 125 (each lot being for 1000 mt). At the end of June, the settlement price is WS 156.15 (calculated as the average of TD7 freight rate assessments over June). The energy trading company as a charterer will have to fix at a higher freight rate in the physical market but at the same time a profit is made in the FFA market of 31.15 WS points ($=156.15 - 125$). In this case, the total payoff from the transaction is calculated as the number of contracts multiplied by the contract size times the Worldscale Flat Rate (that is, the US$/mt rate for WS 100 points). Therefore:

$$\text{Settlement} = \text{contracts} \times \text{lot size} \times \text{flat rate} \times \text{net WS}$$
$$= 80 \times 1000 \,\text{mt} \times \text{US\$4.30/mt} \times 31.15 \,\text{per cent} = \text{US\$107,156.}$$

In addition, the energy trading company has to pay broker's commission which is US\$1075 ($=0.25$ per cent $\times 1.25 \times$ US\$4.30/mt $\times 80,000$).

5.4.5 Hedge-ratio calculation for tanker FFAs

In the previous example, the oil company hedged its freight exposure over a single voyage. There are cases when tanker companies want to hedge their freight income or oil traders want to fix their freight costs over a period of time, rather than for a single voyage. In the dry market this is easily achieved using FFAs on the average of the trip-charter routes. In the tanker market, however, FFAs are for individual voyage routes rather than for a specific voyage duration. To illustrate this, consider the case of a VLCC tanker owner who operates in the Persian Gulf to Japan trade and wants to secure his freight income for the next six months; this can be done by selling TD3 FFAs for a full VLCC load for each of the next six months. However, because the duration of a round trip in TD3 is more than a calendar month, this would result in an overhedged position which may involve more risks than the owner might like to take.[15]

---

[15] In January 2008, the Baltic Exchange commenced reporting on trip-charter earnings for different types of tanker vessels, which were presented in Table 4.8. By trading FFAs on these routes, tanker owners will be able to hedge their earnings for a specific period of time rather than for specific voyages.

In order to address this issue, the number of contracts to sell should be adjusted to reflect the duration of the round-trip voyage; in other words, the owner needs to fit monthly FFA rates into the typical voyage duration for TD3. Since a round trip from the Gulf to Japan takes approximately 43 days, he needs to adjust the number of FFA contracts to sell, accordingly. The hedge ratio thus becomes 0.698, which is calculated as: 30 days (in monthly FFA period)/43 (days of TD3 voyage) = 0.698. Therefore the owner should sell: 260,000 mt × 0.698 = 181,395 mt in TD3 or approximately 181 lots of US$1000 mt for each of the next six months.

5.5   Issues to consider when using FFAs for hedging

In addition to the examples we considered in the previous section, there are a number of additional issues and considerations of which market participants need to be aware when it comes to using FFAs for risk-management purposes. These are 'settlement risk', which is the difference between the average rate used for the settlement of FFAs and the freight rate at which the vessel is fixed in the physical market, and 'basis risk', which refers to the mismatch between the specification of the FFA contract and the exposure of the hedger in the physical market.

5.5.1   Settlement risk

This refers to the difference between the FFA settlement rate and the rate at which the corresponding vessel is actually fixed in the market. The discrepancy between these rates arises because the settlement rate, which is calculated as the average rate over a period of time, can be significantly different from the freight rate on the specific day in the month on which the vessel is fixed. To illustrate the magnitude of these differences, Table 5.10 presents the average percentage differences between the settlement freight rates for different dry routes and the freight rates during the settlement month for the period from January 2003 to April 2007. Depending on the route and the volatility in the market, the difference between the settlement rate and the freight rate on any given day can be as high as 13.4 per cent. For instance, consider the case of the BCI C4 FFA contract, where the settlement rate is calculated as the average over the last seven days of the month; in this case, the average deviation between the settlement rate and the spot freight rate on any specific day of the settlement month is 9.92 per cent. Assuming a freight rate of, say, US$30/mt, this effectively means that the settlement rate can be, on average, different from the spot rate in the market by as much as US$3/mt which, for a Capesize cargo, can mean a difference of US$450,000 in voyage earnings. We also note that the deviation is higher for spot rates during the first half of the month but is only 2.03 per cent during the second half of the month, which is due to the fact that the latter period largely coincides with the averaging period for the calculation of the settlement rate. When

Table 5.10 Average percentage differences between FFA settlement rates and freight rates during the settlement month

Route	Settlement rate	Month	1st half	2nd half
BCI 4	Monthly average	7.05%	5.94%	5.58%
	7-day average	9.92%	12.83%	2.03%
BCI 7	Monthly average	6.09%	5.04%	4.58%
	7-day average	8.40%	10.60%	1.70%
BCI 4TC	Monthly average	8.76%	6.75%	6.22%
BPI 2A	7-day average	10.88%	13.77%	2.09%
BPI 3A	7-day average	13.40%	16.51%	2.99%
BPI 4TC	Monthly average	7.89%	6.21%	6.17%

Notes: The table presents the root mean squared errors (RMSE) between the natural log of the average settlement rate in a month and the natural log of the spot freight rates during the entire month, the first half, or the second half of the month for the period 2 January 2003 to 30 April 2007 for selected routes from the BPI and the BCI Indices.
The RMSE for a given month is calculated as:

$RMSE = \sqrt{\frac{\sum_{i=1}^{n}(S_{average} - S_i)^2}{n}}$ where n is the number of days in the month, $S_{average}$ is the natural log of the average settlement rate for the month and S_i is the natural log of the spot Baltic assessment on day i of the month.

we now consider the settlement rates calculated as monthly averages for the same route, we note that the average deviation across the entire month is lower, at 7.05 per cent, and the difference between the first and second half of the month is not as pronounced as is the case with the seven-day average. A similar pattern emerges when we consider the other dry routes presented in Table 5.10.

Therefore, settlement risk represents a major source of risk for practitioners using the FFA market for risk-management purposes. The results in Table 5.10 indicate that this risk is at its lowest when the date of the fixture is as close as possible to the seven-day averaging window used in the calculation of settlement rates. However, due to the nature of the shipping markets, the point in time at which a vessel is fixed is dictated by a number of parameters – such as the positioning and availability of a ship as well as the availability of cargo – and co-ordinating the period of physical fixing with the FFA settlements may not always be practical. One alternative approach could be to use index-linked physical contracts where a vessel is chartered and her freight earnings are revised periodically on the basis of a Baltic Index. In this way the physical contracts are priced similarly to an FFA, which overcomes the problem of settlement risk. This is quite common in commodity and energy markets in particular, and has already been applied in the dry market by some operators.

5.5.2 Basis risk

Basis is the difference between the spot and the forward or futures price for a commodity. For instance, the basis for the BCI 4TC contract is the difference between the BCI 4TC spot Baltic assessment and the BCI 4TC forward contract for a specific maturity; therefore, for each specific maturity we can have a different basis. Basis risk refers to the uncertainty about the level of the basis when a hedge is lifted and usually arises when the route we want to hedge is not exactly the same as the route underlying the futures contract or when we are uncertain as to the exact date on which a vessel is to be fixed, and we may have to close an FFA position before its expiry. In the latter case, the effectiveness of the hedge is somewhat reduced, because there is uncertainty about the level of the basis when the hedge is lifted; in contrast, if an FFA position is carried until the expiry of the contract then there is no basis risk since – due to the convergence of spot and forward prices – the basis of the contract at maturity will be equal to zero.[16]

Basis risk also arises when there is a mismatch between the FFA contract and the exposure in the physical market. For instance, this could arise when we use Supramax FFAs to hedge exposure in the Handysize sector; when using Panamax FFAs – which are based on a 74,000 mt dwt Panamax vessel – to hedge freight income on a 65,000 mt dwt Panamax; or even using a basket of trip-charter routes, such as BPI 4TC, to hedge exposure on a specific Panamax route, such as route BPI 3A. In all these cases market participants could achieve better hedging results if they were to use the FFA that most closely matches their exposure in the market. However, this may not always be possible: for instance, when liquidity in the FFA market is low, as is the case, for instance, with Handysize FFAs; when the underlying physical route does not have a corresponding FFA market, as is the case particularly in the Handysize market where the underlying physical base is highly fragmented and FFAs are available only for six representative trip-charter routes; finally, when the specification of the vessel to hedge is different from the representative Baltic-type vessel used in the calculation of the indices. In all the above cases, there is a mismatch between the exposure of the hedger in the physical market and the forward contract that is used for hedging; as a result, the hedger will be exposed to a degree of basis risk.

In order to ensure that basis risk is minimised, there are two parameters that need to be considered. First, hedgers need to select an FFA route that has a strong correlation with their exposure in the physical market and then use that FFA route to hedge their physical risk; the higher the correlation between the physical market and the FFA contract the lower

---

[16] Some textbooks also call this type of risk *time basis risk* to distinguish it from basis risk arising from mismatches between the forward and the underlying asset (see Eydeland and Wolyniec, 2003)

the variability of the hedged cash flows and hence the more effective the hedge.

Second, in order to implement the hedge effectively, the hedger also needs to calculate the ratio of the quantity or size of the FFAs to buy or sell to the size of the exposure in the physical market – which is known as the 'hedge ratio'. In most of the hedging examples we presented in the previous section, we implicitly used a hedge ratio of one; in other words, in order to hedge 1000 mt of physical cargo we use 1000 mt of FFAs, which is known as a 'one-to-one' or 'naïve' hedge ratio (Ederington, 1979). However, when the correlation between the FFA and the physical rate is less than perfect, when there is a difference in the level of the average freight rate in the physical and the FFA market, or when volatility of FFA rates is different from volatility of the physical market, this ratio will have to be modified accordingly. For instance, consider Figure 5.12, which presents the Baltic Handysize (BHSI) and Supramax (BSI) TC averages, as well as their ratio (measured on the right-hand axis). It is evident that there is a strong degree of co-movement between the two series, the correlation in levels between the two series being 98.5 per cent. We can also note that the average BHSI/BSI ratio is 70 per cent; in other words, on average, if the BSI increases by US$1000/day, it is expected that the BHSI will increase by US$700/day. In addition, this ratio has been relatively constant during the period of investigation with a range of 10 per cent, a maximum value of 77 per cent and a minimum value of 67 per cent.

Given that liquidity in the Handysize FFA market is relatively low, participants in the Handysize market can use the much more liquid Supramax FFA market to hedge their exposure. In doing so they are exposed to basis risk and, since the average levels of freight rates are different in the two markets, as we can see in Figure 5.12, the use of an appropriate hedge ratio is required for this strategy to be effective. From the analysis presented here it seems that an appropriate hedge ratio is 0.7, which suggests hedging the monthly BHSI exposure using 70 per cent of a monthly BSI contract; this is equivalent to buying $0.70 \times 30 = 21$ days of the BSI contract.[17]

To illustrate the effectiveness of this strategy, consider the case of a Handysize operator in early September 2006, who wants to secure his freight income for the last quarter of 2006 (Q4 2006) and the first quarter of 2007 (Q1 2007). In order to hedge earnings from operating in the charter market for that period he sells 0.7 BSI 5TC FFAs for Q4 2006 and Q1 2007 at US$30,500/day and US$26,000/day respectively – which were the market rates at the time; in other words he sells $30 \times 0.7 \times 21$ days of BSI 5TC contracts per month for each month of Q4 2006 and Q1 2007. In this way he locks in a freight

---

[17] The implementation of this strategy may be restricted by the fact that most of the BSI contracts are traded for a full calendar month and liquidity for buying part of the month is limited. However, a Handysize operator can still use this strategy to hedge, for instance, the monthly earnings of three Handysize vessels using two monthly BSI contracts, which roughly corresponds to a 70 per cent ratio.

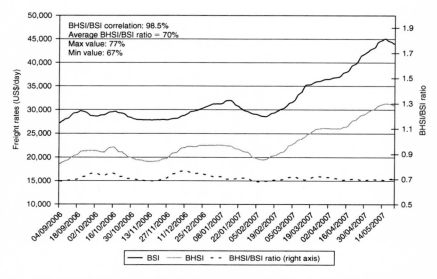

Figure 5.12   Baltic Handysize (BHSI) and Supramax (BSI) Indices and their ratio
Source: Baltic Exchange.

income of US$21,350/day (=30,500 × 0.7) and US$18,200/day (=26,000 × 0.7) for Q4 2006 and Q1 2007, respectively. Table 5.11 presents the outcome of this hedge. The first two columns present the settlement rates, calculated as the monthly averages of the BHI and BHSI spot rates for each maturity month. The following two columns present the profit or loss from the FFA position. For instance, the owner sold the October contract at US$30,500/day and the settlement rate is US$29,018/day, resulting therefore in a profit of US$1482/day per contract or a total profit of US$31,112 (=1482 × 21) for the entire 21-day position. Therefore, for the entire monthly hedge, this translates into an equivalent value of US$1037/day (=US$31,112/30) for the Handysize hedge. Consequently, the total income from the operation in physical income plus the income from the FFA position is US$22,185/day (=US$21,148 + 1037); since the locked value was US$21,350/day, the deviation of the hedged position from the locked value is 3.84 per cent (=22,185/21,350 − 1).[18] If we repeat this process for the remaining maturities,

---

[18] Some differences in the results may be due to rounding. In the example presented here we assume that the monthly Handysize earnings in the physical market are equivalent to the average monthly BHSI rate. Therefore, there is no mismatch between the Baltic Handysize vessel and the earnings of the vessel used in the example. In addition, we also need to consider broker's commission, which is 0.25 per cent of the total freight rate; in other words, 0.25 per cent × 0.7 × 3 × 30 × (US$30,500 + US$26,000)

Table 5.11   Outcome of the BSI/BHSI hedge for Q4 2006 and Q1 2007 using a hedge ratio of 0.7

Sold   0.7 Q4 06 BSI @ 30,500 to lock in an equivalent BHSI rate of US$21,350/day for Q4 06

Sold   0.7 Q1 07 BSI @ 26,000 to lock in an equivalent BHSI rate of US$18,200/day for Q1 07

Settlement rates		P&L		Hedged position	
(Average of month) BSI	BHSI	per contract sold (US$/day)	Total for 21 contracts (US$)	Hedged TC (US$/day)	Deviation from locked value
Oct 29,018	21,148	1,482	31,112	22,185	3.84%
Nov 27,889	19,466	2,611	54,824	21,293	−0.27%
Dec 29,068	21,911	1,432	30,080	22,914	7.07%
Jan 30,936	21,958	−4,936	−103,657	18,503	1.65%
Feb 29,349	20,265	−3,349	−70,325	17,921	−1.55%
Mar 34,404	24,537	−8,404	−176,474	18,655	2.47%

we can see that overall the deviation from the locked value remains at low levels and the maximum deviation in any given month is only 7.07 per cent.

Overall, this strategy seems to have been quite effective; this was due to the fact that the correlation between the two routes is quite strong and the strength of this relationship does not change over the examination period; this is also evidenced by the fact that the ratio between the two routes remains almost constant at a level of 70 per cent, which is perhaps the most important factor in guaranteeing the success of this strategy.

For other routes it could be the case that correlations are less favourable; in these situations the hedge ratios will need to be modified accordingly and alternative techniques such as the 'minimum variance hedge ratio' (MVHR) will have to be used. The MVHR is estimated as the ratio of the covariance between spot and FFA price changes (returns) over the unconditional variance of FFA price returns, as follows (also see Appendix 1.A for the derivation of the MVHR)

$$\gamma^* = \frac{Cov(\Delta S_t, \Delta F_t)}{Var(\Delta F_t)} \tag{5.1}$$

The MVHR is the hedge ratio that minimises the risk of a given position in the physical market (Ederington, 1979). Applications of this methodology in the freight futures (BIFFEX) market by Nomikos (1999) and Nomikos and

---

= US$8,898.75. Finally, for simplicity we also assume that each month has 30 days; in practice, the October settlement would be calculated on the basis of 31 days.

Kavussanos (2000a; 2000b) have shown that hedgers can achieve greater risk reduction by using the MVHR rather than a hedge ratio of 1.0.

An extension of this approach is to estimate 'time-varying hedge ratios' (TVHR). This procedure involves re-estimating the MVHR at frequent intervals, and re-adjusting the position in the forward market accordingly, as shown by Kroner and Sultan (1993) and applied in the freight futures market by Nomikos and Kavussanos (2000a; 2000b) using multivariate GARCH models. The motivation behind this process is the fact that the variance and covariance between spot and FFA prices are time-varying and, consequently, the hedge ratios estimated through equation (5.1) should also be time-varying. Although theoretically the use of TVHR may improve the hedging results even further, in practice its implementation in the market presents some difficulties, most notably the fact that it requires market participants to be able to buy or sell FFAs in smaller quantities than full cargoes. Also, since this strategy requires frequent rebalancing of the FFA position, the level of transaction costs, which may consequently reduce the effectiveness of this strategy, should be considered.

5.6   Uses of forward freight agreements

When the first FFAs were traded, the market was primarily used for risk-management purposes, which is also the primary function of any derivatives market. Therefore, at least initially, in the FFA market there were two distinct groups of market participants: owners and operators that were long on freight and would, therefore, take short FFA positions; and charterers or trading companies that were short of physical tonnage and would thus be buyers of FFAs.

If a derivatives market is used only for the purposes of risk-management and hedging, then the ratio of physical to paper trades should be close to one, assuming that every market participant hedges its exposure in the physical market. In other words, the volume of contracts traded in the derivatives market should be equal to the volume traded in the physical market or, to put it in a slightly different way, the volume of FFA traded, in mt, should be equal to the cargo quantity that has been physically transported by sea. However, if we look at established derivatives markets, the volume in the paper market is a multiple of the volume in the underlying market, and this incremental volume is primarily a result of speculative activity. Defining speculation or identifying a speculator is not always easy. Generally, we can say that a speculator is an individual who enters the futures market in search of profit and, in so doing, willingly accepts a level of risk (Kolb and Overdahl, 2007). The difference between a hedger and a speculator is that the former has a position in the underlying market which he needs to hedge and hence he will take a position in the derivatives market that is opposite to the one he holds in the physical market; that is, a shipowner will be a seller of FFAs, and a charterer will be a buyer of FFAs. A speculator, in contrast, will take a position in the derivatives market on the basis of expectations or beliefs about the future direction of the market. Thus, he will buy FFAs if he anticipates the market increasing, and sell FFAs if he has bearish market expectations.

FFAs are a very useful tool for speculating in the freight market for a number of reasons. First, trading in FFAs is easier than trading in the underlying market. The reason for this is that FFAs are simply a paper transaction on the forward value of an underlying freight index; trading in the physical market, on the other hand, involves chartering a ship and physically moving a quantity of cargo between ports, which requires far greater resources and expertise. In addition, FFAs provide the opportunity to speculate not only on rising but also on falling markets, simply by selling the FFA; in contrast, speculating on a falling market in the physical market may not be so easy to achieve. Finally, transaction costs for FFAs are relatively smaller compared to those in the physical market; also, particularly on certain Panamax and Capesize routes, liquidity in the FFA market tends to be better than in the underlying physical market, which also facilitates speculative activities.

Some of the speculative trades in the FFA market involve ordinary directional trades that is, going long or short on certain routes. In addition, market participants take speculative positions in spread trades by simultaneously entering into a long position in one route and a short position in another, related, route. These spread trades can be between two different routes of the same group (for instance, BCI C4 vs BCI C7 or TD3 vs TD5), between two different groups of routes (for instance, BCI 4TC vs BPI 4TC) or between two different maturities of the same group (for instance, BPI Q1 vs BPI Q2). Spread trades and other speculative trading strategies involving FFAs are discussed in more detail in Chapter 6.

In addition, FFAs provide market participants with the opportunity to arbitrage differences between commodity prices in different geographical locations. The use of physical arbitrage in shipping is not a new concept. From the very early days of shipping, traders would try to identify differences between the price of a commodity in two regions and, if the difference in price was greater than the freight cost of transporting the commodity, they would charter a ship and physically ship the commodity from port to port; for an application of physical arbitrage of crude oil prices between the Continent and the US, see Alizadeh and Nomikos (2004). The same strategy can also be implemented using FFAs. The idea behind this strategy is that commodity derivatives are traded for delivery at different geographical locations and the price difference between these futures contracts determines an implied forward cost of transportation, which should be comparable to the FFA for the particular route and the specific maturity; if this is not the case then the discrepancy can be arbitraged by taking positions in the forward commodity contracts in the two different locations and the FFA market. For instance, consider the price of coal in South Africa and in North Europe; these prices are determined by the two major contracts for coal, which are the API2 contract (for delivery of coal in the ARA region) and API4, for delivery of coal in Richards Bay. The difference between the prices of API2 and API4 forward contracts should be approximately equal to the Richards Bay–Rotterdam (BCI C4) freight rate for the specified maturity; if this is not the case, then an arbitrage opportunity exists in the market that traders can exploit by taking appropriate positions in the forward coal and FFA markets.

Finally, another application of the FFA markets is that they provide key information about expected market conditions through what is known as the 'price discovery function'. This is discussed in the next section.

5.7   Price discovery and forward curves

Physical and financial asset prices are determined through the interaction of supply and demand forces in an economy. Forward markets provide a mechanism through which the supply and demand for an asset are brought into alignment, both in the present and over time. Edwards and Ma (1993) argue that since forward contracts are traded for the delivery of an underlying asset at various points in the future, they should reflect the current expectations of the market about the level of spot prices at those points in the future. For instance, when forward prices are higher than current spot prices, then this reflects the market's expectation that there will be an increased demand or a shortage of supply, or both, for that commodity in the future and vice versa. Therefore, through the discovery of expected spot prices, forward prices can help to smooth the supply and demand for a commodity over time and, as a consequence, help to avoid the economic costs which result from shortages in the flow of goods and services.

As already discussed in the first chapter, spot and futures prices for financial and commodity futures markets are related through the 'cost-of-carry' relationship, which is a no-arbitrage condition that links spot and futures prices for commodities that can be stored and carried forward over time, such as metals, oil, agricultural commodities and even forward ship values. However, the concept of carrying charges does not apply to commodities which are non-storable, such as shipping freight. FFAs trade the expected value of the service of seaborne transportation, which is not practical to store or carry forward in time. As a result, FFA rates and the underlying spot rates are not linked through arbitrage but are driven by the expectations of market agents regarding the spot prices that will prevail at the expiry of the contract. This pricing relationship is also called the 'unbiasedness hypothesis' since it implies that forward prices are unbiased forecasts of the realised spot prices.

Mathematically:

$$F(t, T) = E(S_T | \Omega_t) \qquad (5.2)$$

where $E(. |.)$ is the mathematical conditional expectations operator at time t and Ω_t is the information set available to market participants at the same time, conditional on which the expectation is formed. Equation (5.2) states that the price at time t of a futures contract for delivery at time T equals the spot price that market agents expect to prevail at maturity. In forming their expectations, the market agents consider all the relevant information, available to them at time t. The concept of unbiasedness essentially implies that, over a long period of time, the average forecast error from FFAs will be zero. This does not necessarily mean that FFAs will be the most accurate forecasts of the expected spot prices and will, thus, have the smallest forecast error, but rather that they do not consistently overpredict or underpredict the underlying market; in other words, they tend to produce forecasts that, *on average* across a large number of observations, are not consistently biased.

Therefore, FFAs and the resulting forward curves contain useful information about the current sentiment and, in particular, about the future direction of the market. To illustrate the usefulness of forward curves, consider Figure 5.13, which presents the forward curves for route TD3 for the period March 2003 to December 2007. The continuous line on the graph presents the monthly spot rate for TD3 and, on that, we have superimposed the forward curves for maturities up to four months ahead for different months. The first point to note in Figure 5.13 is that forward rates seem to capture reasonably well the general direction of the market; in particular it seems that when the spot market is at a relatively low level, the forward rates increase with time to maturity; in other words the forward curve is in 'contango', indicating the anticipation of the market of future increases in the spot rates; this can be seen, for instance, in September 2004, January 2005, September 2005 and April 2006. On the other hand, when the spot market is at a high level, the forward curve is downward sloping, or 'backwardated', thus indicating the anticipation of the market of lower freight rates in the future.[19] This pattern in forward curves is consistent with the mean reversion property of freight rates. As already discussed, unlike stock prices or prices

---

[19] The terms backwardation and contango are used to describe the general shape of the forward curve at different points in time. A forward curve is backwardated when it is a decreasing function of maturity and thus forward prices for longer-dated contracts are lower than for shorter-dated contracts; this pattern in forward prices is consistent with the spot rate being currently high but the market anticipating an easing of the demand or higher supply and, hence, lower freight rates in the future. On the other hand, a forward curve is in contango when forward rates are an increasing function of time to maturity (see Geman, 2005, for a more thorough discussion about the concepts of backwardation and contango in commodity markets).

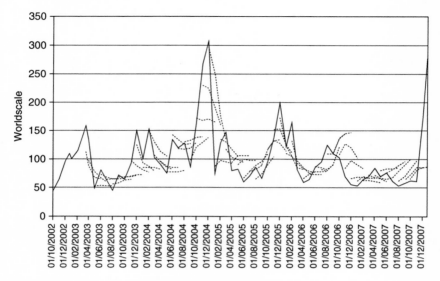

Figure 5.13   TD3 forward curves for March 2003–December 2007
Source: Baltic Exchange (spot data) and Imarex (forward data).

for other financial assets, which follow random walks, freight rates are characterised by mean reversion; in other words, in the long run they tend to
revert to a long-run average level, which reflects the marginal cost of providing the service of seaborne transportation. Mean reversion follows from the
supply and demand dynamics of the freight markets and, in particular, the
constant adjustment of supply to a relatively inelastic demand. For instance,
when freight rates are low, the supply of shipping services will naturally also
be low; however, as the demand for shipping services increases, supply will
gradually increase in response, until excess supply is exhausted. If demand
continues to increase further, due to the delay between the ordering and
delivery of new vessels, freight rates will increase exponentially; however, as
soon as the new vessels are delivered to the market, the increase in supply
will lead to freight rates falling back to their average level.

Table 5.12 presents the directional accuracy for three dirty-tanker routes,
TD3, TD5 and TD7, for the period March 2003 to December 2007. The statistics measure the percentage of times the forward curve can predict correctly
the future direction in the market; for instance, if the one-month forward
curve is in contango, this is a signal that freight rates in the next month
will increase above their current spot level, and vice-versa if the market is in
backwardation. The same table also presents the annualised volatility of the
different forward maturities.

Table 5.12 Directional accuracy of tanker forward curves

		Current month	1-month	2-month	3-month
TD3	Direction	61.40%	59.65%	71.93%	70.18%
	Volatility	105.54%	84.23%	71.18%	56.60%
TD5	Direction	56.14%	66.67%	70.18%	77.19%
	Volatility	81.86%	70.31%	59.61%	53.14%
TD7	Direction	70.18%	68.42%	78.95%	78.95%
	Volatility	73.29%	58.43%	47.82%	45.71%

Notes: The estimation period is from March 2003 to December 2007 (57 observations).
Direction is a test for directional predictability and measures the percentage of times the future change of direction in the spot market can be predicted correctly using the forward curve. Volatility is the annualised volatility of the monthly FFA rates.

Several points can be noted. First we can see that the directional accuracy of forward curves remains at reasonably good levels for short maturities and also increases as time to maturity increases, with directional accuracy of 78.95 per cent for the three-month TD7 FFA; this effectively means that if one is using the three-month TD7 FFA contract as a predictor of the future direction in the market after three months, one will, on average, be correct in one's assessment approximately eight out of ten times. The increase in directional accuracy as time to maturity increases may be due to the fact that seasonality in the market is reflected in the forward rates that, in turn, capture some of the seasonal cycles in the underlying market.

Turning next to the volatilities, we can note the very high level of annualised volatility for tanker rates; for instance, spot month annualised volatility for TD3 is 105 per cent, which is much higher than the typical level of volatility evidenced in financial and other commodity markets. We can also note that volatilities decrease with time to maturity. This pattern in volatilities is known as 'volatility term structure' and indicates that volatilities for long-maturity contracts will be lower than spot volatility; it is also consistent with the fact that spot freight rates follow a mean reverting process. Finally, another interesting observation is that there seems to be a relationship between size and volatility. In other words, FFA rates for larger vessels have greater volatility than FFA rates for smaller vessels and this is also consistent with what we can observe in the underlying physical market.

5.7.1 Baltic Forward Assessments (BFA)

Baltic Forward Assessments are assessments of FFA rates produced by the Baltic Exchange. They are calculated as the average of the assessments received by the Baltic Exchange from the rates submitted by a panel of forward brokers. The reporting forward panellists submit their rates daily, by 16:30 London time, and their assessment reflects a mid price based on what the current bid and offer is. If market price information is not available for the specified maturity, then the panellists take into account all relevant market information available to them at the daily reporting time (for example, how low a seller would go if there were no buyers and vice versa), logically normalised to reflect the characteristics of the FFABA standard contract. The forward panellists are companies whose core business is FFA broking; as such, they should not take positions in the market as principals but they should merely act as intermediaries, bringing together buyers and sellers in the market. As is the case with the underlying route information produced by the Baltic Exchange, the obligations of the panellists and the rules and regulations for the production of the BFA are outlined in the panellists' manual for forward brokers which is known as the *Manual for Forward Panellists* (Baltic Exchange, 2007b). BFAs are primarily used by clearing houses to perform marking-to-market on the open FFA positions and determine margin calls accordingly. They are also used by market participants for the purposes of marking-to-market their daily FFA positions for internal risk-monitoring and -management purposes as well as for measuring counter-party exposure in the FFA market. The BFA rates for BCI C4 and BCI 4TC are shown in Figure 5.1 and Figure 5.2 above.

BFAs produced by the Baltic Exchange are available for a number of dry and wet routes. Table 5.13 presents the reporting routes and periods for the dry BFA. We can see that for individual spot or trip-charter routes (for example, BCI C3 to C7, BPI P2A and BPI 3A) the reported maturities are the nearest months plus the first month of the next nearest quarters and the next three calendar years. Consider, for instance, BCI C4. We can see that on any business day the reported maturities are: the current month and the next seven nearest months; then the first month of the first two nearest quarters (that is, either January, April, July or October); and, finally, the first months of the four quarters for the next three years (that is, January, April, July and October). For instance, in May 2007, the following maturities were reported: May 07 to December 07 (that is the current month up to seven months ahead); then the first months of the next two nearest quarters, that is, January 08 and April 08 covering Q1 and Q2 of 2008, and then Calendar 2008 (which consists of the January, April, July and October 2008 FFAs), Calendar 2009 and Calendar 2010. Each one of these FFAs are settled at the end of their respective maturity month and the settlement rate is calculated as the average of the BCI C4 rate over the final seven days of the settlement month. These maturities are reported until one day before the maturity of the current-month contract, and rollover to the next-nearest maturity takes place on the settlement date of the contract; for instance, in the example presented here, these maturities will be reported until 31 May 2007 and rollover to the next set of maturities will take place on the settlement date of the May contracts, on 30 May 2008, which is the last trading day in May.[20]

Turning next to the basket trip-charter routes (such as BCI 4TC, BPI 4TC, BSI 6TC and BHSI 6TC) the reporting pattern is similar, although the emphasis now is on reporting quarterly contracts as opposed to individual months. Consider, for instance, BCI 4TC. On any given reporting day the following maturities are reported: the current month, the current quarter, the next four quarters and the next three calendar years; a quarter in this case refers to three consecutive FFA monthly contracts covering the respective quarter; similarly a calendar contract refers to a strip of 12 single-month contracts covering the respective calendar year. Each one of these contracts settles at the end of its respective month and the settlement rate is the average of the BCI 4TC rates over the respective calendar months. For instance, in May 2007, the following maturities were reported: current month (May 07); current quarter (Q2 07, which consists of May and June 07 contracts, since the April contract has already expired); the next four consecutive quarters (Q3 07, Q4 07, Q1 08 and Q2 08) and then Calendar contracts for 2008, 2009 and 2010. Each quarterly contract consists of three single-month contracts for the respective maturity; for instance Q4 07 consists of October 2007, November 2007 and December 2007 FFAs; each one of those contracts is settled at the end of its respective month and the settlement rate is calculated as the average BCI 4TC rate over the respective month. Similarly, the Calendar 2008 contract consists of 12 single-month FFA contracts, each maturing at the respective maturity month and settled as above. In addition to these rates, the Baltic Exchange also reports BFA rates for BCI C4 and BCI C7 routes where the settlement rate is calculated as the average of the month (denoted as BCI C4 M and BCI C7 M in Table 5.13), but only a small number of maturities is reported for those routes.

Table 5.14 presents the reporting periods for wet assessments. Overall, BFA are provided for three dirty (TD3, TD5 and TD7) and three clean routes (TC2, TC4 and TC5). For each route the following maturities are quoted: the current month and the next five nearest months; the current quarter and the next four nearest quarters, each quarter consisting of three individual contract months covering the respective quarter; and the next two calendar years – each calendar year consisting of twelve single-month contracts covering the

---

[20] There are some more detailed rules regarding the maturities that are reported at different points in time. For instance, when the reporting month is the first month of each quarter then there will be no reports for six and seven-month contracts because these will be covered by the quarterly maturities. For more details on the general rules of reporting see Baltic Exchange (2007b), also available from the Baltic Exchange website (www.balticexchange.com).

Table 5.13 Reporting periods for dry Baltic Forward Assessments

BCI C3	CM	+1 M	+2M	+3M	+4M				1st M of 1st NQ	1st M of 2nd NQ	1st M of 3rd NQ		
BCI C4	CM	+1M	+2M	+3M	+4M	+5M	+6M	+7M	1st M of 1st NQ	1st M of 2nd NQ	+1 Y	+2Y	+3Y
BCI C5	CM	+1 M	+2M						1st M of 1st NQ	1st M of 2nd NQ	1st M of 3rd NQ		
BCI C7	CM	+1M	+2M	+3M	+4M	+5M	+6M	+7M	1st M of 1st NQ	1st M of 2nd NQ	+1 Y	+2Y	+3Y
BCI C4 M	CM	+1M	+2M										
BCI C7 M	CM	+1M	+2M										
BCI 4TC	CM	CQ	+1Q	+2Q	+3Q	+4Q					+1Y	+2Y	+3Y
BPI P2A	CM	+1M	+2M	+3M	+4M	+5M							
BPI P3A	CM	+1M	+2M	+3M	+4M	+5M							
BPI 4TC	CM	CQ	+1Q	+2Q	+3Q	+4Q					+1Y	+2Y	+3Y
BSI 6TC	CM	CQ	+1Q	+2Q	+3Q	+4Q					+1Y	+2Y	+3Y
BHSI 6TC	CM	CQ	+1Q	+2Q	+3Q	+4Q					+1Y	+2Y	+3Y

Notes: M, Q and Y stand for Months, Quarters and Years, respectively. The numbers in front denote the relevant maturity of the forward contract. For instance +1M denotes the contract that matures next month; similarly +2Q denotes the contracts that matures in the second nearest quarter. 1st M of 1st NQ denotes the first month of the first nearest quarter; this refers to either a January, April, July or October contract. CM and CQ stand for current month and current quarter, respectively.

Source: Baltic Exchange (December 2007).

Table 5.14 Reporting periods for wet Baltic Forward Assessments

TD3	CM	+1M	+2M	+3M	+4M	+5M	CQ	+1Q	+2Q	+3Q	+4Q	+1Y	+2Y
TD5	CM	+1M	+2M	+3M	+4M	+5M	CQ	+1Q	+2Q	+3Q	+4Q	+1Y	+2Y
TD7	CM	+1M	+2M	+3M	+4M	+5M	CQ	+1Q	+2Q	+3Q	+4Q	+1Y	+2Y
TC2	CM	+1M	+2M	+3M	+4M	+5M	CQ	+1Q	+2Q	+3Q	+4Q	+1Y	+2Y
TC4	CM	+1M	+2M	+3M	+4M	+5M	CQ	+1Q	+2Q	+3Q	+4Q	+1Y	+2Y
TC5	CM	+1M	+2M	+3M	+4M	+5M	CQ	+1Q	+2Q	+3Q	+4Q	+1Y	+2Y

Notes: M, Q and Y stand for Months, Quarters and Years, respectively. The numbers in front denote the relevant maturity of the forward contract. For instance +1M denotes the contract that matures in the next month; similarly +2Q denotes the contracts that mature in the second nearest quarter.
CM and CQ stand for current month and current quarter, respectively.
Source: Baltic Exchange (December 2007).

respective year. Each one of those contracts is settled at the end of its respective maturity month and the settlement rate is calculated as the average of the month of the underlying Baltic route.

5.8 Summary and conclusions

In this chapter, devoted to the FFA market, we discussed the practicalities of trading FFAs as well as how FFAs can be used to risk-manage a variety of exposures in the underlying freight market. We also analysed the issues that hedgers need to be aware of in setting up their hedging strategies; finally we discussed the issue of credit risk in the OTC FFA market and how this can be mitigated either by using the FFABA 2007 or ISDA contracts or by having the OTC contract cleared through a clearing house.

Since FFAs' introduction in the early 1990s trading volume has increased constantly on a year-by-year basis. The continuous growth in the market and the influx of new traders, such as investment banks, trading houses and hedge funds, also led to the development of more sophisticated trading strategies using FFAs – such as spread and arbitrage trades – as well as to the increasing use of freight options for hedging and speculative purposes. The major advantage of freight options is that they enable market participants to be hedged if the market moves against them, but also to take advantage of favourable conditions if the market moves to their advantage. The characteristics of freight options are discussed in the next chapter.

Appendix 5.A: FFABA 2007© Forward Freight Agreement contract

Reproduced with the kind permission of the Baltic Exchange and the FFABA.

FORWARD FREIGHT AGREEMENT BROKERS ASSOCIATION ("FFABA")

FORWARD FREIGHT AGREEMENT

FFABA 2007 TERMS

Trade Ref: [•]
Contract Date: [•]

The purpose of this Confirmation is to state the terms and conditions of the Transaction entered into between:

[•] (hereafter, "**Seller**")

Attention: [•]
Postal Address: [•]
Street Address: [•]
Telephone No.:   [•]
Facsimile No.:   [•]
Email Address: [•]

and

[•] (hereafter, "**Buyer**")
Attention: [•]
Postal Address: [•]
Street Address: [•]
Telephone No.:   [•]
Facsimile No.:   [•]
Email Address: [•]

The agreement between the parties set out in this Confirmation is a Confirmation pursuant to the Master Agreement.

In this Confirmation, "**Master Agreement**" has the meaning given to it in clause 9 if that clause applies, and if it does not, means any master agreement by which the Transaction entered into pursuant to and in accordance with this Confirmation is governed.

Until superseded by notice information in a subsequent Confirmation or other communication, the above addresses are hereby recognized as the correct addresses to which any notification under this Confirmation may be properly served.

The terms of this Confirmation are as follows:

1) **Contract Route(s):**
   [•] as defined by the Baltic Exchange on the Contract Date and any route replacing or substituting that route subsequently published by the Baltic Exchange on or before the Settlement Date and with effect from the date of such replacement or substitution.
2) **Contract Rate:**
   [•]
3) **Contract Quantity:**
   (i) Total Quantity: [•]
   (ii) Quantity by Contract Month: [•]
4) **Contract Month(s):**
   [•]
5) **Settlement Dates:**
   The last Baltic Exchange Index publication day of each Contract Month.
6) **Settlement Rate:**
   (a) Each settlement rate (the "**Settlement Rate**") shall be the unweighted average of the rates for the Contract Route(s) published by the Baltic Exchange over the Settlement Period (defined as [•] Baltic Exchange Index publication days of the applicable Contract Month up to and including the Settlement Date).
   (b) If for any reason the Baltic Exchange cannot provide any rate required for establishing the Settlement Rate, then the current chairman of the FFABA may be instructed by either party to form a panel comprising of a minimum of three independent brokers (the "**Panel**") to determine an appropriate rate, which determination will be final and binding on both parties.
   (c) Each party shall bear its own costs and expenses in connection with any determination made pursuant to this clause 6.
   (d) The parties shall severally indemnify and hold harmless each of the members of the Panel, the Baltic Exchange and its members and the FFABA and its members (the "**Indemnified Persons**") against all liabilities, actions, demands, costs and expenses incurred by any of them arising directly or indirectly out of or in connection with the formation of the Panel and any determination made by the Panel.
   (e) As between the parties, each party shall have a right of contribution against the other party in respect of any indemnity payment made pursuant to the preceding paragraph so that their respective liabilities pursuant to that paragraph shall be equal.

7) **Settlement Sum:**
The **"Settlement Sum"** is the difference between the Contract Rate and the Settlement Rate multiplied by the Quantity by Contract Month. If the Settlement Rate is higher than the Contract Rate, the Seller shall pay the Buyer the Settlement Sum. If the Settlement Rate is lower than the Contract Rate, the Buyer shall pay the Seller the Settlement Sum.

8) **Payment Procedure and Obligations:**
   (a) Payment of the Settlement Sum is due on the later of two (2) London business days after presentation of payee's invoice (with complete payment instructions) or five (5) London business days after the Settlement Date and for this purpose a **"London business day"** means a day (other than a Saturday or Sunday on which commercial banks are open for business in London). The Settlement Sum will be deemed "paid" when it has been received into the bank account designated by the payee.
   (b) Payment of the Settlement Sum shall be made telegraphically, in full, in United States dollars. The costs incurred in effecting payment shall be for the account of the payer. Payment may only be effected directly between the parties. The Settlement Sum shall be paid without any deduction or set-off except as permitted pursuant to the Master Agreement or otherwise as agreed by the Buyer and the Seller in writing.

9) **ISDA Master Agreement:**
This clause 9 applies only if either:
   (i) this Confirmation does not already constitute a Confirmation under an existing master agreement entered into by the parties to this Confirmation; or
   (ii) the parties agree, either by virtue of clause 20 or otherwise, that the terms of the Master Agreement that is constituted by this clause are to replace any such existing master agreement.

This Confirmation constitutes and incorporates by reference the provisions of the 1992 ISDA®Master Agreement (Multicurrency – Cross Border) (without Schedule) as if they were fully set out in this Confirmation and with only the following specific modifications and elections:

   (a) Section 2(c)(ii) shall not apply so that a net amount due will be determined in respect of all amounts payable on the same date in the same currency in respect of two or more Transactions;
   (b) Seller is the Calculation Agent except where the Seller is the Defaulting Party in which event Buyer is the Calculation Agent;
   (c) the most current published set of ISDA®Commodity Definitions and ISDA®Definitions shall apply;
   (d) Credit Event Upon Merger is applicable to both parties;

(e) for the purposes of payments on Early Termination, Loss will apply and the Second Method will apply;

(f) Automatic Early Termination will apply to both parties;

(g) the Termination Currency is United States dollars;

(h) the Applicable Rate shall mean the one month USD-LIBOR plus 2%, reset daily and compounded monthly;

(i) Local Business Day or banking day shall each refer to such a day in London;

(j) such other modifications as shall be necessary for such incorporation;

(k) references to "this Master Agreement", "this Agreement", "herein" and other like expressions shall be construed as being references to this Confirmation incorporating such provisions,

and this Confirmation, including such incorporated provisions, shall govern the Transaction referred to in this Confirmation and any other Transaction referred to in clauses 20 and 21.

The agreement constituted and incorporated by the incorporation of the provisions of the 1992 ISDA®Master Agreement (Multicurrency – Cross Border) (without Schedule) pursuant to this clause is referred to in this Confirmation as the "**Master Agreement**".

10) **Capacity and Good Standing:**

In line with and in addition to (as appropriate) the representations contained in Section 3 of the Master Agreement, each party represents to the other party that:

(a) it is duly organized and validly existing under the laws of the jurisdiction of its organization or incorporation, and is solvent and in good standing;

(b) it has the power to execute, deliver, and perform this Confirmation;

(c) all governmental and other consents that are required to have been obtained by it with respect to this Confirmation have been obtained and are in full force and effect and all conditions of any such consents have been complied with;

(d) in the event that a party to this Confirmation is a person organized under, domiciled in, or having its principal place of business in, the United States, each party represents to the other party that it is an "eligible contract participant" as defined in §1a(12) of the Commodity Exchange Act (7 U.S.C. §1a(12), as amended).

11) **Telephone Recording:**

Each party consents to the recording of telephone conversations in connection with this Confirmation.

12) **Commission:**

Each of the parties agrees to pay brokers' commission to any broker (a "**Broker**") as agreed with any Broker.

13) **Non-Assignability:**
Except as provided in Section 7 of the Master Agreement, this Confirmation is non-assignable unless otherwise agreed in writing between the parties to this Confirmation.

14) **Principal To Principal:**
This Confirmation is a principal to principal agreement with settlement directly between the two parties. Both parties agree that any Broker shall be under no obligation or liability in relation to this Confirmation. Both parties agree jointly and severally to indemnify and hold harmless any Broker against all actions, including but not limited to all claims, demands, liabilities, damages, costs and expenses both from the two parties and any third party. Claims, demands, liabilities, damages, costs and expenses suffered or incurred are to be settled directly by or between the two parties.

15) **Law and Jurisdiction:**
This Confirmation shall be governed by and construed in accordance with English law and shall be subject to the exclusive jurisdiction of the High Court of Justice in London, England. The terms of Section 12(a) of the Master Agreement notwithstanding, proceedings may be validly served upon either party by sending the same by ordinary post and/or by fax to the addresses and/or fax numbers for each party given above.

16) **Entire Agreement:**
This Confirmation and the Master Agreement set out the entire agreement and understanding of the parties with respect to the subject matter of this Confirmation and supersede all oral communication and prior writings with respect thereto.

17) **Payment Account Information:**
For Seller: For Buyer:

Bank address: Bank address:

Aba: Aba:

Swift address: Swift address:

Account no.:   Account no.:

Sort code: Sort code:

18) **Third party rights**
(a) Unless provided to the contrary in this Confirmation, a person who is not a party to this Confirmation has no rights under the Contracts (Rights of Third Parties) Act 1999 to enforce or enjoy the benefit of any term of this Confirmation.

(b) Any Indemnified Person and any Broker shall have the right to enjoy the benefit of and enforce the terms of clause 6(d) in the case of any Indemnified Person and clause 14 in the case of any Broker.

(c) Notwithstanding any term of this Confirmation, the consent of any person who is not a party to this Confirmation is not required to rescind or vary this Confirmation.

19) Partial Invalidity

If, at any time, any provision of this Confirmation or the Master Agreement is or becomes illegal, invalid or unenforceable in any respect under any laws of any jurisdiction, neither the legality, validity or enforceability of the remaining provisions nor the legality or enforceability of the provision under the laws of any other jurisdiction will in any way be affected or impaired.

20) Inclusion of historical Confirmations under Master Agreement

(a) **Unless the parties to this Confirmation specifically agree otherwise in writing, this clause 20 shall apply in accordance with its terms.**

(b) This clause 20 applies to this Confirmation and to every agreement entered into between the parties to this Confirmation (and no other persons) before the date of this Confirmation that is in respect of a forward freight swap, option or derivative:

(i) that is expressly stated to be subject to, or is subject to substantially the same terms as, either the FFABA 2000 terms, the FFABA 2005 terms or the FFABA 2007 terms, with or without amendment; and

(ii) in the case of a Confirmation that is stated to be subject to, or subject to substantially the same terms as, the FFABA 2007 terms that does not incorporate a clause substantially in the same form as this clause 20.

(c) Each agreement to which this clause 20 applies shall be treated as a Confirmation under the Master Agreement constituted pursuant to clause 9 as if such agreement had been entered into between the parties on the terms of the Master Agreement on the date of the first such Confirmation.

(d) If there is any inconsistency between the provisions of any agreement constituted pursuant to paragraph (c) above and the agreement constituting a Transaction to which this clause 20 applies, the provisions of the agreement constituting the Transaction to which this clause 20 applies will prevail for the purposes of the Transaction under such agreement.

(e) This clause 20 shall not affect any rights or obligations of the parties under any Transaction accrued before the date of this Confirmation.

(f) This clause 20 is effective notwithstanding any entire agreement clause or similar provision in any such agreement relevant to any such Transaction.

21) Inclusion of subsequent Confirmations under Master Agreement

(a) **Unless the parties to this Confirmation specifically agree otherwise in writing, this clause 21 shall apply in accordance with its terms.**

(b) This clause 21 applies to every Confirmation that is in respect of a forward freight swap, option or derivative entered into between the parties to this Confirmation (and no other persons) subsequent to an agreement incorporating a Master Agreement (as defined in and pursuant to a clause substantially in the same form as and equivalent to clause 9) having been entered into by them.

(c) Each such subsequent Confirmation shall constitute a Confirmation under the Master Agreement on the terms of clauses 20(c), (d), (e) and (f) as if they were incorporated and fully set out in this clause 21 with appropriate and necessary modifications for such incorporation.

Signed for the Seller by   **Signed for the Buyer by**

....

Duly Authorized Signatory   **Duly Authorized Signatory**

6
Technical Analysis and Freight Trading Strategies

6.1 Introduction

Technical analysis is a relatively modern technique in detecting and projecting trends and patterns in the time series of asset prices and is used extensively for establishing trading strategies in commodity, stock and foreign exchange markets. Until recently, technical analysis was not widely used in the shipping industry. However, since the expansion of the freight derivatives market and an increase in freight trading liquidity as well as market depth, some traders have started to use technical analysis to investigate and exploit trading opportunities in the FFA market. The aim of this chapter is to present and discuss a number of technical analysis methods and trading rules applied to shipping freight and FFA markets as well as to the market for ships. In addition, we provide examples of how technical trading rules can be applied to the physical market in the form of establishing chartering strategies or even to the timing of investment in the market for ships.

There have been a number of previous attempts to apply technical analysis to shipping markets. For instance, Norman (1981), Adland (2000), and Adland and Koekebakker (2004) apply technical trading rules to investment decisions in the second-hand market, while Adland and Strandenes (2006) investigate market efficiency in the tanker freight market using technical trading strategies. Finally, Alizadeh and Nomikos (2006; 2007a) combine technical and fundamental analysis in order to determine the optimum timing of investment and divestment in the market for second-hand ships.

6.2 Technical analysis

'Technical analysis' is a generic term used to define analysis of patterns and trends in asset prices, using methods such as Chart analysis, Candle Stick Patterns, Filter and Moving Average Trading Rules, and Momentum Index Strategies. Murphy (1998) defines technical analysis as 'the study of market action, primarily through the use of charts, for the purpose of forecasting future price trends'. The term 'market action' includes three principal sources of information available to the technical analyst, these being: price, volume, and open interest. Technical analysis is primarily conducted by studying charts of past price action. Many different methods and tools are used, but they all rely on the assumption that price patterns and trends exist in markets, and that they can be identified and exploited. Technical analysis is based on three main premises: i) market action discounts everything; ii) price moves in trends; and iii) history repeats itself.

The statement 'market action discounts everything' is regarded as being fundamental to the concept of technical analysis. This concept needs to be fully understood in order to yield any fruitful result or to even make sense of the process. Technical analysts believe that anything which could possibly affect the price of an asset – be it fundamental, political, psychological or anything else – should already be reflected in that price. This effectively means that price action should reflect shifts in supply and demand. Therefore, if demand exceeds supply, prices should rise. Likewise, should supply exceed demand, prices should fall. The charts representing trends do not cause markets to move up or down; rather they represent the bullish or bearish psychology of the marketplace. As a rule, chartists do not concern themselves with the fundamental analysis of why prices rise or fall. They believe that if everything that affects the market price is ultimately reflected in the market place, the market price itself is all that should be studied.

The concept of trend is fundamental to the understanding of the technical approach. If the premise of the market following a trend is not accepted, there is no point in applying technical analysis. The purpose of charting the price action of a market is to identify trends in the early stages of their development in order to capitalise, by trading in the forecasted direction of these trends. Most technical analysis techniques are trend-following although some could pursue an anticipation of a change in trends.

Finally, human psychology plays a pivotal role in much of the reasoning behind technical analysis and the study of the market. Chart patterns which have been identified and characterised represent certain features of human psychology at that point in time. The price charts displayed as patterns reveal the bullish or bearish psychology of the market. The reasoning of analysts is that, since human psychology tends not to change, these patterns have worked well in the past, and that they will continue to work well in the future. This leads technical analysts to conclude that the key to understanding the future lies in a study of the past.

6.2.1   Chart analysis

In very fast markets with high-frequency trading, such as foreign exchange or certain types of commodities, traders do not use fundamental analysis for their day-trading activities. They simply recognise certain patterns that the asset price may follow by studying the time-series graph of the asset price,

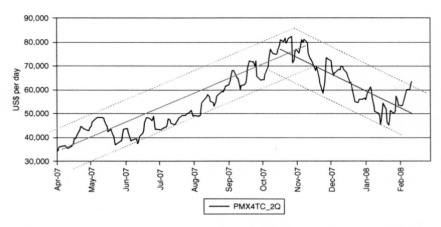

Figure 6.1 Linear trend lines with upper and lower bands for Panamax 4TC Q2 FFA prices

and base their trading strategies on the repetition of these patterns. There are many different patterns which technical analysts have identified and applied; these include: 'trend lines', 'head and shoulders', 'triangle patterns', 'support and resistance', and many others.[1]

'Trend lines' are simple linear directional indicators which can be drawn on a price series to assess its growth or decline over time. Trend lines do not have any predictive power as to how the asset price may evolve, but they can merely be used to see in which direction the prices have moved so far. For instance, Figure 6.1 plots Panamax Q2 (i.e., second-nearest quarter) basket 4TC FFA prices over the period April 2007 to February 2008. It seems that there are two clear trend patterns in the series: that is, Panamax 4TC FFA prices steadily increased over the period April 2007 to November 2007, and declined at similar rate over the next five months until February 2008. It is important to note that when time series show high volatility with a stochastic trend, as is the case in Figure 6.1, use of a linear trend line for future prediction, directional projection, and investment purposes could be inappropriate and misleading.

The 'head and shoulders' patterns are used in technical analysis to assess whether prices have reached their peak and whether there might be a decline or a downward correction in the market. For instance, Figure 6.2 presents the second-quarter FFA prices for Panamax average 4TC over the period August 2007 to December 2007. It can be seen that the rates peaked in mid-October (head) with several smaller peaks (shoulders) before and after October.

---

[1] In this chapter we focus on some patterns and rules that can be applied to the freight market and prices. For more on charts and technical patterns see Kahn (2006) and Murphy (1998) for a variety of technical charts, analysis and trading rules.

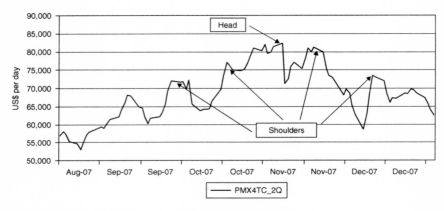

Figure 6.2   Head and shoulders pattern in Q2 Panamax 4TC FFA rates

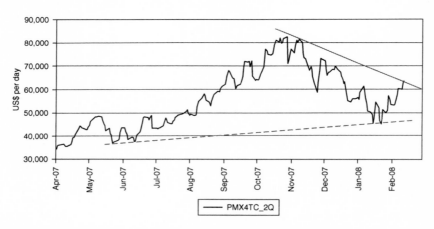

Figure 6.3   Triangle pattern in second-quarter Panamax 4TC FFA rates

The 'triangle patterns' (symmetric or asymmetric) are less observed in FFA rates; however, they show that prices oscillate within a band that narrows over time and converge to a single point. After that, prices may move in any direction. This pattern can be seen in Figure 6.3 where second-quarter Panamax 4TC FFA rates are converging over the period June 2007 to February 2008 to a level of around US$50,000/day.

'Support and resistance' is a technical analysis method which is used extensively by commodity traders. To apply this method, one needs to have a good understanding of supply and demand as well as the interaction between the two in a competitive market. The argument is that prices cannot fall below a level at which suppliers are not prepared to supply the commodity.

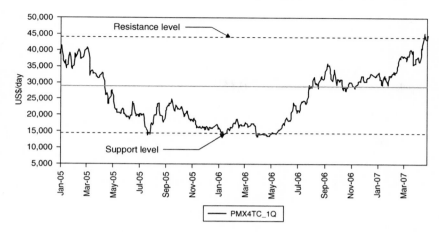

Figure 6.4 Support and resistance bands for Panamax 4TC first-quarter FFA prices

Also, prices are expected not to exceed a level above which consumers are not prepared to pay for the commodity. Therefore, the technical analyst identifies boundaries for price fluctuations which he believes will not be breached or exceeded, and hence prices will not move outside this band. The resistance level (R-L) can be set as the level that the prices have hit a few times before but never exceeded. Similarly the support level (S-L) can be set by choosing the level below which the prices have not fallen to before. While historical values of price levels are used to define the support and resistance levels, it should also be noted that support and resistance levels may evolve over time as supply and demand conditions in the market change.

As a trading rule, a trader can sell (short) freight contracts if the price approaches or goes above the resistance level and buy (long) freight contracts when the price approaches or falls below the support level. Although there is a good economic argument for the existence of support and resistance levels in shipping freight markets, freight movements in the past few years have shown that these boundaries can be reached and passed. Therefore, freight-trading strategies based on support and resistance chart analysis can be extremely risky. Figure 6.4 presents a typical support and resistance level for Panamax first-nearest quarter 4TC FFA price over the period January 2005 to April 2007. Over that period, FFA prices moved between the lower bound of US$15,000/day to an upper resistance bound of US$45,000/day, which was considered an extremely high hire rate for Panamax ships. However, a few months later, over September 2007 to January 2008, first-quarter FFA rates exceeded the resistance level and reached highs of US$85,000/day. Thus, although theoretically, we assume that shipping freight rates do have upper and lower boundaries, these are breached at times, especially during extremely tight supply and demand conditions.

The number of chart patterns is by no means limited to what has been discussed here. There are many chart and price patterns that are proposed and applied by technical analysts in different markets. Kahn (2006) provides a detailed description of many different chart patterns proposed and used by technical analysts and traders in FX, financial and commodity markets.

6.3 Technical trading rules

Theoretically, the methods and combinations of technical trading rules can be unlimited. Along with the increase in computational power and availability of high-frequency data – on price, volume, open interest, and the like – in recent years there has been a parallel growth in the number of technical analysis methods and techniques. In addition, the availability of electronic trading and fast trade executions have contributed to the popularity of technical analysis and trading rules among investors in many financial and commodity markets. The empirical evidence on the effectiveness of different technical analysis techniques in producing superior trading profit is mixed. Researchers using a variety of methods and a range of sample periods and markets, report different conclusions on the performance of technical analysis and trading rules. In the following sections, we present some technical trading rules that can be used to set up trading strategies in forward freight markets and examine the performance of some of these techniques.

6.4 Moving averages (MA)

A moving average (MA) of an asset price or a variable shows the changes in the average value of the price or the variable over a period of time. MAs are generally used to measure a variable's trend and momentum, and to define areas of possible support and/or resistance. Depending on the number of observations used in the averaging window, a variety of MAs can be constructed. In general, if the number of observations in the averaging window is relatively small, then the MA is called a 'short' or a 'fast' MA, whereas if the number of observations in the averaging window is relatively large it is called a 'slow' or 'long' MA. For instance, Figure 6.5 presents Panamax basket 4TC second-quarter FFA prices along with 10-, 20- and 40-day MA series. It can be seen that the MA10 series follows the FFA prices more closely compared to the MA20 or MA40 series. In fact, these long MA series seem to be smoother than the short MA10 series.

6.4.1 The moving average crossover trading rule

MA series and their comparisons are widely used to detect turning points and changes in price trends and, therefore, for establishing trading rules. The simplest MA trading rule, which is used by most technical analysts, is the

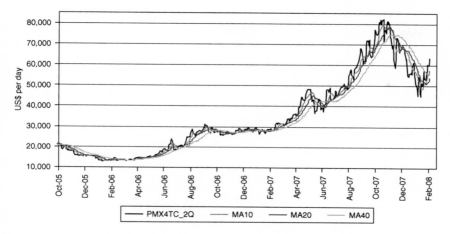

Figure 6.5 Plot of Panamax 4TC Q2 FFA prices and moving average series

'MA crossover rule' – also known as 'MA convergence-divergence' (MACD). The standard MA crossover trading rule indicates a buy (sell) signal when the fast/short MA cuts the slow/long MA from below (above). In other words, the rule signals a future price increase when the fast/short MA cuts the slow/long MA from below, and signals a future price drop when the fast MA cuts the slow MA line from above. Two most popular combinations of the double MA crossover method for futures traders are the MA5–20 and MA10–50. The technique of using two MAs lags the market slightly more than the single MA rule, but it reduces the so-called 'whipsaw' effects.[2] However, one criticism of this method is that all prices receive the same weighting throughout the averaging window. Some analysts believe that a heavier weighting should be assigned to the more recent price action using exponential moving averages (EMA).

An alternative, and relatively more complicated, approach is to use what is known as the 'triple MA trading rule'. The most widely used triple crossover MA technique is the popular MA4–9–18 combination. This combination is mainly used in futures trading. A buying alert takes place in an uptrend when the MA4 cuts both the MA9 and MA18 from below. A confirmed buy signal occurs when the MA9 then cuts the MA18 from below. This places the MA4 above the MA9, which is above the MA18. However, since the frequency of trading and speed of price changes in freight markets are relatively low compared to other commodity and financial markets, the triple crossover

---

[2] A whipsaw occurs when a buy or sell signal is reversed in a short time or too frequently within a period. Volatile markets and sensitive indicators can cause whipsaws.

Table 6.1   Risk-return comparisons of static buy-and-hold and MA trading strategies

	Buy-and-hold	MA 10–20	MA 20-40	MA 10–20–40	MA 10–20–60
Total sample: 11 April 2005 to 14 February 2008					
Annual return	24.88%	65.72%	50.05%	51.82%	54.74%
Overall return	71.15%	188.24%	143.15%	148.19%	156.55%
Annualised StDv	47.76%	47.74%	47.81%	45.94%	44.38%
Sharpe ratio	0.521	1.376	1.047	1.128	1.233
First sub-sample: 11 April 2005 to 30 April 2007					
Annual return	15.41%	73.10%	60.11%	60.77%	69.09%
Overall return	31.68%	150.30%	123.60%	124.95%	142.04%
Annualised StDv	40.64%	40.45%	40.66%	38.67%	37.75%
Sharpe ratio	0.379	1.807	1.479	1.572	1.830
Second sub-sample: 1 May 2007 To 14 February 2008					
Average return	49.3%	48.7%	24.4%	29.1%	18.1%
Overall return	39.5%	38.9%	19.6%	23.2%	14.5%
Standard deviation of returns	62.5%	62.8%	62.6%	60.8%	58.0%
Sharpe ratio	0.789	0.775	0.391	0.478	0.313

trading rule should be adjusted accordingly in terms of the averaging period (for example, to MA10–20–40).

MA is considered a solid tool which may be used simultaneously with chart analysis. Chart analysis is considered subjective and difficult to test, whereas MA crossover rules are seen as less subjective and more robust. To clarify, two technical analysts may disagree on the interpretation of a given price pattern, whether it is a triangle or a wedge, while with MA the trend signals are precise and not open to debate. However, the MA does not work all the time; one such case in which MA does not prove to be helpful is when the market does not display a trending phase, that is to say when the prices trade sideways in a horizontal price band or trading range.

To illustrate the application of the MA crossover trading rule on FFAs, consider the Panamax second quarter 4TC FFAs presented in Panel A of Figure 6.6. We implement two MA crossover trading rules, namely MA10–20 and MA20–40, over the period 11 April 2005 to 14 February 2008. The rule is based on a 'buy' signal when short MA is greater than long MA, and a 'sell' signal when the short MA is less than the long MA series. We also assume that any trade or change in the position incurs a 1 per cent transaction cost. The results are presented in Table 6.1. It seems that the MA10–20 trading exercise performs better that any other MA crossover combinations, with an overall return of 188.24 per cent, an average annualised return of 65.72% per cent, an annualised standard deviation of 47.74 per cent, and a return-to-risk ratio (that is a Sharpe ratio) of 1.376. The return and risk of MA10–20 is also better than the outright 'buy-and-hold' strategy which yields an average annualised return of 24.88 per cent, a standard deviation of 47.76 per cent, and a return-to-risk ratio of 0.521. The return on the MA10–20 trading rule is almost three times higher than the return on the buy-and-hold strategy while the standard deviation of returns are similar for both strategies over the whole sample.

In addition to double MA crossover rules, we use two triple MA crossover strategies. These are MA10–20–40 and MA10–20–60. In this case, the rule is based on a 'buy' signal when a short MA is greater than two long MA series and a 'sell' signal when the short MA is less than the two long MA series. No position is taken if the short MA is between the two long MA series; we also assume 1 per cent transaction costs for any change in position. The results of triple MA crossover trading rules suggest that this strategy outperforms buy-and-hold and other double MA rules with the exception of MA10–20. The overall cumulative profit of the three double MA crossover trading rules and two triple crossover rules on a Panamax second-quarter 4TC FFA are presented in Panel B of Figure 6.6.

However, it should be noted that the profitability of MA trading rules can be very much dependent on the sample chosen and there is no guarantee of their performance. For instance, while this MA10–20 rule produced significant profits over whole sample period (11 April 2005 to 14 February 2008), it may well be the case that applying this rule to a different sample period produces a completely different set of results. This can be seen when we split the sample into two sub-periods: the first period covers 11 April 2005 to 30 April 2007; and the second is between 1 May 2007 and 14 February 2008. Results of the trading rules in the two sub-samples seem to be completely different. For instance, while the MA10–20 performs much better than the buy-and-hold strategy in the first sub-period, yielding an average return of 73.1 per cent with a standard deviation of 40.45 per cent, the performance of the model in the second sub-sample is hardly as good as the buy-and-hold rule, with an average return of 48.7 per cent and a standard deviation of 62.8 per cent. This change in performance seems to be consistent across all models. In the case of the triple MA10–20–60 crossover rule also, the decrease in the performance in the second sub-sample is quite significant, while the model produced superior results in the first sub-period. The main reason for this is because MA trading – and any other technical trading rules – do not take into account market fundamentals; they are purely backward-looking rules. As a result, these rules cannot incorporate any additional market information or expectations into the trading strategy and buy-or-sell decisions.

6.4.2 Stochastic oscillators

'Stochastic oscillators', sometimes known as 'stochastics', are another set of popular indicators and trading rules used in technical analysis. A stochastic oscillator shows where the price is trading relative to the recent high-low range. For instance, a ten-period stochastic compares the current price against

Panel A: Panamax second-quarter basket 4TC FFAs and MA10, 20 and 40 series

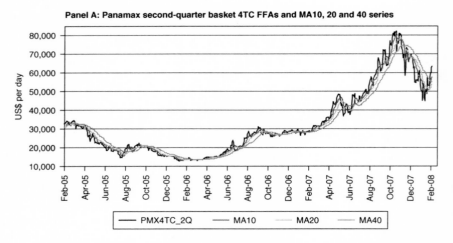

Panel B: Cumulative profit of double and triple MA crossover trading rule on second-quarter Panamax 4TC FFAs

Figure 6.6   MA crossover trading rule on a Panamax second-quarter 4TC FFAs

the highest and lowest price over the previous ten days, to see where the current price falls within that range. The oscillator takes a value of 100 when the current price is at the top of the lagged period range (10-day High-Low), and a value of 0 when the current price is at the bottom of the range. This is essentially an indication of price momentum over the window and can be used for setting up a trading strategy. The trading rule can be set up on the oscillator or its moving average. For instance, when the MA of the oscillator is above 80 it can be considered as a 'buy' signal, when the value of the MA series is below 20 points it is a 'sell' signal; anything between 20 and 80 is a neutral position.

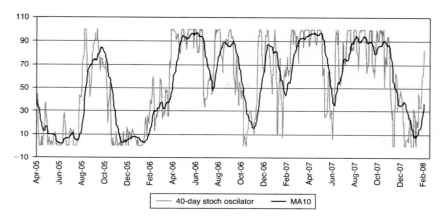

Figure 6.7 40-Day stochastic oscillator and its MA10 on Q2 Panamax 4TC FFA

To illustrate how a trading strategy based on a stochastic oscillator works, consider Q2 Panamax 4TC FFA prices. We first build a stochastic oscillator with a window of 40 days and construct a 10-day MA on this oscillator, as shown in Figure 6.7. Next we set up trading strategies based on 20–80, 30–70, and 40–60 lower-upper bands on the MA oscillator; that is, a long position when the MA on the oscillator is greater than the upper band, a short position when the oscillator is less than lower band, and a neutral position when it is between the upper and lower bands. We also assume transaction costs of 1 per cent for each trade. Results are presented in Table 6.2 for the total sample period of 11 April 2005 to 14 February 2008, as well as for two sub-sample periods; 11 April 2005 to 30 April 2007, and 1 May 2007 to 14 February 2008. It can be seen that over the whole sample period the 40–60 stochastic oscillator outperforms buy-and-hold and other strategies, with an average annualised return of 42.13 per cent, a total return of 120.5 per cent, a standard deviation of 44.79 per cent, and a return-to-risk ratio of 0.941. However, when we look at the performance over the two sub-samples, we notice that while the stochastic oscillators significantly outperform the buy-and-hold trading rule with return-to-risk ratios of more than 1.2 in the first sub-sample, their performance is not better than the buy-and-hold strategy over the second period. In fact, in two out of the three trading rules, the return is negative whereas the buy-and-hold method yields a return of 49.3 per cent. This shows that stochastic oscillators can perform well when there is no significant trend in prices and volatility is relatively low, as in the first period when the volatility of the buy-and-hold is 40.64 per cent. However, when prices tend to have significant trend and high volatility, as in the second period when volatility is 62.5 per cent, stochastic oscillators cannot be used as effective trading rules. This is perhaps due to a high frequency of trading signals and the ensuing higher transaction costs.

Table 6.2 Comparison of return and risk of static buy-and-hold and stochastic oscillator trading strategies

	Buy-and-hold	40-day SO 20–80	40-day SO 30–70	40-day SO 40–60
Total sample: 11 April 2005 To 14 February 2008				
Annual return	24.88%	30.44%	38.72%	42.13%
Overall return	71.15%	87.06%	110.74%	120.50%
Annualised StDv	47.76%	38.32%	41.32%	44.79%
Sharpe ratio	0.521	0.794	0.937	0.941
First sub-sample: 11 April 2005 to 30 April 2007				
Annual return	15.41%	42.89%	42.50%	59.04%
Overall return	31.68%	88.18%	87.38%	121.39%
Annualised StDv	40.64%	33.90%	36.31%	38.31%
Sharpe ratio	0.379	1.265	1.170	1.541
Second sub-sample: 1 May 2007 to 14 February 2008				
Annual return	49.3%	−1.4%	29.2%	−1.1%
Overall return	39.5%	−1.1%	23.4%	−0.9%
Annualised StDv	62.5%	47.9%	52.1%	58.2%
Sharpe ratio	0.789	−0.029	0.561	−0.019

6.5   Filter rules

Filter rules are another set of technical trading tools used by traders to establish trading strategies based on deviation of prices from certain trends or patterns that they are assumed to follow. According to Fama and Blume (1966) an x percent standard filter rule can be defined as follows:

> If the daily closing price of a particular security moves up at least x percent, buy and hold the security until its price moves down at least x percent from a subsequent high, at which time simultaneously sell and go short. The short position is maintained until the daily closing price rises at least x percent above a subsequent low at which one covers and buys. Moves less than x percent in either direction are ignored.

Filter rules may also complement other trading rules, such as MA, if there is a need for an adjustment indicator, to reduce overtrading. When transaction costs are high, overtrading can cause slippage and reduce or eliminate profits. Slippage refers to the reduction in trading profits that arises from the cost of trading; this includes bid-offer spreads, commissions and fees. Therefore it is necessary to find adjustments to the indicator in order to reduce the number of trades, without reducing the returns from the profitable trades. This may be achieved by applying filter rules, which filter the buy/sell signals, specifying

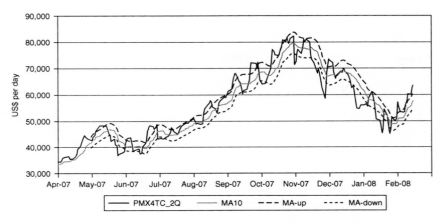

Figure 6.8 Plot of MA10 and 5 per cent envelope for Panamax 4TC Q2 FFA

that you want the software to generate a buy or sell signal only if the price is *a* percentage point above or below the MA or has been above or below the MA by *z* amount of time. Two popular types of filter rules are 'MA envelopes' and 'Bollinger Bands'. Both consist of a mean, normally expressed as a moving average (MA) series with two upper and lower trading bands.

6.5.1 Moving average envelopes

A moving average (MA) envelope, also known as 'percentage envelope', is a band of two series that follow a particular MA series with slightly higher and lower values than the MA series. These two lines form a band around the MA series and can be used as trading indicators. To construct an MA envelope, we first calculate the MA series based on *k* number of days, then we calculate two series which are *x* per cent (for example, 5 per cent or 10 per cent) above and below the MA values. This is illustrated in Figure 6.8 for Panamax Q2 4TC FFA, where the MA10 is plotted along with the 5 per cent up-and-down bands (envelope). Setting up trading strategies based on MA envelopes or bands involves following a rule where a 'sell' signal is indicated when actual prices exceed the upper envelope/band and the position is held until prices reach the MA series (or the lower band); conversely a 'buy' signal is indicated when prices fall below the lower envelope/band and the position is held until prices reach the MA series (or the upper band). Using an MA envelope for trading reduces the number of trades substantially, which in turn lowers the slippage and transaction costs.

MA envelopes can also be applied to an MA crossover strategy. In this case, we calculate the difference between a fast and a slow MA series, and construct a new MA series using the two bands on the difference between the MA series. Again the trading rule can be based on whether the MA

Table 6.3 Comparison of return and risk of buy-and-hold against MA envelope trading rules on Q2 Panamax 4TC FFA

Statistics	Buy-and-hold	MA10 ± 15%	MA20 ± 15%
Total sample: 11 April 2005 to 14 February 2008			
Annual return	24.88%	24.65%	23.65%
Overall return	71.15%	70.51%	67.65%
Annualised StDv	47.76%	20.07%	31.01%
Sharpe ratio	0.521	1.228	0.763
First sub-sample: 11 April 2005 to 30 April 2007			
Annual return	15.41%	14.00%	8.72%
Overall return	31.68%	28.79%	17.92%
Annualised StDv	40.64%	17.31%	25.28%
Sharpe ratio	0.379	0.809	0.345
Second sub-sample: 1May 2007 to 14 February 2008			
Annual return	49.3%	52.2%	62.2%
Overall return	39.5%	41.7%	49.7%
Annualised StDv	62.5%	25.8%	42.2%
Sharpe ratio	0.789	2.022	1.471

difference exceeds or falls below the two MA bands. Once again the aim is to reduce the number of trading signals, avoid frequent trading and reduce slippage.

Table 6.3 presents the performance of MA10 and MA20 envelope strategies with 15 per cent upper and lower bands used for trading indicators. The trading results are reported for the whole sample as well as for the two sub-periods within the sample. Both MA10 and MA20 envelope strategies seem to outperform the buy-and-hold strategy when comparing return-to-risk (that is, Sharpe) ratios. However, it can be noticed that while trading rules do not significantly improve the average returns over the buy-and-hold rule, they significantly reduce the standard deviation of returns. This is because using an MA envelope, or any filter rule, reduces the number of trades substantially. As a result, fewer trading positions are taken that are normally profitable, thus reducing the variation in returns. In addition, comparison of results of buy-and-hold and MA envelope trading rules over the two sub-samples suggests that there is not much difference in terms of performance of MA envelope models when we change the sample period.

6.5.2 Bollinger Bands

'Bollinger Bands' are similar to MA envelopes, in that they are constructed by defining upper and lower bands on the MA series. However, in the case of the Bollinger Band, the trading range is variable because it is calculated by the standard deviation over the same window (data points) as the

MA. Therefore, Bollinger Bands expand and contract based on the volatility over the window. The Bollinger Band at any point in time is constructed by adding and subtracting the standard deviation of the MA series over a window, to and from the MA value at that point in time. The standard deviation is added to the MA series to obtain the upper envelope and subtracted from the MA series to obtain the lower envelope. The formula is as follows;[3]

$$U_t = MA_t + a\,\sigma_t; \quad D_t = MA_t - a\,\sigma_t; \quad \sigma_t = \sqrt{\dfrac{\displaystyle\sum_{i=t-k}^{t}(x_i - \overline{x})^2}{k-1}}$$

Where, U_t is the upper envelope, D_t is the lower envelope, MA_t is the k-period moving average, a is the number of standard deviations to add or subtract for the moving average (integers or fractions are permissible). σ_t is the standard deviation of the MA series over a window of let us say k observations.

The rationale for construction of the Bollinger Band is that during a period of rising price volatility, the distance between the two bands increases (when bands are unusually far apart, that is often a sign that the current trend may be in the process of ending, and this is usually evident in spiked peaks). Conversely, during a period of low market volatility, the band narrows. The reduced distance between the upper and the lower band is often a sign that a market may be about to initiate a new trend; the number of standard deviations also ensures that the data falls within the trading range with a given probability (for example, two standard deviations correspond to a 95 per cent confidence interval). The simplest way to use Bollinger Bands is to use the upper and lower bands as price targets and signal generators. In a strong uptrend, prices will usually fluctuate between the mean and the upper band. In this case, a price crossing below the mean would be a warning of a trend reversal of the downward trend.

As an example, consider the second-nearest quarter (Q2) Panamax 4TC FFAs presented in Figure 6.9, where the 20-day moving average along with ±1.5 standard deviation bands are also shown. It can be seen that the FFA series crosses the upper and lower bands at several points. A simple trading rule that can be devised here is to buy the contract when the FFA series falls below the lower Bollinger Band, and close it when the series reaches the MA series from below. On the other hand, when the FFA series exceeds the upper band it can be considered a sell signal and the position can be closed when the FFA price reaches the MA from above.

---

[3] The Bollinger Band was devised by John Bollinger of Bollinger Capital Management; see www.bollingerbands.com

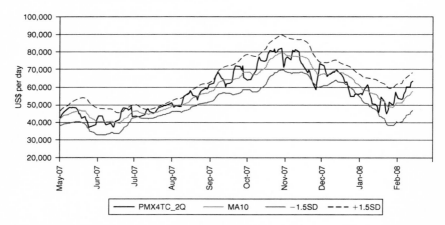

Figure 6.9 Plot of moving average (MA10) and Bollinger Bands for second-quarter Panamax 4TC FFA

Table 6.4 Comparison of return and risk of buy-and-hold against Bollinger Band trading rules on Q2 Panamax 4TC FFA

Statistics	Buy-and-hold	MA10 ± 0.5SD	MA10 ± 1SD	MA10 ± 1.5SD
Total sample: 11 April 2005 to 14 February 2008				
Annual return	24.88%	2.90%	17.99%	0.53%
Overall return	71.15%	8.30%	51.46%	1.51%
Annualised StDv	47.76%	41.39%	34.71%	25.14%
Sharpe ratio	0.521	0.070	0.518	0.021
First sub-sample: 11 April 2005 to 30 April 2007				
Annual return	15.41%	−21.36%	0.72%	−11.95%
Overall return	31.68%	−43.91%	1.49%	−24.57%
Annualised StDv	40.64%	34.42%	29.44%	24.54%
Sharpe ratio	0.379	−0.620	0.025	−0.487
Second sub-sample: 1 May 2007 to 14 February 2008				
Annual return	49.3%	65.3%	62.5%	32.6%
Overall return	39.5%	52.2%	50.0%	26.1%
Annualised StDv	62.5%	55.3%	45.5%	26.6%
Sharpe ratio	0.789	1.181	1.374	1.226

We implemented three Bollinger Band trading rules to Q2 Panamax 4TC FFA rates over the sample period 11 April 2005 to 14 February 2008 and the two sub-samples; 11 April 2005 to 30 April 2007, and 1 May 2007 to 14 February 2008, assuming 1 per cent round-trip transaction costs. The trading rules are based on an MA10 series with 0.5, 1 and 1.5 standard deviation bands. The results, presented in Table 6.4, reveal that the performance of these filter strategies is heavily dependent on the selection of the band width as well as the sample period. Over the whole sample, none of the Bollinger Band trading rules seem to be outperforming the static buy-and-hold strategy. When the sub-samples are examined, it can be seen that, while the Bollinger Band trading rules underperform the buy-and-hold strategy in the first sub-sample, they all outperform the static trading rule in the second sub-sample. This could be because of higher volatility during the second sub-period which offers more trading opportunities when a Bollinger Band trading rule is applied. Also, as will be presented later, these trading rules perform better when they are applied to spreads.

6.6 The momentum trading model

The momentum trading strategy is based on an index which reflects the relative strength or momentum of 'up' or 'down' movements in asset prices. The momentum index is constructed as the ratio of average (or sum of) positive price changes to average (or sum of) negative price changes over a period of time. Therefore the index value at time t can be written as

$$M_{t+1} = \frac{1}{K}\sum_{t=1}^{K} u_t \left/ \frac{1}{K}\sum_{t=1}^{K} d_t \right. \tag{6.1}$$

Where M_{t+1} is the measure of momentum, and u_t and d_t represent up and down movements in prices over the previous k-periods. The momentum measure can be used to construct an index which takes values from 0 to 100, known as the 'relative strength index' (RSI).

$$RSI_{t+1} = 100 - \frac{100}{(1 + M_{t+1})} \tag{6.2}$$

It can be seen that when average ups and downs over a K period are equal, then the value of RSI will be 50, whereas if the average up movement is greater (less) than average down movements over K period, RSI will be greater (less) than 50. The RSI trading rule indicates a buy signal due to an increase in upward momentum when the RSI is above an upper threshold (say, 60) and a sell signal due to a downward momentum in the market when RSI is below a lower threshold (say, 40). There will be no trade when the RSI is between the two upper and lower bands. Obviously, the trader can test the performance of different bands for RSI trading, and widening the band should reduce the number of trades and lower transaction costs, but profitability may also be reduced.

Table 6.5   Return and risk of RSI trading with different lower and upper bands for Q2 Panamax 4TC FFA

Statistics	Buy-and-hold	RSI (40–60)	RSI (42.5–57.5)	RSI (45–55)
Total sample: 11 April 2005 to 14 February 2008				
Annual return	24.88%	34.17%	49.60%	49.97%
Overall return	71.15%	97.73%	141.85%	142.91%
Annualised StDv	47.76%	39.5%	41.5%	43.4%
Sharpe ratio	0.521	0.87	1.20	1.15
First sub-sample: 11 April 2005 to 30 April 2007				
Annual return	15.41%	50.71%	67.76%	55.36%
Overall return	31.68%	104.26%	139.32%	113.82%
Annualised StDv	40.64%	34.67%	35.65%	37.92%
Sharpe ratio	0.379	1.463	1.901	1.460
Second sub-sample: 1 May 2007 to 14 February 2008				
Annual return	49.3%	−8.2%	3.2%	36.4%
Overall return	39.5%	−6.5%	2.5%	29.1%
Annualised StDv	62.5%	49.7%	53.5%	55.1%
Sharpe ratio	0.789	−0.164	0.059	0.660

In order to illustrate how RSI trading works, consider once more the second-quarter Panamax 4TC FFA. The 40-day RSI[4] for this contract is constructed and presented in Panel A of Figure 6.10, along with 40–60 lower and upper bands. Tracking the index, it can be observed that there are several periods over which the index stays above 60, indicating an upward momentum and suggesting a buy signal. Also there are several periods where the index remains below 40, which means that the RSI is indicating a downward momentum and suggesting a sell signal. We have followed this trading rule using different upper and lower bands (RSI40–60, RSI42.5–57.5, and RSI 45–55) over the sample period, and calculated the average return, risk, overall return, and return-to-risk ratio of different strategies. We also assumed transaction costs of 1 per cent for each trade.

The results are presented in Table 6.5 and the cumulative profit of each trading strategy over the whole sample is presented in Panel B of Figure 6.10. In general, it seems that RSI trading rules perform better than the static buy-and-hold strategy. The best RSI rule is found to be the 42.5–57.5 upper and lower bands with an average return of 49.6 per cent and a return-to-risk ratio of 1.20. The cumulative profit index of the three RSI trading models is shown in Panel B of Figure 6.10.

---

[4] The RSI in this case is calculated based on sum of positive movements against sum of negative movements as opposed to average of positive or negative movements of prices; that is $M_{t+1} = \sum_{t=1}^{K} u_t / \sum_{t=1}^{K} d_t$.

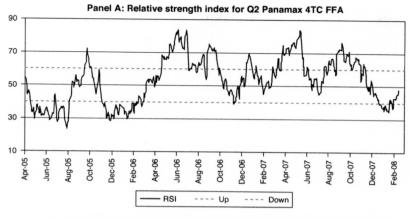

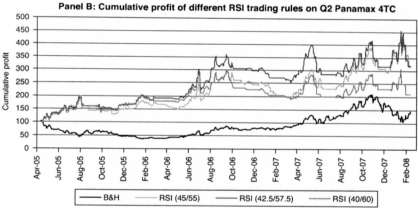

Figure 6.10 Trading relative strength index (RSI) for Q2 Panamax 4TC FFA

6.7 Spread trading in FFA markets

Spread (or 'pair') trading is a term given to transactions based on the difference between asset prices. When assets are highly correlated or they move together over long periods, it might be possible to take opposite positions in these assets simultaneously, and thus profit from the divergence or convergence in prices. Spreads are widely traded in oil, equity and fixed-income markets. For instance, traders in the oil market take opposite positions in crude and gasoline futures prices depending on their expectations about future spread between the two commodities. Depending on the type of underlying assets, the maturity of contracts, and the location of markets where assets are traded, spread trades can be classified into different types.

These are: 'commodity' or 'quality' spreads such as crude vs. gasoline, crude vs. gas, or gas vs. electricity; 'time spreads' such as near-month vs. second-month futures contracts; and 'market' or 'geographical' spreads such as WTI crude vs. IPE crude.

Spread trading in freight markets is becoming more popular as liquidity in the market increases and opportunities for trading across different routes and further down the forward curve increase. For instance, one particular spread trade in the dry market is the Capesize-Panamax average 4TC spread. Another interesting spread is Panamax P2A–P3A, which represents the profitability differential between Atlantic and Pacific basins. In the tanker market the most popular spread is TD5–TD3. There are several benefits in trading FFA spreads instead of outright FFA trading. Firstly, volatility and price-risk exposure can be substantially lower when trading spreads, as correlation between the underlying in the spread position increases. Obviously, having simultaneous short-long positions on contracts with high correlation ensures that large gains in one position can be offset by losses in the second position, due to correlation and co-movements between the underlying assets. Also, lower price-risk exposure in turn means lower margin requirements in cleared contracts due to netting agreements. Finally, it might be easier to devise technical trading rules on spreads as they tend not to deviate from their long-run mean and can be more predictable. At the same time, there are also several disadvantages when trading spreads. Firstly, since liquidity concentrates on a few routes and front-month contracts, the combination of routes and maturities that can be traded is somehow limited. Low liquidity and market depth also increase bid-ask spreads which, in turn, reduce further the profitability of trading and mean that it may be difficult to get in and out of positions fast enough before a price move. Finally, counter-party risk increases in the OTC FFA market as the number of open trading positions increases.

For setting successful freight spread trading, one has to examine the long- and the short-term correlation between contracts. A necessary condition for successful and profitable spread trading is to have high long-term correlation and low short-term correlation between the two contracts. The long-term correlation is defined as the correlation between price levels and it ensures high degree of co-movement between prices over the long run. The short-term correlation, on the other hand, measures the degree of co-movement between price changes (returns) and indicates how much prices diverge in the short term. The second important issue in setting up spread trading, as with any other trade, is the timing of transactions (that is, identifying the right point in time to buy or sell a spread). This can be achieved using technical analysis or applying trading rules based on the historical behaviour of the spread, although knowledge about the underlying market and interaction between routes, sizes and events is crucial. Finally, as with any other trading strategy, bid-ask spreads, transaction costs and commissions should also be considered.

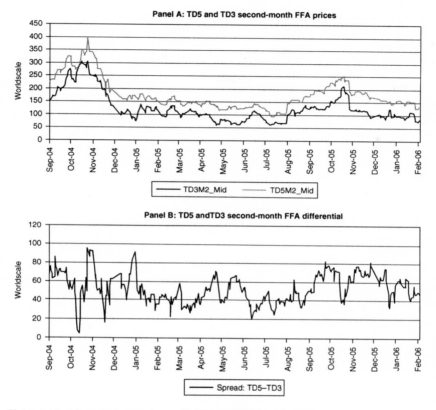

Figure 6.11   Historical second-month TD3 and TD5 tanker FFAs

6.7.1   Tanker spread trading

To illustrate how spread trading can be applied to the FFA market, consider TD3 against TD5 prices. TD3 FFA is a contract for a VLCC (260,000 mt crude oil) cargo from Persian Gulf to Japan, while TD5 FFA is a contract for a Suezmax (130,000 mt crude oil) cargo from West Africa to Philadelphia. The two markets are highly correlated as they both reflect large cargoes of crude oil from the sources of supply of crude oil to industrial demand regions. Panel A in Figure 6.11 presents the historical values of second-month TD3 and TD5 FFA contracts over the period September 2004 to February 2006. It can be seen that TD3 and TD5 FFAs seem to move close together in the long run, with TD3 at a relatively constant discount to TD5. The correlation between the price levels for these two contracts is estimated as 0.965 over the sample period, while the estimated correlation between price changes is 0.560. Panel B of the same figure presents the spread between the second-month FFA prices in the two routes. In contrast to price levels, one can argue that the spread between TD5 and TD3 seems to fluctuate within a smaller band with a mean of around 45 Worldscale (WS) points. The fact that the spread follows a constant mean and reverts to this mean after any deviation indicates that some form of trading strategy can be devised to exploit such behaviour. For instance, when the TD5-TD3 second-month FFA spread is significantly greater than 45 WS points (as was the case, for instance, in mid-November 2004 or mid-January 2005), this can be viewed as an indication that the market expects a shortage of Suezmax tankers on the TD5 route relative to VLCC tankers on the TD3 route. As a result, the difference between TD5 and TD3 FFAs is relatively higher than what it should be under normal conditions. However, this might be due to a temporary supply-demand imbalance and the market could revert to normal levels in a few weeks if not days. Therefore, a spread trader can enter into a short TD5–TD3 spread position, that is, combine a long second-month TD3 FFA and a short second-month TD5 FFA, and wait for the market to revert to normal condition and the spread to narrow. If this happens and the spread reverts to 45 WS points or thereabouts, then the trader can close the two positions and take the profit.

On the other hand, there might be occasions when the TD5–TD3 second-month FFA spread is significantly lower than 45 WS points (for example, in mid-July 2005). This can be regarded as an indication that the market expects a shortage of VLCC tankers on the TD3 route, relative to Suezmax tankers on the TD5 route. As a result the difference between TD5 and TD3 FFAs is relatively low compared to its value under normal market conditions. This time, a 'long-spread' position is the combination of a short second-month TD3 FFA and a long second-month TD5 FFA. Again, the trader expects the market to revert to normal condition; that is, for the spread to widen to 45WS points or thereabouts. Then the position can be closed and profits realised.

Let us look at a TD5–TD3 spread trading example. On 22 June 2005, a trader compares the second-month TD3 and TD5 prices as shown in Table 6.6. The spread stands at 49 WS points (119 WS – 70 WS). According to the trader's analysis this is considered a high spread level, therefore, she enters into a short TD5–TD3 spread; that is, long TD3 and short TD5. The trader keeps this position until either TD3 rises or TD5 falls, or both, and the spread narrows sufficiently. Let us say that on 11 July 2005, the trader sees that the spread has narrowed enough to 34 WS points and closes the position by buying the TD5–TD3 spread; that is, selling TD3 at 116 WS and buying TD5 at 150 WS. This results in a profit of US$6159 per contract in the TD3 transaction and a loss of US$3212 per contract in the TD5 transaction, which means a total profit of US$2947.80 per contract.[5]

---

[5] In this spread trading example, we use 2005 Worldscale flat rates of US$13.39/mt for TD3 and US$10.36/mt for TD5.

Table 6.6 The TD5–TD3 spread narrows from 49 to 34

	TD3		TD5	
	Bid	**Ask**	**Bid**	**Ask**
21 June 2005	67	71	117	128
22 June 2005	66	*70*	*119*	129
Position: long Aug TD3 @70 WS and short Aug TD5 @119 WS				
10 July 2005	114	118	138	147
11 July 2005	*116*	120	140	*150*
Position: short Aug TD3 @116 WS and long August TD5 @150 WS				
Profit & loss 46 WS for TD3 & −31 WS for TD5 US$6159/cont & −US$3212/cont Final result => US$2947.80				

Source of data: Imarex.

Obviously, in this example we did not adjust the trade for contract size and the difference in flat rates. A more precise trade could be built on a US$/mt basis by converting the rates from WS to US$/mt and then executing trades in order to have comparative positions on both the long and short legs of the transaction.

6.7.2 Dry-bulk spread trading

The combination of pairs for spread trading in the dry-bulk FFA market is also quite large as the correlations between many Capesize routes (such as C4–C7, C3–C5), Panamax routes (such as P2A–P3A) and Supramax routes are relatively strong. However, since liquidity in individual routes is less than in basket routes, spread trading may be more effective in pairing basket FFAs such as Capesize-Panamax 4TCs or Panamax-Supramax 4TCs.

To illustrate how basket spread trading can be used in the dry market, consider Calendar FFA contracts for the average 4TC of Capesize and Panamax vessels. Panel A in Figure 6.12 presents the historical values of Calendar FFA for the average 4TC of Capesize and Panamax vessels over the period February 2005 to February 2008.[6] The correlation between the price levels for these two contracts is estimated as 0.997 over the sample period, while the estimated correlation between price changes is 0.833. It can be seen that the two

---

[6] Calendar 4TC FFA series are Baltic Forward Assessments published by the Baltic Exchange. Also, note that in constructing continuous calendar 4TC FFA series, prices are rolled over once the contract enters the delivery period. In the case of Calendar FFAs, the rollover is in January of the delivery year.

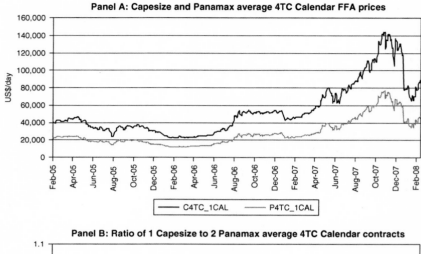

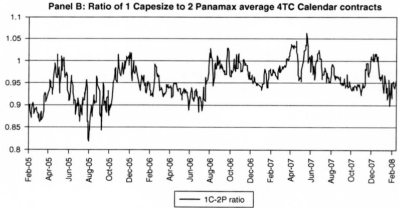

Figure 6.12   Historical Capesize-Panamax average 4TC Calendar FFAs and 1-2 Capesize-Panamax FFA ratio

contracts tend to move very close together in the long run, with Capesize 4TC trading almost twice as high as Panamax 4TC.

Panel B of the same figure presents the ratio of 1-Capesize to 2-Panamax 4TC Calendar FFA contracts. It can be seen that the ratio (spread) seems to fluctuate within a small band with a mean of about 0.95.[7] The fact that the

---

[7] Note that we made the monetary sizes of contracts comparable by using a '1 to 2' ratio of the Capesize against Panamax FFAs. That is to say, for every one Capesize position we take two Panamax positions. The monetary difference between one Capesize and two Panamax contracts will constitute the spread.

Table 6.7   Capesize-Panamax Calendar 4TC ratio widens from 0.818 to 1.001

Date	Capesize Cal_06 4TC FFA US$/day	Panamax Cal_06 4TC FFA US$/day	1:2 Cape-Panamax ratio
29 July 2005	23,938	14,538	0.823
01 August 2005	23,813	14,554	0.818
Position: long Cal06 Capesize @US$23,938/day and short 2xCal06 Panamax @US$14,538/day			
12 December 2005	29,345	14,913	0.983
13 December 2005	28,875	14,429	1.001
Position: short Cal06 Capesize @ US$28,875/day and long 2xCal06 Panamax @ US$14,429/day			
Profit & loss			
{[−23,813 + 2 × (14,554)] + [28,875 − 2 × (14,429)]} × 365 days Final result => US$1,938,880			

ratio follows a constant mean and reverts to this mean following any divergence indicates that spread or differential trading strategies can be devised to exploit such behaviour. For instance, when the 1-2 Capesize-Panamax calendar 4TC ratio is significantly greater than 0.95, it can be regarded as deviation from the normal ratio suggesting a short Capesize-Panamax spread position (simultaneous short position on 1-Capesize Cal 4TC FFA and long position on 2-Panamax Cal 4TC FFA). The trader can keep this spread position until the ratio reverts back to 0.95, or thereabouts, when the position can be closed to profit from the trade. On the other hand, there might be occasions when the 1-2 ratio of Capesize-Panamax Calendar 4TC is significantly less than 0.95, which can again be regarded as a deviation from the long-run ratio, suggesting a long Capesize-Panamax spread position (simultaneous long position on Capesize Cal 4TC FFA and short position on 2 Panamax Cal 4TC FFA). Once again the trader can keep this position until the ratio reverts back to 0.95 or thereabouts, when the position is closed and the profit can be realised.

A trading example is presented in Table 6.7. Here the trader enters into a long 1-2 Capesize-Panamax Cal_06 4TC contract on 29 July 2005, when the ratio is 0.823. A ratio of 0.823 means that Capesize FFA is relatively undervalued compared to Panamax FFA and the trader believes that this offers a good opportunity. The trader holds the position until 13 December, when the ratio has increased to 1.001. On that day, the trader closes the position by selling Capesize Cal_06 4TC FFA and buying 2 Panamax Cal_06 4TC FFA. Thus, by executing this spread trade, on 13 December 2005, the trader locks into an overall profit of US$1.938m, or US$5312 per day.

Table 6.8 Comparison of performance of different trading rules on 1–2 ratio of Capesize-Panamax FFA contracts

Statistics	CSZ Cal FFA	PMX Cal FFA	MA(20) BB	MA(40) BB	MA(10) Env	MA(20) Env
Total sample: 1 February 2005 To 14 February 2008						
Annual return	48.54%	44.54%	24.68%	32.21%	32.15%	42.03%
Overall return	146.58%	134.50%	74.53%	97.27%	97.09%	126.91%
Annualised StDv	39.35%	39.25%	20.20%	19.08%	21.79%	21.80%
Sharpe ratio	1.234	1.135	1.222	1.688	1.475	1.928

Notes: CSZ Cal FFA and PMX Cal FFA are the nearest 1-year Calendar FFAs for Capesize and Panamax, respectively.
MA20 and MA40 Bollinger Bands are for ±1 standard deviation.
MA10 and MA20 envelopes are constructed with ±1.5% upper and lower bands.

In order to investigate the performance of this type of trade over a period of time, we implement a spread trade strategy over the period 1 February 2005 to 14 February 2008. The timing of spread trades (long-short positions) can be determined using different technical trading strategies such as MA envelope and crossover rules, filter rules or even RSI momentum strategies. The rules that we employ here are MA20 and MA40 Bollinger Bands with one standard deviation bands on the 1-2 Capesize-Panamax Calendar 4TC FFA ratio, as well as MA10 and MA20 envelopes with 1.5 per cent bands. For instance, Panel A of Figure 6.13 presents the 1-2 Capesize-Panamax Calendar 4TC FFA ratio as well as the MA20 ±1.5 per cent envelope-on ratio. The ratio seems to fluctuate at a constant range around the mean value of 0.95, but there are some cyclical movements which reflect periodic adjustment in supply and demand between the (and within each of) Capesize and Panamax markets.

The results of spread trading models are presented in Table 6.8 along with the statistics on the buy-and-hold strategy on both Capesize and Panamax calendar FFAs. A close look at the statistics reveals that, while average annualised returns of spread trades are lower than the static buy-and-hold, their standard deviation or risk is much lower, at almost half. For instance, the standard deviations of outright buy-and-hold for both FFAs are 39.35 per cent and 39.25 per cent for Capesize and Panamax FFA prices, respectively, whereas the standard deviations of spread trading rules are below 21.8 per cent. This reduction in risk in trading positions also reduces the return-to-risk ratio of the trading strategies, making them more attractive.

Finally, Panel B of Figure 6.13 plots the cumulative returns of spread trading strategies against the static buy-and-hold rule. It can be seen that spread trading models yield steady cumulative profit with low fluctuations, whereas the outright positions seem to be losing value over the first half of the sample

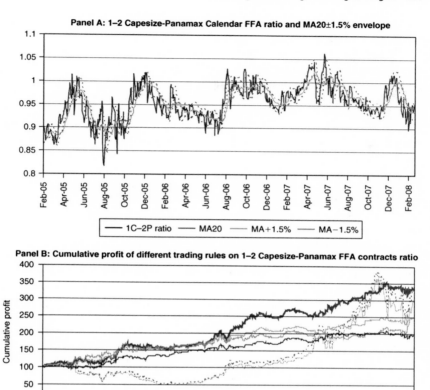

Figure 6.13 1-2 Capesize-Panamax Calendar 4TC FFA ratio and cumulative profit of technical trading rules

but increase significantly in the second period. Such erratic behaviour in profit patterns might not be attractive to some investors. Thus, setting up spread trading models can enhance the risk-return profile of portfolios if appropriate pairs and trading models are selected.

6.8 Time-charter and implied forward rates

The existence of freight contracts with different maturities (durations) in the shipping industry offers both shipowners and charterers flexibility in their decisions regarding chartering and operational activities. As discussed in Chapter 2, short-term or spot charter rates are determined through the interaction between current supply and demand for shipping services (see, for example, Stopford, 1997), whereas long-term period rates are believed to be determined through agents' expectations about future short-term rates. Several studies have investigated the relationship between spot and long-term charter contracts (see, for example, Hale and Vanags, 1989; Veenstra, 1999; Kavussanos and Alizadeh, 2002b, among others). The general focus of these studies is how time-charter rates are formed through expected spot rates and whether such a relationship is in line with the notion of the 'efficient market hypothesis' (EMH).[8]

The most important implication of EMH in relation to the shipping freight market is that charter contracts, with different maturities, should be related in such a way that charterers/shipowners are indifferent to operating under a period contract or a series of consecutive short-term contracts over the life of the long-term contract. Otherwise, there will be instances where the difference between the two chartering strategies can be exploited by agents to make excess profit without taking additional risk. The relationship between short-term and long-term contracts, known as the 'term structure relationship', is embedded in theories such as the 'expectations hypothesis of the term structure' (EHTS). According to the EHTS, long-term time-charter rates, say for one year, should reflect the weighted average of expected monthly (spot) freight contracts over the next 12 months. Furthermore, any deviation from such a relationship is explained through the existence of time-varying risk premia.

Let TC_t^T denote the time-charter rate at a given time t with maturity T. If we observe two time-charter rates with different maturities, say T and T_1 with $T = T_1 + T_2$, and assume that the EMH holds, the implied forward time-charter rate for period T_2 can be calculated. This is due to the fact that if EMH holds, agents should be indifferent in chartering a vessel for the T period or chartering the vessel for T_1 period and renew the contract for another T_2 period at the expiry of the first contract, that is, T_1. Therefore, using the present-value model and assuming a constant discount rate, r, we can write

$$\sum_{i=1}^{T} \delta^i (TC_{t+i}^T) = \sum_{i=1}^{T_1} \delta^i (TC_{t+i}^{T_1}) + \sum_{i=T_1+1}^{T} \delta^i (E_t TC_{t+i}^{T_2}) \qquad (6.3)$$

where δ^i is i period discount factor, $\delta^i = 1/(1 + r)^i$, and E_t is the expectations operator. Rearranging the above equation, it is possible to derive the forward

---

[8] See Kavussanos and Alizadeh (2002b) for more details on the EMH and its implications for shipping markets.

Table 6.9 Forecasting performance of implied forward time-charter rates against alternative econometric models

		Random walk	ARIMA	VAR	VECM	Implied TC rates
Handymax	RMSE	0.19057	0.18029	0.17919	0.16117	0.09254
	Theil's U		0.9461	0.9403	0.8457	0.4856
Panamax	RMSE	0.26971	0.25542	0.25322	0.24639	0.13589
	Theil's U		0.9470	0.9389	0.9135	0.5038
Capesize	RMSE	0.44519	0.43717	0.43656	0.41471	0.19571
	Theil's U		0.9820	0.9806	0.9315	0.4396

Note: Forecast horizon is 26 weeks (six months) ahead in all cases.

time-charter rate, $E_t TC_{T_1}^{T_2}$ as

$$E_t TC_{T_1}^{T_2} = \left(\sum_{i=1}^{T} \delta^i (TC_{t+i}^T) - \sum_{i=1}^{T_1} \delta^i (TC_{t+i}^{T_1}) \right) \bigg/ \sum_{i=T_1+1}^{T} \delta^i \qquad (6.4)$$

For example, the present value of a 12-month time-charter contract at time t, TC_t^{12m}, should be equal to the present value of a six-month contract at time t, TC_t^{6m}, plus the present value of another six-month contract which starts six months later, $E_t TC_{t+6}^{6m}$. This in turn implies that, provided the EMH holds, the implied (expected) forward rate for a six-month time-charter contract would be

$$IFTC_{t,t+6}^{6m} = E_t TC_{t+6}^{6m} = \left(\sum_{i=1}^{12} \delta^i (TC_{t+i}^{12m}) - \sum_{i=1}^{6} \delta^i (TC_{t+i}^{6m}) \right) \bigg/ \sum_{i=6+1}^{12} \delta^i \qquad (6.5)$$

where $IFTC_{t,t+6}^{6m}$ is the implied forward six-month time-charter rate at time t for $t+6$.

Alizadeh et al. (2007) investigated the predictive power of the implied forward TC rates as a forecast of future TC rates in comparison with other statistical models in the dry-bulk market. Their results, reproduced here in Table 6.9, indicate that the implied TC rates (IMTC) outperform the forecast from competing time-series models such as the 'autoregressive integrated moving average' (ARIMA), 'vector autoregressive' (VAR) and the 'vector error correction' (VECM) models. They estimate these models over the period 6 January 1989 to 29 March 1996 (378 observations) and use the period of 4 April 1996 to 27 June 2003 as the forecast evaluation period. Both 'root mean squared forecast error' (RMSE)[9] and 'Theil's U'[10] statistics indicate that implied forward TC rates provide the most accurate forecasts for future six-month TC rates compared to alternative models across all vessel sizes, as shown in Table 6.9. For instance, in the case of Capesize vessels, the lowest RMSE for predicting six-month TC, six months from the present, is obtained for the implied TC rates (0.19571) which is less than half that of the alternative models. This means that forecasts produced by implied forward TC rates are significantly more accurate than those of other models.

In addition, Alizadeh et al. (2007) find that these implied forward time-charter rates are unbiased predictors of time-charter rates observed in the future; that is, the average forecast error of implied TC rates is zero and there is no systematic pattern in their behaviour. This finding is important because it can be regarded as additional evidence as to the reliability of the forecasts produced by implied forward TC rates in the dry-bulk market.

Finally, Alizadeh et al. (2007) also investigated whether agents can make excess profit by simple chartering strategies based on technical trading rules. This is interesting because if the notion of EMH is valid, then there should not be any possibility for making excess profit through chartering strategies. They examined whether hiring-in vessels for long-period charters (12 months) and re-letting them over shorter periods (two consecutive six-month periods) is profitable. The trading strategy is based on application of technical analysis on the differential between short-term and long-term charter rates (the spread). For instance, they use a simple moving average (MA) chartering strategy defined as follows: charter in a vessel on a 12-month TC and simultaneously re-let the vessel on a six-month TC if the current spread between the two TC rates exceeds the average of the spread over the last Y weeks.

The study also reports that the simple MA trading rules generate substantial profit when they are implemented in an out-of-sample evaluation period and that technical trading models perform better on the basis of a rolling or continuously expanding estimation sample.[11]

---

[9] The RMSE is based on a symmetric loss function and is calculated as $RMSE = \sqrt{\sum_{i=1}^{N}(TC_i^a - TC_i^f)^2/N}$, where TC_i^a are the realised/actual values of the TC rates, TC_i^f are the forecast values of TC rates at time i, and N is the number of forecasts.

[10] Theil's U is the ratio of RMSE of the model and the RMSE of a 'random walk' model and indicates how accurate are the forecasts compared to forecasts from a random walk (that is, no change) model.

[11] It is worth pointing out that, from a practical point of view, it may not be possible for a ship-operator to take the opposite position, that is, charter a vessel in on two consecutive six-month charters and re-let the same vessel on a 12-month charter, but one can use six-month time-charter contract with an option to extend for a further six months. Moreover, this strategy would also be feasible for an owner (that is, charter in vessels on two consecutive six-month time-charter contracts and charter out an *owned* vessel on a 12-month charter). However, in their simulations they take the view of

6.8.1 The relative value trading rule

As another chartering strategy, consider a relative value trading rule which is based on the slope of the TC curve. Under this rule we generate a relative value index using the ratio of the natural log of six-month and 12-month time-charter rates [Index = ln(6mTC)-ln(12mTC)]. This log difference is essentially the premium or discount of six-month TC to 12-month TC, which reflects the degree of backwardation or contango in the TC market. The trading strategy is then constructed on the basis of how large is the value of this index with respect to an assumed ratio, say x per cent (5 per cent, 10 per cent or 15 per cent). If the index is greater than x per cent, charter in 12-month and sublet for two consecutive six-month contracts, and if the index is less than x per cent, do nothing.[12]

We have constructed these indices for three sizes of dry-bulk carriers over the period January 1992 to May 2007 on a weekly basis, as illustrated in Figure 6.14, Panel A. It can be seen that relative value indices vary between −15 per cent to +15 per cent across, with an average of almost zero, for differently sized dry-bulk carriers. The results of the relative value trading strategy over the period January 2002 to May 2007 are presented in Table 6.10 for different levels of x varying from 5 per cent to 20 per cent. It is not surprising to see that the relative value strategy works quite well over the period under investigation. It generates profits of US$431.76m, US$260.26m, and US$171.52m for the Capesize, Panamax and Handymax markets respectively, when trading is based on a benchmark relative value of x = 5 per cent.

One possible restriction to this trading model is that it may not be possible to hire in a vessel every week and hire her out immediately. Also, one might argue that the above results can be evidence against the EMH and if every shipowner or operator attempts to trade based on such a strategy, then such profit-making opportunities may disappear.

6.9 Technical trading rules and shipping investment

Alizadeh and Nomikos (2007a) investigate the performance of trading strategies for investment decisions in the market for second-hand ships, based on signals indicated by fundamental market-price indicators such as the price-earnings (P/E) ratio. They begin by arguing that the ratio of ship prices to operating earnings (log price-earnings ratio) is a measure of whether the

---

a ship-operator and impose the restriction that vessels can only be chartered in on a 12-month TC basis and then re-let. This is likely to underestimate the profitability of the technical chartering strategies, and is similar to a short-sale restriction in financial markets.

[12] We mentioned in footnote 11 that a reverse chartering strategy may not be practical.

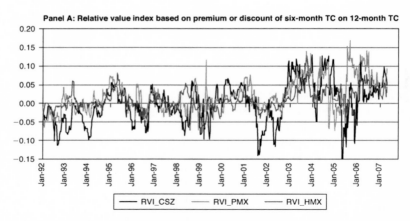

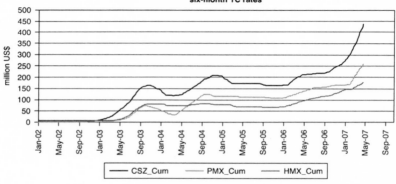

Figure 6.14   Relative value index based on premium or discount of 6m TC on 12m TC

market for second-hand ships is under- or overvalued, relative to its fundamentals.[13] If so, investors might be able to use the spread between price and operational earnings to identify the timing for sale and purchase of merchant ships. They use the historical spread between price and earnings as a benchmark and set up a trading strategy which signals a 'sell decision' if the spread is higher than its historical average and a 'buy decision' if the spread is lower than its historical average. This is because when the spread at time t is greater than its long-run value, it can be regarded as an indication that

---

[13] In fact, they derive the relationship between price and earnings based on the argument that the price of a ship should reflect the discounted present value of the future earnings of the vessel.

Table 6.10   Profitability of technical chartering strategies based on the period January 2002 to May 2007

x		Capesize	Panamax	Handysize
5%	Average profit US$m/w	1.564	0.943	0.621
	Total profit US$m	431.76	260.26	171.52
	Standard deviation	23.68	15.58	8.73
10%	Average profit US$m/w	1.423	0.977	0.418
	Total profit US$m	392.65	269.54	115.25
	Standard deviation	21.54	13.89	6.75
15%	Average profit m$/w	1.000	0.734	0.103
	Total profit m$	276.00	202.45	28.46
	Standard deviation	17.86	11.83	4.10
20%	Average profit m$/w	0.559	0.414	0.007
	Total profit m$	154.19	114.37	1.97
	Standard deviation	11.19	8.37	0.86

Notes: x represents the percentage premium of the six-month over the 12-month TC rate.
Average profit is the average profit of trading rule, measured in US$m per week over the whole sample.
Standard deviation is the standard deviation of the average profit following the trading strategy.

ships are overvalued relative to their future potential earnings. On the other hand, when the spread is lower than the long-run average, it can regarded as indication that prices are low and vessels are undervalued relative to their potential future earnings.

To identify the investment timing, Alizadeh and Nomikos (2007) used two simple technical trading rules on the log difference of price and earnings (log P/E ratio). The proposed moving average trading strategy is mainly based on the MA crossover rule on the P/E ratio; that is, comparison of a fast (short) and a slow (long) MA series. For instance, in a given month, a positive difference between the 12-month MA and the one-month MA of the P/E ratios is considered as a 'buy' signal; similarly, a negative difference signals a 'sell' decision.[14]

Using a data set of monthly five-year-old ship prices for three different sizes of dry-bulk carriers (Capesize, Panamax and Handysize) and operating profits (earnings less operating costs), Alizadeh and Nomikos (2007) constructed

---

[14] For the strategy implemented, a sell decision will be executed only if the investor has already bought a ship. In other words short-selling is not permitted since practically it is not possible for an investor to take a short position in a vessel. However, the development of 'paper' contracts on ship prices, such as the Forward Values on the Baltic Sale & Purchase Assessments (BSPA) may allow investors to short-sell the vessel values and benefit from falling ship prices. These contracts are discussed in Chapter 13.

Table 6.11   Results of empirical simulation of trading strategies

	Handysize	Panamax	Capesize
MA12,1 on P/E ratio			
Mean return	0.08611	0.14814	0.16127
St dev	0.12907	0.15083	0.20209
Sharpe ratio	0.66713	0.98216	0.79800
MA6,1 on P/E ratio			
Mean return	0.07332	0.14017	0.15751
St dev	0.13346	0.15353	0.20197
Sharpe ratio	0.54936	0.91296	0.77983
Buy and Hold			
Mean return	0.08487	0.11459	0.08097
St dev	0.18406	0.20967	0.25288
Sharpe ratio	0.46109	0.54651	0.32019

Notes: Mean return and standard deviation are the annualised mean returns (monthly mean return x 12) and standard deviation of returns (monthly standard deviation x $\sqrt{12}$) respectively for the different trading strategies. Sharpe ratio is the ratio of mean returns over the standard deviation of returns.
Sample period is January 1976 to September 2004 for Handysize and Panamax series and April 1979 to September 2004 for the Capesize series.

the log P/E ratios for three sizes of bulk carriers and used the MA crossovers to identify investment timing. The results of their analyses are reproduced in Table 6.11, where the annualised mean returns, annualised standard deviations of returns and Sharpe ratios are reported for the different strategies. It can be noted that both the MA6,1 and MA12,1 strategies outperform the buy-and-hold strategy, as indicated by the Sharpe ratios across all markets. For example, when the MA12,1 trading rule was applied, the Sharpe ratios for Handysize, Panamax and Capesize investments increased to 0.667, 0.982 and 0.798 respectively, reflecting the joint effect of the increase in mean returns and the reduction in standard deviations of return on the investment in each market. It can also be seen that the gain through such investment strategies and trading rules is greater in the markets for larger vessels because of the higher volatility in these markets compared to the market for Handysize vessels, and because of better or more frequent trading opportunities arising from such variations in prices.

Panel A of Figure 6.15 presents the plot of a fast MA1 and a slow MA12 series on the log of the P/E ratio of Panamax ships, while Panel B of the same figure plots the cumulative returns of the two buy-and-hold and the MA technical trading rule on the log P/E ratio of Panamax ships. The significant increase in cumulative returns when the active MA12,1 trading rule is employed, compared to a buy-and-hold strategy, is evident. In fact, it is also interesting to note that the proposed trading model correctly identifies

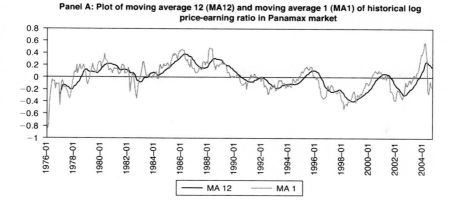

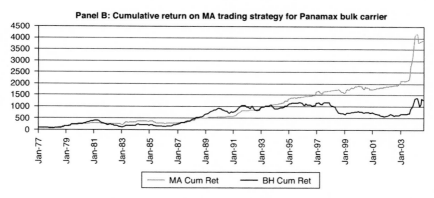

Figure 6.15 MA trading rule on log P/E ratio and its cumulative returns in the Panamax sector

the buy signal during the lucrative shipping markets of 2003–2004, when earnings increased sharply compared to ship prices.

In order to assess the robustness of their proposed methodology, Alizadeh and Nomikos (2007) also use the stationary bootstrap technique of Politis and Romano (1994) to re-generate the underlying series and hence replicate the trading results from the different strategies in a simulation environment. The result of the bootstrap testing exercise provides further support that their proposed model significantly outperforms the static buy-and-hold strategy.

6.10   Summary and conclusions

With the expansion of the freight derivatives market and increase in freight trading liquidity and market depth, traders in shipping markets have started to use technical analysis to investigate and exploit trading opportunities in the FFA market. In this chapter, we reviewed a number of technical analysis methods and trading rules which could be applied to shipping freight and FFA markets as well as to the market for ships. We also investigated the effectiveness of several technical trading rules, including MA crossovers, filter rules and momentum indices in the FFA market. In addition, we highlighted the opportunities, advantages and disadvantages of spread, or pair, trading, in forward freight markets. Furthermore, using the relationship between freight contracts with different durations, we illustrated how implied forward TC rates can be estimated and also examined their predictive power. It was also shown that the relative value of contracts can be used as an effective indicator for physical freight trading. Finally, we discussed the application of technical trading rules to the timing of investment in shipping markets, where it was argued that technical analysis can be combined with fundamental analysis to capture the turning points of fundamental indicators in the market for ships.

7

Options on Freight Rates

7.1 Introduction

As we saw in the previous chapter, the use of FFAs as a trading and speculative instrument has been increasing constantly since their introduction in the early 1990s. As the market grows and becomes more mature, market participants also look at exploring the usefulness of other derivatives instruments, most notably options. Although FFAs provide reasonable hedging strategies and enable participants to lock in a given freight rate over a period of time, they lack the flexibility that would enable their users to maintain the hedge if the market moves against them, and to be able to participate in the market when market conditions are favourable. Option contracts, on the other hand, offer this flexibility. Freight options are traded as OTC instruments, in the same fashion as FFAs, and over recent years they have become more popular with shipping-market practitioners. Shipping-freight options were first introduced in 1990 when trading options on BIFFEX started. Like the BIFFEX contracts however, trading on these options never picked up and eventually they were de-listed in April 2002.

In this chapter we are going to discuss freight options and their use in freight-rate risk management and speculation. First, we consider the properties of freight options and present the profit patterns from buying or selling call-and-put options; we also discuss the practicalities of trading freight options. We then examine the risk-management applications of freight options by considering the use of caps, floors and collars. One of the attractions of options is that by combining them we can create a wide range of different payoff profiles which, in turn, can be used for trading, speculation and risk-management purposes in the market. Some of these trading strategies are presented in the last section of this chapter.

7.2 A primer on options

There are two types of option contracts: 'call options' and 'put options'. A call option is a contract that gives its holder (or buyer) the right, but not the

Table 7.1   Imarex option quotes for TD3 route on 23 August 2005

Strike price (WS)	Calls			Puts		
	Sep 05	Oct 05	Nov 05	Sep 05	Oct 05	Nov 05
70	14.4	15.3	20.1	3.4	9.2	13.4
80	8.9	11.0	15.9	7.8	14.8	19.1
90	5.2	7.8	12.5	14.1	21.6	25.7

Source: Imarex.

obligation, to buy an underlying asset (such as freight rate) from the seller (or 'writer') of the call option at a certain price, known as the 'strike price' or 'exercise price' and, at a certain point in time, known as the 'expiration date' or the 'maturity'. On the other hand, a put option gives its holder the right, but not the obligation, to sell an underlying asset to the writer of the put option at a certain strike price and at the expiration date. In order to have such a right, the buyer of the option pays a 'premium' to the writer of the option. The premium is also known as the 'option price'. Option contracts are also classified according to the date on which they can be exercised: a 'European' option can only be exercised at the maturity of the option; an 'American' option can be exercised at any time during the life of the option, including the maturity. Options give their holders the flexibility of buying or selling an underlying asset at a certain pre-specified price during – or at – a certain period. This is important because the holder is under no obligation to settle the contract, in contrast to futures, forward and swap contracts; the writer, however, is obliged to transact if the holder decides to do so.

Table 7.1 presents the option premia (in Worldscale points – WS) for call and put options written on route TD3 of the BDTI (260,000 mt of crude oil from the Persian Gulf to Japan) from Imarex, across three different maturities and three different strike prices. Consider, for instance, the September 2005 call option with a strike price of 80 WS. The buyer of this option has the right, but not the obligation, to buy (settle) the freight rate for TD3, at the end of September 2005, as the difference between the strike price and the average of TD3 in September. For instance, if the average TD3 rate in September is 90 WS, the buyer of the option will exercise the option and receive 10 WS points per contract. If, on the other hand, the market goes down and the average freight rate is, say, 70 WS points, the option holder will let the option expire worthless, forfeits the premium, and will fix in the spot market at a reduced rate of 70 WS. Therefore, the holder of a call option essentially has the same positive payoff as a long FFA contract on TD3 but without the downside if the spot rate goes below the strike price. The payoff of the call option can thus be described mathematically as:[1]

$$\text{Call payoff} = \max(0, S - X) \tag{7.1}$$

where S is the spot freight rate and X is the strike price. In order to buy the contract, the option buyer has to pay the option premium of 8.9 WS points per ton of cargo to be hedged, upfront on 23 August 2005; assuming a flat rate for TD3 of US\$12.15/mt, the total premium is: US\$281,151(=US\$12.15 × 8.9/100 × US\$260,000). The payoff of the strategy is shown in Figure 7.1, Panel A. We can see that if the freight rate at expiry is less than 80 WS points, the option expires worthless and the call-option buyer loses the premium. If the freight rate is more than 80, then the option is exercised and for every WS point increase of the freight rates in the market, the call option buyer makes a corresponding WS point profit in the payoff, as shown by the 45-degree line on the payoff diagram.[2] For the option buyer to recover the cost of buying the option, the underlying market (TD3 rates) must rise above 88.9 WS points, which is the strike price plus the cost of the option premium, that is, the break-even rate for the option.

Consider next the September 2005 put option with a strike price of 80 WS. The buyer of this option has the right, but not the obligation, to sell or short the TD3 freight rate at the end of September 2005. For instance, if the average TD3 rate in September is 70 WS, the buyer of the put will exercise the option and receive 10 WS points per contract. If, on the other hand, the freight rate increases to 90 WS points, then the option holder will let the option expire worthless in the market, as shown in Figure 7.1, Panel B. The payoff of the put option can thus be described mathematically as:

$$\text{Put payoff} = \max(0, X - S) \tag{7.2}$$

Similarly, we can construct the payoff profiles for a short-call or short-put option contract. There are two parties for every option contract; the buyer (or long), and the writer (or short). This also implies that the buyer's and seller's payoffs from entering into an option agreement are reversed. For instance, the payoff of the short call will be: $-\max(0, S - X)$ and is presented in Figure 7.2, Panel A. We can see that if the call option is not exercised, the option seller keeps the option premium, which is also the maximum profit he can make by selling the option. However, if the option is exercised, then

---

[1] The options described here are settled using the average freight rate over the settlement month instead of the freight rate on the last day of the month. These are called 'average price' or 'Asian' options and are discussed in more detail in the next chapter.
[2] Since these graphs present the payoff of the option at expiry and the premium is paid upfront, the graphs reflect the compounded future value of the option premium from the time the option was bought until its maturity.

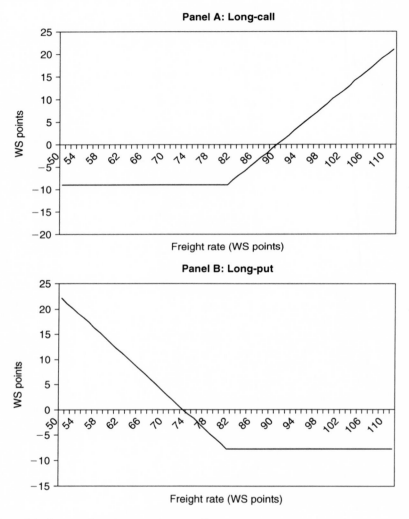

Figure 7.1   Long-call and put-option payoffs

the seller of the option is obliged to transact at the price specified by the contract and this potentially may lead to very large losses. This therefore implies that the position of an option seller can be very risky due to potentially large and unbounded losses. This is also the reason why traditionally in the OTC option markets there tends to be a larger number of option buyers than sellers. In addition, the very risky profile of a short-option position also means

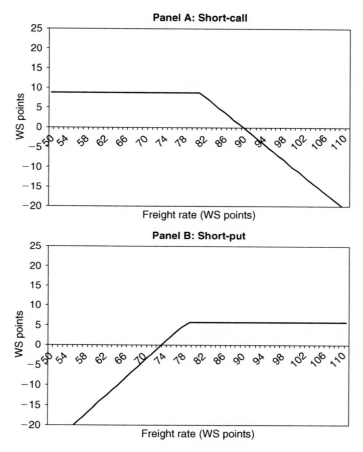

Figure 7.2   Short-call and put-option payoffs

that traders need to somehow hedge their exposure.[3] Finally Figure 7.2, Panel B presents the payoff profile of a short-put option.

Another important parameter of options is their 'moneyness', which measures the exercise value of the option. An 'at-the-money' (ATM) option is an option whose strike price is very close to the price of the underlying. An 'out-of-money option' (OTM) is an option which has no exercise value if

---

[3] This is normally done using the option price sensitivities, known as 'Greeks', which are discussed in the next chapter.

Table 7.2 Moneyness conditions for call and put options

	Call	Put
In-the-money (ITM)	S > X	S < X
At-the-money (ATM)	S = X	S = X
Out-of-the-money (OTM)	S < X	S > X

it is exercised immediately, and an 'in-the-money option' (ITM) is an option which has an exercise value if it is exercised immediately. In other words, a call option is ITM when the strike price is below the price of the underlying and OTM when the strike price is above the price of the underlying. By the same token, a put option is ITM when the strike price is above the price of the underlying and OTM when the strike price is below the price of the underlying.

7.3 Properties of option prices

In this section we introduce the boundary conditions that characterise rational option prices; in other words the upper and lower limits of option prices. Next, we identify the factors that affect the price of an option and discuss their impact on put- and call-option premia. Finally, we explore how put and call prices are related through the relationship that is known as 'put-call parity'. Before we start our analysis, we must introduce the notation that will be used throughout this book to define options. For this purpose we denote:

C: European call-option price
P: European put-option price
S_0: Underlying asset price today
X: Strike price
T: Time to expiration of the option expressed as fraction of a year
σ: Annualised volatility of the underlying asset
S_T: Underlying asset price at the maturity of the option at T
r: Risk-free rate.

7.3.1 Boundary conditions for European call prices

Generally, there are some boundary conditions (upper and lower limits) that the price of an option cannot violate. For European call options on an asset that pays no dividend, for instance, we can identify the following conditions:

1. *The value of a call cannot be negative.* Therefore, $C_0 \geq 0$. Even if a call option is deep OTM, the option will still have some positive value. This is because

a call option is an instrument with limited liability. If the call holder sees that it is advantageous to exercise it at maturity, the call will be exercised. The call therefore will have positive value because its holder cannot be forced to exercise it.

2. *The value of a call option will always be less than the value of the underlying*: $C_0 \leq S_0$. A call option gives its holder the right to buy the underlying asset and this right can never be worth more than the underlying; if this were the case then nobody would buy the option and there would be an arbitrage opportunity to exploit.

3. *The value of a call at expiration is*: $C_T = max(0, S_T - X)$. This is the payoff of the option when the option is exercised.

4. *At any point prior to expiry, the value of a European call must at least equal the greater of zero or the underlying price minus the present value of the exercise price*: $C_0 \geq max(S_0 - Xe^{-rT}, 0)$; this also follows from the third condition above. If at expiry the value of the call is worth the maximum of zero or the underlying price less the exercise price, before expiration the call must be worth at least the stock price less the present value of the exercise price.

At this point it is also worth mentioning the difference between the 'intrinsic value' and the 'time value' of an option. The intrinsic value is the payoff that the call-option holder receives if the option is exercised immediately; for a call option the intrinsic value is therefore: $C_T = max(0, S_T - X)$. There are options that may have zero intrinsic value but their premium is still positive. The premium in this case reflects what is known as the time value of an option; this is the part of the option's premium that reflects the possibility of future favourable movements in the value of the underlying and the option being in the end at-the-money. In general, the value of an option equals the intrinsic value and the time value; an option that still has some time to run will, in general, have a positive time-value.[4]

Figure 7.3 shows the expiration-date payoffs of a plain vanilla call option as the dotted line. In the same figure we also plot the value of the same call option two and six months before maturity. We can see that option values before maturity have a convex payoff – but as the time to maturity approaches, the payoff becomes linear and converges with the expiration-date payoff. The figure also presents the time value and intrinsic value of the six-month option when the underlying rate is 90 WS. We can also note that while the two options have the same intrinsic value, the time value of the option with six months to maturity is greater than the time value of the option with two months to maturity.

---

[4] The exception to that is when we have an American option that may be optimal to exercise early. In this case the time value of the option is equal to zero.

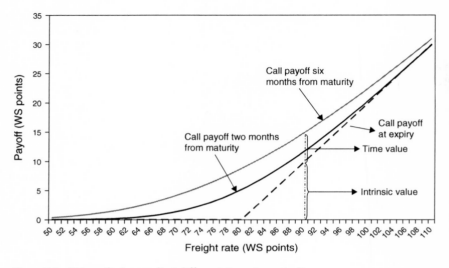

Figure 7.3   Value of a long call at different times to maturity

7.3.2   Boundary conditions for European put prices

For put options the upper and lower limits are similar to those for calls.

1. *The value of a put cannot be negative.* Therefore, $P_0 \geq 0$. Even if a put option is deep OTM, the option will still have some positive value as there is always a chance – even if very small – that the option may expire ITM.
2. *The value of a European put option will be less than the discounted present value of the strike price:* $P_0 \leq Xe^{-rT}$. The reason for this is that a put option gives its holder the right to sell the underlying asset at the strike price; this right can never be worth more than the discounted present value of the strike.
3. *The value of the put at expiration is:* $P_T = max(0, X - S_T)$. This is the payoff of the put when the option is exercised at maturity.
4. *At any point prior to expiry, the value of a European put must at least equal the greater of zero, or the present value of the exercise price minus the stock price:* $P_0 \geq max(Xe^{-rT} - S_0, 0)$.

7.3.3   Put-call parity

Based on the no-arbitrage argument in asset pricing, there is a relationship that links the price of a European call to the price of a European put option. This is known as the 'put-call parity relationship'. Consider a European call (C_0) and a European put option (P_0); both have the same underlying asset, same time to maturity (T) and same strike price (X). The formula that links the price of the put and call is:

$$C_0 + Xe^{-rT} = S_0 + P_0 \qquad (7.3)$$

The put-call parity relationship shows that the price of a European call with a certain exercise price and time to maturity can be derived from the value of a European put with the same exercise price and date and vice versa. If this relationship does not hold then there are arbitrage opportunities in the market (see Hull, 2007, for an arbitrage example when put-call parity is violated). Although the formula shown applies to European options it should also be applicable to Asian options as well – and hence, options on freight. The put-call parity relationship can also be extended to accommodate cases when we have options on futures. In the case, the relationship becomes:

$$C_0 + Xe^{-rT} = Fe^{-rT} + P_0 \quad \Rightarrow \quad C_0 = P_0 + (F - X)e^{-rT} \qquad (7.4)$$

7.3.4 Factors affecting the value of calls and put options

Overall, we can identify five factors that affect the price of an option:

1. S_0: The price of the underlying asset
2. X: The strike price
3. T: The time to expiration of the options expressed as fraction of a year
4. σ: The volatility of the underlying asset
5. r: The risk-free rate.

We examine each one of these factors in more detail next.[5]

Underlying asset price and strike price

At maturity, the payoff of a call option will be the greater of the amount by which the underlying exceeds the strike price or zero; in other words: $C_T = max(0, S_T - X)$. Call options therefore, become more valuable as the underlying increases and less valuable at the strike price increases. The opposite is true for put options. The payoff from a put option will be the greater of the amount by which the strike price exceeds the underlying or zero; in other words: $P_T = max(X - S_T, 0)$. Put options therefore, become less valuable as the underlying increases and more valuable at the strike price increases.

The time to expiry of the option

Both put and call options become more valuable as time to expiry increases. The reason for this is that the greater the time to maturity of the option

---

[5] There is also a sixth factor affecting the value of options which are dividend payments. However, this is not relevant when it comes to freight options and hence is not discussed here.

the higher the chance that the option has to expire ITM and, hence, the more valuable the option. This is always the case for American options, and is generally the case for European options; however, there are cases when a European call with shorter time to maturity may be more valuable than a similar call with longer time to maturity. This could be the case, for instance, when there are expectations of (downward) jumps in prices after the maturity of the first option that will affect the value of the second option.

The risk (or volatility) of the asset

The volatility of the underlying is a measure of the uncertainty about future movements in the price of the asset (see also the discussion in Chapter 3 on the role of volatility and how it is calculated). Volatility is perhaps the most important factor when it comes to options pricing; this also explains why options trading is also called 'volatility trading'. As volatility increases the chance that there will be larger movements in the value of the underlying increases; as a result, the likelihood that an option will expire ITM increases, which means that both call and put options become more valuable.

The risk-free rate

The risk-free interest rate also affects the price of an option. In general, as a proxy for the risk-free rate we use the return on Treasury bills with a maturity which is comparable to that of the option. Generally, if interest rates increase, the present value of any future cash flow received by the holder of the option decreases. This implies that as interest rates increase, the value of calls will increase and the value of puts will decrease.

7.4   Practicalities of trading options in the freight market

Freight options are traded in almost exactly the same way that the underlying FFAs are transacted, and have similar maturities. Buyers and sellers of options agree on a strike price, and then negotiate a premium. The premium is quoted in US$/day for trip-charter routes, in US$/ton for voyage routes and in WS points for tanker routes. Option contracts are executed between two counterparties through a broker, either as an OTC contract, or through a clearing house. In addition, freight options on certain routes are also available for trading through the Imarex screen.

For options traded in the OTC market, the option premium is payable by the option buyer within five business days after the confirmation of the trade. At the settlement of the option, which is the last day of the maturity month, if the option expires ITM the option seller must pay the settlement sum to the option buyer within five business days after the settlement date. The broker in an OTC option trade will receive commission which is agreed in advance with the principals; it is typically 5 per cent of the option premium. The contract documentation choices for freight options are similar to those available for the FFA market. There is a separate FFABA contract for trading freight options, known as the FFABA 2007 Freight Option Agreement. The contract is similar to the FFABA 2007 FFA contract, discussed in Chapter 5, with some additional clauses which are specific to freight options trading. A specimen contract is presented in Appendix 7.A; its main terms are as follows:

- Clause 1: The agreed contract route (such as BCI C4)
- Clause 2: The option type: whether the traded option is a call, a put, a straddle or a strangle (see Sections 7.6.5 and 7.6.6)
- Clause 3: The strike price(s)
- Clause 4: The option premium – expressed in US$/ton or US$/day multiplied by the total quantity
- Clause 5: The total contract quantity and quantity by contract month. The distinction between total quantity and quantity by month is useful in cases when contracts are traded for the duration of more than one month or when the total quantity is spread across a range of months. This is similar to Clause 3 in the FFABA 2007 FFA contract (see Section 5.9)
- Clause 6: Contract months – these are the settlement months that will be traded (for example, January 2008)
- Clause 7: Settlement dates – this is the last Baltic Index publication date of the contract month
- Clause 9: Settlement rate – this clause specifies how the settlement rate will be calculated (for example, the average of the underlying route over the entire calendar month) and is similar to Clause 6 of the FFABA 2007 FFA contract
- Clause 10: Settlement sum – this specifies the amount that the option seller will pay the buyer if the option is exercised
- Clause 12: ISDA® Master Agreement – this clause incorporates the ISDA® Master Agreement by reference and is similar to clause 9 of the FFABA 2007 FFA contract.

Finally, options may also be cleared through a clearing house. For the option buyer, the maximum loss is the amount of premium paid which, as discussed earlier, will have to be paid within five business days after the option agreement. Since this is the maximum loss for a buyer, he is not required to maintain a margin and his position will not be marked to market. The option seller, on the other hand, will have to deposit in his clearing account the amount of premium that he receives, and then the short option position will be marked-to-market accordingly.

7.5 Risk-management strategies using options

Due to their flexibility and asymmetric risk profile, options are very effective hedging instruments since they enable hedgers to be covered on the downside, and participate in the market on the upside.[6] Hedging positions

---

[6] This is also why in the literature options are called as one-sided forwards or swaps.

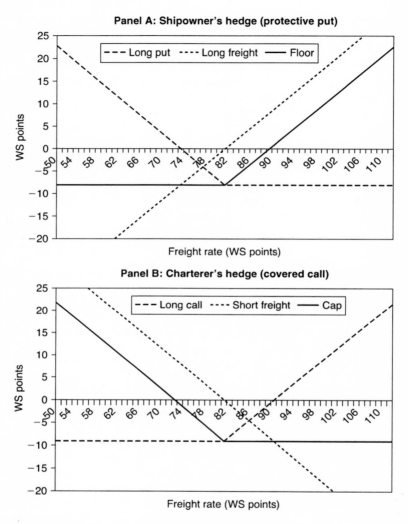

Figure 7.4 Hedging positions using long calls and puts

can be established by entering into long call or put option positions. For instance, a shipowner who wants to protect his freight income against a decline in freight rates will be buying put options; in this case, if freight rates decrease then the put option will expire in-the-money and will compensate the owner for the decline in freight rates and loss of earnings in the physical market. Similarly, a charterer who wants protection against an increase in the cost of transportation will buy call options. The profile of these positions is shown in Figure 7.4, panels A and B respectively.

Consider, for instance, the shipowner's hedge. The shipowner is long on freight so the risk is that freight rates in the market may fall. Assuming that he does not want his freight income for September to fall far below 80 WS, he buys a September TD3 put with a strike price of 80, paying a 7.8 WS premium. If he combines the long-freight with the long-put position, the payoff will be similar to a long call as shown in Panel A above. This essentially means that if the freight rate in the market is below the strike price of 80 WS points in September, the option will be exercised and, as a result, the owner's income will remain at 80 WS points, less the premium of 7.8 WS. Therefore, in this case the owner has created a floor at 72.2 WS. On the other hand, if freight rates in the market increase above the level of the strike price the put option will expire out-of-the-money and the owner will be able to take advantage of the higher freight rates in the market. In any case, his effective freight rate will be reduced by the level of the option premium, 7.8 WS points, that he paid in order to buy the put. This strategy is also called a 'protective put'.

Similarly, a charterer who is short in physical freight can hedge his freight exposure using a long-call position. A combination of the charterer's short freight with the long-call position results in a payoff that looks like a put option as shown in Figure 7.4, Panel B. In this case, the maximum freight cost will be the strike price plus the cost of the option premium; if the option expires OTM the charterer will take advantage of the lower rates in the market. This strategy is also called a 'covered call'. We can see, therefore, that in both cases the long-call or -put positions are very similar to an insurance policy. The hedger pays the insurance premium upfront; if the option expires ITM, the insurance policy will indemnify the hedger. If, on the other hand, the market moves in favour of the hedger the option is not exercised and it expires worthless. Therefore, the maximum loss is limited to the option premium; in this case, the hedger can take advantage of the more favourable conditions in the spot market.

In the previous examples we considered the long-call and long-put positions. It is also interesting to examine the positions that the sellers of these options would have. These are shown in Figure 7.5. Consider for instance Panel A; an individual who sells a call option will be exposed to unbounded losses if the underlying market rises. He therefore has to cover this potentially risky position by owning the underlying asset; hence the name 'writing-covered call'.[7] In the case of freight, this essentially means that the seller of the call should have a long position in the underlying freight route, either by holding tonnage or by having a long FFA, to cover the potential exercise

---

[7] In contrast, one who sells a call without owning the underlying is said to sell a 'naked call'. It is not always the case that the call seller will have to maintain the full underlying in order to cover his short-call position. His holding of the underlying will be determined by the sensitivity of the option price to changes in the underlying in what is known as the 'delta' of the option. This is discussed in Chapter 8 below.

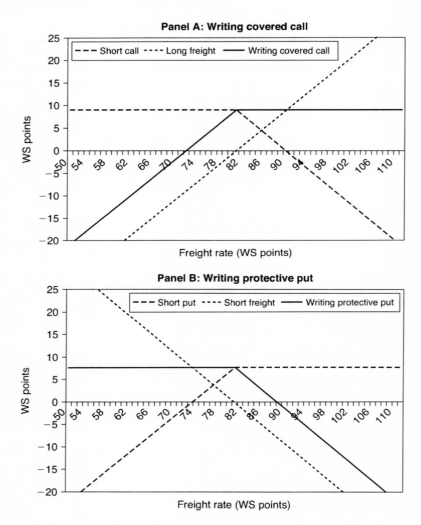

Figure 7.5   Writing covered and protective positions

of the option. 'Covered' therefore means that the call seller owns the under-lying asset that he can deliver, if the call is exercised, without incurring any further cost – apart from an opportunity cost in delivering it for less than the market price. Similarly, a short-put position will be protected using a short-freight position; that is, by selling FFAs; this strategy is known as a 'writing protective put'.

The above strategies can also be used to enhance the return of a given position. Generally, call-options sellers would prefer to sell OTM calls. A call being OTM means that the underlying must rise before the call is exercised against the seller; thus, the seller of an OTM call receives the premium, which is the maximum profit, along with some potential for profit from the underlying. For instance, consider again the case presented in Figure 7.5, Panel A. Assume that a trader has bought an FFA contract at say, 80 WS points. He also has a subjective, maximum return that he would like to make on this position; this would depend on his risk-return profile and on his expected return on the market and, of course, this is subjective and varies from trader to trader. In this example, we assume that the trader is happy to sell the FFA at, say, 100 WS and thus realise a 'maximum' desired gain of 20 WS. He can then sell an OTM call option with a strike price of 100 WS. In doing so he receives the option premium which enhances the return on his investment. If the market rises above 100 WS, then the call option will be exercised and his profit will be capped at 100 WS plus the option premium received up-front. Therefore, in following this strategy, the investor has 'enhanced' the yield of the investment; however, it should be noted that what is being enhanced are not the objective risk-return characteristics but, instead, the *subjective* expected returns of the investor. These strategies are also called 'yield-enhancement' or 'call-overwriting' strategies and are frequently used by investors, particularly in stagnant markets, to enhance the yield on their investment (see also Neftci, 2007).

7.5.1 An example of hedging using options

Consider the following example illustrating the use of options on FFAs. It is late August 2005 and an oil-trading company has sold a VLCC cargo of crude oil (2m barrels or approximately 260,000 mt) to receivers in the Far East, for shipment in November. Shipment will take place in late November and under the sale agreement the seller of the cargo will be responsible for paying the transportation costs; the cargo will be shipped from the Persian Gulf to the Far East. The oil trading company is therefore worried over its exposure to freight risk because an appreciation in freight rates over the coming months will increase the transportation costs.

In an effort to control the freight-rate costs, the charterer considers the use of freight derivatives. FFAs could be used to 'lock in' a certain freight cost; however, there is a concern that such an approach is inflexible and does not enable advantage to be taken of a potential fall in freight rates. For that the charterer decides to buy an October 2005 call option for route TD3 of the BDTI (260,000 mt of crude from the Gulf to Japan);[8] the choice of the October contract is due to the fact that the 'laycan' (see Section 5.4.3

---

[8] The cargo size of route TD3 at the time was 250,000 mt which was then changed to 260,000 mt on 3 January 2006; therefore, in this example we consider the more recent definition of this route.

above) for the route is 30–40 days ahead of the index, so the settlement in October should match cargo liftings at the end of November. A broker advises that there is a counter-party willing to 'write' an October 2005 call option with a strike price of 90 WS at a premium of 7.8 WS points. Therefore, the total premium that the trader will pay to the seller of the call is $7.8/100 \times US\$260,000 \times 12.15 = US\$246,402$. In addition, the trader will have to pay a broker's commission of 5 per cent of the total option premium paid, that is, US\$12,320.

Table 7.3 presents the outcome of this hedge under two different scenarios. In the first case, the average freight rate in October is below the strike price; in this case, the option expires OTM and is not exercised and the trader takes advantage of the lower freight rates in the market. On the other hand, if the freight market increases to say, 110 WS, the option expires ITM and the total freight cost is then capped to 90 WS plus the cost of the option premium (97.8 WS or a total of US\$3,089,502) irrespective of how far above the strike price the level of freight rates in the market is.

Therefore, options are a flexible hedging instrument because they enable the charterer to cap transportation costs when freight rates increase, and to fix vessels at the prevailing spot rate when freight rates decrease. More specifically, if the spot rate is greater than the strike price at the expiration of the call option, then the option is exercised and as a result the effective freight rate for the company is the strike price plus the option premium. Similarly, if the spot rate is lower than the strike price, the option expires worthless, and the effective freight rate is the current spot rate in the market plus the option premium.

7.5.2   Hedging using a collar

Although options provide an effective form of hedging, the fact that the hedger has to pay the option premium upfront may sometimes be a factor that decides against the use of the options as a hedging tool. For instance, in the previous example, the charterer would have to pay an upfront premium of US\$246,402. One way of reducing this cost would be for the charterer to 'sacrifice' some of his upside potential when the market goes down in return for protection against possible freight rate upturns. That would, therefore, involve the charterer selling an OTM put option with a low strike price, say at 70 WS, on the same underlying and with the same maturity as the call option. Selling a put provides income which the charterer can use to offset the cost of the call. This strategy is known as a 'collar strategy'. The most popular type of a collar is a 'zero cost collar', where the cost of the call is offset fully by the premium received from the short put so that the overall cost of the hedge is zero. By following this strategy, the charterer has a maximum freight cost of 90 WS. If the market falls below the strike price of the put, then the put will be exercised against him and his total cost will be 'floored' to the put strike price of 70 WS. Thus, the charterer has financed the downside protection

Table 7.3 An example of hedging freight rates using freight-rate options

TD3 call-option hedge

Physical market	Options market
August 2005	
TD3 Freight Rate : 70 WS Freight cost: US$2,211,300 (=70/100 × 12.15 × US$260,000) Charterer **buys** October 2005 call at a total cost of US$246,402	Option details: October 2005 call with a strike Price of 90 WS. Premium: 7.8 WS (=7.8/100 × 12.15 × US$260,000)
31 October 2005 – falling market	
Average TD3 in October: 75 WS Actual freight cost: US$2,369,250 (=75/100 × 12.15 × US$260,000)	Strike price (90 WS) > spot price (75 WS) Therefore option is not exercised
Total freight cost (including option premium) = US$2,615,652 (=US$2,369,250 + 246,402) or 82.8 WS	
31 October 2005 – alternative scenario – rising market	
Average TD3 in October: 110 WS Actual freight cost: US$3,474,900 (=110/100 × 12.15 × US$260,000)	Strike price (90 WS) < spot price (110 WS) Therefore option is exercised Payoff from the options transaction (110 − 90) × 260,000 × 12.15 − US$246,402 = US$385,398
Total freight cost (inc. option premium) = $3,474,900 − $385,398 = US$3,089,502 or 97.8 WS	

provided by the long call by selling part of the upside potential of the freight market with a short put. Similarly, an owner could construct a collar by buying a put and selling an OTM, high strike price call.[9]

7.5.2.1 Constructing a zero-cost collar in the dry-bulk market

In mid-June 2007, a Panamax owner is concerned about the volatility in the freight market and wants to secure freight income for 2008. There are a number of hedging choices available: first, the shipowner could sell a Calendar 2008 FFA contract for the BPI 4TC average, currently quoted at US$36,500/day; however, he is uncertain about the direction of the market and hence does not want to lock in a forward rate, in case the market rises further than that. The second option would be to buy Calendar 2008 BPI 4TC put options. There is a quote for Cal-08 puts with a strike price of US$33,500/day for a premium of US$3,000/day. This is essentially a strip of 12 options for each of the 12 months of 2008. Each option will be settled separately at the end of each month and the settlement rate will be calculated as the average of the month for BPI 4TC; the total payoff for each month will therefore be:

$$max(33,500 - S_{ave}, 0) \times number\ of\ days\ in\ the\ month \qquad (7.5)$$

where S_{ave} is the average freight rate over the settlement month. For instance, if the average freight rate in January is US$30,000/day the payoff of the option would be US$108,500 (=US$3,500/day × 31). Although such a hedge would effectively guarantee the owner a minimum income of US$33,500/day – minus the option premium – for 2008, this is also a rather expensive hedge since, in order to buy the options, the owner would have to pay an upfront premium of US$1,098,000 (=US$3,000/day × 366 days). The third hedging option would thus be for the owner to 'sacrifice' some upside potential by selling an OTM call option at a higher strike price. The broker has identified a counter-party for this trade, who is willing to sell to the owner the Cal-08 4TC puts with a US$33,500/day strike, and buy from the owner the Cal-08 4TC calls at a strike of US$41,000/day. Since the premia from the long-put and short-call positions match exactly, this strategy would effectively be a zero-cost strategy.

The outcome of this strategy is shown on Figure 7.6. Panel A presents the payoff from the combined options and physical positions for any given maturity and Panel B shows the owner's possible net freight income

---

[9] Another way market participants can reduce the cost of the option premia is to use exotic options that have more complex payoffs than those of standard European or Asian options. One example here are barrier options with knock-in features where the option contract comes into existence only if the underlying price crosses a predetermined price level. For more on the use of exotic options for trading and hedging, see Zhang (1998).

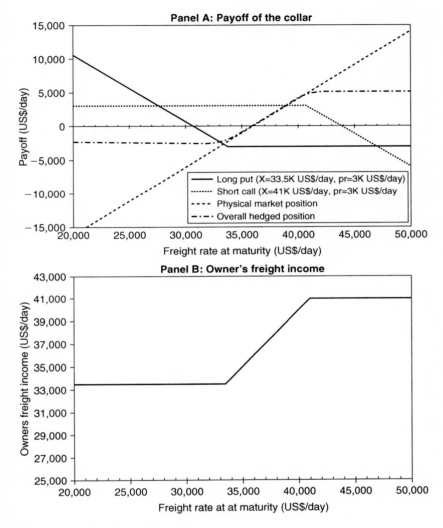

Figure 7.6 An owner's zero-cost collar

from the collar hedge; we can see therefore, that the income is guaranteed to be between US$33,500/day and US$41,000/day for every month of 2008. This strategy guarantees that the shipowner's income will not fall below US$33,500/day but at the same time the income is also capped at US$41,000/day. If, on the other hand, the owner had opted for the FFA hedge, then the income would have been US$36,500/day. Thus, the collar strategy provides more flexibility and also allows the owner to take advantage of any potential upside in the market while at the same time being protected on the downside. We can also note that there is a link between the collar strategy and the FFA hedge. In fact, if the strike prices for the call and the put are identical then the collar hedge is identical to an FFA hedge and the strikes in that case should be equal to the FFA rate; this argument follows directly from the put-call parity relationship of equation (7.4) above which links the prices of calls and puts that are written on the same asset and have the same maturity.

7.6 Option-trading strategies

In the previous section, we considered the payoffs from either long or short positions in single-option contracts. We also examined strategies where positions in an option contract are combined with FFA positions; for instance, in the construction of covered calls or protective put positions, as well as in structuring collar transactions. In this section, we will examine the profit profiles obtained when we have positions in two or more different options on the same underlying asset. One of the interesting features of option contracts is that they can be used to create a wide range of different payoff functions. By trading option combinations, traders can shape the risk-and-return characteristics of their option positions which allow more advanced and complex speculative strategies.

We will start our analysis by looking at directional strategies which generate profit if the market moves in one direction. Such strategies include 'bear' and 'bull' spreads, constructed using calls or puts, which take a speculative view on the direction in the underlying risk. We will also examine the use of a 'box-spread' which generates a risk-free return by combining bull and bear spreads. Then we will look at volatility strategies which generate profit if there is large movement in the market irrespective of the direction. Such strategies include 'straddles' and 'strangles', as well as 'strips' and 'straps'. We then combine these portfolios in order to get more complicated volatility positions and reduce costs and risk in the form of 'butterfly' strategies. We will present examples for each of these strategies using the option quotes in Table 7.4.

7.6.1 Bull spreads

This popular spread can be created by buying an ITM call option, with a low strike price and higher premium, and selling an OTM call option with a high strike price and hence a low premium. Both options are on the same underlying with the same maturities. This strategy will generate a positive payoff in a bullish market because the low exercise price call will bring a higher payoff than the high exercise price call; hence, the name 'bull call spread'. Overall, this strategy offers the advantage of being less expensive than an outright call purchase; it also limits the downside in case the market falls. This also implies that the profit potential is also limited and less than

Table 7.4 Imarex option quotes for TD3 route on 23 August 2005

CALLS		Strike			Premium		
Maturity	FFA rate	−WS 10	ATM	+WS 10	−WS 10 (ITM)	ATM	+WS 10 (OTM)
Sep 05	80.5	70	80	90	14.4	8.9	5.2
Oct 05	95	90	100	110	15.3	11.0	7.8
Nov 05	115	110	120	130	20.1	15.9	12.5
Dec 05	120	110	120	130	26.2	21.8	18.0
Q4 05	110	100	110	120	20.6	16.2	12.8

PUTS		Strike			Premium		
Maturity	FFA rate	+WS 10	ATM	−WS 10	+WS 10 (ITM)	ATM	−WS 10 (OTM)
Sep 05	80.5	90	80	70	14.1	7.8	3.4
Oct 05	95	110	100	90	21.6	14.8	9.2
Nov 05	115	130	120	110	25.7	19.1	13.4
Dec 05	120	130	120	110	25.8	19.6	14.2
Q4 05	110	120	110	100	24.3	17.8	12.3

Source: Imarex

what it would have been with an outright long-call position. In addition, this strategy requires an initial upfront payment of premium, albeit a lower one than an outright long call option, since the long ITM call is more expensive than the short OTM call.

To illustrate how we can construct a bull call spread, suppose we construct a strategy using the 90 WS and 110 WS strike October 2005 TD3 calls, presented in Table 7.4. The payoff of this strategy is shown in Figure 7.7.[10] In order to set up this strategy we need to pay an upfront premium of 7.5 WS points [15.3 − 7.8]. If, at maturity, freight rates are below the lower strike price of 90 WS, then this strategy will result in a net loss which is equal to the net premium paid of 7.5 WS points; in this case, therefore, both options expire OTM and the trader forfeits the premium paid. The breakeven rate is 97.5 WS which is the lower strike plus the net premium paid. If the market is greater than that then this strategy will generate a positive payoff. The maximum profit for this strategy will be 12.5 WS points and this is calculated as: *higher strike − lower strike − premium paid* (110 − 90 − 7.5) WS. Notice also that for rates below 117.8 WS, the bull call spread will outperform the outright

---

[10] For ease of exposition, all the payoff diagrams in this section ignore the time value of money in the option premia. Therefore, the payoff for each contract is calculated as the final payoff minus the initial cost of the option contracts; in theory, we should use the final payoff minus the compounded future value of the option premium at the maturity of the contract.

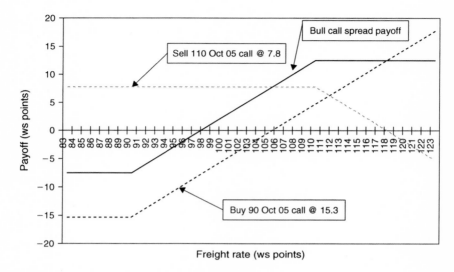

Figure 7.7   Payoff from bull spread using call options

call-purchase strategy, which also implies that a call spread may be a more effi-cient speculative strategy for relatively smaller movements in the underlying market.[11]

Overall, a bull spread strategy limits the investors' upside as well as down-side risk. The strategy can be described by saying that the investor has a call option with a strike price equal to X_1 and has chosen to give up some upside potential by selling a call option with a higher strike price, X_2, which partly finances the purchase of the more expensive lower strike call. Overall, we can identify three different types of bull call spreads:

1. Both calls are OTM
2. One call is ITM and the other is OTM – similar to the one presented in Figure 7.7
3. Both calls are initially ITM.

The first type of bull call spread has the lowest cost in terms of setting up, since both options are OTM; at the same time it also has a low probability of ending up with a positive payoff. At the other end, the third strategy is the

---

[11] This is calculated as: *lower strike + ITM premium paid + bull call spread profit* $(90 + 15.3 + 12.5 = 117.8 \text{ WS})$ and represents the point at which the ITM call payoff crosses the bull call spread.

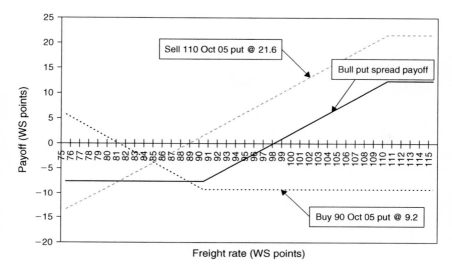

Figure 7.8 Payoff from bull spread using put options

most expensive to set up but also has the highest probability of a positive exercise value. Finally the second strategy comes between the other two in terms of cost and chance of positive exercise.

One can also construct bull spreads using puts. This strategy involves simultaneous sale and purchase of put options on the same underlying and same maturities and with strikes X_1 and X_2, respectively, where $X_1 < X_2$. For instance, we can construct a bull spread with puts by buying the 90 WS and selling the 110 WS strike October 2005 TD3 puts. The payoff from this strategy is shown in Figure 7.8. Compared to the bull call spread this strategy will generate a net positive upfront cash flow of 12.4 WS points since the premium from the sale of the option is more than the cost of purchase of the put. This will also be the maximum profit from this strategy which will be materialised if freight rates are higher than 110 WS points, in which case both put options expire OTM and the trader keeps the option premium. On the other hand, if freight rates decrease below that level, the payoff from the strategy will drop accordingly. The breakeven rate is 97.6 WS which is the higher strike minus the net premium received. Finally, if freight rates drop below the lower strike price of 90 WS then the strategy will generate the maximum loss, which is 7.6 WS ($= 110 - 90 - 12.4 = 7.6$), calculated as: *higher strike price − lower strike price − max profit*. Therefore, this strategy is very similar, in terms of its payoff, to a bull call spread. However, the fact that there is an upfront cash inflow means that both the maximum loss and profit are slightly less than what it would have been with the bull call spread.

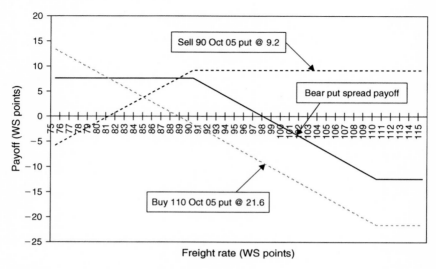

Figure 7.9 Payoff from bear spread using put options

7.6.2 Bear spreads

An investor who enters into a bull spread is hoping that the underlying price will increase. By contrast, an investor who enters into a bear spread is hoping that the underlying price will decline. A bear put spread can be constructed as an inverse bull put spread by selling a put option with strike X_1 and buying a put option with strike X_2, where $X_1 < X_2$. The strike price of the option purchased is greater than the strike price of the option sold. The payoff of a bear put spread constructed by buying the 110 WS October 2005 TD3 put and selling the 90 WS October 2005 TD3 put in Table 7.4 is shown in Figure 7.9. Initially this strategy requires the payment of an upfront premium of 12.4 WS points (21.6 − 9.2). If TD3 freight rate at expiry is higher than the strike price of 110 WS points, then this strategy will result in a net loss which is equal to the net premium paid of 12.4 WS points. As freight rates in the market decrease, we can see that the payoff increases. The breakeven rate is 97.6 WS, which is calculated as: *high strike − net premium paid*. The maximum profit from this strategy will be realised when the freight rate at expiry is below 90 WS points. In this case the profit will be 7.6 WS points (110 − 90 − 12.4), calculated as: *higher strike − lower strike − premium paid*. Therefore, a bear put spread is very similar to a long-put position where the trader has sacrificed some of the profit potential by selling an OTM put option.

This strategy is cheaper to set up than a straight put purchase and will outperform the put purchase, in terms of the final payoff, if freight rates in the market stay above 80.8 WS points, which is calculated as: *high strike put − ITM*

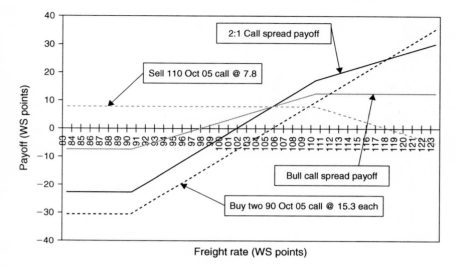

Figure 7.10 Payoff of a 2:1 call spread

put premium paid — bull call spread profit (110–21.6–7.6). Therefore, like bull spreads, bear spreads limit both the upside potential and the risk. Bear spreads can also be created using calls instead of puts by buying a high-strike–low-premium call and selling a low-strike–high-premium call; unlike bear put spreads, bear spreads created using calls involve an initial cash inflow.

7.6.3 Ratio spreads

These are spread transactions in which two or more related options are traded in a specified proportion. For example, a trader might buy two calls with a low strike price and sell one call with a high strike which gives a 2:1 ratio spread. As the ratio of one instrument to the other can be varied without limit, there are infinite combinations of ratio spreads that can be constructed. Therefore, since we cannot provide examples for each different type of call spread, we are going to consider the two types of spreads which seem to be the most commonly used in the shipping industry. These are the 2:1 call spread, comprising two long- and one short-option positions, and the 1:2 call spread, comprising one long- and two short-option positions. To illustrate how we can construct a 2:1 call spread, we consider the bull call spread example in Figure 7.7. The bull call spread was constructed by buying the 90 WS October 05 TD3 call and by selling the 110 WS October 05 TD3 call. We can construct a 2:1 spread by buying two 90 WS October 05 TD3 calls and selling one 110 WS October 05 TD3 call. The payoff from this strategy is shown in Figure 7.10. For comparison purposes we also present on the same graph the payoff from the bull-call spread from Figure 7.7.

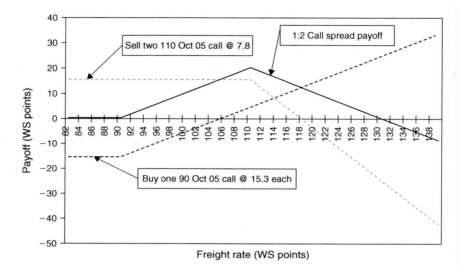

Figure 7.11   Payoff of a 1:2 call spread

We can see that if the freight rate at expiry is less than the lower strike price of 90 WS then both options will expire OTM and the trader will lose the premium paid in order to set up the strategy; this is equal to 22.8 WS points ($2 \times 15.3 - 7.8$). For higher freight rates both long-call positions will be exercised and the breakeven rate will be equal to 101.4 WS; this is calculated as the lower strike price minus half the premium paid ($90 + 22.8/2$); the reason why we use half the premium is that for this range of freight rates we have two options, which means that a one-WS-point change in the freight market will result in a two-WS-point change in the options position. When the freight market rises above 110 WS points then the short call will be exercised against the trader. In this case, the slope of the payoff will become flatter and there will be a one-to-one relationship between changes in the freight market and the payoff of the option. Compared to the bull call spread, we can see that the 2:1 spread costs more to set up but also offers much higher profits if the market rises significantly.

By varying the ratio between the options in the spread, it is possible to create a wide variety of payoff patterns. For instance, Figure 7.11 presents the payoff of a 1:2 spread consisting of a long-position in one 90 WS October 05 TD3 call and a short position in two 110 WS October 05 TD3 calls. We can see that this strategy has initially a small cash inflow of 0.3 WS points, reflecting the difference between the option premia sold vs. the option premia bought. For freight rates higher than 90 WS points, the long-call option will be exercised and the trader will have a positive payoff. The payoff reaches its maximum when the freight rate is 110 WS and the short-call positions

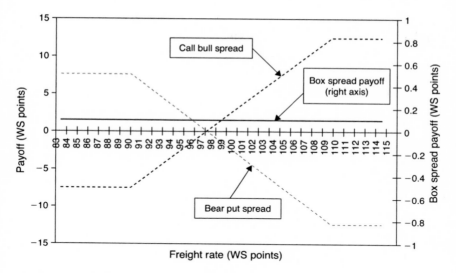

Figure 7.12   Payoff of a box spread combination

become ITM; the maximum profit in this instance is 20.3 WS points, which is the difference between the two strikes plus the net premium received. For higher freight rates the short calls will be exercised and will erode the profits from this strategy. Finally, for freight rates higher than 130.3 WS, this strategy will generate a loss since both short calls will be deep ITM.[12] Despite the fact that this strategy leaves the trader exposed to high risk if freight rates increase, by shorting calls that are sufficiently OTM the trader can reduce the cost of the outright call purchase.

7.6.4   Box spread

A box spread is a combination of a bull call spread and a bear put spread. Overall, the strategy consists of two simultaneous spread positions: A bull call spread, constructed by buying a call option with strike price X_1 and selling a call option with strike X_2, where $X_1 < X_2$; and a bear put spread, constructed by selling a put option with strike X_1 and buying a put option with strike X_2. All options are written on the same underlying, and have the same maturity.

Figure 7.12 shows the payoff of a box spread constructed using the bull spread in Figure 7.7 and the bear put spread in Figure 7.9. Overall we can see that this strategy will generate a risk-free payoff of 0.1 WS points (the payoff

---

[12] This is calculated as high strike price plus maximum profit, i.e., $110 + 20.3 = 130.3$ WS points.

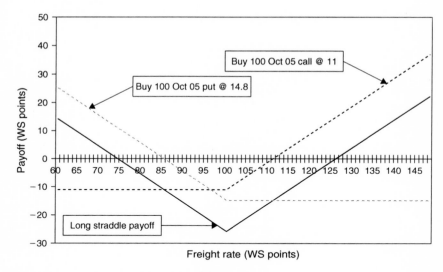

Figure 7.13 A long straddle combination

from the box spread is measured on the right axis) irrespective of the level of freight rates at expiry. This is calculated as the differences between the two strike prices minus the net premium paid ($110 - 90 - 7.5 - 12.4$). The value of the box spread at expiration will be equal to the difference between the two strike prices ($110 - 90$); since this amount will be received irrespective of the freight rate at expiry, this payoff will be riskless and its value today should be its present value discounted at the risk-free rate, that is, $e^{-rt}(X_2 - X_1)$. In other words, the value of the combined bull call and bear put spreads should be equal to the discounted present value of the difference in strike prices, discounted at the risk-free rate. This is also presented in Figure 7.12 where the payoff of 0.1 is effectively the time value of the net premium paid until the expiry of the option. If the price of the box spread today is different from $e^{-rt}(X_2 - X_1)$ then traders can make arbitrage profits by selling or buying the spread respectively. Therefore, box spreads also provide a quick method for calculating whether calls and puts with different strikes and the same maturity are correctly priced.

7.6.5 Straddle combinations

Straddles are constructed by buying a call and a put with the same strike, X, and same expiration date, T. A long straddle is in fact a volatility strategy; the greater the volatility in the market the greater the profit from the position. If, at expiration, the underlying is close to the strike price X, then this strategy leads to a loss of the total premium paid for the two options. However, a sufficiently large move in either direction can result in a large profit.

Figure 7.13 presents a long straddle combination, using the 100 WS strike October 2005 TD3 call and the 100 WS strike October 2005 TD3 put, as shown in Table 7.4. As we can see in the graph the maximum loss in this strategy is the total premium paid, which is 25.8 WS (14.8 + 11.0). For the strategy to generate positive payoff, the straddle holder needs the freight rate to either rise more than 125.8 WS (which is the strike price plus the premium paid) or the freight rate to drop below 74.2 WS (which is the strike minus the premium paid). A long straddle is appropriate if the investor expects a large move in the market but is uncertain as to which direction the market will move. One example here is the impact that a hurricane may have on freight rates in the US Gulf region. If it disrupts the supply facilities, it is likely that freight rates will increase, hence, there will be an upward trend in the market. It is also likely that the market anticipates that and freight rates are also higher than normal given the current market conditions. Therefore, if the hurricane does not disrupt the supply facilities, chances are that freight rates will decrease. In this setting, the strategy that enables investors to profit from the move in the market is a straddle. The problem in the example presented above, however, is that if your view about the freight rates is very much similar to the view of other participants in the market, this collective view will also be reflected in the prices of the options, which will be much higher than normal due to the anticipation of a jump. Therefore, the V shape of the straddle will move downward so that a bigger move in the freight market will be necessary to make the strategy profitable (see Hull, 2006). Therefore, for the long straddle to be effective, you must believe that there will be a substantial move in the market (prices will either increase or decrease significantly) and these beliefs must be different from those of other investors.

Similarly, one may also construct a short straddle by selling a call and a put with the same strike and expiration date. The payoff of the short straddle using the same options as above is shown in Figure 7.14. We can see that in the case of a short straddle the maximum profit is the net premium received. However, this is a highly risky strategy since the loss arising from a large price move can be unlimited.

7.6.6 Strangle combinations

A major disadvantage of using straddles for speculation is that they involve the purchase of options that are near ATM and hence are more expensive. One way of reducing the premia involved is to buy calls and puts with strike prices that are further apart; since in this case the options may be OTM the total premium will be lower. Therefore, to set up this strategy, which is called a 'strangle', the trader buys a call and a put with the same expiration date and strike prices $X_2 > X_1$, respectively.

Figure 7.15 presents the payoff of a long strangle constructed by buying the 110 WS strike October 2005 TD3 call and the 100 WS strike October 2005 TD3 put, as shown in Table 7.4. We can see that the total premium paid is 22.6 WS

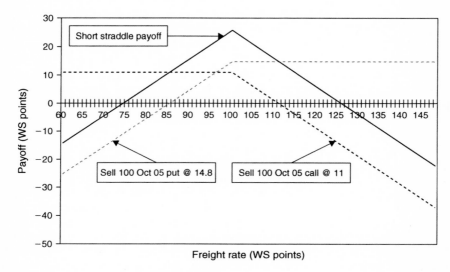

Figure 7.14   A short straddle combination

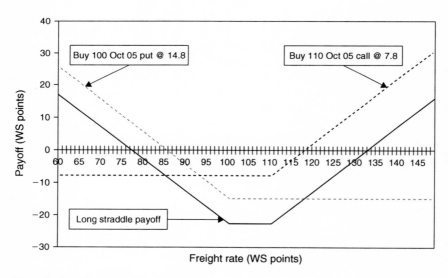

Figure 7.15   A long strangle combination

points $(14.8 + 7.8)$ which is less than the premium for the straddle strategy in the previous example. This implies that the upside potential is also less than that of the straddle. As we can see in the graph, for the strategy to generate positive payoff, the freight rate must either rise above 132.6 WS (which is the

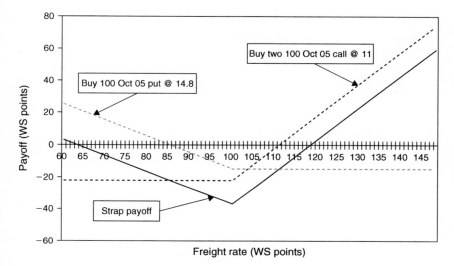

Figure 7.16 Payoff of a strap strategy

higher strike price plus the premium paid: 110 + 22.6) or drop below 74.2 WS. Generally, the overall payoff of the strangle depends on how far apart are the two strike prices; the further apart, the lower the premium paid and the further the underlying price must rise or fall for a profit to be realised. Similarly, one can construct a short strangle by selling the corresponding calls and puts.

7.6.7 Strips and straps

These strategies are also volatility strategies, and are very similar to straddles. A 'strip' consists of a long position in one call and two puts with the same strike price and expiration date. A 'strap' consists of a long position in two calls and one put with the same strike and expiration date. Therefore, both strategies are very similar to straddles and will generate positive payoffs if there is a large movement in the market; however, unlike a straddle, there is asymmetry in their payoffs. A strip generates a higher payoff when there is a price decrease and is suitable when a price move in the underlying is expected and a price decrease is more likely than a price increase. A strap, on the other hand, generates a higher payoff when there is a price increase. Figure 7.16 presents the payoff of a strap constructed by buying two 100WS strike October 2005 TD3 calls and one 100 WS strike October 05 TD3 put. We can see in Figure 7.16 that the payoff line on the upside is much steeper, due to the purchase of the two options; this means that when there is a price increase, for every WS point increase in the underlying the payoff will increase by two WS points. As expected, this strategy is more expensive than the straddle since the total premium paid is 36.8 WS (14.8 + 2 × 11.0).

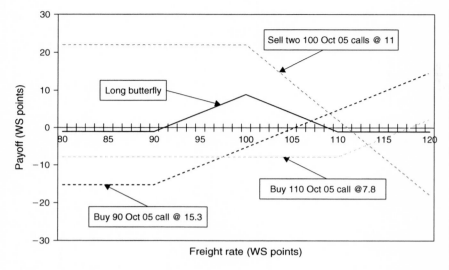

Figure 7.17   A long butterfly spread

7.6.8   Butterfly spreads

One way of reducing the risk profile of a short strangle is to reduce the losses which the strategy can potentially generate by putting a floor on the payoff if the market rises or falls by more than a specified level. Such a payoff can be constructed by buying two calls with strike prices X_1 and X_3 and selling two calls with strike price X_2, where $X_1 < X_2 < X_3$ and all options have the same maturity date. As an example, consider the long butterfly spread in Figure 7.17, constructed by buying the 90 WS and 110 WS October 2005 TD3 calls and selling two 100 WS October 2005 TD3 calls, shown in Table 7.4. We can see that when there is a large movement in the market, the losses are capped. For instance, if the market drops below the lower strike price of 90 WS or rises above the highest strike price of 110 WS, the losses will be capped and the maximum loss will be the net premium paid, which is 1.1 WS point ($15.3 + 7.8 - 2 \times 11$). On the other hand, if the market does not change much from its current level, and the underlying at expiration is at the middle strike price of 100 WS, then we obtain the maximum profit which is equal to the difference between the middle and the lower strike prices minus the net premium paid: that is, the maximum profit in this example will be 8.9 WS points ($100 \times 90 \times 1.1$). In general the strategy will generate a positive payoff for as long as the freight rate is above the lower strike plus the premium paid ($91.1 \text{ WS} = [90 + 1.1]$) or below the high strike minus premium paid ($108.9 \text{ WS} = [110 - 1.1]$). Compared to the straddle, the butterfly spread reduces the risk of a very large loss – at the expense of a lower chance of profits.

We can also construct the long butterfly spread in Figure 7.17 by shorting an ATM straddle and going long on a strangle with strikes that are equal to the two outer strikes of the butterfly. In addition, as is the case with bear and bull spreads, butterfly spreads can also be constructed using puts instead of calls. In this case, a long butterfly would be constructed by buying a put with a low and a high strike price and shorting two puts in the middle. For European options, the long butterfly with puts constructed like this will give the same payoff as the long butterfly with calls, due to the put-call parity relationship. Finally, a trader may also write a butterfly spread by buying the middle options and selling the two calls with strikes of 90 WS and 110 WS. This strategy would be used if the market is expected to be volatile and would thus fall outside the two breakeven points of 91.1 WS and 108.9 WS points. This strategy will be cheaper to set up compared to a straddle but it will also cap the maximum profit to the net premium received.

7.7   Summary and conclusions

Freight options are becoming more and more popular with market practitioners and are increasingly used for both risk-management and speculation purposes. We considered the profit patterns from buying or selling call-and-put options as well as the practicalities of trading freight options. We then examined risk-management applications of freight options as well as some speculative strategies making use of options that are practised by traders in the freight market. There are of course numerous ways one can combine different options positions in order to create unique payoffs and there are a number of textbooks that discuss more extensively trading strategies using options; these include Chance (2006), Kolb and Overdahl (2007), Neftci (2007) and Hull (2006). Perhaps the major issue in the freight options market today is the issue of determining the fair premium to pay for freight options and how to hedge a short position in an option. These issues are discussed in the next chapter.

Appendix 7.A: FFABA 2007© Freight Options Contract

Reproduced with the kind permission of the Baltic Exchange and the FFABA.

FORWARD FREIGHT AGREEMENT BROKERS ASSOCIATION ("FFABA")

FREIGHT OPTION AGREEMENT

FFABA 2007 TERMS

Trade Ref: [•]
Contract Date: [•]

The purpose of this Confirmation is to state the terms and conditions of the Transaction entered into between:

[•] (hereafter, '**Seller**')
Attention: [•]
Postal Address: [•]
Street Address: [•]
Telephone No.:   [•]
Facsimile No.:   [•]
Email Address: [•]

and

[•] (hereafter, '**Buyer**')
Attention: [•]
Postal Address: [•]
Street Address: [•]
Telephone No.:   [•]
Facsimile No.:   [•]
Email Address: [•]

The agreement between the parties set out in this Confirmation is a Confirmation pursuant to the Master Agreement.

In this Confirmation, '**Master Agreement**' has the meaning given to it in clause 12 if that clause applies, and if it does not, means any master agreement by which the Transaction entered into pursuant to and in accordance with this Confirmation is governed.

Until superseded by notice information in a subsequent Confirmation or other communication, the above addresses are hereby recognised as the correct addresses to which any notification under this Confirmation may be properly served.

The terms of this Confirmation are as follows:

1) **Contract Route(s):**
   [•] as defined by the Baltic Exchange on the Contract Date and any route replacing or substituting that route subsequently published by the Baltic

Exchange on or before the Settlement Date and with effect from the date of such replacement or substitution.

2) **Option Type:**
   [•]: [Call] [Put] [Straddle] [Strangle] Option.

3) **Strike Price[s]:**
   [•] US$ [•] [per day] [ton[ne]].

4) **Option Premium:**
   US$ [•] [per day] [ton[ne]], times the Total Quantity.

5) **Contract Quantity:**
   (i) Total Quantity: [•].
   (ii) Quantity by Contract Month: [•].

6) **Contract Month(s):**
   [•]

7) **Settlement Dates:**
   The last Baltic Exchange Index publication day of each Contract Month.

8) **Payment of the Option Premium**
   (a) Payment of the Option Premium by the Buyer is due on the later of two (2) London business days after presentation of Seller's invoice (with complete payment instructions) or five (5) London business days after the date of this Confirmation Agreement and for this purpose a '**London business day**' means a day (other than a Saturday or Sunday) on which Commercial banks are open for business in London). The Option Premium will be deemed 'paid' when it has been received in to the bank account designated by the Seller.
   (b) Payment of the Option Premium shall be made telegraphically, in full, in United States dollars. The cost incurred in effecting payment shall be for the account of the Buyer. Payment may only be effected directly between the parties. The Premium Option shall be paid without any deduction or set off except as permitted pursuant to the Master Agreement or otherwise as agreed by the Buyer and the Seller in writing.

9) **Settlement Rate:**
   (a) Each settlement rate (the '**Settlement Rate**') shall be the unweighted average of the rates for the Contract Route(s) published by the Baltic Exchange over the Settlement Period (defined as [•] Baltic Exchange Index publication days of the applicable Contract Month up to and including the Settlement Date).
   (b) If for any reason the Baltic Exchange cannot provide any rate required for establishing the Settlement Rate, then the current chairman of the FFABA may be instructed by either party to form a panel comprising of a minimum of three independent brokers (the '**Panel**') to determine an appropriate rate, which determination will be final and binding on both parties.

(c) Each party shall bear its own costs and expenses in connection with any determination made pursuant to this clause 9.

(d) The parties shall severally indemnify and hold harmless each of the members of the Panel, the Baltic Exchange and its members and the FFABA and its members (the '**Indemnified Persons**') against all liabilities, actions, demands, costs and expenses incurred by any of them arising directly or indirectly out of or in connection with the formation of the Panel and any determination made by the Panel.

(e) As between the parties, each party shall have a right of contribution against the other party in respect of any indemnity payment made pursuant to the preceding paragraph so that their respective liabilities pursuant to that paragraph shall be equal.

10) Settlement Sum:

(a) In the case of a Call Option, if the Settlement Rate is higher than the Strike Price, the '**Settlement Sum**' is an amount equal to the product of (i) the difference between the Settlement Rate and the Strike Price expressed as a positive amount multiplied by (ii) the Quantity by Contract Month, and the Seller shall pay the Buyer the Settlement Sum. If the Settlement Rate is lower than or equal to the Strike Price, the Settlement Sum shall be zero and no payment shall be due.

(b) In the case of a Put Option, if the Settlement Rate is lower than the Strike Price, the '**Settlement Sum**' is an amount equal to the product of (i) the difference between the Strike Price and the Settlement Rate expressed as a positive amount multiplied by (ii) the Quantity by Contract Month, and the Seller shall pay the Buyer the Settlement Sum. If the Settlement Rate is higher than or equal to the Strike Price, the Settlement Sum shall be zero and no payment shall be due.

(c) In the case of a Straddle Option, if the Settlement Rate is higher or lower than the Strike Price, the '**Settlement Sum**' is an amount equal to the product of (i) the difference between the Settlement Rate and the Strike Price multiplied by (ii) the Quantity by Contract Month, and the Seller shall pay the Buyer the Settlement Sum. If the Settlement Rate is equal to the Strike Price, the Settlement Sum shall be zero and no payment shall be due.

(d) In the case of a Strangle Option, if the Settlement Rate is higher than the higher Strike Price or lower than the lower Strike Price, the '**Settlement Sum**' is an amount equal to the product of (i) the difference between the Settlement Rate and the relevant Strike Price multiplied by (ii) the Quantity by Contract Month, and the Seller shall pay the Buyer the Settlement Sum. If the Settlement Rate is equal to or lower than the higher Strike Price or is equal to or higher than the lower Strike Price, the Settlement Sum shall be zero and no payment shall be due.

11) **Payment Procedure and Obligations:**
    (a) Payment of the Settlement Sum is due on the later of two (2) London business days after presentation of payee's invoice (with complete payment instructions) or five (5) London business days after the Settlement Date and for this purpose a '**London business day**' means a day (other than a Saturday or Sunday) on which commercial banks are open for business in London). The Settlement Sum will be deemed 'paid' when it has been received into the bank account designated by the payee.
    (b) Payment of the Settlement Sum shall be made telegraphically, in full, in United States dollars. The costs incurred in effecting payment shall be for the account of the payer. Payment may only be effected directly between the parties. The Settlement Sum shall be paid without any deduction or set-off except as permitted pursuant to the Master Agreement or otherwise as agreed by the Buyer and the Seller in writing.

12) **ISDA Master Agreement:**
This clause 12 applies only if either:
    (i) this Confirmation does not already constitute a Confirmation under an existing master agreement entered into by the parties to this Confirmation; or
    (ii) the parties agree, either by virtue of clause 23 or otherwise, that the terms of the Master Agreement that is constituted by this clause are to replace any such existing master agreement.

This Confirmation constitutes and incorporates by reference the provisions of the 1992 ISDA® Master Agreement (Multicurrency – Cross Border) (without Schedule) as if they were fully set out in this Confirmation and with only the following specific modifications and elections:

    (a) Section 2(c)(ii) shall not apply so that a net amount due will be determined in respect of all amounts payable on the same date in the same currency in respect of two or more Transactions;
    (b) Seller is the Calculation Agent except where the Seller is the Defaulting Party in which event Buyer is the Calculation Agent;
    (c) the most current published set of ISDA® Commodity Definitions and ISDA® Definitions shall apply;
    (d) Credit Event Upon Merger is applicable to both parties;
    (e) for the purposes of payments on Early Termination, Loss will apply and the Second Method will apply;
    (f) Automatic Early Termination will apply to both parties;
    (g) the Termination Currency is United States dollars;

(h) the Applicable Rate shall mean the one month USD-LIBOR plus 2 per cent, reset daily and compounded monthly;

(i)   Local Business Day or banking day shall each refer to such a day in London;

(j)   such other modifications as shall be necessary for such incorporation;

(k) references to 'this Master Agreement', 'this Agreement', 'herein' and other like expressions shall be construed as being references to this Confirmation incorporating such provisions,

and this Confirmation, including such incorporated provisions, shall govern the Transaction referred to in this Confirmation and any other Transaction referred to in clauses 23 and 24.

The agreement constituted and incorporated by the incorporation of the provisions of the 1992 ISDA® Master Agreement (Multicurrency – Cross Border) (without Schedule) pursuant to this clause is referred to in this Confirmation as the '**Master Agreement**'.

13) **Capacity and Good Standing:**
In line with and in addition to (as appropriate) the representations contained in Section 3 of the Master Agreement, each party represents to the other party that:

(a) it is duly organised and validly existing under the laws of the jurisdiction of its organization or incorporation, and is solvent and in good standing;

(b) it has the power to execute, deliver, and perform this Confirmation;

(c) all governmental and other consents that are required to have been obtained by it with respect to this Confirmation have been obtained and are in full force and effect and all conditions of any such consents have been complied with;

(d) in the event that a party to this Confirmation is a person organised under, domiciled in, or having its principal place of business in, the United States, each party represents to the other party that it is an 'eligible contract participant' as defined in §1a(12) of the Commodity Exchange Act (7 U.S.C. §1a(12), as amended).

14) **Telephone Recording:**
Each party consents to the recording of telephone conversations in connection with this Confirmation.

15) **Commission:**
Each of the parties agrees to pay brokers' commission to any broker (a '**Broker**') as agreed with any Broker.

16) **Non-Assignability:**
Except as provided in Section 7 of the Master Agreement, this Confirmation is non-assignable unless otherwise agreed in writing between the parties to this Confirmation.

17) Principal to Principal:
This Confirmation is a principal to principal agreement with settlement directly between the two parties. Both parties agree that any Broker shall be under no obligation or liability in relation to this Confirmation. Both parties agree jointly and severally to indemnify and hold harmless any Broker against all actions, including but not limited to all claims, demands, liabilities, damages, costs and expenses both from the two parties and any third party. Claims, demands, liabilities, damages, costs and expenses suffered or incurred are to be settled directly by or between the two parties.

18) Law and Jurisdiction:
This Confirmation shall be governed by and construed in accordance with English law and shall be subject to the exclusive jurisdiction of the High Court of Justice in London, England. The terms of Section 12(a) of the Master Agreement notwithstanding, proceedings may be validly served upon either party by sending the same by ordinary post and/or by fax to the addresses and/or fax numbers for each party given above.

19) Entire Agreement:
This Confirmation and the Master Agreement set out the entire agreement and understanding of the parties with respect to the subject matter of this Confirmation and supersede all oral communication and prior writings with respect thereto.

20) Payment Account Information:

For Seller:	For Buyer:
Bank address:	Bank address:
Aba:	Aba:
Swift address:	Swift address:
Account no.:	Account no.:
Sort code:	Sort code:

21) Third party rights
(a) Unless provided to the contrary in this Confirmation, a person who is not a party to this Confirmation has no rights under the Contracts (Rights of Third Parties) Act 1999 to enforce or enjoy the benefit of any term of this Confirmation.

(b) Any Indemnified Person and any Broker shall have the right to enjoy the benefit of and enforce the terms of clause 9(d) in the case of any Indemnified Person and clause 17 in the case of any Broker.

(c) Notwithstanding any term of this Confirmation, the consent of any person who is not a party to this Confirmation is not required to rescind or vary this Confirmation.

22) Partial Invalidity
If, at any time, any provision of this Confirmation or the Master Agreement is or becomes illegal, invalid or unenforceable in any respect under

any laws of any jurisdiction, neither the legality, validity or enforceability of the remaining provisions nor the legality or enforceability of the provision under the laws of any other jurisdiction will in any way be affected or impaired.

23) Inclusion of historical Confirmations under Master Agreement

   (a) **Unless the parties to this Confirmation specifically agree otherwise in writing, this clause 23 shall apply in accordance with its terms.**

   (b) This clause 23 applies to this Confirmation and to every agreement entered into between the parties to this Confirmation (and no other persons) before the date of this Confirmation that is in respect of a forward freight swap, option or derivative:

      (a) that is expressly stated to be subject to, or is subject to substantially the same terms as, either the FFABA 2000 terms, the FFABA 2005 terms or the FFABA 2007 terms, with or without amendment; and

      (b) in the case of a Confirmation that is stated to be subject to, or subject to substantially the same terms as, the FFABA 2007 terms that does not incorporate a clause substantially in the same form as this clause 23.

   (c) Each agreement to which this clause 23 applies shall be treated as a Confirmation under the Master Agreement constituted pursuant to clause 12 as if such agreement had been entered into between the parties on the terms of the Master Agreement on the date of the first such Confirmation.

   (d) If there is any inconsistency between the provisions of any agreement constituted pursuant to paragraph (c) above and the agreement constituting a Transaction to which this clause 23 applies, the provisions of the agreement constituting the Transaction to which this clause 23 applies will prevail for the purposes of the Transaction under such agreement.

   (e) This clause 23 shall not affect any rights or obligations of the parties under any Transaction accrued before the date of this Confirmation.

   (f) This clause 23 is effective notwithstanding any entire agreement clause or similar provision in any such agreement relevant to any such Transaction.

24) Inclusion of subsequent Confirmations under Master Agreement

   (a) **Unless the parties to this Confirmation specifically agree otherwise in writing, this clause 24 shall apply in accordance with its terms.**

   (b) This clause 24 applies to every Confirmation that is in respect of a forward freight swap, option or derivative entered into between the parties to this Confirmation (and no other persons) subsequent to an agreement incorporating a Master Agreement (as defined in and pursuant to a clause substantially in the same form as and equivalent to clause 12) having been entered into by them.

(c)   Each such subsequent Confirmation shall constitute a Confirmation under the Master Agreement on the terms of clauses 23(c), (d), (e) and (f) as if they were incorporated and fully set out in this clause 24 with appropriate and necessary modifications for such incorporation.

Signed for the Seller by   **Signed for the Buyer by**

....

Duly Authorised Signatory   **Duly Authorised Signatory**

8
Pricing and Risk Management of Option Positions

8.1 Introduction

In the previous chapter we discussed the properties and characteristics of freight options. Freight options are becoming increasingly popular with practitioners and are used both for risk-management and speculation purposes. From the point of view of traders in the market and particularly for option sellers, there are two important considerations that have to be examined. The first is the issue of determining a fair option premium to charge when selling a freight option. This should reflect, among other things, the risks option sellers face in the market and should provide a fair level of compensation for those risks. The premium should be fair because if it is too high then the option will be overpriced; on the other hand, if the premium is too low then the premium will not provide an adequate level of compensation for the risks the seller is facing. The second important consideration is how to manage or hedge a short-option position. As was shown in the previous chapter, a short position in a call or put option that is exercised against its seller may lead to potentially very big losses and option sellers therefore need to have offsetting positions in either the FFA or the physical market in order to reduce their exposure.

In this chapter we discuss these two important issues. In the first part we discuss the challenges practitioners face in pricing freight options and the models and techniques that have been developed for their valuation. Then, in the second part, we discuss the hedging techniques that option sellers can use in order to reduce the risk of their short positions.

8.2 Pricing freight options

In general, the following methods can be used to price options: 'analytical' or 'closed-form' solutions; 'Monte Carlo simulation'; and the 'tree-building methodology'. A closed-form solution is the solution to a differential equation that expresses the change in option value relative to all the key variables which affect its value, and results in an exact equation that provides the value of the option; examples of closed form-solution include the Black-Scholes (1973), Merton (1973) and Black (1976) models. The major advantage of closed-form solutions is their flexibility and the fact that they are easy to use and quick to give the option value. On the other hand, the more complicated the underlying process and the more complicated the type of option to be priced, the more difficult – if not impossible – it becomes to arrive at a closed-form solution. Hence, solving for closed-form solutions often remains an ultimate and yet also an unattainable option-valuation technique (see also Pilipovic, 2007).

The second approach is Monte Carlo simulation. This involves simulating the underlying market variables and calculating the expected option payoff at the expiry of the contract. By performing a large number of simulations, one can obtain an empirical distribution of the option payoffs; the average of these payoffs across a large number of simulations is then discounted back to obtain the present value of the option. The advantage of this technique is that it can accommodate very easily path-dependent options, such as average price freight options, which can only be valued approximately using closed-form solutions. In addition, it is relatively easy to modify the underlying process by incorporating additional stochastic factors, which results in a more realistic model for the underlying prices and, hence, more accurate option prices. However, Monte Carlo simulation is a computer-intensive method and hence may not be practical to use in real-life trading situations when one wants to, say, price a portfolio of options or perform mark-to-market calculations and time is of the essence.

The third strategy for options pricing is the building of underlying price trees. In this setting, at each time-step, there is a probability of the asset moving up by a certain amount and a probability of it moving down by another amount. Trees provide a means for pricing American-style options which is more complicated to implement using Monte Carlo. This is also why tree methods are widely used in the evaluation of real options, where there are many early exercise features. On the other hand, trees cannot accommodate easily path-dependent options such as average price freight options. The trees can also be extended to become trinomial trees where, at each time step, there are three possible outcomes. Tree methods and their applications for real options valuation are discussed in Chapter 14.

The topic of options pricing is vast and there are numerous papers on the subject. Hence, necessarily, the discussion in this chapter focuses on the applications and models that are applicable to pricing freight options. We discuss both closed-form solutions and the use of Monte Carlo simulation for pricing freight options.

8.2.1   Which approach is better for pricing freight options?

Pricing freight options presents a number of challenges for researchers. First, the underlying asset of the option, which is the freight rate produced by the

Baltic Exchange, is not a tradable asset because freight rates reflect the cost of providing the service of seaborne transportation which, by its own nature, cannot be stored or carried forward in time. As a result, arbitrage between the underlying spot freight market and options across time and space is limited. Although the spot Baltic rates are not tradable assets, the FFAs on these routes are regularly traded contracts that can be used in a replicating strategy, that is, when delta hedging a short option position (see Section 8.9.1 for more on delta hedging). Therefore the information contained in the FFA rates should be used when pricing derivatives on freight and, hence, the pricing model used for freight options should be based on the Black (1976) model for pricing options on futures.

Second, freight options are settled as 'average price Asian options'. These are options whose final payoff is based on the average level of the underlying asset price over a period of time. There are two basic styles of Asian options: 'average price options' – when the average spot price over a specified period prior to maturity is used as the underlying price for the payoff calculation; and 'average strike options' – when the average spot price over some period prior the maturity is used as strike price. In addition, both arithmetic and geometric averages can be used in the calculation of settlement rates, with the arithmetic average being the more popular. The options used in the FFA market are 'arithmetic average price options'; therefore, the payoff at expiry of an average price Asian call to the holder of the option is $\max\left(\sum_{i=1}^{n} S_i/n - X, 0\right)$ while the payoff at expiry of an average price Asian put is $\max\left(X - \sum_{i=1}^{n} S_i/n, 0\right)$ where S_i is the underlying spot rate at time i, and n denotes the number of days used in the calculation of the average, which for FFA options is usually the number of trading days in the settlement month.[1] Like European options, these options can only be exercised on the settlement date of the contracts.

As is the case with FFAs, the calculation of an average settlement rate is used in order to ensure that settlement rates are not susceptible to large moves due to very high volatility or market manipulation on any specific trading day. For instance, an attempt to manipulate the underlying price just before settlement will have little impact on the settlement price if this is calculated as the average of the month and consists of 21 individual data points. This also explains why Asian options are quite popular in either thinly traded markets, or in markets where there is very high volatility, such as the market for freight. In addition, since the volatility of the average price is less than the volatility of the underlying, the premium for an Asian option will

---

[1] Similarly, the payoffs of average strike options are $\max\left(S - \sum_{i=1}^{n} S_i/n, 0\right)$ and $\max\left(\sum_{i=1}^{n} S_i/n - S, 0\right)$ for calls and puts respectively.

generally be lower than the premium for an otherwise identical European option.[2]

Pricing Asian options is more complicated than pricing 'plain vanilla' European options. There are two types of average options: 'geometric' and 'arithmetic'. For geometric average price options there is a closed-form solution for calculating their price, developed by Kemna and Vorst (1990). However these options are rarely traded in commodity markets and are not traded at all in the freight markets and hence are not discussed here (see Haug, 2007, for more details on the pricing of geometric average options).

Regarding the more popular arithmetic-average price options, it is very difficult to develop a closed-form solution for their valuation. The main reason for this is that when the asset is assumed to be lognormally distributed, the arithmetic average of a set of lognormal distributions does not have analytically tractable properties. However, the distribution is approximately lognormal and this leads to a number of analytical approximations for the valuation of these options (Hull, 2006). In the next section, we will consider some of those approximations that have been proposed in the literature and will analyse their application in pricing options on freight. Alternatively, arithmetic-average options can also be priced, perhaps more easily, using Monte Carlo simulation, which is discussed in Section 8.5.

We commence our discussion on option pricing models with the Black-Scholes (1973), Merton (1973) and Black (1976) models; although these models are not directly applicable for pricing Asian options on freight they nevertheless provide a valuable benchmark – particularly the Black model – against which other models may be compared and implied volatilities may be calculated. Then we discuss option-pricing models that have been developed for the valuation of average-price Asian options, such as the Turnbull and Wakeman (1991), Lévy (1997) and Haug et al. (2003) and Curran (1992) approximations, as well as the valuation model of Koekebakker et al. (2007), for the valuation of average-price freight options; we also compare the option premia generated from the different models. Finally, we discuss and present an example of the use of Monte Carlo simulation for pricing average-price freight options.

8.2.2 The Black-Scholes-Merton (BSM) model (1973)

The breakthrough in options-pricing theory came with the famous papers by Black and Scholes (1973) and Merton (1973) (henceforth BSM). They were the first to show that options could be priced by constructing a risk-free hedge through dynamically managing a simple portfolio consisting of the underlying asset and cash. They assumed that the underlying asset, S, follows

---

[2] One exception is when the option is in the averaging period in which case the value of an average-rate option can naturally be higher than that of a similar standard option, depending of the realisation of the asset price (Haug, 2007).

the following stochastic differential equation:

$$\frac{dS}{S} = \mu dt + \sigma dz \tag{8.1}$$

Where: dS represents an increment in the asset price process during an infinitesimal interval of time, dt; μ and σ are the drift and volatility of S, respectively; dz is the underlying uncertainty driving the model; dz presents an increment in a standard normal random variable over an infinitesimal interval of time, $dz = \varepsilon\sqrt{dt}$, where $\varepsilon \sim N(0,1)$. Equation (8.1) implies that the percentage changes (that is, returns) in the value of the underlying asset are completely random and independent of the past price behaviour of the asset. We call this process for the behaviour of the underlying variable a geometric Brownian motion (GBM).

BSM showed that, assuming the underlying asset follows the GBM process of equation (8.1), one can construct a portfolio consisting of a short position in a call option, C, and a certain number of units of the underlying asset, S, which is instantaneously riskless and hence earns the risk-free rate. In addition, they also showed that in this case, the derivatives contract, C, must satisfy the following partial differential equation:

$$\frac{\partial C}{\partial t} + rS\frac{\partial C}{\partial S} + \frac{1}{2}\sigma^2 S^2 \frac{\partial^2 C}{\partial S^2} = rC \tag{8.2}$$

Any derivative whose payoff is contingent on the level of the asset price following equation (8.1) must satisfy equation (8.2). In order to evaluate the value of a derivative, equation (8.2) must be solved with the appropriate boundary conditions, which are the option's payoff at expiry ($C_T = max(S_T - X, 0)$ for European calls, and $P_T = max(X - S_T, 0)$ for European puts), which yields the Black-Scholes (1973) option-pricing formula for calculating the values of European calls, C, and European puts, P[3]:

$$C = SN(d_1) - Xe^{-rT}N(d_2)$$

$$P = Xe^{-rT}N(-d_2) - SN(-d_1) \tag{8.3}$$

Where $N(d_1)$ is the cumulative normal distribution function measuring the area under the standard normal curve that lies to the left of d_1, and d_1 and

---

[3] The derivation of the Black-Scholes option-pricing formula requires some background knowledge on solving partial differential equations and, hence, is outside the scope of this book. For more on the derivation of the Black-Scholes (1973) model see Haug (2007), Hull (2006) and Wilmott et al. (1997).

d_2 are given by:

$$d_1 = \frac{\ln(S/X) + \left(r + \frac{\sigma^2}{2}\right)T}{\sigma\sqrt{T}} \quad \text{and} \quad d_2 = d_1 - \sigma\sqrt{T} \tag{8.4}$$

where: S is the underlying asset; X is the strike price of the option; r is the risk-free rate; σ is the annualised volatility of the underlying asset; and T is the time to maturity of the option, measured as a fraction of a year. The use of the risk-free rate for discounting is based on the notion of the risk-neutral valuation and the fact that the portfolio of the derivative and the underlying is risk-free and should thus earn the risk-free rate. We can see that as pricing inputs in the formula we have all those parameters identified in Chapter 7 as being the determinants of the option's price – namely, the current spot price for the underlying asset, S, the strike price, X, the time to expiry of the option, T, the interest rate (risk-free rate) over the time to maturity of the option, r, and the volatility of the underlying asset, σ.

It can be seen from the formulae for d_1 and d_2 in equation (8.4), that as T approaches zero ($T \to 0$, that is, as the option approaches its expiration) and $S \geq X$, then both d_1 and d_2 approach infinity ($d_1, d_2 \to \infty$). As a result, both $N(d_1)$ and $N(d_2)$ approach one, while $N(-d_1)$ and $N(-d_2)$ approach zero. This in turn suggests that the call-option value becomes $S - X$, while the put-option value becomes zero. On the other hand, as ($T \to 0$) and $S < X$, then both d_1 and d_2 approach negative infinity ($d_1, d_2 \to -\infty$). As a result, both $N(d_1)$ and $N(d_2)$ approach zero, while $N(-d_1)$ and $N(-d_2)$ approach one, which in turn implies that the call-option value becomes zero, while the put-option value becomes $X - S$. These two conditions are also the boundary conditions necessary for the derivation of the Black-Scholes model. It should also be mentioned that, for a call option, $N(d_1)$ is the option's delta (see Section 8.9) while $N(d_2)$ reflects the probability that a call option will expire in-the-money at maturity.

8.2.3 The Black Model (1976)

The Black (1976) model (also known as 'Black 76') is an extension of the Black-Scholes model that gives the value of a European option written on a futures or forward contract F_0, which matures at some time s in the future where $s > T$. In this case the underlying asset is the forward contract and this is also the contract we use in order to delta hedge a short-option position. Assuming that the underlying forward rate is lognormally distributed, the value of the call and put options is calculated as:

$$C = e^{-rT}[F_0 N(d_1) - X N(d_2)]$$

$$P = e^{-rT}[X N(-d_2) - F_0 N(-d_1)] \tag{8.5}$$

where
$$d_1 = \frac{\ln(F_0/X) + \sigma^2 T/2}{\sigma\sqrt{T}}$$

$$d_2 = \frac{\ln(F_0/X) - \sigma^2 T/2}{\sigma\sqrt{T}} = d_1 - \sigma\sqrt{T}$$

where σ is the volatility of the futures contract. Typically this depends on the maturity of the contract due to the volatility term structure of forward rates, as well as its seasonal behaviour. Generally, the maturity of the option T should be less than or equal to the maturity of the futures contract. In the case where both expire at the same time, for a lognormal forward price for an asset that pays no dividends, an option written on the futures is equivalent to an option written on the spot. To illustrate this, consider the spot-forward relationship $F_0 = Se^{rT}$. Substituting this in the Black (1976) model results in:

$$C = e^{-rT}[Se^{rT}N(d_1) - XN(d_2)] = C = SN(d_1) - Xe^{-rT}N(d_2)$$

8.2.4   The Turnbull and Wakeman approximation (1991)

Turnbull and Wakeman adjust the mean and variance of the underlying process so that they are consistent with the exact moments of the arithmetic average. The adjusted mean, b_A, and variance σ_A are then used as inputs in the Black 76 version of equation (8.5):

$$C \approx Se^{(b_A - r)T}N(d_1) - Xe^{-rT}N(d_2)$$

$$P \approx Xe^{-rT}N(-d_2) - Se^{(b_A - r)T}N(-d_1) \tag{8.6}$$

$$d_1 = \frac{\ln(S/X) + (b_A + \sigma_A^2/2)\,T}{\sigma_A\sqrt{T}} \quad d_2 = d_1 - \sigma_A\sqrt{T}$$

The volatility and adjusted mean are given by:

$$\sigma_A = \sqrt{\frac{\ln(M_2)}{T} - 2b_A}$$

$$b_A = \frac{\ln(M_1)}{T} \tag{8.7}$$

where M_1 and M_2 are the first and second moments of the arithmetic average, under risk neutrality. In the case where the cost of carry is zero, as is the case with freight options which are effectively options on forwards, the underlying asset price in equation (8.6) will be the FFA rate, so that the formula is similar to the Black (1976) model, and M_1 and M_2 are calculated as:

$$M_1 = 1 \quad \text{and} \quad M_2 = \frac{2e^{\sigma^2 T} - 2e^{\sigma^2 t_1}[1 + \sigma^2(T - t_1)]}{\sigma^4(T - t_1)^2}$$

where T is the time to maturity of the option and t_1 is the time to the beginning of the averaging period and, since $M_1 = 1$, $\beta_A = 0$ in equation (8.7). In this case, σ_A is the volatility of the average on the futures σ_A.

If the option is in the averaging period, the strike price must be replaced by $\hat{X}$, and the option value must be multiplied by T/T_2, where $\hat{X} = \dfrac{T_2}{T}X - \dfrac{\tau}{T}S_A$, T_2 is the time-span of the (original) averaging period, $\tau = T_2 - T$ is the realised average period so far and S_A is the average asset price during the realised or observed time period so far. If we are into the averaging period, $\tau > 0$, and $\dfrac{T_2}{T}X - \dfrac{\tau}{T}S_A < 0$, then a call option will certainly be exercised and is equal to the expected value of the average at maturity under risk neutrality, minus the strike price $e^{-rT}(E[S_A] - X)$. Similarly, the put in this case will be out-of-the-money and will have a value of zero.

8.2.5 Lévy (1997) and Haug et al. (2003) Discrete Asian Approximation

The Turnbull and Wakeman approximation is based on the assumption that the arithmetic average of the underlying rate is calculated on a continuous basis. In practice, all traded Asian options have discrete fixings on their average – for instance, every day of the week. This is also the case for freight options which are settled as the average of the daily observations of the underlying index over the settlement month. For that, it is more appropriate to use the discrete time approximation of the formulae to value Asian options. For instance, Lévy, (1997) and Haug et al. (2003) extend the Turnbull and Wakeman approximation to value Asian options with discrete time fixings as follows:

$$C_A \approx e^{-rT}[F_A N(d_1) - X N(d_2)]$$

$$P_A \approx e^{-rT}[X N(-d_2) - F_A N(-d_1)] \tag{8.8}$$

where

$$d_1 = \frac{\ln(F_A/X) + T\,\sigma_A^2/2}{\sigma_A\sqrt{T}} \quad \text{and} \quad d_2 = d_1 - \sigma_A\sqrt{T}$$

F_A is defined as $E[A_T]$, and, if the cost-of-carry is zero, σ_A in equation (8.9) is calculated as:

$$\sigma_A = \sqrt{\frac{\ln(E[A_T^2]) - 2\ln(E[A_T])}{T}}$$

$$E[A_T] = S$$

$$E[A_T^2] = \frac{S^2 e^{\sigma^2 t_1}}{n^2}\left[\frac{1 - e^{\sigma^2 hn}}{1 - e^{\sigma^2 h}} + \frac{2}{1 - e^{\sigma^2 h}}\left(n - \frac{1 - e^{\sigma^2 hn}}{1 - e^{\sigma^2 h}}\right)\right]$$

where: T is the time to maturity expressed as a fraction of a year; t_1 is the time remaining to the first averaging point, also expressed as a fraction of a calendar year; n is the number of averaging points (such as the number of days in a month, if averaging takes place over a calendar month); and, $h = \dfrac{(T - t_1)}{(n - 1)}$ reflects the time-span of one averaging period. If the option is in the averaging period, then the strike price must be replaced by $\hat{X}$ as follows:

$$\hat{X} = \frac{nX - mS_A}{n - m} \tag{8.9}$$

and the option value must be multiplied by $\dfrac{m}{n - m}$, where m represents the number of averaging points which have already been realised, so that $m > 0$ and S_A is the average asset price during the realised or observed time period so far. Moreover, if $S_A > \dfrac{n}{m}X$ then the exercise is certain for a call and, in the case of a put, it must end up out-of-the-money. So the value of the put must be zero, while the value of the call must be $C_A = e^{-rT}(\hat{S}_A - X)$ where $\hat{S}_A = S_A \dfrac{m}{n} + E[A] \dfrac{n - m}{n}$.

8.2.6   Curran's approximation (1992)

Curran (1992) developed an approximation method for pricing Asian options. This approach uses the mathematical technique known as 'conditioning' to compute the expected discounted risk-neutral payoff of the option, and involves calculating the expected payoffs of the Asian options conditional on the risk-neutral distribution of the geometric average of the underlying asset. Curran (1992) shows that this method gives more accurate results compared to other closed-form solutions (see also Eydeland and Wolyniec, 2003):

$$C_A \approx e^{-rT}\left[\frac{1}{n}\sum_{i=1}^{n} e^{\mu_i + \sigma_i^2/2} N\left(\frac{\mu - \ln(\hat{X})}{\sigma_x} + \frac{\sigma_{x_i}}{\sigma_x}\right) - X N\left(\frac{\mu - \ln(\hat{X})}{\sigma_x}\right)\right]$$

$$\tag{8.10}$$

$$P_A \approx e^{-rT}\left[X N\left(-\frac{\mu - \ln(\hat{X})}{\sigma_x}\right) - \frac{1}{n}\sum_{i=1}^{n} e^{\mu_i + \sigma_i^2/2} N\left(-\frac{\mu - \ln(\hat{X})}{\sigma_x} - \frac{\sigma_{x_i}}{\sigma_x}\right)\right]$$

where

$$\mu_i = \ln(S) + (b - \sigma^2/2)t_i$$

$$\sigma_i = \sqrt{\sigma^2[t_1 + (i - 1)h]}$$

$$\sigma_{x_i} = \sigma^2\{t_1 + h[(i - 1) - i(i - 1)/(2n)]\}$$

$$\mu = \ln(S) + (b - \sigma^2/2)[t_1 + (n-1)h/2]$$

$$\sigma_x = \sqrt{\sigma^2[t_1 + h(n-1)(2n-1)/6n]}$$

and

$$\hat{X} = 2X - \frac{1}{n}\sum_{i=1}^{n} \exp\left\{\mu_i + \frac{\sigma_{x_i}[\ln(X) - \mu]}{\sigma_x^2} + \frac{\sigma_i^2 - \sigma_{x_i}^2/\sigma_x^2}{2}\right\}$$

where b is the cost-of-carry of the asset which, in the case of freight, is zero and all the other parameters are the same as used in equation (8.8). If the option is in the averaging period, that is, $m > 0$, then the strike price must be replaced by $X = \dfrac{nX - mS_A}{n - m}$ and the option price must be multiplied by $\dfrac{m}{n - m}$ as discussed in Section 8.2.5.

8.2.7 Applications for freight markets

In addition to the models presented earlier, there are also options-pricing models which have been developed specifically for the pricing of freight options. For instance, Tvedt (1998) derives a formula for pricing freight options on the BIFFEX contract and develops a modified Black 76 model that takes into account the statistical properties of the freight markets, in particular the fact that freight rates are mean-reverting and that they have an 'absorbing' level which reflects the lay-up level of freight rates. However, the model is only applicable to pricing ordinary European options and hence cannot be applied to price options on FFAs.

More recently, Koekebakker et al. (2007) propose an extension of the Black 76 model that deals with average price options, and adapt it for freight. They assume that FFA rates are lognormally distributed; however, when the contract enters the averaging period, lognormality no longer applies and, thus, they propose a lognormal approximation during the settlement period. In general, assuming equidistant observations, the volatility of an FFA contract can be approximated as:

$$\sigma_F^2 = T_1 \cdot \sigma^2 + R(N) \cdot (T_N - T_1) \cdot \sigma^2$$

$$\text{where} \qquad R(N) = \frac{1 - \dfrac{3}{2N} + \dfrac{3}{N^2}}{3 - \dfrac{3}{N}} \tag{8.11}$$

where: σ is the volatility of the underlying spot rate; T_1 is the time remaining before averaging starts; T_N is the time to maturity of the option; $T_N - T_1$ is the averaging period; and, N is the number of days in the averaging period. Assuming that the FFA settles against a continuous average of the freight rates (by letting $N \to \infty$) then $R(N) \to 1/3$.

The first part of the volatility formula, $T_1\sigma^2$, reflects the volatility prior to the averaging period while the second part, $R(N)(T_N - T_1)\sigma^2$, reflects the volatility during the averaging period. Koekebakker et al. (2007) point out that this approximation is better the shorter the delivery period and the further in the future delivery takes place. The formula suggests that during the settlement period, volatility will also decrease as more of the realised freight in the averaging period is known. This is expected, since large movements in the market during the averaging period will have a smaller impact on the FFA rates; the further we progress in the averaging period, the smaller this impact is going to be.

The volatility plug-in calculated above can then be used as the volatility input in the Black 76 model. To illustrate why this is the case, consider an FFA contract: the price of that contract, $F(t, T_1, T_N)$, is the price set today, at time t, to deliver at time T_N, the arithmetic average of the underlying freight during the period (T_1, T_N). For instance, in the case of an FFA on the average of the 4 TC routes, which is settled as the average of a month, T_1 and T_N are the first and last trading days of the settlement month respectively. Similarly, the payoff of an Asian call option on freight will be: $C(t, T_1, T_N) = \max(F(T_N, T_1, T_N) - X, 0)$. Therefore, this Asian option can be considered as a European option on an FFA, since the payoff of the option is identical to that of an FFA. Therefore, one can use the volatility plug-in as an input in the Black 76 model, as follows:

$$C(t, T_1, T_N) = e^{-rT}[F(t, T_1, T_N)N(d_1) - XN(d_2)]$$

$$P(t, T_1, T_N) = e^{-rT}[XN(-d_2) - F(t, T_1, T_N)N(-d_1)]$$

$$\text{where} \quad d_1 = \frac{\ln(F(t, T_1, T_N)/X) + \frac{1}{2}\sigma_F^2}{\sigma_F} \tag{8.12}$$

$$d_2 = \frac{\ln(F(t, T_1, T_N)/X) - \frac{1}{2}\sigma_F^2}{\sigma_F} = d_1 - \sigma_F$$

where σ_F is the volatility plug-in of equation (8.11). When we are in the averaging period $(t > T_1)$ we have to adjust the strike price and the FFA price, which will be used as the inputs in the Black 76 formula, as follows:

$$\overline{X} = X - \frac{t - T_1}{T_N - T_1}A_R \quad \text{and} \quad \overline{F}(t, t, T_N) = \frac{T_N - t_1}{T_N - T_1}F(t, t, T_N)$$

where A_R is the realised average spot freight rate from T_1 to t. Thus the strike price is replaced by the realised spot freight rate average; similarly, the FFA price input is weighted by the time to settlement relative to the original settlement period.

Using equation (8.12), caps and floors can be valued as sums of individual calls and puts. In addition, multi-period call-and-put options such as, for instance, calendar option contracts, can be valued as the sum of 12 individual

Table 8.1   Comparison of option premia for TD3 (in WS points)

		Panel A: ATM options								
		Calls					Puts			
T	FFA	TW	LV	CR	KK	BL	TW	LV	CR	KK	BL
Oct 07	78	4.68	4.64	4.64	4.65	6.83	4.68	4.64	4.64	4.65	6.83
Nov 07	92	9.20	9.17	9.17	9.17	10.90	9.20	9.17	9.17	9.17	10.90
Dec 07	94	12.00	11.98	11.98	11.98	13.39	12.00	11.98	11.98	11.98	13.39
Jan 08	90	13.51	13.49	13.49	13.49	14.64	13.51	13.49	13.49	13.49	14.64
Feb 08	86	14.56	14.55	14.54	14.55	15.52	14.56	14.55	14.54	14.55	15.52

		Panel B: 10 per cent OTM options								
		Calls					Puts			
T	FFA	TW	LV	CR	KK	BL	TW	LV	CR	KK	BL
Oct 07	78	1.97	1.94	1.95	1.94	3.94	1.59	1.57	1.55	1.57	3.32
Nov 07	92	5.75	5.73	5.73	5.73	7.43	4.90	4.88	4.87	4.88	6.40
Dec 07	94	8.46	8.45	8.44	8.45	9.87	7.32	7.30	7.30	7.31	8.58
Jan 08	90	10.15	10.13	10.13	10.13	11.31	8.84	8.83	8.83	8.83	9.89
Feb 08	86	11.39	11.38	11.37	11.38	12.38	9.97	9.96	9.96	9.96	10.86

		Panel C: 10 per cent ITM options								
		Calls					Puts			
T	FFA	TW	LV	CR	KK	BL	TW	LV	CR	KK	BL
Oct 07	78	9.38	9.35	9.33	9.35	11.11	9.75	9.72	9.73	9.73	11.72
Nov 07	92	14.07	14.05	14.04	14.05	15.56	14.92	14.89	14.89	14.90	16.60
Dec 07	94	16.67	16.65	16.65	16.66	17.93	17.81	17.80	17.79	17.80	19.22
Jan 08	90	17.78	17.77	17.76	17.77	18.82	19.09	19.07	19.07	19.07	20.25
Feb 08	86	18.50	18.49	18.48	18.49	19.39	19.92	19.90	19.90	19.90	20.90

Note: TD3 FFA rates, in WS points, are provided by Imarex (24 September 2007) and are the underlying rates for the calculation of the relevant options.

call-and-put options for each one of the 12 months during the settlement year.

8.2.8   An option-pricing example

In order to compare the different models, we calculate the option premia for call and puts from the different models presented in the previous section. The option premia are calculated using the Imarex TD3 forward curve on 24 September 2007 and the results are presented in Table 8.1. The first column presents the forward curve for TD3 on 24 September 2007 for the next five nearest maturities, which are used as the underlying rates for the different option-pricing models. We then calculate option premia using the following models, discussed in the previous sections: the Turnbull and Wakeman (1991) approximation of equation (8.6) with continuously calculated average, denoted as TW; the discrete time approximation of TW by Lévy (1997) and Haug et al. (2003) of equation (8.8), denoted as LV; the Curran (1992) approximation of equation (8.10), denoted as CR; and the Koekebakker et al. (2007) approximation of equations (8.11) and (8.12), denoted as KK. Finally, for comparison purposes we also calculate the option prices generated by the Black 76 model of equation (8.5), denoted as BL.

The underlying asset in each case is the FFA forward curve at the relevant maturity. The first option, which expires on October 2007, will enter the averaging period in four trading days and the settlement rate will be calculated as the average of the month, assuming that we have 21 averaging points for each monthly contract. In addition, we assume a flat volatility term structure of 70 per cent per annum; although this contrasts with the fact that we expect volatility term structure to prevail in the market and thus volatilities to gradually decrease as we consider more distant FFA contracts, we make this assumption in order to compare consistently the option premia across different maturities and strike prices. In Section 8.3 we discuss how a volatility term structure can be incorporated into the models discussed here. We also assume an interest rate of 2 per cent in all cases. Finally, we consider three different sets of options: ATM options, presented in Panel A, where the strike price for each maturity is set equal to the FFA rate for the specified maturity; 10 per cent OTM options in Panel B, where the strike price is 10 per cent above the FFA rate for the relevant call maturity and 10% below the FFA rate for the put; and 10 per cent ITM in Panel C, where the strike is 10 per cent below the FFA rate for calls and vice-versa for the puts.

Several points are worth noting. In all cases, we can note that the Black 76 model results in higher call-and-put option premia, due to the fact that the volatility used is higher because there is no adjustment for the impact of the averaging period. However, the difference in the premia between Black 76 and the other approximations becomes relatively smaller as the maturity of the options increases. As time to maturity increases, then the fixed averaging period of one calendar month becomes a relatively smaller proportion of the option maturity horizon; this results in the premium of an average price option to be relatively closer to the premium of a standard European option for the corresponding period, compared to options that are nearer to maturity. In fact, at the limit, as the averaging period becomes an infinitesimal time period prior to expiry, the premium of an average price option becomes approximately equal to that of a European option (see Lévy and Turnbull, 1992).

We can also note that all the discrete-time approximations (such as LV, CR and KK) generate option premia which are very similar, and this pattern seems to be consistent for both calls and puts, and across all maturities and different levels of option moneyness. It also appears that any discrepancies between the option premia become smaller as we move into longer-maturity contracts. Comparing the premia calculated using the Turnbull and Wakeman (TW) approximation we can see that, in all cases, the TW model slightly overvalues the option premia compared to the other discrete-time approximations, and this seems to be the case for both calls and puts across all maturities and strike levels. This is due to the fact that in general the volatility of the continuous-time average is slightly higher than the volatility of the discrete-time average. This difference in volatilities becomes smaller as we move into longer-maturity contracts, since the averaging period becomes a smaller proportion of the total time-to-maturity of the option; this results in the option premia, calculated using the TW approximation, getting closer to the premia calculated from the other models.

Finally, we can also note that at-the-money calls and puts have the same value, reflecting the forward put-call parity relationship, $C = P + (F - X)e^{-rT}$, discussed in Chapter 7. We can see that when the options are ATM ($F = X$), then $C = P$ and the call-and-put premia will be the same. This is generally the case for options before the averaging period. When the options enter the averaging period, the put-call parity relationship is modified to take into account the calculation of the average, as shown in Lévy and Turnbull (1992).

8.3 Asian options with volatility term structure

In the previous example, we assumed that the volatility term structure was flat. However, as already discussed, because the underlying spot freight rates are mean-reverting, we expect a volatility term structure in the FFA rates; in other words, volatility becomes a function of time to maturity and declines the longer the time to maturity of the FFA contract. To illustrate why this is the case, consider the following example. If the spot market experiences a sudden drop in the level of freight rates below the normal or long-run average freight rate, then this is going to primarily affect the FFA contracts with short time to maturity, which are expected to decrease in value. Longer-maturity contracts, on the other hand, are also expected to decrease, but to a much lesser extent. This is due to the mean reversion of the spot freight rates, which implies that, despite the decrease in the spot market, freight rates are expected to revert back to their normal levels before the maturity of the longer-dated FFA contract. The opposite will happen when there is a positive shock in the freight market. Therefore, due to the mean reversion of the spot freight rates, we expect the volatility of the short-dated contracts to be higher than the volatility of the longer-dated contracts and also expect the volatility of an FFA contract to increase as the contract approaches settlement.

Volatility term structure has a number of implications for market participants. For instance, it explains why margin curves are a decreasing function of time to maturity, as discussed in Chapter 5. Volatility term structure is also important when it comes to options pricing. If we ignore volatility term structure and assume a flat volatility irrespective of the maturity of an option, then we would tend to undervalue short-maturity options and overvalue long-dated ones; this has important consequences for trading and risk managing short option positions. Therefore, volatility term structure becomes an important factor which should be considered in options pricing.

Using the approximations for pricing average price options that we considered in the previous section, volatility term structure can be incorporated by modifying the volatility input in the relevant options-pricing model. For instance, Haug et al. (2003) propose calibrating the volatility of the arithmetic discrete average to the term structure of implied volatilities, using the following formulae:

$$\sigma_A = \sqrt{\frac{\ln(E[A_T^2]) - 2\ln(E[A_T])}{T}} \tag{8.13}$$

where

$$E[A_T] = \frac{1}{n} \sum_{i=1}^{n} F_i$$

$$E[A_T^2] = \frac{S^2}{n^2} \sum_{i=1}^{n} e^{(2b+\sigma_i^2)t_i} + 2 \sum_{i=1}^{n} \sum_{j=i+1}^{n} e^{(b+\sigma_i^2)t_i} e^{bt_j}$$

where F_i is the forward price at fixing i, and σ_i is the plain vanilla volatility for an option with expiration t_i where t_i is the time to fixing i. In the case of an option on futures, $b = 0$, in which case $E[A_T] = S$, we can then approximate the value of the arithmetic call option as:

$$C_A \approx e^{-rT}[F_A N(d_1) - X N(d_2)]$$

$$P_A \approx e^{-rT}[X N(-d_2) - F_A N(-d_1)]$$

where

$$d_1 = \frac{\ln(F_A/X) + T\sigma_A^2/2}{\sigma_A\sqrt{T}} \quad \text{and} \quad d_2 = d_1 - \sigma_A\sqrt{T} \tag{8.14}$$

This is essentially the Black 76 formula with modified asset price and volatility. Empirical evidence suggests that this model works best for reasonably low volatility – for instance, spot volatility less than 30 per cent (Haug, 2007). However, it is in general far better to use a relatively simple approximation which takes into account the term structure of volatility than to use a more accurate model that does not calibrate to the term structure.

Another approximation is the one proposed by Koekebakker and Ollmar (2005). Although published earlier, this is in effect an extension of the Koekebakker et al. (2007) volatility plug-in designed to take into account the volatility term structure of FFA contracts. In this case, volatility decreases with time to maturity due to mean reversion, thus creating a volatility term structure. Then, as the contract enters into the averaging period, volatility gradually decreases due to the effect of averaging. Their approach is different from the Haug et al. (2003) model because they do not calibrate the option prices on the traded implied volatilities in the market, but instead estimate the volatility plug-in on the basis of the speed of mean reversion, which is estimated from spot prices or from the observed forward curve.

8.4 Implied volatility

Any closed-form solution model offers an easily computable formula to calculate the fair price of an option, simply by inputting the five available pricing ingredients, namely: the price of the underlying asset; the strike price of the option; the time to maturity; the risk-free rate; and the volatility. Of all these pricing inputs the one parameter which cannot be directly observed in the market is the volatility of the underlying asset. In Chapter 3 we discussed how volatility can be estimated and forecasted from past or historical freight rates using a variety of techniques. The availability of traded options also provides another source of volatility, which is the market volatility implied by the prices of traded options and is simply known as 'implied volatility'.

This reflects the market's view about the volatility of the underlying asset over the time-to-maturity of an option contract and is the value of σ in the option-pricing formula that when substituted in the closed-form solution will give the market value of the option. However, it is not possible to invert the option-pricing formula so that volatility can be expressed as a function of S, X, r, T and C, and, as a result, implied volatility is calculated using iterative search procedures such as, for instance, using the solver function in Excel.[4] To illustrate this procedure, consider the following example: on 24 September 2007, the ATM October 2007 TD3 option is quoted on the Imarex screen at 6.1 WS points. The underlying FFA rate is 78 WS points, the option will enter the averaging period in four trading days and averaging will take place over each trading day in September (21 days in total). Assuming that interest rates are 2 per cent, we use the Lévy (1997) approximation of equation (8.8) with the following pricing parameters: $F_A = X = 78$, $C_A = 6.1$, $r = 2$ per cent, $T = 25/252 = 0.099$, $t_1 = 4/252 = 0.020$ and $n = 21$. Therefore, given these pricing parameters, the objective is to find the value of σ_A in equation (8.8) which, when substituted in the model, will give the market

---

[4] For a discussion of other more advanced and faster procedures for extracting implied volatilities from quoted option prices see Haug (2007) and Hull (2006).

Table 8.2 Imarex TD3 implied volatilities on 24 September 2007

	FFA rate	−10 WS points	ATM	+10 WS points
Oct 07	78.0	94.3%	92.0%	94.3%
Nov 07	92.0	75.9%	74.0%	75.9%
Dec 07	94.0	60.5%	59.0%	60.5%
Jan 08	90.0	56.4%	55.0%	56.4%
Feb 08	86.0	51.3%	50.0%	51.3%

Source: Imarex.

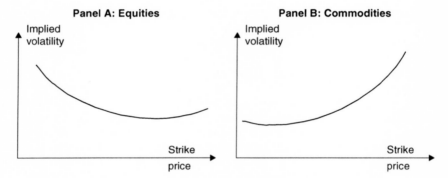

Figure 8.1 Empirical volatility smiles for equities and commodities

option value of 6.1 WS points. Using the solver function in Excel we find the implied volatility to be approximately 92 per cent.

Table 8.2 presents the implied volatilities for TD3. These are calculated by Imarex based on market quotes for these options on that day using the Lévy (1997) approximation of equation (8.8). The volatilities are available for ATM options, +10 and −10 WS points from the ATM strikes. Two important observations can be made by looking at this report. The first is that, as the time to maturity of the option increases, implied volatilities decrease. This pattern is consistent with the volatility term structure in the FFA market and, as discussed in the previous section, is due to the mean reversion of spot freight rates. The second and perhaps more important observation is that we can note that, in general, low- and high-strike implied volatilities are higher than ATM implied volatilities.

This variability in implied volatilities across different strikes can be observed in most financial and commodity markets and is called a 'volatility smile' because when implied volatilities are plotted against the strike prices, we generally observe a pattern which looks like a smile, as shown in Figure 8.1. We generally observe that volatilities for ITM or OTM options are higher than those for ATM options and this difference, in general, increases the further away we are from the ATM range.

If the assumptions underlying the BSM, Black 76 or the other models that we considered in the previous section were correct, then we would expect implied volatilities for same-maturity options to be the same across the different strikes and hence the graph of the implied volatilities across strikes to be a flat line. One of the reasons for the observed volatility smile is that the actual distribution of the underlying asset has fatter tails than the lognormal distribution, which is the prevailing assumption in the Black 76 model and its approximations used in the valuation of average price options. For instance, descriptive statistics presented in Chapter 3 indicate that freight rates exhibit a higher degree of kurtosis than that which a lognormal distribution would imply. Therefore, because a lognormal distribution understates the probability of extreme movements in the markets, the occurrence of very low or very high prices is higher than that which is implied by a lognormal distribution. As a result, deep OTM calls and puts are more likely to be exercised and hence their premium should be higher than the premium calculated using the Black 76 model. In order to compensate for this discrepancy in the Black 76 model, a trader in the market would need to use a higher implied volatility to price an OTM call or put. In fact, it is established market practice to quote the price of an option in terms of its implied volatility and, effectively, traders adjust the price of the option by assigning different volatility values for options with identical underlying and expiration but different strikes. The dependence of implied volatility on the strike price for options on the same maturity is referred to as 'the smile'. It should also be mentioned that because of the put-call parity relationship, the implied volatility of a European call option is the same as the implied volatility of a European put option when the two have the same strike and maturity. This relationship also holds for average price options and implies that when traders quote implied volatilities they do not need to specify whether they are referring to calls or puts, since the relationship is the same for both.

In practice the volatility strike structure does not have to be a smile. It can take on various shapes, depending on what the actual price distribution of the underlying is, compared to the lognormal distribution. At the other extreme, if the pricing model is built in a way that exactly matches the exact price distribution, the volatility term structure would be flat, that is, it would be the same across all strikes. For instance, the volatility smile used by traders to price equity options (either on individual stocks or stock indices) has the general form shown in Figure 8.1, Panel A. We can see that the volatility decreases as the strike price increases; however, the shape of the smile is not symmetric around the ATM strikes and it seems that the volatility used to price a low strike option (either a deep ITM call or deep OTM put) is significantly higher than that used to price a high strike option (either a deep ITM put or deep OTM call). This is because the implied distribution for equity options has a heavier left tail and a less heavy right tail compared to a lognormal distribution, which is often attributed to the impact of leverage in equity options. As a company's equity declines in value, its leverage – that is, the debt-to-equity ratio – increases as a proportion of the total market value of the company. As a result, the likelihood of default for the company increases, which in turn causes volatilities to increase, making even lower stock prices more likely. On the other hand, as a company's equity increases in value, leverage decreases and, in turn, the volatility of its equity decreases. This is known as the 'leverage effect', and implies that, in general, the implied volatility of equity options should follow the pattern shown in Figure 8.1, Panel A (see as well Section 3.4 and Hull, 2006). This pattern in volatilities no longer presents a smile, since implied volatilities are no longer symmetric around the ATM strikes; this is often known as the 'volatility skew'.

Turning next to commodities, it seems that volatility skew in their case has the opposite direction to that observed in equity markets. For instance, Geman and Nguyen (2003) analysed a database of futures options traded on four energy commodities on NYMEX and found that the volatility smile derived from option prices is skewed to the right and has a shape similar to that presented in Figure 8.1, Panel B, showing that the market is more risk-averse to a rise in commodity prices. Such a pattern is known in the literature as an 'inverse leverage effect'. This reflects the negative impact on the world economy of higher energy and commodity prices in general, and is consistent with the empirical fact that the historical volatility of commodities tends to increase when prices are high and, if there were a wide range of strikes traded in the market, this is also possibly the pattern that one would expect to see in the freight options market. Given the supply and demand fundamentals of the freight market that were analysed in Chapter 2, we expect higher volatility in the market when freight rates are high and supply and demand conditions are very tight. In this case, the fleet is utilised at full capacity and there is very little that can be done to increase the stock of fleet in the short run. As a result, because the market operates at the steep part of the supply curve, volatility in the market will be higher, since even a small change in the supply or demand for shipping services will have a comparatively larger impact on the level of freight rates. It should also be noted, however, that this theoretical conjecture is not supported by the news impact curves for freight, presented in Chapter 3, that indicate the presence of leverage effects in freight markets.

8.5 Pricing Asian options using Monte Carlo simulation

Monte Carlo simulation provides a flexible method for valuing complex derivatives for which analytical formulae are difficult or impossible to obtain. The method is particularly useful for the valuation of complex path-dependent options, such as average-price Asian options. In addition, the method can easily accommodate more realistic underlying price processes for freight rates which may incorporate jumps in prices, mean reversion, seasonality, stochastic volatility and so on. This is also relevant for the freight market because the descriptive statistics and the statistical analysis of the freight rates, discussed in Chapter 2, indicate that freight rates are leptokurtic with a far higher probability of extremely high or low values than that which a lognormal distribution would imply. In this section we describe how Monte Carlo can be used for the valuation of options, and present an example for the valuation of a freight option when the underlying freight rate follows a GBM process.

In general, the value of an option is the discounted payoff of its expectation under some appropriate pricing measure; for instance, in the case of a call option:

$$C = e^{-rt}E^Q[\max(S_T - X, 0)].$$

We can obtain an estimate of this expectation by computing the average of a large number of discounted payoffs, estimated using Monte Carlo simulation. This technique involves simulating the possible paths which the asset price can take from today until the maturity of the option. To illustrate how Monte Carlo simulation can be implemented, consider for instance the GBM process of equation (8.1). The solution of this equation in discrete-time form under the pricing measure Q can be written as:

$$S(t + \Delta t) = S(t)e^{(\lambda - \sigma^2/2)\Delta t + \sigma \varepsilon_t \sqrt{\Delta t}} \tag{8.15}$$

Where: Δt is a small time increment, ε is a random sample from a standard normal distribution $\varepsilon \sim N(0,1)$; $\lambda = \mu - \sigma\gamma$ and γ is a real valued function, often interpreted as the market price of risk, that measures the risk-return trade-off for derivative securities dependent on S; at any given point in time λ should be the same for all derivatives which are only dependent on S and t. If the underlying asset, S, is a tradable security that pays no income, such as, for instance, a stock that pays no dividends, then $\gamma = (\mu - r)/\sigma$ in which case $\lambda = r$ in equation (8.15). In the case of freight options, S is a non-tradable spot freight rate and, hence, one must assume a market price of risk in order to price derivative instruments. Usually, this may be inferred from the market prices of other traded instruments in the market; or, alternatively, one can assume a given value as the market price of risk. For simplicity, in our example we assume that $\gamma = (\mu - r)/\sigma$ and thus set $\lambda = r$. In order to implement Monte Carlo simulation for the purposes of pricing freight options, we can consider the following steps:

Step 1: Simulate one path for the freight rates using the risk-neutral dynamics of equation (8.15). This involves choosing an appropriate time step in equation (8.15), say, for instance, one trading day, so that $\Delta t = 1/252$. In order to price the options we have to simulate the paths of freight rates under the pricing measure which, in our example, involves setting $\lambda = r$. Finally, we use random drawings from a standard normal distribution for the values of ε; these can be calculated easily using the normsinv(rand()) function or the random-number generator add-in in Excel.

Step 2: Calculate the payoff of the option at expiry. For a European call option, this involves calculating max $(S_T - X, 0)$ at the option-expiration date. For an average price Asian option, we calculate the average of the spot freight rates, over the averaging period, and then use that average in the calculation of the payoff.

Step 3: Repeat steps 1 and 2 many times to get a number of sample payoffs. A minimum of 10,000 simulations are typically necessary in order to price an option with satisfactory accuracy, although in real-life applications typically 100,000 or even 1 million simulations may be required. It should be noted that the standard error of the simulations is given by $\dfrac{sd}{\sqrt{n}}$ where sd is the standard deviation of the payoff and n is the number of simulations. Therefore, given a number of iterations, n, in order to double the accuracy of the simulations we need to increase the number of iterations by a factor of four. Therefore, increasing the accuracy of simulations comes at the expense of more computation time required to calculate the results. A number of techniques, such as 'antithetic variables' and 'control variates', are available to speed up the simulation process (see also Hull, 2006).

Step 4: Calculate the mean payoff across all the simulated paths at the option expiration date and discount it at the risk-free rate to get an estimate of the value of the option. Therefore, the eventual value for an average price call option will be calculated using the formula shown below:

$$C = \frac{e^{-rT}}{n} \sum_{i=1}^{n} \max \left[\sum_{j=1}^{m+1} \left[S_{T-j+1} e^{(r-\sigma^2/2)\Delta t + \sigma \varepsilon_{j,i} \sqrt{\Delta t}} \right] \middle/ m - X, 0 \right]$$

Where T is the time to maturity of the option, n is the total number of simulated paths, m is the number of time-steps over which the average rate will be calculated and Δt is the time-step between each averaging point or trading day.

For instance, suppose that we want to price a BPI 4TC call option with a strike price of US$50,000/day. The option expires in three months (63 trading days) and the settlement rate is calculated as the average freight rate over the last trading month, with 21 averaging points in total. The current spot BPI 4TC rate is US$50,000/day ($S = 50,000$), the underlying volatility is

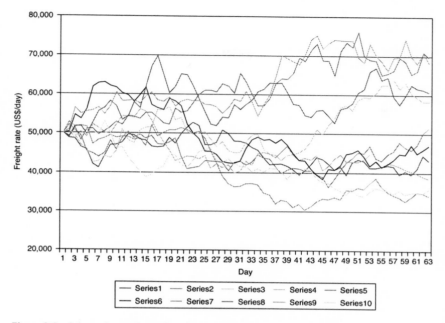

Figure 8.2 Selected sample paths of BPI 4TC Monte Carlo simulation

60 per cent ($\sigma = 0.6$) and the risk-free interest rate in the market is 5 per cent. For the Monte Carlo simulation, we use time-steps of one-day, assuming that there are 252 trading days in a year (that is, $\Delta t = 1/252$). Figure 8.2 presents the paths of ten randomly selected simulated freight rates for the underlying BPI 4TC rates over the next three months.

We then calculate the settlement rate which is the average rate over the last 21 simulated trading points, as shown in Table 8.3. Finally, we calculate the mean payoff across the ten simulated paths which is US\$5787/day. Its discounted present value is the value of the call option today; this is $C = 5787 \, e^{-0.05(63/252)} = \text{US\$5715/day}$. In the example presented here, we estimated the value of the option as the average across only ten simulated paths. In practice, we should be using a larger number of simulations in which case the price of the option changes accordingly. For instance, as we increase the number of simulations to 10,000 the value of the option becomes US\$5462/day; for 100,000 simulations the option becomes US\$5486/day and for 1 million simulations the value of the option is US\$5521/day.

Monte Carlo simulation is easy to implement and works particularly well for path-dependent options, such as Asian options, when analytic solutions are only approximate. The main drawback is that it is a computer-intensive process and thus lacks the speed one gets with closed-form solutions.

Table 8.3 Calculation of call-option payoffs for 10 randomly sample paths

Day	Series 1	Series 2	Series 3	Series 4	Series 5	Series 6	Series 7	Series 8	Series 9	Series 10
1	50,000	50,000	50,000	50,000	50,000	50,000	50,000	50,000	50,000	50,000
2	48,748	52,075	50,839	50,331	48,900	50,254	52,782	49,128	50,875	50,522
⋮	⋮	⋮	⋮	⋮	⋮	⋮	⋮	⋮	⋮	⋮
43	42,127	40,566	48,087	43,375	71,384	41,033	31,298	54,191	74,160	40,598
44	43,946	39,602	51,066	44,471	73,159	39,576	32,592	55,908	75,235	38,657
⋮	⋮	⋮	⋮	⋮	⋮	⋮	⋮	⋮	⋮	⋮
62	44,444	50,143	58,290	39,167	70,946	45,910	34,853	61,320	70,833	34,819
63	43,142	51,505	58,265	38,570	69,714	47,008	34,223	60,684	68,317	35,940
Settlement rate	41,862	44,026	57,747	42,162	69,288	43,304	34,647	59,539	71,294	35,869
Payoff: max(S_{ave}-X,0)	5,787	–	7,747	–	19,288	–	–	9,539	21,294	–

Averaging period (Days 43–63)

Average payoff 5,787

In addition, in the simple GBM case we presented here, the option price should be very close to the prices one gets from some of the approximations we discussed earlier, thus making the benefits of this process less obvious; for instance, in the example presented here, using Curran's approximation in equation (8.10) and setting $b = r$, since the underlying asset is assumed to be the spot freight rate, we get an option premium of US\$5516/day which is less than 0.1 per cent different from the premium we calculated using Monte Carlo.[5] However, the major advantage of Monte Carlo is that it is relatively easy to add additional complexity to the underlying process, by introducing, for instance, stochastic volatility or jump terms. More complex models can capture the underlying properties of freight rates more accurately than a simple GBM model and hence may lead to more accurate option prices. When more complex processes are introduced, it may be very difficult – or impossible – to obtain closed-form solutions for freight options and hence Monte Carlo provides the only method for pricing options. For more on the use of Monte Carlo to price options using more complex underlying processes, compared to GBM, see Clewlow and Strickland (2000).

8.6 Risk management of option positions

A financial institution which sells an option to a client in the OTC market is faced with the problem of managing its risk. As we saw in the previous chapter, a short position in a call or put option that is exercised against its seller may lead to potentially very large losses and hence option sellers need to have offsetting positions in either the FFA or the physical market in order to reduce their exposure.

In this section we discuss the hedging techniques that option sellers can use in order to reduce the risk of their short positions. Although selling protective puts or covered calls covers the risk of exercise, these strategies are not efficient because, for instance, the seller of a call always needs to maintain a long position in the FFA market. For a company selling an option in the market, the most complete hedge is in an exactly offsetting position, for example, long calls bought against short calls sold. The long position is then held as a static hedge, meaning that the hedge need not be changed over

---

[5] Monte Carlo simulation for freight options is usually implemented by simulating the underlying spot freight rate under the risk-neutral measure. Since the underlying asset is non-tradable, we need to incorporate in the simulation the market price of risk. By setting $\lambda = r$ in equation (8.15), implicitly we assume that the underlying is now a tradable asset that pays no dividends, similar, for instance, to a stock index. In order to make the results from the closed-form solution comparable to the option premium calculated using Monte Carlo, we also need to make the same assumption for the underlying asset used in the option-pricing formula, by setting $b = r$ in equation (8.10).

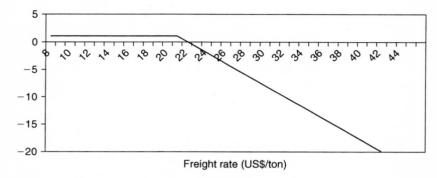

Figure 8.3 Payoff of a short-call option position

time. However, in many cases, particularly when liquidity is low as is the case in the freight market, it may not be possible to trade such a position. In practice, traders in the market use sophisticated hedging strategies using the so-called 'Greek letters' or simply 'Greeks'. Each Greek letter measures the sensitivity of the option price with respect to the fundamental factors which affect its value. Each Greek letter therefore measures a different dimension to the risk of an option position, and the aim of a trader is to manage the Greeks so that all the risks are acceptable. In this section, therefore, we will consider option price sensitivities and how one may set up effective hedging strategies for the management of risk arising from short option positions.

8.7   Hedging a short-call position: an example

Consider the case of an investment bank which has sold a European call option on BCI C4 (150,000 mt coal from Richards Bay to Rotterdam). In mid-November 2006, the underlying freight rate trades at US$20/mt and the option expires in ten weeks' time, at the end of January 2007. The underlying volatility $\sigma = 42$ per cent and the risk-free rate is 5 per cent. Finally, the strike price of the option is $X = US\$21/mt$. The option was sold for US$1.1/mt, representing a total premium of $150,000 \times 1.1 = US\$165,000$. Figure 8.3 shows the payoff of the short-call option position at the option expiration date.

We can see that overall this position leaves the bank exposed to substantial risk at expiry, if the option is eventually exercised, and the bank must take the necessary steps to reduce its risk in this event. One strategy is for the bank to leave the downside open and do nothing for hedging. In this case we say that the bank has adopted a 'naked' position. For instance, if the bank maintains a naked position, and freight rate at expiry is below US$21/mt, the option is not exercised and the bank keeps the premium of US$165,000. On the other hand, if the freight rate at expiry is US$25/mt, then the option is

Table 8.4 Option-price sensitivities with respect to different inputs

Input	Input symbol	Greek parameter	Greek symbol
Underlying price	S	Delta	Δ
Delta	Δ	Gamma	Γ
Time to maturity	T	Theta	Θ
Volatility	σ	Vega	Λ
Interest rate	r	Rho	P

exercised and the bank has to pay the option buyer US$4/mt or US$600,000 in total, which is far greater than the premium the bank received when it sold the option. An alternative approach would be for the bank to fully cover the possibility of an exercise by adopting a 'covered' strategy. This involves buying a January 2007 BCI C4 FFA at a rate of US$20/mt. If the option is exercised the loss will be offset by the higher settlement of the long FFA position. On the other hand, if the freight rate drops to, say, US$15/mt, and the option expires out-of-the-money, then there is a loss of US$5/mt (US$750,000) from the long FFA position, which is considerably greater than the US$1.1/mt premium received.

We can see therefore, that neither approach provides a satisfactory hedge. The option premium is US$1.1/mt which also suggests that the fair cost of setting up a hedging strategy for the short-call option position should be on average equal to that amount; but on any occasion, the cost is liable to range from zero to more than US$750,000. In practice, when selling options, traders in the market use sophisticated hedging techniques involving the Greeks. These are discussed next.

8.8   Option-price sensitivities: 'Greeks'

The sensitivities of an option-pricing formula with respect to the pricing inputs are commonly called Greeks and are usually denoted by letters of the Greek alphabet. These are the partial derivatives of call-and-put prices with respect to the underlying parameters that are used as price inputs in the option-pricing formulae. The following table shows the standard Greeks, with reference to the Black-Scholes (1973) option-pricing formula.

Delta (Δ): The most important Greek is 'Delta', denoted as Δ. This measures the sensitivity of the option value to changes in the value of the underlying asset.

Gamma (Γ): Gamma measures the rate of change of Delta and is, therefore, the second partial derivative of the option with respect to the underlying.

Theta (Θ): Theta measures the change in the value of the option with respect to time. Options are assets whose value decays with the passage of time, and

Table 8.5 Option-price sensitivities for the Black-Scholes (1973) model

Call option	Put option
$\Delta = \dfrac{\partial C}{\partial S} = N(d_1)$	$\Delta = \dfrac{\partial P}{\partial S} = N(-d_1)$
$\Gamma = \dfrac{\partial^2 C}{\partial S^2} = \dfrac{N'(d_1)}{S\sigma\sqrt{T}}$	$\Gamma = \dfrac{\partial^2 P}{\partial S^2} = \dfrac{N'(d_1)}{S\sigma\sqrt{T}}$
$\Theta = \dfrac{\partial C}{\partial T} = -\dfrac{SN'(d_1)\sigma}{2\sqrt{T}} - rXe^{-rT}N(d_2)$	$\Theta = \dfrac{\partial P}{\partial T} = -\dfrac{SN'(d_1)\sigma}{2\sqrt{T}} + rXe^{-rT}N(-d_2)$
$\Lambda = \dfrac{\partial C}{\partial \sigma} = S\sqrt{T}N'(d_1)$	$\Lambda = \dfrac{\partial P}{\partial \sigma} = S\sqrt{T}N'(d_1)$
$P = \dfrac{\partial C}{\partial r} = XTe^{-rT}N(d_2)$	$P = \dfrac{\partial P}{\partial r} = -XTe^{-rT}N(-d_2)$

Note: N'(.) denotes the standard normal distribution function and N(.) is the cumulative standard normal distribution function.

so the theta is (usually) negative for long positions and positive for short positions.

Rho (P): Measures the change in the value of the option with respect to interest rates. Calls rise in value and puts fall as interest rates increase.

Vega (Λ): Vega measures the rate of change of the price of the option with respect to changes in volatility. It is generally positive for long positions and negative for short positions.

Table 8.5 summarises the formulae for the Greeks for European call and put options, calculated from the Black-Scholes (1973) model (see Neftci, 2007, for the derivations). In the next section, we consider each of the Greek parameters in more detail:[6]

8.9 Delta (Δ)

Delta, also known as the 'hedge ratio', shows the change in value of the option in response to a change in the value of the underlying variable. It is the slope of the curve that relates the option price to the price of the underlying asset. Suppose, for instance, that $\Delta = 0.4$; this means that when

---

[6] The Greeks presented here are not the only option price sensitivities of interest. In fact, market traders also calculate the sensitivities of these Greeks with respect to S, σ, T and r. These are higher-order cross partial derivatives that under certain circumstances will be quite relevant to trades. For more details on these additional Greeks see Neftci (2007). Also, our analysis focuses on the Greeks from the Black-Scholes (1973) model since this model provides an established benchmark for traders in the market.

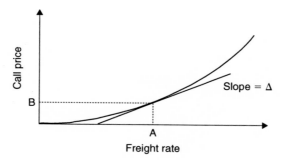

Figure 8.4   Call-option delta calculation

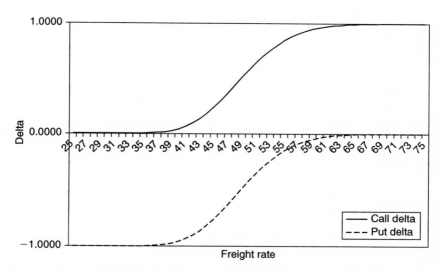

Figure 8.5   Variation of call and put option delta with respect to the value of the underlying ($X = 50$, $r = 5$ per cent, $\sigma = 20$ per cent, $T = 20$ weeks)

the underlying asset changes by, say, US$1/mt, the option will change by 40 per cent of that amount. Figure 8.4 shows the relationship between the call price and the underlying freight rate. When the underlying rate corresponds to point A, the option price corresponds to point B, and Δ is the slope of the line which is tangent to the curve at that point.

Figure 8.5 shows the variation of European call-and-put option deltas with respect to changes in the underlying asset; the parameters of the option are: ($X = 50$, $r = 5$ per cent, $\sigma = 20$ per cent and $T = 20$ weeks). For the European call, $\Delta = N(d_1) \geq 0$ and the call delta will always take values between 0 and 1. More specifically, it will be close to 0 for deep out-of-the-money calls; this is

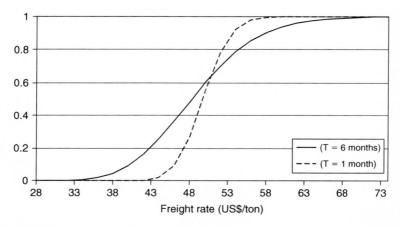

Figure 8.6   Variation of call-option delta with respect to remaining time to expiration ($X = 50$, $r = 5$ per cent, $\sigma = 20$ per cent)

due to the slim chance of profitable exercise, which means that a large shift in the underlying is required for the value of the option to change significantly. As the underlying asset increases, the call delta increases as well and gets close to 0.5 for at-the-money options.

Finally, as the underlying increases further and the option becomes ITM, the call delta will increase accordingly. For a deep ITM option, the call delta will be close to 1, because in this case the option 'behaves' like the underlying asset due to the certainty that the option will be exercised. Similarly, the delta for European puts is: $\Delta = -N(-d_1) = N(d_1) - 1 < 0$. We can see now that $\Delta \rightarrow -1$ when the put is deep in the money and $\Delta \rightarrow 0$ when the put is deep out-of-the-money. For ATM puts, Δ will be close to -0.5. Figure 8.6 shows the variation of the call-option delta as time to maturity approaches by comparing the deltas of two calls with six- and one-month to maturity. We can see that the call-option delta becomes steeper as the option maturity approaches because the probability of the option ending up ITM becomes more sensitive to small changes in the underlying price close to the strike price.

8.9.1   Delta hedging

The delta of an option measures the rate of change in the price of the option caused by a small change in the value of the underlying asset. Thus, in order to offset a change in the option price, we must take a position in the underlying asset which is equal to the negative of the call-option delta. For instance, suppose we have written a call option; the delta of a short position in the call option is equal to $-\Delta C/\Delta S$ and, therefore, to delta hedge this position we must buy $\Delta C/\Delta S$ of the underlying asset. If Π denotes the value of the hedged portfolio, then we have: $\Pi = -C + (\Delta C/\Delta S)S$. If the underlying were to change by a small amount ΔS, the change in the value of the portfolio would be: $\Delta\Pi = -\Delta C + (\Delta C/\Delta S)\Delta S = 0$. The change in the value of the portfolio is, therefore, zero and the portfolio is immune to small changes in the value of the underlying. By considering very small changes in the value of the underlying, this may lead to:

$$\frac{\Delta C}{\Delta S}\bigg|_{\Delta S \to 0} = \frac{\partial C}{\partial S} = delta$$

Since delta changes continuously as the underlying changes (see as well Figure 8.5) this implies that we must continuously trade the underlying asset in order to keep our portfolio completely neutral to changes in the market. In this case the overall delta of the portfolio will be zero and we call this a 'delta-neutral' portfolio.

To illustrate how this works in practice, let us revisit the example in Section 8.7. Suppose that the delta of the short call is $\Delta = 0.4271$. The bank that has sold the call option will need to buy $0.4271 \times 150,000\,\mathrm{mt} = 64,064\,\mathrm{mt}$ of FFA in order to hedge its exposure in the market; in this way, if, for instance, the FFA contract increases by US\$1/mt (US\$64,064 in total) the call-option price will go up by US\$0.4271/mt ($0.4271 \times 1 \times 150,000 = \mathrm{US\$64,064}$ in total) so that the overall value of the portfolio does not change. Therefore, the portfolio of 0.4271 FFA and one call option is immune to small changes in freight rates and is delta neutral.

In order to maintain delta neutrality the portfolio needs to be 'rebalanced' frequently because Δ changes continuously as the underlying changes. For instance, having established the position described above, assume that in the following week, the January 2007 FFA rate has increased to US\$20.770/mt. The new option value is US\$1.329/mt.[7] Therefore, the value of the FFA position has now increased by US\$49,329 [$=(20.770 - 20) \times 64,064$] which more than offsets the decrease of US\$42,591 in the call-option position [$=(1.329 - 1.044) \times 150,000$]. There is a discrepancy of US\$6738, which is the hedging error.

Figure 8.7 graphs the performance of the delta hedge for a wide range of FFA rates. We can see that the hedge works reasonably well when the underlying moves by a small amount compared to the current FFA rate of US\$20/mt, but declines in effectiveness as the FFA rate moves further away from that value. This discrepancy arises because FFAs are linear instruments in terms of their sensitivity to changes in the underlying asset, while call options are non-linear. As such, a delta hedge will work effectively for small changes in the value of the underlying. This means that as the underlying moves, the call-option delta will change accordingly and, in order to maintain the

---

[7] The option premium and the option's delta presented in this example and in Table 8.6 are calculated using the Black (1976) option-pricing model.

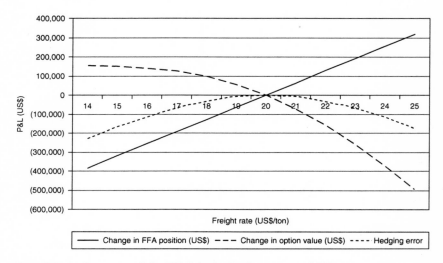

Figure 8.7   Performance of the FFA delta hedge for a range of FFA rates

effectiveness of the strategy, the holding in the FFA position needs to be rebalanced accordingly. The bigger the move, the bigger the change in the value of the delta and hence the larger the required rebalancing of the portfolio. Such a strategy is called a 'dynamic delta hedge' because the holdings in the FFA market will need to be rebalanced as the underlying changes.

To illustrate how dynamic hedging can be implemented, we extend the example presented above by considering the evolution of FFA rates over the following ten weeks until the expiry date of the option. The hedge is assumed to be rebalanced weekly. The results are presented in Table 8.6. For instance, in the second week, the FFA rate has increased to 20.77 and the delta of the call option has increased to 0.505. This means that we must rebalance our FFA position and buy $(0.505 - 0.4271) \times 150,000 = 11,723$ mt of C4 FFA contracts (some differences in the results are due to rounding), so that the total FFA holding becomes 75,787 $(=64,064 + 11,723)$. The following week (Week 2) the market goes down to US\$19.705/mt and the option value is also reduced to US\$116,868. Overall, the value of the option position has decreased by US\$82,388 $(=199,256 - 116,868)$ and at the same time the value of the FFA position has decreased to US\$80,713, thus reducing the overall hedging error to US\$1675. As we continue in this fashion, towards the end of the life of the option, it becomes apparent that the option will expire ITM and as such, the delta approaches 1.0. At that stage, the option writer will have a fully covered position. Similarly, if the option was to expire OTM, the delta would tend to go to zero and, as such, the option writer would leave his position naked. It is also interesting to note that the discounted present value of all the costs

Table 8.6 Simulation of dynamic delta hedging

Week	Freight rate (US$/mt)	Call-option delta	Change in FFA position (mt)	Total FFA size (mt)	Change in FFA value (US$)	Call-option value (US$)	Change in option value (US$)	Hedging error (US$)
0	20.000	0.4271	64,064	64,064		156,665		
1	20.770	0.505	11,723	75,787	49,329	199,256	42,591	6,738
2	19.705	0.377	(19,175)	56,612	(80,713)	116,868	(82,388)	1,675
3	20.923	0.518	21,040	77,651	68,953	185,868	69,000	(47)
4	19.874	0.374	(21,551)	56,100	(81,456)	101,893	(83,975)	2,519
5	21.129	0.542	25,204	81,304	70,406	172,852	70,959	(553)
6	22.302	0.715	25,901	107,205	95,370	266,929	94,077	1,293
7	23.085	0.837	18,271	125,476	83,942	342,795	75,866	8,076
8	23.094	0.883	6,913	132,388	1,129	330,144	(12,651)	13,780
9	24.667	0.996	17,080	149,469	208,247	549,691	219,547	(11,301)
10	25.346	1.000	530	149,999	101,489	651,900	102,209	(719)

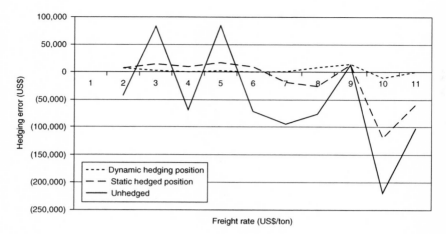

Figure 8.8   Hedging error from the dynamic, static and naked hedging strategies

that the hedger incurs in order to set up this strategy should be very close to the option premium.

Finally, Figure 8.8 presents the hedging error for the ten-week period when we use dynamic hedging, constant hedging (by assuming that delta = 0.427 throughout the life of the option and we do not rebalance the portfolio) and by taking a naked position in the market. We can see that the dynamic hedging strategy provides the lowest hedging error across the different strategies, ignoring transaction costs.

It is also interesting to examine how frequently a portfolio has to be rebalanced. The critical factor here is by how much the underlying has moved from the point where it was when the hedge was set up. One could set the hedge rebalancing triggers to be an upper limit on the hedging error as mentioned by Clewlow and Strickland (2000); for instance, to rebalance whenever the hedging error is more than 10 per cent of the initial position. One additional consideration is the level of transaction costs. Every time the FFA position is rebalanced, costs are incurred in trading the underlying. These costs comprise both the broker's commission in trading the FFA contract and also liquidity costs when there is thin trading in the market. Efficient hedging, therefore, requires a trade-off between risk reduction by minimising the hedging error and trading costs.

8.9.2   Delta hedging of Asian options

The example we presented earlier refers to the case of ordinary European options. Since freight options are Asian options it is interesting to see how delta hedging can be implemented in their case. Before the averaging period there are not many differences between delta hedging Asian and European

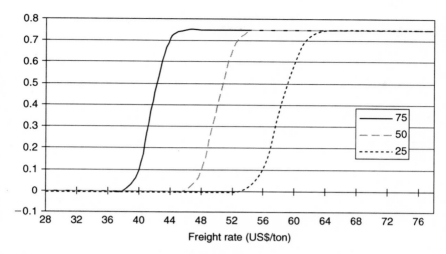

Figure 8.9   Average price-call deltas for different average price levels

options, but as we enter into the averaging period, Asian options are in fact easier to hedge than ordinary plain vanilla options. The reason for that is that, as time passes, we observe more of the prices that will be used to calculate the final average price and, as a result, uncertainty regarding the final payoff decreases and the option becomes progressively easier to hedge.

This can be seen by looking at Figure 8.9 which plots the deltas for three average price options. All three options have the same underlying charac-teristics ($X = 50$, $\sigma = 25$ per cent, $r_f = 5$ per cent) and expire in three weeks; the averaging period is four weeks and we are already in the first week of averaging. We consider three different cases corresponding to different aver-age levels of freight rates that prevailed during the first week. We can see, for instance, that when the average in the first week is US\$75/mt, then the delta is near one for a wide range of underlying prices, reflecting the higher probability that this option has to expire ITM. In this case, freight rates will have to drop below US\$44/ton for deltas to start decreasing and the option delta will become close to zero if the market drops below US\$36/mt. Simi-larly, if the average in the first week is US\$25/mt, then it is more likely that the option will expire OTM and the market has to increase above US\$64/mt for the option to expire ITM. Overall, irrespective of the average freight level in the first week, we can see that deltas remain close to zero or 1 for a wider range of underlying values and their movements are confined to a narrow range of approximately US\$10/mt. Therefore, deltas in this case exhibit lower variability and are thus easier to hedge.

It is also interesting to see how the delta of an average price option will change as we approach the maturity of the option. Figure 8.10 presents the

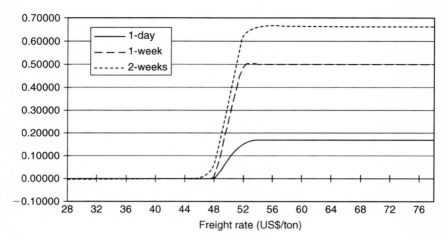

Figure 8.10   Average price deltas for different times to maturity

deltas of the same average price options as before, assuming that the average rate so far is US$50/mt and under three different times to maturity. We can see that as the option maturity approaches, the deltas tend to zero because price movements during the remaining time period until the expiry of the option will have little impact on the final payoff. In general, as pointed out by Lévy (1997), as more of the fixings in the averaging period are recorded, both the delta and the gamma (the sensitivity of delta to the spot price, discussed in the next section) diminish to zero in a stepped manner. As a result, at the moment each fixing is recorded a portion of the outstanding delta hedge will need to be unwound.

8.10   Gamma (Γ)

Gamma measures the rate of change of delta. It is therefore the second partial derivative of the option with respect to the underlying. Deltas change all the time; if an out-of-the-money option becomes in-the-money, its delta will rise and, as a result, gamma will change as well. As such, gamma has important implications for hedging an options position. For a European call option on a non-dividend paying stock, the gamma for calls and puts, based on the Black-Scholes (1973) model, are shown below

$$\Gamma = \frac{\partial^2 C}{\partial S^2} = \frac{N'(d_1)}{S\sigma\sqrt{T}}$$

Since gamma is the sensitivity of the delta to the underlying, it is a measure of by how much, or how often, a position must be rebalanced in order to

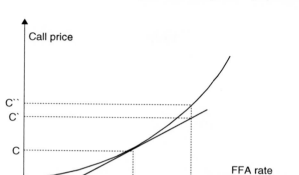

Figure 8.11   Hedging error induced by option-price curvature

maintain a delta-neutral position. If gamma is small, delta changes slowly and adjustments to keep a portfolio delta neutral need only to be made infrequently. However, if gamma is large in absolute terms, delta is highly sensitive to the price of the underlying asset and it is then quite risky to leave a delta-neutral portfolio unchanged for any length of time.

Figure 8.11 illustrates this point. When the FFA rate moves from S to S', delta hedging assumes that the option price will move from C to C', when in fact it moves from C to C″. The difference between C' and C″ gives rise to the hedging error we saw in Figure 8.7. Therefore, gamma also measures the curvature of the relationship between the option price and the underlying price. The gamma of a long position for a call or put option will always be positive and varies with respect to the price of the underlying and to delta as shown in Figure 8.12. We can see that gamma takes its maximum value when the option is ATM. This is due to the fact that the delta is most sensitive for ATM options. Similarly, gamma takes its lowest values when the option is deep ITM or OTM; this is due to the fact that, for this range of prices, deltas show very little sensitivity to changes in the value of the underlying.

Figure 8.13 also shows the variation in the value of gamma for different time-to-maturity options by comparing the gammas of two calls with six months and one month to maturity. We can see that for the longer time-to-maturity options, the distribution of gamma is flatter, which means that gamma is more sensitive to a wider range of changes in the value of the underlying. In contrast, as the time to maturity approaches, the range of prices affecting gamma narrows significantly. This is also consistent with the call-option delta graphs in Figure 8.6; there we saw that call-option deltas becomes steeper as the option maturity decreases, since the probability of the option ending up ITM becomes more sensitive to small changes in the underlying price close to the strike price.

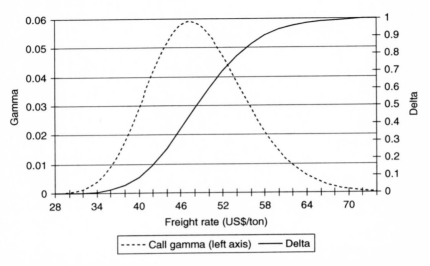

Figure 8.12 Relationship between call-option gamma and delta ($X = 50$, $r = 5$ per cent, $\sigma = 20$ per cent, $T = 6$ months)

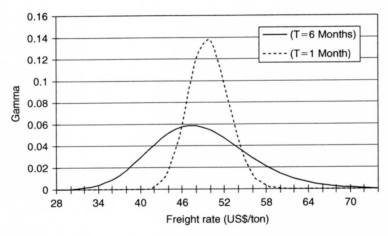

Figure 8.13 Variation of call option gamma with respect to time to maturity ($X = 50$, $r = 5$ per cent, $\sigma = 20$ per cent)

8.10.1 Gamma-neutral strategies

Because transaction costs can be large and because one wants to reduce exposure to hedging error, it is natural to try to minimise the need to rebalance the portfolio too frequently in order to maintain delta neutrality. Since gamma is a measure of sensitivity of the hedge ratio to the movement in the underlying asset, the need to rebalance may be reduced by using a 'gamma-neutral' strategy, that is, by setting the gamma of a portfolio to zero.

A position in the underlying asset or a forward contract both have a gamma of zero and hence cannot be used to change the gamma of a portfolio. What is then required is a position in an instrument that is not linearly dependent on the underlying asset, such as an option. Therefore, in order to maintain gamma neutrality one needs to buy or sell more options, not just the underlying. To illustrate how this is achieved, suppose that a delta-neutral portfolio has a gamma equal to Γ and another traded option has a gamma of Γ_T. If the number of options added to the portfolio is w_T, the gamma of the portfolio is $w_T \Gamma_T + \Gamma$. Hence the position in the traded option necessary to make the portfolio gamma neutral is $w_T = -\Gamma/\Gamma_T$. Of course, by including more options, the delta of the portfolio will change and so the position in the underlying will have to be changed in order to maintain delta neutrality. In addition, the portfolio is gamma neutral only instantaneously. As time passes, gamma neutrality can be maintained only if the position in the traded option is adjusted so that it is always equal to Γ/Γ_T. Consider the following example: suppose that a portfolio is delta neutral and has a gamma of -3000. The delta and gamma of a particular traded option are 0.62 and 1.5 respectively. The portfolio can be made gamma neutral by including a long position of $3000/1.5 = 2000$ call options. However, the delta of the portfolio will then change from zero to $2000 \times 0.62 = 1240$. A quantity of 1240 units of the underlying asset must therefore be sold from the portfolio to keep it delta neutral.

Making a delta-neutral portfolio gamma-neutral can be regarded as a first correction for the fact that the position in the underlying cannot be changed continuously when delta hedging is used. Delta neutrality provides protection against relatively small price moves between rebalancing, while gamma neutrality provides protection against larger movements in the underlying price between rebalancing (see Hull, 2007)

8.11 Theta (Θ)

Theta (Θ) measures the rate of change in the value of the option with respect to the passage of time with all else remaining constant. The thetas for calls and puts, based on Black-Scholes (1973), are shown below

$$\Theta_{Call} = \frac{\partial C}{\partial T} = -\frac{SN'(d_1)\sigma}{2\sqrt{T}} - rXe^{-rT}N(d_2)$$

$$\Theta_{Put} = \frac{\partial P}{\partial T} = -\frac{SN'(d_1)\sigma}{2\sqrt{T}} + rXe^{-rT}N(-d_2)$$

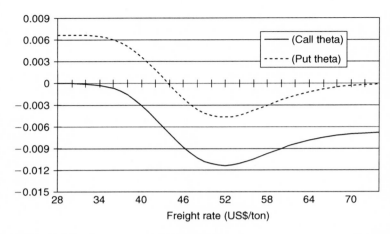

Figure 8.14   Variation of call and put options theta (X = 50, r = 5%, σ = 20%, T = 6 months)

Options are time-decaying assets, and so theta is (usually) negative for long positions and positive for short positions.[8]   This is because as the time to maturity decreases with all else remaining the same, options tend to become less valuable. In the formulae shown above, theta measures the time decay in years and this can be converted into the theta per trading day by dividing it by the number of trading days. For instance, the theta of a put option is $\Theta = -18.15$; this means that if 0.01 years (or approximately 2.5 trading days) pass with no change to any other factor, the value of the option will decline by 0.1815.

Figure 8.14 presents the variation of a call and put theta with respect to changes in the price of the underlying. We can see that for ATM options, thetas tend to be large and negative, which indicates that time decay is larger for these options. For call options, as the underlying price decreases theta goes to zero and as the underlying increases call theta approaches $-rXe^{-rt}$. On the other hand for put options, as the option moves OTM, theta tends to zero. Finally for deep ITM puts, thetas can be positive, as is shown on the graph. This is due to the fact that there is a lower limit to the price of the underlying – which is the price going to zero – and, as such, the possibility of further profits from a reduction in the value of the underlying is limited.

Figure 8.15 presents the variation of call-option thetas as time to maturity approaches for an ATM option (X = US$50/mt), an ITM option

---

[8] There some exceptions to that rule; for instance, the theta of an in-the-money European put on an asset that does not pay any dividends can be positive (see Hull, 2007).

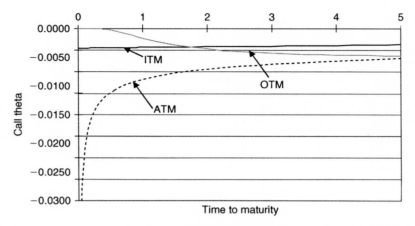

Figure 8.15 Variation of call-option theta with respect to time to maturity $(S = 50,$ $r = 5$ per cent, $\sigma = 20$ per cent) for ITM, OTM and ATM options

$(X = US\$25/mt)$ and an OTM option $(X = US\$75/mt)$. We can see that ATM options exhibit the highest time decay in their value and as maturity approaches, the rate of time decay increases as well. Theta is not the same type of hedge parameter as delta or gamma. There is always uncertainty about the future level of freight rates but there is no uncertainty about the passage of time. Hence, although it makes sense to hedge deltas and gammas, it does not make any sense to hedge against the effect of the passage of time in the value of our portfolio. Despite this, theta is a very useful parameter; for option writers, for instance, it makes sense to write options with high time decay as they will benefit more from the passage of time. In addition, in a delta-neutral portfolio, theta is a proxy for gamma, as we shall see in the next section.

8.11.1 The relationship between theta, delta and gamma

Theta is a very important factor for delta-hedged portfolios because it ensures that the portfolio earns the risk-free rate. To illustrate this point, consider the Black-Scholes-Merton Partial Differential Equation which dictates that a derivative contract, C, must satisfy the following partial differential equation (see as well Hull, 2007, for more details).

$$\frac{\partial C}{\partial t} + rS\frac{\partial C}{\partial S} + \frac{1}{2}\sigma^2 S^2 \frac{\partial^2 C}{\partial S^2} = rC$$

$$\text{Since } \Theta = \frac{\partial C}{\partial T} \quad \Delta = \frac{\partial C}{\partial S} \quad \Gamma = \frac{\partial^2 C}{\partial S^2}$$

$$\text{it follows that } \quad \Theta + rS\Delta + \frac{1}{2}\sigma^2 S^2 \Gamma = rC$$

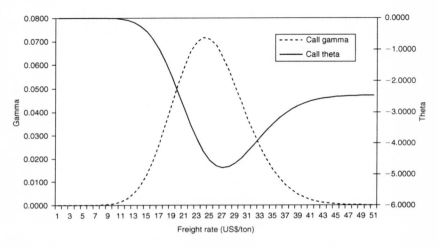

Figure 8.16 Relationship between gamma and theta with respect to changes in the underlying (X = 50, r = 5 per cent, σ = 20 per cent, T = 6 months)

For a delta-neutral portfolio, $\Delta = 0$ and $\Theta + \frac{1}{2}\sigma^2 S^2 \Gamma = rC$. This shows that when Θ is large and negative, gamma tends to be large and positive – and vice-versa.

This can also be seen in Figure 8.16 which plots the gamma (on the left axis) and the theta (right axis) for a call option and also explains why theta can be regarded as a proxy for gamma in a delta-neutral portfolio. Therefore, if theta is negative and gamma is positive, a delta-hedged portfolio will decline in value, if there is no change in S, due to the theta effect; but will increase in value if there is a large negative or positive change in S, due to the gamma effect.

8.12   Vega (Λ)

As we saw in Chapter 3, volatility in the market changes over time. Although there is a positive association between market volatility and the price of an option, what is also important is the sensitivity of the option to changes in the level of volatility. Vega (also called kappa and usually denoted by the Greek letter lambda, Λ) measures the rate of change of the price of the option with respect to changes in volatility. It is generally positive for long positions, and negative for short positions. If vega is high the option is very sensitive to changes in volatility; the formula for the vega of European call-and-put options, based on the Black-Scholes (1973) model, is shown below:

$$\Lambda = \frac{\partial C}{\partial \sigma} = \frac{\partial P}{\partial \sigma} = S\sqrt{T}N'(d_1)$$

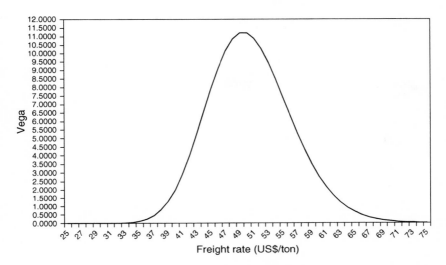

Figure 8.17 Variability of vega with respect to underlying price ($X = 50$, $r = 5$ per cent, $\sigma = 20$ per cent, $T = 20$ weeks)

Figure 8.17 shows the variation of vega with respect to changes in the value of the underlying price for a call or put option. We can note the similarity between the vega and the option gamma in Figure 8.12. We can also note that vega is greatest when the option is at-the-money, which also implies that ATM options are the most sensitive to changes in volatility. Option traders use vega to calculate the 'new' option price when implied volatilities change; vega is also important because it enables traders to keep track of their exposure to implied volatilities. For instance, a trader long on vega will benefit from an increase in implied volatilities and will see the value of his position decline if volatility in the market decreases.

As is the case with gamma hedging, to obtain vega neutrality one needs to take a position in an option. Gamma neutrality thus protects against large changes in S; vega neutrality protects against change in σ. The issue is whether it is better to use the available option to obtain gamma or vega neutrality. Hull and White (1987) show that this depends on the time between hedge rebalancing as well as the rate of change in the volatility. For instance they show that for a delta and gamma-neutral position, an increase in σ will increase the volatility of the securities in the portfolio as time to maturity increases, which may outweigh the benefits of gamma hedging.

8.13 Rho (P)

Rho (P) measures the change in the value of the option with respect to interest rates. Calls will rise in value and puts will fall as interest rates increase.

For European call-and-put options, Rho, following the Black-Scholes (1973) model, is calculated as:

$$P_{Call} = \frac{\partial C}{\partial r} = XTe^{-rT}N(d_2) \quad P_{Put} = \frac{\partial P}{\partial r} = -XTe^{-rT}N(-d_2)$$

In general, options are not very sensitive to interest rates. For instance, consider the following data: $S_0 = 49$, $X = 50$, $r = 5$ per cent, $s = 20$ per cent, $T = 20$ weeks. Using the BS model we find that the value of the call is 2.396 and the rho value is $= 8.880$; this implies that if rates increase by 1 per cent, the value of the call will increase by 0.0888 ($= 0.01 \times 8.880$) to 2.4848. Similarly, the value of the put is 2.446 and the put rho -9.933; that is, if rates increase by 1 per cent the value of the put will decrease by 0.09933.

8.13.1   Interpretation of Greek parameters: reading the Greeks

Consider the following information for a call option written on an FFA contract. The FFA rate is $S = US\$28/mt$, the strike price is $X = US\$30/mt$; the underlying volatility is $\sigma = 40$ per cent; the option expires in 15 days ($T = 15$ days) and the risk-free rate is 5 per cent. The price of the option is US\$0.405mt and the option has the following option price sensitivities (Greeks): delta $= 0.26107$; gamma $= 0.12083$; theta $= -5.64434$; vega $= 2.18612$; rho $= 0.39836$.

These option price sensitivities can be interpreted as follows:

Delta $= 0.26107$: means that if the FFA rate increases by US\$1/mt, the option price should increase approximately by 26.107 cents/mt

Gamma $= 0.12083$: means that when the FFA rate increases by US\$1/mt, the delta of the option will change by 0.12083 of that amount

Theta $= -5.64434$: this represents the decay in the value of the option over one year. Over the period of one day the theta effect is going to be US\$–0.021709/mt per day ($= 1/260 \times -5.64434$)

Vega $= 2.18612$: this means that if the volatility in the market increases by 1 per cent (from 40 per cent to 41 per cent) then the option price will increase by US\$0.021861/mt ($= 1$ per cent $\times 2.18612$)

Rho $= 0.39836$: if interest rates increase by 1 per cent (from 5 per cent to 6 per cent) then the price of the option will increase by US\$0.00398/mt ($= 1\% \times 0.39836$)

8.14   Dynamic hedging in practice

In practice a trader responsible for options trading, involving a particular asset, must keep delta, gamma and vega within limits set by risk management.

Typically, the delta limit is expressed as the equivalent maximum position in the underlying asset. For instance, the delta limit on BCI C4 can be US$10m. If the BCI C4 rate is US$20/mt then this means that the absolute value of delta must be 500,000 mt. The vega limit is typically expressed as maximum dollar exposure per 1 per cent change in volatility. Traders usually ensure that their portfolios are delta-neutral at least once a day. Gamma and vega are also monitored but, particularly if the options market is not very liquid, they are not usually managed on a daily basis. Typically, and this is what can be observed in the freight market as well, a number of investment banks write options to their customers; in doing so, they accumulate negative gamma and vega. One way of reducing this exposure is to buy options at competitive prices (see also Hull, 2007).

Another point worth noting is that if options are sold near ATM, both gammas and vegas are relatively high. As time passes and the market moves, it is likely that these options will move either ITM or OTM, which implies that gammas and vegas will become smaller. On the other hand, if the underlying asset does not move significantly and the options stay near ATM, then, as time to maturity approaches, gamma will increase, which means that the traders need to take extra care with hedging their positions. This type of risk is also called 'pin risk' (Kolb and Overdahl, 2007), because the underlying rate is 'pinned' to the options exercise price. Pin risk means that the option is very sensitive to extremely small changes in the value of the underlying. As the expiration date approaches, changes in the value of the asset from below to above the strike price will cause the call option's delta to abruptly change from being near zero to being near 1, meaning that the gamma will be extremely large. Thus, forming an effective hedge in the presence of pin risk can be extremely challenging. Finally, it should also be noted that there may as well be economies of scale in managing a larger option's portfolio since, for instance, delta hedging would involve building a larger FFA position, which may be easier to accomplish.

In an ideal world, traders should rebalance their portfolios frequently in order to maintain delta, gamma and vega neutrality. In the FFA market this may be more difficult to achieve compared to other options markets. Delta hedging rests on the ability to be able to buy and sell fractions of an FFA contract (for example, a quarter of a cargo for voyage routes, or ten days of a monthly contract for trip-charter routes) as we saw in Table 8.6, which may not be always possible to do; as such, any delta hedge will be only approximately efficient. In addition, one also needs to consider the liquidity costs which may be involved in rebalancing the FFA portfolio at the frequencies required. Vega and gamma neutrality, on the other hand, require taking positions in other traded options; however, given the relatively low liquidity in the market it may be difficult to find options that can be traded in the volumes required at competitive prices.

8.14.1 Greeks and trading strategies

The Greek parameters are also used to guide speculative trading strategies using options. By using the Greeks a trader can create strategies to exploit certain expectations efficiently. For instance, large positive gammas imply that large shifts in the price will be beneficial for long straddles and strangles. Similarly, long straddles and strangles will also have large positive vegas, which implies positive exposure to increases in volatility. Although large positive gammas and vegas work favourably for long straddles, they have the opposite impact for short positions. Finally, large positive thetas are beneficial for option sellers, since they reduce the liability of potential exercise as time passes.

8.15 Summary and conclusions

In this chapter we discussed the issues of options pricing and the risk management of short-options positions. Determining the option premium is important and should reflect a fair level of compensation for the risks that option sellers face in the market. Since freight options are settled as average price options their valuation is more complicated than that of ordinary European options; closed-form solutions are available but these only provide an approximation of the true option price. We also discussed how to incorporate in the pricing models the volatility term structure prevailing in the FFA rates as well as the use of Monte Carlo simulation for pricing freight options. Finally, we discussed the hedging techniques that option sellers can use in order to reduce the risk of their short positions. Naked and covered positions still leave the option sellers exposed to high levels of risk and, as a result, traders have to rely on sophisticated hedging strategies, using the sensitivity of option positions with respect to pricing inputs, known as Greeks. We identified the most important Greeks and also examined how we can use them to hedge a short position on FFA options.

9
Value-at-Risk in Shipping and Freight Risk Management

9.1 Introduction

Shipping market participants have always been faced with important and difficult investment decisions because of the complex and volatile nature of the shipping industry. While volatility in ship prices and freight rates offers the opportunity for large profits, it can also lead to huge losses. Therefore, as with any other business, assessing and monitoring volatility is an important part of shipping investment and risk-management activities, for several reasons. First, being aware of the magnitude of risk exposure, *shipping companies* can employ risk-management techniques to reduce and/or control the overall financial risk of the firm. Second, lenders (*banks*) financing ships can assess their risk in providing funds to shipowners. Third, *traders* can assess any changes in the value of their portfolios under the small probability that the market crashes. Finally, when trading FFAs and freight options it is always helpful to know the potential expected loss of each position and of the portfolio as whole, especially when contracts are cleared and margins should be maintained. Within this setting, risk measurement and assessment is of utmost importance for market participants and accurate risk quantification is critical for evaluating investment decisions as well as for the development of effective trading and hedging strategies.

One relatively new proactive risk assessment and measurement tool is the estimated potential loss or the 'value-at-risk' (VaR). Nowadays, many firms use VaR to measure market risk exposure, mainly because this method summarises risk in a single number which can easily be used to present and communicate information effectively to company management, shareholders, regulators and others.

The origins of VaR can be traced back to 1922 with the implementation of the minimum capital requirements imposed by the New York Stock Exchange (NYSE). For banks, the first regulatory capital requirements were imposed in the Great Depression era that followed the stock market crash (29 October 1929), with the establishment of the Securities and Exchange

Commission (SEC) in the US in 1934.[1] Later, following a series of financial disasters involving derivatives transactions (for example, Barings Bank, 1995; Metallgesellschaft, 1993; and the municipality of Orange County, California, 1994), as well as tighter capital requirements by regulatory bodies (the Basle Accord), financial institutions are obliged to maintain minimum capital requirements in order to ensure that potential losses cannot cause any major crises. As a result of these requirements, different risk-assessment methodologies were developed and used to quantify and assess the overall risk of financial institutions. In the late 1980s JP Morgan laid down internally the first set of standardised assumptions for calculating the potential loss that a firm is exposed to. Releasing the RiskMetrics methodology in October 1994 and publishing the risk-assessment method and procedure behind it, JP Morgan provided the foundation for estimation of VaR, which attracted the interest of both industry and academics. Since then, the RiskMetrics approach for estimating VaR and its variants has been adapted and implemented extensively by many financial institutions and companies.

Although VaR methodology for assessing risk exposure has been adapted by many financial institutions, investment houses and trading companies for many years, it has only been used in shipping very recently, following the growth in the FFA market and the involvement of shipping companies in trading FFAs. As a result, research in the area of the application, relevance and importance of VaR in shipping and FFA markets has been very limited. Angelidis and Skiadopolous (2008) investigate the performance of a number of VaR-estimation techniques for different Baltic tanker and dry-bulk routes as well as for two Panamax and Capesize basket routes. They estimate VaR using different GARCH models and nonparametric methods, and conclude that a simple filtered historical simulation method (see Section 9.3.2.1) seems to perform better than other models in estimating the VaR for most shipping routes. Alizadeh and Nomikos (2007c) also examine the performance of regime-switching volatility models in freight markets and find that incorporating regime changes in volatility models improves VaR estimates.

The aim of this chapter is to present and discuss different methodologies used to estimate VaR and illustrate different applications of VaR in assessing and monitoring risk in the shipping freight market. The structure of this chapter is as follows. Section 9.2 describes the VaR measure and demonstrates how to calculate VaR using different volatility-estimation techniques. Several examples are used to illustrate how VaR of single, double and multiple asset portfolios can be estimated. Section 9.3 is divided into two parts. The first explains parametric VaR estimation techniques, while the second discusses

---

[1] For a thorough historical review of the birth and development of the VaR theory and practice, see Holton (2003).

nonparametric VaR estimation procedures, where different methodologies are clearly illustrated using analytical examples. Section 9.4 demonstrates how to handle nonlinear instruments such as options, while Section 9.5 introduces the use of 'principal component analysis' in VaR estimation for portfolios of FFAs. Finally, Section 9.6 is devoted to procedures and techniques used to assess the performance of VaR estimation methodologies such as backtesting and stresstesting.

9.2 Simple VaR estimation

Value-at-risk refers to a particular amount of money which is likely to be lost due to changes in the market over a certain period of time and given some probability – known as confidence level. For example, if the VaR of an asset is US\$2m, given a 99 per cent confidence level over a ten-day investment horizon, it means that the probability that the value of the asset falls by more than US\$2m in ten days is only 1 per cent. In other words, there is only a 1 per cent chance that the value of the asset drops by US\$2m or more in ten days. In order to show this mathematically, let r_{t+k} be the (log) return on an asset over the period t to $t + k$ and $(1 - \alpha)$ the confidence level. Then, conditional on the information set at t, (Ω_t), the VaR can be defined as the solution to the following expression:

$$\Pr(r_{t+k} \leq VaR^{\alpha}_{t+k} | \Omega_t) = \alpha \tag{9.1}$$

This means that the VaR estimate is a single measure of the expected or potential loss in the value of a portfolio over a certain period and its particular likelihood. Consequently, VaR estimates depend on two important parameters; first, the chosen confidence level (CL = $1 - \alpha$) and second, the holding period (HP) or VaR horizon. There is a positive and nonlinear relationship between the VaR and the confidence level chosen; that is, the VaR increases at an increasing rate as a higher CL is chosen. This is shown in Panel A of Figure 9.1. There is also a positive and non-linear relationship between the VaR and the holding period; that is, the VaR increases at a decreasing rate, as the holding period increases. This is because, as the holding period increases, the volatility of the underlying asset increases by a square root of time factor, as shown in Panel B of Figure 9.1.

Confidence level is typically chosen to be 99 per cent or 95 per cent depending on how confident the firm, the trader or the investor would like to be about risk exposure and potential loss.[2] The market risk amendment to the Basle Capital Accord (originally released in January 1996, modified

---

[2] Assuming normally distributed returns, confidence levels of 99 per cent and 95 per cent are equivalent to 2.326 and 1.645 standard deviation moves to either side of the mean of the distribution, respectively.

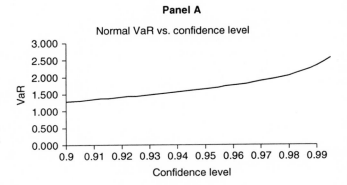

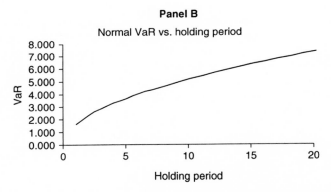

Figure 9.1   The relationship between VaR, confidence level and holding period

in September 1997, and further revised on 14 November 2005) instructs a 99 per cent confidence level over a ten-day period to calculate VaR for regulatory capital requirements. However, apart from regulatory purposes, banks and other firms may be interested in different confidence levels and holding periods depending on the asset or the structure of the portfolio under study. For instance, for some investors a 99 per cent confidence level may not be useful since it implies a tighter and more cautious assessment of risk compared to a 95 per cent confidence level. Similarly, the holding period should represent the time required to unwind the holding portfolio, raise cash to compensate losses, or implement contingencies. For instance, a one-day or one-week VaR for highly illiquid assets, such as a portfolio of ships or shipping loans, may not be appropriate because changes in the market may not be very significant over a one-day or one-week horizon. On the other hand, for FFA and freight portfolios, it is more appropriate to estimate daily and weekly VaR because the market is relatively liquid and one-day or one-week changes in the market can be quite significant.

Example 1: Single-asset VaR calculation using volatilities

To illustrate how a simple VaR can be estimated for a single asset, suppose a freight trader maintains a portfolio which consists of one long TD3 FFA position of 5000 mt with four months to maturity. The current value of the FFA position is 70 WS or US$47,250, given a flat rate of US$13.5/mt (=5000 × 0.70 × US$13.5/mt). The historical volatility of the four-month TD3 contract is 62 per cent per annum.

When calculating the VaR of FFA contracts, it is useful to measure time in days rather than years because we are mainly interested in the potential loss level of shorter periods. Assuming there are 252 trading days in one year, the daily volatility of the contract is approximately 3.91 per cent (=62%/$\sqrt{252}$). Therefore, one standard deviation change in the value of the contract in one day will result in a US$1845.40 (=US$47,250 × 3.91 per cent) drop in the value of portfolio, which is also known as the one-day dollar standard deviation. By the same token, the ten-day dollar standard deviation of this FFA contract will be US$5835.70 (=US$1845.4 × $\sqrt{10}$), while the three-month dollar standard deviation will be US$14,647.5 (=US$1845.4 × $\sqrt{252/4}$), and so on. In order to calculate the VaR of the long TD3 position, we further assume that the successive daily changes in TD3 FFA rates are independent and returns are normally distributed with zero mean; then, the 1 per cent one-day and ten-day value-at-risk of the long TD3 FFA position would be:

$$VaR_{1d}^{1\%} = Z_\alpha * \sigma_{1day} = 2.326 * US\$1,845.4 \Rightarrow VaR_{1day} = US\$4,293.07$$

$$VaR_{10d}^{1\%} = Z_\alpha * \sigma_{1day} * \sqrt{10} = 2.326 * US\$1,845.4 * \sqrt{10}$$

$$\Rightarrow VaR_{10day} = US\$13,575.87$$

where Z_α represents the critical value for the 99 per cent confidence level of the standard normal distribution. According to the example, the 1 per cent ten-day VaR suggests that there is only a 1 per cent chance that the value of the FFA contract drops by US$13,575.78 or more in ten days. Alternatively, we can say that we are 99 per cent confident that the value of the long TD3 position will not drop by more than US$13,575.78 in ten days. Figure 9.2 presents the probability distribution of the TD3 FFA portfolio value after ten days along with the 1 per cent ten-day VaR.

Nevertheless, this might not be the most accurate and appropriate way of calculating VaR. The assumptions that: a) FFA price changes are normally distributed; b) the volatility of FFA price changes is constant; c) there is no growth, depreciation, mean reversion, and seasonality in the FFA contract; and d) that FFA prices take negative values under a normal distribution, might not be valid or appropriate when estimating the VaR. Therefore, these issues

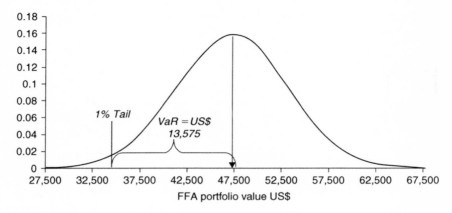

Figure 9.2   Probability distribution of TD3 FFA value after ten days

must be addressed in order to obtain a better and more accurate estimate of VaR. More specifically, we need to investigate the actual distribution of returns and prices and use better volatility estimates (such as time-varying, RiskMetrics or GARCH, as discussed in Chapter 3) if necessary. In addition, we must consider and incorporate any appreciation or depreciation in the value of the asset as well as the distributional properties of the underlying returns.

Example 2: Single-asset VaR calculation using volatilities

Following Example 1, suppose that the portfolio consists of a single contract that is a long position on a TD7 FFA with four months to maturity for 5000 mt. The current value of this long position is 140 WS, or US$31,150 (=5000 × 1.40 × US$4.45/mt), based on a WS flat rate of US$4.45/mt. The historical volatility of TD7 FFA contract with four months to expiry is 50 per cent per annum. Once again, assuming that the successive daily changes in TD7 FFA prices are independent and normally distributed with zero mean, the daily and ten-day dollar SD of TD7 FFA can be estimated as:

$$\sigma_{1d} = \sigma_y/\sqrt{252} = 50\%/\sqrt{252} = 3.15\%$$

$$\text{US\$ } \sigma_{1d} = \text{US\$}31,150 \times 3.15\% = \text{US\$}981.1$$

$$\text{US\$ } \sigma_{10d} = \text{US\$}31,150 \times 3.15\% \times \sqrt{10} = \text{US\$}3102.6$$

while the 1 per cent one-day and ten-day VaR of this portfolio can be calculated as

$$VaR_{1d}^{1\%} = Z_\alpha * \sigma_{1d} = 2.326 * \text{US\$}981.1 \Rightarrow VaR_{1d} = \text{US\$}2282.5$$

$$VaR_{1d}^{1\%} = Z_\alpha * \sigma_{10d} = 2.326 * \text{US\$}3,102.6 \Rightarrow VaR_{10d} = \text{US\$}7217.8$$

Hence, there is 1 per cent chance that the value of the FFA contract drops by US$7217.80 or more in ten days.

Example 3: Two-asset VaR calculation using volatilities and correlation

Now consider a portfolio consisting of two long FFA contracts, one TD3 (5000 mt) and one TD7 (5000 mt), each with four months to maturity, and current values of US$47,250 and US$31,150 respectively. The estimated volatility of the TD3 contract is 62 per cent (that is, 3.91 per cent per day) and the estimated volatility of the TD7 contract is 50 per cent (or 3.15 per cent per day), while the correlation between the two is 41 per cent. Assuming that the two FFA prices follow a bivariate normal distribution, we can use the following expression to calculate the ten-day dollar standard deviation of the portfolio of the two assets:

$$
\begin{aligned}
\sigma_P &= \sqrt{\sigma_{TD3}^2 + \sigma_{TD7}^2 + 2(\rho)(\sigma_{TD3})(\sigma_{TD7})} \\
&= \sqrt{(5835.7)^2 + (3102.6)^2 + 2(0.41)(5835.7)(3102.6)} \\
&= US\$7605.4
\end{aligned}
\tag{9.2}
$$

Note that the standard deviations used in the formula are dollar values and thus the weights are not included. Having obtained the dollar standard deviation of the portfolio, assuming 99 per cent confidence level, the VaR of the portfolio of the two FFA positions can be estimated as:

$$
VaR_{1d}^{1\%} = Z_\alpha * \sigma_{10d} = 2.326 * US\$7650.4 \Rightarrow VaR_{10d} = US\$17,797.5
$$

It can be seen that the ten-day VaR for the two-asset portfolio is substantially lower than the sum of the two ten-day VaR estimated for individual FFA positions, which is US$20,793.60. This is direct result of diversification, which reduces the VaR of portfolios of multi assets provided that the correlation between the assets is less than one. According to the portfolio theory, the lower the correlation between the individual assets, the greater is the reduction in the volatility of the portfolio risk (see Chapter 13 for more on the benefits of diversification in shipping).

Example 4: Two-asset VaR calculation using volatilities and correlation

Consider again the FFA contracts presented in the previous example. Suppose that this time the portfolio consists of one long TD3 (5000 mt) position and one short TD7 (5000 mt) position. Assuming that the two FFA rates follow a bivariate normal distribution, we can use the following expression to calculate the ten-day dollar standard deviation of the portfolio of the two

FFAs, noting that in the case of long-short (opposite) positions, the sign of the correlation coefficient changes:

$$\sigma_P = \sqrt{(5835.7)^2 + (3102.6)^2 - 2(0.41)(5835.7)(3102.6)} = US\$5369.8$$

Therefore, the ten-day dollar volatility of the portfolio and the two asset portfolio VaR, assuming 99 per cent confidence level, will be:

$$VaR_{1d}^{1\%} = Z_\alpha * \sigma_{10d} = 2.326 * US\$5369.8 \Rightarrow VaR_{1\%,10d} = US\$12,492.0$$

which is again substantially less than the long-long portfolio presented in Example 3.

9.2.1   VaR of multi-asset portfolios

The above results can be extended to multiple-asset portfolios as long as changes in the value of portfolio are linearly related to changes in the value of the underlying market variables (assets). These are portfolios which do not include non-linear derivatives instruments such as options. If the change in the value of the portfolio is linearly related to the changes in the market variables, then the return and the variance of the portfolio can be estimated as:

$$r_p = \sum_{i=1}^{n} w_i r_i \tag{9.3}$$

and

$$\sigma_p^2 = \sum_{i=1}^{n} w_i^2 \sigma_i^2 + 2\sum_{i=1}^{n} \sum_{j<i} \rho_{ij} w_i w_j \sigma_i \sigma_j \tag{9.4}$$

where r_p is the return of portfolio, r_i is the return on asset i included in the portfolio, w_i is the weight of asset i, and ρ_{ij} is the correlation between returns on asset i and j in the portfolio. Once the variance and standard deviation of the portfolio is estimated, it is not difficult to estimate the VaR, assuming a certain confidence level as well as a distribution for the value of the underlying portfolio.

An alternative way to estimate the VaR of a portfolio is to use the 'correlation matrix of returns', C. In this method, first we estimate individual VaR levels given a certain confidence level and stack them in vector **V**. Then we pre- and post-multiply the correlation matrix with **V**, to estimate the VaR of the portfolio as:

$$VaR_d^{\alpha\%} = (\mathbf{V}'\mathbf{C}\mathbf{V})^{1/2} \tag{9.5}$$

where

$$V' = (\text{VaR}_1 \ \text{VaR}_2 \ \cdots \ \text{VaR}_n), \quad C = \begin{pmatrix} 1 & \rho_{1,2} & \cdots & \rho_{1,n} \\ \rho_{1,2} & 1 & \cdots & \rho_{2,n} \\ \vdots & & \ddots & \vdots \\ \rho_{n,1} & \rho_{n,2} & \cdots & 1 \end{pmatrix}$$

Example 5: Multi-asset VaR calculation using volatilities and correlation

To illustrate how this method can be used to estimate the VaR of a portfolio of FFAs, consider a portfolio of four TD3 FFA positions (one, two, three and four months to maturity) on 17 March 2003. Each FFA contract is for 5000 mt. The current value of each position, along with the 1 per cent one- and ten-day VaR estimates and the correlation matrix of returns on these FFA contracts, are presented in Table 9.1.

Table 9.1 Individual VaRs and correlation matrix

Panel A: VaR calculation one, two, three and four months to maturity

TD3 FFA	WS	Current value	Volatility	One-day volatility	Z	One-day VaR	Ten-day VaR
1M	112.5	75,937.5	113.50%	7.15%	2.326	12,630.7	39,941.7
2M	88.0	59,400.0	86.70%	5.46%	2.326	7,547.1	23,866.0
3M	67.5	45,562.5	74.40%	4.69%	2.326	4,967.7	15,709.2
4M	65.0	43,875.0	62.00%	3.91%	2.326	3,986.4	12,606.2

Panel B: Correlation matrix

$$C = \begin{pmatrix} 1 & 0.724 & 0.593 & 0.426 \\ 0.724 & 1 & 0.826 & 0.667 \\ 0.593 & 0.826 & 1 & 0.774 \\ 0.426 & 0.667 & 0.774 & 1 \end{pmatrix}$$

Using equation (9.5), the 10-day 1 per cent VaR of the portfolio can be calculated as:

$$VaR_{10d}^{1\%} = (V'CV)^{1/2}$$

$$= \left((39{,}941 \ 23{,}866 \ 15{,}709 \ 12{,}606) \begin{pmatrix} 1 & 0.72 & 0.59 & 0.43 \\ 0.72 & 1 & 0.83 & 0.67 \\ 0.59 & 0.83 & 1 & 0.77 \\ 0.43 & 0.67 & 0.77 & 1 \end{pmatrix} \begin{pmatrix} 39{,}941 \\ 23{,}866 \\ 15{,}709 \\ 12{,}606 \end{pmatrix} \right)^{1/2}$$

$$= \text{US\$80{,}315}$$

Therefore, the 1 per cent ten-day VaR for this portfolio is US\$80,315, which is substantially lower than the sum of VaR estimates of individual FFA positions (US\$92,123). This is again the result of diversification.

9.3 VaR estimation methodologies

The accuracy of the VaR estimate depends heavily on the method used for estimating the volatility of the underlying asset, the behaviour of the variable, as well as the assumptions regarding the distributional properties of the price changes (returns). Factors such as volatility clustering, leptokurtosis, fat-tails and skewness are stylised facts of freight rates that can affect the accuracy of VaR estimates and the performance of VaR procedures. Therefore, a number of alternative methodologies have been proposed to incorporate deviations from normality, as well as the time-varying volatility of returns, when estimating VaR. The following sections are devoted to discussing some of these methods, which are broadly classified into parametric and non-parametric approaches.

9.3.1 Parametric VaR estimation

The parametric approach to estimating the VaR explicitly assumes that returns follow a defined parametric distribution, such as the 'normal', 'student-t' or 'generalised error' distributions, among others. Based on this approach, parametric models are used to estimate the unconditional and conditional distribution of returns, which is then used to calculate VaR. These methods are usually preferred and used frequently in estimating VaR because they are simple to apply and produce relatively accurate VaR estimates (see, for example, Jorion, 1995; 2002). To illustrate, let us assume that the dynamics of log-returns of freight rates r_t can be described by a stochastic process of the form:

$$r_t = \kappa(x) + \varepsilon_t; \quad \varepsilon_t = z_t \sigma_t; \quad z_t \overset{iid}{\sim} f(0, 1; \theta_1)$$
$$\sigma_t^2 = g(\theta_2 | \Omega_{t-1}) \tag{9.6}$$

where $k(x)$ is a function describing the conditional mean equation, ε_t is a white-noise process with time-varying variance σ_t^2 conditioned on the information set available at $t-1$, (Ω_{t-1}), and $f(.)$ is the probability density function of z_t which corresponds to a distribution function F. θ_1 and θ_2 represent the vector of the parameters to be estimated for the conditional mean and the variance process, respectively. The mean equation can be specified to best capture the dynamics of the asset returns. For instance, 'autoregressive moving average' (ARMA), 'mean reversion' (MR), or 'mean reversion with jump diffusion' (MRJD) processes can be used to explain r_t. Then, conditional on the information set at t (Ω_t), if $(F^a)^{-1}(z_t)$ is the ath quantile of the assumed distribution F, and σ_{t+1} the forecasted volatility, the one-period-ahead VaR given a specific confidence level $(1-a)$ can be calculated as:

$$VaR_{t+1}^a = k(x) + (F^a)^{-1}(z_t)\sigma_{t+1} \tag{9.7}$$

9.3.1.1 The sample variance and covariance method

A simple and straightforward method of calculating VaR is to use the historical constant variance and covariance between the return series, and find the difference between the mean and the α per cent percentile of the distribution of the asset or the portfolio; that is, $VaR_{t+1} = Z_\alpha \sigma_t$. Based on this method, forecasts of variances of returns are usually generated using a rolling window of a specified size, say, 1000 data points. The 'variance-covariance' method is a simple and fast means of estimating the VaR, but is believed to be efficient only in the short term. Its main disadvantage is that it does not take into account the dynamics of volatility of the underlying asset because it applies equal weights to past observations in the variance calculation.

9.3.1.2 The exponential weighted average variance and RiskMetrics methods

RiskMetrics uses a weighted average of the estimated volatility and the last price changes at any point in time to estimate future volatility and VaR.[3] The weighting factor, which determines the decay in the importance of past observations, could be estimated from historical data. However, usually it is set as constant between 0.9 and 0.98. JP Morgan RiskMetrics, for instance, uses a weighting multiplier of 0.97 which is argued to be the optimal decay factor in variance calculation. Thus the RiskMetrics exponentially weighted average variance estimator can be obtained using the following equation.

$$\sigma_{t+1}^2 = \lambda \sigma_t^2 + (1 - \lambda) r_t^2 \qquad (9.8)$$

It is obvious that the higher the decay factor, the longer the memory assigned to past observations. In case of a portfolio of assets, the covariance and correlation of two assets, say X and Y, can be estimated respectively as:

$$\sigma_{XY,t+1}^2 = \lambda \sigma_{XY,t}^2 + (1 - \lambda) r_t^X r_t^Y \qquad (9.9)$$

$$\rho_{XY,t+1} = \frac{\sigma_{XY,t}}{\sigma_{X,t} \sigma_{Y,t}} \qquad (9.10)$$

Again, once the variance and covariance are calculated, the α per cent VaR can be estimated assuming an appropriate parametric distribution.

9.3.1.3 GARCH models and VaR estimation

A relatively more advanced parametric method for VaR estimation is to use the volatility input estimated through GARCH-type models. In the simple GARCH (1,1) specification the variance is a function of the most recent

---

[3] For more details on this approach the reader is referred to JP Morgan, *RiskMetrics Technical Manual* (1996) as well as Chapter 3 of this book.

error terms and the previous period's variance. Hence, $\sigma_t^2 = g(\theta_2 | \Omega_{t-1})$ can be formulated as:

$$\sigma_t^2 = \beta_0 + \beta_1 \varepsilon_{t-1}^2 + \beta_2 \sigma_{t-1}^2 \tag{9.11}$$

where $\theta_2 = (\beta_0 \; \beta_1 \; \beta_2)$ is a vector of parameters to be estimated, subject to the non-negativity constraints $\beta_0 \geq 0$, β_1 and $\beta_2 > 0$, in order for the variance to be positive definite. GARCH models can also be extended in a multivariate framework to model the variance/covariance matrix of a portfolio of assets (see Chapter 3 for more details on multivariate GARCH models).

9.3.1.4 Monte Carlo simulation and VaR estimation

This method of estimating the VaR of an asset or a portfolio is based on the assumption that prices follow a certain stochastic process (geometric Brownian motion, jump diffusion, mean reversion, mean reversion jump diffusion and so on), or a multivariate process in the case of portfolios. Once the stochastic mathematical process for the underlying asset is determined, it can be used to generate many possible paths for the evolution of the asset price through Monte Carlo simulation. Simulating the stochastic processes of the underlying assets will yield the distribution of the portfolio value at given point in the future, and the VaR of the portfolio can be estimated as the difference between the expected value (mean) of the distribution of the portfolio and the α per cent lower percentile of the distribution.

The advantage of this method is that it allows for certain properties of the underlying asset price, such as seasonality and mean reversion, to be considered and incorporated in the simulation exercise. This is quite important because such dynamics in asset price have direct impact on the accuracy of estimated VaR. For example, if the price of an asset is mean-reverting and current prices are above their long-run mean, then there is a higher likelihood that prices will drop (Figure 9.3, Price path 1). On the other hand, when current prices are below their long-run mean, then there is a higher likelihood of a price increase (Figure 9.3, Price path 2).

Another advantage of Monte Carlo simulation is that due to its flexibility it can be used to estimate the VaR of portfolios containing short-dated as well as non-linear instruments such as options and option portfolios. In addition, sensitivity analysis can be performed in a simple way by changing market parameters. For instance, by changing the variances and correlations of a portfolio, we can assess the sensitivity of the portfolio and examine the effect of different volatility regimes on VaR estimates. However, simulation techniques are highly dependent on the accuracy and quality of the processes chosen for the behaviour of the underlying asset prices, and their complexity and computational burden increases with the number of assets in the portfolio.

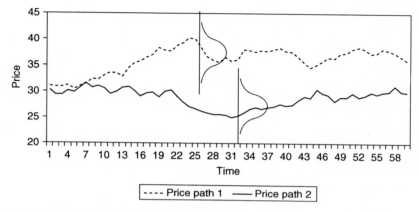

Figure 9.3   Mean reversion and VaR estimation

The steps in MCS for VaR calculation include:[4]

Step 1: Specify the dynamics of the underlying processes.

Step 2: Generate N sample paths by sampling changes in asset prices over the required horizon. A minimum of 10,000 simulations is typically necessary for satisfactorily accurate estimates.

Step 3: Evaluate the portfolio at the end of horizon for each generated sample path. The N outcomes constitute the distribution of the portfolio values at the required time horizon.

Step 4: Finally, VaR can be estimated as the difference between the mean of the simulated distribution and the lower α per cent percentile of the ordered simulated outcomes at the point in time for which the VaR is considered; for instance, see Figure 9.4 for the 1 per cent VaR.

Example 6: Estimating VaR using Monte Carlo simulation

Consider Portfolio A consisting of two long FFA contracts on two different hypothetical shipping routes (Routes 1 and 2), and Portfolio B, which consists of a long position in Route 1 and a short position in Route 2. The current value for Route 1 is US$30/mt for 54,000 mt and daily volatility of 2.52 per cent,

---

[4] In Chapter 8, we used Monte Carlo simulation to price options. Although the underlying methodology remains the same, there is an important difference between the two applications. In particular, when using MCS to price options, simulations must be carried out under the risk-neutral measure by taking into account the market price of risk. When we use MCS for VaR estimation on the other hand, simulations are carried out by using the real drift of the underlying series, which can be estimated from historical data.

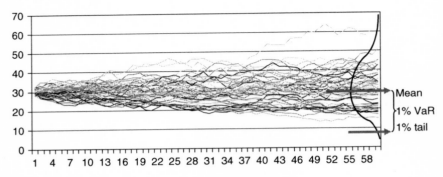

Figure 9.4 Calculating VaR from the simulated distribution

while the current value for Route 2 is US$10/mt for 150,000 mt of cargo and daily volatility of 1.89 per cent. The long-run mean of freight rates for Routes 1 and 2 are US$25/mt and US$8/mt respectively, while the estimated historical correlation between the two routes is 0.8. In addition, it is assumed that freight rates on both routes are mean-reverting with mean-reversion rates of 0.33 and 0.4 for routes one and two respectively.[5] The estimated one-day 5 per cent VaR of the two portfolios using the variance covariance method would be:

$$\text{Route 1}: VaR_{1d}^{5\%} = Z_\alpha \sigma_{daily} = 1.645 \times (30 \times 54{,}000 \times 0.0252) = \text{US\$}67{,}143$$

$$\text{Route 2}: VaR_{1d}^{5\%} = Z_\alpha \sigma_{daily} = 1.645 \times (10 \times 150{,}000 \times 0.0189) = \text{US\$}46{,}627$$

and therefore
Portfolio A:

$$VaR_{1d}^{5\%} = \left((67{,}143 \quad 46{,}627) \begin{pmatrix} 1 & 0.8 \\ 0.8 & 1 \end{pmatrix} \begin{pmatrix} 67{,}147 \\ 46{,}627 \end{pmatrix} \right)^{1/2} = \text{US\$}108{,}127$$

---

[5] A mean-reverting process is defined as a process in which prices tend to revert back to their long-run mean. A discrete version of a bivariate mean-reverting process can be written as

$$\Delta s_{1,t} = [\alpha_1(\mu_1 - s_{1,t}) - \tfrac{1}{2}\sigma_1^2]\Delta t + \sigma_1\sqrt{\Delta t}\varepsilon_{1,t}$$
$$\Delta s_{2,t} = [\alpha_2(\mu_2 - s_{2,t}) - \tfrac{1}{2}\sigma_2^2]\Delta t + \sigma_2\sqrt{\Delta t}\varepsilon_{2,t} \qquad \boldsymbol{\varepsilon}_t \sim N(0, \boldsymbol{\Sigma})$$

where $s_{1,t}$ and $s_{2,t}$ are log of asset prices and $\Delta s_{1,t}$ and $\Delta s_{2,t}$ are log price changes at time t; μ_1 and μ_2 are the log price levels to which prices of assets 1 and 2 revert over the long run respectively; α_1 and α_2 are the coefficients of mean-reversion measuring the speed at which prices revert to their mean; σ_1 and σ_2 are the standard deviation of prices, and $\boldsymbol{\varepsilon}_t$ is a (2×1) vector of stochastic terms which follow a bivariate normal distribution with zero mean and variance-covariance $\boldsymbol{\Sigma} = \begin{pmatrix} \sigma_1^2 & \sigma_{1,2} \\ \sigma_{2,1} & \sigma_2^2 \end{pmatrix}$.

Portfolio B:

$$VaR_{1d}^{5\%} = \left((67{,}143 \quad 46{,}627) \begin{pmatrix} 1 & -0.8 \\ -0.8 & 1 \end{pmatrix} \begin{pmatrix} 67{,}143 \\ 46{,}627 \end{pmatrix} \right)^{1/2} = US\$40.905$$

Using Monte Carlo simulation, we estimate 5 per cent VaR for each route as well as Portfolios A and B for different time horizons; namely, one, ten, 20 and 40 days. Panel A of Table 9.2 presents the parameters of the underlying routes whereas Panel B presents the estimated VaR for both the individual routes and the two portfolios. It can be seen that VaR estimated for Portfolios A and B through MCS are slightly lower that those estimated using the simple variance-covariance method. This is because MCS incorporates the assumed mean-reversion property of freight-rate processes and, as a result, the estimated portfolio VaRs are marginally less than those estimated through the simple variance-covariance method. Although the difference in VaRs is relatively small for short horizons, this increases as we consider longer VaR periods, consistent with the fact that the impact of mean-reversion increases as we consider longer periods; for instance, the estimated 5 per cent 40-day VaR for Portfolio A using MCS is US\$601,538, while the estimated 5 per cent 40-day VaR for Portfolio A using the variance-covariance method is US\$683,854 (=US\$108,127 × $\sqrt{40}$).

9.3.1.5 Recent advances in parametric VaR models

In addition to the techniques discussed earlier, recent empirical evidence also indicates the usefulness of new modelling approaches for estimating VaR in the presence of conditional volatility. These new approaches include 'extreme value theory', 'regime-switching GARCH models', and 'stochastic volatility models'.

Extreme value theory (EVT) deals with the effect of extreme events in the market and adjusts the tails of the distribution from which VaR is calculated. One of the main underlying assumptions in estimating VaR relates to the shape of the distribution of changes in the underlying asset. So far, we have assumed that asset returns follow a normal distribution. However, this assumption is frequently violated and conventional VaR models may provide poor estimates of VaR when return distributions exhibit fat tails and skewness. This effectively implies that large movements in the market, particularly on the tails of the distribution, are more frequent than what a normal distribution would predict. EVT provides a framework for handling the tail behaviour of a distribution and is used to estimate the VaR by adjusting the tails to capture deviations from normality.[6]

---

[6] See Tsay (2002), Christoffersen (2003), and Dowd (2002) for more details of extreme value theory and VaR estimation.

Table 9.2   VaR calculation using Monte Carlo simulation

Panel A: Assumptions

Route	Maturity	Rate (US$/mt)	Contract size (tonnes)	Daily volatility	Mean reversion rate	Long-run mean
1	60 days	30	54,000	2.52%	0.33	US$25/t
2	60 days	10	150,000	1.89%	0.40	US$8/t

Route	Current value (US$)		Current value (US$)		
			Port A	Port B	Correlation
1	1.62 m	(=US$30 × 54,000 mt)	3.12 m	0.12 m	0.8
2	1.50 m	(=US$10 × 150,000 mt)	Long route 1	Long route 1	
			Long route 2	Short route 2	

Panel B: Estimated 5 per cent VaR using MC simulation (US$)

	Route 1	Route 2	Portfolio A	Portfolio B
1-day VaR	66,121	44,863	105,428	41,106
10-day VaR	201,509	139,890	333,136	125,630
20-day VaR	279,375	190,127	451,969	175,951
40-day VaR	372,858	251,517	601,538	245,969

Regime-switching GARCH models are an extension of GARCH models that condition volatility on the state of the market. A common feature of GARCH models is that they tend to impose a high degree of persistence on the conditional volatility. This means that shocks to the conditional variance that occurred in the distant past continue to have a nontrivial impact on the current estimate of volatility. Lamoureux and Lastrapes (1990) associate these high levels of volatility persistence with structural breaks or regime shifts in the volatility process. Allowing volatility to switch between two state processes can also facilitate the mitigation of the non-normalities that the data exhibit (see, for instance, Li and Lin, 2004). Volatility-switching models are discussed more extensively above in Chapter 3 and their application to freight-rate VaR can be found in Alizadeh and Nomikos (2007c).

Finally, the motivation of stochastic volatility (SV) models stems from the fact that volatility is unobservable and thus it is more appropriate to model volatility as a random variable rather than define it as a specific process, as GARCH models do. Section 3.5.7 above provides a more detailed explanation and an estimated example of a SV model for freight rates; Shephard (2005) also provides a comprehensive survey of SV models.

9.3.2 Nonparametric VaR estimation methods

The non-parametric approach for estimating VaR uses the historical distribution of returns to determine the tail of the distribution and the relevant VaR estimate rather than making assumptions regarding the probability distribution that returns should follow.[7] Therefore, non-parametric VaR estimation methods allow for asymmetries, fat-tails and other deviations from normality which might be unique to a particular asset. Approaches for non-parametric VaR estimation include 'historical simulation', 'bootstrap' and 'quantile regressions'.

9.3.2.1 Historical simulation

The historical simulation (HS) approach allows for a distribution to be determined through past observations. This method uses the percentile of the historical returns to estimate the VaR. Hence, the α per cent one-period VaR is equal to the corresponding percentile of past N returns:

$$VaR_t^a = (F^a)^{-1}(\{r_{t-i}\}_{i=t-i-N}^{t-1}) \tag{9.12}$$

where $(F^a)^{-1}(\{r_{t-i}\}_{i=t-i-N}^{t-1})$ represents the α per cent percentile of past N return observations. An extension of HS, referred to as the 'filtered historical simulation' (FHS) method, uses the percentiles of the historical distribution of standardised returns. FHS is a semi-parametric method because it combines non-parametric HS with a parametric model in VaR estimation. In that sense, if $z_t (= \varepsilon_t/\sigma_t)$ are the standardised residuals of the parametric model, VaR is calculated as:

$$VaR_t^a = (F^a)^{-1} \left(\{z_{t-i}\}_{i=t-i-N}^{t-1} | \theta \right) \sigma_t \tag{9.13}$$

where σ_t is the standard deviation of the returns series based on historical values.

Example 7: Estimating VaR using historical simulation

To illustrate how FHS can be used to estimate VaR, consider one long TD3 FFA position with four months to maturity. The current value of this FFA position, given a market rate of 70 WS and a flat rate of US\$13.50/mt, is US\$47,250 (=5000 × 0.70 × US\$13.5/mt). The historical volatility of the TD3 contract with four-month maturity is 62 per cent per annum. Now, consider the distribution of standardised historical returns (log-changes) of the four-month TD3 FFA over the period December 2002 to December 2005, presented in Figure 9.5, versus a standardised normal distribution. It can be seen that

---

[7] The only assumption needed is that of stationarity of the distribution of returns or volatility.

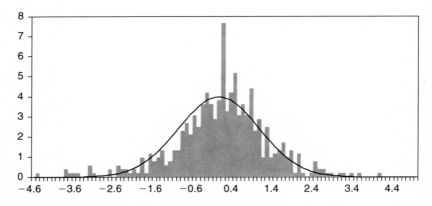

Figure 9.5   Historical vs. normal distribution of four-month TD3 FFA returns
Sample: December 2002 to December 2005.
Source: Imarex.

the distribution of standardised FFA returns has fatter tails than the normal distribution. Thus, assuming that returns are normally distributed may not be appropriate for estimating the VaR, and may lead to inaccurate results.

In order to address this issue we can use the filtered historical simulation method of data to find the percentiles of the standardised price changes. For that, first we standardise the returns over a certain time interval, 766 past observations in this case. For the 1 per cent tail value we find the value of observation 8 (out of 776 ranked standardised r_t); for 5 per cent tail value we find the value of observation 39; and for 10 per cent tail value, the value of observation is 78. The 1 per cent, 5 per cent and 10 per cent percentiles of the standardised returns on TD3 FFA are thus -3.221, -1.652, and -0.967 respectively. These percentiles are quite different from those of a normal distribution (that is, -2.326, -1.645 and -1.282 respectively). The FHS percentiles can be considered as the estimated non-parametric Z_a'; that is, the number which should be multiplied by the volatility of the FFA prices to obtain the VaR.

Since the daily volatility is 3.91 per cent ($=62\%/\sqrt{252}$), the daily dollar standard deviation is US\$1845.40 ($=$US\$47,250 $\times$ 3.91%). Hence, the one- and ten-day VaRs can be calculated as:

$$VaR_{1d}^{1\%} = Z_\alpha' * \sigma_{1day} = 3.221 \times US\$1845.40$$

$$\Rightarrow VaR_{1day} = US\$5944.07$$

$$VaR_{1d}^{1\%} = Z_\alpha' * \sigma_{1day} \times \sqrt{10} = 3.221 \times US\$1845.40 \times \sqrt{10}$$

$$\Rightarrow VaR_{10day} = US\$18,796.81$$

which is higher than the corresponding values with normal Z_a that is, US\$4293.07 and US\$13,575.87 for one- and ten-day VaRs respectively, reflecting the existence of fat-tails in the series.

9.3.2.2 The bootstrap method of estimating VaR

The bootstrap method, introduced by Efron (1979), uses historical observations to derive the distribution of asset returns and estimate the percentile of the empirical distribution. This is done by using random draws, with replacements, from past return series to construct the distribution of the asset prices and estimate the VaR. In Monte Carlo simulation the data are generated artificially based on an underlying process and a given distribution for the stochastic variable(s), whereas the bootstrap method uses the actual data and allows the distribution of the returns to be determined by historical asset-price changes. In this way, the distributional properties of the data are maintained. Bootstrapping methods can also be combined with parametric models to estimate VaR. This natural extension of bootstrap is referred to as 'semi-parametric bootstrap'. Hence, instead of bootstrapping the log-differenced series, the bootstrap is applied to the standardised residuals of the parametric model to generate the distribution of the dependent variable of the model (returns) and to estimate the VaR.

The main advantage of the bootstrap approach is that it can approximate the properties of the sampling distribution of the underlying statistic even when such a distribution is not parametrically defined, or when the underlined statistic is complex and not easy to obtain. This flexible method allows for deviations from normal distribution (skewness and fat-tails) and non-linearities since it is based on the actual distribution of the data. The major disadvantage of this method is that it is based on the principle that the past repeats itself and fairly represents the future, which may not always be the case. Another disadvantage is the impracticality of dealing with possible structural breaks and changes in the behaviour of the series. In addition, this method requires relatively large data sets of historical data in order to produce reliable results.

Finally, the ordinary bootstrap method is not valid in the case of serially dependent observations or when the data exhibit severe outliers, as is the case for freight rates. This is because the re-sampled series will not retain the statistical properties of the original data set and bootstrap will yield inconsistent results and VaR estimates. In view of that, several non-parametric methods dealing with serially dependent data have been developed. One such method is the 'stationary bootstrap' method developed by Politis and Romano (1994). This procedure is based on re-sampling random-length blocks from the original data, where the length of each block follows a geometric distribution. This procedure generates random samples that preserve the serial-dependence property of the original series and that are also stationary.

9.3.2.3 The quantile regression method

Based on the assumption and the empirical evidence that financial time series are autocorrelated, Engle and Manganelli (2004) developed a new method of calculating VaR using quantile regression techniques. They argue that since volatility evolves in clusters, the same clustering effect should occur in the VaR process itself. Hence, the quantile of the returns distribution can be modelled explicitly by using an autoregressive term and a 'shock' similar to the GARCH process. In the most simple case, the 'conditional autoregressive VaR model' (CAViaR) can be expressed as:[8]

$$VaR_t^a = \beta_0 + \sum_{i=1}^{p} \beta_i VaR_{t-i}^a + \sum_{j=1}^{q} \beta_j |r_{t-j}| \tag{9.14}$$

The inclusion of lagged VaR terms ensures that VaR changes smoothly over time whereas the absolute return links returns with VaR. The above model responds symmetrically to positive and negative returns. Different specifications have been proposed in the literature, such as:

Asymmetric absolute value: $VaR_t^a = \beta_0 + \beta_1 VaR_{t-1}^a + \beta_2 |r_{t-1}|^+ + \beta_3 |r_{t-1}|^-$

and

Indirect GARCH : $VaR_t^a = \sqrt{\beta_0 + \beta_1 (VaR_{t-1}^a)^2 + \beta_2 r_{t-1}^2}$

The motivation for CAViaR models stems from the fact that since we are interested in the quantile of a distribution we can model this quantile directly without making any assumption regarding the distributional properties (*iid*) of the data or returns. The main disadvantage of this method is that sometimes, if certain restrictions are not imposed, it may generate irrational quantiles (for example: $VaR_t^{1\%} < VaR_t^{5\%}$).

9.4 VaR for non-linear instruments

So far we have discussed how to estimate the VaR of FFA portfolios, which are linear instruments with regards to changes in the underlying asset (freight rates). Options, on the other hand, are non-linear instruments in that, first, their value is not linearly linked to the value of the underlying asset and

---

[8] The parameters of such models can be estimated by minimising the quantile loss function (see Koenker and Basset; 1978): $\arg \min_{\theta} \dfrac{1}{T} \sum_{t=1}^{T} (r_t - VaR_t^a)((1-a)I\{r_{t+1} < VaR_{t+1}^a\} + aI\{r_{t+1} \geq VaR_{t+1}^a\})$, where I is an indicator function that takes the value of 1 if the condition in $\{\cdot\}$ is met, and 0 otherwise.

second, they are driven by the underlying assets' volatility, which in turn is unobserved. Hence, portfolios that include assets with nonlinear payoff structures, such as options, impose an additional challenge in the computation of VaR.

To illustrate this, consider the distribution of the value of a long-call position, shown in Panel A of Figure 9.6. It can be seen that the distribution of the option value is positively skewed due to the unlimited upside potential gain and the limited downside loss equal to the option premium. Similarly, the distribution of the value of a short-call position is presented in Panel B of Figure 9.6. This time the distribution of short-call option positions is negatively skewed because of the unlimited downside (loss) potential and the limited upside gain equal to the option premium.

The non-linear structure in the payoff of options means that special techniques are used in the estimation of options VaR, including mapping.

9.4.1 Mapping VaR for options

The fundamental assumption in the Black-Scholes-Merton option-pricing model is that the underlying asset follows a geometric Brownian motion (GBM); that is, returns are normally distributed with constant variance. Moreover, as seen in Chapter 8, the option price is a function of the underlying asset price, the strike price, the volatility of the underlying asset, time to maturity and interest rates. Using a Taylor-series expansion, the change in the price of the option ($dC \equiv df$) can be written as the following partial differential equation:

$$dC \equiv df = \frac{\partial f}{\partial S}dS + \frac{1}{2}\frac{\partial^2 f}{\partial S^2}(dS)^2 + \frac{\partial f}{\partial \sigma}d\sigma + \frac{\partial f}{\partial r}dr + \frac{\partial f}{\partial t}dt \qquad (9.15)$$

where

$\frac{\partial f}{\partial S} = \Delta =$ is the delta of the option $\quad \frac{\partial^2 f}{\partial S^2} = \Gamma =$ is the gamma of the option

$\frac{\partial f}{\partial r} = \rho =$ is the rho of the option $\quad \frac{\partial f}{\partial \sigma} = \Lambda =$ is the vega of the option

$\frac{\partial f}{\partial t} = \Theta =$ is the theta of the option

and C is the option premium, S is the current price of the underlying, r is the risk-free rate, X is the strike price, σ is the volatility, and T is the time to maturity. The interpretation of each of the Greek parameters and option sensitivities are discussed in Chapter 8, Sections 8.8–8.13.

There are several ways to estimate the VaR of an option position. Delta approximation and delta-gamma approximation belong to the parametric

Panel A
Distribution of the value of a long-call position

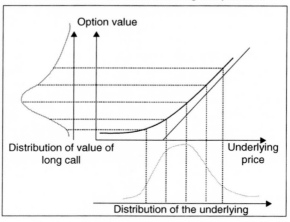

Panel B
Distribution of the value of a short-call position

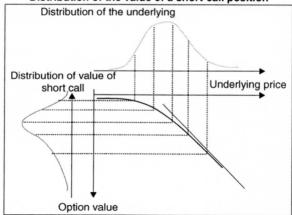

Figure 9.6   Distribution of changes: long- and short-call positions

family, where the normal distribution or the Cornish-Fisher expansion is used along with the Greek parameters to approximate the profit and loss (P&L) of the option position and obtain the VaR. The non-parametric and simulation techniques generate a number of scenarios in order to revalue the option portfolio and then approximate the P&L distribution of the option position or the portfolio, which can then be used to estimate the VaR. Alternatively, the simulated paths of the option portfolio can be used for delta or delta-gamma approximations in order to obtain the VaR of the option portfolio. We consider some of the parametric approximations next.

9.4.2 Delta approximation

This method, also referred to as 'local' approximation, focuses only on the first derivative of the option price with respect to the underlying, that is, the delta (Δ) of the option. In other words, it is assumed that the only sources of risk are first-order changes in the value of the underlying, and the effects of Γ; Θ, ρ and Λ are ignored. To estimate the VaR of an option position we need to obtain the volatility σ of the underlying asset and scale it by the delta of the option to obtain an approximation for the VaR of the option as:

$$VaR^{option} \approx VaR^{S}\Delta \approx (Z_{\alpha}\sigma S)\Delta \qquad (9.16)$$

Although this approach is computationally very easy and relatively fast to implement, it is extremely simplistic and at best is an approximation. In particular, since first-order approximations are reasonably accurate only for small price changes, and since we are interested in extreme events, this may suggest that delta approximations should not be relied on so much. In addition, for non-linear instruments such as options (which have convex pricing functions), this approximation may only be valid over short periods of time as well as for small changes in the underlying asset price.

Example 8: Delta approximation for estimating VaR of options

Consider a European one-year TC option with $S_0 = $ US\$22,500/day, $X = $ US\$25,000/day, $\sigma = 30$ per cent, time to maturity of three months, and r_f of 3 per cent. The premium for this option is US\$547.60/day, while the delta of the option is $\Delta = 0.2818$. Using the delta approximation, the 1 per cent one-day VaR can be computed as:

$$VaR_{1d}^{1\%} \approx (Z_{\alpha}\sigma S)\Delta \approx \left(2.326(0.3/\sqrt{252})22,500\right)0.2818 \approx US\$278.70$$

The above VaR approximation means that there is only a 1 per cent chance that the value of this long-call option will drop by US\$278.70, or more in one day.

9.4.3 Delta-gamma approximation

A more accurate way of estimating the VaR of an option position is to use delta-gamma approximation. This methodology is a natural extension of the delta-normal method which also assumes that the major source of risk in holding the option is due only to changes in the underlying. Then, in addition to the delta of an option position, we also consider the gamma and the change in the option value is approximated in equation (9.15) as:

$$dC \equiv df = \frac{\partial f}{\partial S} dS + \frac{1}{2} \frac{\partial^2 f}{\partial S^2} (dS)^2 = \Delta dS + \frac{1}{2} \Gamma (dS)^2 \qquad (9.17)$$

Thus, the linear term of dS is assumed to be normally distributed, whereas if this is the case the quadratic term dS^2 would follow a (non-central) chi-squared distribution. However, making a further assumption that the distribution of the option value is normal, that is, dS and dS^2 are jointly normally distributed (which actually contradicts empirical evidence), the VaR of an option position can be calculated as:

$$VaR^{option} \approx VaR^S \sqrt{\Delta^2 + (1/4)\Gamma^2\sigma^2} \approx (Z_\alpha \sigma S)\sqrt{\Delta^2 + (1/4)\Gamma^2\sigma^2} \qquad (9.18)$$

It can be seen that if the Γ is zero then (9.18) collapses to (9.16), and delta approximation might be a good enough estimate of the VaR of the option position.

Alternatively, assuming that returns are normally distributed with zero mean and standard deviation σ, we can write the first three moments of df as:

> 1st moment: $E(df) = (1/2)S^2 \Gamma \sigma^2$
> 2nd moment: $E(df^2) = S^2 \Delta^2 \sigma^2 + (3/4)S^4 \Gamma^2 \sigma^4$
> 3rd moment: $E(df^3) = (9/2)S^4 \Delta^2 \Gamma \sigma^4 + (15/8)S^6 \Gamma^3 \sigma^6$

Then, VaR can be calculated as:

$$VaR^{option} \approx Z_\alpha \sigma^{option} \approx Z_\alpha \sqrt{[E(df^2) - E(df)^2]} \qquad (9.19)$$

Several versions of the delta-gamma method have been developed to improve the accuracy of the approximation (see also Dowd, 2002). One of the most popular is the 'delta-gamma Monte Carlo method' which assumes hypothetical changes in the portfolio value df. In particular, after each random draw of the Monte Carlo simulation (see section 9.3.1.4) of the returns of the underlying asset, the conventional delta-gamma method is applied and df distribution is approximated.

Another widespread methodology is the 'delta-gamma Cornish-Fisher method' which uses a Cornish-Fisher expansion to obtain the ath percentile of the standardised df distribution using the first three moments $E(df^i)$ for $i = 1, 2, 3$. This involves an adjustment in the calculation of the quantile where we replace the normal Z_a with Z'_a. The latter is calculated as follows:

$$Z'_a = Z_\alpha - \frac{1}{6}(Z_\alpha^2 - 1)\frac{1}{\sigma_{df}^3}E[(df - \mu_{df})^3]$$

$$= Z_\alpha - \frac{1}{6}(Z_\alpha^2 - 1)\frac{E[(df)^3] - 3E[(df)^2]\mu_{df} + 2\mu_{df}^3}{\sigma_{df}^3}$$

$$= Z_\alpha - \frac{1}{6}(Z_\alpha^2 - 1)Q_{df} \tag{9.20}$$

where Q_{df} is a measure of skewness. Note that this method is applicable to all variance-covariance VaR methods discussed in this chapter (such as RiskMetrics, GARCH and so on).

Example 9: Delta-gamma approximation for estimating VaR of options

Consider the previous example with the additional assumption that the gamma of the option is $\Gamma = 0.0001$. Using the delta-gamma approximation, the 1 per cent one-day VaR of the long-call option can be computed as follows:

$$VaR_{1d}^{1\%} \approx Z_\alpha \sigma S\sqrt{\Delta^2 + (1/4)\Gamma^2\sigma^2}$$

$$\approx 2.326(0.3/\sqrt{252})22,500\sqrt{0.2818^2 + (1/4)0.0001^2(0.3/\sqrt{252})^2}$$

$$\approx US\$278.70$$

The difference between the delta and the delta-gamma approximations seems to be negligible because the gamma of this option position is very small.

Alternatively, we can approximate the VaR of the option position by calculating the first two moments of df, and use the moments to calculate the variance ($[E(df^2) - E(df)^2]$) and the VaR of the option position as follows:

1st moment: $E(df^1) = (1/2)S^2\Gamma\sigma^2 = 9.04$
2nd moment: $E(df^2) = S^2\Delta^2\sigma^2 + (3/4)S^4\Gamma^2\sigma^4 = 14,603.01$

$$VaR_{1d}^{1\%} \approx Z_\alpha \sigma^{option} \approx Z_\alpha\sqrt{[E(df^2) - E(df)^2]}$$

$$\approx 2.326\sqrt{14603.01 - 9.04^2} = US\$280.30$$

Finally, using the Cornish-Fisher expansion, we can obtain the ath percentile of the standardised df distribution by replacing Z_a (2.326) of the normal distribution with Z'_a, and estimate the 1 per cent one-day VaR as:

$$Q_{df} = \frac{1{,}179{,}258.70 - 3(14{,}603.01)(9.04) + 2(9.04)^3}{(120.519)^3} = 0.449$$

$$Z'_\alpha = Z_\alpha + (1/6)(Z_\alpha^2 - 1)Q_{df} = 2.326 + (1/6)(2.326^2 - 1)(0.449) = 2.656$$

$$VaR_{1d}^{1\%} \approx \mu_{df} + Z'_a\sigma_f = 9.04 + 2.656 \times \sqrt{14{,}603.01 - 9.04^2} = US\$329.10$$

Figure 9.7 presents the differences in the option VaR estimates using the different methods. The differences in the option VaR depends on the option premium and the underlying price. The curves represent the delta-normal (from Example 8), delta-gamma and delta-gamma Cornish-Fisher methods. It can be seen that the largest difference in the option VaRs estimated using different methods is when the option is at-the-money or close to that point. It is around ATM options that the gamma is at its maximum and delta is about 0.5. Therefore, gamma effects in VaR have a higher impact for near ATM options.

9.5   Principal component analysis and VaR estimation

Principal component analysis (PCA) is a powerful statistical tool for estimating the VaR of multi-asset portfolios of relatively large dimensions. PCA is in fact a decomposition technique which is used to analyse correlation structures, express relationship patterns and, in a way, capture the most important factors that determine the volatility dynamics of the data set. PCA deals with 'the curse of dimensionality' by tracking a few factors (principal components) that can explain a large proportion of the variation of the portfolio, without any significant loss of information. Consider a portfolio of k assets with the returns input in $R_{(t \times k)}$, where t is the number of observations, and covariance and correlation matrix $H_{(k \times k)}$ and $C_{(k \times k)}$, respectively:

$$R_t = \left(r_{1,t} \;\cdots\; r_{k,t} \right), H = \begin{bmatrix} \sigma_{11} & \sigma_{12} & \cdots & \sigma_{1k} \\ \sigma_{21} & \sigma_{22} & \cdots & \sigma_{2k} \\ \cdots & \cdots & \cdots & \cdots \\ \sigma_{k1} & \sigma_{k2} & \cdots & \sigma_{kk} \end{bmatrix} and\; C = \begin{bmatrix} 1 & \rho_{12} & \cdots & \rho_{1k} \\ \rho_{21} & 1 & \cdots & \rho_{2k} \\ \cdots & \cdots & \cdots & \cdots \\ \rho_{k1} & \rho_{k2} & \cdots & 1 \end{bmatrix}$$

In order for the PCA to work properly, each column of matrix **R** should be stationary with zero mean and unit variance; otherwise, the asset with the highest volatility will be spuriously identified as the most significant principal component. The goal is to derive a new matrix, **H***, which approximates **H**, with fewer uncorrelated components and consequently a smaller dimension (see Appendix 9.A below for a detailed explanation of PCA).

Panel A
Option-VaR against underlying price

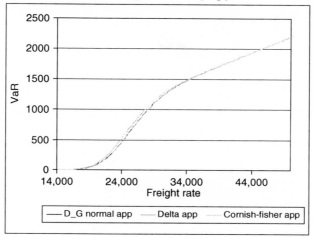

Panel B
Option-VaR against option premium

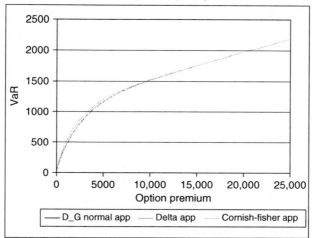

Figure 9.7   Plot of differences in option VaR-estimation methods

Empirical evidence suggests that for most portfolios two or three components could be used to summarise the exposure of the portfolio because they
might be sufficient to explain more than 90 per cent of the variation in **R**.
The first principal component (PC) normally corresponds to a 'parallel shift'

in the asset values; the second PC corresponds to 'twist' in the movement of the value of the assets; the third PC explains the bending effect and so on (see Figure 9.8). To estimate the VaR of a relatively large portfolio of assets using PCA, the following steps are involved:

Step 1: Applying the PCA technique to the historical returns of assets which are included in the portfolio. As explained above, this step involves identifying the factors that have the highest explanatory power regarding the volatility of the return series in the data set.
Step 2: Determining the exposures of portfolio values to those risk factors.
Step 3: Calculating the standard deviation of the portfolio using exposures to the principal components. Once we have the volatility of the portfolio, calculation of VaR is straightforward. Or, alternatively, generate the distribution of the portfolio values from the distribution of the identified risk factors, and hence calculate the VaR from the latter distribution.

Example 10: Estimating VaR using principal component analysis

To illustrate how PCA can be used to estimate the VaR of a portfolio of FFA contracts, consider a portfolio which consists of 4 TD3 FFA positions with one, two, three and four months to maturity. Each contract is for 5000 mt and, given a flat rate of US$13.5/mt, the total value of the portfolio is US$224,775 (see Table 9.3 for the calculations). Panel A of Table 9.3 also reports the size of each contract as well as the weights of each position in the portfolio, which are calculated as:

$$\text{Contract size}_{(\text{1M-TD3})} = \frac{WS}{100} \times Flat\ rate \times Size = \frac{112.5}{100} \times 13.5 \times 5,000 = 75,937.5$$

$$\text{Weights}_{(\text{1M-TD3})} = \frac{Contract\ size}{Total\ value\ of\ portfolio} = \frac{75,397.5}{224,775} = 33.78\%$$

Panel B of Table 9.3 presents the variance proportions. It can be seen that the first factor can explain more than 75 per cent of the portfolio variation, while the first two factors can explain more than 90 per cent, and so on. Thus, we can use the first two PCs to estimate VaR – because these explain more than 90 per cent of the variation in the rate. For more accurate estimation of VaR, we can use the first three factors, which explain 96.5 per cent of the variation of the portfolio. The eigenvectors of the PCA are also reported in Panel B of Table 9.3.

We can calculate the effect on the portfolio of a one WS-point change in each of the FFAs. This corresponds to an increase of US$675 (= 0.01 × US$13.5/mt × 5000 mt) for every single FFA position. Therefore, the exposure of portfolio value to each PC can be estimated as the product of the

Table 9.3 Using principal component analysis to calculate VaR

Panel A: Assumptions for one, two, three and four months to maturity

Flat rate	TD3 FFA	WS	Cont size	Weights
13.5	1M	112.5	75,937.5	0.3378
	2M	88.0	59,400.0	0.2643
CL	3M	67.5	45,562.5	0.2027
99%	4M	65.0	43,875.0	0.1952
			224,775.0	

Panel B: Components and eigenvectors

	Comp 1	Comp 2	Comp 3	Comp 4
Eigenvalue	3.020	0.611	0.228	0.141
Variance prop.	0.755	0.153	0.057	0.035
Cumulative prop.	0.755	0.908	0.965	1.000
SD of component	86.9%	39.1%	23.9%	18.8%

	Vector 1	Vector 2	Vector 3	Vector 4
1M-TD3 returns	−0.4490	−0.7442	−0.4608	−0.1795
2M-TD3 returns	−0.5360	−0.1459	0.4989	0.6652
3M-TD3 returns	−0.5333	0.2282	0.4224	−0.6965
4M-TD3 returns	−0.4761	0.6106	−0.6003	0.2005

Panel C: VaR calculation US$

WS change	1	1	1	1
US$ change in FFA	675	675	675	675
Exposure to PC1	−1,346.23			
Exposure to PC2	−34.70			
SD per annum	116,984.2			
SD per day	7,369.3			
1-day VaR	17,143.58			
10-day VaR	54,212.76			

eigenvector of each factor and the vector of US$ change in each FFA position due to a unit change in WS:

$$Exposure\ PC_1 = (675\ \ 675\ \ 675\ \ 675) \begin{pmatrix} -0.4490 \\ -0.5360 \\ -0.5333 \\ -0.4761 \end{pmatrix} = -US\$1,346.23$$

$$Exposure\ PC_2 = (675\ \ 675\ \ 675\ \ 675) \begin{pmatrix} -0.7442 \\ -0.1459 \\ 0.2282 \\ 0.6106 \end{pmatrix} = -US\$34.70$$

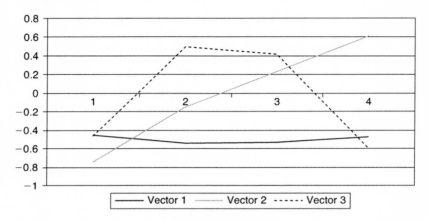

Figure 9.8   Eigenvectors from principal components analysis on freight rates

Then we calculate the standard deviation of the portfolio, using the standard deviation of each component (presented in Panel B) and the PC exposures, as:

$$\sigma_{year} = \sqrt{(Exposure\ PC_1)^2(SD_1)^2 + (Exposure\ PC_2)^2(SD_2)^2}$$

$$= \sqrt{(-1,346.23)^2(86.9)^2 + (-34.7)^2(39.1)^2} = US\$116,984$$

which yields approximate daily and ten-day standard deviations of

$$\sigma_{daily} = \sigma_{year}/\sqrt{252} = US\$116,984/\sqrt{252} = US\$7369$$

$$\sigma_{10d} = \sigma_{daily} \times \sqrt{10} = US\$7369 \times \sqrt{10} = US\$23,303$$

Finally, we estimate the ten-day 1 per cent VaR as US\$54,212.76 ($= 2.326 \times US\$7369 \times \sqrt{10}$). Note that this is significantly smaller than the estimate in Example 5 in Section 9.2.1, which is US\$80,314. This is expected because here we used only two out of four factors to estimate the VaR of the portfolio; as a result, part of the variation in the value of the portfolio – which is due to the third and fourth sources of risk – is not considered, hence the lower VaR estimate.

The impact of the eigenvectors of three factors extracted through PCA on the portfolio of TD3 FFAs is presented in Figure 9.8. It can be seen that the response of all FFAs to the first factor is negative through a parallel downward shift; the response of the FFAs to the second factors is such that the far end of the curve moves up and the front end moves down, that is, there is a tilt in the curve; and the response of the FFA to the third factor is that the middle of the curve rises and the two ends move down, that is, there is a bend in the curve.

9.6 Backtesting and stresstesting of VaR models

VaR models have to be tested for their performance to ensure their results are reliable and robust. This is done through answering questions such as:

1. How many times were the actual (individual) returns less than the VaR forecast?
2. How big are the actual returns in the lower 5th percentile compared to the *size* of those for the distribution considered?
3. Do violations of the model forecasts occur in clusters or they are independent?
4. How accurate are VaR predictions?

These questions can be answered through a set of procedures and statistical validation techniques known as 'backtesting' and 'stresstesting'.

Backtesting procedures are essential because unrealistic assumptions and flawed VaR models could be more damaging than helpful to the business because they may underestimate risks and may thus lead to unjustified investment decisions. This is also of particular importance to external regulators such as auditors, creditors, investors and credit-rating agencies which require accurate estimates of risk and demand sound validation of the risk-quantification techniques employed.

The simplest means of backtesting is by running the model through the historical sample and testing whether the VaR values correspond to the proportion of times that changes in the variable/portfolio exceeded the VaR level. If this occurs say, α per cent of the time, then we can be assured that the method chosen to estimate the α per cent VaR is relatively accurate. On the other hand, if changes in the portfolio significantly exceed the α per cent VaR level, then we cannot be confident about the predictive performance of the VaR methodology used. However, the predictive accuracy and effectiveness of VaR models must be verified using appropriate statistical tests. The most commonly used framework in backtesting VaR models was developed by Christoffersen (1998). A sequence of out-of-sample VaR estimates is said to be efficient with respect to the information set available at $t - 1$, Ω_{t-1}, if the following condition holds:

$$E[\Phi_t | \Omega_{t-1}] = a \quad \text{with } \Phi_t = \begin{cases} 1, & R_t < VaR_t^a \\ 0, & R_t \geq VaR_t^a \end{cases} \tag{9.21}$$

The above equation implies that the expected VaR failures Φ_t should be first, on average, equal to the nominal confidence level and second, uncorrelated with any function/variable in the information set available at $t - 1$. The above property is tested using intermediary statistics of unconditional coverage, independence and conditional coverage (see Christoffersen, 1998).

In addition, various loss functions that deal with the magnitude of errors (violations) can also be constructed as supplementary measures to backtest VaR models. Backtesting VaR models using loss functions was first introduced by Lopez (1999). Traditionally, the loss functions employed are asymmetric in view of the fact that underprediction and overprediction of VaR estimates have diverse implications. For instance, underprediction of risk might lead to liquidity problems and thus reoccurring underprediction can lead to insolvency. On the other hand, overprediction will lead to a higher capital charge, which does not represent a bankruptcy risk, but results in higher opportunity cost from tied-up capital.

The power of these tests is mainly affected by the horizon over which the VaR is estimated and by the confidence level. In particular, longer horizons and higher confidence levels reduce the power of the tests. For instance, a 30-day VaR is expected to reduce any dependencies in the time series, thus reducing the power of the test. Similarly, high confidence levels (say, 99.5 per cent) imply that we have to wait for at least 200 observations, on average, to validate the model, which leads to a reduction in power.

Besides backtesting, which verifies the accuracy of different VaR models by systematically comparing projected VaR estimates with historical returns, stresstesting is also an essential part of the design and validation of the appropriate VaR model. Stresstesting involves examining the model's responsiveness and its sensitivity to some extreme events (hypothetical or real). For instance, if one or several variable(s) change by a large magnitude, or some extraordinary and extreme events take place (such as a hurricane in US Gulf waters), what will happen to the value of portfolio? What would be the magnitude of loss, and does this fall within the VaR limit?

Stresstesting is normally carried out via scenario analysis. Sets of different scenarios might be constructed by subjecting the model (VaR) to some extreme events, recording the impact on the portfolio value and comparing it to the estimated VaR. A relatively simple way to search for worst-case scenarios is the so-called 'factor-push method'. Within this setting, changes in the individual risk factors are followed by an evaluation of the portfolio value. However, in this case, correlations and data interdependencies are neglected, since it may not make sense to consider scenarios in which strongly positively correlated risk factors move in opposite directions. A solution is to use the 'conditional scenario method' which adds the constraint of given correlations. The scenarios can be created by:

1. Simulating shocks based on historical data (such as the oil crisis of the 1970s, Black Monday/the 1987 stock market crash, the 1997–8 Asian financial crisis, the 2008 'credit crunch', and so on).
2. Simulating predefined changes in the individual risk factors. For instance, what is the impact on a portfolio P&L if there is a rise/fall of two or three

standard deviations in an FFA position which constitute k per cent of the portfolio?

3. Simulating shocks based on potential changes to the risk factors. For instance, what would be the impact on the P&L of a portfolio if a war breaks out, oil production in a country is disrupted, or a seaway or canal is closed due to political conflict, or even if there is a hurricane or an earthquake?

However, stresstesting suffers from a number of problems. First, it is highly subjective because the scenarios chosen depend on the individual. Second, inferences concerning those tests are not an easy task because probabilities are difficult to assign to extreme events. Third, they cannot be combined in a quantitative manner with the actual risk measure, that is, VaR. Finally, such procedures are difficult to test; hence, their performance cannot be assessed. As Berkowitz (2000) puts it: 'stresstesting is a statistical purgatory. We have some loss numbers but who is to say whether we should be concerned about them?'

9.7 Summary and conclusions

In this chapter we presented and discussed an important part of the modern risk-management process that deals with the assessment of the magnitude of potential loss due to market-risk exposure. This method of risk measurement, which is becoming an integral part of the risk-management process in the shipping industry, summarises the market risk exposure in a single number, known as VaR. The VaR is used to express the potential or maximum possible loss, given a certain probability that the market moves, over a specified time horizon. The most important use of VaR in shipping business is when trading FFAs and dealing with portfolios of freight derivatives, including freight options. In such cases, it is always helpful to know the potential expected loss of each position and of the portfolio as whole, especially when contracts are cleared and margins should be maintained.

We explored and reviewed different VaR-estimation techniques and approaches, providing real examples for single positions as well as for multi-asset portfolios. It was argued that the distributional properties as well as dynamics of the price changes of underlying assets (FFAs) should be taken into account to increase the accuracy of VaR estimates for FFA positions. This can be achieved using nonparametric approaches or simulation techniques. In addition, we showed how the VaR of large freight portfolios can be estimated using a simple variance-covariance method or principal component analysis. For estimating the VaR of non-linear freight derivatives instruments such as options, we presented different methods, including delta and delta-gamma approximations, and compared their performances. Finally, we discussed approaches such as backtesting and stresstesting in the context of assessing the performance of various VaR estimation techniques.

Appendix 9.A: Principal component analysis

Using a linear combination of a set of time series (price changes or returns of assets in a portfolio), a principal component can be expressed as a weighted sum of all price changes. Let $\mathbf{w}_1 = (w_{11}, \ldots w_{k1})'$ serve as a column vector which summarises the *weights* assigned to each asset included in the portfolio.[9] Subject to the constraint that $\mathbf{w}_1$ is normalised, that is, $\mathbf{w}_1'\mathbf{w}_1 = 1$, the first principal component with dimensions $(t \times k)$, is as follows:

$$\mathbf{F}_1 = w_{11}r_{1t} + \cdots + w_{k1}r_{kt}$$
$$\sigma^2(\mathbf{F}_1) = \mathbf{w}_1'\mathbf{H}\mathbf{w}_1 = \mathbf{w}_1'(\mathbf{F}_1'\mathbf{F}_1)\mathbf{w}_1 \qquad (9.22)$$

Performing PCA on portfolio $\mathbf{R}$ involves calculating the eigenvalues and eigenvectors of the covariance matrix in order to determine the factors. The highest eigenvalue is related to the first principal component (PC) that can explain the majority of variation in $\mathbf{R}$, the second highest eigenvalue is related to the second PC that can explain the second source of variation in $\mathbf{R}$, and so on. Factors are determined by ordering the eigenvectors from the highest to the lowest according to the corresponding eigenvalues. In the above equation, $\mathbf{w}_1$ is actually an eigenvector. This is chosen in such a way that it maximises the variance of $\mathbf{F}_1$, $\sigma^2(\mathbf{F}_1)$. Then, according to eigenvector theory,[10] if $\mathbf{w}_1$ satisfies $\mathbf{H}\mathbf{w}_1 = \lambda_1\mathbf{w}_1$, λ_1 is the largest eigenvalue of $\mathbf{H}$ with the corresponding eigenvector $\mathbf{w}_1$. After the first PC is determined, we move on to the second PC as the one that maximises the variance of $\mathbf{F}_2$, $\sigma^2(\mathbf{F}_2)$, subject to the constraints that $\mathbf{w}_2$ is both normalised ($\mathbf{w}_2'\mathbf{w}_2 = 1$) and orthogonal to the first, that is, $\mathbf{w}_2'\mathbf{w}_1 = 0$. Then, λ_2 is the largest eigenvalue of $\mathbf{H}$ with corresponding eigenvector $\mathbf{w}_2$. λ_2 indicates the PC that can explain the majority of the remaining variation in $\mathbf{R}$.

In short, the principal components are *the maximum variance* linear combinations of the original variables subject to the constraint that each of the components is independent of the other. Generally, we can obtain k individual principal components, as the number of assets in the portfolio. This

---

[9] Note that the term weight here has nothing to do with how the capital of the investor is allocated to the portfolio assets.

[10] Let $\mathbf{A}$ be a square matrix and λ a scalar. If there exists a vector $\mathbf{B} \neq 0$ such as: $\mathbf{A} \times \mathbf{B} = \lambda \times \mathbf{B}$, then λ is called the eigenvalue of $\mathbf{A}$ with corresponding eigenvector $\mathbf{B}$. Eigenvalues are the solution to the following equation: $(\mathbf{A} - \lambda \times \mathbf{I}) \times \mathbf{B} = 0$

implies that the variance-covariance matrix **H** can be decomposed as (singular value decomposition):

$$\mathbf{H} = \mathbf{WDW'} = (\mathbf{w}_1 \quad \dots \quad \mathbf{w_k}) \begin{pmatrix} \lambda_1 & \dots & 0 \\ \dots & \dots & \dots \\ 0 & \dots & \lambda_k \end{pmatrix} \begin{pmatrix} \mathbf{w'_1} \\ \dots \\ \mathbf{w'_k} \end{pmatrix}$$

$$= \begin{pmatrix} w_{11} & \dots & w_{1k} \\ \dots & \dots & \dots \\ w_{k1} & \dots & w_{kk} \end{pmatrix} \begin{pmatrix} \lambda_1 & \dots & 0 \\ \dots & \dots & \dots \\ 0 & \dots & \lambda_k \end{pmatrix} \begin{pmatrix} w_{11} & \dots & w_{k1} \\ \dots & \dots & \dots \\ w_{1k} & \dots & w_{kk} \end{pmatrix} \quad (9.23)$$

However, in practice we use only the first few of these components. That is exactly the purpose of PCA: to transform a high number of correlated variables into a smaller number of uncorrelated variables. So, instead of working with all the components, that is, k, we would choose the first l components that can explain the majority of variation in **R**. Let **z** be a vector containing weights on each asset of a portfolio comprising k assets. The expected return and variance of the portfolio would then be $\mathbf{z'R}$ and $\mathbf{z'Hz}$, respectively. After identifying the l (with $l < k$), most significant components that can adequately describe the variance of a portfolio, the original covariance matrix of the portfolio can instead be approximated with $\mathbf{z'H^*z}$, where:

$$\mathbf{H^*} = \mathbf{w_1 w'_1} \lambda_1 + \dots + \mathbf{w_l w'_l} \lambda_l \quad (9.24)$$

10
Bunker Risk Analysis and Risk Management

10.1 Introduction

In general, ships use fuel oil (bunker) for propulsion, and diesel oil for manoeuvring in ports and for electricity generators. Fuel oil is essentially the 'residual oil' that was originally defined as whatever liquid was left behind in the petroleum distillation unit after the removal of more valuable products such as kerosene, diesel and naphtha (Percy, et al., 1996). There are two basic grades of bunker fuel, heavy fuel oil (HFO) 180 centistokes (cst) and the more widely used HFO 380 cst.[1] Centistokes is the unit of measurement of fuel viscosity and the distinction between the two grades is the distillate content: Grade 180 cst has a 7 per cent to 15 per cent distillate content, while Grade 380 cst has 2 per cent to 5 per cent distillate content (Visweswaran, 2000). The higher the distillate content, the more energy the fuel has; 60 per cent of the world bunker trade is in HFO380cst while HFO180cst and other grades account for about 30 per cent, with the remaining 10 per cent of world trade being in marine diesel oil. Bunker fuel is also classified according to its sulphur content into low (1 per cent) and high (3.5 per cent) sulphur. Low-sulphur fuel oils are less corrosive and hence more expensive compared to high-sulphur fuels, even though the corrosion process caused by high-sulphur fuel can be counteracted by using special cylinder lubricants. Although recent technological advances have enabled ships to use lower-grade bunkers more efficiently, high-grade bunkers are still used by more sophisticated ships, especially cruise ships and fast ferries.

The aim of this chapter is to first illustrate and assess the fluctuations of bunker prices and to highlight the importance of bunker price risk to shipping operations. Second, we discuss different derivatives instruments available to

---

[1] Bunker fuel is a term which has been used for many years to define the most thick and sticky of the residual fuel oils. When steamships were coal-fired, 'bunkers' were the home for the bins used to hold the coal. As marine diesel engines became prevalent, the term was carried over to include the liquid fuel tanks.

shipowners, operators and bunker suppliers to control their exposure to risk involved in bunker prices. Further, we analyse the pros and cons of different contracts used in bunker risk management and provide examples of how they can be used effectively.

10.2 The world bunker market

Although marine bunkers are bought and sold in almost every port in the world, the world bunker market can be broadly divided into three major regional markets where the bulk of physical bunkering activities take place. These markets are Asia (Singapore), Europe (Rotterdam) and the Americas (US Gulf). Other relatively important geographical markets include New York, Fujairah, Yokohama and Hamburg. The Singapore bunker market is by far the largest marine fuel market in the world, with a turnover of around 28.5 million tonnes in 2006. In Europe, the Amsterdam–Rotterdam–Antwerp (ARA) area is a prime benchmark bunkering region. The heart of the ARA region is Rotterdam, with a hub of oil-refining and storage facilities sited in its Europort complex, which handles around 100 million tonnes (metric ton or mt) of crude oil annually. The bunker trade in Rotterdam alone reached 13.4 million mt in 2006. In the Americas, the US Gulf bunker market has an annual turnover of around 10 million mt while the trade in New York market is just less than 3 million mt per year.

Since bunker fuel is a low derivative of petroleum, its price is closely related to world oil prices. It is also well documented that oil prices are very volatile and depend upon many factors, including political and economic events around the world. As a result, disturbances and shocks to the world oil market are transmitted to the bunker market, causing large fluctuations in bunker prices. This is evident from Figure 10.1 which presents the historical bunker prices in five major bunker regions, namely: Rotterdam, Houston, Singapore, Fujairah and Japan. Two important observations can be made here. First, bunker prices in these geographical regions move together in the long run due to the fact that they are driven by crude-oil prices and fundamentals; however, there are short-term deviations between these prices due to local factors such as supply and demand imbalances, seasonality and local competition. Second, historical prices indicate large fluctuations and high volatility in bunker prices, which is expected because bunker prices are linked to world oil prices and shocks and large swings in the world oil market directly affect the world bunker market.

Table 10.1 presents descriptive statistics of spot bunker prices in five major bunkering ports around the world. It can be seen that average bunker prices show significant variation across different ports, with Japan and Rotterdam being the most and the least expensive bunkering ports respectively. While the range of variation seems to be between a minimum of US$49/mt to a maximum of US$578/mt, average growth rates have been 5 per cent to

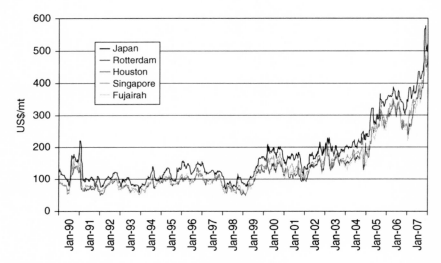

Figure 10.1   Weekly spot bunker prices in five major ports
Source: Clarkson's SIN.

Table 10.1   Descriptive statistics of bunker prices in major bunkering ports

		Rotterdam	Houston	Singapore	Fujairah	Japan
Average price	US$/mt	138	140	151	147	176
Minimum price	US$/mt	51	49	52	51	59
Maximum price	US$/mt	495	499	513	513	578
Annualised mean return	%	5.2	5.2	5.7	5.7	6.2
Annualised standard devn.	%	42.0	44.9	42.7	40.7	33.0
Skewness		−0.295	−0.453	−0.141	−0.159	0.084
Kurtosis		3.764	3.298	3.593	4.728	7.238

Sample period: 1991–2007.

6 per cent per annum over the past 16 years. This reflects the significant increases in bunker prices since 2005 in line with oil-price rises. Historical volatility of bunker prices also seems to be different across these bunkering ports, with Japan showing the lowest volatility (33 per cent) and Houston the highest (44.9 per cent). The average annualised standard deviation of 40 per cent indicates that the bunker market is in general a very volatile market where a 10 per cent to 20 per cent price change in one month is quite common.

10.3   Bunker-price risk in shipping operations

The structure and definition of costs in shipping operations were discussed in Chapter 2, where it is argued that perhaps the most important source of risk on the costs side of the shipping operation is fluctuations in fuel-oil or bunker prices. Bunker cost varies depending on the duration of the voyage, the age of the ship as well as the size of the vessel's engine and its efficiency. For example, for a long-haul voyage, bunker expenses may be more than 75 per cent of the total voyage costs, whereas for a short-haul voyage, bunker expenditure could be as low as 20 per cent of the total costs. However, on average, bunker-fuel costs account for more than 50 per cent of the total voyage costs and, as a result, sharp and unanticipated changes in bunker prices have a major impact on the operating profitability of shipping companies and ship operators. This is because bunker prices are naturally related to world oil prices, which have been shown to exhibit substantial variability both in the short and long term. Therefore, it is of utmost importance for shipping companies and ship operators to control and minimise their exposure to bunker-market fluctuations in order to secure their operating profit.

To illustrate this point, consider a Panamax operator who fixes a contract of affreightment (CoA) for 150,000 mt of cargo today; the contract requires three shipments, one every two months, at a rate of US$25/mt. This means that the freight contract generates US$1,250,000 (US$25/mt × 50,000 mt) every two months. If the current bunker price is US$300/mt, and the ship consumes 2500 mt of bunker per voyage, the expected profit for the shipowner from each voyage, assuming that port charges are US$150,000, will be US$350,000. Now consider the case where bunker prices increase by 20 per cent to US$360/mt within two months. This results in an overall reduction in profits of US$150,000 for each voyage and US$450,000 for the entire contract. Therefore, fluctuations in bunker prices can indeed have an adverse impact on the profitability and hence viability of shipping ventures.

In the past, there were not many options available to shipowners for controlling bunker-price uncertainty. As a result, shipowning and ship-operating companies had difficulty in securing their bunker costs and profit margins, which is an important part of their operation. One way of managing bunker-price risk, which was and still is used mainly by larger liner companies, is to include a bunker adjustment clause in the shipping contract, known as the 'bunker adjustment factor' (BAF).[2] BAF is essentially an agreement

---

[2] Bunker adjustment factor (BAF) can be defined as a surcharge that is designed to take into account fluctuations in fuel prices in a shipping contract. BAF is quite common in liner shipping contracts and CoAs, because these contracts are usually agreed on a long-term basis, whereas fuel prices can fluctuate dramatically over short periods. Therefore, BAFs allow for the uncertainty with regards to fuel price to be accounted for

between the carrier (ship operator) and the shipper where the latter agrees to pay additional charges if there is significant change in bunker prices, according to a preset formula. In this way, the carrier passes the bunker-price risk to the shipper. However, in recent years many shipping companies have found that BAF is not the most efficient method for managing bunker risk, for two main reasons. First, there is always a time lag between the increase in market price of bunker and application of BAF for freight calculation. Second, the increase in bunker price should be sufficient for the BAF to take effect. In addition, charterers may not find shipping contracts with BAF clauses very attractive.

During the early 1980s, shipowners, charterers and other parties involved in shipping realised that risk-management techniques which had been applied successfully in commodity and financial markets – such as hedging using futures, options and swaps – could also be applied to risk management in the shipping industry. This initially led to the development of exchange-traded bunker futures contracts. For example, in 1988 the Singapore Futures Exchange launched a bunker futures contract and, in 1999, the International Petroleum Exchange launched a similar contract in London. However, both contracts failed to attract trading interest by market participants and were eventually withdrawn from the market due to very low trading activity.[3] This was primarily due to the nature of the bunker market because physical bunker is traded in different geographical locations around the world, whereas futures contracts are for the delivery of bunker fuel in specific locations. Consequently, futures prices do not follow accurately the movement of bunker fuel prices in different locations, which in turn reduces the effectiveness of the contract as a hedging instrument.

In the absence of bunker futures contracts, and due to the close association between bunker prices and petroleum prices, futures contracts on the latter are alternative candidates for bunker-price risk management. However, Alizadeh et al. (2004) show that these instruments do not provide significant benefits in terms of hedging and risk reduction. In fact, they report that correlation between petroleum futures prices and bunker prices in Rotterdam, New York, Singapore and Houston are relatively low (below 70 per cent) in most cases, which means that the effectiveness of hedging using such futures contracts would not be as high as required (for example, 50 per cent at highest).

---

in a manner agreed between the carrier and the shipper. BAFs are normally calculated with reference to bunker market prices (for example, Platts reports in major import locations such as Rotterdam) against the price in reference year (for example, the year in which the BAF formula was set). The surcharge is then calculated and applied if the difference exceeds a certain, predetermined, level.

[3] The Singapore bunker futures contract was withdrawn in the early 1990s while trading on London IPE futures bunker contract lasted only for six months.

10.4   Hedging bunker risk using OTC instruments

The non-availability of reliable exchange-traded bunker futures contracts led in the 1990s to the development and trade in tailor-made over-the-counter (OTC) instruments for bunker risk-management purposes. Nowadays, many financial institutions and commodity trading houses, such as BNP Paribas, Barclays Capital, Morgan Stanley and Calyon amongst others, offer OTC bunker derivative products such as forward contracts, swaps and options. Shipping companies have also realised the benefits of OTC bunker contracts for risk-management purposes and have started using these products. As a result, there has been a large growth in trade in bunker derivative contracts, the most important of which are discussed in the next section.

10.5   Hedging bunker prices using forward contracts

A forward bunker contract is defined as an agreement between a seller and a buyer to exchange a *specified quantity* of bunker of *certain quality*, at an *agreed price*, at a *certain delivery location* and a specified *time in the future*. Forward contracts are OTC cash-settled paper contracts in the sense that settlement is made on the difference between the contracted price and the price for bunker at the delivery point, although physical delivery may also be possible. The settlement price for forward bunker agreements is normally calculated as the average of the underlying spot price over the settlement period which, depending on the terms of the contract, can be a month in most cases, or a week. These spot prices are normally reported by an independent price-reporting agency such as Platts or Bunkerworld. Depending on the physical position of the hedger, forward contracts can be used to construct a 'long hedge' or a 'short hedge'. Shipowners are naturally short of physical bunker and, therefore, for a hedging strategy should buy forward bunker contracts. Bunker suppliers, on the other hand, have a naturally long physical bunker position and, in order to hedge, should sell forward bunker contracts. For a discussion of the statistical properties and applications of forward bunker prices see Alizadeh and Nomikos (2003a; 2004a).

10.5.1   Long hedge using forward bunker contract

To illustrate how shipowners can use forward bunker agreements in a long-hedge strategy to manage bunker-price risk, consider the following example. In December 2006 a Panamax operator fixes a contract of affreightment (CoA) for 120,000 mt of cargo to be shipped from the US Gulf to the Far East, which requires two shipments (in January and March 2007), at a rate of US$25/mt. The current bunker price in US Gulf is US$300/mt, and the ship consumes

5000 mt of bunker per voyage. The owner is worried that bunker prices in the US Gulf may increase in March and thus reduce or eliminate the profit from the second voyage of the contract. Therefore, the owner decides to hedge the bunker cost for March 2007. His bunker broker advises him that 5000 mt March forward bunker contracts for Houston are trading at US$310/mt. By buying the forward bunker contract the owner therefore locks his bunker price for March at US$310/mt, irrespective of the eventual bunker price in Houston in March.

The outcome of this long-hedge risk-management strategy is presented in Table 10.2. In March 2007, the market price for fuel oil delivered in Houston to the shipowner was US$332/mt; therefore, taking 5000 mt of bunkers costs US$1,660,000. On the other hand, the settlement price, calculated as the average bunker price in Houston in March, is US$333/mt. Therefore, according to the forward contract, the shipowner is entitled to receive US$23/mt ($333 − $310): that is, a profit of US$115,000 ($23 × 5000 mt), which, combined with the bunker price paid in March, yields a total bunker cost of US$1,545,000 for the voyage in March.

In this case, the shipowner's profit of US$115,000 from the forward contract compensated his loss in the physical market due to the increase in bunker prices from December 2006 to March 2007.

Consider now an alternative scenario; suppose that average bunker prices at the end of March in Houston fall to say, US$290/mt. In this case, since the market price is lower than the forward agreement price (US$310/mt), the shipowner has to pay the seller of the contract the difference between the settlement price (US$290/mt) and the forward price; that is, US$20/mt or a total of US$100,000. However, at the same time, the shipowner buys bunkers in the physical market at a lower price of say, US$292/mt, which compensates his loss in the forward market. Therefore, the overall cost for bunkers will be US$312/mt, or US$1,560,000.

10.5.2 Short hedge using forward bunker contract

The example above can also be extended to the case of a bunker supplier. In this case, because the supplier is long in the physical market, he has to sell (short) forward bunker contracts in order to hedge the selling price of the bunker at some time in the future. Let us consider a Singapore bunker supplier on 20 July 2006, who is going to sell 30,000 mt of bunker inventories in two months' time. The current spot bunker price is US$318/mt and the supplier is thus worried that bunker prices may soften over the next few months and affect his profit margin for this inventory. Therefore, he decides to sell 30,000 mt September 2006 Singapore forward bunker at US$325/mt, which is the current forward rate.

The outcome of this short-hedge risk-management strategy is presented in Table 10.3. Assuming the hedged position is carried until the maturity and

Table 10.2   Long hedge using a forward bunker contract

Forward bunker hedge for March 2007	
Physical market	**Forward market**

28 December 2006

Spot bunker price: US$300/mt	March forward bunker price:
Total current bunker cost:	US$310/mt
US$1,500,000(= 5000 mt × $300/mt)	Expected total bunker cost:
	US$1,550,000(= 5000 mt × $310/mt)

Shipowner **buys** 5000 mt Houston March forward bunker for US$310/mt

31 March 2007 – First scenario: rising bunker prices

Spot bunker price bought on	Settlement: average of spot price in
20 March = US$332/mt	March = US$333/mt
Total bunker cost:	Shipowner settles the difference
US$1,660,000(= 5000 mt × $332/mt)	between forward bunker price and
	March average price with the seller
	of the forward contract: profit
	from forward transaction
	($333 − $310) × 5000 mt =
	US$115,000

Net result from hedging

Overall cost of bunker for the	$1,660,000 − $115,000 = US$1,545,000
hedged position	

31 March 2007: second scenario: falling bunker prices

Spot bunker price bought on	Settlement: average of spot price in
20 March = US$292/mt	March = US$290/mt
Total bunker cost:	Shipowner settles the difference
US$1,460,000(= 5000 mt × $292/mt)	between forward bunker price and
	March average price with the seller of
	the forward contract: profit from
	forward transaction ($310 − $290) ×
	5000 mt = US$100,000

Net result from hedging

Overall cost of bunker for	$1,460,000 + $100,000 = US$1,560,000
the hedged position	

Table 10.3 Short hedge using a forward bunker contract

Forward bunker hedge for September 2006	
Physical market	**Forward market**
20 July 2006	
Spot bunker price: US$318/mt	September forward bunker price: US$325/mt
Total current bunker revenue:	Expected total bunker revenue:
US$9,540,000 (= 30,000 mt × $318/mt)	US$9,750,000 (= 30,000 mt × $325/mt)
Bunker supplier **sells** 30,000 mt Singapore September forward bunker at US$325/mt	
30 September 2007	
Spot bunker price sold in September = US$291.5/mt	Settlement: average of spot price in September = US$291.5/mt
Total bunker sales: US$8,745,000 (= 30,000 mt × $291.5/mt)	The supplier settles the difference between forward bunker price and September average price with the buyer of the forward contract: profit from forward transaction ($325 − $291.5) × 30,000 mt = US$1,005,000
Net result from hedging	
Overall revenue of the hedged position $8,745,000 + $1,005,000 = US$9,750,000	

given the September Singapore settlement price of US$291.50/mt, the supplier should receive US$1,005,000 [30,000 × ($325/mt − $291.5/mt)] which will compensate for the lower bunker-selling prices in the physical market. Therefore, the overall selling price of bunkers will be around US$325/mt and the total revenue of the supplier through this trade will be US$9,750,000, which is what the supplier was expecting. Also, note that if Singapore bunker prices had risen to a higher level than the forward price, then the supplier could sell the bunker in the physical market at the higher price, but he would have settled the September forward contract at a loss. Therefore, this again would result in an overall selling price of US$325/mt.

10.6 Bunker swap contracts

Swap contracts are perhaps the most popular instruments for bunker-price risk management and nowadays many commodity trading houses, as well as financial institutions, actively participate in trading bunker swaps. Bunker swaps are also OTC arrangements, which involve no transfer of physical commodity, and are settled in cash at the maturity date(s). Swap contracts are usually arranged through a third party known as a 'swap facilitator', a broker or a dealer. The role of the swap facilitator is to help the two counter-parties

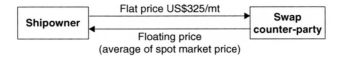

Figure 10.2 Plain vanilla swap contract between shipowner and swap counter-party

identify each other and assist them in completing the swap-contract trans-action. Therefore, swap facilitators act as intermediaries.

10.6.1 Plain vanilla bunker swap

A simple swap contract, sometimes called a 'plain vanilla bunker swap', is an agreement between two parties where a floating price for a certain grade of bunker at a given location is exchanged for a fixed price over a specified period based on a notional volume. The floating price is normally the average of the prevailing spot market prices over the settlement period(s) and the fixed price is the price which is negotiated and agreed before the initiation of the swap contract. For example, in December 2006, a shipowner enters into a plain vanilla fixed-for-floating bunker swap contract with a counter-party, in which he agrees to pay US$325/mt for 5000 mt of fuel oil at the end of each month in 2007. In return, the counter-party agrees to pay a floating price, calculated as the average of the month, for 5000 mt of a certain grade of bunker at a specified port (such as Singapore) at the end of each month during 2007. Therefore, at the end of every month during the life of the bunker swap contract, the shipowner pays US$1,625,000 (5000 mt × US$325) to the swap counter-party and receives the monthly average of the market price of that particular grade of bunker at the specified location, multiplied by 5000. However, in practice, the parties exchange only the differences. By entering into this swap contract, the shipowner has a fixed purchase price of bunker at US$325/mt over the next 12 months, whatever the spot bunker price in the market. Figure 10.2 presents the cash flow for the above plain vanilla swap example.

It can be seen that although the shipowner agrees to a 5000 mt swap con-tract, this does not necessarily mean that he purchases the same amount of fuel oil in the physical market at the end of each month because the amount of bunker taken depends on the vessel's requirements. However, the swap contract is settled between the two parties in cash, based on the notional amount of 5000 mt, until the contract ends.

Table 10.4 presents the realised settlement prices calculated as the average of the month over the life of the bunker swap, and the monthly cash settle-ments calculated based on the notional volume of 5000 mt. For example, whenever the settlement price is below the swap price of US$325/mt, the shipowner pays the difference multiplied by 5000 to the seller of the swap,

Table 10.4   Cash flows between counter-parties in a 12-month bunker swap contract

	Floating/ settlement price US$/mt	Fixed swap price US$/mt	Swap volume mt	Settlement amount US$
January	229.13	325.00	5000	−479,375
February	251.50	325.00	5000	−367,500
March	274.25	325.00	5000	−253,750
April	312.00	325.00	5000	−65,000
May	325.88	325.00	5000	4,400
June	331.13	325.00	5000	30,650
July	359.88	325.00	5000	174,400
August	347.50	325.00	5000	112,500
September	374.00	325.00	5000	245,000
October	412.50	325.00	5000	437,500
November	480.50	325.00	5000	777,500
December	448.38	325.00	5000	616,900

Note: Settlement reflects the shipowner's cash inflow (when positive) or outflow (when negative) from using the swap. It is calculated as the difference between the floating price (monthly average of the spot market price) and the fixed price (or swap price) times the notional swap amount of 5000 mt.

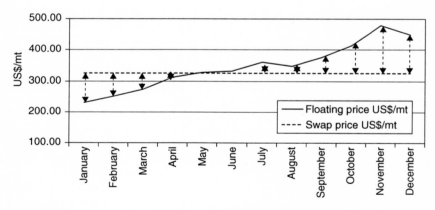

Figure 10.3   Comparison of one-year fixed for floating swap price

and whenever the settlement price is above the swap price the shipowner receives the difference multiplied by 5000 from the seller of the swap. Figure 10.3 illustrates the cash settlements between the shipowner and the swap counter-party over the life of the contract.

Plain vanilla bunker swaps can be priced directly from forward bunker curves using the no-arbitrage argument between a swap contract and a series of forward contracts, because the appropriate portfolio of forward contracts

Table 10.5 Bunker forward curve and spot interest rate yield curve

30 Dec 2006	Jan 2007	Feb 2007	Mar 2007
Forward price US$/mt	230	250	262
Interest rates %	5.0%	4.75%	4.5%
Fixed price US$/mt	K	K	K

is a hedge for the swap contract. Therefore, by selecting a series of forward contracts for which the maturities are the same as the reset dates of the swap contract, one can set the discounted present value of the forward curve equal to the discounted present value of the fixed swap price and solve the equation to obtain the fair price of the swap. The discount rate can be inferred from the spot yield curve with maturities similar to the forward contracts. Mathematically,

$$K = \frac{\sum_{k=1}^{m} [P(t, s_k)F(t, s_k)]}{\sum_{k=1}^{m} [P(t, s_k)]} \tag{10.1}$$

where K is the fixed swap price at the initiation of the swap, $F(t, s_k)$ is the forward price today (t) for settlement at period s_k, $P(t, s_k)$ is the discount factor from period s_k to today, and m is the number of swap periods (resets). Using the forward prices $F(t, s_k)$ and appropriate discount factors $P(t, s_k)$, the above swap-pricing formula can be solved to obtain K as the fair value for fixed price. This is because of the no-arbitrage argument which requires that any difference between the forward prices and the swap price that could lead to potential riskless arbitrage be eliminated immediately by agents and the relationship restored. It should be noted that the above formula can be used to obtain the price of the swap at the initiation of the contract but, as time passes, the swap might be in-the-money or out-of-the-money depending on the changes of the forward curve and the interest rates. That is, the value of the swap contract can increase or decrease during the life of the swap.

As an example consider a series of Rotterdam forward bunker prices in December 2006 for January, February and March 2007 trading at US$230/mt, US$250/mt and US$262/mt respectively. At the same time one-, two- and three-month interest rates are 5 per cent, 4.75 per cent and 4.5 per cent per annum respectively, as shown in Table 10.5.

In order to find the fair value of the swap contract, equation (10.1) is solved for K. Since the pricing model can be highly non-linear, the equation can be set up in Excel and then the solver function used to find the value for K, which satisfies the equality. In this case, using the Excel solver, we find that a fair value for a fixed price of Rotterdam three-month plain vanilla bunker swap in December 2006 is US$247.30/mt.

10.7 Exotic bunker swaps

So far we have discussed the properties of simple or plain vanilla swap contracts. In addition, there are swap contracts with more complex payoffs which can fulfil specific hedging requirements and risk-management strategies of shipowners and operators in a more effective or efficient way. Among these are; 'differential swap', 'variable volume swap' or 'swing', 'participation swap', 'double-up swap' and 'extendable swap'. We describe each contract next.

10.7.1 Differential swap

A differential swap is a contract where the parties agree to exchange the difference between two floating prices, known as the floating differential, for a fixed differential price. In other words, differential swap can be regarded as a spread swap where the floating spread between two asset prices is exchanged for a fixed price. For example, a trader can enter into a US$30/mt Singapore–Rotterdam 380 cst differential bunker swap for 10,000 mt. Under this contract the buyer pays a fixed price and receives the floating differential price between Singapore and Rotterdam bunker prices at the reset dates, based on the notional volume. Since this is a cash-settled contract, the two parties exchange only the difference in cash flows. As a result, when the differential between Singapore and Rotterdam prices is greater than US$30/mt, the seller pays the actual differential minus US$30 multiplied by 10,000 mt to the buyer of the contract. On the other hand, if the differential between Singapore and Rotterdam prices is less than US$30/mt, the buyer pays the differential minus US$30 multiplied by 10,000 mt to the seller.

Differential swap contracts can be used when a shipowner needs to transfer a bunker hedge, which uses the plain vanilla swap contract based on one location to another. Suppose that a shipowner who is operating a vessel in the Atlantic has entered into a 10,000 mt plain vanilla Rotterdam bunker swap at a fixed price of US$400/mt with monthly resets for each month of 2007. Halfway into the year, the shipowner decides to relocate the vessel to the Pacific due to a stronger freight market in that region. The shipowner expects to take bunkers in Singapore but is worried that the hedge with the Rotterdam swap may not be suitable. Therefore, he can enter into a Singapore–Rotterdam differential swap for the rest of 2007.

For pricing differential swaps, again we use the forward bunker curves for the two markets of interest and the no-arbitrage argument between a swap contract and two series of forward contracts, since the appropriate portfolio of forward contracts is a hedge for the swap contract. Therefore, by selecting two series of forward contracts with the same maturity as the reset dates of the swap, we set the discounted present value of the difference in forward curves equal to the discounted present value of the fixed differential swap price.

$$K = \frac{\sum\limits_{k=1}^{m} P(t, s_k)[F_1(t, s_k) - F_2(t, s_k)]}{\sum\limits_{k=1}^{m} P(t, s_k)} \tag{10.2}$$

where $F_1(t, s_k)$ and $F_2(t, s_k)$ are the two forward bunker prices, K is the fixed-price for the spread at the initiation of the swap, and $P(t, s_k)$ is the discount factor. By solving equation (10.2) one can obtain the fair price of the differential swap.

10.7.2 Extendable swap

An extendable swap is another useful instrument in bunker risk management. In an extendable swap contract the buyer, or fixed-rate payer, has the option to extend the contract for a pre-specified period with the same fixed-for-floating price and notional volume. This is essentially like buying an option on the swap (swaption) at the time of entering the swap, with the maturity of the swaption being at the expiry of the initial swap, and with similar strike price. The extension period could be less than, or equal to, the initial swap contract period and the option is normally exercised prior to the maturity of the initial swap contract. Therefore, during the exercise period, the fixed-price payer compares the price of the extendable swap with the market price of a swap contract with equivalent terms, and decides whether or not to exercise the option to extend the contract. Obviously, the fact that under the extendable swap the seller grants the extension option to the fixed-price payer entails that the price of this swap is higher than the price of a plain vanilla swap. The difference essentially reflects the premium of the swaption.

As an example consider the following 12-month extendable fixed-for-floating Singapore bunker swap on a notional amount of 10,000 mt at US\$350/mt at the end of December 2006. By entering into this extendable swap contract, the buyer purchases the right – but not the obligation – to extend the contract for another six months, from January 2008 to June 2008. At the maturity of the swap, if the price of the six-month plain vanilla Singapore 380 cst bunker swap is higher than US\$350/mt, the buyer will exercise the option and extend the swap for another six months. On the other hand, if in December 2007 the then price of a six-month plain vanilla Singapore 380 cst bunker swap is less than US\$350/mt, the buyer will leave the option unexercised and enter into a six-month plain vanilla Singapore 380 cst bunker swap at a lower market rate.

Sometimes, depending on the contract, the option to extend is granted by the fixed-rate payer to the swap seller, to achieve cheaper swap prices. Under such an agreement, the seller has the right – but not the obligation – to extend

Table 10.6   Terms of an extendable fixed-for-floating swap

• Initial swap:	12-month fixed-for-floating
• Swap period:	January 2007 to December 2007
• Fixed price:	US$350/mt
• Floating price:	average of daily Platts assessment in calendar month
• Grade:	HS 380 cst
• Pricing location:	Singapore
• Notional volume:	10,000 mt
• Extension:	six-month
• Exercise:	the last settlement month

the contract depending on the prevailing market condition at the exercise period. This means that the seller exercises the option and extends the swap if the market price of similar swap at maturity is less than the extension price, and vice versa.

10.7.3   Forward bunker swap

Under a forward bunker swap, as the name suggests, the two parties agree today to enter into a swap contract which starts at some time in the future. Therefore, the fixed price and other terms in the contract, including settlement period, grade, volume and pricing location, are agreed some time before the start of the first pricing period. For example, on 20 January 2007 a shipowner has just negotiated and fixed a CoA for carrying six shipments of iron ore, each of 120,000 mt, from Australia to China at a rate of US$20/mt, starting from April 2007.[4] The shipowner's plan is to take bunkers in Singapore on a monthly basis. Current bunker price in Singapore is US$278.50/mt, but the owner is worried about future bunker price movements and would therefore like to hedge his bunker exposure for this CoA. Since the shipments will commence in three months, the owner can enter into a three-month forward six-month Singapore bunker swap in January 2007. Let us say that the price of this six-month bunker swap starting in three months' time is US$300/mt based on 5000 mt notional volume. This strategy allows the owner to fix the bunker cost for the entire CoA contract at a price of US$300/mt. Table 10.7 presents the realised settlement prices and cash flows of the forward bunker swap contract.

In fact, the owner calculated the voyage estimate for the CoA based on this forward swap price and, hence, arrived at a competitively priced freight rate which he has then negotiated with the charterer. Once the CoA is fixed

---

[4] Although some CoAs include bunker adjustment factors (BAFs) to pass on the bunker price risk to the charterer, in this case we assume that the shipowner is prepared to manage the risk himself in order to make the contract more attractive to the charterer.

Table 10.7   Settlement and cash flows of the forward bunker swap contract

		Floating price	Swap price	Quantity	Settlement
Month		US$/mt	US$/mt	mt	US$
	January				
	February				
	March				
1	April	340.87	300.00	5000	204,350
2	May	340.00	300.00	5000	200,000
3	June	354.75	300.00	5000	273,750
4	July	384.00	300.00	5000	420,000
5	August	367.13	300.00	5000	335,650
6	September	389.88	300.00	5000	449,400

the shipowner decides to hedge the bunker using a forward bunker swap, in order to cover his exposure to bunker price fluctuations in Singapore.

Over the settlement period, according to the realised prices, it can be seen that the shipowner made a good decision to enter into this forward bunker swap agreement, as bunker prices in Singapore increased significantly in the period from April to September 2007. As a result of this hedge, the shipowner's swap contract was in-the-money and the bunker cost remained at US$300/mt, thus protecting the profit margin of the CoA.

10.7.4   Participation swap

A participation swap is a plain vanilla swap where one party has the option to decide whether the settlement is calculated on the full notional quantity or on part of it, let us say 50 per cent. The notional quantity on which the settlement is calculated for a single month has to be nominated prior to the settlement period. For example, consider a simple six-month participation bunker swap based on a 5000 mt notional amount, with 50 per cent participation at fixed-price payer's (that is, shipowner's) option. This contract gives the shipowner the right to exercise full participation each month if he expects to receive settlement for that month, but to exercise 50 per cent participation in any month if he expects to pay for that settlement month. However, normally the shipowner should announce the quantity prior to the start of the settlement period. Obviously, having such an option is valuable and therefore this type of participation bunker swap in which the fixed price payer has the option on notional quantity is more expensive than a plain vanilla bunker swap where the quantity is constant. On the other hand, if the participation option is granted to the floating price payer, the fixed price would be lower than in a plain vanilla bunker swap.

10.7.5   Double-up swap

Under a double-up swap contract, one party has the right – but not the obligation – to double up the underlying notional amount before the pricing period; that is, before the averaging period starts. Therefore, if the fixed-price payer has the option, when he expects that the next settlement is going to be in his favour, he exercises the option and doubles the notional volume. On the other hand, when the fixed-price payer expects that the market in the next settlement is going to be against him, he leaves the option unexercised and stays with the initial notional volume. In order to benefit from the double-up option, the fixed-price payer has to pay a premium which is normally implied and added to the fixed price of the swap contract. Furthermore, it can be seen that both a participation and a double-up swap can be regarded as a portfolio of a plain vanilla bunker swap on a notional volume, with a series of long bunker options with similar expiry dates as the reset dates of the swap, and the same notional volume. In the case of a participation swap, these are put options (floors) while for double-up swaps these are call options.

10.7.6   Variable volume swap or swing

A variable volume swap or swing is similar to a plain vanilla swap, but the notional volume based on which the contract is settled is not known and can be variable within a range at the buyer's (or the seller's) option. Normally, the notional volume is nominated prior to settlement or average pricing period. In some contracts, the exchange is based on the realised volume, on the reading on a meter, of the amount of consumption, or a similar measurement. Again in this type of swap, the holder of the volumetric option will increase the volume whenever he expects the market to be in his favour, and will reduce the volume if he expects the market price to be against him. In return the grantor receives a premium which is again embedded in the fixed swap price. Therefore, if the fixed-price payer has the volumetric optionality, then the fixed price will be more expensive than in a plain vanilla swap, while if the floating-price payer has the volumetric optionality, then the fixed price will be less than in a plain vanilla swap.

10.8   Hedging bunker price using options

Although option contracts have been used extensively for risk management in energy markets since the early 1980s, it was not until the 1990s that options were first used as a means of hedging bunker-price risk in shipping. Nowadays, several financial institutions and commodity trading houses offer numerous types of options on bunker prices to shipowners and shipping companies.

The most common type of option contracts used in the bunker market are 'average price Asian' options, where the settlement price is calculated as the average spot bunker price over a period of time based on a specified location and grade. The rationale behind using averaging in calculating the settlement price is, firstly, to eliminate or reduce any possibility of market manipulation by a single participant (or a group of them) during the settlement period. Secondly, the average pricing over the settlement period might be better suited to the needs of the hedger as he may not know exactly when the physical commitment will take place over the settlement period. Finally, average price Asian options are in general cheaper than European options, due to the fact that the volatility of the underlying price is reduced by using the average price over the settlement period; that is, the price behaviour of the underlying asset can be smoothed by averaging the price series.

The general definition, types, trading strategies, and payoffs of different option contracts were discussed in Chapter 7. The aim of this section is, therefore, to discuss the types of options contracts and hedging strategies that are used to manage bunker price fluctuations.

10.8.1 Bunker caps and floors

A 'caplet' is defined as a long call position to hedge a short physical position on the underlying bunker price. Therefore, a caplet gives its holder (for example, the shipowner) the opportunity to limit any possible future losses caused by an increase in the bunker price for one period. The purchase of the call option compensates the owner in the case of a price rise, and provides an upper bound on the price that the owner has to pay for bunkers at expiry. A 'floorlet', on the other hand, is defined as a long-put option position to hedge a long physical position of the underlying bunker price at maturity. Therefore, a floorlet gives its holder (for example, the bunker supplier) the opportunity to limit any possible future losses caused by bunker price decrease for a single period in the future. In other words, the put option compensates the holder in the case of a bunker price fall over the delivery period and provides a lower bound on the selling price that the supplier receives for bunkers at maturity.

By the same token, a 'cap' can be defined as a long position on a portfolio of two or more caplets with the same exercise price, but different maturity dates. As a result, a cap gives its holder (for example, the shipowner) the opportunity to limit any possible future losses due to an increase in bunker prices over a time period. Similarly, a 'floor' is a portfolio of two or more floorlets with the same exercise price, but different maturities. Therefore, the pricing and hedging techniques for caps and floors are the same as those used in the case of caplets and floorlets.

To illustrate how a caplet can be used by a shipowner to manage bunker price risk, consider the following example. On 20 December 2006 the spot bunker price in Fujairah is US$302/mt. The tanker Ocean Star is scheduled to load cargo in the Persian Gulf and sail for Rotterdam in the last week of January 2007. Her owner fears that Fujairah bunker prices at the end of January 2007, when the ship is going to take on 10,000 mt of fuel oil, may rise substantially and hence cause cash-flow problems for this voyage. In order to avoid this, the owner decides to hedge his bunker cost using a caplet. Through a broker, the owner finds out that the following call option contract is available.

Call option quote	
Expiry	End of January 2007
Premium	US$10/mt
Strike price	US$310/mt
Settlement	Average of the month
Grade	Fujairah 380 cst
Volume	10,000 mt

The shipowner agrees to buy the US$310 strike January option and pay the premium of US$100,000 (= $10/mt × 10,000 mt) to the option writer on 20 December 2006. The outcome of this hedging strategy is presented in Table 10.8. Under the first scenario, January bunker prices in Fujairah have fallen and the shipowner will not exercise the option because the settlement price, US$280/mt, is less than the strike price, US$310/mt. This leaves the shipowner out of pocket for the premium paid. In this case the amount paid for bunker is US$2,800,000 and, adding to that the option premium, the total bunker cost is US$2,900,000. Under the second scenario, the bunker price in January has risen to US$350/mt. Thus, the shipowner can exercise the option, because the settlement price is greater than the strike price, and the owner is entitled to receive US$40/mt from the writer of the option; that is, a sum of US$400,000 [($350 − $310) × 10,000 mt]. This will compensate the owner against the rise in bunker prices in the physical market. However, the premium paid for buying the option should be deducted from this amount, which leaves the shipowner with US$300,000 profit from the option contract. Therefore, the total bunker cost for the shipowner will be US$3,200,000 ($3,500,000 − $300,000).

Panel A of Figure 10.4 illustrates the payoff of the above caplet hedge in a graphical form, while Panel B presents the final bunker price to the shipowner under a caplet hedge. It can be seen that by buying the call option, the shipowner has hedged the bunker cost up to a maximum of US$320/mt (a total of US$3,200,000), regardless of how much bunker prices increase in January.

10.8.2   Collars or cylinder options

Collars are very effective risk-management instruments designed to confine the gains and losses of the holder of the instrument. They are generally a combination of caps and floors, which allows the profit/loss of the investor to be limited to a maximum (cap) and minimum (floor). A collar is a combination of a long call and short put, or vice-versa, combined with a short or long

Table 10.8   Hedging against bunker price fluctuations using a cap

Caplet hedge for January 2007	
Physical market	**Options market**
20 December 2006	
Bunker price in Fujairah: US$302/mt Bunker cost: US$3,020,000 (= 10,000 × $302)	Option details: January 2007 Call with a strike Price of US$310/mt, Premium = US$10/mt
Shipowner **buys** January 2007 call at a total cost of US$100,000 (= $10 × 10,000)	
31 January 2007 – first scenario **Falling bunker market**	
Bunker price in Fujairah: US$280/mt Actual bunker cost: US$2,800,000	Strike price (US$310) > Settlement price (US$280) Therefore option is not exercised
Total bunker cost (including option premium) **= $2,800,000 + $100,000 = US$2,900,000**	
31 January 2007 – alternative scenario **Rising bunker market**	
Bunker price in Fujairah: US$350/mt Actual bunker cost: US$3,500,000	Strike price (US$310) < Settlement Price (US$350) Therefore option is exercised Payoff from the options transaction ($350 − $310) × 10,000 − $100,000 = US$300,000
Total bunker cost (including option premium) **= $3,500,000 − $300,000 = US$3,200,000**	

physical position, respectively. For example, to construct a collar hedge, a shipowner who is short on bunkers in the physical market and has to purchase fuel oil at certain time in the future can buy a call option and sell a put option for the same amount of bunker, with both options expiring at the same time as the physical market settlement. Very often collars are designed and used when hedgers do not want to incur any upfront cost for hedging their positions; they are appropriately known as 'zero-cost collars'.

Collars are used in a variety of markets. For instance, in Chapter 7 we discussed the applications of collars in the FFA market. In this section, we discuss the use of collars for hedging bunker-price risk. To illustrate how a zero-cost collar can be used by a shipowner to manage bunker price risk, consider the caplet example presented previously. The owner of the tanker Ocean Star whose vessel is scheduled to load cargo in the Persian Gulf and

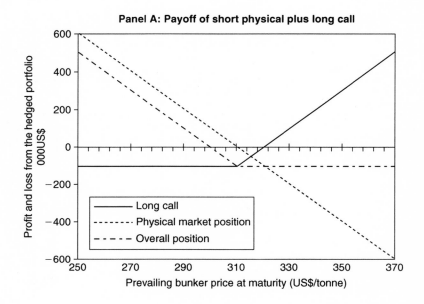

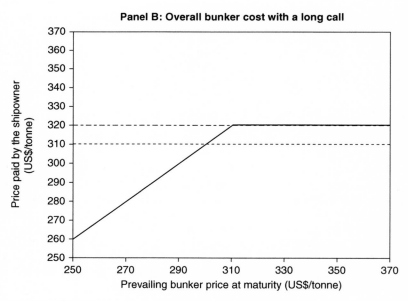

Figure 10.4   Bunker price to be paid by a caplet holder

sail for Rotterdam in the last week of January 2007 fears that Fujairah bunker prices at the end of January 2007 may rise substantially and reduce or eliminate his profit margin on the voyage. However, the owner is also concerned about the upfront cost of hedging with a call option and would prefer a hedging strategy with less or no upfront cost. He thus, decides to construct a collar hedge using the following January 2007 call and put options on Fujairah fuel oil prices.

	Call option:	Put option:
Expiry	End of January 2007	End of January 2007
Premium	US$10/mt	US$10/mt
Strike price	US$310/mt	US$290/mt
Settlement	Average of the month	Average of the month
Grade	Fujairah 380 cst	Fujairah 380 cst
Volume	10,000 mt	10,000 mt

To achieve this, the owner can sell the January 2007 put option and receive the premium (US$100,000) and, at the same time, buy the call option which has the same premium, maturity and quantity. Therefore, there will not be any upfront cost for participating in the options market and constructing the hedged position. Panel A of Figure 10.5 plots the payoff of a zero-cost collar to the holder against different spot bunker prices at maturity, while

Table 10.9 Payoff of the zero-cost collar and overall cost of bunkers for a shipowner

Settlement price at expiry US$/mt	Call-option payoff US$/mt		Put-option payoff US$/mt		Collar payoff US$/mt	Overall bunker cost for shipowner US$/mt
270	(No exe)	−10	(Exe)	−10	−20	290
275	(No exe)	−10	(Exe)	−5	−15	290
280	(No exe)	−10	(Exe)	−0	−10	290
285	(No exe)	−10	(Exe)	+5	−5	290
290	(No exe)	−10	(No Exe)	10	0	290
295	(No exe)	−10	(No Exe)	10	0	295
300	(No exe)	−10	(No Exe)	10	0	300
305	(No exe)	−10	(No Exe)	10	0	305
310	(No exe)	−10	(No Exe)	10	0	310
315	(Exe)	−5	(No Exe)	10	5	310
320	(Exe)	0	(No Exe)	10	10	310
325	(Exe)	+5	(No Exe)	10	15	310
330	(Exe)	+10	(No Exe)	10	20	310

Note: 'No exe' indicates that the option is not exercised and 'Exe' indicates that the option is exercised.

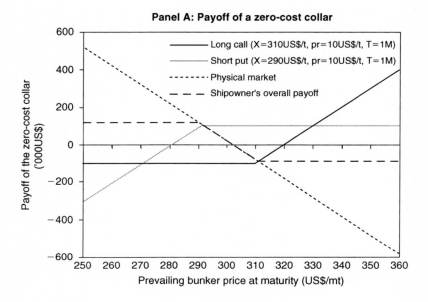

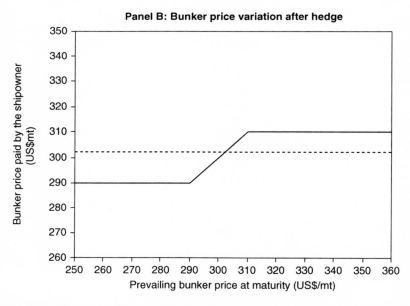

Figure 10.5 Zero-cost collar payoff to the shipowner and purchase prices after hedge against different bunker prices at expiry

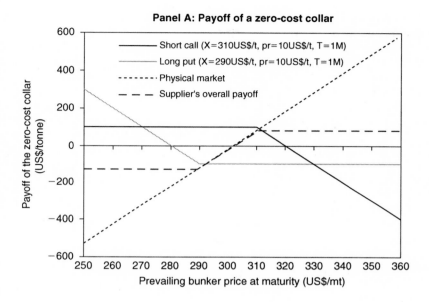

Panel A: Payoff of a zero-cost collar

- —— Short call (X=310US$/t, pr=10US$/t, T=1M)
- —— Long put (X=290US$/t, pr=10US$/t, T=1M)
- ------- Physical market
- – – – Supplier's overall payoff

Payoff of the zero-cost collar (US$/tonne)

Prevailing bunker price at maturity (US$/mt)

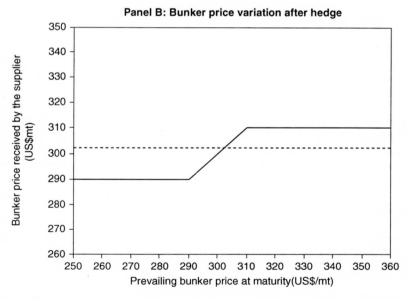

Panel B: Bunker price variation after hedge

Bunker price received by the supplier (US$mt)

Prevailing bunker price at maturity(US$/mt)

Figure 10.6 Zero-cost collar payoff to the bunker supplier and bunker selling price against different bunker prices at expiry

Panel B plots the fuel cost paid by the holder of the collar against possible spot bunker prices at expiry.

It can be seen that the payoff of the collar strategy is limited to between US$120,000 and –US$80,000 and the overall cost of bunker remains within certain limits; that is, the strike price for the put (US$290/mt) and the strike price for the call (US$310/mt). Using the zero-cost collar, the owner has essentially sacrificed some of the benefits in case of a drop in bunker prices in January by writing the put option in order to be able to finance the protection against an increase in bunker prices in the same month through buying a call option. Table 10.9 presents the payoffs of the long-call, short-put and the short physical (shipowner's) positions in the zero-cost collar hedge example. The overall results indicate that the bunker cost for the shipowner is confined within the US$290/mt to US$310/mt limits, regardless of any extreme swings in bunker prices at the expiry.

A similar collar hedge can also be designed for a bunker seller who is long in the physical market in January 2007 and would like to protect his selling price in case the market falls in January. To achieve this, the supplier should sell the January call option and use the premium to buy the January put option. With this zero-cost collar strategy the supplier will be protected in the case of a bunker price drop in January but he cannot benefit from price increases, since the call option will be exercised and he has to compensate the buyer of the call option. This is shown in Figure 10.6, Panel A, which illustrates the position of the bunker supplier using a zero-cost collar. The final outcome of the collar ensures that whatever the price for the bunker at maturity, the supplier's selling price can only fluctuate between US$290/mt and US$310/mt.

10.9   Summary and conclusions

In this chapter, we discussed the world bunker market and analysed bunker-price fluctuations in major bunkering ports. Our analysis indicates that bunker-price levels and their volatility have increased recently and there are significant differences in the behaviour of prices across different bunkering regions. This is mainly attributed to local supply and demand imbalances, which cause sharp price movements. It was also established that changes in bunker prices can have a serious impact on the profitability of shipping operations. The development of OTC bunker derivatives products and the mechanics of using instruments, such as forward bunker agreements, bunker swaps and options on bunker prices, for hedging bunker-price risk from the points of view of both the shipowner and bunker supplier were also discussed. Finally, it seems that while shipowners are becoming more aware of the importance of bunker risk management in shipping operations, the availability of bunker derivatives for a limited number of bunkering ports makes regular bunker hedging more difficult and costly for shipowners who operate in a variety of routes.

11
Financial and Interest Rate Risk in Shipping

11.1 Introduction

In addition to fluctuations of freight rates, bunker prices and asset prices, unanticipated interest rate changes justify a substantial fraction of the shipping risk management function. Vast amounts of capital are required for the financing needs of shipping companies, the majority of which are provided through loans via international commercial banks. Shipping finance structure has changed as the industry evolves and becomes more mature, with sophisticated financial instruments and well-informed market participants. Indeed, apart from debt financing, instruments such as bank loans, asset-backed mortgages, bond issues, private placements and shipyard financing, a shipping company may raise funds through equity (retained profits, rights issues, public offerings) or even mezzanine funds (convertible bonds, unsecured debt). The latter strategy assumes more risk and is less popular in the maritime business, due to the capital-intensive nature of the industry which gives rise to highly leveraged companies. The inverse effect, which interest-rate volatility may have on the assets and liabilities of a company, can lead to severe liquidity problems and mismatching of cash inflows and outflows, especially in the shipping markets where business-cycle dynamics are proved to be catastrophic during periods of 'troughs'.

The terms of ship financing depend on various factors. To name a few: the operational and financial capabilities of shipping companies, creditworthiness, reputation and fleet size, current and prevailing market conditions at the time the vessel was purchased, and so on.[1] For example, highly reputable shipowners with a large fleet which can be used as collateral may enjoy better financing terms than a shipowner with relatively lower levels of credit and collateral. Interest-rate risk is directly related to the individual debt structure

---

[1] For example, when freight rates are high and the shipowner has a secure long-term time-charter contract, providers of funds may relax their terms of finance compared to periods when the market is tight and the purchaser does not have a secure contract.

of the company (debt-to-equity ratio, cost of capital/equity, timing of cash inflows-outflows, and so on), since the elevated gearing ratios of shipping companies involve liabilities susceptible to interest-rate instability. Furthermore, most shipping loans are quoted in US dollars. If debt and revenues are denominated in different currencies, this exposes the borrower to exchange-rate risk. In the absence of hedging, this behaviour is speculative; for a loan denominated in a foreign currency, if the latter appreciates against the domestic currency, the loan amount will increase. Similarly, if the foreign currency depreciates against the domestic, the loan amount will decrease. Hence, shipping companies face another aspect of risk, namely currency risk, which is directly related to interest-rate exposure, since each currency is linked with a different interest rate yield curve. These facts provide evidence that interest-rate risk measurement and mitigation is an indispensable aspect of shipping risk management.

The aim of this chapter is to review interest-rate risk hedging strategies, using the available financial instruments. Specifically, we concentrate on managing interest-rate risk of ship-financing projects and highlight the pros and cons of different contracts used in interest-rate risk management. The structure of this chapter is as follows. Section 11.2 presents an overview of the term loans under which banks lend funds. Section 11.3 describes the risk management of interest rates on the shipowner's side, using forwards, futures, swaps and option contracts. The hedging procedure for each of those derivatives contracts is clearly illustrated using analytical examples. The pricing function of these tools is also explained. Finally, Section 11.4 makes a reference to currency risk, explaining the hedging and pricing function of currency swaps derivative contracts.

11.2 Reference rates and international financial markets

Shipping loans are mainly US-dollar denominated and are issued in international financial markets. One very important and active element of the latter is the Eurocurrency market. Eurocurrencies are foreign currencies that are borrowed and lent in domestic markets: for instance, a Eurodollar deposit is an offshore US-dollar deposit and the bank accommodating the funds may be a non-US-based bank or the overseas branch of a US bank. Eurodollar deposit maturities range from overnight to several years, but volumes are primarily concentrated in the short end of the yield curve. The international nature of maritime business and the benefits of the Eurodollar market over domestic borrowing are the core incentives of US-dollar denominated debt. As one of the largest unregulated markets, it has gained competitive advantage over the domestic markets through sophistication, economies of scale due to the large amounts of deposits and loans to finance governments and multinationals, and diversification of risk through the process of syndication.

Most 'Euro-bank' loans in the Eurocurrency market bear interest at the London Interbank Offered Rate (LIBOR) floating rate. LIBOR is the most widely used and quoted benchmark interest-rate index at which banks borrow funds from each other, within London, for a specified period of time. It is used in standardised quotations, loan agreements, derivative transactions in both major exchanges and OTC markets. The LIBOR rate is a function of local interest rates, banks' expectations of future rates, the profile of contributor banks (such as their credit rating), liquidity in the London markets in the currency concerned, maturity and so on. It is officially defined by the British Bankers Association (BBA) and compiled in conjunction with Reuters.[2] For instance, the US-dollar LIBOR is the average rate of 16 multinational banks' interbank offered rates as sampled by the BBA shortly after 11.00am in London. In a similar way, BBA calculates the euro LIBOR, Japanese yen LIBOR, sterling LIBOR and other currency LIBOR rates from samples of banks (the contributor banks' list is annually reviewed).

Another international reference rate is the EURIBOR (Euro Interbank Offered Rate) which is the rate at which euro-denominated interbank term deposits within the euro zone are offered by one prime bank to another. Apart from LIBOR, most major domestic financial centres construct their own interbank offered rates for local loan agreement purposes. These rates include PIBOR (Paris Interbank Offered Rate), FIBOR (Frankfurt Interbank Offered Rate), SIBOR (Singapore Interbank Offered Rate) and so on.

Figure 11.1 presents the evolution of the three-, six-, and 12-month US LIBOR rates for the period from April 1993 to February 2007. The data are monthly annualised rates. The volatility in interest rates introduces a great amount of risk considering the fluctuations of future cash flows, particularly during a depressed shipping market. To illustrate the importance of interest-rate risk management, consider a shipping company that enters into a US$100m loan agreement to finance part of a vessel acquisition. The agreed borrowing rate is the one-year LIBOR plus a spread of 25 basis points (100 basis points is equal to 1 per cent) and the maturity of the loan occurs in five years with annual reset periods, resulting in five interest payments for the period 2003–2007. LIBOR rates for the specific period rose from 1.4 per cent per annum in January 2003 to 5.4 per cent per annum in January 2007.

The majority of ship finance is carried out through plain vanilla term loans. These loans are financial products of international commercial banks and refer to a specified amount of money, called drawdown, for a specific maturity (usually above three years) depending on the qualitative and quantitative characteristics of the asset to be financed, such as whether it is a newbuilding or a second-hand vessel, the vessel's age or market conditions.

---

[2] Eurodollar deposits with maturities longer than a year are not quoted by the BBA. Typically, interest rate swap rates can be used as an approximation for longer periods.

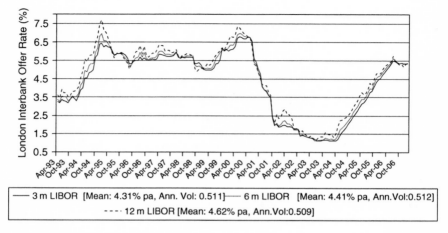

Figure 11.1 Evolution of LIBOR rates
Source: British Bankers Association.

The borrower makes periodic interest payments plus repayments of capital according to a pre-specified amortisation schedule. The most common reference rate is either the three-, six-, and 12-month LIBOR rates and is reset at regular intervals, every three or six or 12 months, respectively. In addition to LIBOR rates, borrowers pay a spread of usually 50 to 300 basis points (0.5 per cent to 3 per cent) over the floating rate which reflects the creditworthiness, terms of credit, general business and financial risk as well as the bank's profit margin.

11.3 Term loans

The contractual structure of term loans is negotiated on the basis of the credit-worthiness of the shipping company and the financier's confidence in the company's corporate management and investment plan. The financial status of the potential borrower is cautiously examined, through conducting full credit analysis, because the probability of default of the candidate company will determine the decision and the terms of funding. Moreover, from a financier's perspective, other criteria of the loan approval are the obtainable 'collaterals' (such as the mortgage on the vessel, guarantees, assignment of earnings or additional cash collateral) and the 'covenants' granted (that is, legal clauses that authorise the lender to regulate borrower's actions). For more information on the topic of credit risk in the shipping industry, see Grammenos (2002).

Term loans are flexible and the repayment schedule can be arranged to meet the demands of the borrower. A fixed-rate loan has a uniform interest rate until maturity, whereas a floating-rate loan has an interest rate reset at predetermined time intervals. A common repayment plan involves 'equal instalments', consisting of constant payments. Each payment includes an amount of the principal plus the accrued interest on the unpaid balance; thus, the capital portion repaid increases as time to maturity approaches. A more frequent repayment schedule is to assume 'unequal instalments' because yields on shipping loans are attached to the benchmark LIBOR. Moreover, a 'balloon repayment' may be arranged; that is, a large lump-sum payment of the outstanding capital due at or near the maturity date of the loan. The main purpose of the balloon payment is to reduce substantially the size of the periodic payments, whereas the balloon payment will usually be covered by the resale or scrap value of the vessel at the end of the loan. Obviously, this strategy generates residual value risk and as an alternative, if market expectations permit, it is not uncommon to spread out the balloon payment by refinancing and/or restructuring the loan. If the balloon repayment refers to the payment of the entire capital upon maturity, this payment is known as 'bullet repayment'. However, due to the capital-intensive nature of the shipping industry, bullet payments are not common. Other clauses may include a 'moratorium', where the lender is authorised to permit suspension of capital repayments for a period known as grace or holiday period, which may often last one or two years immediately following the commencement of the loan agreement.

11.3.1 A fixed-rate loan example

Table 11.1 presents some examples of fixed-rate term loans under different repayment schedules. Suppose a shipping company borrows US$10m for ten years at a fixed rate of 7 per cent, plus a spread of 100 basis points (bp); that is, a fixed rate of 8 per cent per annum; the fixed rate of 7 per cent is effectively the swap rate for the period (as will be discussed in Section 11.7). The fixed payment at the end of each period is an annuity and, for the example presented in Panel A, is calculated as:

$$PV = C\left[1 - \frac{1}{(1+r)^n}\right] \Big/ r \Rightarrow \$10m = C\left[1 - \frac{1}{(1+0.08)^{10}}\right] \Big/ 0.08$$
$$\Rightarrow C = \$1.490m$$

Interest payment in the first period is simply US$800,000 (=8 per cent × US$10m) and the capital repayment is US$690,000 (= US$1.49m − US$0.8m). Then, the remaining capital to be repaid is US$9.31m (= US$10m − US$1.49m). Interest payment in the second period is now US$745,000 (8 per cent on the US$9.31m principal) and the capital repayment is US$746,000 (= US$1.49m − US$0.745m). Outstanding capital reduces to US$8.56m (= US$9.31m − US$1.49m), and so on, until the

Table 11.1 Fixed-rate term loans repayment examples

Interest rate: 8% fixed – Amounts in US$'000s

Drawdown	$10m									
Term	10 years									
Period	**1**	**2**	**3**	**4**	**5**	**6**	**7**	**8**	**9**	**10**
Panel A: Equal instalments										
Total payment	1,490	1,490	1,490	1,490	1,490	1,490	1,490	1,490	1,490	1,490
Interest payment	800	745	685	621	551	476	395	307	213	110
Capital repayment	690	746	805	870	939	1,014	1,095	1,183	1,278	1,380
Remaining capital	9,310	8,564	7,759	6,889	5,950	4,936	3,841	2,658	1,380	0
Panel B:Moratorium: 2-year holiday period										
Total payment	800	800	1,740	1,740	1,740	1,740	1,740	1,740	1,740	1,740
Interest payment	800	800	800	725	644	556	461	359	248	129
Capital repayment	0	0	940	1,015	1,097	1,184	1,279	1,381	1,492	1,611
Remaining capital	10,000	10,000	9,060	8,044	6,948	5,764	4,485	3,103	1,611	0
Panel C:Balloon repayment: 20% of the capital is due at maturity										
Total payment	1,600	1,536	1,472	1,408	1,344	1,280	1,216	1,152	1,088	3,024
Interest payment	800	736	672	608	544	480	416	352	288	224
Capital repayment	800	800	800	800	800	800	800	800	800	800
Balloon payment	0	0	0	0	0	0	0	0	0	2,000
Remaining capital	9,200	8,400	7,600	6,800	6,000	5,200	4,400	3,600	2,800	0
Panel D:Bullet repayment: 100% of the capital is due at maturity										
Total payment	800	800	800	800	800	800	800	800	800	10,800
Interest payment	800	800	800	800	800	800	800	800	800	800
Capital repayment	0	0	0	0	0	0	0	0	0	0
Bullet payment	0	0	0	0	0	0	0	0	0	10,000
Remaining capital	10,000	10,000	10,000	10,000	10,000	10,000	10,000	10,000	10,000	0

outstanding capital at expiry is zero. When a moratorium is granted for the first two years (Panel B), only interest is paid during that period. From year three onwards, the entire amount of capital and the repayments from years three to ten can be calculated using the eight-period annuity formula as follows:

$$\$10m = C\left[1 - \frac{1}{(1+0.08)^8}\right]\bigg/0.08 \Rightarrow C = \$1.740m$$

Next, consider the case where we have a balloon repayment (Panel C). If 20 per cent of the capital is due at maturity, that is US\$2m, the remaining capital to be paid during the tenure of the loan is US\$8m, which will be repaid in equal instalments of US\$0.8m per year. As the interest is proportional to the outstanding amount of the loan, the overall instalments will decrease as time to maturity approaches. Finally, in the case of bullet repayment, presented in Panel D, interest payments are fixed at a rate of 8 per cent, and the entire capital is due at maturity. Overall, we can note that fixed-rate loans are beneficial for borrowers if interest rates in the market increase above the fixed rate; similarly, fixed-rate loans are beneficial for lenders if interest rates in the market decrease below the fixed rate level.

11.3.2 Floating-rate loan examples

Now let us consider the effects of a floating borrowing rate. Following from the previous example, suppose that the company is borrowing at a floating borrowing rate of LIBOR plus a spread of 100bp. Consider two simple cases where interest rates either increase (Table 11.2, Panel A) or decrease (Table 11.2, Panel B) by 20bp per period so that at the outset of the loan the LIBOR rate is 7 per cent, the next period is either 7.2 per cent or 6.8 per cent, and so on. Due to the impact of changes in the rates, instalments do not remain equal from period to period because each instalment is determined on the basis of the new interest rate. Therefore, interest payments are calculated separately upon each instalment and capital payments are calculated according to the chosen amortisation schedule.

The payment for each period is calculated again as the present value of an annuity which results in the capital to be amortised throughout the remaining life of the loan.

$$C_i = [\text{Remaining capital}]\bigg/\left(\left[1 - \frac{1}{(1+r_i)^i}\right]\bigg/r_i\right), \text{ for } i = \{1\ldots 10\}$$

Overall, borrowers can benefit from falling LIBOR rates. On the other hand, if interest rates increase, borrowers will be exposed to higher interest payments. Uncertainty of the level of cash payments may create cash-flow and liquidity problems, if interest rates increase above expectations. Figure 11.2 presents

Table 11.2 Floating-rate term loans examples

Drawdown	US$10m									
Spread over LIBOR	1%									
Term	10 years									
Period	1	2	3	4	5	6	7	8	9	10

Panel A: Increasing interest rates – amounts in US$'000s

LIBOR	7%	7.20%	7.40%	7.60%	7.80%	8%	8.20%	8.40%	8.60%	8.80%
Total payment	1,490	1,503	1,514	1,524	1,533	1,542	1,548	1,554	1,558	1,561
Interest payment	800	763	720	669	609	540	459	367	261	139
Capital repayment	690	739	794	856	925	1,002	1,089	1,187	1,297	1,422
Remaining capital	9,310	8,570	7,776	6,921	5,996	4,994	3,905	2,719	1,422	0

Effective borrowing cost: $10m = \sum_{t=1}^{10} \dfrac{(C_t)_t}{(1 + IRR)^t} \xrightarrow{IRR} y = 8.55\% pa$

Panel B: Decreasing interest rates – amounts in US$'000s

LIBOR	7%	6.80%	6.60%	6.40%	6.20%	6%	5.80%	5.60%	5.40%	5.20%
Total payment	1,490	1,478	1,467	1,457	1,448	1,440	1,433	1,428	1,424	1,422
Interest payment	800	726	650	573	494	413	332	249	166	83
Capital repayment	690	752	816	884	954	1,027	1,102	1,179	1,258	1,339
Remaining capital	9,310	8,558	7,742	6,858	5,904	4,877	3,776	2,597	1,339	0

Effective Borrowing Cost: $10m = \sum_{t=1}^{10} \dfrac{(C_t)_t}{(1 + IRR)^t} \xrightarrow{IRR} y = 7.45\% pa$

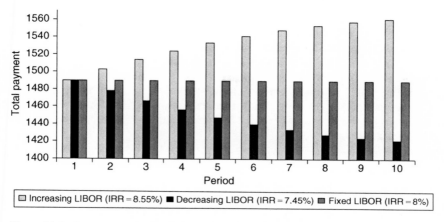

Figure 11.2 Sensitivity of cash flows to changes in interest rates

the sensitivity of the floating-rate cash flows to interest-rate fluctuations, against the fixed rate cash flows.

11.4 Hedging interest-rate risk

In finance, hedging is the strategy of mitigating risk exposure by establishing an offsetting position in the derivatives markets. Consider the example demonstrated in the previous section. Fluctuations in the LIBOR rates between the LIBOR reset periods result in uncertainty regarding the future level of loan-interest payments. Derivative markets allow market agents to minimise their exposure to risk by reducing the variance of their portfolio; hence risk-management tools and their effectiveness in terms of hedging are of utmost importance. The hedging techniques and instruments used to hedge interest rate risk are similar to those used for freight and bunker risk management, namely: 'interest-rate forwards', called 'forward rate agreements' (FRAs); 'interest-rate futures'; 'interest-rate swaps'; and 'interest-rate options' ('caps', 'floors' and 'collars'). We discuss each of these instruments next.

11.5 Forward-rate agreements

A forward-rate agreement (FRA) is a bilateral contract to exchange interest-rate payments on a notional principal amount, at a certain future date, over a specified time interval. The underlying asset for the FRA contracts is usually a LIBOR rate with a specified maturity, but other reference rates such as EURIBOR can be agreed as well. FRA contracts are over-the-counter (OTC) cash-settled contracts on the difference between the interest rate stipulated in the contract and the prevailing interest rate at maturity. Hence, FRAs are off-balance-sheet transactions; there are no up-front margin requirements and they are not marked-to-market. A wide range of maturities is available, starting from a few days up to terms of several years. However, three, six, nine and 12 months are usually more liquid.

Each payment on the differential between FRA rate and current spot rate is settled at the beginning of each period. Because interest payments accrue from the loan's commencement date and are not due until maturity, each payment should be discounted accordingly. Assuming LIBOR as the reference rate and Q as the notional principal amount, each interest payment can then be calculated as:

$$\text{Interest payment} = Q \frac{(LIBOR - FRA\ rate)\frac{days}{360}}{1 + LIBOR\frac{days}{360}}$$

where FRA rate refers to the agreed rate, and days represent the number of days in the future interest period. The day count convention (that is, days/360) for short-term lending differs between different currencies and determines how interest accrues over a period of time in a variety of trans-actions, such as bonds, swaps and loans. For instance, in the US-dollar and Eurodollar markets the convention factor of *(actual number of days)/360* applies; this effectively means that interest is accrued by considering the actual number of days over which the money is invested, assuming that there are 360 days in a year. In the sterling or pound (GBP) market, the portion of a year over which the rates are calculated, becomes *(actual number of days)/365*. Throughout our analysis we will follow the *actual/360* convention since we deal mainly with the US-dollar money markets.

Turning next to the mechanics of FRAs, if interest rates rise above the agreed rate then the seller of the FRA pays the buyer the increased interest expense. Similarly, if interest rates fall below the agreed rate the buyer of the FRA pays the seller the increased interest-rate cost. Consider for instance, the case of a shipowner who knows that he will need to borrow US$10m in two months for the period from 20 December 2005 to 20 March 2006. The owner fears that interest rates may rise by December, thus increasing interest costs. A way to hedge this exposure is by using FRA contracts. Suppose the company obtains FRA quotes from several banks and finally enters into an FRA agreement trading at 6 per cent for settlement in December. By buying the forward contract the owner effectively locks in a borrowing rate of 6 per cent, irrespective of the eventual three-month LIBOR rate in December. On the settlement date, the pre-fixed rate of 6 per cent is applied to a notional amount of US$10m, taken out for three months. The outcome is illustrated in Table 11.10, where we consider two separate scenarios for the level of interest rates in December.

In the first scenario, the three-month LIBOR rate in December increases to 7 per cent. The shipowner is entitled to receive the amount of US$24,838.28

Table 11.3 Hedging interest-rate risk using FRAs

Two-month LIBOR hedge for the period 20 October 2005 to 20 December 2005	
LIBOR market	FRA market
20 October 2005	
90-day LIBOR rate: 6%	3-month FRA rate for December settlement: 6% Notional principal: US$10m
Shipowner **buys** FRA with settlement on 20 December at 6% on a notional principal of US$10m	
20 December 2005 – rising market	
Shipowner **borrows** US$10m for 3 months priced at current LIBOR rate	
90-day LIBOR rate: 7% Additional cost of borrowing: $10,000,000\dfrac{(0.06-0.07)\dfrac{91}{360}}{1+0.07\dfrac{91}{360}}=-\$24,838.28$	FRA rate: 6% Profit in the FRA market: $10,000,000\dfrac{(0.07-0.06)\dfrac{91}{360}}{1+0.07\dfrac{91}{360}}=\$24,838.28$
Net result from hedging = $0	
20 December 2005 – alternative scenario – falling market	
90-day LIBOR rate: 5% Profit in the LIBOR market: $10,000,000\dfrac{(0.06-0.05)\dfrac{91}{360}}{1+0.05\dfrac{91}{360}}=\$24,962.28$	FRA rate: 6% Loss in the FRA market: $10,000,000\dfrac{(0.05-0.06)\dfrac{91}{360}}{1+0.05\dfrac{91}{360}}=-\$24,962.28$
Net result from hedging = $0	

from the bank. On the other hand, in the LIBOR spot market the shipowner has to pay US$24,838.28 additional interest due to the increase in interest rates. Therefore, by buying the forward agreement the loss of US$24,838.28 due to the 1 per cent increase in the LIBOR rate is offset, and as a result the effective borrowing rate is 6 per cent because the amount of US$10m will have to be borrowed at the actual rate of 7 per cent, but the borrowing cost is decreased by the compensating payment in the FRA market. The discount factor $(1+0.07[91/360])$ reflects the fact that the FRA payment is set at the beginning of the period (settlement date) and paid after 91 days.

In the second scenario, the LIBOR rate declines to 5 per cent. Now, the amount of US$24,962.28 will be refunded from the bank to the company. In this case the effective borrowing rate is also 6 per cent because the amount of US$10m will have to be borrowed at the actual rate of 5 per cent, but the borrowing cost is increased by the additional payment from the FRA.

In both scenarios the company effectively locked in a fixed borrowing rate of 6 per cent. The shipowner/borrower (the buyer of the FRA) is by this method hedged against a rise in interest rates. The example above can also be extended to accommodate the case of a shipowner who wants to invest/deposit an amount of the operating revenues of the company. The only difference is that the shipowner will be a seller of FRAs with a position in the LIBID market.[3] Finally, this example can be extended to allow for multiple interest-rate reset periods. Because an FRA contract is used to hedge a single-period interest payment, usually a strip of FRAs is required to fully hedge a term loan. A portfolio of FRAs is equivalent to a plain vanilla swap and this link will be demonstrated in the discussion of swap valuation in section 11.11.1 below.

11.6   Interest-rate futures

Futures contracts on interest rates are extremely liquid, with high traded volumes and open interest, because interest-rate volatility affects a wide range of market participants. Interest-rate futures are standardised contracts, traded in organised exchanges and thus do not incorporate credit risk as do OTC derivatives contracts. The most liquid interest rate futures contract is the Chicago Mercantile Exchange (CME) Eurodollar future, especially in the front months of the forward curve. Other liquid contracts include the Short Sterling and Euribor futures contracts traded at NYSE Euronext.

Futures contracts on interest rates are quoted as 100 minus the implied interest rate or yield. Therefore, when interest rates increase, interest rate futures decrease and vice-versa. Consequently, borrowers in the market wishing to hedge their interest-rate risk will be sellers of futures and lenders will be buyers.

11.6.1   Eurodollar futures contracts

The most heavily traded short-term interest-rate futures contract is the CME's Eurodollar Futures Contract, launched in 1982. The underlying asset of the contract is the interest on a three-month US-dollar LIBOR deposit on a notional principal of US$1m. The contract expires on the second business day in London preceding the third Wednesday of the settlement month. Table 11.4 presents an indicative range of Eurodollar futures prices with maturities up to almost two years.

Prices are quoted as 100 less the LIBOR; for example, for the June 07 contract the annual yield on the three-month Eurodollar deposit is 5.34 per cent (100 − 94.66). This gives the notional right to borrow at 5.34 per cent for three months. Each tick on the price is equal to 1 basis point and is worth US$25 per contract (calculated as 0.01 per cent × 1,000,000 × 90/360). Eurodollar

---

[3] LIBID stands for London Interbank Bid rate and is the rate bid by banks in Eurocurrency deposits.

Table 11.4 Eurodollars futures prices

Maturity	Open	High	Low	Settle	Yield	Open interest
March	94.64	94.64	94.63	94.64	5.36	1,281,965
June	94.65	94.67	94.65	94.66	5.34	1,359,704
Sept	94.74	94.76	94.74	94.76	5.24	1,377,287
Dec 07	94.85	94.88	94.84	94.87	5.13	1,403,983
March	94.94	94.97	94.93	94.95	5.05	917,590
June	94.98	95.01	94.97	95.00	5.00	699,680
Sept	95.02	95.04	95.00	95.03	4.97	617,458

Source: Financial Times, 25 January 2007, p. 37. Only regular quarterly maturities are shown. All contracts are for a notional US$1m, three-month deposit; yields are in percentage terms. Open interest is the number of contracts outstanding.

futures trade in half (US$12.50 per contract) and quarter (US$6.25 per contract) ticks. The main delivery months are March, June, September and December, with contract expirations up to ten years out. Hedging with interest-rate futures works in the same way as it does with FRA contracts. The main advantage compared to the FRA market is that because the contracts are exchange-traded, credit risk is reduced. On the other hand, FRA contracts do not require any cash outflows prior to maturity whereas for futures contracts both initial-margin requirements and daily marking-to-market have to be considered because they may cause liquidity problems if the participant cannot meet margin call payments.

11.7 Interest-rate swaps

As already discussed, because a single-maturity FRA contract can only hedge a single reset period, a strip of FRAs is required to fully hedge a term loan. In this case, it is common to 'bundle' this strip of FRAs as a single contract with a common price across all maturities. Such a contract is called an interest-rate swap. These are a very popular class of financial derivatives for both trading and hedging interest-rate risk. At the end of June 2006 the notional amount of interest-rate swaps outstanding was estimated to be more than US$200 trillion.[4] An interest-rate swap is a bilateral OTC contractual agreement to exchange streams of interest payments for a specific maturity, called the tenor, based on a notional principal. The notional principal is only used for the purposes of calculating interest payments and is not exchanged between the two parties. In its basic form, also called a plain vanilla swap, the contract involves the exchange of a fixed-for-floating interest payment. However, 'floating-for-floating' swaps, called 'basis swaps', are also possible.

---

[4] Source: Bank for International Settlements (www.bis.org/statizstics/derstats.htm). The figure is based on semi-annual data.

Figure 11.3 Swap structure for the shipowner

To demonstrate how swaps work, consider the case of a shipping company that enters into a five-year loan of US$100m in order to finance the purchase of a second-hand vessel. Under the terms of the loan, the company undertakes the obligation to pay the six-month LIBOR plus a spread of 20bp every six months for the next five years. The first interest payment is known in advance because it is based on the LIBOR rate at the outset of the loan and is due six months later. If the shipping company is concerned about the possibility of an increase in the LIBOR rates, it may enter into a fixed-for-floating swap which will transform the floating-rate payments to fixed. Suppose, for instance, that the shipping company agrees to pay a 5.5 per cent fixed rate in exchange for the six-month LIBOR, on a notional principal of US$100m, every six months for the next five years; the structure of the swap is illustrated in Figure 11.3.

The LIBOR received from the swap is offset by the LIBOR paid for the loan. In fact, the company borrows on a fixed rate, which is effectively locked in at 5.7 per cent per annum ($=$ LIBOR $+$ 0.2 per cent $+$ 5.5 per cent $-$ LIBOR), irrespective of movements in LIBOR rates. Swap payments are settled on a net basis; therefore the shipping company will receive the differential when LIBOR rises above 5.5 per cent and pay the differential when LIBOR falls below 5.5 per cent.

Table 11.5 displays the resulting cash flows throughout the tenor of the swap, given the realized six-month LIBOR rates in the market. For instance, in July 2003, the interest due is US$3.05m ($=$ US$100m [6.1%][180/360]). However, the swap's contract cash flows net out to US$300,000 and therefore the overall interest expense for the owner, including the spread of 20bp, is reduced to US$2.85m, resulting in a borrowing rate of 5.7 per cent per annum.[5]

Swap transactions involve intermediaries, usually banks, that get commission and brokerage fees for their services. Financial intermediaries usually act as brokers who find counter-parties to swap transactions. Alternatively, they may act as swap dealers by taking the other side of the swap in order to benefit from favourable movements in the market. In this case, which is also presented in Figure 11.3, swap dealers warehouse the credit risk of the other party and are compensated for that by asking for a spread over the swap rates, as shown in Table 11.6, which presents the quoted interest swap rates for

---

[5] For simplicity of exposition, we assume that the loan is not amortised.

Table 11.5 Cash flows for the shipowner in a five-year interest-rate swap contract

Date	LIBOR rate	in US$'000s		
		Floating cash flow	Fixed cash flow	Net cash flow
Jan 5, 2001	5.1%			
Jul 5, 2001	6.3%	2550	(2750)	(200)
Jan 5, 2002	6.7%	3150	(2750)	400
Jul 5, 2002	7.0%	3350	(2750)	600
Jan 5, 2003	6.1%	3500	(2750)	750
Jul 5, 2003	5.0%	3050	(2750)	300
Jan 5, 2004	4.3%	2500	(2750)	(250)
Jul 5, 2004	5.2%	2150	(2750)	(600)
Jan 5, 2005	7.1%	2600	(2750)	(150)
Jul 5, 2005	7.2%	3550	(2750)	800
Jan 5, 2006	6.3%	3600	(2750)	850

Table 11.6 Interest-rate swaps

	Euro €		GBP £		SFR		US$		Yen ¥	
	Bid	Ask	Bid	Ask	Bid	Ask	Bid	Ask	Bid	Ask
1 year	4.12	4.15	5.86	5.88	2.46	2.52	5.41	5.44	0.68	0.71
2 year	4.18	4.21	5.76	5.80	2.58	2.66	5.26	5.29	0.85	0.88
3 year	4.18	4.21	5.71	5.75	2.63	2.71	5.20	5.23	1.01	1.04
4 year	4.18	4.21	5.64	5.69	2.66	2.74	5.19	5.22	1.16	1.19
5 year	4.18	4.21	5.58	5.63	2.69	2.77	5.19	5.22	1.30	1.33
6 year	4.19	4.22	5.51	5.56	2.72	2.80	5.20	5.23	1.42	1.45
7 year	4.20	4.23	5.44	5.49	2.75	2.83	5.22	5.25	1.52	1.55
8 year	4.22	4.25	5.38	5.43	2.78	2.86	5.24	5.27	1.62	1.65
9 year	4.23	4.26	5.32	5.37	2.81	2.89	5.26	5.29	1.71	1.74
10 year	4.25	4.28	5.26	5.31	2.83	2.91	5.27	5.30	1.79	1.82
12 year	4.28	4.31	5.16	5.23	2.87	2.97	5.31	5.34	1.93	1.96
15 year	4.33	4.36	5.02	5.11	2.91	3.01	5.36	5.39	2.10	2.13
20 year	4.36	4.39	4.81	4.94	2.93	3.03	5.39	5.42	2.29	2.32
25 year	4.36	4.39	4.67	4.80	2.92	3.02	5.40	5.43	2.42	2.45
30 year	4.34	4.37	4.55	4.68	2.92	3.02	5.40	5.43	2.48	2.51
LIBOR	**3.9045**		**5.7144**		**2.2700**		**5.3600**		**0.5944**	

Source: *Financial Times*, 25 January 2007, p. 37. Bid-and-ask spreads are as of close of London business. US$ is quoted against three-month LIBOR; Japanese yen against six-month LIBOR; Euro and Swiss franc against six-month LIBOR.

major currencies for tenors up to 30 years. For instance, the fixed rates for a five-year plain vanilla interest rate swap in Swiss francs against the floating six-month Swiss franc LIBOR are 2.69 per cent and 2.77 per cent for the seller and buyer of the swap, respectively. These are the rates available for investment-grade companies and bid-ask spreads will usually be wider for less creditworthy companies.

Swap dealers hedge their positions by taking appropriate long or short positions in the futures or forwards markets or by arranging offsetting swaps with other counter-parties; however, in the latter case, it may not always be possible to plan equal opposing swap positions and swap dealers face mismatched risk in terms of the of quantity and timing of the swap cash flows. Finally, it should be noted that usually for a shipping company, the swap will be arranged directly though the lending bank and in most cases, the shipowner will simply be paying the fixed rate instead of paying or receiving the offsetting cash flows, as described in Table 11.5.

11.7.1 Pricing and unwinding of interest-rate swaps

Valuation of financial derivatives is vital from a risk-management perspective and any portfolio of derivatives contracts should be valued on a daily basis. The value of the swap today shows the net cash flow that has to be incurred if the swap is terminated early. Although not all swaps can be settled prior to expiry, they can change hands under the approval of the swap facilitator who has to verify the creditworthiness of the new counter-parties. In either case, the swap value describes how much the swap is worth today and thus the amount of money the counter-parties have to pay or receive in order to terminate the contract early. A common alternative way to unwind the swap is to neutralise the swap payments by reversing the position and agreeing another offsetting swap contract. Of course nowadays, cancellable swaps exist, but the embedded option to cancel makes these transactions more complex and more expensive. Cancellable swap contracts are called 'break' or 'cancellable' forwards. They are divided into 'callable', which give the right to the fixed-rate payer to unwind the agreement prior to expiry, and 'puttable' which give the right to the fixed-rate receiver to unwind the agreement. For instance, the shipping company in the previous example could have purchased a callable swap in order to be able to terminate the deal early. However, exotics like callable swaps are beyond the scope of this section; instead we focus on plain vanilla swaps pricing, which provides the basis for swap valuation.

At the initiation of the swap agreement, the value of the contract will have zero market value; this is a no-arbitrage condition and implies that in order for the deal to be fairly priced, the present values of the expected floating and fixed stream of payments should be equal. We can thus consider the value of an interest-rate swap as the difference between the value of a fixed-rate bond and the value of a floating-rate bond. For instance, for the party that pays the floating rate and receives the fixed rate, the value of the swap will be the value of a portfolio consisting of a long position in a fixed-rate bond and a short position in a floating-rate bond, as follows:

$$V_{Swap} = B_{fixed} - B_{floating} \qquad (11.1)$$

where B_{fixed} is the fixed-rate bond that pays, say *FC*, for a sequence of dates $t_1 < \cdots < t_n$ and $B_{floating}$ is the floating-rate bond that pays a single payment, say *VC*, at the next reset period and its value reverts to par immediately afterwards. Calculation of the fixed rate takes place at the beginning of the deal, as the rate that sets the NPV of floating and fixed payments equal to zero. To illustrate this procedure, consider a swap dealer who has to determine the fixed rate in order to construct a fixed-for-floating swap. The swap tenor is four years with annual resets and the 12-, 24-, 36- and 48-month LIBOR rates with continuous compounding are 6.3 per cent, 6.8 per cent, 7.3 per cent and 8 per cent respectively. The value of the floating leg at inception equals the par value, say US$10m. The fixed payment *FC* is then calculated as:

$$V_{Swapt=0} = 0 \Rightarrow B_{fixed} = B_{floating} \Rightarrow$$

$$e^{-0.063(1)}FC + e^{-0.068(2)}FC + e^{-0.073(3)}FC + e^{-0.08(4)}FC$$

$$+ e^{-0.08(4)}US\$10m = US\$10m \Rightarrow$$

$$3.341FC + 7.261 = US\$10m \Rightarrow FC = 0.8196$$

It follows that $FC \approx US\$819,600$, resulting in an annual fixed rate of 8.2 per cent $(=FC/\$Q)$. Therefore, if the fixed leg is set equal to 8.2 per cent the NPV of the swap will be zero as will be the expected profit to the swap dealer. In practice, the rate will be higher than 8.2 per cent to cover the dealer's market risk from the position as well as commission and brokerage fees. As time passes and interest rates change, the swap value will change accordingly. In this case, the value of the swap can be calculated using equation (11.1). The value of the fixed-rate bond is estimated by discounting the future cash flows to present using continuously compounded spot rates:

$$B_{fixed} = \sum_{i=1}^{N} e^{-r_i t_i} FC + e^{-r_n t_n} \$Q \qquad (11.2)$$

The floating leg depends only on the next payment and the notional principal, because after each payment date, future payments are set to par:

$$B_{floating} = e^{-r_1 t_1}(VC + \$Q) \qquad (11.3)$$

For instance, consider the interest-rate swap example presented in Table 11.5. The shipping company decides to terminate the swap agreement on 5 April 2004. The remaining life of the swap is 1.75 years. The continuously compounded LIBOR rates with three-, nine-, 15- and 21-month maturities are 5.3 per cent, 5.8 per cent, 6.2 per cent and 6.3 per cent, respectively. The six-month LIBOR rate at the last payment date was 4.3 per cent with semiannual compounding. Given that the fixed payment at each period is US$2.75m, (=$100m[5.5%][180/360]), the fixed and floating legs of the swap are priced, respectively, as:

$$B_{fixed} = e^{-0.053(0.25)}2.75 + e^{-0.058(0.75)}2.75 + e^{-0.062(1.25)}2.75$$
$$+ e^{-0.063(1.75)}102.75 = US\$99,915,615$$

$$B_{floating} = e^{-0.053(0.25)}100(1 + 0.043\frac{180}{360}) = US\$100,805,440$$

The overall value for the shipowner who receives floating and pays fixed is: $V_{Swap} = B_{floating} - B_{fixed} = US\$100,805,440 - US\$99,115,615 = US\$889,825$; similarly, the value of the swap to the party paying floating and receiving fixed will be $-US\$889,825$. Calculating the value of the swap in this way is important because it enables companies to mark-to-market their positions and also calculate their counter-party exposure for each swap transaction. It also determines that each counter-party needs to pay or receive in order to terminate the swap early.

Alternatively, the swap can also be valued as a portfolio of FRAs by calculating the FRA rates for the relevant reset periods, as discussed by Cuthbertson and Nitzsche (2001). Similarly, an interest-rate swap can be priced as a portfolio of interest-rate futures. However, because futures are standardised, with specific expiration months and mark-to-market settlement, forwards are considered to be a more accurate tool for swap valuation. In addition, the methods described here can also be applied for the valuation of basis (floating-for-floating) swaps, by decomposing the swap into a portfolio of two fixed-for-floating swaps; for example, a 'LIBOR for EURIBOR' swap is equivalent to a portfolio of 'LIBOR for fixed' and 'fixed for EURIBOR' swaps. Then the two swaps can be valued separately using the above methods. Finally, in the examples presented we discussed the case of non-amortising swaps; in other words, the swap notional amount remains the same throughout the swap tenor. Since in most cases part of the loan capital is repaid during the life of the loan, the swap notional amount must be reduced accordingly to reflect the reduction in the loan capital. These swaps are called 'amortising swaps' and are most commonly used to hedge interest-rate risk in term loans. Their pricing is based on the same principle as discussed here, assuming the fact that the loan capital is repaid according to some predetermined schedule; for more on the pricing of amortising swaps see Kolb and Overdahl (2007).

11.8 Interest-rate options

Swaps are very useful hedging tools and provide an effective hedge against fluctuations in interest rates. However, a borrower is locked into a fixed rate and cannot take advantage of any decrease in the level of interest rates in the market. Interest-rate options provide a more flexible alternative. These are traded either on organised exchanges or over-the-counter. Exchange-traded options are mainly options on interest-rate futures, rather than simple rates; they include options on Eurodollar futures traded in the Chicago Mercantile Exchange (CME) or options on Short Sterling futures traded in NYSE Euronext. In this section we discuss hedging strategies using interest-rate options contracts.

11.8.1 Interest-rate caplets and floorlets

'Caplets' and 'floorlets' are risk-management tools, designed to provide insurance by setting a maximum (cap) and a minimum (floor) floating rate respectively for a certain interest-rate period. A caplet is defined as a long position on a single call option on an underlying interest rate. An interest rate caplet gives its holder the opportunity to limit any possible future losses due to an increase in interest rates. The purchase of the call option compensates the floating-rate borrower in the case of an interest-rate rise and provides an upper bound on the spot interest-rate payment which the borrower has to pay at expiry. A floorlet, on the other hand, is defined as a long position on a single put option on an underlying asset. An interest-rate floorlet gives its holder the opportunity to limit any possible future losses due to a drop in interest rates. The purchase of the put option compensates the floating-rate lender/investor in the case of an interest-rate fall and provides a lower bound on the spot interest-rate payment that the investor receives at expiry.

A 'cap' is a portfolio of two or more caplets with the same exercise price but different maturity dates, while a 'floor' is a portfolio of two or more floorlets with the same exercise price but different maturities. Therefore, both pricing and hedging techniques for caps and floors are the same as those used in the case of caplets and floorlets. Caps and floors are structured on the basis of a specific reference rate, for example, three-month LIBOR, which is reset at regular intervals, say every three months. A caplet (long call) with maturity date T and strike rate K_c pays at expiry (T) an amount equal to the difference between the spot interest rate (say $LIBOR_T$) and the strike rate K_c, if this amount is positive, and zero otherwise. In the same way, a floorlet (long put) with maturity date T and strike rate K_{FL} pays at expiry (T) an amount equal to the difference between the strike rate K_{FL} and spot interest rate, if this amount is positive, and zero otherwise. The payoffs are:

$$\text{Caplet: } \$Q \left\{ \max(0, \text{LIBOR}_T - K_c) \frac{\text{days}}{360} \right\} \text{ and,}$$

$$\text{Floorlet: } \$Q \left\{ \max (0, K_{FL} - \text{LIBOR}_T) \frac{\text{days}}{360} \right\}$$

11.8.1.1   An example of a caplet option hedge

On 10 November 2001, the LIBOR interest rate is at 6 per cent. A shipowner knows that he will need to arrange short-term financing, until he completes the sale of one of his vessels in four months; he will need to borrow around US$100m on 10 December 2001, for three months, until 10 March 2002. The rate for the loan will be the three-month LIBOR rate on 10 December plus a spread of 25bp. The owner is concerned that LIBOR rates may rise and hence cause cash-flow problems from the required interest payments on the loan. In order to avoid this, the owner decides to hedge his borrowing cost; he finds that the following call option on the three-month LIBOR for a notional amount of $100m is available:

option premium = US$250,000 (=0.25% of the notional principal of $100m)
strike rate = 6.5%
expiry date = 10 December 2001

If the shipowner agrees to buy the option, then by paying US$250,000 to the call writer on 10 November 2001, he buys the right – but not the obligation – to receive the December 90-day LIBOR rate on a notional principal of US$100m on 10 March 2002 at the fixed strike rate of 6.5 per cent. The outcome of this hedging strategy is presented in Table 11.7.

Under the first scenario, in December, the 90-day LIBOR rate has fallen to 3 per cent and the shipowner will not exercise the option because the market LIBOR rate is lower than the strike rate. This leaves the shipowner with a loss of US$250,000 for the premium paid in November. In this case the effective amount borrowed in December is US$99.749m, that is, the loan less the amount paid for the premium in November, compounded one month ahead (US$251,302). Moreover, the effective interest rate on borrowing in December 2001, US$99.75m and paying out the amount of US$100m plus the interest of US$812,500 [=US$100m(3.25%)(90/360)]on 10 March 2002, is 4.4 per cent per annum. Effectively by subtracting the option premium from the amount borrowed, we have incorporated the cost of the option premium in the cost of borrowing.

Table 11.7 Hedging against interest-rate fluctuations using a caplet

One-month caplet hedge for the period 10 November to 10 December 2001	
LIBOR market	Options market
10 November 2001	
Current interest rate : 6% Shipowner **buys** December 2001 call at a total cost of US$250,000	Option details: December 2001 Call with a Strike rate of 6.5%. Premium: US$250,000 Notional principal: US$100m
10 December 2001	
Shipowner **borrows** US$100m at **90-day LIBOR plus 0.25%** for the period December 2001–March 2002 Compounded call premium = US$250,000 [1 + (0.06 + 0.0025)(30/360)] = US$251,302 Effective amount borrowed = US$100m − US$251,302 = US$99,748,698	
First scenario: falling interest rates	
10 December 2001	
90-day LIBOR = 3%	Strike rate (6.5%) > Spot rate (3%) Therefore option is not exercised
10 March 2001	
Actual borrowing cost US$812,500 = US$100m (3% + 0.25%) 90/360	Payoff from the options transaction US$0
Total borrowing cost (not including option premium) = US$812,500	

Effective interest rate (including option premium) $= \left(\dfrac{100,812,500}{99.748,698}\right)^{360/90} - 1 = 4.335\%$

Second scenario: rising interest rates	
10 December 2001	
90-day LIBOR$_t$ = 9%	Strike rate (6.5%) < spot rate (9%) Therefore option is exercised
10 March 2001	
Actual borrowing cost US$2,312,500 = US$100m (9% + 0.25%) 90/360	Payoff from the options transaction US$625,000 = US$100m (9% − 6.5%) 90/360
Total borrowing cost (not including option premium) = **US$2,312,500 − US$625,000 = US$1,687,500**	

Effective interest rate (including option premium) $= \left(\dfrac{101,687,500}{99,748,698}\right)^{360/90} - 1 = 8.004\%$

Under the second scenario, the December 90-day LIBOR has risen to 9 per cent. Then, the shipowner can exercise the option, as the market rate is higher that the strike rate, and is entitled to receive US$625,000 from the writer of the option. This will compensate the owner against the rise in interest rates. Consequently, the interest-rate payment in the spot market is US$2,312,500 minus the profit from the call payout, US$625,000, which amounts to US$1,687,500. The effective interest rate on borrowing in this case is 8.1 per cent per annum instead of 9 per cent.

Panel A of Figure 11.4 shows the result of the above hedge using a caplet. It can be seen that by buying the call option, the shipowner has hedged the borrowing cost up to a maximum of 8 per cent per annum (a total interest payment of US$1,687,500 on a borrowing capital equal to US$99.749m) regardless of by how much interest rates increase in December. We can also note that the owner can take advantage of lower interest rates in the market by not exercising his options, when interest rates are below the strike price. In this case, however, the cost of borrowing will be slightly higher than the cost of borrowing if the owner had not hedged, reflecting the cost of the option premium, as can be seen in Panel A.

Panel B of Figure 11.4 shows the possible interest-rate payments received for a lender/investor once a floorlet hedge is used. This may be the case for a shipping company expecting to receive funds, for example, operating revenues or the resale or scrap value of a vessel. Suppose that a shipowner has agreed to sell one of his vessels for US$100m. The sale will tale place in three months' time and the owner would like to deposit the funds from the sale for a period of six months until he decides how best to use the sale proceeds. However, since the sale will take place in three months, interest rates may be lower than their current level so the owner buys a put option (floorlet) to lock in a lower bound, or floor, on the return on his deposit. Panel B presents the interest rate received by the owner when he buys a three-month-to-maturity put option, with a strike price of 6 per cent and a premium of US$250,000. The lower bound in this case is equal to 5.15 per cent.

11.8.2   Interest-rate caps and floors

Caplets and floorlets are used to hedge interest-rate risk over a single reset period. In practice, in order to hedge a term loan with multiple resets, we require multiple caplets that cover successive interest-rate periods. Consider the following example. Suppose that on 10 December 2001, a tanker owner wishes to borrow US$100m for the purchase of a second-hand vessel. The term of the loan will be five years and the reference rate will be the US-dollar LIBOR with semi-annual resets, on 10 December and 10 June of each year. The owner is concerned that adverse movements in the level of LIBOR rates might cause cash-flow problems from the interest payments on the loan.

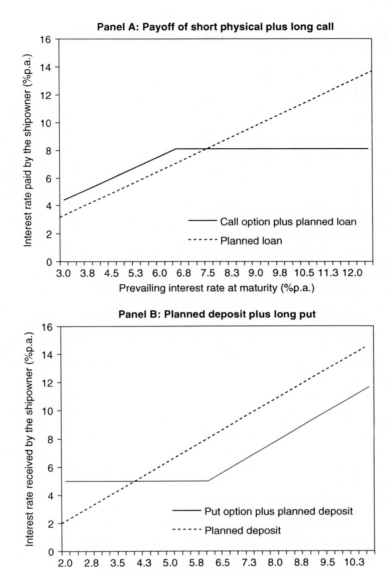

Figure 11.4 Interest rate to be paid or received by a caplet and a floorlet holder

In order to avoid this, the owner decides to hedge his borrowing cost; he finds that the following cap (portfolio of caplets) is available:

option premium = US$400,000 (=0.4% of the principal of US$100m)
strike rate = 6.5 per cent
expiry dates = semi-annually on loan reset periods

If the shipowner agrees to buy this portfolio of caplets, then by paying US$400,000 up-front to the call writer on 10 December 2001, he buys the right – but not the obligation – to receive the 180-day LIBOR rate on a notional principal of US$100m semi-annually over the next five years regardless of the LIBOR rate at that time, and pay the fixed strike rate of 6.5 per cent (note that the first interest payment is based on the current rate). If the 180-day LIBOR on each interest payment date has fallen below 6.5 per cent the shipowner will not exercise his right because the market LIBOR rate will be cheaper than the strike rate. If the 180-day LIBOR on each interest payment date is higher than 6.5 per cent the shipowner will exercise his right because the market LIBOR rate will be more expensive than the strike rate. In the latter case, actual cash payments occur after each expiry date.

Table 11.8 summarises the outcome of the loan repayment schedule along with the cash flows from undertaking a long position in the above interest-rate cap. We can see that interest rates are above the strike price in most cases apart from one interest-rate period. For example, on 10 June 2003, the LIBOR rate is equal to 9.1 per cent, therefore the loan interest payment six months later is equal to US$4.626m (=$100m [9.1%] 183/360). The corresponding cap payoff is equal to US$1.322m (=$100m [9.1% – 6.5%] 183/360), resulting in a cash outflow of US$3.304m. On the other hand, in December 2005, where LIBOR is 5.2 per cent, the option is not exercised and the cap payoff is zero. The effective cost of borrowing will be the internal rate of return (IRR), which represents the cost of capital or, in other words, the rate at which future cash flows are discounted to today's value of dollars; the higher the IRR, the higher the cost of borrowing. Mathematically:

$$100 - 0.400 = \frac{3.033}{(1+y)} + \frac{3.304}{(1+y)^2} + \frac{3.286}{(1+y)^3} + \cdots + \frac{3.304}{(1+y)^8} + \frac{2.629}{(1+y)^9}$$
$$+ \frac{100 + 3.304}{(1+y)^{10}}$$

which gives a semi-annual rate of $y = 3.26$ per cent and an annualised rate of $(1.0326)^2 - 1 = 6.62$ per cent per annum. If the cap had not been purchased the relevant borrowing rate would have been 7.93 per cent per annum. Consequently, the cap-hedge is equivalent to an upper bound to interest rate payments of US$3.286m to US$3.304m. Small deviations occur because a six-month period sometimes covers 182 days and sometimes 183 days.

Table 11.8 Hedging against interest-rate fluctuations using a cap

Five-year cap hedge for the period December 2001-2006

LIBOR market	Options market
10 December 2001	
Current interest rate: 6%	Cap option details: Cap with a strike rate of 6.5%
Loan = US$100m	Premium: US$400,000
Reset periods = 180 days	Notional principal: US$100m
Maturity = 5 years	Semi-annual exercise dates

Shipowner **borrows** US$100m at the rate of 180-day LIBOR for the period 2001-2006 with semi-annual reset periods
Shipowner **buys** a cap interest-rate option at a total cost of US$400,000
Effective amount borrowed = US$100m – US$400,000 = US$99,600,000

Date	Days	LIBOR (%)	Interest paid	Cap payoff	Principal repayment	Net cash flows	
						With cap	Without cap
10 December 2001		6.0		-400,000	0	99,600,000	100,000,000
10 June 2002	182	6.7	3,033,333	–	0	-3,033,333	-3,033,333
10 December 2002	183	7.3	3,405,833	101,667	0	-3,304,167	-3,405,833
10 June 2003	182	9.1	3,690,556	404,444	0	-3,286,111	-3,690,556
10 December 2003	183	10.0	4,625,833	1,321,667	0	-3,304,167	-4,625,833
10 June 2004	183	8.7	5,083,333	1,779,167	0	-3,304,167	-5,083,333
10 December 2004	183	9.3	4,422,500	1,118,333	0	-3,304,167	-4,422,500
10 June 2005	182	7.5	4,701,667	1,415,556	0	-3,286,111	-4,701,667
10 December 2005	183	5.2	3,812,500	508,333	0	-3,304,167	-3,812,500
10 June 2006	182	6.9	2,628,889	0	0	-2,628,889	-2,628,889
10 December 2006	183		3,507,500	203,333	100,000,000	-103,304,167	-103,507,500

Effective interest rate (with cap)

$$\$100m - \$0.4m = \sum_{t=1}^{10} \frac{(Net\ Cash\ Flows)_t}{(1+IRR)^t} \xrightarrow{IRR(with\ Cap)} y = 3.26\%\ semi-annually\ or\ y = 6.62\%\ p.a.$$

Effective interest rate (without cap)

$$\$100m = \sum_{t=1}^{10} \frac{(Net\ Cash\ Flows)_t}{(1+IRR)^t} \xrightarrow{IRR(without\ Cap)} y = 3.89\%\ semi-annually\ or\ y = 7.93\%\ p.a.$$

Finally, also note that the cap is not exercised for the first reset on 10 June 2001 because the interest rate that will be paid on that period is known at the initiation of the contract. Furthermore, when a floor hedge is considered – for example, for a shipping company expecting to receive a vessel's scrap or resale price that wishes to make a five-year deposit to receive interest – the shipowner should buy a portfolio of floorlets (floor) to hedge against falling interest rates.

11.8.3   Interest-rate collars

Collars are very effective risk-management instruments designed to confine the gains and losses of the potential holder of the instrument within certain limits. As discussed in Chapter 7, collars are a combination of caps and floors, which allow the profit/loss of the investor to be limited to a maximum (cap) and minimum (floor). For example, a shipowner who plans to borrow a certain amount of capital in the future can buy an interest-rate call option (cap) and sell an interest-rate put option (floor) with a notional principal equal to the amount of the loan and expiration dates that match the tenor of the loan. If the shipowner is borrowing money at a floating LIBOR rate, the cap will limit any possible future losses due to an increase in interest rates by compensating the borrower to the amount of $Q\{\max(0, LIBOR_T - K_c)days/360\}$ at each reset. For this insurance, the shipowner will pay a cap premium. A way to offset the higher premium is to sell a put option for the same maturity but lower strike and receive the floor premium. However, by doing so, potential profits are limited if interest rates fall. The purpose of collars is to limit the effective borrowing cost by setting upper and lower bounds. Mathematically, the collar payoff at each reset can be expressed as (using the day count convention actual/360) can be expressed as:

$$Collar\ payoff\ =\ C_{cap} - C_{floor} = \$Q[\ \max\{0, LIBOR_t - K_C\}$$
$$- \max\{0, K_{FL} - LIBOR_t\}]\frac{days}{360}$$

where T is the expiry date, and days are the days remaining for the options to expire. It is clear that the effective borrowing cost with collar, at time $t = T - days$, is:

$$Effective\ borrowing\ cost_T\ =\ \$Q[LIBOR_t - \max\{0, LIBOR_t - K_C\}$$
$$+ \max\{0, K_{FL} - LIBOR_t\}]\frac{days}{360}$$

Therefore:

If $LIBOR_t > K_C$ the payoff is $\$Q\ K_C\ (days/360)$
If $LIBOR_t < K_{FL}$ the payoff is $\$Q\ K_{FL}\ (days/360)$
If $K_{FL} < LIBOR_t < K_C$ the payoff is $\$Q\ LIBOR_t\ (days/360)$

Very often collars are designed as zero-cost collars and used when hedgers do not want to incur any upfront cost for hedging their positions. By adjusting the strike prices of the caps and the floors accordingly, the cap premium matches the put premium and the overall cost of the collar is zero.

11.8.3.1 An example of a zero-cost collar

To illustrate how a zero-cost collar can be constructed to hedge interest-rate risk, consider the following example. On 10 December 2001, a shipowner knows that he will need to arrange short-term financing until he completes the sale of one of his vessels in six months' time; he will thus need to borrow around US$100m on 10 June 2002 for six months until 10 December 2002. The current six-month LIBOR rate is at 7 per cent. The owner is concerned that LIBOR rates may rise and hence cause cash-flow problems from the required interest payments on the loan. At the same time, he does not want to incur any upfront cost for the hedge so he considers buying a zero-cost collar option, which limits the fluctuations of interest rates within certain limits. Assume that the following option contracts are available to him in December 2001:

> A June call option (cap) on 180-day LIBOR with a strike rate of 8 per cent and a premium of US$250,000
> A June put option (floor) on 180-day LIBOR with a strike rate of 5.5 per cent and a premium of US$250,000.

By selling the put option, the owner can raise the money to buy the call option and there will not be any cost for participating in the options market. Therefore, by constructing a zero-cost collar, the shipowner ensures that his interest expenses will remain within certain limits; the minimum payment, should interest rates drop, is US$2.750m (Table 10) while, in the case of a rise in interest rates, the owner will not pay more than US$4m. For instance, if LIBOR rates rise to 10 per cent, the interest due from the loan is US$5m [=$100m(10%)(180/360)]. The US$1m cash inflow from the collar will reduce the total interest payment to US$4m. The collar payoff in that case is calculated as:

$$Collar\ payoff = C_{cap} - C_{floor} = US\$10m[\max\{0, 10\% - 8\%\}$$
$$- \max\{0, 5.5\% - 10\%\}]\frac{180}{360} = US\$10m[2\% - 0]\frac{180}{360}$$
$$= US\$1,000,000$$

Table 11.9 presents the payoffs of the long call, short put and the planned loan in the collar hedge example. The overall results indicate that the borrowing cost for the shipowner is confined within the 5.58 per cent to 8.16 per cent limit regardless of the level of LIBOR rates at expiry.

Table 11.9 The payoff of the collar hedge and overall borrowing cost

LIBOR at expiry (%)	Call option payoff (US$m)		Put option payoff (US$m)	Collar payoff (US$m)	Overall cost for shipowner (US$m)	Effective interest rate (%)
3	(No exe)		(Exe)	−1.250	2.750	5.58
3.5	(No exe)		(Exe)	−1.000	2.750	5.58
4	(No exe)		(Exe)	−0.750	2.750	5.58
4.5	(No exe)		(Exe)	−0.500	2.750	5.58
5	(No exe)		(Exe)	−0.250	2.750	5.58
5.5	(No exe)		(No exe)	0	2.750	5.58
6	(No exe)		(No exe)	0	3.000	6.09
6.5	(No exe)		(No exe)	0	3.250	6.61
7	(No exe)		(No exe)	0	3.500	7.12
7.5	(No exe)		(No exe)	0	3.750	7.64
8	(No exe)		(No exe)	0	4.000	8.16
8.5	(Exe)	+0.250	(No exe)	0.250	4.000	8.16
9	(Exe)	+0.500	(No exe)	0.500	4.000	8.16
9.5	(Exe)	+0.750	(No exe)	0.750	4.000	8.16
10	(Exe)	+1.000	(No exe)	1.000	4.000	8.16
10.5	(Exe)	+1.250	(No exe)	1.250	4.000	8.16

Notes: No exe indicates that the option is not exercise and Exe indicates that the option is exercised. Premia are not included since they cancel each other.

Panel A of Figure 11.5 shows the plot of the collar to the holder against different LIBOR rates at maturity, while Panel B plots the borrowing cost of the shipowner against possible LIBOR rates at expiry. It can be seen that the final borrowing cost can only vary between 5.58 per cent and 8.16 per cent regardless of the variation of interest rates at maturity.

Now suppose that the shipowner needs to borrow US$100m for five years, starting from 10 December 2001, with semi-annual reset periods. The shipowner finds the following option contracts available to him in December 2001:

A cap on 180-day LIBOR with a strike rate of 8% and a premium of US$950,000.
A floor on 180-day LIBOR with a strike rate of 5.5% and a premium of US$1.15m.

In this case, the shipowner receives a net premium of US$200,000. The result of the strategy is presented in Table 11.10 based on a specific path for LIBOR rates. With this collar, the shipowner ensures that his interest expenses throughout the maturity of the loan will remain within certain limits. The procedure is the same as before, only that now we have a strip of caplets and a strip of floorlets. The effective borrowing rates, calculated using the IRR, are also presented in the same table. We can see that the effective cost of borrowing for the unhedged strategy is 7.81 per cent per annum whereas for the cap it is 7.43 per cent per annum. The collar strategy proves to be the best method with a 7.23 per cent annual borrowing rate. This is because the premium received offsets the future cash payouts from the floor as well as part of the upfront payment for the purchase of the cap.

11.9 Pricing caps and floors using Black's model

For interest-rate options the cash payoff is determined at expiry of the option but the actual cash payout takes place later. For instance, recall the example with the caplet hedge in section 11.8.1.1. The shipowner buys the 'right' on 10 November 2001 to receive on 10 March 2002 the 90-day LIBOR rate prevailing in December on a notional principal of US$100m at the fixed strike rate of 6.5 per cent. Graphically, this is represented in Figure 11.6.

Let a sequence of dates $t_1 < \cdots < t_n$ cover the tenor of the swap and $t_{k+1} - t_k$ represent the period between two successive resets. The strike rate of each caplet (floorlet) is denoted by K_C (K_{FL}) and L_k denotes the reference rate that is observed at time t_k for settlement at t_{k+1}. If we assume that L_k is log-normally distributed with annualised standard deviation $\sigma_k \sqrt{t_k}$, the value of a single caplet (floorlet) can be calculated using a modified version of the [to p. 394]

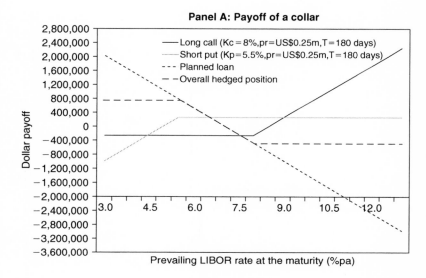

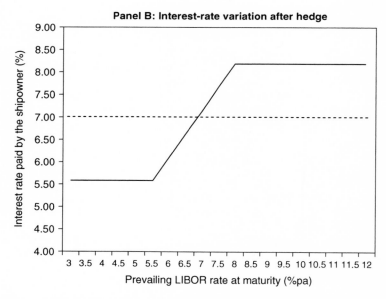

Figure 11.5 Collar-hedge payoff to the shipowner and effective interest rates after hedge against different LIBOR rates at expiry

Table 11.10 Hedging against interest-rate fluctuations using a collar

Five-year cap hedge for the period December 2001–2006

LIBOR market	Options market
	10 December 2001
Current interest rate: 8% Loan = US$100m Reset periods = six months Maturity = 5 years	Notional principal: US$100m. Semi-annual exercise dates Cap with a strike rate of 8% and premium of US$950,000 Floor with a strike rate of 5.5% and premium of US$1.15m

Shipowner **borrows** US$100m at the LIBOR rate for the period June 2002–December 2006 with semi-annual reset periods
Shipowner **buys** a cap interest-rate option at a total cost of US$950,000
Shipowner **sells** a floor interest-rate option at a total benefit of US$1,150,000

Effective amount borrowed = US$100m − US$950,000 + US$1.150m = US$100.20m

Date	Days	LIBOR (%)	Interest paid	Cap payoff	Floor payoff	Principal payment	Net cash flows with Collar	Cap only
10 Dec 01		8.0		-950,000	1,150,000	0	100,200,000	99,050,000
10 Jun 02	182	6.5	3,989,041	-	-	0	-3,989,041	-3,989,041
10 Dec 02	183	8.8	3,258,904	0	0	0	-3,258,904	-3,258,904
10 Jun 03	182	9.1	4,387,945	398,904	0	0	-3,989,041	-3,989,041
10 Dec 03	183	11.0	4,562,466	551,507	0	0	-4,010,959	-4,010,959
10 Jun 04	183	8.7	5,515,068	1,504,110	0	0	-4,010,959	-4,010,959
10 Dec 04	183	5.4	4,361,918	350,959	0	0	-4,010,959	-4,010,959
10 Jun 05	182	4.9	2,692,603	0	-49,863	0	-2,742,466	-2,692,603
10 Dec 05	183	5.3	2,456,712	0	-300,822	0	-2,757,534	-2,456,712
10 Jun 06	182	8.1	2,642,740	0	-99,726	0	-2,742,466	-2,642,740
10 Dec 06	183		4,061,096	50,137	0	100,000,000	-104,010,959	-104,010,959

Effective interest rate (with collar) = 7.23%
Effective interest rate (with cap only) = 7.43%
Effective interest rate (without cap and without floor) = 7.81%

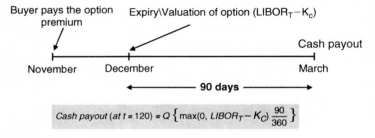

Figure 11.6 The timing of interest-rate option payoff
Source: Cuthbertson and Nitzsche (2001)

[from p. 391] Black 76 model discussed in Chapter 8. The formula is modified to allow for the fact that the payoff is calculated at t_k but the actual payoff takes place at t_{k+1}; using the actual/360-day-count convention, the value of a caplet or floorlet can be calculated as:

$$V_{Caplet} = \$QP(0, t_{K+1})[L_k N(d_1) - K_C N(d_2)]\frac{days}{360}$$

$$V_{Floorlet} = \$QP(0, t_{K+1})[K_{FL} N(d_2) - L_k N(d_1)]\frac{days}{360}$$

$$\text{where } d_1 = \frac{\ln(L_k/K_{C\,(or\,FL)}) + \sigma_k^2 t_k/2}{\sigma_k \sqrt{t_k}} \text{ and } d_2 = d_1 - \sigma_k \sqrt{t_k}$$

Where $P(0, t_{k+1})$ is the price of a zero coupon bond at time 0 paying \$1 at time t_{k+1}, thus covering the entire period from the time the option is bought until the actual cash payout; σ the annualised interest rate volatility and $N(\cdot)$ is the standard normal cumulative distribution function. Assuming that the cap (floor) comprises n individual caplets (floorlets), the value of the cap (floor) will be calculated as the sum of the n individual caplets (floorlets) as follows:

$$V_{Cap} = \sum_{i=1}^{n} V_{Caplets,i} \text{ and } V_{Floor} = \sum_{i=1}^{n} V_{Floorlets,i}$$

For instance, consider a contract that caps the interest rate on a US\$10m loan at 8 per cent per annum (with quarterly compounding) for three months starting in one year. Suppose that the yield curve is flat at 7 per cent per annum with quarterly compounding and that the volatility for the three-month rate underlying the caplet is 20 per cent per annum.

The spot interest rate with continuous compounding is 6.93 per cent ($= 4\ln[1 + 0.07(0.25)]$). Therefore:

$$d_1 = \frac{\ln(L_k/K_C) + \sigma_k^2 t_k/2}{\sigma_k \sqrt{t_k}} = \frac{\ln(0.07/0.08) + 0.2^2 \times 1/2}{0.2\sqrt{1}} = -0.5677$$

$$d_2 = d_1 - \sigma\sqrt{t_k} = -0.5677 - 0.2 = -0.7677$$

$$P(0, t_{k+1}) = e^{-r\Delta t} = e^{-0.0693(1.25)} = 0.9169$$

Replacing d_1, d_2 and $P(0, t_{k+1})$ in the Black 76 model we calculate the value of the cap as:

$$\$QP(0, t_{k+1})[F_k N(d_1) - KN(d_2)]\frac{days}{360}$$

$$= US\$10m \times 0.9169 \times [0.07N(-0.5677)$$

$$- 0.08N(-0.7677)]\frac{90}{360} = US\$5,612$$

11.10 Forward swaps and swaptions

A forward swap is a bilateral contractual agreement whereby two counter-parties enter into a swap agreement on a notional specified capital commencing on a pre-determined future date, at a specified swap rate; it is, in other words, an interest-rate swap with a forward start date. Forward swaps are useful for securing the future level of swap rates and can also be used for speculation on the future value of the underlying reference rates. On the other hand, in a forward swap, the purchaser has the obligation – rather than the right – to enter into a specified swap agreement with the issuer on a specified future date.

It is for this reason that forward swaps are usually traded with embedded options that provide flexibility with respect to exercising the forward swap. These instruments are called 'swaptions' (swaps with an option). A swaption is an OTC contract which gives the purchaser the right – but not the obligation – to enter into a specified swap agreement with the issuer, on or by a specified future date, either as a fixed-rate payer and floating-rate receiver, called a 'payer swaption', or as a fixed-rate receiver and floating-rate payer, called a 'receiver swaption'. Therefore, a payer swaption is exercised when interest rates increase and a receiver swaption when the opposite occurs; in other words, a payer swaption is a call option on a forward swap and a receiver swaption is a put option on a forward swap. The terms of the underlying swap contract are predetermined, as are the option's maturity date, strike rate and notional amount. Swaptions can be American, European or Bermudan – if the holder has the right of multiple potential exercise dates; for example, semi-annually between two specified reset dates.

Suppose, for instance, that a shipping company will need to borrow US$100m in six months' time, for a five-year period at a floating rate, for the acquisition of a vessel. Hedging this exposure to rising interest-rate movements would require a five-year swap contract, beginning in six months' time, whereby the floating interest-rate payments will be exchanged for fixed-rate payments on a notional amount of US$100m. In this case the shipping company can hedge its position by purchasing a payer swaption that gives the right to enter into a five-year swap agreement with the issuer after six months as a fixed-rate payer and floating-rate receiver at a fixed strike price of, say, 6 per cent. If five-year swap rates in six months' time rise above 6 per cent, then the shipping company can exercise the swaption and either enter into the plain vanilla swap with a swap rate of 6 per cent or settle the swap in cash and receive the payout from the swaption. On the other hand, if swap rates fall below 6 per cent, then the company will not exercise the option and instead will initiate a new swap agreement at a rate lower than the option's strike price. In the latter case the swaption's premium, received by the issuer, is the only cash outflow from the swaption.

Swaptions are also used to offset the payments on an existing swap in later years. For instance, a company that has a long position on a pay fixed receive floating swap for five years and wants to terminate the swap after two years can do so by entering into a three-year receiver swaption, expiring in two years. Swaptions can also be valued using the Black 76 model; for more information on the valuation of swaptions see Cuthbertson and Nitzsche (2001).

11.11 Hedging using currency swaps

In shipping markets, most cash inflows and outflows are US-dollar denominated. For instance, freight rates and bunker prices are quoted in US dollars, while most shipping loans are issued in US dollars in Eurocurrency markets. However, there are also cases where shipping companies undertake debt issued in currencies other than US dollars. In these cases the corporate management is interested in matching the interest-rate payments to the same currency as their revenues, that is, US dollars. Such an exposure can be managed using 'currency swaps'. A currency swap is a bilateral OTC contractual agreement to exchange the principal and streams of interest payments from one currency to another for a specified time horizon. Unlike interest-rate swaps, the principal actually changes hands, both at the inception and redemption of the deal. Since the cash flows of the two parties are not in the same currency, the counter-parties' respective payments are made in full.

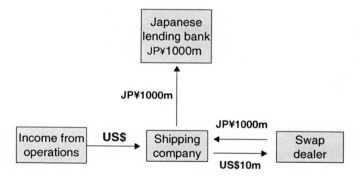

Figure 11.7 Structure of the currency swap

Table 11.11 Cash flows for the shipowner in a four-year currency swap contract

	(amounts in millions)				
Year	2007	2008	2009	2010	2011
US$ cash flow	+10.00	−0.522	−0.522	−0.522	−10.522
JP¥ cash flow	−1,000	+1.16	+1.16	+1.16	+1,001.16

To illustrate how a currency swap can be used by a shipping company, consider the following example. In 2001, a shipping company borrows 10 billion Japanese yen (JP¥) for four years to finance a vessel acquisition. Since the company's cash inflows are in US dollars, a way to match the firm's cash inflows and outflows is by using a plain vanilla 'pay US$, receive JP¥' swap. The rationale behind such a contract is to pay off the Yen-denominated debt with the proceeds from the operation of the vessel, as shown in Figure 11.7.

The rates for the currency swap are provided from the interest-rate swap rates presented in Table 11.6 by selecting the relevant bid and ask rates across the preferred maturity. For instance, assuming the spot exchange rate to be US$/JP¥ = 100 so that the equivalent US-dollar amount of debt is US$10m, under the terms of the four-year 'pay US$ receive JP¥' swap, the shipping company will pay 5.22 per cent on a US-dollar principal of US$10m and receive 1.16 per cent on a yen principal of ¥1billion every year for the next four years. Table 11.11 presents the cash flows from the swap agreement. The principal amount is exchanged both at initiation and redemption of the contract and a fixed interest payment is made each year.

11.11.1 Pricing currency swaps

In order to price currency swaps we follow an approach that is similar to that used for interest-rate swaps which are priced as the difference between the value of a fixed-rate bond and the value of a floating-rate bond. Thus, fixed-for-fixed currency swaps are simply the difference between the value of a fixed-rate domestic bond and the value of a fixed-rate foreign bond. This is equivalent to a synthetic bond portfolio consisting of a long (short) position in a domestic bond and a short (long) position in a foreign bond. If S_0 is the spot exchange rate, for the counterparty that pays in domestic currency and receives foreign payments, the value of the swap is:

$$V_{Swap} = B_{domestic} - S_0 B_{foreign}$$

Suppose that in 2008, the shipping company wants to terminate the swap shown in Table 11.11 early. If the current exchange rate is US\$/JP¥ = 90, the continuously compounded US-dollar and Japanese yen rates are 7 per cent per annum and 3 per cent per annum respectively and assuming a flat yield curve, the value of the swap is:

$$B_{domestic} = e^{-0.07(1)}0.522 + e^{-0.07(2)}0.522 + e^{-0.07(3)}10.522 = US\$9,469,462$$

$$B_{foreign} = e^{-0.03(1)}1.16 + e^{-0.03(2)}1.16 + e^{-0.03(3)}1,001.16 = JP¥917,209,509$$

$$V_{Swap} = S_0 B_{foreign} - B_{domestic} = \frac{JP¥917,209,509}{\left(90\frac{JP¥}{US\$}\right)}$$

$$- US\$9,469,462 = US\$721,735$$

11.12   Summary and conclusions

In this section we discussed the issue of financial risk in shipping operations and management. Due to the capital-intensive nature of shipping and the fact that most vessel acquisitions are financed through term loans priced on a floating-rate basis, unanticipated changes in interest rates may have an adverse impact on the assets and liabilities of a company and can lead to severe liquidity problems and cash-flow mismatch, especially given the business-cycle dynamics of shipping markets. Consequently, interest-rate risk measurement and mitigation is an indispensable aspect of shipping risk management.

The hedging instruments used for the management of interest-rate risk are similar to the ones used for freight and bunker-risk management. Therefore, we have forwards (forward rate agreements – FRAs), futures (Eurodollar futures), swaps, options (caps, floors and collars) and options on swaps (swaptions). We discussed and reviewed interest-rate risk hedging strategies, using analytical examples from the point of view of the borrower (that is, the shipowner); the pricing function of those tools was also explained. Finally, we also referred to the issue of currency risk by explaining the hedging and pricing function of currency swaps.

12
Credit Risk Measurement and Management in Shipping

12.1 Introduction

One of the most important types of risk to which market practitioners in shipping are exposed is credit risk. Credit risk arises because most of the deals, trades and contracts in shipping are on a principal-to-principal basis, which means that two parties agree to do business with each other and rely on each other's ability to honour the agreement. The agreement could be a simple charter contract between a shipowner and a charterer, a newbuilding contact between an investor and a shipyard, or even a bunker transaction between a shipowner and a bunker supplier. In any case, parties to contracts can be exposed to each other's ability to perform the contract, or to credit risk.

The issue of credit risk is especially important in the shipping industry as shipping by nature is a risky business. Agents involved are usually exposed to extreme freight-rate, ship-price, and cash-flow fluctuations and, as a result, there is always a possibility that parties to contracts can fail to fully meet their contractual agreements and therefore default. The aim of this chapter is to discuss the issue of credit risk in the shipping industry along with methods that are used traditionally to manage such exposure, as well as new developments in measuring and managing credit risk.

Therefore, in what follows, we first define what credit risk is and how it is expressed. Next we present different methods of measuring credit risk with examples from the shipping industry; we also discuss the role of credit-rating agencies and present historical credit ratings of shipping companies. Finally, we present various methods of managing credit risk, with particular emphasis on newly developed credit-risk-management products known as credit derivatives.

12.2 What is credit risk?

Credit risk can be defined as the possibility of a loss occurring for a party due to the other party's failure to meet its contractual obligations in accordance with the agreed terms of a deal. It is important to note that the loss due to credit risk may be due to not only the incomplete fulfilment of the counterparty's obligation, but also to delay or postponement in fulfilling the contractual obligation, even if it is eventually completely fulfilled. Therefore, before entering into a deal/contract, firms evaluate their counter-party in terms of its capacity to fulfill the contractual obligation by assessing their credit risk and creditworthiness.

Credit risk can be further classified into three types; namely, 'default risk', 'downgrade risk', and 'credit-spread risk'.

- *Default risk* is the risk of a party to a deal failing to fulfil its contractual obligations, such as repayment of a debt obligation or payments of coupons and redemption values of a bond.
- *Downgrade risk* is the financial loss to a party to a deal caused by the deterioration of the counter-party's credit status – normally reported by credit-rating agencies – and of the counter-party's capacity to honour its contractual obligations. Although, a downgrade may not lead to default it may result in a reduction in the value of contracts such as loans that are drawn, or bonds that are issued by the counter-party.
- *Credit-spread risk* is the risk of change in the yield premium of a debt obligation or an instrument (bond or loan) due to changes in market conditions. Again, changes in credit spread and credit-spread risk may result in financial losses, but this does not necessarily mean that the counter-party to the deal will default.

12.3   What is the source of credit risk in shipping?

Shipping is a risky business, and agents involved in it are exposed to freight and price fluctuations due to market risk. Therefore, there is always a possibility that agents may not be able to fully meet their contractual agreements and therefore default. Credit risk in shipping can be viewed from the point of view of a financier (banker) who provides funds to a shipowner to purchase a new ship, an investor who purchases shipping bonds, a private investor who provides private equity for shipping companies, a supplier who provides credit for purchases to shipowners and operators, or even a derivatives trader who enters into a derivatives contract with a shipowner. By the same token, credit risk can be viewed from the shipowner's side when he enters into a charter contract with a charterer who may not perform the required contractual obligations and make payments on time, or when a shipowner places a newbuilding order and the shipyard fails to deliver the vessel on time, or even when the shipowner enters into a derivatives contract with a counter-party who fails to settle the contract at its maturity.

In what follows we focus on credit risk in general, but we consider *default risk* as the major component of credit risk, especially in shipping markets and transactions. Credit risk is usually expressed in one of the following terms:

- *Probability of default*, which is defined as the likelihood of the counter-party failing to meet its contractual obligations fully on time;
- *Loss-given default*, which is defined as the financial loss which could occur in the case of the counter-party failing to meet its contractual obligations fully on time.
- *Distance to default*, which is a pure statistical measure of credit risk and is defined as the number of standard deviations drops in the asset value that can trigger a default.

The three expressions above, although stating credit risk in different forms, are interrelated in one way or another. For instance, there is a direct relationship between 'probability of default' and 'distance to default' since the greater the distance to default, the lower the probability of default, and vice-versa. 'Loss-given default' depends mainly on the size of transaction and the recovery rate if the default occurs. Naturally, investors try to estimate and recognise appropriate levels of loss-given default in their transactions that are related to the probability of default. In other words, if the probability of default of the counter-party is high the transaction is designed to have a lower loss-given default by reducing the value of the deal.

There are a number of methodologies that have been proposed and developed to assess or measure credit risk, in the forms of probability of default, loss-given default and distance to default. These range from simple assessments to highly sophisticated mathematical models. Broadly speaking, credit-risk analysis can be classified into 'qualitative' and 'quantitative' credit-risk assessment methods depending on the methodology and variables used. The common denominator in both methods – while they differ in the type of information and processing method – is the information about the counter-party, company or the claim.

12.3.1 Qualitative vs. quantitative credit-risk analysis

Perhaps one of the most difficult tasks facing a party to a transaction is the evaluation of the counter-party's creditworthiness and default risk. This is because creditworthiness is an unobservable factor and something that cannot be measured directly. Another reason could be the fact that there are many factors that can influence, in one way or another, the performance of the counter-party to the deal. These factors can be qualitative and/or quantitative.

Qualitative credit-risk analysis is based on firm specific factors that are not quantifiable, which include: the business history and reputation of the firm; managerial expertise, experience and ethics; relative standing in the market

Table 12.1 Important variables in qualitative and quantitative credit-risk analyses

Sample qualitative variables	Sample quantitative variables
• Reputation/business history	• Financial health of the firm
• Managerial expertise and track record	• Firm size
• Relative standing in the market	• Earnings (interest coverage)
• Financial flexibility and capital structure	• Gearing (debt-to-equity ratio)
• Strength and operating flexibility	• Turnover and ROC
• Strategic plans and contingencies	• Market conditions
	• Interest rates
	• Cash-flow uncertainty

and the business share of the company; financial flexibility and structure in terms of accessibility to cash or other types of assets to cover any losses; strength and operational flexibility to change and adapt under difficult market conditions in order to cut losses; and strategic plans and contingencies for bad days and financial distress. Overall, although these variables cannot be directly measured, companies can be assessed and compared given such information.

Quantitative risk analysis, on the other hand, utilises variables that can be measured to assess the credit risk and capability of an entity to honour its financial obligations. These variables include firm-specific factors such as: financial health in terms of profitability, return on assets, turnover, return on capital, etc.; earnings and interest coverage; the firm's size and its market share; and its capital structure in terms of leverage and balance-sheet items. Other quantitative variables to consider are market factors such as: general market and economic conditions; the level of long-term and short-term interest rates; and, most importantly, the cash flow and revenue uncertainty of the firm. Quantitative risk analysis generally involves statistical or mathematical models which use quantifiable factors to estimate the probability of default.

12.4 Credit ratings and rating agencies

Credit risk and credit-risk assessment have been used by investors, lenders and market participants for many centuries. The modern credit-risk analysis and reporting system has been developed to evaluate corporations in terms of their ability to meet their obligations to investors who purchase corporate bonds, or lenders who provide funds for corporations. Over time, independent rating agencies (such as Moody's, Standard & Poor's, and Fitch – and many others) were set up to assess the credit risk of companies and to publish their findings for the benefit of investors. Rating agencies use a variety of techniques and models to assess the relative creditworthiness of corporations

Table 12.2 Fitch, Standard & Poor's and Moody's rating scales

	Fitch	Standard & Poors	Moody's
Investment grade	AAA+	AAA+	Aaa1
	AAA	AAA	Aaa2
	AAA−	AAA−	Aaa3
	AA+	AA+	Aa1
	AA	AA	Aa2
	AA−	AA−	Aa3
	A+	A+	A1
	A	A	A2
	A−	A−	A3
	BBB+	BBB+	Baa1
	BBB	BBB	Baa2
	BBB−	BBB−	Baa3
Speculative grade	BB+	BB+	Ba1
	BB	BB	Ba2
	BB−	BB−	Ba3
	B+	B+	B1
	B	B	B2
	B−	B−	B3
	CCC+	CCC+	
	CCC	CCC	Caa
	CC	CC	Ca
	C	C	C
		CI	
Default	DDD		
	DD		
	D	D	

Source: Data from rating agencies.

and companies, and provide objective, consistent and simple measures to indicate the likelihood of a company honouring its debt obligations.

To provide a simple and consistent way of reporting their views on the creditworthiness of corporations, rating agencies developed rating scales or classifications which are more or less similar. The rating classifications of Fitch, Standard & Poor's, and Moody's are presented in Table 12.2. Corporate bonds and, in general, listed corporations are classified into eight main credit classes; AAA is the highest, D the lowest, and there are 24 other sub-classes in-between. Moreover, bonds are divided into two categories: 'investment grade' and 'non-investment grade' (speculative grade or high yield) bonds. Any bond or company rated BBB− and better is regarded as investment grade and any bond or company rated BB+ or worse is considered speculative grade. It should also be noted that despite the fact that rating agencies use different notation, their classifications are based on a standard rating scale and are thus comparable.

In the fixed-income market, the yield of an instrument is defined as the percentage return on the instrument (such as a bond, certificate of deposit, Treasury bill, and so on) over a period of time. When the return of the instrument is calculated based on the assumption that the instrument is held until maturity with no default, the yield is known as the 'yield to maturity' (YTM). The YTM of a corporate instrument contains important information regarding the creditworthiness of the issuer. This is because, as the creditworthiness of the issuer declines, the cash flow from the bond/claim will become more uncertain, that is, the probability of default increases, and investors demand a higher rate of return in order to purchase or invest in that instrument. In other words, investors discount the cash flow from the claim at a higher rate and therefore the yield of the instrument increases.

When a bond or a claim is risk-free, then it should have the lowest yield to maturity in comparison to all other instruments which carry some form of risk or uncertainty regarding future cash flows.

12.4.1   Shipping high-yield bond issues

The first high-yield bond issue for ship finance was in 1992 when Sea Containers Ltd issued US$125m of subordinated debentures. By 1998, US$5,437m had been raised in the high-yield bond market for shipping companies, through 40 issues of various types of bonds (these are presented in Table 12.3). Companies such as Sea Containers, Trans Maritima and Overseas Shipholding Group were at the forefront of tapping the bond market for ship finance. Despite the decline in the number of shipping high-yield bond issues after 1999 – mainly due to a number of downgrades and some shipping companies defaulting in their debt obligations – the market has seen an increase of new issues (15 in the US debt-capital market during 2003 and 2004) primarily due to strong shipping market conditions.[1]

The difference between the YTM of a bond issued by a corporation and the YTM on a government bond of the same maturity is known as yield premium. Yield premium can be viewed as a reflection of the likelihood of the failure of the firm to meet its contractual obligations to the investor. However, the yield premium does not only reflect default risk but also incorporates liquidity risk. This is because government bonds, especially those with short maturity, are more liquid in comparison to corporate bonds with similar maturities and terms. Figure 12.1 presents the average yield premium on shipping high-yield bonds with different ratings over the period 1998 to 2002. It can be seen that

---

[1] During depressed shipping market conditions – where spreads are high in order to reflect the riskiness of the issues – the costs of issuing new high yield bonds are high and investors are not usually attracted to this market. On the other hand, in good shipping conditions the issuance costs are lower and the shipping high-yield bond market attracts more investors.

Table 12.3 Shipping high-yield bond offerings by year of issue (1992–2002)

Year	Number of issues	Total float (US$m)	Average float (US$m)	Average coupon (%)	Average term (years)	Average rating (S&P/Moody's)
1992	1	125.00	125.00	12.500	12.00	BB−/Ba3
1993	8	1135.0	141.88	9.172	9.625	BB−/Ba3
1994	1	175.00	175.00	11.250	10.00	BB/Ba2
1995	1	175.00	175.00	10.500	10.00	BB/Ba2
1996	3	490.00	163.33	9.607	9.66	BB−/Ba3
1997	8	1083.00	135.37	10.438	9.00	B/B2
1998	15	2254.00	150.26	10.099	9.53	B+/B1
1999	1	115.00	115.00	10.750	7.00	BB−/Ba3
2000	0	0.00	0.00	0.00	0.00	−
2001	1	350.00	350.00	8.880	10.00	BB−/Ba3
2002	1	200.00	200.00	10.380	10.00	BB+/Ba3
Total	40	6102	152.55	10.35	9.681	B+/B1

Source: Grammenos et al. (2007).

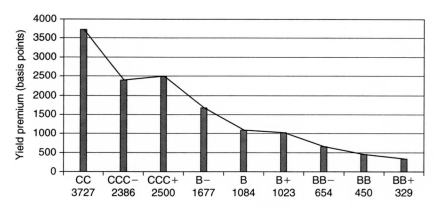

Figure 12.1 Historical yield spread of shipping bonds with different ratings
Source: Grammenos et al. (2007).

the average yield premium for shipping bonds varies from 3.29 per cent for BB+ bonds to 37.27 per cent for CC rated bonds.

The yield premium can change over time for a variety of reasons, including market conditions and changes in the firm's cash flow and creditworthiness. This can be seen in Figure 12.2 where the Merrill Lynch shipping high-yield bond index (ML_SHIP) is plotted against Lehman Brothers' B and BB-rated corporate bond indices (LB_B and LB_BB, respectively). Several observations can be made here. First, as one would expect, the yield premium for BB-rated

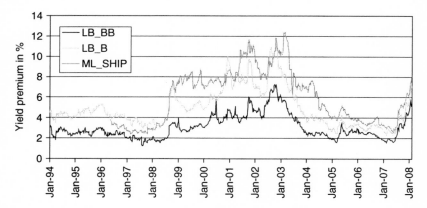

Figure 12.2   Dynamic behaviour of credit premium of the shipping bond index
Source: Datastream.

bonds is less than that for B-rated and shipping high-yield bond indices. Second, while there seems to be some form of co-movement in the long run, there are significant short-run deviations amongst these indices. The long-run co-movements could be due to the fact that the yield premium of corporate bonds depends on general economic conditions while, in the short run, yield premia may change due to supply and demand conditions as well as the perceived risk differences between these bonds. Finally, the average yield premium of shipping high-yield bonds changed dramatically, from low values of 3 per cent between 1994 and 1998, to high values of 10 per cent to 12 per cent between 1999 and 2003, due to the downturn in shipping markets and general economic conditions. After 2003, once conditions in the shipping market improved significantly and shipping freight rates increased to substantially high levels, the credit spread on shipping bonds narrowed again and many companies decided to issue bonds.

Several studies in the literature are devoted to finding the determinants of credit premium. For example, Grammenos et al. (2007) find that variables such as a firm's capital structure (leverage), freight-market conditions and time to maturity of bonds are important variables in determining the credit premium of shipping bonds. In another study Grammenos et al. (2008) develop a model to measure probability of the default of shipping high-yield bond issues using macroeconomic factors along with factors specific to the firm. They argue that gearing ratio, the amount raised over total-assets ratio, the working capital over total-assets ratio, the retained earnings over total-assets ratio and an industry specific variable capturing the shipping market conditions at the time of issuance, are the best estimates for predicting the default of shipping high-yield bonds at the time of issuance.

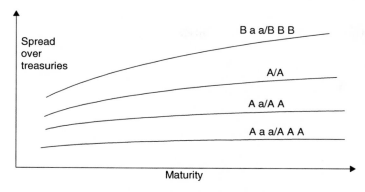

Figure 12.3 Theoretical credit premium of bonds with different rating and maturity

There is also a clear relationship between the yield premium of corporate bonds and their maturity. This is shown graphically in Figure 12.3, where it can be observed that as the maturity of bonds increases, so does their yield premium. This is because, in general, the probability of a company failing to perform its contractual obligations increases with time. Hence, investors demand a higher rate of return on their investment; that is, they discount the cash flows from claims with longer term to maturity at higher rates, leading to lower current prices for those securities and thus higher yield.

12.5 Estimating probability of default

Due to the fact that credit risk is an unobservable variable and because of the complexity of the variables involved in the determination of credit-worthiness of a counter-party or a transaction, we normally tend to estimate credit risk by extracting the probability of default of a counter-party using other observable variables. In general, there are three different methods for estimating the probability of default. The first method is based on comparing the yield premium of bonds or debt obligations with a risk-free bond or debt obligation; the second approach is based on historical information about performance and default of companies; finally, the third and the most sophisticated method, which is based on option-pricing theory, uses information about the companies' or individuals' assets and liabilities along with the variation in asset values to estimate the probability of default.

12.5.1 Extracting default probabilities from traded bonds

As mentioned, one method for estimating probability of default of a firm is to use the yield premium of a bond issued by the company. To illustrate how the yield premium can be used to estimate default risk of a firm, consider the following example. Assume that a BB-rated listed shipping company has issued a one-year zero-coupon bond with a YTM of 7 per cent, while a one-year risk-free US Treasury bond has a YTM of 5 per cent. This means that every US$1 face value of the shipping company's bond is selling at 93.239 cents and every US$1 face value of the government bond is selling at 95.123 cents:

$$\text{Present value of US\$1 shipping bond} = 1 \times e^{-0.07} = 0.93239$$
$$\text{Present value of US\$1 Treasury bond} = 1 \times e^{-0.05} = 0.95123$$

Comparing the present values, we can see that the shipping bond is selling at 1.98 per cent [(95.123 − 93.239)/95.123] discount to the government bond. This means that investors are demanding a 1.98 per cent discount on a shipping bond compared to a government bond with similar terms in order to invest in bonds issued by the shipping company. In other words, investors expect to lose 1.98 per cent of the value of the investment when they invest in the shipping bond due to their expectations about the likelihood of default by the company; therefore, they demand a higher rate of return in order to invest in the bond issued by the company. However, if the shipping company defaults, entities that are owed money can file claims against the assets of the company. The assets are then sold by the liquidator and are used to meet the claims as far as possible, according to the order of seniority of the claims. Hence, part of any claim or bond issued by the company can be recovered, while the rate of recovery of the claim depends on the value of company's assets at the time of liquidation and the seniority of the claims on them. Table 12.4 presents historical average recovery rates and their dispersion around the mean for claims with different seniority levels. It can be seen that, for example, the historical average recovery rate for a senior secured claim or bond is 45.8 per cent, while a subordinated claim has an average recovery rate of 15.0 per cent.

Using expected loss – calculated previously as 1.98 per cent – and the recovery rate, one can work out the probability of default as follows:

$$P(\text{default}) = \frac{\text{Expected loss\%}}{1 - \text{Recovery rate}}$$

In our example, assuming a 50 per cent recovery rate, we can estimate the one year probability of default for this BB-rated company as:

$$P(\text{default}) = \frac{0.0198}{1 - 0.5} = 0.0396 = 3.96\%$$

Table 12.4   2003 average ultimate recovery rates

Instrument type	Discounted ultimate recovery rate (%)	Standard deviation (%)	Observations
Bank debt	74.1	32.4	331
Senior secured bonds	45.8	36.5	42
Senior unsecured bonds	36.8	35.1	198
Senior subordinated bonds	21.3	30.8	116
Subordinated bonds	15.0	24.7	55
Junior subordinated bonds	2.5	4.1	4

Source: 2003 Recovery Highlights, S&P LossStat Database (www2.standard and poors.com).

Table 12.5   Historical cumulative probability of default

	1	2	3	4	5	7	10
AAA	0.00	0.00	0.04	0.07	0.12	0.32	0.67
AA	0.01	0.04	0.10	0.18	0.29	0.62	0.96
A	0.04	0.12	0.21	0.36	0.57	1.01	1.86
BBB	0.24	0.55	0.89	1.55	2.23	3.60	5.20
BB	1.08	3.48	6.65	9.71	12.57	18.09	23.86
B	5.94	13.49	20.12	25.36	29.58	36.34	43.41
CCC	25.26	34.79	42.16	48.18	54.65	58.64	62.58

Source: Hull (2006).

The probability of default of 3.96 per cent is therefore the likelihood of this shipping company failing to fulfil its contractual obligations of repaying the face value of the bond to investors in full and on time.

12.5.2   Historical default probabilities

Probability of default can also be measured based on historical figures. For example, based on historical data on defaults, one can estimate the percentage of claims and obligations issued by companies with different credit ratings that defaulted. Rating agencies with access to such data sets analyse them and report their results on a regular basis. Table 12.5 presents the historical cumulative default probabilities for companies with different ratings and across a range of maturities, reported by Standard & Poor's in January 2001. For instance, the cumulative default probability figures indicate that the likelihood of an AAA-rated firm defaulting on its obligation in the first or second year is almost zero, while the probability of the same company defaulting on its obligation in 10 years has been 0.67 per cent. In other words, historically, almost none of the bonds/claims issued by AAA companies defaulted in the first two years, while 0.67 per cent of bonds/claims issued by AAA companies

Table 12.6   Year-on-year historical probabilities of default

	1 to 2	2 to 3	3 to 4	4 to 5	5 to 7	7 to 10
AAA	0	0.04	0.03	0.05	0.2	0.35
AA	0.03	0.06	0.08	0.11	0.33	0.34
A	0.08	0.09	0.15	0.21	0.44	0.85
BBB	0.31	0.34	0.66	0.68	1.37	1.6
BB	2.4	3.17	3.06	2.86	5.52	5.77
B	7.55	6.63	5.24	4.22	6.76	7.07
CCC	9.53	7.37	6.02	6.47	3.99	3.94

defaulted within 10 years. By the same token, historical figures show that the likelihood of a CCC company defaulting on its obligation in the first year is 25.26 per cent and this could increase to 62.58 per cent for a 10-year obligation. Although historical default probabilities are an easy way to assess the likelihood of companies fulfilling their obligation, they should also be considered with special care. This is because these probabilities are based on historical data and do not take into account changes in market conditions or specific information about the company and its current financial performance. In other words, they do not capture the dynamic nature of default probabilities over time.

Although the table reports cumulative historical default probabilities, one can also interpolate year-on-year default probabilities. For example, a company with an initial credit rating of BBB has a probability of 0.24 per cent of defaulting by the end of the first year, 0.55 per cent by the end of the second year, and so on. Therefore, the probability of default between year one and two for this company is simply the difference between the two – that is, 0.31 per cent (0.55 per cent – 0.24 per cent). Table 12.6 presents historical estimates of year-on-year probability of default for different rating classes. It can be seen that while year-on-year probability of default for AAA-rated companies (or debt obligation) increases with time, the year-on-year probability of default of CCC companies tends to decrease. One explanation for such a difference in the pattern of year-on-year default probabilities across ratings is that, if companies with poor initial ratings survive for some period, then the chances of their survival will improve with time; on the other hand, the creditworthiness of companies with the best credit ratings can only deteriorate over time.

Finally, let us compare the probability of default that we estimated for the BB-rated shipping company using its bond and the historical default probability of a BB company over one year. The one-year probability of default of the shipping company based on yield premium is 3.96 per cent while the historical probability of default is 1.08 per cent. This comparison reveals a large difference between historical probabilities and those calculated based on yield premia. In fact, default probabilities estimated on the basis of yield premia are significantly higher than historical values.

12.5.3 Estimating default probabilities using Merton's model

The idea of estimating the probability of default of an entity using the option-pricing theory of Black-Scholes (1973) and Merton (1973) was proposed by Vasicek (1984).[2] This model assumes that a company can default if, and when, the value of its assets is less than its liabilities. In other words, the value of the company to the shareholders at time t, E_t, is like the payoff of a call option with a strike price equal to the face value of its debt (X).

$$E_t = \max [A_t - X, 0] \tag{12.1}$$

where A_t is the market value of the total assets of the company. This also implies that the value of the debt to the lender at maturity (T), D_T, could be the asset value when the value of a company's assets is less than its debt and the company is in default, or X when the company's assets are worth more than its debt and the company is not in default. Therefore:

$$D_T = \min [A_T, X] \tag{12.2}$$

The same argument can be used to explain the position of the lender of the debt as a short put option on the assets of the company and a risk-free debt X, as follows:

$$D_T = X - \max [X - A_t, 0] \tag{12.3}$$

This is because if the value of the company's assets at the maturity of the debt is greater than its debt, the debt holder receives X in full, but when the company's asset value is less than its debt $[X > A_T]$, then the holder of the debt only receives the asset value A_T. Also, at any point in time, total assets A_t should be equal to the sum of the market value of $D(t, T)$ at time t for maturity T, and equity E_t of the company.

$$D(t, T) + E_t = A_t \tag{12.4}$$

Since it is established that the value of the company's equity to shareholders is a call option on the company's assets, we can use the Black-Scholes-Merton option-pricing model to evaluate the fair price of the option as follows:

$$E_t = A_t N(d_1) - e^{-r(T-t)} X N(d_2) \tag{12.5}$$

---

[2] This was developed for the KMV Corporation in 1984, subsequently became the KMV credit monitor and was then acquired by Moody's.

where, as usual, $N(d_1)$ and $N(d_2)$ are cumulative normal probability for d_1 and d_2 respectively, r is the risk-free rate, and d_1 and d_2 are calculated as

$$d_1 = \frac{\ln\left(\frac{A_t}{X}\right) + \left(r + \frac{\sigma_A^2}{2}\right)(T - t)}{\sigma_A\sqrt{T - t}}$$

$$\text{and } d_2 = d_1 - \sigma_A\sqrt{T - t}$$

where σ_A is the standard deviation of the firm's asset value. Once the value of equity at time t, E_t, is estimated using equation (12.5), it can be deducted from the asset value of the firm at time t, A_t, to obtain the debt value.

$$D(t, T) = A_t - E_t \qquad (12.6)$$

It can be noted that $N(d_2)$ is the risk-neutral probability that at the maturity of the debt the company's asset value is greater than its debt, and the company does not default. Similarly, $1 - N(d_2)$, is the risk-neutral probability that at maturity, the company's asset value will be less than its debt, and the company defaults. Furthermore, having obtained the value of debt at time t for maturity T, $D(t, T)$, we can calculate the yield on the debt, $y(t, T)$ as:

$$y(t, T) = \frac{\ln(X) - \ln(D_{(t,T)})}{T - t} \qquad (12.7)$$

The yield on the debt can be compared with the yield on a risk-free instrument with the same maturity to obtain the credit premium and default probability. Alternatively, one can directly calculate the risk-neutral probability of default from $N(d_2)$. Figure 12.4 presents the evolution of the asset value over time and its distribution at the time of maturity of the debt along with the probability of default as the proportion of the area of the asset-value distribution, which represents the possibility that the asset value is less than the face value of the debt at maturity.

To illustrate how this methodology works, consider a one-vessel shipping company with a total market asset value of US$120m, of which US$100m is debt with one year to maturity.[3] The volatility of the vessel's price is

---

[3] It has to be pointed out that since we have the volatility of the asset value (ship) we do not need to use the volatility of the firm's equity to estimate the asset volatility. This is not always the case as in general what is available is the volatility of the firm's equity which should be used to derive the firm's assets' volatility using the relationship between assets and equity value and their respective volatilities $\sigma_E = \frac{V_0}{E_0}\frac{\partial E}{\partial V}\sigma_V$. (see Hull, 2006).

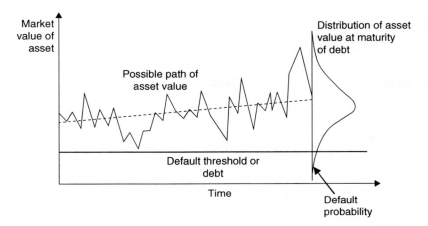

Figure 12.4   Distribution of asset value at maturity of debt and probability of default

30 per cent, while the current one-year risk-free rate is 5 per cent. Based on the information, we can estimate the current value of the company's equity, current value of debt, the yield on the debt, and the probability of default. Using the Black-Scholes-Merton model, we first calculate d_1, d_2, and corresponding cumulative probabilities.

$$d_1 = \frac{\ln\left(\dfrac{120}{100}\right) + \left(0.05 + \dfrac{0.3^2}{2}\right)(1)}{0.3\sqrt{1}} = 0.9244 \Rightarrow N(d_1) = 0.8224$$

$$d_2 = d_1 - \sigma_A\sqrt{T-t} = 0.9244 - 0.3(1) = 0.6244 \Rightarrow N(d_2) = 0.7338$$

Using the above probabilities and the option-pricing formula in equation (12.5), current equity value and debt can be calculated as

$$E_t = A_t N(d_1) - e^{-r(T-t)} X N(d_2) = 120(0.8224) - e^{(-0.05*1)}(100)(0.7338)$$

$$= \text{US\$28.88m}$$

$$D(t, T) = A_t - E_t = \text{US\$120m} - \text{US\$28.88m} = \text{US\$91.12m}$$

Moreover, the yield and the credit premium for this debt can be calculated using equation (12.7) as 9.3 per cent and 4.3 per cent respectively, and the default probability based on $[1 - N(d_2)]$ will be 26.62 per cent. In addition, the present value of no default debt is US$95.123m, which means that the expected loss on this debt is 4.21 per cent $[(95.123 - 91.12)/95.123]$; therefore, we can estimate the expected recovery in the event of default of the debt as

$$\text{Expected recovery} = 1 - \frac{\text{Expected loss\%}}{P(\text{default})} = 1 - \frac{0.0421}{0.2662} = 84.19\%$$

In addition, one can use the current value of the asset, (A_t), its volatility, σ_A, and the face value of debt, D, to estimate the distance to default as $Z = [(A_t - D)/(\sigma_A * A_t)]$. Distance to default is, in fact, the number of standard deviations which the asset value has to move to trigger the default, if we assume asset values are normally distributed. Using the values of volatility, asset price and face value of debt considered earlier, the distance to default is $0.55 = [(120 - 100)/(0.3 \times 120)]$.

The above example is simplified for illustration purposes and is based on several assumptions, many of which may not hold in reality. For instance, the maturity of the debt is usually longer than one year and the company may even have several debt obligations. In addition, the company may have other assets in its portfolio with different risk levels; therefore, estimating the total asset value and asset volatility could also add to the challenge. However, the basic model presented here can be and has been extended to accommodate different, more complex situations. For example, Geske and Johnson (1984) and Black and Cox (1976) extend the approach to the case of multi-period debt obligations by considering defaults as a series of contingent events (see Anson et al., 2004, for more detailed discussion on complex credit-risk models).

12.6   Credit-risk management and credit derivatives

Having discussed credit-risk analysis and measurement, the next natural question is: how can credit or default risk be managed or controlled? This question arises because losses due to counter-party default can have a severe impact on the financial health of any business. For example, the failure of a charterer to adhere to the terms of a time-charter contract due to a drop in freight rates and possible early termination could have serious implications for the shipowner, who has an obligation to the bank/lender that has financed the ship. Therefore, the non-performance of the charterer as counter-party and any change in the freight income due to renegotiation and possible early termination of the contract can cause serious cash-flow problems for the shipowner.

The main objective of credit-risk management is to eliminate or minimise the credit-risk exposure of a party to a deal. There are a number of methods which can be used for such a purpose and some of them have been used by practitioners for a long time. For example, for many centuries, lenders, even after careful consideration of the reputation of their borrower, preferred to have some sort of collateral in case the borrower could not return the item or amount borrowed in full or on time. Alternatively, lenders could ask for an endorsement from a third person with a very good reputation, which is now quite commonly issued by bank as a 'bank guarantee' or 'letter of credit'. Although, risk analysis and management have evolved over the years, the methods and tools used remain relatively similar.

However, in recent years the introduction of credit derivative instruments has revolutionised the credit-risk management process to the extent that credit is now considered an asset that can be traded like any other commodity, stock or bond. In the following section, we will discuss different methods used for credit-risk management – both traditional methods, such as collateralisation, downgrade triggers, contract design and netting and diversification, as well as recently developed instruments such as credit derivatives.

12.6.1 Collateralisation

Collateralisation is perhaps the oldest and most effective method of credit-risk management. Under such an agreement the party exposed to the default risk of the counter-party takes some form of collateral for security. The collateral can be any valuable asset – a vessel under a ship mortgage-finance agreement, cash or other marketable securities required by the clearing house for a cleared derivative contract, or even a letter of credit (LC) requested by a bunker supplier in a bunker transaction. The value of the collateral is used, in part or full, as compensation when and if the counter-party fails to perform the contractual obligations. The benefit of having collateral on the back of a deal is that it reduces the cost of recovery and litigation procedures in the case of default. In addition, collateralised debt is preferred to unsecured debt since its recovery rate is normally higher compared to unsecured claims or debt obligations. However, when a party agrees to assign an asset as collateral, it is normally at the expense of the other terms in the contract, including the yield or return in the case of loans. For instance, in the case of bonds, normally the yield on senior secured bonds is lower than that of comparable bonds (in terms of issuer risk, maturity and coupon) that have lower security levels, such as junior subordinated bonds.

12.6.2 Downgrade triggers

Including downgrade triggers in contracts allows a party to close out or change the terms of the contract if there is a downgrade in the level of the counter-party's creditworthiness or if the credit rating of the counter-party falls below a certain level. This approach requires a clear definition of what is regarded as a downgrade or credit threshold level as well as of how the value of the contract should be determined in such cases. For instance, consider a BB-rated shipping company entering into a derivative contract with an AAA-rated bank, with an agreement that if the credit rating of the company falls below B, the bank may reserve the right to close out the contract at its market value. Another example is a term loan provided by a bank to a shipping company which normally includes a downgrade clause in relation to the value of the ship. Under the terms of this contract, the borrower (shipping company) agrees to provide additional security (cash or additional collateral) if the hull-to-debt (HTD) ratio falls below a pre-specified level.

12.6.3   Contract design and netting

Another approach to controlling and mitigating counter-party credit risk in a transaction is to design the contract in such a way that it incorporates clauses for default and non-performance compensations. For instance, netting of outstanding contracts is a clause that states that in a bilateral transaction, if a party defaults on one contract, then all outstanding contracts will also be considered in default. This means that the innocent party can use the netting clause and offset part of its losses against the other contracts. Netting is also used increasingly in OTC contracts between parties to mark-to-market each other's contracts if there is more than one agreement between the two parties. For instance the FFABA© 2007 contract incorporates a close-out netting clause in the event of a default (see Chapter 5, Section 5.9 above).

To illustrate how netting works, consider a shipping company that has three FFA contracts with counter-party XYZ. The contracts are OTC and their settlement dates are in two, six and 12 months. The current outstanding value of the contracts are +US$2m, +US$5m and −US$4m to the shipping company. Suppose the counter-party XYZ runs into financial difficulty due to losses in its operation and defaults on the first settlement of +US$2m to the shipping company. The shipping company can then use the netting clause and consider all contracts at default. Therefore, the loss to the shipping company with netting will reduce to US$3m. Without the netting, counterparty XYZ defaults on the first two contracts and claims the third contract, which means a loss of US$7m to the shipping company.

12.6.4   Diversification

The overall credit risk of a portfolio and potential losses due to defaults can be reduced if contracts and/or claims are well diversified. Indeed the most important factor for the effectiveness of diversification in credit-risk reduction is once more the low correlation between the default probabilities of contracts included in the portfolio. As an example, consider a bank that has a large portfolio of shipping loans, all of which have been given to tanker owners. Since all tanker owners are exposed to fluctuations in the tanker market, the correlation between the probabilities of default on these loans is very high because any downturn in the tanker market may trigger several defaults at the same time. On the other hand, if the bank designs a well-diversified shipping loan portfolio across different sectors of the shipping industry (for example, dry bulk, cruise shipping, fishing, offshore) the overall credit risk may be reduced, because the correlation between the default probabilities of borrowers would be lower or even negative. Moreover, lenders can diversify their loan portfolio in terms of credibility, industry, country and so on to reduce overall exposure to credit and default risks. However, it should be noted that credit exposure diversification can eliminate risk only to a certain extent and certainly not completely. Therefore, one has to analyse the correlation between default probabilities and changes in credit risk of counter-parties in order to dynamically control and minimise the overall credit risk of the portfolio. One technique of assessing the credit risk of a portfolio of contracts (bonds, claims or loans) is 'Credit Value-at-Risk' (CVaR).[4]

12.6.5 Credit derivatives

Credit derivatives, although in existence implicitly for a long time in the form of guarantees and letters of credit, are said to be the most innovative products in finance and risk management. The credit derivative market was developed in the 1990s and the growth in trade in these instruments has been increasing ever since. According to the British Bankers Association, the global trade in the credit derivatives market (excluding asset swaps) had reached US$1.2 trillion by the end of 2001 and US$20 trillion in 2006.

A credit derivative is a financial instrument whose payoff depends upon the performance and/or creditworthiness of one or more commercial or sovereign entities in meeting their contractual agreements. Thus, credit derivatives allow credit risks to be exchanged, or even traded, without the underlying assets being exchanged. As a result, managers and investors who do want to enter into certain deals or invest in certain assets but do not want to be exposed to the credit exposure of the counter-party to the deal can use credit derivatives to control or eliminate their default-risk exposure. In addition, credit derivatives have opened the way for speculators to bet on credit events such as upgrades and downgrades as well as defaults by commercial or sovereign entities. In the following sections we discuss some of the instruments that can be used for risk management in shipping by private

---

[4] Credit Value-at-Risk (CVaR) or CreditMetrics was developed by JP Morgan (along with co-sponsors such as Bank of America, KMV Corporation, UBS and others) in 1997. The method follows the VaR approach of RiskMetrics, but it estimates the potential loss in the value of a portfolio due to changes in the credit risk of the assets in the portfolio instead of using only changes in the market-price movement of the assets. For a detailed explanation of how CVaR is estimated as well as other alternative portfolio credit-risk measurement approaches, see Cuthbertson and Nitzsche (2001).

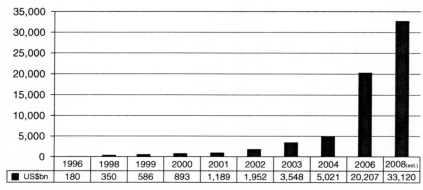

	1996	1998	1999	2000	2001	2002	2003	2004	2006	2008(est.)
■ US$bn	180	350	586	893	1,189	1,952	3,548	5,021	20,207	33,120

Global credit derivatives market US$bn

Figure 12.5   The global trend in the credit derivatives market
Source: British Bankers Association.

investors, banks providing funds for ship finance, hedge funds and private equity fund managers. These derivatives include 'credit default swaps', 'total return swaps' and 'credit default option'.

12.6.5.1   Credit default swap (CDS)

This is a contract under which an investor buys protection from a protection seller (Company B) against default on a reference bond or a claim issued by a reference entity (Company C). Under this contract the protection buyer makes regular (annual, semi-annual or quarterly) payments, known as the premium, to the protection seller over the period for which the protection is bought. In the event of default by reference entity C, the protection buyer has the right to sell the reference bond to B for its face value, or the protection seller pays the buyer the difference between the market value and the face value of the claim or bond. Therefore, credit default swaps simply work like an insurance policy on the reference bond or claim and financially indemnify the protection buyer in the case of default.

As an example consider the case where a hedge fund, Fund A, has purchased US$10m of bonds, with a five-year term to maturity issued by a shipping company, Company C. However, the fund is worried about the credit risk of the shipping company and would like to protect itself against possible non-performance and default of the bonds, and therefore enters into a credit default swap with a financial institution, the CDS seller, Bank B. Under this agreement the fund pays a flat fee of, for example, 90 basis points on US$10m each year for five years. This means a quarterly premium payment of US$22,500 [$10m × 0.009/4] every quarter. The premium is paid until the default or credit event occurs, in which case the fund hands in the

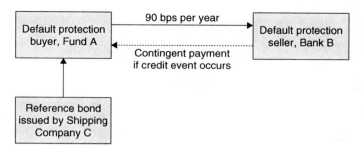

Figure 12.6 Cash flow of a credit swap deal

bonds and receives US$10m. Alternatively, the difference between the market price of the bonds and the US$10m notional value is paid by the protection seller to the fund. Figure 12.6 presents a diagram of the cash flows of this CDS agreement.

Note that the notional value of US$10m is not the redemption value of the bonds. For example, if the redemption value of the bonds in the example was US$12m but at the time of the CDS agreement they were selling at US$10m (the notional value), the fund would receive only US$10m from the protection seller in the event of default while handing back bonds with par value of US$12m. Also note that by using the CDS the fund lowers its credit exposure from a counter-party with a relatively low credit rating (the shipping company) to a counter-party with a relatively high credit rating (the bank). This means that the CDS should reflect the credit spread between the shipping company and the CDS seller.

Table 12.7 shows CDS quotes for a sample of investment-grade companies in January 2008. It can be seen that credit-default swap prices are directly related to the credit rating of the companies as well as to the time horizon over which the default swap is quoted. Since these prices are quoted for trade between large institutions with high credit ratings, quotes might be different for counter-parties with lower credit ratings and smaller capitalisations.

Sometimes investors bundle more than two (typically three to five) bonds or reference entities into a basket and secure a credit default swap on the basket. The payoff of the CDS is then dependent on whether the contract is an 'Nth to default swap', a 'subordinated basket default swap', or a 'senior basket default swap'. In an Nth to default swap, the protection seller guarantees protection only after there has been a default on the Nth reference entity and no payout for the first N-1 reference entities. In other words, the payout is triggered only when the Nth claim defaults, and compensation is paid on all N previously defaulted reference entities. However, once the payout is made, the swap contract terminates and if any of the rest of the reference entities in the basket defaults following the payout, there will not be any protection.

Table 12.7 Sample CDS quotes for different companies in different sectors on 23 January 2008

Sector	Company	Rating	Period in years				
			1	3	5	7	10
Financial	Merrill Lynch	A+	230.0	195.0	156.6	160.0	144.2
	Citi Group	AA−	74.5	78.5	87.8	90.2	89.1
Car manufacturing	Daimler Chrysler	BBB+	53.2	62.4	71.3	75.3	77.4
	Toyota Motors	AAA	11.3	16.3	21.0	23.3	26.8
Retail	Wal-Mart Stores	AA	28.9	34.4	40.5	46.2	53.8
	Home Depot	BBB+	111.8	121.9	152.0	131.9	137.1
Cruise shipping	Carnival Corp.	A−	31.2	60.2	89.0	106.2	132.0
	Royal Caribbean	BBB	109.8	187.8	310.0	311.3	315.8
Oil & Gas	Exxon Mobil	AAA	6.5	16.6	26.2	34.8	50.6
	Chevron	AA	14.5	26.5	38.0	43.7	53.2

Note: Figures are basis points.
Source: Datastream.

In a subordinated basket default swap, the protection seller sets limits on payouts on individual reference entities in the basket as well as on an aggregate payout over the life of the swap for the basket. For instance, a basket of five reference entities is insured by a protection seller for a maximum of US$10m for each item in the basket and an overall maximum of US$$20m. This means that if the first and second reference entities each result in a loss of US$15m during the life of the swap, then the protection seller is liable for US$20m and the swap is terminated. However, if the losses of the first two reference entities are US$15m, then the swap is alive and if the third reference entity's default results in a US$8m loss, the protection seller has to compensate the protection buyer for US$5m, which is what remains of the maximum swap protection over the life of the swap.

Finally, under a senior basket default swap there is a maximum payout for each reference entity, but the payout is not triggered until after a pre-specified threshold is reached. For instance, if there are five reference entities in the basket, each with a maximum protection level of US$10m, and the aggregate protection level is US$40m, then there will not be any payout if the total loss is below $40m, while the individual reference entity's loss considered for calculation of the total loss is a maximum of US$10m, regardless of the actual loss.

12.6.5.2 *Total return swap (TRS)*

Under a total return swap the two parties agree to exchange the returns on two assets or portfolios of assets with a similar notional amount. For example, in its simplest form, the counter-parties may agree to exchange the returns

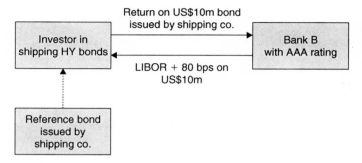

Figure 12.7 Cash flow of a simple total return swap

of a corporate bond (coupons and change in the price) and a reference rate (say, LIBOR) plus a margin. In more complex cases, for example, two banks may agree to exchange the return on two portfolios of loan or debt obligations with the same notional value at the initiation of the deal. Since at the initiation the assets/portfolios have the same market value, the value of a total return swap is zero initially but may change due to changes in risk and return on assets and portfolios.

To illustrate, consider an investor who has purchased US$10m worth of bonds issued by a shipping company, with five years to maturity. The investor is concerned about the future performance of the company and would like to reduce the credit risk involved in this deal over the next five years. Thus, he decides to enter into a five-year total return swap with Bank B, which is an AAA-rated company. Under the total return swap, the investor agrees to pay Bank B the total return on the US$10m shipping bonds, and in return receive one-year LIBOR plus 80 basis points on US$10m every year. The cash flow of this simple total return swap is shown in Figure 12.7.

If the shipping company performs its debt obligation over the five years, the bank receives the coupons and par value, and the investor receives LIBOR+80 basis points on US$10m. However, in the event of default by the shipping company, the bank will not receive anything, while the investor still receives LIBOR+80 basis points on US$10m. It can be argued that by using a total return swap the investor has upgraded the counter-party risk of the bond portfolio from the creditworthiness of the shipping company to the credit-worthiness of an AAA-rated bank, but has paid the price through accepting a lower return as LIBOR+80 basis points on US$10m. Moreover, in order to hedge the swap return further, the investor can enter into a five-year fixed-for-floating interest-rate swap of, say, 5 per cent per annum. This will ensure that the investor receives a fixed return of 5.8 per cent per annum over five years with a lower credit risk compared to that of shipping bonds.

To illustrate how a total return swap on two reference portfolios can be used, consider a ship finance Bank (Bank A) with a large loan portfolio concentrated

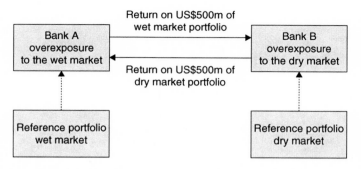

Figure 12.8   Cash flows of a total return swap on two reference portfolios

in one sector, say, the tanker sector. Since the bank is overexposed to the tanker market, the chances of several of their borrowers failing to meet their debt obligations, if conditions in the tanker market deteriorate, could be high. Therefore, Bank A decides to enter into a total return swap with Bank B, which has a large portfolio of loans in the dry sector and is overexposed to the dry market. Assuming both banks have similar credit ratings, under the contract the two banks agree to exchange returns on US$500m of their portfolios over a certain period, say three years. It has to be mentioned that counterparties to a TRS deal normally choose the TRS deals that effectively diversify their exposure. Therefore, TRS can be designed to have any type of underlying portfolio of assets and returns (residential, industrial, stocks, or even fixed income). In many cases, one leg of the swap is a floating rate (LIBOR or FRN) plus a margin on a notional value.

12.6.5.3   Credit spread options (CSO)

These are instruments with payoffs contingent on the yield on two reference assets, normally a risky asset and a risk-free asset. In other words, these are options on the yield spread of an asset or debt obligation and their payoffs depend on the yield spread and strike yield spread (K) at or before the maturity of the option. For example, a credit spread call option pays off when at maturity or exercise period the yield spread $(Y_1 - Y_{rf})$ exceeds some level K, mathematically:

Call option payoff $= Q^* \max [0, (Y_1 - Y_{rf}) - K]$
Put option payoff $= Q^* \max [0, K - (Y_1 - Y_{rf})]$

where Q is the notional value on the basis of which the option is settled.

Credit spread options are useful instruments for managing the risk of downgrade in ratings and losses in values of corporate bonds or debt obligations. To illustrate this, consider an investor who has bought US$10m of bonds

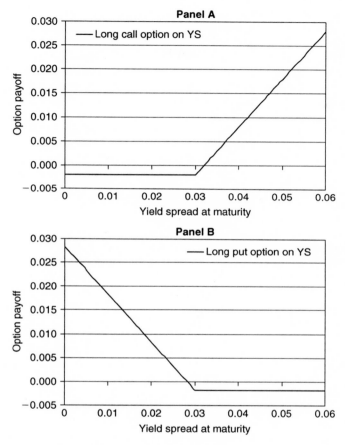

Figure 12.9 Payoffs of long-call and long-put positions on credit spread options

issued by a shipping company, C, with five years to maturity. Currently the rating of the issuer is BB and the yield to maturity of the bonds is 6 per cent, which is 2 per cent above the risk-free government bond ($Y_{rf} = 4\%$) with similar maturity. The investor is concerned about the possibility of losses due to the deterioration of the performance of the shipping company and subsequent downgrades in the company's credit rating. Hence, the investor decides to protect himself against such losses by buying a credit spread call option on a US$10m portfolio of company C bonds with a yield spread strike of $K = 3\%$ for one year, from an option writer (say, Bank B). As with any other option, the credit default option premium is paid upfront and, for simplicity, let us assume that the option can be exercised at maturity, like a European option.

If the company performs well and its credit rating remains at such a level that the difference in the bond yield and the base yield (Y_{rf}) does not exceed 3 per cent, the option expires unexercised. On the other hand, if during the life of the option the company's credit rating deteriorates and is consequently downgraded, the difference between the yield on the bond and the base yield will exceed $K = 3\%$, and the investor can exercise the option. For instance, assume that after one year market conditions are such that the company is downgraded to CCC and the yield on its bond increases to 10 per cent, while the yield on the base government bond is now 5 per cent. This means that the yield spread is 5 per cent and the option is in-the-money; therefore, the investor can exercise the option and receive US$200,000 [2% × $10m], which should compensate for part of the loss in the value of the bond due to change in the credit rating of the shipping company.

Panels A and B of Figure 12.9 present payoffs of long-call and long-put positions on credit spread options, both with a strike of 3 per cent. It can be seen that a long-call option position can be used as a hedging position against downgrade risk exposure, where the option payoff protects the holder from losses due to deterioration in the credit rating of the debt obligation and a widening of credit spread. The long-put position, on the other hand, can protect a short position on debt obligations against any credit upgrade risk.

12.7   Summary and conclusions

In this chapter we highlighted credit risk as one of the most significant types of risk to which practitioners in the shipping markets are exposed to. This is because most of the deals, trades and contracts in this industry are on a principal-to-principal basis, which means that the two parties agree to do business with each other and rely on each other's capability of honouring the agreement. In addition, the risky and volatile nature of shipping markets also means that there is always a possibility that parties to contracts fail to fully meet their contractual agreements and thus default.

We defined credit risk and explained how it is expressed. Different methods of measuring credit risk, with examples from the shipping industry along with credit rating and historical credit ratings of shipping companies, were discussed in detail. For the purposes of managing credit risk, we presented different approaches used by the counter-parties to control their credit exposure. These include traditional contractual terms such as collateralisation, downgrade triggers, credit limits and diversification. Finally, we reviewed the recently developed credit derivative instruments that can be used to effectively and efficiently manage credit exposure and default risk.

13
Ship Price Risk and Risk Management

13.1 Introduction

Investors in shipping markets have always been faced with important and difficult decisions about timing of investment and divestment because of the complex and volatile nature of the shipping industry. Volatility of ship prices has also been of concern to banks, shipyards and shipping companies, because changes in ship prices over short periods of time have serious impact on their businesses. For this reason, banks financing ships, investors providing equity to shipowners and operators, shipyards building new ships, and asset players in shipping markets all tend to monitor the volatility of the market for ships and incorporate such information in their lending, investment, portfolio construction and divestment decisions.

From the academic point of view, several studies are devoted to assessing, modelling and forecasting the volatility of ship prices, while others are focused on the importance of ship-price volatility in the decision-making process of market participants, as well as pricing of assets and derivatives. For instance, Kavussanos (1997) investigates the dynamics of volatility of second-hand dry-bulk carriers and argues that there is a positive relationship between price volatility and vessel size. Alizadeh and Nomikos (2003b) examine the relationship between ship-price volatility and trading activities in the sale and purchase market for dry-bulk carriers and find that volatility of ship prices is inversely related to trading volume in the sale and purchase market. Alizadeh (2001) and Kavussanos and Alizadeh (2002b) suggest that there is a direct relationship between price volatility and investment returns in the dry-bulk sector, and that the market for ships is efficient in the sense that profit-making opportunities, in excess of what is implied by the market according to the level of risk taken, are limited or do not exist. From the practical point of view, market participants pay particular attention to the volatility of ship prices in order to design and to set terms of credit for ship finance; asset players monitor changes in ship price for investment timing and portfolio management, while shipyards follow conditions in the market for ships to expand or slow down production, or offer deals to attract new clients and secure contracts.

The aim of this chapter is to first discuss how ship prices are determined and highlight important factors influencing ship prices. We then examine the volatility of ship prices and compare them across different sizes and types of ships. Next, we review the risk involved in investing in ships and holding them in portfolios, as well as how the portfolio risk can be optimised, providing examples from the tanker and the dry-bulk market. Finally, we present and discuss recently reported ship-price indices as well as derivatives which are developed to trade ship values. In this respect, we show how such derivative contracts can be structured and used for ship-price risk management as well as trading purposes, and extend the discussion on how such derivatives can be priced.

13.2   Ship-price formation

Traditional approaches for modelling ship prices are based on general and partial equilibrium models which explain ship prices using structural relationships between a number of variables such as orderbook, newbuilding deliveries, scrapping rates, freight rates and bunker prices (see Strandenes, 1984, Beenstock and Vergottis, 1989 and Tsolakis et al., 2003, among others). More recent studies have applied real options analysis for determining ship prices. This valuation framework takes explicitly into account the operational flexibility in ship management, in terms of choosing between entry and exit from the market, spot and period time-charter operations, and switching between lay-up and trading modes (see Dixit and Pindyck, 1994, Tvedt, 1997, and Bendal and Stent, 2003, among others).

The price formation in the second-hand market for ships has also been examined to determine whether markets for ships are efficient and whether prices are formed rationally. For example, Kavussanos and Alizadeh (2002b), Hale and Vanags (1992) and Glen (1997) test the validity of the Efficient Market Hypothesis (EMH)[1] in the formation of second-hand dry-bulk prices. These studies argue that the failure of the EMH may either be attributed to the existence of time-varying risk premia, or reflect arbitrage opportunities in the market. The latter suggests that if prices for vessels are found to deviate consistently from their rational values, then trading strategies can be adapted

---

[1] The concept of market efficiency has been used in several contexts to characterise a market in which rational investors use all the relevant information to evaluate and price assets traded in that market and arbitrage away any excess profit-making opportunities. This definition of the efficient market implies that prices fully and instantaneously reflect all the relevant information. As a result, there is no opportunity for agents to make profits in excess of what the rational investors expect to make, considering the level of risk and transaction costs involved.

to exploit excess profit-making opportunities.[2] For example, when ship prices are lower than their fundamental values, then buying and operating these vessels may be profitable because they might be under-priced compared to their future profitability (that is, the earnings from freight operations). On the other hand, when prices are higher than their corresponding rational values, it may be more profitable to charter in vessels rather than buying and operating them, since they might be overpriced in comparison to their expected future profitability.

Investors in the shipping industry, like investors in any other sector of the economy, are not only interested in the income generated from the day-to-day operation of ships but also in gains from capital appreciation in the value of the vessels. Therefore, from the investors' point of view, the expected one-period return, $E_t r_{t+1}$, on shipping investments is equal to the expected one-period capital gains between time t and $t + 1$, $(E_t P_{t+1} - P_t)/P_t$, plus the expected return from operation, $E_t \Pi_{t+1}/P_t$, where $E_t P_{t+1}$ is the expected ship price at time $t + 1$ and $E_t \Pi_{t+1}$ is the expected operating profit between period t and $t + 1$[3]. Mathematically,

$$E_t r_{t+1} = \left(\frac{E_t P_{t+1} - P_t + E_t \Pi_{t+1}}{P_t} \right) \quad (13.1)$$

Equation (13.1) can be rearranged to arrive at a present-value model, where the current ship price, P_t, is expressed in terms of the expected price of the vessel, expected operational profits and the expected rate of return, as in the following expression.

$$P_t = \left(\frac{E_t P_{t+1} + E_t \Pi_{t+1}}{1 + E_t r_{t+1}} \right) \quad (13.2)$$

Through recursive substitution and some algebraic manipulation, P_t can be written as the sum of the present values of future profits plus the present value of the expected terminal or resale price, P^{sc}_{t+n}, of the vessel, assuming a discount rate equal to the required rate of return. Mathematically,

$$P_t = \sum_{i=1}^{n} \frac{E_t \Pi_{t+i}}{(1 + r_i)^i} + \frac{E_t P^{sc}_{t+n}}{(1 + r_n)^n} \quad (13.3)$$

Equation (13.3) is in fact a discounted present-value model which explains the price of a ship in terms of her expected operational earnings and resale value, which could be the terminal or scrap value or second-hand value of the ship if she is sold as second-hand. This model can thus be regarded as

---

[2] Here, by fundamental or rational value of the asset we mean the discounted present value of the expected stream of income that the asset generates over its lifetime.

[3] See Chapter 2 for the description of operating profits and TC earnings.

the theoretical price of the vessel at time t, based on assumptions about her expected operating revenue, discount rate and expected resale value. It can be seen that in the formation of ship prices, any error in expected values can lead to potential mis-pricing, and when uncertainty about future freight market conditions and resale value of the vessel increases, so does the potential pricing error. In practice, when the discounted present value model is used for asset pricing, uncertainty about the future income generated by the asset and its resale value is incorporated in the discount factor as a risk premium. Thus, the discount factor, r_i, is adjusted in such a way as to reflect the risk involved in holding the asset as $r_i = r_f + r_p$, where r_f is risk-free rate and r_p is risk premium. Therefore, r_i is in fact the rate of return required by the investor to hold the asset.

13.3 Comparison of ship-price risk across sectors

The volatility of ship prices can vary across the size, the type and the age of vessel due to the nature of the trade and transportation of commodities in which each type of vessel is involved. In general, as mentioned in Chapter 2, larger ships are involved in transportation of fewer commodities and across a smaller number of routes. For instance, VLCCs are employed in carrying crude oil in four or five routes from the Persian Gulf to Europe, the US and the Far East, as well as from West Africa to the US and the Far East. Therefore, these vessels are highly sensitive to changes and disturbances in the international trade in crude oil. By contrast, smaller ships such as Aframax and Handysize tankers are mainly employed in carrying oil products, and to a lesser extent crude oil, in several routes around the world. As a result, their operating revenue is less sensitive to changes in world economic activity, trade in wet-bulk commodities and overall market conditions. Thus, it is expected that the price of smaller ships, whether operating in the tanker, dry-bulk or container/liner sectors, would be less volatile than the price of larger ships in each sector, due to their operational flexibility.

Risk-and-return statistics of dry-bulk and tanker-ship prices across three different age groups (newbuilding, five-year-old second-hand, and scrap), over the period February 1981 to May 2008 are presented in Table 13.1, Panels A and B respectively. There are several interesting points which emerge from these statistics. First, it can be seen that the average ship price in each sector is directly related to the vessel age, across different size classes. For instance, while the average price for a newbuilding Capesize dry-bulk carrier over the sample period is US\$43.9m, the average price for a second-hand Capesize is US\$35.94m, and the average scrap value for this type of ship is US\$4.07m. This pattern can be observed in all sectors. Second, prices for larger vessels seem to show higher volatility than prices for smaller vessels, across the age spectrum. For example, in the dry-bulk sector, the annualised volatility of newbuilding prices declines from 11.19 per cent for Capesize

Table 13.1 Comparison of ship-price risk across dry-bulk carriers of different sizes

Panel A: Dry-bulk sector

		Newbuilding	Second-hand	Scrap value
Capesize	Average price $USm	43.90	35.94	4.07
	Mean price change	0.0410	0.0682	0.0357
	StDev of price change	0.1119	0.1957	0.2175
Panamax	Average price $USm	26.26	21.31	2.60
	Mean price change	0.0301	0.0572	0.0390
	StDev of price change	0.0994	0.1978	0.2176
Handysize	Average price $USm	19.75	13.77	1.48
	Mean price change	0.0255	0.0570	0.0508
	StDev of price change	0.0921	0.1783	0.2468

Panel B: Tanker sector

		Newbuilding	Second-hand	Scrap value
VLCC	Average price $USm	78.69	57.06	6.89
	Mean price change	0.0254	0.0748	0.0471
	StDev of price change	0.0962	0.1986	0.1978
Suezmax	Average price $USm	51.51	38.55	4.93
	Mean price change	0.0235	0.0608	0.0471
	StDev of price change	0.0932	0.1578	0.2110
Aframax	Average price $USm	37.84	31.36	3.45
	Mean price change	0.0276	0.0540	0.0470
	StDev of price change	0.0922	0.1453	0.2109
Handysize	Average price $USm	28.92	19.92	1.74
	Mean price change	0.0254	0.0351	0.0472
	StDev of price change	0.0791	0.1860	0.2110

Sample period: January 1980 to May 2008.
Source of data: Clarkson's SIN.

vessels to 9.94 per cent and 9.21 per cent for Panamax and Handysize ships respectively. In the second-hand market, the volatility of ship prices declines from 19.57 per cent and 19.78 per cent for Capesize and Panamax vessels to 17.83 per cent for Handysize ships. Also, in the tanker sector, the volatility of newbuilding prices decreases from 9.62 per cent for VLCCs to 9.32 per cent, 9.22 per cent and 7.9 per cent for Suezmax, Aframax and Handysize tankers respectively. Volatility of second-hand price of tankers also declines from 19.86 per cent for VLCCs to 15.78 per cent and 14.53 per cent for Suezmax and Aframax tankers. The only exception is the price volatility of Handysize tankers, which, at 18.60 per cent, is higher than those for Suezmax and Aframax tankers. The volatility of scrap price for ships in different sectors ranges between 19.78 per cent and 24.68 per cent, with no particular pattern across size or type of ship, due to the fact that these prices are strongly related to world scrap steel prices rather than to the fundamentals of trade for each vessel type. In general, the higher volatility of larger vessels compared to smaller ones can be attributed to the fact that they are less versatile than smaller vessels in terms of the commodities they carry and the routes they serve. Finally, second-hand prices seem to show higher volatility than newbuilding prices across the size spectrum. This might be due to the fact that second-hand vessels are generally available for immediate delivery and trading and, as a result, their prices are more sensitive to current market conditions and more volatile (see Chapter 2 for more details).

13.3.1   Dynamics of volatility of ship prices

The importance of shipping-market conditions in freight-rate determination, and the fact that shipping freight rates and their volatilities can vary depending on the supply and demand schedules for shipping service, were discussed in Chapter 2. The relationship between freight rates and ship prices was also presented in Section 13.2 of this chapter. Based on these relationships, it can be argued that volatility of ship prices can also be time-varying and dependent on changes in freight-market conditions. In other words, the uncertainty and volatility of freight rates can be transmitted to ship prices through the discounted present-value model for ship-price determination, as shown in equation (13.3).

The first study to investigate the dynamics of volatility of ship prices was Kavussanos (1997). In this paper, the author uses GARCH-type models to examine and model time-varying volatility of second-hand dry-bulk vessels. Reported results suggest that changes in second-hand prices for Handysize and Panamax bulk carriers are positively related to changes in time-charter rates, while their time-varying volatilities are positively related to the levels of interest rates. In the case of second-hand prices for Capesize vessels, both level and volatilities are positively related to changes in time-charter rates. Also, it is reported that price volatilities are positively related to the size of vessel; that is, prices of larger vessels show higher volatilities compared to those of smaller ones.

As shown in Chapter 3, the time-varying volatility of a variable can be captured using a variety of techniques, including exponentially weighted average volatility estimates, as well as GARCH and stochastic volatility models. To illustrate the time-varying behaviour of the volatility of prices for different types of ships in the tanker and dry sectors, we estimate EGARCH(1,1) models and present the results in graphical form in Figures 13.1 and 13.2 respectively. Visual inspection of the volatility graphs reveals that, over the period January 1976 to May 2008, ship-price risk for vessels of different sizes in both sectors fluctuated between 5 per cent and 65 per cent. The highest level of price volatility for tanker and dry-bulk carriers was observable in the first half of the 1980s when the market was heading towards a prolonged recession. There

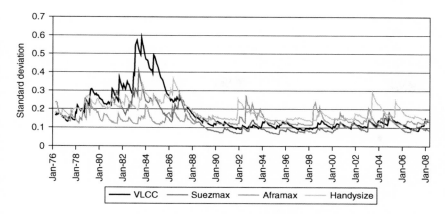

Figure 13.1 Plot of dynamics of price volatility of tankers of different sizes

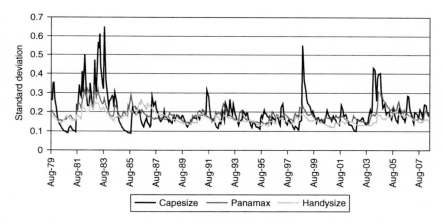

Figure 13.2 Plot of dynamics of price volatility of dry-bulk carriers of different sizes

have also been several shorter periods when ship-price volatilities increased substantially. For instance, volatility of Capesize bulk carriers increased sharply in the middle of 1998 and in late 2003. In addition, although price volatilities seem to show some degree of co-movement across vessel type and size, due to overall market conditions, the dynamics of volatilities seem to be different. The idiosyncratic nature of price volatilities can be attributed to the unique risk and specific characteristics and conditions in each market.

Therefore, we can conclude that in general ship prices show time-varying volatility and the dynamics of volatilities are different across different sizes and types of vessels. From a practical point of view, time-varying volatilities can be used to estimate value-at-risk for the value of each ship or the value of a portfolio of vessels. For instance, in a shipping finance term loan, a bank can use the time-varying volatility of ship prices to estimate the likelihood that the hull-to-debt ratio for a term credit deal falls below one. In this case, the value of the loan will be less than the value of the collateral and the bank may require additional security from the borrower.

13.4   Ship-price risk management

Traditionally, shipowners and asset players in shipping markets employed physical asset diversification methods to manage ship-price risk and the fluctuation in the value of their portfolio of assets, which could consist of ships of different size, type or age. However, this method of risk management can have a limited effect because of the positive correlation between prices of different vessel types. An alternative method used by ship-operators is to eliminate ship-price risk altogether from the portfolio by not owning ships, but leasing or chartering them on a long-term time-charter or bareboat-charter basis. The downside of this method is that investors in these companies cannot benefit from any capital gain or ship-price appreciation. More recently, with the development of derivative contracts on ship values, such as forward ship value agreements, not only can investors manage the asset-price risk and overall risk of their portfolio/fleet, but can also benefit from falling market prices by speculating and selling these contracts. In the following sections we discuss the methods that can be used for ship-price risk management, and present examples for each case to highlight both their advantages and limitations.

13.4.1   Portfolio theory and diversification

The concept of portfolio theory in finance was first discussed by Markowitz (1952) where he pointed out that combining assets into portfolios can reduce the standard deviation of the portfolio below the level obtained from a simple weighted average calculation. This is possible only if the prices of assets in the portfolio do not move exactly together; that is, prices should not be perfectly and positively correlated. According to portfolio theory, as the number of assets in a portfolio – that are not perfectly and positively correlated – increases, the fluctuation in the value of the portfolio should decrease. Therefore, portfolio construction involves finding the weighted combination of diversified assets which yields the lowest standard deviation for a pre-specified level of expected return, or highest return for a given level of risk. We call these portfolios 'efficient portfolios'.

The reason for the reduction of the overall risk of a portfolio is because when risky assets are combined into portfolios, changes in prices of assets in the portfolio tend to cancel each other out, provided that they are not perfectly and positively correlated. This means that when there is drop in the value of one of the assets in the portfolio, there might be one or more other assets which increase in value and compensate the loss occurred in the value of the first asset. Thus, the variance of a portfolio of risky assets is not merely the sum of their separate variances; it also includes the covariances between the asset returns. The return of a portfolio of N assets can be calculated as the weighted average of returns and the risk (variance) of the same portfolio can be calculated as the weighted average of variances and correlations (or covariances) using the following formulae:

$$E(r_p) = \sum_{i=1}^{N} w_i r_i \qquad (13.4)$$

and

$$Var(r_p) = \sum_{i=1}^{N} w_i^2 \sigma_i^2 + \sum_{\substack{i=1 \\ i \neq j}}^{N} \sum_{j=1}^{N} w_i w_j \rho_{ij} \sigma_i \sigma_j \qquad (13.5)$$

where $E(r_p)$ is the expected return on the portfolio, w_i represents the weight of asset i in the portfolio, $Var(r_p)$ is the variance of the portfolio, σ_i^2 is the variance of asset i, and ρ_{ij} is the correlation between returns of i and j.

Combining assets in a portfolio with appropriate weights to manage risk can only eliminate the 'unique' or 'diversifiable risk'. This is the risk that is unique to each asset and related to the factors affecting that particular asset. The 'market' or 'systematic risk', on the other hand, is that part of the fluctuation in the value of the portfolio of assets which cannot be eliminated through diversification, regardless of how many assets are included in the portfolio. The systematic risk is due to the economy-wide sources of risk which affect the overall value of assets and the market as a whole. Therefore, for a well-diversified investor, only market risk matters and the investor would want to be compensated for the risk that cannot be eliminated by diversification. The effect of diversification in terms of decline in portfolio risk, when the number of assets which are not perfectly and positively correlated increases, can be seen in Figure 13.3.

To illustrate the effect of diversification and how the risk and return on a portfolio varies with the allocation of different weights to each asset, consider a portfolio of two assets; an investment on a VLCC tanker with an expected return of 14 per cent and a variance of 0.22 (SD = 47 per cent), and an investment on a Handysize tanker with an expected return of 5 per cent and a variance of 0.12 (SD = 34.6 per cent). We assume the covariance between the returns on VLCC and Handysize tanker investment is −0.01 (correlation = −6 per cent). Using different investment proportions (weights) for VLCC and Handysize tankers, we calculate the portfolio risk and return in each case. The results, presented in Table 13.2, indicate that the lowest portfolio variance of 0.0771 is obtained when 62.5 per cent of the value of

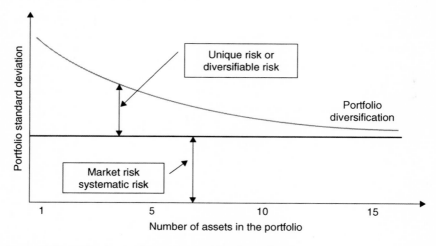

Figure 13.3   Risk reduction through portfolio diversification

Table 13.2   Risk and return of a two-asset portfolio with different weights

Investment	in HANDY	in VLCC	Var(Rp)	E(Rp)	SR
A	100.00%	0.00%	0.12	5.00%	0.144
B	87.50%	12.50%	0.095	6.10%	0.201
C	75.00%	25.00%	0.0806	7.30%	0.260
D	62.50%	37.50%	**0.0771**	8.40%	0.310
E	50.00%	50.00%	0.0842	9.50%	0.336
F	37.50%	62.50%	0.1021	10.60%	**0.339**
G	25.00%	75.00%	0.1306	11.80%	0.329
H	12.50%	87.50%	0.17	12.90%	0.314
I	0.00%	100.00%	0.22	14.00%	0.298

the portfolio is invested in Handysize and 37.5 per cent in VLCC tankers. Moreover, the risk-and-return relationship of different portfolios of VLCC and Handysize tankers is plotted in Figure 13.4. The line segment connecting point D to point I on the graph, is known as the 'efficient frontier', because all the portfolios that lie on that line segment are efficient portfolios. In terms of the Sharpe ratio, the optimum portfolio is portfolio combination F, which has the highest Sharpe ratio across any other combination.

Having discussed the risk-and-return profile of a two-asset portfolio, we now examine the risk-and-return profile of a multi-asset portfolio of vessels in the dry and the tanker sectors as well as a combination of them using historical returns, variances and correlations. Starting with the market for tankers, we estimate the correlations between price changes of different size tankers, as well as their standard deviations over the period February 1981

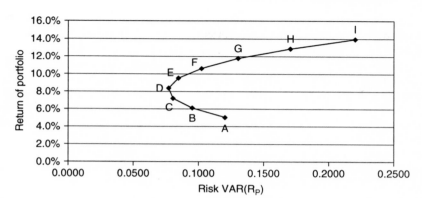

Figure 13.4   Risk-and-return graph of a two-asset portfolio with different weights

Table 13.3   Correlation matrix and distribution of returns on tankers of different sizes

Panel A

Correlation matrix of returns on tankers of different sizes

	VLCC	Suezmax	Aframax	Handysize
VLCC	1			
Suezmax	0.519	1		
Aframax	0.301	0.337	1	
Handysize	0.026	0.225	0.256	1

Panel B

Distribution of returns for tankers of different sizes and an equally weighted portfolio of these vessels

	VLCC	Suezmax	Aframax	Handysize	Portfolio
Mean	0.074	0.061	0.054	0.035	0.056
StDev	0.201	0.158	0.145	0.186	0.116
Skewness	−0.893	0.623	−0.299	1.149	−0.001
Kurtosis	19.078	10.611	7.473	12.568	5.348
Sharpe ratio	0.368	0.385	0.372	0.189	0.483

Sample period: February 1981 to May 2008.

to April 2008. These statistics are reported in Panels A and B of Table 13.3, along with the average return, skewness, kurtosis, and the Sharpe ratio for each type of tanker. First, we can see that price changes of VLCC and Suezmax vessels show the highest correlation, 51.9 per cent, while the lowest correlation is between price changes of VLCC and Handysize tankers, 2.6 per cent.

This is expected because VLCC and Suezmax prices tend to move more closely together than prices for VLCC and Handysize tankers. This is due to the fact that the underlying driver for the price of large tankers is the international trade in crude oil; therefore, any change in crude trade should affect the operational profitability of both vessels and consequently their prices. On the other hand, the underlying price driver for Handysize product tankers is the trade in oil products; therefore, changes in crude oil trade may have a lesser impact effect on the price for these vessels. As a result, VLCC and Handysize tanker prices show the lowest degree of co-movement. Second, coefficients of kurtosis for all tankers indicate significant excess kurtosis, while coefficients of skewness indicate significant asymmetry in the distribution of price changes. More precisely, price changes of VLCC and Aframax tankers seem to be negatively skewed, whereas the distribution of price changes for Suezmax and Handysize tankers show positive skewness.

To illustrate the effect of diversification on the risk and return of a portfolio of ships, we construct an equally weighted portfolio which constitutes a 25 per cent investment in each type of tanker. The statistics representing the distributional properties of the return on this portfolio are presented in Panel B of Table 13.3. The statistics suggest that while the expected return on the portfolio of 5.6 per cent is somewhere between the highest average return (VLCC = 7.4 per cent) and the lowest average return (Handysize = 3.5 per cent), the standard deviation of the portfolio, 11.6 per cent, is lower than the standard deviation of returns on individual tankers. Moreover, the portfolio seems to have the highest return-to-risk or Sharpe ratio (0.483) compared to all single-asset investments. The coefficients of skewness and kurtosis indicate that the distribution of portfolio returns is closer to a normal distribution compared to the distribution of returns on individual ships, which is a direct result of diversification.

The second example involves constructing an equally weighted portfolio of three differently sized dry-bulk vessels; that is, Capesize, Panamax and Handysize. The correlation matrix of price changes for these ships, presented in Panel A of Table 13.4, reveals that the highest correlation is between the Capesize and Panamax returns (51 per cent) and the lowest correlation is between Capesize and Handysize vessels (37 per cent). The results suggest that the correlation between returns on dry-bulk carriers are generally higher than those for tanker vessels, due to higher degree of substitution amongst dry-bulk carriers, both in terms of the cargoes they carry and the routes they operate in.

Panel B of Table 13.4 presents the distributional properties of returns on each type of ship, as well as an equally weighted portfolio of dry-bulk ships. Once more, it can be seen that while the portfolio return is the average of the return on three types of ships, the standard deviation of portfolio returns is 15.3 per cent, which is lower than the standard deviations of individual ships. The Sharpe ratio of the portfolio (0.363) is also higher than that of individual

Table 13.4 Correlation matrix and distribution of returns on dry-bulk carriers of different sizes

Panel A		
Correlation matrix of returns on dry-bulk carriers of different sizes		
	Capesize	Panamax	Handysize
Capesize	1		
Panamax	0.510	1	
Handysize	0.370	0.447	1

Panel B			
Distribution of returns for dry-bulk carriers of different sizes and an equally weighted portfolio of these vessels			
	Capesize	Panamax	Handysize	Portfolio
Mean	0.063	0.050	0.054	0.055
StDev	0.198	0.199	0.179	0.153
Skew	1.583	−0.056	−0.068	0.171
Kurtosis	15.212	6.013	5.562	5.251
SR	0.318	0.249	0.301	0.363

Sample period: February 1981 to May 2008.

investments, which means that diversifying the fleet in the dry-bulk market can yield a better risk-to-return ratio. Coefficients of skewness and kurtosis also point to the fact that the distribution of returns of the portfolio of dry-bulk ships can be closer to a normal distribution than the distribution of returns on individual ships.

Finally, we construct an equally weighted portfolio and an optimally weighted portfolio of all types of ships (dry-bulk and tankers), and estimate the expected return, risk, skewness, kurtosis and the Sharpe ratio of each portfolio. The optimum portfolio is constructed by finding the appropriate investment allocation weights for each sector, which maximise the Sharpe ratio. This is done using an optimiser (such as the Excel solver) subject to certain restrictions, such as no short selling or positivity of asset weights. The results, presented in Table 13.5, suggest that diversifying investment across tanker and dry-bulk shipping sectors can reduce the risk further and enhance the risk-to-return ratio. For example, returns on both equally weighted and optimally weighted portfolios of all ship types show lower standard deviations compared to the single-sector portfolios. Furthermore, the overall return-to-risk (Sharpe) ratio of the portfolio with optimum weights, 0.551, is higher than that of other portfolios, highlighting the benefits of correct asset

Table 13.5   Comparison of risk and return of different portfolios of ships

	Portfolio of ships			
	Equally weighted Tanker	Equally weighted Dry-bulk	Equally weighted All ships	Optimally weighted All ships
Mean	0.056	0.055	0.056	0.059
StDev	0.116	0.153	0.109	0.107
Skew	−0.001	0.171	−0.050	0.062
Kurtosis	5.348	5.251	4.733	5.151
SR	0.483	0.363	0.510	0.551

Sample period: February 1981 to May 2008.

allocation and efficient portfolio construction. It should be noted that diversification can be extended further to more sectors, as well as across the age spectrum in each sector, to achieve even better results. In practice, investors tend to diversify their portfolio of assets across different types, sizes and ages of ships.

In financial markets, portfolio and fund managers constantly asses the risk, return and correlation between assets in their portfolio, and rebalance them in order to optimise the return-to-risk ratio of the portfolio and enhance the overall performance of the fund. This is known as 'dynamic portfolio optimisation'. This method, although theoretically sound, may not be economically and practically applicable to the market for ships because of lack of liquidity and market depth, high transaction costs and brokers' commissions, and the length of time required to complete an S&P transaction due to inspection, survey, preparation of documentation and so on. Therefore, although such dynamic asset allocation strategies may not be applied continuously to adjust a portfolio of ships, investors and owners can still benefit from portfolio optimisation by rebalancing their fleet less frequently.

Another important issue raised by some owners who are against fleet diversification and portfolio optimisation is that of specialisation and operational expertise. The problem of lack of expertise in the operation of vessels of different types can be addressed by outsourcing the commercial and operational activities of those vessels. For instance, investors may use management companies and shipping pools to operate their vessels, and even share the ownership through joint ventures in order to diversify. After all, the objective of investors and shipping companies should be optimising the risk and return of investment and firm value over and above what can be achieved through providing freight services.

13.4.2 Derivatives on ship values

As explained in Chapter 1, a derivative instrument is a contract whose value is derived and depends on the value of an underlying asset, commodity, or on an index. Therefore, in order to design and trade derivative contracts on the value of a merchant ship, there should be a reliable ship-price index and an independent price-reporting system. Since ships are not homogenous assets, due to differences in age, size, design, structure, equipment, hull condition and so on, a standard ship – of certain type, size, age, condition – has to be nominated and prices on that type of ship must be regularly reported. This idea was first developed by Clarkson Securities through initiation of reporting second-hand price assessments on four standard-type five-year-old vessels. The task of collecting and processing the brokers' assessments of the vessel values was handed over to the Baltic Exchange in April 2003. As a result, the index was renamed the Baltic Ship Value Assessment (BaSVA), and then more recently changed to the Baltic Sale and Purchase Assessments (BSPA). The BSPAs are bi-monthly ship value indices, produced for standard-type vessels, based on average price assessments reported by an international and independent panel of sale and purchase brokers on prices of standard-type ships.

In order to have a more accurate and representative price indicator, vessels with standard specifications were chosen as the underlying asset for the index; these are ships with a comparatively high turnover in the physical sale and purchase market. The standard-type vessels used for reporting BSPA prices and their specifications are given in Table 13.6. These are VLCC, Aframax and medium-range product tankers, as well as Capesize, Panamax and Supramax dry-bulk carriers. The BSPA panellists report their assessments under the guidelines issued by the Baltic Exchange to maintain consistency and pricing accuracy, as outlined in the Baltic Exchange panellist's manual (Baltic Exchange, 2008). Figure 13.5 plots the values of BSPA for six standard vessels over the period September 2003 to February 2008. It can be seen that there has been an overall upward trend in standard ship indices, reflecting the growth in the freight-rate market, as well as a high degree of co-movement between prices of vessels of different sizes both in the tanker and the dry-bulk sectors.

13.4.3 Forward Ship Value Agreements (FoSVA)

The introduction of BSPA indices has given investors, shipowners, asset players, financiers, shipyards and other participants in the shipping industry the opportunity not only to trade and speculate on ship prices, but also to manage ship-price risk. An instrument developed for this purpose is the Forward Ship Value Agreement (FoSVA). This is a simple cash-settled forward contract on the value of the BSPA. As with any other forward contract, under a FoSVA the buyer and the seller agree to exchange the fixed (contract) price with the BSPA (settlement) price at some point in the future. Therefore, if the

Table 13.6   BSPA Standard-type ship specifications

Vessel type	Specification
VLCC tanker	305,000 dwt double hull built in 'first class competitive yard' – European-standard B&W main engine – about 15.5 knots service speed laden on about 90 tons, length overall (loa) about 332m, beam about 58m. Non-coated. Not ice-classed. Five years old. Special survey passed. Delivery prompt (two-three months), charter free, 2 per cent total commission.
AFRAMAX tanker	105,000 dwt double hull built in 'first-class competitive yard' – European standard B&W main engine – about 15.5 knots service speed laden on about 50 tons, loa about 248m, beam about 42m. Non-coated. Not ice-classed. Five years old. Special survey passed. Delivery prompt (two-three months), charter free, 2 per cent total commission.
MR product tanker	45,000 dwt, double hull, built in 'first-class competitive yard' – European standard B&W main engine, about 14.5 knots service speed on about 35/32.8 mt fuel oil (laden/ballast), loa about 182m, beam about 32m, draft about 12m. Non-coated. Not ice-classed. Five years old. Special survey passed. Delivery prompt (two-three months), charter free, 2 per cent total commission.
CAPESIZE (Dry)	172,000 dwt, 'built in first-class competitive yard' 190,000 cbm grain, max, loa 289m, max beam 45m, draft 17.75m, 14.5 knots laden, 15 knots ballast on 56 mt fuel oil, no diesel at sea. Non-coated. Not ice-classed. Five years old. Special survey passed. Delivery prompt (two-three months), charter free, 2 per cent total commission.
PANAMAX (Dry)	74,000 dwt, 'built in first-class competitive yard', 89,000 cbm grain, max, loa 225m, draft 13.95m, 14 knots on 32/28 fuel oil laden/ballast and no diesel at sea. Non-coated. Not ice-classed. Five years old. Special survey passed. Delivery prompt (two-three months), charter free, 2 per cent total commission.
'Tess 52' SUPRAMAX (Dry)	52,454 dwt. 'built in first-class competitive yard', European standard B&W main engine, 66,500 cbm grain, loa 190m, beam 32.26m, draft 12.02m, 14.8 knots on 30.0 mt 390 at sea, five holds/five hatches, 4 × 30 mt cranes. Not iced-classed. Five years old. Special survey passed. Delivery prompt (two-three months), charter free, 2 per cent total commission.

Source: Baltic Exchange, February 2008.

settlement price at maturity exceeds the contract price, then the seller pays the difference to the buyer and vice versa. While the underlying BSPA vessels are standardised, OTC FoSVAs can be tailored to the needs of principals in terms of the agreed settlement period, maturity and type of vessel.

As with any other derivative, FoSVAs can be used either for hedging, arbitrage or speculation. For the purpose of hedging, natural sellers of FoSVAs could be those who are most at risk in case of a fall in the asset values of

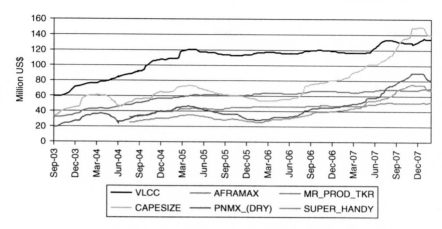

Figure 13.5 Plot of Baltic Exchange Sale and Purchase Assessment (BSPA) indices for different types of ships

ships – owners, shipyards, lending banks and asset underwriters. Natural buyers of FoSVA contracts include the traditional shipping investors and asset players, as well as non-shipping investors seeking exposure to the shipping industry without having to buy the vessel, for example, hedge funds, financial institutions and private investors. The benefit of participation to non-shipping investors is that they can not only speculate and benefit from movement in the market for ships but can also diversify their portfolio of assets further and construct more efficient asset portfolios. For instance, investors looking for a commodity or asset that correlates strongly with the state of the world economy, industrial production and international trade can trade FoSVAs. They can also be used by banks, which are exposed to shipping markets due to their ship-finance activities, to manage their risk or offer resale value guarantees to their clients. An additional benefit of the FoSVA is that, traditionally, speculators and asset players could only use the long position in the market for ships to speculate on ship prices; however, the introduction of derivatives on ship values gives investors the opportunity to speculate and benefit from falling ship prices by selling forward contracts on ship values.

To illustrate how a FoSVA can be used to hedge the resale value of a vessel at a certain time in the future, consider a shipping investor who has the opportunity to purchase a four-year-old 305,000 dwt VLCC for US$120m, financed with 20 per cent equity and 80 per cent debt with 6 per cent interest. Let us also assume that the daily operating costs for this vessel are US$10,000/day, including dry-docking and special survey allowance, and that the investor has the opportunity to lock in freight rates at around US$55,000/day either by fixing the vessel on a 12-month time-charter or by using a Calendar FFA contract and operating the vessel in the spot market. However, the investor

Table 13.7 Results of hedging resale value for a VLCC using FoSVAs

1-year short FoSVA hedge	
Physical market	**Forward market**
20 July 2006	
Four-year-old VLCC price: US$120m	July 2007 VLCC FoSVA: US$115m
Investor sells 1 VLCC FoSVA at US$115m	
July 2007 – rising ship prices	
Five-year-old VLCC price = US$130m	Settlement: Average of VLCC BSPA July 2007 = US$130m
The investor sells the vessel at market price of US$130m	The investor settles the FoSVA at a loss of US$15m
	Loss from forward transaction ($115m – $130m) = –US$15m
Net result from hedging: US$115m = ($130m – $15m)	
July 2007 – falling ship prices	
5 year old VLCC price = $95m	Settlement: Average of VLCC BSPA July 2007 = $95m
The investor sells the vessel at market price of $95m	The investors settles the FoSVA at a profit of $20m
	Profit from forward transaction ($115m – $95m) = $20m
Net result from hedging: = $115m = ($95m + $20m)	

is concerned about the exposure to residual/resale value risk, which could potentially lead to a low return or a loss on the equity if the market price for this vessel declines significantly after one year, which is the investor's investment horizon.

Now consider that the investor has the opportunity to enter into a forward ship value agreement for a five-year-old VLCC, with maturity of one year. Let us say the price of this contract is US$115m. In order to secure or hedge the resale value of the vessel after one year, the investor decides to sell a 12-month FoSVA contract, equivalent to one VLCC vessel. Following this strategy, the investor hedges the exposure to fluctuations in the second-hand market value of the vessel and, if credit risk is ignored, he is guaranteed a residual value of US$115m – or very close to it – after one year. The result of the hedge is presented in Table 13.7. It can be seen that if the market price of the VLCC after one year increases, let us say to US$130m, the investor can sell the vessel at the market price, while incurring a loss of US$15m (US$115m – US$130m) in settling the FoSVA, which leaves the overall resale value of the VLCC as US$115m. On the other hand, should the price of the five-year old VLCC fall to US$95m, the investor would sell the vessel for US$95m in the market but makes a profit of US$20m on the FoSVA, which once again means an overall resale value of US$115m. Hedging the resale value of the ship can secure the overall return on this shipping investment project. It is not difficult to perform a simple calculation, with guaranteed net freight earnings of US$19.8m over the next year (assuming five days off-hire), a locked-in vessel depreciation of US$5m, and a sale and purchase commission of 2 per cent, to arrive at a guaranteed return on equity (ROE) of 12.45 per cent.

Although we used the July 2007 BSPA for settlement, in a real deal investors and traders may prefer to use a settlement rate based on the average BSPA over a longer period of time, say, a quarter. Having the settlement as an average of a period can reduce hedging mismatch due to price spikes and the likelihood of market manipulation. This is particularly important because the sale and purchase market for ships is relatively illiquid compared to freight or commodities, because there are a limited number of ships that are traded in the sale and purchase market at any point in time. In addition, the relatively small size of fleet in certain sectors suggests that the market could potentially be controlled by large investors.

Despite the apparent benefits of FoSVA, trading in these contracts has been very limited and has not exceeded a few transactions so far. This can be due to several reasons. First, investors and traders might be reluctant to participate in this market and trade derivatives on ship values because of their views on the transparency and liquidity in the market. Second, the size of the contract and potential credit risk could be another obstacle that prevents traders from using FoSVAs, although OTC deals can be designed on fractions of vessel values. Finally, and perhaps more importantly, it could be the case that due to the high correlation between FFAs and ship prices, and relatively higher liquidity in the FFA market, investors find it easier to use FFAs to trade, hedge or speculate in shipping markets, rather than using the less liquid FoSVAs. To illustrate the correlation between the FFAs and BSPA, we plot the historical BSPA and 1st, 2nd and 3rd calendar 4TC FFA rates for Capesize and Panamax dry-bulk carriers in Figures 13.6 and 13.7, respectively. The visual inspection of these graphs points to a high correlation between FFA rates and ship price for both vessel sizes. This is confirmed by the correlation coefficients presented in Table 13.8. Both Capesize and Panamax Baltic ship-value assessments seem to be highly correlated with 1st, 2nd and 3rd calendar 4TC FFA rates with correlation coefficients of more than 90 per cent. This is in line with the theory of ship-price determination as ship values should reflect the expected future profitability in that sector.

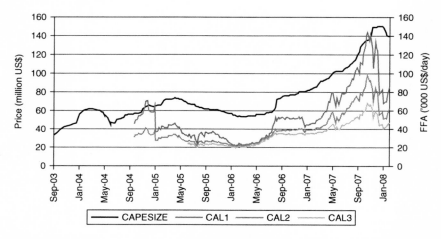

Figure 13.6   Baltic Ship Value Assessments and 1st, 2nd and 3rd Calendar 4TC FFA rates for Capesize dry-bulk carriers

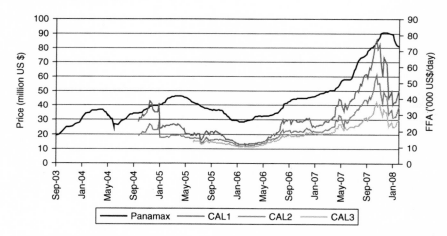

Figure 13.7   Baltic Ship Value Assessments and 1st, 2nd and 3rd Calendar 4TC FFA rates for Panamax dry-bulk carriers

13.4.4   Forward curves for ship prices

The next natural question is that of how forward ship values can be determined. We argued that merchant ships are considered as physical capital assets that generate income through freight operations and appreciate or depreciate in value depending on current and expected freight-market conditions. Therefore, in order to determine the forward value of ships we can use the cost-of-carry and no-arbitrage model used for determining the fair

Table 13.8 Average ship prices, 4TC FFA rates, and their correlations for Capesize and Panamax dry-bulk carriers

	Capesize sector			
	Ship price	FFA Cal +1	FFA Cal +2	FFA Cal +3
Average (US$m)	84.4	20.24	15.30	12.64
Correlation		0.914	0.913	0.914
	Panamax sector			
	Ship price	FFA Cal +1	FFA Cal +2	FFA Cal +3
Average (US$m)	49.46	10.52	8.08	6.66
Correlation		0.930	0.936	0.940

forward value of a storable commodity, which was presented in Chapter 1. To do this we need to make certain assumptions regarding the freight income, cost of financing, insurance and maintenance, as well as the rate of depreciation. The rate of depreciation must be considered because if a ship is bought today to be delivered against a forward ship value contract in a year's time, under the cost-of-carry model, everything else assumed to be constant, the vessel will tend to lose part of its value due to increase in age and wear-and-tear. The rate of depreciation can be estimated using differences in the average value of newbuild, five-year-, ten-year- and 20-year-old second-hand vessels. The freight income can also be estimated from FFA forward curves (for example, average 4TC contracts). Therefore, according to the cost-of-carry model, we can write the forward value of a vessel $F(t, T)$, at time t for delivery at time T, as

$$F(t, T) = S_t e^{(r+w-\delta)(T-t)} \qquad (13.6)$$

where S_t is the current price of the vessel, r represents the cost of financing, insuring and maintaining the vessel, w is the rate of depreciation, and δ is the freight income minus operating cost, presented in the form of percentage of asset price.

Using the BSPA for three sizes of dry-bulk carriers at the end of April 2008 and their respective forward freight curves, we construct the implied forward ship values over the next five years. The calculation is based on operating costs of US$12,000, US$10,000 and US$9,000 per day for Capesize, Panamax and Supramax ships respectively, as well as 8 per cent interest and insurance, and a 5 per cent depreciation rate per year. The implied forward ship values are presented in Panel B in Figure 13.8, while FFA prices which are used for their calculation are presented in Panel A of the same figure. As expected, there is a high correlation between the FFA prices and implied forward ship values, and both prices series (markets) seem to be in backwardation. The implied forward ship value curve for Capesize vessels indicates that prices are expected to decline sharply over the next three to four years and settle around a US$55m to US$60m range in 2012 and 2013. Similarly, the implied forward ship values for Panamax and Supramax vessels indicate that prices for these vessels are expected to decline and settle around US$40m in 2012 and 2013.

Adland et al (2004) estimate the implied forward prices from historical data for vessel prices and the term structure of freight rates under the assumption that the cost-of-carry relationship holds and investigate whether the implied forward prices have been unbiased predictors of realised prices. Their results suggest that forward ship prices implied by the cost-of-carry relationship are not unbiased predictors of future second-hand prices and such deviation from unbiaseness hypothesis might be due to the the presence of a risk premium.

An alternative way to derive forward ship values is to use the newbuilding contracts for different delivery dates and adjust these prices considering the investment costs, newbuilding contract specification premium or discount (for example, for multiple ships or extension options), and the price differential between a newbuilding and a second-hand vessel at the time of delivery (maturity of forward contract). For instance, in March and April 2008, the newbuilding price for a standard Baltic Capesize bulk carrier for delivery in May or June 2011 was quoted at US$85m. Assuming a 6 per cent interest rate and a 5 per cent depreciation rate per annum, as well as an adjustment for technological advances of a newbuild compared to a five-year-old second-hand ship, the implied three-year forward price of a standard Baltic Capesize will be about US$61m, which is close to the value that we derived though the cost-of-carry model, US$60m. Similarly, one can use a series of newbuilding quotes to construct implied forward ship value curves.

13.4.5 The Baltic Demolition Index (BDA)

In addition to BSPA, the Baltic Exchange produces assessment indices on the demolition price of different types of ships. These are known as Baltic Demolition Assessments (BDA), which are intended to be used for trading derivatives on the demolition price of ships as well as for hedging the residual value of ships; this could be useful in managing the risk involved in financing relatively old ships or when there is a balloon payment on shipping loans and the balloon may be covered by the scrap value of the vessel. Currently, BDAs are compiled and reported for three types of ships and delivery in two different locations. These are dirty tanker, clean tanker and bulk carriers delivered in China and the Indian subcontinent. BDA prices are in US dollar per 'light displacement' (ltd) tonnage of the ship. Light displacement is the weight of

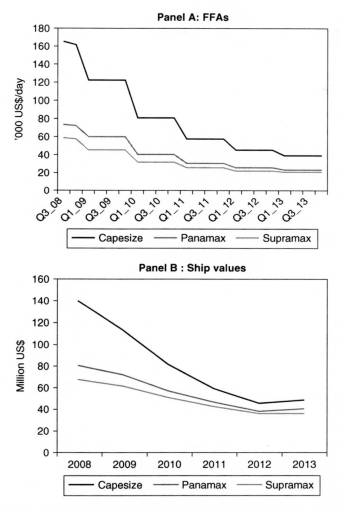

Figure 13.8 Forward freight curves and implied forward ship values for different types of dry-bulk carriers in May 2008

the ship with no cargo or fuel on board; it essentially represents the steel content of the ship.[4]

---

[4] Although vessels contain other items and materials (navigational equipment, engine(s), generators, cranes, cables and so on), these are normally stripped and sold separately during the dismantling process.

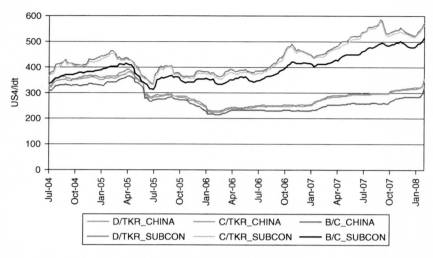

Figure 13.9   Baltic Exchange Demolition Assessment indices for different types of ships and delivery locations

Note: D/TKR is dirty tanker, C/TKR is clean tanker, and B/C is bulk carrier, with delivery locations in China and the Indian subcontinent.

Vessel demolition prices are closely linked with world scrap-steel prices, although the supply and demand for scrap ships may also have some impact on prices. Figure 13.9 plots the reported BDA values over the period July 2004 to February 2008. It can be seen that BDA prices move close together in the long run, reflecting the fact that they are driven by the same fundamental driver – namely, the condition of the world scrap-steel market. However, since July 2005 it seems that demolition prices in the subcontinent and China have been diverging to some extent. This might be due to the increase in the number of scrapyards and scrapping activity in the subcontinent compared to China as the demand for scrap steel in India increases. Also, it seems that tanker BDAs are relatively higher than those for bulk carriers both in the subcontinent and China, perhaps due to their structure, steel content or steel quality.

Currently, there are no derivatives traded on BDA. Theoretically, BDA forwards could be used to hedge the scrap price of a ship, especially when the project involves a relatively old vessel. This type of derivative has been used in the past in the form of residual value insurance in shipping projects, but to trade residual value of the ship or speculate on the BDA is something that can be developed further. To see how forward contracts on BDA can be used for hedging, consider an investor who is planning to invest in a relatively old, 20-year-old, Panamax vessel which has a current value of US$25m. The investor is planning to operate the vessel for the next five years and sell the vessel as scrap at the end of the fifth year. The freight revenue of the ship

Table 13.9 Results of hedging the scrap price of a vessel using BDA forward contracts

1-year short BDA hedge	
Physical market	**Forward market**
20 July 2008	
Panamax scrap value: US$500/ldt Total value: US$5m ($500/ltd × 10,000 t)	July 2013 Panamax BDA: US$5m
Investor sells 1 Panamax BDA at US$5m	
July 2013 – rising scrap prices	
Panamax scrap value = US$700/ldt	Settlement: Average of BDA in July 2013 = US$700/ldt
The investor sells the vessel at market price of: US$7m ($700/ldt × 10,000 t)	The investors settles the BDA forward at a loss of US$2m Loss from forward transaction ($5m − $7m) = −US$2m
Net result from hedging: ($7m − $2m) = US$5m	
July 2013 – falling scrap prices	
Panamax scrap value = US$350/ldt	Settlement: Average of BDA in July 2013 = US$350/ldt
The investor sells the vessel at market price of: US$3.5m ($350/ldt × 10,000 t)	The investors settles the BDA forward at a profit of US$1.5m Profit from forward transaction ($5 m − $3.5m) = US$1.5m
Net result from hedging: $3.5m + $1.5m = US$5m	

can be hedged through a series of FFA contracts, while the capital costs can also be managed using interest-rate swaps. All other costs can be considered to be either constant or to increase at the rate of inflation. The only uncertain variable in this project is the resale value of the ship. In five years' time, if the resale value of the vessel, which is going to be 25 years old at that time, increases, then the investor's project can be profitable, but if the resale value of the vessel declines, the project can end up at a loss. However, a simple forward BDA agreement can be used to hedge the scrap (or resale) value of this ship in year 5. This strategy allows the investor to lock into a scrap value of, say US$5m (e.g. US$500/ldt × 10,000 mt) in five years' time (that is, the maturity of the forward BDA agreement and the project). To hedge the scrap price of the vessel, the investor sells a BDA contract on a whole Panamax value for US$5m with five years to maturity.

Results of this short BDA hedge under different possible outcomes for scrap value of the ship in July 2013 are presented in Table 13.9. Under a rising market scenario, scrap price and BDA for Panamax vessels in July 2013 is assumed to be US$700/ldt. This means that the investor can sell the vessel at a relative high scrap value of US$7m in the market, but has to settle the BDA forward contract with a loss of US$200/ltd, that is a total loss of US$2m. Thus the overall scrap price for investor will be US$5m. On the other hand, should the scrap price for Panamax ships in July 2013 drop to US$350/ltd, the investor sells the vessel for US$3.5m for demolition, but settles the BDA forward contract at a profit of US$1.5m [(US$500/ltd – US$350/ltd) × 10,000 mt], thus ending up with an overall demolition value of US$5m.

In terms of pricing, forward contracts on BDA are more complicated to price, compared to FoSVAs, as the BDA is linked primarily to the steel price. Although, the cost-of-carry-relationship-and-no-arbitrage argument can also be used to price forward demolition values, the success of such a model might be limited due to the strong linkage between demolition price and world scrap-steel price.

13.5　Summary and conclusions

The volatility in the market for ships is directly related to the volatility in the freight market. This is because ship prices are believed to be determined through a discounted present value model in which revenue from freight operations is the main pricing factor. Since freight-rate levels and volatilities are different across sizes and types of vessel, ship-price volatilities also vary across size and sector and over time. Moreover, we reviewed the risk involved in holding ships as assets in portfolios and how the risk of the portfolio can be managed through diversification.

Given the limited effectiveness of diversification in ship-price risk management, we discussed the available ship price indices as well as the derivative contracts on those indices. Examples of how such derivatives can be used for ship-price risk management and trading purposes were presented, while the limitations of their trading and liquidity were also highlighted. It was argued that low liquidity, size of the contract and potential credit risk can be obstacles to the growth of trade in FoSVAs. In addition, the high correlation between FFAs and asset prices and higher liquidity in the FFA market means that participants might prefer to use FFAs for hedging ship price because the FFA market is more liquid compared to BSPA. Finally, we discussed the Baltic Demolition Indices (BDA) of scrap market prices for different types of ships and how derivatives on the BDA can be traded and used to hedge the residual value of ships.

14
Real Options and Optionalities in Shipping

14.1 Introduction

In Chapters 7 and 8, we discussed options on shipping freight rates, hedging with freight options, as well as their pricing and trading strategies. In this chapter we explore the natural extension of these instruments for valuing flexibility and optionality in investment and operational projects using 'real option analysis' (ROA). Since there are a number of strategic and managerial flexibilities embedded in shipping investment and operations projects, we focus on the use of real option analysis in evaluating such optionalities in shipping. We also discuss several of the options that are embedded in shipping contracts such as the option to extend a time-charter contract, the option to place a newbuilding order, or a purchase option on a time-charter contract. These options and optionalities are used extensively in the shipping industry; however, in many cases they are granted for free or for a nominal fee without being properly valued. The issue of identifying and then pricing these options is the topic of this chapter.

14.2 Financial versus real options

According to Trigeorgis (1995) real option analysis (ROA) is a methodology for valuing flexible strategies in an uncertain world. In fact, the purpose of real option valuation methodology is to quantify the management's ability to expand, delay, switch or contract a project depending on changes in factors determining the value of the project. Real options are important not only in identifying and evaluating different investment decision pathways or projects that management can navigate given the highly uncertain business environment, but also in comparing strategic decision pathways and examining their financial viability and feasibility. In addition, real option analysis can be used to assess the timing of the effective execution of investment decisions and to find the optimal trigger values and cost or revenue drivers of projects. For a review of real option analysis and its relevance to maritime and shipping investment, see Bendall (2002) and Bendall and Stent (2003).

Table 14.1   Financial options versus real options

Financial options	Real options
– Relatively short maturities	– Relatively longer maturities
– Underlying variable is a tradable asset	– Underlying variables are cash flows affected by managerial decisions
– Cannot control option price	– Strategic option value can increase through flexibility
– Smaller values	– Higher values
– Competitive and traded in secondary markets	– Not tradable
– Priced using closed-form solutions, trees and simulation methods	– Priced using closed-form solutions, trees and simulation methods
– Management assumptions and actions have no effect on the value of the option	– Management assumptions and actions drive the value of the option

Source: Mun (2002).

There are a number of differences between financial options and real options, which are presented in Table 14.1. For instance, while for a financial option the underlying variables are tradable financial assets, in real options the underlying variables are cash flows affected by managerial decisions. In terms of maturity and marketability, financial options normally have short maturities and can be traded in a secondary market, whereas real options are embedded values in projects with a longer life which cannot be traded. The value of financial options (that is, the option premium) cannot be controlled by investors, while real option values depend on the embedded flexibility and strategic optionality of projects. Furthermore, for financial options, investors' actions and assumptions have no effect on the values of options. This is not the case for real options, where values of real options depend on or can be influenced by investors' actions and assumptions. Finally, while financial options can be relatively small in value, values of embedded real options can be relatively high. Despite the differences between financial options and real options, they both can be valued using closed-form solutions, tree methods and simulation techniques.

14.3   Conventional NPV versus real option valuation

The traditional approach in valuing projects has been the discounted cash flow model in which the net cash flow of a project is discounted, using an appropriate discount rate[1] to the present time in order to find the net present

---

[1] The appropriate discount rate is the risk-adjusted rate. In practice, this is normally considered to be the rate of return on a project with a similar risk profile. There are

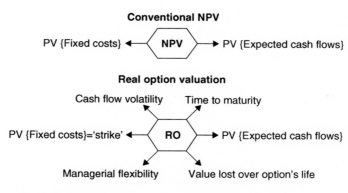

Figure 14.1 'Drivers' of NPV and real option valuation techniques
Source: Cuthbertson and Nitzsche (2001).

value (NPV) of the project. The NPV, which is a static measure of the profitability of the project, is then assessed and the project is selected if the NPV is positive, and rejected if the NPV is negative. A major disadvantage of NPV analysis in investment appraisal and project evaluation is that it does not incorporate several other factors that can influence the success of the project or the venture, including managerial flexibility, different paths that might be available once the project is undertaken, as well as uncertainty around the project's cash flows. Although the last can be incorporated in the discount rate used in the NPV analysis, the dynamics of such volatility in the outcome of the underlying factors cannot be effectively incorporated in a conventional NPV model.

In contrast to a conventional NPV analysis where the value drivers are present values of expected cash flows and costs, in real option analysis other factors that can influence the investment profitability are also considered. These additional factors or value drivers are: uncertainty about future cash flows; the life of the project or investment; managerial and operational flexibility; and the time value of such flexibility or optionality itself. A comparison of different value drivers in NPV and real option valuation methods is presented in Figure 14.1. Therefore, considering the value drivers in project evaluation, it can be argued that ROA becomes more important and worth

different methods proposed in the literature to estimate the discount rate: the Capital Asset Pricing Model (CAPM), Arbitrage Pricing Theory (APT), or the Multifactor Asset Pricing Model (MAPT). The most common method is based on CAPM, which yields the cost of equity which can then be used to calculate the weighted average cost of capital (WACC) if the project is leveraged (see Brealey et al., 2007, for more details on the calculation of WACC).

Table 14.2   NPV calculation of shipping acquisition

Year	0	1	2	3	4	5	6
Purchase price (US$m)	−10.0						
Expected operating profit		1.50	1.50	1.50	1.50	1.50	1.50
Expected scrap value							4.00
PV of cash flows	−10.0	1.41	1.32	1.24	1.17	1.09	3.77
NPV	0.00						

Note: all figures in US$m.

using when, for instance, the conventional NPV is close to zero, or when there is great flexibility – to expand, contract, delay or switch – embedded in the project. Also, ROA becomes more appropriate and better reflects the true value of the project as uncertainty about the future outcome of the underlying factors increases. Finally, for projects with a relatively long life span, ROA can determine the value of the project more efficiently compared to a conventional NPV analysis.

14.3.1   Valuation of a shipping project

To illustrate the difference between the conventional NPV and real option analysis in investment appraisal, consider a shipping investment project where the investor is planning to purchase a small 20-year-old ship with a market price of US$10m. The investor expects to operate the vessel for six years and sell her, possibly for scrap, at an expected value of US$4m at the end of the sixth year. The operating profit, that is, freight revenue minus operating costs for this vessel is expected to be US$1.5m a year and the cost of capital (discount factor) is estimated to be 6.5 per cent, which reflects the risk-free rate of 5 per cent plus a risk premium of 1.5 per cent. Given the cash-flow projection and the discount rate, we can calculate the NPV of this project, as presented in Table 14.2.

It can be seen that the NPV of this project is approximately zero and, hence, the investor is indifferent as to whether to accept or reject this project. Now consider that the investor has the option to sell the vessel for US$4m and exit (abandon) the project at any point during its life. Assuming that the price volatility of the vessel is 30 per cent, and the risk-free rate is 5 per cent, we can calculate the value of this 'option to exit' which is available to the investor once the project is under way. Since the option can be exercised at any time during the project this is an American option; the value of this option, calculated using the Binomial Option Pricing Model (BOPM) with six steps, is US$91,850 (see Appendix 14.A).

Therefore, by considering and adding the value of this 'option to exit', once the project is under way, the investor can reassess the NPV and the profitability of the project. The combined values of static NPV and the option on the project is known as the 'expanded NPV' which, in this case, is US$91,850 (US$0 + US$91,850). Thus, although based on the conventional NPV, the investor may not be able to decide on the execution of the project, the expanded NPV is positive and indicates that the project can be profitable. Of course, in this example we assumed that the resale value of the vessel throughout the life of the project is known and remains constant at US$4m, but in reality this value can change. There are, however, methods that can take the stochastic behaviour of the resale value into account, as will be seen in Section 14.6. Furthermore, the option to exit is one of the many options available to the investor; each option may add to the overall value of the project and must be taken into account during the valuation process.

14.4 Real options in shipping

Given the number of strategic optionalities available to participants in the shipping industry, the topic of application of real options in shipping investment and operations has been the focus of much academic research. This was first proposed by Dixit (1988; 1989) where decisions to lay up and enter and exit the market were evaluated. Several other studies extend the application of real options to other strategic aspects of shipping investment and operations, including: Bjerksund and Ekern (1995), who value the option to extend a time-charter shipping contract; Sodal et al. (2008a) who investigate options available for a combined carrier to switch between dry and wet markets; Sodal et al. (2008b) who evaluate the options available to shipping investors to switch between tanker and dry markets; and Bendall and Stent (2001) who apply real option analysis to evaluate an investment in a fast-cargo service in South East Asia. The aim of the following sections is to discuss and provide examples of applications of real options to shipping investment and operations. We use an option valuation technique known as the Binomial Option Pricing Model (BOPM) developed by Cox et al. (1979), for its simplicity and ability to price American options; the methodology of the BOMP is described in more detail in the appendix.

14.4.1 Option to abandon/exit

As mentioned in Section 14.3.1 one of the options available to a shipowner or a shipping company is to sell the assets and exit the market. Such a strategic optionality can have substantial value, especially when the volatility in the market is high and there is a lot of uncertainty about its future direction. In this section we show how such an exit option can be evaluated using a simple example. Again, assuming that the current price of the vessel is US$10m, the annualised volatility of ship prices is 30 per cent, the risk-free rate is 5 per cent, and the life of the project is six years, we can construct a six-step asset price evolution lattice (see the Appendix, Section 14.8) using up (u)

and down (*d*) multipliers, and calculating the risk-neutral probability (*p*), as follows:

$$u = e^{\sigma\sqrt{\Delta t}} = e^{0.3\sqrt{6/6}} = 1.3499 \quad d = e^{-\sigma\sqrt{\Delta t}} = \frac{1}{u} = 0.7408$$

$$p = \frac{e^{r\Delta t} - d}{u - d} = \frac{e^{0.05 \times 6/6} - 0.7408}{1.3499 - 0.7408} = 0.5097$$

Underlying price lattice

	Steps					
	1	**2**	**3**	**4**	**5**	**6**
						60.50
					44.82	
				33.20		33.20
			24.60		24.60	
		18.22		18.22		18.22
	13.50		13.50		13.50	
10.00		10.00		10.00		10.00
	7.41		7.41		7.41	
		5.49		5.49		5.49
			4.07		4.07	
				3.01		3.01
					2.23	
						1.65

Now assume that the investor can sell the vessel for US$4m any time during the life of the project. This is therefore a put option on the vessel with a strike price of US$4m and, since the option can be exercised at any time, it is an American option. We can construct, first, the end nodes in the option valuation lattice, using the payoff formula for a put option, i.e., max(*X* − *S*, 0), and then solve for the intermediate nodes to get the option value, using the backwards induction method, adjusted for the possibility of early exercise. To value the intermediate nodes, we begin with nodes in step 5 and calculate the one-step discounted present value of the risk-neutral probability-weighted average of the two outcomes attached to the node. This is then compared to the intrinsic value of the option in this node, i.e., max(*X* − *S*, 0), and the greater of the two is then selected; for instance, node A in step 5 is calculated as

$$\text{node A} = \max\{(X - \$2.231), [p(\$0.99) + (1 - p)(\$2.35)]e^{-r\Delta t}\}$$
$$= \max\{(\$4 - \$2.231), [(0.5097)(\$0.99) + (1 - 0.5097)(\$2.35)]e^{-0.05(1)}\}$$
$$= \max\{\$1.77, 1.57\} = \text{US}\$1.77$$

Option valuation lattice

	Steps					
	1	2	3	4	5	6
						0.00
					0.00	
				0.00		0.00
			0.00		0.00	
		0.00		0.00		0.00
	0.02		0.00		0.00	
0.092		0.05		0.00		0.00
	0.17		0.10		0.00	
		0.33		0.21		0.00
			0.59		0.46	
				1.05		0.99
					1.77	→ node A
						2.35

Notice that the backwards induction is set up in such a way that early exercise is allowed; that is, in each node the expected value of continuing the project is compared to the value of terminating the project and, if the latter is higher, the project is terminated and vice versa. For instance, in node A, the option is exercised early (that is, the vessel is sold in the market) since the intrinsic value of the option is greater than the value if we do not exercise. This procedure can be applied to find the value of all intermediate nodes back to the first, which is the value of the option to sell the vessel at any time for US$4m and abandon the project. The value of this option is therefore US$91,850.

In a more realistic case, Bendall and Stent (2001) apply real option analysis to evaluating investment in a fast cargo service in South East Asia. Their model calculates the optimum number of ships required to meet the given distribution task, the most profitable deployment of the fleet, and the profitability of the service. Their results demonstrate that ROA is more appropriate in valuing flexibility, in their case the abandonment option, in such investment projects.

14.4.2   Option to expand

The possibility of expansion in operational and investment projects can be quite valuable to firms because expansion possibilities give them the flexibility to have limited involvement initially and subsequently increase their involvement once conditions are right. For instance, consider a company that might be able to increase its capacity by expanding its fleet by, say, z per cent (for example, by chartering in and operating more ships in one route) at time T in the future, for a given cost of, say, X. It can be seen that this strategic expansion potential is an embedded call option on the project, which has a strike price of X. Assuming that the value of the project with no expansion potential at time T is V_T, the payoff of this expansion option can be written as

$$\text{payoff} = \max[0, zV_T - X]$$

It can be seen that the value of the firm is V_T, if the cost of expansion, X, at maturity is greater than the added value to the firm zV_T, while the value of the firm is $V_T + zV_T - X$, if the cost of expansion is less than the added value of the expansion. Therefore, there is a value for such an expansion option and this value can be estimated using the BOPM.

As an example consider a liner company, which has an exclusive right to operate on a specific route. This firm is planning to invest in a small container vessel. The revenue from this operation depends on the demand for container transportation and varies over time. However, while the NPV of the current operation is estimated to be US$10m, the firm believes that the estimated NPV has a volatility of 40 per cent. In addition, the company has the option to add a second vessel to this route at the end of the year if the demand increases, but such expansion requires an additional investment of US$15m for acquiring the second vessel. To price the 'option to expand' on this project, we first construct the lattice for the evolution of NPV using the up and down multipliers, calculated using 40 per cent volatility and five time steps during the life of the project (1 year).

$$u = e^{\sigma\sqrt{\Delta t}} = e^{0.4\sqrt{1/5}} = 1.1959 \quad and \quad d = e^{-\sigma\sqrt{\Delta t}} = \frac{1}{u} = 0.8362$$

$$p = \frac{e^{r\Delta t} - d}{u - d} = \frac{e^{0.05 \times 1/5} - 0.8362}{1.1959 - 0.8362} = 0.483$$

Price evolution lattice

Steps					
1	2	3	4	5	6
					24.46
				20.45	
			17.10		17.10
		14.30		14.30	
	11.96		11.96		11.96
10.00		10.00		10.00	
	8.36		8.36		8.36
		6.99		6.99	
			5.85		5.85
				4.89	
					4.09

To calculate the terminal nodes (payoffs) in the option valuation lattice we simply use the "=max()" function in Excel to define the payoff considering the expansion option of doubling up, less the cost of expansion (US$15m); thus we can write:

$$\text{node A} = \max\,[\$24.46m, (2 * \$24.46m - \$15m)]$$
$$= US\$33.92m$$
$$\text{node B} = \max\,[\$4.09m, (2 * \$4.09m - \$15m)]$$
$$= US\$4.09m$$

Option valuation lattice

		Steps				
	1	2	3	4	5	
					33.92	node A
		node C		26.06		
			20.30		19.21	
		16.08		15.31		
	12.93		12.44		11.96	
10.52		10.23		10.00		
	8.47		8.36		8.36	
		6.99		6.99		
			5.85		5.85	
				4.89		node B
					4.09	

Next we use the backwards induction method to evaluate the intermediate nodes back to the first, which is the value of the option to expand the operation. Since there is no early exercise, we can evaluate each node by discounting the risk-neutral probability-weighted outcome of each node using risk-free rate. For instance, the value of the top node in step 4 of the option valuation lattice is

$$\text{node C} = [p(S_0u^5) + (1-p)(S_0u^4d)]e^{-r\Delta t}$$
$$= [(0.483)(\$33.92m) + (1-0.483)(\$19.21)]e^{-0.05(1)}$$
$$= US\$26.06m$$

Once the backwards induction process is complete, it can be seen that the value of the expansion option to the firm is US$0.52m (US$10.52m − US$10m), and the expanded NPV of the project is US$10.52m.

14.4.3 Option to contract

Another valuable type of strategic flexibility available to shipping companies is the option to reduce or contract their operations. For instance, a liner shipping company can choose to reduce its services or take some ships out of operation if the market declines. Similarly, a port operator can reduce its operations in terms of hours or cargo work, or the number of berths used in the terminal. In such cases, the option to contract has a value to the firm which depends on future cash flows and the contraction costs. To illustrate, let us assume that, by reducing operations, the firm value reduces by z per-cent, at time T in future, while the amount of savings is X dollars. Thus, the payoff of the option to contract to this firm at time T will be:

$$\text{payoff} = \max[0, X - zV_T]$$

$$\text{firm's value} = \max[V_T, V_T + X - zV_T]$$

It can be seen that the value of the firm is V_T, if the savings through con-traction, X, at some point in the future are less than the reduction in the value of the firm zV_T, while the value of the firm will be $(V_T + X - zV_T)$, if the savings through contraction are greater than the loss in the value of the firm in the case of contraction. Therefore, this is similar to a put option with a strike price of X: the value of such an option depends on the underlying factors and their uncertainty, and can be estimated using BOPM.

14.4.4   Option to switch

The availability of different modes of operation and chartering contracts in shipping offers a certain level of flexibility to shipowners, ship operators and charterers. For instance, a Panamax owner can choose to switch between spot and the time-charter contracts or switch between different routes depending on the level of profitability on each route. Moreover, combined carriers offer their owners the flexibility to switch between the wet and dry makets in order to maximise their operating profit. In addition, these ships could be employed in carrying backhaul cargoes when possible, to increase profitabil-ity. Although the market for such vessels has diminished over recent years, they were designed to offer switching and cargo-carrying flexibility. One pos-sible reason for their demise could be their smaller cargo-carrying capacity compared to a normal dry-bulk carrier or a tanker.

In order to evaluate the option to switch, one can use the present value of expected earnings under each mode of operation (V_1 and V_2) as well as the cost of switching from mode 1 to mode 2 (CS) to find the payoff of the option in the following form:

$$\text{payoff} = \max[0, V_1 - V_2 - CS]$$

However, if the firm has the option to switch between the modes more than once, the above formula must be modified to take into account the dynamics of variables that influence the switching decision as well as the additional cost involved in switching to and from a mode. Furthermore, there might be more than two modes that the firm can choose to operate, which makes the payoff and valuation of the option to switch even more complex.

Sodal et al. (2008a) use real option analysis to value the option to switch between the dry and wet-bulk markets for a combination carrier. They suggest a mean-reverting (Ornstein-Uhlenbeck) version of a standard entry-exit model with stochastic prices for implementing the real option valuation, and derive a closed-form solution for the value of flexibility. They find that the estimated value of flexibility is related to historical price differentials between combination carriers and oil tankers of comparable size. They also examine the sensitivity of their result with respect to changes in input variables such as switching costs, mean freight differential in dry and wet sectors, discount rates and market volatility. Based on the results, their main conclusion is that the operational flexibility of combination carriers has significant value.

In another study, Sodal et al. (2008b) use a real options valuation model with stochastic freight rates to investigate market efficiency and the economics of switching between the dry-bulk and tanker markets in international shipping. They suggest and value a strategy that allows the shipowner to replace a Capesize dry-bulk carrier with a Suezmax tanker when the expected net present value of such a switch is optimal, and vice versa, using real options analysis. Considering cost and demand parameters, as well as the stochastic characteristics of freight rates throughout a 12-year time period from 1993 to 2005, Sodal et al. show that there is a value in switching between the sectors.

14.4.5 Option to lay-up

Perhaps one of the most relevant optionalities available to shipowners is the option to stop operating the vessel temporarily, known as the 'option to lay-up'. This option is normally exercised when the revenue of operating the vessel does not cover the cost of running her. When freight markets are in recession, freight rates are low and freight income may be less than total costs so the vessel may be operating at a loss. There are even instances when freight rates are so low that freight income does not even cover all voyage costs. In such instances, the shipowner has the strategic option of laying-up the vessel. This strategy enables the shipowner to minimise potential losses during the market recession and to reactivate the vessel when the market recovers. Hence, when evaluating ship prices, it is important to incorporate such operational flexibility in NPV calculations. Figure 14.2 presents a schematic diagram of the evolution of freight revenue, voyage costs and operating expenses, and the decision to lay-up a vessel.

Obviously laying-up a vessel and reactivating her later when the market recovers involves some costs. These are deactivation and reactivation costs, respectively, while operating and capital costs have also to be paid when

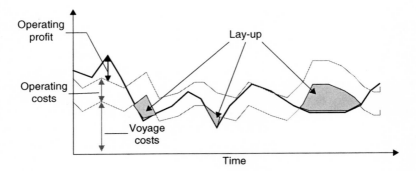

Figure 14.2   Evolution of freight revenue, voyage costs and operating expenses, and the decision to lay-up a vessel

the vessel is in lay-up, but these may be lower than when the vessel is fully operational. The decision to lay-up should be made when the present value of the expected losses of remaining in the market is higher than the cost of laying-up. Therefore, the decision depends on the level of lay-up costs and the level and volatility of the freight market as well as expectations about the laying-up period. Thus, the option to lay-up should be valued as an option on lay-up costs. Dixit and Pindyck (1994) provide an example of how to price the option to lay-up for a tanker vessel.

14.4.6   Option to delay (wait)

Another useful and valuable form of flexibility available to managers, shipowners, operators or charterers is the option to delay certain decisions and projects. For example, on many occasions a ship arrives at a certain load-ing region when freight rates are relatively low because the number of vessels available for trading is greater than the number of cargoes available for trans-portation. This is known as momentary supply-demand imbalance, which causes freight rates in that region to be lower than the freight rate levels globally (see Stopford, 1997). The reverse situation may also develop when the number of cargoes available for transportation is greater than the number of ships ready for trading, hence causing a momentary freight surge. In such situations, depending on the case, either the charterer or the shipowner has the option to delay fixing the ship and to wait for more favourable market conditions. For instance, the shipowner, whose vessel arrives in a loading region where the number of cargoes is less than the number of ships avail-able, can opt to delay fixing the ship and hope for freight rates to recover. On the other hand, a charterer who finds the rates to be high, due to the limited availability of ships, can choose to withhold the cargo until the mar-ket gets back to normal. Naturally, delaying a fixture has its own cost for the shipowner or the charterer, but either party should assess the expected costs and benefits of the delay and make the optimum decision.

14.5 Other options in shipping

In addition to real options discussed in previous sections, there are other implicit options which are embedded in many shipping contracts. Some of these options are used quite frequently by practitioners in shipping without proper valuation. These options include: period TC extension options, options to place one or more newbuilding orders on the back of a newbuilding contract, and purchase options on a time-charter contract, among others. The aim of the following sections is to discuss and provide examples of how such options can be evaluated using BOPM.

14.5.1 Option to extend a period time-charter contract

It is a relatively common practice in time-charter contracts to include an extension clause which gives the charterer the option to extend the TC contract for a pre-specified period (say, two, three or six months) once the original agreement/period expires. In many cases, shipowners grant charterers such options at no cost or at a very small incremental premium, but these options can be quite valuable to charterers. Sometimes, a shipowner may consider the credibility of the charterer as a desirable factor and throw such an option for free to make the contract more attractive to the charterer, or perhaps to maintain a good working relationship with a credible charterer. In such a case, the shipowner in fact accepts an implicit premium in the form of a reduction in the counterparty's credit risk.

In order to explore how one can price such options, consider a 12-month US$20,000/day period TC contract with a three-month extension option. Under this agreement the charterer is granted the option to extend the 12-month period TC for another three months at the same rate. We assume that the option can only be exercised at the end of the 12-month TC period but, in reality, the option may have an exercise period just prior to the end of the 12-month TC contract. Although, this is not actually a real option, in the sense discussed in Section 14.4, we can price this using BOPM, if we treat this as an option on the three-month TC with a strike price of US$20,000/day and 12 months to maturity.

To price this option, it is important to note that we should use the volatility of the three-month TC rate as the volatility of the underlying asset. If such a volatility estimate is not directly available, we can use the volatility term structure to interpolate the volatility of a three-month TC. Let us assume that the annualised volatility of the three-month rate is currently at 50 per cent and the risk-free rate is 5 per cent per annum, while the current three-month TC rate is US$18,000/day. We can estimate u, d and p assuming a six-step binomial process ($\Delta t = 1/6$) and construct the tree for the three-month TC.

$$u = e^{\sigma\sqrt{\Delta t}} = e^{0.5\sqrt{1/6}} = 1.2265 \quad d = e^{-\sigma\sqrt{\Delta t}} = \frac{1}{u} = 0.8153$$

$$p = \frac{e^{r\Delta t} - d}{u - d} = \frac{e^{0.05 \times 1/6} - 0.8153}{1.2265 - 0.8153} = 0.470$$

Underlying price lattice

			Steps			
	1	**2**	**3**	**4**	**5**	**6**
						61259
					49949	
				40726		40726
			33206		33206	
		27075		27075		27075
	22076		22076		22076	
18000		18000		18000		18000
	14677		14677		14677	
		11967		11967		11967
			9757		9757	
				7956		7956
					6487	
						5289

Next we construct the corresponding tree for option valuation and find the payoff of the option at each end node; that is, at expiry. As this is effectively a call option on the three-month TC rate, the option payoff is the three-month TC rate at expiry is less than US$20,000/day, if the three-month TC is greater than US$20,000/day or zero otherwise; in other words, the payoff is: max(3-month TC – US$20,000/day, 0). We thus calculate the payoffs for each end node as:

Option valuation lattice

			Steps			
	1	**2**	**3**	**4**	**5**	**6**
			Node A			41259
				30114		
				21057		20726
			13991		13372	
		8889		7959		7075
	5442		4513		3294	
3232		2477		1534		0
	1328		714		0	
		333		0		0
			0		0	
				0		0
					0	
						0

Once the values of the end nodes are calculated, we use the risk-neutral probability-weighted discounting procedure to calculate the interim nodes backwards to get the value of the option. For instance, the value of the top interim node in step 5 (node A) is calculated as

$$\text{node A} = [p(S_0u^6) + (1 - p)(S_0u^5d)]e^{-r\Delta t}$$
$$= [(0.47)(\$41,252) + (1 - 0.47)(\$20,726)]e^{-0.05(1/6)}$$
$$= \text{US\$30,114}$$

Therefore, using a six-step binomial tree, the fair value of this extension option is US\$3232/day for three months; that is, US\$290,880 in total (some differences may be due to rounding). However, this premium should be spread over 12 months; this results in a premium of US\$808/day over the initial time-charter contract.

14.5.2 Option on newbuilding orders

Under the option on newbuilding orders, shipyards grant shipowners or investors the option – but not the obligation – to place one or more orders for sister ships, on the back of the first order, at a specified price over a period of time in the future. This means that the shipowner can decide whether to exercise the right of placing more orders by comparing the contract price and the prevailing market price for newbuilding vessels at the time of the exercise. If the newbuilding price in the market is above the contract price, the shipowner can exercise the option by placing the order or sell this right to another investor who is interested in placing an order for this type of ship. On the other hand, if the newbuilding price in the market is below the contract price, the shipowner can leave the option to expire, and either places an order at a lower market price, or does not place any order at all. Therefore, these types of options can be quite valuable for shipowners, especially when the volatility of newbuilding prices is relatively high, the shipyard's order-books are relatively full, or the shipowner is uncertain about the future prospects of his project.

A newbuilding option essentially can be considered as a call option on the price of the underlying newbuild vessel, with a strike price equal to the contract price. This option can be priced as a normal option on the value of the new ship given the current newbuilding price, volatility, maturity and agreed strike price. Indeed, to grant this option the shipowner has to pay a premium which is normally implicit in the price of the first order. Also, shipyards sometimes grant such options to make the newbuilding contract more attractive, to remain competitive, or even to secure future employment and contracts.

As an example, consider a shipowner who places an order for a newbuild vessel at US\$50m and is granted the option – but not the obligation – to place another order for a sister ship at any time over the next year for the same price. Since the option can be exercised at any time prior to the delivery of the first ship, it is an American option. Thus, assuming that the newbuilding price volatility for this type of vessel is 15 per cent, the risk-free rate is 5 per cent, and time to maturity is one year, the value of this option can be calculated using BOPM. To do this we estimate u, d and p assuming a six-step binomial tree and construct the newbuilding price evolution lattice using u, d and the time step $\Delta t = 1/6$.

$$u = e^{\sigma\sqrt{\Delta t}} = e^{0.15\sqrt{1/6}} = 1.0632 \quad d = e^{-\sigma\sqrt{\Delta t}} = \frac{1}{u} = 0.9406$$

$$p = \frac{e^{r\Delta t} - d}{u - d} = \frac{e^{0.05 \times 1/6} - 0.9406}{1.0632 - 0.9406} = 0.553$$

Underlying price lattice

	Steps					
	1	2	3	4	5	6
						72.20
					67.91	
				63.88		63.88
			60.08		60.08	
		56.51		56.51		56.51
	53.16		53.16		53.16	
50.00		50.00		50.00		50.00
	47.03		47.03		47.03	
		44.24		44.24		44.24
			41.61		41.61	
				39.14		39.14
					36.81	
						34.63

Next, we construct the corresponding option valuation tree and find the payoff of the option for each end node at expiry as the difference between the newbuilding price at the end node of the price evolution lattice and the strike price (US$50m) if the newbuilding price is greater than the strike price, or zero otherwise; that is, max(newbuilding price – 50, 0). Finally, we use the backwards induction method to find the values of intermediate nodes and to get the option value at the initiation of the contract, bearing in mind that we need to allow for the possibility of early exercise.[2]

---

[2] It should be noted that one of the assumptions behind the use of BOPM for the valuation of the newbuilding order options is that the underlying asset, that is, the vessel, is tradable in the market and hence the expected return of the hedged portfolio is the risk-free rate. Also, in this case it will never be optimum to exercise early an American call and, hence, its value will be the same as that of a European call.

Option valuation lattice

Steps					
1	2	3	4	5	6
		Node A			22.20
				18.33	
			14.70		13.88
		11.32		10.50	
	8.38		7.34		6.51
5.99		4.89		3.57	
4.17	3.16		1.96		0.00
1.99		1.07		0.00	
	0.59		0.00		0.00
		0.00		0.00	
			0.00		0.00
				0.00	
					0.00

To value the intermediate nodes, we begin with nodes in step 5 and calculate the one-step discounted present value of the risk-neutral probability-weighted average of the two outcomes attached to the node, and compare it with the value of early exercise; that is, placing an order, which is the difference between the corresponding node in the price lattice and strike price. For instance, the value of the top node in step 5 (node A) is calculated as:

$$\text{node A} = \max\{(\text{US\$}67.91 - X), [p(\text{US\$}22.20) + (1 - p)(\text{US\$}13.88)]e^{-r\Delta t}\}$$

$$= \max\{(\text{US\$}67.91 - \text{US\$}50), [(0.553)(\text{US\$}22.20)$$

$$+(1 - 0.553)(\text{US\$}13.88)]e^{-0.05(1/6)}\}$$

$$= \max\{17.91, 18.33\} = 18.33$$

This procedure is then applied to find the value of all intermediate nodes back to the first, which yields the value of this option as US$4.17m. As already discussed, on many occasions, especially when shipbuilding activity is relatively low, shipyards offer such options at no cost in order to secure a deal, to ensure the possibility of future employment or simply to remain competitive. While such options can be quite valuable to shipowners and quite costly to shipyards, the lattter can recover part of the value of the option through savings on the design process which would be cheaper for a second sister ship.

14.5.3 Purchase option on a time-charter contract

Perhaps one of the most valuable options in shipping markets is the purchase option on the back of a period TC contract. Under this agreement, the shipowner (investor) grants the charterer the option – but not the obligation – to purchase the vessel at a pre-specified price (strike) over a certain period during the life of the time-charter contract. These options are normally granted with long-term TC or bare-boat contracts to make them more attractive to charterers. The option premium might be embedded in the charter contract or might be considered as an offset towards the credibility of the charterer. Obviously, such options can be quite valuable to charterers especially when ship price volatility is high and options can end up in-the-money and hence be exercised. Under these option contracts, the charterers can exercise the right by purchasing the vessel at an agreed price, or receive the differential between market price and the contract price, at maturity or during the exercise period. Several companies have made large profits in recent years by exercising their purchase options on contracts that they entered into in the early part of the 2000s when the dry-freight market and ship prices were at relatively low levels. Once the market peaked, ship prices increased along with freight rates and the purchase options ended up in-the-money.

As an example, consider a shipowner who enters into a five-year TC contract with a purchase option with an operating company. Under this agreement the operating company has the option to purchase the vessel for US\$30m during the fourth or fifth year of the TC contract. Assuming that the price volatility of this type of ship is 20 per cent and the risk-free rate is 5 per cent, we can construct a five-step price-evolution lattice, with the following parameters.

$$u = e^{\sigma\sqrt{\Delta t}} = e^{0.2\sqrt{1}} = 1.2214 \quad d = e^{-\sigma\sqrt{\Delta t}} = \frac{1}{u} = 0.8187$$

$$p = \frac{e^{r\Delta t} - d}{u - d} = \frac{e^{0.05 \times 1} - 0.8187}{1.2214 - 0.8187} = 0.5775$$

Underlying price lattice

	Steps				
	1	2	3	4	5
					54.37
				44.51	
			36.44		36.44
		29.84		29.84	
	24.43		24.43		24.43
20.00		20.00		20.00	
	16.37		16.37		16.37
		13.41		13.41	
			10.98		10.98
				8.99	
					7.36

Once again we start pricing the option by finding the values of end nodes in the option-valuation lattice. Next, the intermediate nodes are calculated using the backwards induction method, but this time we only allow early exercise in years 4 and 5.[3] Therefore, the value of this purchase option is US$2.4m.

$$\text{node A} = \max\{(\text{US}\$44.50 - X), [p(\text{US}\$24.37) + (1 - p)(\text{US}\$6.44)]e^{-r\Delta t}\}$$

$$= \max\{(\text{US}\$44.50 - \text{US}\$30), [(0.5775)(\text{US}\$24.37)$$

$$+(1 - 0.5775)(\text{US}\$6.44)]e^{-0.05(1)}\}$$

$$= 15.97$$

Option valuation lattice

	Steps				
	1	2	3	4	5
			node A		24.37
		node B		15.97	
			10.20		6.44
		6.38		3.54	
	3.94		1.94		0.00
2.40		1.07		0.00	
	0.59		0.00		0.00
		0.00		0.00	
			0.00		0.00
				0.00	
					0.00

$$\text{node B} = [p(\text{US}\$15.97) + (1 - p)(\text{US}\$3.54)]e^{-r\Delta t}$$

$$= [(0.5775)(\text{US}\$15.97) + (1 - 0.5775)(\text{US}\$3.54)]e^{-0.05(1)}$$

$$= 10.20$$

In this valuation process we have made the assumption that there will be no depreciation in the vessel value, which is not realistic. It is known that vessel values depreciate over time due to wear and tear and, as a result, we may have overestimated the option value. We can incorporate depreciation in the binomial tree by adjusting the compounding factor in the calculation of the risk-neutral probabilities to reflect the impact of depreciation; in this

---

[3] This type of option, when early exercise is allowed only at certain, and not all, intervals, is called a 'Bermudan option'.

case, the expected return of a hedged position should be the risk-free rate plus the expected depreciation rate, to compensate the investor for the loss of value in the position due to depreciation.

14.5.4 Option on writing-off part of a debt

It is well known that the most traditional and still prominent method of ship finance is through bank loans. Normally, under a term loan for ship finance, the lender (bank) takes the vessel as collateral and includes several clauses and covenants in the contract to protect itself against non-performance and default by the borrower. In addition, the lender normally uses the hull-to-debt ratio (HTD) or value-to-loan ratio to monitor the security of the transaction. This is important because any drop in the value of the vessel will lower the HTD and can thus be used as an indicator of the possibility of the borrower running into difficulty. If the HTD falls below a certain level that the lender no longer considers acceptable, additional collateral may be required to bring back the HTD to a level acceptable by the lender.

Historically, cyclical shipping markets and the high volatility of ship prices have very often caused the initial HTD ratio to get close to one or even less than one, when borrowers have lost all their equity. Such a situation can be very difficult for the borrower not only because the value of the asset has eroded, but also because the lender may ask for additional collateral or equity, the access to which might be very difficult or even not possible. One way to avoid such situations is to set up an option on the HTD ratio, which, once exercised, brings back the HTD ratio to its initial level. Essentially, under such an agreement, the lender grants an option to the borrower to write off part of the debt under certain conditions and over a certain period. This option is therefore a put option on part of the outstanding loan amount. The option could be triggered when the value of the collateral reaches a certain level which does not cover the loan. When the value of the ship drops below the trigger level then the option is exercised and the part of the outstanding loan is written off to bring back the HTD ratio to its initial level (for example, 120 per cent).

To illustrate, consider a lender who provides a five-year US$50m term loan to a shipowner, for the purchase a US$60m Panamax vessel; thus, the initial HTD is 120 per cent. At the same time, the lender grants the option to write off part of the debt and bring back the HTD ratio to 120 per cent should the value of the vessel fall below the outstanding amount of the debt, only once over the life of the loan. In other words, the option can be exercised when the HTD drops below one, as shown in Figure 14.3, and gives the owner the right to ask the lender to write off part of the debt and bring the HTD ratio back to 120 per cent.

To illustrate how such an option can be valued, assume that the price volatility of this vessel is 20 per cent, the risk-free rate is 5 per cent, the term

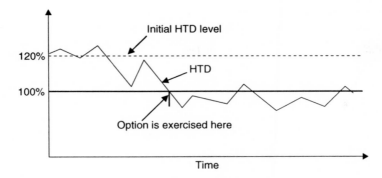

Figure 14.3   Evolution of the HTD ratio of the term loan

of the loan is five years, and the borrower has been granted the option of writing off part of the loan to bring back the HTD ratio to 120 per cent once during the term of the loan. Also, for simplicity, assume that there is no amortisation in the loan; that is, the loan will be repaid in full at the end of the term. Therefore, this is like an American put option on the value of the vessel, with a payoff which depends on the value of the vessel at exercise. Once again we can use a binomial tree to price this option, using a five-year five-step tree. First, we construct the price evolution lattice, given u, d and p.

$$u = e^{\sigma\sqrt{\Delta t}} = e^{0.2\sqrt{1}} = 1.2214 \quad d = e^{-\sigma\sqrt{\Delta t}} = \frac{1}{u} = 0.8187$$

$$p = \frac{e^{r\Delta t} - d}{u - d} = \frac{e^{0.05\times1} - 0.8187}{1.2214 - 0.8187} = 0.5775$$

Underlying price lattice

	Steps				
	1	2	3	4	5
					163.10
				133.53	
			109.33		109.33
		89.51		89.51	
	73.28		73.28		73.28
60.00		60.00		60.00	
	49.12		49.12		49.12
		40.22		40.22	
			32.93		32.93
				26.96	
					22.07

Next, using the values of the terminal nodes in the price lattice, we calculate the terminal nodes in the option valuation lattice. One important point here is that the terminal payoffs in the option valuation lattice are calculated to allow no payoff, if the price in the corresponding cell in the price lattice is greater than the loan value, or 20 per cent of the difference between the loan and the price, if the price is less than the loan value (US$50m). In other words the payoff function is:

$$payoff = \begin{cases} 0 & S > X \\ X - S/1.2 & S < X \end{cases}$$

where S is the value of the vessel and X is the strike price (loan value). The intermediate nodes in the backward induction are also calculated using the same approach.

Option valuation lattice

			Steps		
	1	2	3	4	5
					0
				0.00	
			0.00		0
		0.59		0.00	
	2.11		1.46		0
4.80		4.45		3.64	
	9.07		9.06		9.06
		16.48		16.48	
			22.56		22.56
				27.53	
					31.61

It can be seen that the value of this option is US$4.80m. Although, this option seems to be expensive, given the ship-price volatility and time to maturity, it can be financed by the lender and added to the amount of the loan. One way of reducing the option premium is by structuring this option as a barrier option with knock-in features where the option comes into existence only when the ship price reaches a certain level. By setting the barrier sufficiently low, the option premium will be less than would be the case with an ordinary put option.

14.6   Pricing real options using simulation

The use of simulation techniques in pricing options was discussed in Chapter 8. Simulation method can also be used to evaluate real options in the same manner as for financial options. To illustrate how simulation techniques can be used in valuing real options, consider the example on 'option to expand' in section 14.4.2. A firm, with exclusive rights to operate in a route, has the option to add a new vessel and expand its operation at the end of the year if the demand increases, for an additional US$15m. We assume that the current static operation NPV is US$10m, the estimated volatility is 40 per cent,

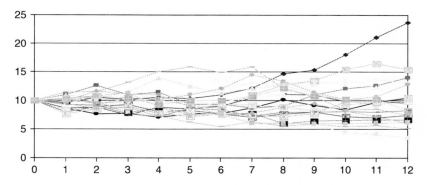

Figure 14.4 Simulated paths for NPV of a project with an expansion option

and the risk-free rate is 5 per cent. Since the expansion option can only be exercised at the end of the current life of the project (first year), the option is European. We start building the simulation model under the assumption that the NPV of this project follows a GBM process for which the discrete time model can be written as

$$NPV_t = NPV_0 \, e^{[(\mu - 0.5\sigma^2)t + \sigma\varepsilon\sqrt{\Delta t}]}$$

where σ is the volatility, μ is the growth rate, and ε is a random variable which follows a standardised normal distribution. In order to find the value of the option, we need to have an estimate of the market price of risk; as in the example of the freight options in Chapter 8, we set μ equal to the risk-free rate. We use 12 time steps to simulate the paths that the NPV may follow until the end of the project; a random sample of possible NPV trajectories over the life of the project is presented in Figure 14.4.[4]

Moreover, Panels A and B in Figure 14.5 present the distribution of possible NPVs with no expansion option, and also with the expansion option based on 10,000 simulations. The mean of the simulated distribution of NPV with no expansion option is US$10.52, whereas the mean of the simulated distribution with expansion is slightly higher at US$11.04m. Also, it can be observed that the project value can take very high values, for example, US$40m or US$45m, when the expansion option is exercised.

Finally, we can find the payoff of the option at maturity under each possible path and discount the average payoff using the risk-free rate. The value of the option to expand is estimated to be US$494,000, which is roughly comparable to what we found when we used the binomial option-pricing

---

[4] The simulations and the resulting output are estimated using @risk from www.palisade.com.

Panel A

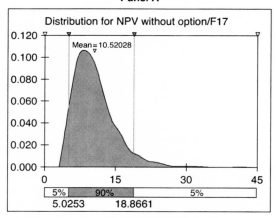

Panel B

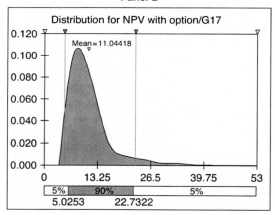

Figure 14.5 Probability distributions of possible project values at maturity

model, US$520,000. Furthermore, the 90 per cent interval estimate of the value of the option to expand on this project is estimated to be between US$0 and US$3.7m.

14.6.1 Sensitivity analysis and interval estimates

As with discounted cash flow and NPV models, results of real option valuation depend heavily on the assumptions made about the inputs that were used in their estimation – volatility of the underlying asset, risk-free rate, fluctuations in strike price, and so on. Therefore, once again simulation analysis may be used not only to construct the distribution of the option value based on the distributional properties assumed for input factors, but also to investigate the sensitivity of real option values to changes in the input factors. Simulation can be set up on a binomial option-pricing model, where the inputs can be drawn from appropriate distributions or stochastic models, and output will be the distribution of the option value. Based on this distribution, interval estimates for the real option value can also be constructed.

For instance, consider the example of the option to abandon a project: that is, selling the vessel and terminating the project at any time after it is under way. We can use a probability distribution or stochastic model for the strike price, which is the resale value (or scrap value) of the vessel. Previously we assumed that this price is constant. Relaxing the assumption of having a fixed resale value of US$4m is more realistic because the investor may not know today how much the vessel will be sold for at the time of abandoning the project. Moreover, different probability distributions or stochastic models can also be used for calculating the volatility of the NPV of the project (asset price) to obtain a range of possible option values and the confidence interval.

We can incorporate these parameters into the option-to-abandon/exit example by assuming, for instance, that the resale value follows a lognormal distribution with a mean of US$4m and standard deviation of US$1m; and the estimate of NPV volatility follows a lognormal distribution with a mean of 0.3 and a standard deviation of 0.05. Then we simulate these values, which are subsequently used as inputs in the binomial tree. Performing 10,000 simulations, we obtain the distribution of the value of the abandonment option, which is presented in Panel A of Figure 14.6. The mean of the distribution is US$124,100, which is slightly higher than the option value we obtained through a binomial tree with no simulation. This is expected, because allowing input factors to be random also increases the value of the option to abandon.

Furthermore one can investigate the sensitivity of the option value with respect to the underlying pricing factors such as volatility, strike level, etc. In this example, the sensitivity of the option value to the two stochastic factors (resale value and volatility) can be seen through the tornado graph presented in Panel B of Figure 14.6. As expected, changes in the resale value and volatility have a positive impact on the value of the option. It can also be seen that option values are more sensitive to changes in the resale value compared to the volatility of the project's cash flows; on average, if the resale value increases by US$1m, the value of the option will increase by US$724,000.

14.7   Summary and conclusions

In this chapter we discussed real option analysis in relation to project valuation and highlighted the advantages of this valuation approach compared to static NPV analysis. We also discussed different types of real options that

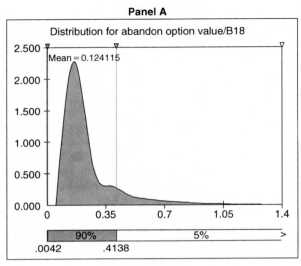

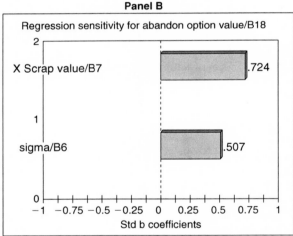

Figure 14.6   Distribution and sensitivity of the exit option value calculated using a binomial tree when input factors are simulated

exist in shipping and maritime projects. Using a simple example, the valuation of each type of real option and embedded optionalities in shipping investment, projects and contracts were demonstrated through the binomial option pricing model (BOPM). Furthermore, we discussed how simulation techniques can be used to value real options and measure the sensitivity of their values to underlying factors.

Appendix 14.A: The binomial option pricing model (BOPM)

The binomial option pricing model proposed by Cox et al. (1979) is a flexible tool for pricing a variety of options, in particular real options. BOPM is based on the principle of constructing a risk-neutral portfolio consisting of an option and the underlying asset which is assumed to follow a binomial process. To construct the risk-neutral price evolution tree, we divide the life of the option into several small steps, each with a length Δt. Therefore, we assume that over a small interval Δt, the asset price (S_0) can increase by a multiple of u ($u > 1$) to $S_0 u$, or decline by a multiple of d ($d < 1$) to $S_0 d$. These two possible movements in price in a small time interval cause both up and down movements. Also, assuming the probability of a price increase to be p, then the probability of a down movement in asset price will be $(1 - p)$. Therefore, the one-step price evolution can be shown as

The up (u) and down (d) multipliers, as well as the risk-neutral probability (p), can be determined using the assets' volatility and the risk-free rate. Calculation of these parameters is based on the assumption that in a risk-neutral world the expected return on any asset should be the risk-free rate of interest, r. Therefore, the expected return on the above asset over Δt period should be r. Hence, we can write

$$S_0 e^{r\Delta t} = pS_0 u + (1 - p)S_0 d \qquad (14.1)$$

or

$$e^{r\Delta t} = pu + (1 - p)d \qquad (14.2)$$

To determine values of unknown parameters u, d, and p, we need to define three relationships amongst them. We also know that the variance of the asset price over a small fraction of time can be written as $\sigma^2 \Delta t$, where σ^2 is the annualised variance of the asset price. Since the expected return is $e^{r\Delta t}$, the variance of expected return ($\sigma^2 \Delta t$) over a small period Δt can be written as[5]

$$\sigma^2 \Delta t = pu^2 + (1 - p)d^2 - [pu + (1 - p)d]^2 \qquad (14.3)$$

Then we can substitute p from equation (14.2) in (14.3) to obtain

$$\sigma^2 \Delta t = e^{r\Delta t}(u + d) - ud - e^{2r\Delta t} \qquad (14.4)$$

---

[5] This is because $\text{var}(x) = E(x^2) - [E(x)]^2$. Also, $E[(e^{r\Delta t})^2] = pu^2 + (1 - p)d^2$, and $E[(e^{r\Delta t})]^2 = [pu + (1 - p)d]^2$. See also Hull (2006).

Furthermore, assuming $u = 1/d$, one can calculate u, d and p as

$$u = e^{\sigma\sqrt{\Delta t}}, \quad d = e^{-\sigma\sqrt{\Delta t}}, \quad p = \frac{e^{r\Delta t} - d}{u - d}$$

As an example, assume that $S = $ US\$100, $X = $ US\$100, T $= 1$ year, $r = 5$ per cent, $\sigma = 25$ per cent. We can construct a one-step binomial tree or lattice for the price evolution as:

$$u = e^{0.25\sqrt{1}} = 1.284, \quad d = e^{-0.25\sqrt{1}} = 0.779, \quad p = \frac{e^{0.05\times1} - 0.779}{1.284 - 0.779} = 0.539$$

Underlying price lattice

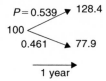

Once the two outcomes of the underlying price evolution (the binomial tree or lattice) are estimated, the values of the end nodes can be determined. We can then construct another lattice with two end outcomes which represent the corresponding payoffs of the option at the end nodes of the price evolution lattice. This is done by comparing the possible asset price at the end nodes and the strike price using the call payoff functions: that is, max($S - X, 0$) for a call and *max(X − S,0)* for a put. For instance, in our example, assuming a strike price of US\$100, the payoff of a European call option at node A is 28.4 because the option can be exercised *max*(US\$128.4 − US\$100,0); and at node B is 0 because the option cannot be exercised *max*(US\$77.9 − US\$100,0). The final step is known as the 'backwards induction'; here the value of the previous node C is calculated as the risk-neutral probability-weighted average of option values at nodes A and B, discounted for one step. Therefore the value of the option is US\$14.57.

Option valuation lattice

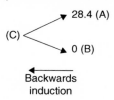

$$c = [p(\text{payoff A}) + (1 - p)(\text{payoff B})]e^{-r\Delta t}$$
$$= [0.539(28.4) + (1 - 0.539)(0)]e^{-0.05(1)} = \text{US\$14.57}$$

Of course, this example was based on a one-step price evolution in one year; therefore, the option value obtained is not very accurate. In order to increase the accuracy of the binomial option-pricing model we need to increase the number of steps in the binomial tree over the life of the option. For instance, we can price the same option using a two-step binomial tree for the asset, but this time the time step will be $\Delta t = 0.5$; that is, half a year. This results in new values for u, d and p, as follows:

$$u = e^{0.25\sqrt{0.5}} = 1.193, \quad d = e^{-0.25\sqrt{0.5}} = 0.838, \quad p = \frac{e^{0.05 \times 0.5} - 0.838}{1.193 - 0.838} = 0.527$$

Underlying price lattice

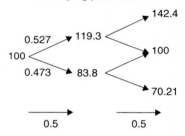

This process can be continued to construct a binomial tree for asset-price evolution with, for instance, n steps. Once the binomial tree is constructed and the values of end nodes are determined ($142.40, $100 and $70.21), we can evaluate the payoff of the option at the end nodes by comparing the possible asset price at maturity and the strike price. Once again the payoffs are noted in the option valuation lattice as end nodes, and the backwards induction method is used to calculate the one-step discounted present value of the risk-neutral probability-weighted average of the nodes back to the first node as follows:

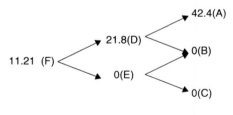

where

$$\text{node D} = [p(\text{payoff A}) + (1 - p)(\text{payoff B})]e^{-r\Delta t}$$
$$= [0.527(42.4) + (1 - 0.527)(0)]e^{-0.05(0.5)} = \text{US}\$21.80$$
$$\text{node E} = [p(\text{payoff B}) + (1 - p)(\text{payoff C})]e^{-r\Delta t}$$
$$= [0.527(0) + (1 - 0.527)(0)]e^{-0.05(0.5)} = \text{US}\$0$$
$$\text{node F} = [p(\text{payoff D}) + (1 - p)(\text{payoff E})]e^{-r\Delta t}$$
$$= [0.527(21.8) + (1 - 0.527)(0)]e^{-0.05(0.5)} = \text{US}\$11.21$$

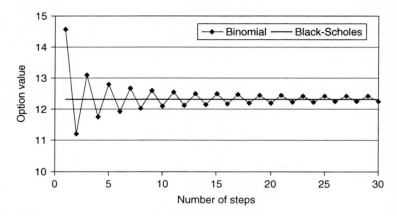

Figure 14.7 Convergence of binomial to Black-Scholes option prices

We can notice that this time the value of the call option is US$11.21 which is lower than US$14.57 calculated using a single-step tree. As mentioned, the accuracy of the binomial option-pricing method increases as the number of steps increases. This value converges to the value obtained using the Black-Scholes model as the number of steps increases, as shown in Figure 14.7.

The binomial option pricing model is a very flexible method that can be used for pricing American options as well. The basic BOPM can be extended to accommodate changing volatility, mean reversion in asset prices, three-dimensional trees and price spread options, as well as trinomial trees and non-recombining trees (as opposed to the recombining trees introduced here). Indeed, the more complexity introduced into the binomial tree construction, the more accurate will be the results of the option price; at the same time, however, the valuation can become more complex and difficult.[6]

---

[6] See Mun (2002) for more discussion on complex tree-based option pricing models and the valuation of real options.

References

Quoted statistical and news sources

Astrup Fearnley (*Fearnleys World Bulk Trade/Dry Bulk Quarterly*): www.fearnresearch.no
Baltic Exchange: www.balticexchange.com
Bank for International Settlements: www.bis.org/statizstics/derstats.htm.
Bunkerworld: www.bunkerworld.com
Clarkson's Shipping Intelligence Network (SIN): www.clarksons.net
Clarkson's Shipping Research Services, *Shipping Review and Outlook* (London: CSRS)
Clarkson Research Studies: www.clarksonresearch.com/acatalog
Datastream: www.datastream.com
Drewry Shipping Consultants: www.drewry.co.uk
Euronext.LIFFE: www.euronext.com
FFABA (Forward Freight Agreement Brokers' Association): www.balticexchange.com/ffaba
Fitch Ratings: www.fitchratings.com
Freight Investor Services (FIS): www.freightinvestorservices.com
Heidmar Group: www.heidmar.com
Imarex: International Maritime Exchange: www.imarex.com
Institute of Shipping Economics and Logistics (ISL): www.isl.org
ISDA (International Swaps and Derivatives Association): www.isda.org
LCH.Clearnet: www.lchclearnet.com
Lloyds Maritime Information Unit (LMIU): www.lloydsmiu.com
Lloyd's Register of Shipping, *World Fleet Statistics*: www.lr.org
Lloyd's List: www.lloydslist.com
Lloyd's Ship Manager (LSM): www.lloydsshipmanager.com
Lloyd's Shipping Economist: www.shipecon.com
Moody's: www.moodys.com
NYMEX: www.nymex.com
Platts: InfoStore: www.platts.com
SGX (Singapore Exchange): www.sgx.com
Simpson, Spence and Young Consultancy and Research Ltd (SSY): www.ssyonline.com
Standard & Poor's: www2.standardandpoors.com

Books and articles

Adland, R. (2000) 'Technical Trading Rule Performance in the Second-hand Asset Markets in Bulk Shipping', Foundation for Research in Economics and Business Administration, Bergen, Norway, working paper No. 04/2000.
Adland, R. and S. Koekebakker (2004) 'Market Efficiency in the Second-hand Market for Bulk Ships', *Maritime Economics and Logistics*, Vol. 6., No. 1, pp. 1–15.
Adland, R. and Strandenes, S.P. (2006) 'Market Efficiency in the Bulk Freight Market Revisited', *Maritime Policy and Management*, Vol. 33, No. 2, pp. 107–17.

Adland, R., H. Jia and S. Koekebakker (2004) 'The Pricing of Forward Ship Value Agreements and the Unbiasedness of Implied Forward Prices in the Second-Hand Market for Ships', *Maritime Economics and Logistics*, Vol. 6, No. 2, pp. 109–21.

Alizadeh A. H. (2001) 'Econometric Analysis of Shipping Markets; Seasonality, Efficiency and Risk Premia', PhD Thesis, City University Business School, London.

Alizadeh, A H., N. K. Nomikos and P. Pouliasis (2008) 'A Markov Regime Switching Approach for Hedging Energy Commodities', *Journal of Banking and Finance*, Vol. 32, No. 9, pp. 1970–83.

Alizadeh, A. H, R. Adland and S. Koekkebaker (2007) 'Predictive Power and Unbiasedness of Implied Forward Charter Rates,' *Journal of Forecasting*, Vol. 26, No. 6, pp. 385–403.

Alizadeh, A. H. and N. K. Nomikos (2002) 'The Dry Bulk Shipping Market', in C. Th. Grammenos (ed.) *The Handbook of Maritime Economics and Business* (London: LLP/Informa), pp. 227–50.

Alizadeh, A. H. and N. K. Nomikos (2003a) 'Bunker Risk Management using Forward and Swap Contracts', *Lloyds Shipping Economist*, May, pp. 25–8.

Alizadeh, A. H. and N. K. Nomikos (2003b) 'The Price-volume Relationship in the Sale and Purchase Market for Dry Bulk Vessels', *Maritime Policy & Management*, Vol. 30, No. 4, pp. 321–37.

Alizadeh, A. H. and N. K. Nomikos (2004a) 'The Efficiency of the Forward Bunker Market', *International Journal of Logistics – Research and Applications*, Vol. 7, No. 3, pp. 281–96.

Alizadeh, A. H. and N. K. Nomikos (2004b) 'A Markov Regime Switching Approach for Hedging Stock Indices', *Journal of Futures Markets*, Vol. 24, No. 7, pp. 649–74.

Alizadeh, A. and N. K. Nomikos (2006) 'Trading Strategies in the Market for Tankers', *Maritime Policy and Management*, Vol. 33, No. 2, pp. 119–40.

Alizadeh, A. H. and N. K. Nomikos. (2007a): 'Investment Timing and Trading Strategies in the Sale and Purchase Market for Ships', *Transportation Research*, Vol. 41, No 1, Part B, pp. 126–43.

Alizadeh, A. H. and N. K. Nomikos (2007b) 'The Slope of Forward Curve and Volatility of Shipping Freight Rates', mimeo, Cass Business School, City University, London, UK.

Alizadeh, A. H. and N. K. Nomikos (2007c) 'Dynamics of the Term Structure and Volatility of Shipping Freight Rate', INFORMS Annual Conference, Seattle, Washington, USA.

Alizadeh, A. H., M. Kavussanos and D. Menachof (2004) 'Hedging Against Bunker Price Fluctuations Using Petroleum Futures Contracts; Constant versus Time-varying Hedge Ratios', *Applied Economics*, Vol. 36, No. 12, pp. 1337–53.

Andersen, T. G. and T. Bollerslev (1998) 'Answering the Sceptics: Yes, Standard Volatility Models do Provide Accurate Forecasts', *International Economic Review*, Vol. 39, pp. 885–905.

Angelidis, T. and G. S. Skiadopolous (2008) 'Measuring the Market Risk of Freight Rates: A Value-at-Risk Approach', *International Journal of Theoretical and Applied Finance*, Vol. 11, No. 5, pp. 447–69.

Anson, M. J. P., F. J. Fabozzi, M. Choudry and R. Chen (2004) *Credit Derivatives Instruments, Applications and Pricing* (Hoboken: John Wiley Finance).

Baba, Y., R. Engle, D. Kraft and K. Kroner (1987) 'Multivariate Simultaneous Generalised ARCH', Unpublished Manuscript, University of California, San Diego.

Baillie, R. T., T Bollerslev and H. O. Mikkelsen (1996) 'Fractionally Integrated Generalized Autoregressive Conditional Heteroskedasticity', *Journal of Econometrics*, Vol. 74, pp. 3–30.

Baltic Exchange (2003) *Guide to Market Practice for Members of the FFABA*, September.

Baltic Exchange (2007a) *A History of the Baltic Indices*, December.

Baltic Exchange (2007b) *Manual for Forward Panellists: Baltic Forward Assessments*, December.

Baltic Exchange (2008) *Manual for Panellists: A Guide to Freight Reporting and Index Production*, January.

Beenstock, M. (1985) 'A Theory of Ship Prices', *Maritime Policy and Management*, Vol. 12, No. 3, pp. 215–25.

Beenstock, M. and A. Vergottis (1989) 'An Econometric Model of the World Market for Dry Cargo Freight and Shipping', *Applied Economics* Vol. 21, No. 3, pp. 339–56.

Bendall H. B. (2002) 'Valuing Maritime Investments Using Real Options Analysis', in C. Th. Grammnos (ed.) *The Handbook of Maritime Economics and Business* (London: LLP/Informa), pp. 623–41.

Bendall, H. B. and A. F. Stent (2001) 'A Scheduling Model for High Speed Container Service: A Hub and Spoke Short Sea Application', *International Journal of Maritime Economics*, No. 3, pp. 262–77.

Bendall, H. B. and A. F. Stent (2003) 'Investment Strategies in Market Uncertainty', *Maritime Policy & Management*, Vol. 30, No. 4, pp. 293–303.

Bera, A. K. and M. L. Higgins (1993) 'ARCH Models: Properties, Estimation and Testing', *Journal of Economic Surveys*, Vol. 7, No. 4, pp. 305–66.

Berkowitz, J. (2000) 'A Coherent Framework for Stress-Testing', *Journal of Risk*, Vol. 2, No. 2, pp. 5–15.

Bjerksund, P. and S. Ekern (1995) 'Contingent Claims Evaluation of Mean Reverting Cash Flows in Shipping', in L. Trigeorgis (ed.) *Real Options in Capital Investment* (London: Praeger), pp. 207–21.

Black, F and J. Cox (1976) 'Valuing Corporate Securities: Some Effects of Bonds Indenture Provisions', *Journal of Finance*, Vol. 31, No. 2, pp. 351–67.

Black, F. (1976) 'The Pricing of Commodity Contracts', *Journal of Financial Economics*, Vol. 3, pp. 167–69.

Black, F., and M. Scholes (1973) 'The Pricing of Options and Corporate Liabilities', *Journal of Political Economy*, Vol. 81, No. 3, pp. 637–59.

Bollerslev, T. (1986) 'Generalized Autoregressive Conditional Heteroskedasticity', *Journal of Econometrics*, Vol. 31, No. 3, pp. 307–27.

Bollerslev, T. (1987) 'A Conditional Heteroskedastic Time Series Model for Speculative Prices and Rates of Return', *Review of Economics and Statistics*, Vol. 69, No. 3, pp. 542–7.

Bollerslev T., R. F. Engle and J. M.Wooldridge (1988) 'A Capital Asset Pricing Model with Time Varying Covariances', *Journal of Political Economy*, Vol. 96, No.1, pp. 116–31.

Bollerslev, T. and J. M. Wooldridge (1992) 'Quasi-maximum Likelihood Estimation of Dynamic Models with Time-varying Covariances,' *Econometric Reviews*, Vol. 11, No. 2, pp. 143–72.

Bollerslev, T., R. Y. Chou, and K. F. Kroner (1992) 'ARCH Modelling in Finance: A Review of Theory and Empirical Evidence,' *Journal of Econometrics*, Vol. 52, Nos 1–2, pp. 5–59.

Brealey, R., S. Myers and F. Allen (2007) *Corporate Finance*, 9th edition (New York: McGraw Hill).

Broto, C. and E. Ruiz (2004) 'Estimation Method for Stochastic Volatility Models; A Survey', *Journal of Econometric Surveys*, Vol. 18, No. 5, pp. 613–49.

Cai, J. (1994) 'A Markov Model of Switching Regime-ARCH', *Journal of Business and Economic Statistics*, Vol. 12, No. 3, pp. 309–16.

Chance, D. (2006) *An Introduction to Derivatives and Risk Management*, 6th edition (Mason: Thomson South-Western)

Christoffersen, P. (1998) 'Evaluating Interval Forecasts', *International Economic Review*, Vol. 39 No. 4, pp. 841–64.

Christoffersen, P. F. (2003) *Elements of Financial Risk Management* (London, New York: Academic Press).

Clewlow, L. and C. Strickland (2000) *Energy Derivatives: Pricing and Risk Management* (Houston: Lacima Publications).

Claughton, T., and P. Undseth (2002) 'Clearing: A Potential White Knight', *Energy in the News*, Volume 2, available at www.nymex.com

Cox, J. C., S. A. Ross and M. Rubinstein (1979) 'Option Pricing: A Simplified Approach', *Journal of Financial Economics*, Vol. 7, No. 3, pp. 229–63.

Curran, M. (1992) 'Beyond Average Intelligence', *Risk*, November, p. 60.

Cuthbertson, K. and D. Nitzsche (2001) *Financial Engineering: Derivatives and Risk Management*, 1st edition (Chichester: John Wiley & Sons).

Denning, K. C., W. B. Riley and J. P. Delooze (1994) 'Baltic Freight Futures: Random Walk or Seasonally Predictable?', *International Review of Economics and Finance*, Vol. 3, No. 4., pp. 399–428.

Ding, Z., C. W. J. Granger and R. F. Engle (1993) 'A Long Memory Property of Stock Market Returns and a New Model', *Journal of Empirical Finance*, Vol. 1, No. 1, pp. 83–106.

Dixit, A. K. (1988) 'Optimal Lay-up and Scrapping Decisions', unpublished manuscript (July), Princeton University.

Dixit, A. K. (1989) 'Entry and Exit Decisions under Uncertainty', *Journal of Political Economy*, Vol. 97, No. 3, pp. 620–38.

Dixit, A. K. and R. S. Pindyck (1994) *Investment under Uncertainty* (New Haven: Princeton University Press).

Dowd, K. (2002) *An Introduction to Market Risk Measurement* (Chichester: John Wiley & Sons).

Dueker, M. J. (1997) 'Markov Switching in GARCH Processes and Mean Reverting Stock Market Volatility', *Journal of Business and Economic Statistics*, Vol. 15, No. 1, pp, 26–34.

Ederington, L. H., (1979) 'The Hedging Performance of the New Futures Markets', *The Journal of Finance*, Vol. 34, No. 1, pp. 157–70.

Edwards F. and C. Ma (1992) *Futures and Options*, International Edition (Singapore: McGraw-Hill).

Efron, B. (1979) 'Bootstrap Methods: Another Look at the Jackknife', *Annals of Statistics*, Vol. 7, pp. 1–26.

Embechts, P., C. Klüppelberg and T. Mickosh (1997) *Modelling Extremal Events for Insurance and Finance* (Berlin: Springer).

Engle, R. F. (1982) 'Autoregressive Conditional Heteroskedasticity with Estimates of the Variance of United Kingdom Inflation', *Econometrica*, Vol. 50, No. 4, pp. 987–1008.

Engle, R. F. (1993) 'Statistical Models for Financial Volatility', *Financial Analysts' Journal*, January–February, pp. 72–8.

Engle, R. F. and G. Gonzales-Rivera (1991) 'Semiparametric ARCH Models', *Journal of Business and Economics Statistics*, Vol. 9, No. 4, pp. 345–59.

Engle, R. F. and K. F. Kroner (1995), 'Multivariate Simultaneous Generalized ARCH', *Econometric Theory*, Vol. 11, pp. 122–50.

Engle, R. F. and S. Manganelli (2004) 'CaViaR: Conditional Autoregressive Value at Risk by Regression Quantiles', *Journal of Business and Economic Statistics*, Vol. 22, pp. 367–81.

Engle, R. F., D. M. Lilien and R. P. Robins (1987) 'Estimating Time-varying Risk Premia in the Term Structure: the ARCH-M Model', *Econometrica*, Vol. 55, No. 2, pp. 391–407.

Engle, R. F. and V. K. Ng (1993) 'Measuring and Testing the Impact of News on Volatility,' *Journal of Finance*, Vol. 48, pp. 1749–78.

Eydeland, A. and K. Wolyniec (2003) *Energy and Power Risk Management* (New Jersey: Wiley Finance).

Fama, E. and M. E. Blume (1966) 'Filter Rules and Stock-Market Trading', *The Journal of Business*, Vol. 39, No. 1, Part 2: Supplement on Security Prices, pp. 226–41.

Financial Times (2008) 'Freight Futures Surge as Funds Seek Refuge', 24 February.

Fong, W. M. and K. H. See (2002) 'A Markov Switching Model of the Conditional Volatility of Crude Oil Prices', *Energy Economics*, Vol. 24, No. 1, pp. 71–95.

Geman, H. (2005) *Commodities and Commodity Derivatives* (Chichester: John Wiley & Sons).

Geman, H. and V. N. Nguyen (2003) 'Analysing Volatility Surfaces for Energy Commodities', ESSEC Working Paper Series.

Geman, H. and M. Yor (1993) 'Bessel Processes, Asian Options and Perpetuities', *Mathematical Finance*, Vol. 3, pp. 349–75.

Geske, R. (1979) 'Valuation of Compound Options', *Journal of Financial Economics*, Vol. 7, No. 1, pp. 63–81.

Geske, R. and H. E. Johnson (1984) 'The American Put Option Valued Analytically', *Journal of Finance*, Vol. 39, No. 5, pp. 1511–24.

Geweke, J. (1986) 'Modelling the Persistence of Conditional Variances: A Comment', *Econometric Reviews*, Vol. 5, No.1 , pp. 57–61.

Glen, D. (1997) 'The Market for Second-hand Ships: Further Results on Efficiency Using Cointegration Analysis', *Maritime Policy and Management*, Vol. 24, No. 3, pp. 245–60.

Glen, D., M. Owen and R. Van der Meer (1981) 'Spot and Time Charter Rates for Tankers, 1970–1977', *Journal of Transport Economics and Policy*, Vol. 13, No. 1, pp. 45–58.

Glosten, L., R. Jagannathan and D. E. Runkle (1993) 'On the Relation between the Expected Value and the Volatility of the Nominal Excess Return on Stocks,' *Journal of Finance*, Vol. 48, No. 5, pp. 1779–1801.

Grammenos, C. T., A. H. Alizadeh and N. Papapostolou (2007) 'Factors Affecting the Dynamics of Yields Premia on Shipping Seasoned High Yield Bonds', *Transportation Research*, Part E, pp. 549–64.

Grammenos, C. T., N. K. Nomikos and N. Papapostolou (2008) 'Estimating the Probability of Default for Shipping High Yield Bond Issues', *Transportation Research*, Part E: Logistics and Transportation Review, Vol. 44, No. 6, pp. 1123–38.

Grammenos, C., Th. (2002) 'Credit Risk Analysis and Policy in Bank Shipping Finance', in *The Handbook of Maritime Economics and Business* (London: Lloyd's of London Press).

Gray, J. (1990) *Shipping Futures* (London: Lloyd's of London Press).

Gray, S. F. (1996) 'Modelling the Conditional Distribution of Interest Rates as Regime Switching Process', *Journal of Financial Economics*, Vol. 42, No. 1, pp. 27–62.

Gujarati, D. H. (2005) *Basic Econometrics*, 4th edition (London: McGraw-Hill).

Haigh, M., N. Nomikos and D. Bessler (2004) 'Integration and Causality in International Freight Markets – Modelling with Error Correction and Directed Acyclic Graphs', *Southern Economic Journal*, Vol. 71, No. 1, 145–63.

Hale, C. and A. Vanags (1989) 'Spot and Period Rates in the Dry Bulk Market: Some Tests for the Period 1980–1986', *Journal of Transport Economics and Policy*, Vol. 23, No. 3, pp. 281–91.

Hale, C. and A. Vanags (1992) 'The Market for Second-hand Ships: Some Results on Efficiency Using Cointegration', *Maritime Policy and Management*, Vol. 19, No.1, pp. 31–40.

Hamilton, J. D. (1989) 'A New Approach to the Economic Analysis of Nonstationary Time Series and the Business Cycle', *Econometrica*, Vol. 57, No. 2, pp. 357–84.

Hamilton, J. D. (1994) *Time Series Analysis* (Princeton: Princeton University Press).

Hamilton, J. D. and R. Susmel (1994) 'Autoregressive Conditional Heteroskedasticity and Changes in Regime', *Journal of Econometrics*, Vol. 64, No. 1/2, pp. 307–33.

Harrington, S. E. and G. R. Niehaus (2003) *Risk Management and Insurance*, 2nd edition (New York: McGraw Hill).

Haug, E. G. (2007) *The Complete Guide to Option Pricing Formulas*, 2nd edition (New York: McGraw Hill).

Haug, E. G., J. Haug and W. Margrabe (2003) 'Asian Pyramid Power', *Willmott Magazine*, March.

Heston, S. L. (1993) 'A Closed Form Solution for Options with Stochastic Volatility with Applications to Bonds and Currency Options', *Review of Financial Studies*, Vol. 6, No. 2, pp. 327–43.

Holton, A. G. (2003) *Value-at-Risk: Theory and Practice* (St Louis: Academic Press).

Hull, J. (2006) *Options, Futures and Other Derivatives*, 6th edition (Saddle River: Prentice Hall International).

Hull, J. and A. White (1987) 'Hedging Risks from Writing Foreign Currency Options', *Journal of International Money and Finance*, Vol. 6, No. 2, pp. 131–52.

JP Morgan (1996) *RiskMetrics*, Technical Document, JP Morgan.

Jensen, M. and G. A. Bennington (1970) 'Random Walks and Technical Theories; Some Additional Evidence', *Journal of Finance*, Vol. 25, No. 2, pp. 469–82.

Johansen, S. (1988) 'Statistical Analysis of Cointegrating Vectors', *Journal of Economic Dynamics and Control*, Vol. 12, pp. 231–54.

Johansen, S. (1991) 'Estimation and Hypothesis Testing of Cointegration Vectors in Gaussian Vector Autoregressive Models', *Econometrica*, Vol. 59, pp. 1551–80.

Jorion, P. (1995) *Big Bets Gone Bad: Derivatives and Bankruptcy in Orange County* (San Diego: Academic Press).

Jorion, P. (2002) *Value-at-Risk: The New Benchmark for Managing Financial Risk*, 2nd edition (New York: McGraw-Hill).

Kahn, M. N. (2006) *Technical Analysis Plain and Simple: Charting the Markets in Your Language*, 2nd edition (Saddle River: Prentice Hall).

Kavussanos, M. and N. Nomikos (1999) 'The Forward Pricing Function of the Shipping Freight Futures Market', *Journal of Futures Markets*, Vol. 19, pp. 353–76.

Kavussanos, M. and N. Nomikos (2000a) 'Constant vs. Time-Varying Hedge Ratios and Hedging Efficiency in the BIFFEX Market', *Transportation Research*, Vol. 36, No. 4, pp. 229–48.

Kavussanos, M. and N. Nomikos (2000b) 'Dynamic Hedging in the Freight Futures Market', *Journal of Derivatives*, Vol. 8, No. 1, pp. 41–58.

Kavussanos, M. and N. Nomikos (2000c) 'Futures Hedging Effectiveness when the Composition of the Underlying Asset Changes; the Case of the Freight Futures Contract', *The Journal of Futures Markets*, Vol. 20, No. 6.

Kavussanos, M. G. (1997) 'The Dynamics of Time-varying Volatilities in Different Size Second-hand Ship Prices of the Dry-cargo Sector', *Applied Economics*, Vol. 29, No. 4, pp. 433–44.

Kavussanos, M. G. and Alizadeh, A.H. (2001) 'Seasonality Patterns in the Dry Bulk Shipping Spot and Time-charter Freight Rates,', *Transportation Research*, Part E, Vol. 37, pp. 443–67.

Kavussanos, M. G. and A. Alizadeh (2002a) 'Seasonality Patterns in Tanker Spot Freight Rate Markets', *Economic Modelling*, Vol. 19, No. 5, pp. 747–83.

Kavussanos, M. G. and A. Alizadeh (2002b) 'The Expectations Hypothesis of the Term Structure and Risk Premia in Dry Bulk Shipping Freight Markets; An EGARCH-M Approach', *Journal of Transport Economics and Policy*, Vol. 36, Part 2, pp. 267–304.

Kavussanos, M. G. (1996) 'Comparisons of Volatility in the Dry-cargo Ship Sector: Spot versus Time Charters, and Small versus Larger Vessels', *Journal of Transport Economics and Policy*, January, pp. 67–82.

Kemna, A. and A Vorst (1990) 'A Pricing Method for Options Based on Average Asset Values', *Journal of Banking and Finance*, Vol. 14: pp. 113–29.

Kennedy, D. J. and R. T. Califano (n.d.) 'Forward Freight Agreements', Carter, Ledyard and Milburn LLP Client Alert, available from www.clm.com

Klein, B. (1977) 'The Demand for Quality-adjusted Cash Balances: Price Uncertainty in the US Demand for Money Function', *Journal of Political Economy*, Vol. 85, No. 4, pp. 692–715.

Koekebakker, S. and R. Adland (2004) 'Modelling Forward Freight Rate Dynamics – Empirical Evidence from Time-charter Rates', *Maritime Policy and Management*, Vol. 31, No 4, pp. 319–35.

Koekebakker, S. and F. Ollmar (2005) 'Clarkson Securities Freight Options Model', from www.clarksons.com

Koekebakker, S., R. Adland and S. Sødal (2007) 'Pricing Freight Rate Options', *Transportation Research: Part E*, Vol. 43, No. 5, pp. 535–48.

Koenker, R. and G. Bassett (1978) 'Regression Quantiles', *Econometrica*, Vol. 46, No. 1, pp. 33–50.

Kolb, R. W. and J. A. Overdahl (2007) *Futures, Options and Swaps*, 5th edition (Oxford: Blackwells Business Publishers).

Koutmos, G. and M. Tucker (1996) 'Temporal Relationships and Dynamic Interactions Between Spot and Future Stock Markets', *Journal of Futures Markets*, Vol. 16, No. 1, pp. 55–69.

Kroner, K. and J. Sultan (1993) 'Time-Varying Distributions and Dynamic Hedging with Foreign Currency Futures', *Journal of Financial and Quantitative Analysis*, Vol. 28, No. 4, pp. 535–51.

Lamoureux, C. G. and W. D. Lastrapes (1990) 'Persistence in Variance, Structural Change, and the GARCH Model', *Journal of Business & Economic Statistics*, Vol. 8, pp. 225–34.

LCH.Clearnet (2008) 'Initial Margin Calculation on Derivative Markets: SPAN© Method', accessed at www.lchclearnet.com, February 2008

Lévy, E. (1997) 'Asian Options', in L. Clewlow and C. Strickland (eds), *Exotic Options: The State of the Art* (Washington DC: International Thomson Business Press).

Lévy, E. and Turnbull, S. M. (1992). 'Average Intelligence', *Risk Magazine*, Vol. 5, No. 2, pp. 53–9.

Li, M.-Y. L, and H.-W. W. Lin (2004) 'Estimating Value-at-risk via Markov-switching ARCH Models – an Empirical Study of Stock Index Returns', *Applied Econometrics Letters*, Vol. 11, pp. 679–91.

Ljung, M. and G. Box (1978) 'On a Measure of Lack of Fit in Time-series Models', *Biometrika*, Vol. 65, pp. 297–303.

Lloyd's Register of Shipping (1996) *World Fleet Statistics* (London: Lloyd's Register).

Lo, A. W. and C. MacKinlay (1990) 'Data-snooping Biases in Tests of Financial Asset Pricing Models', *The Review of Financial Studies*, Vol. 3, No. 3, pp. 431–67.

Lopez, J.A. (1999) 'Methods for Evaluating Value-at-Risk Estimates', Federal Reserve Bank of New York, *Economic Policy Review*, Vol. 2, pp. 3–17.

Mandelbrot, B. (1963) 'The Variation of Certain Speculative Prices', *Journal of Business*, Vol. 36, No. 4, pp. 394–419.

Marcucci, J. (2005) 'Forecasting Volatility with Regime-switching GARCH Models', *Studies in Nonlinear Dynamics & Econometrics*, Vol. 9, No. 4, pp. 1–53.

Markowitz, H. M. (1952) 'Portfolio Selection', *Journal of Finance*, Vol. 7, No. 1, pp. 77–91.

McConville, J. (1999) *Economics of Maritime Transport: Theory and Practice*, 1st edition (London: Witherby).

Merton, R. C. (1973) 'Theory of Rational Option Pricing', *Bell Journal of Economics and Management Science*, Vol. 4, No.1, pp. 141–83.

Merton, R. C. (1974) 'On the Pricing of Corporate Debt: The Risk Structure of Interest Rates', *Journal of Finance*, Vol. 29, No. 2, pp. 449–470.

Milhoj, A. (1987) 'A Multiplicative Parameterization of ARCH Models', Research Report, No 101, Institute of Statistics, University of Copenhagen.

Mun, J. (2002) *Real Option Analysis: Tools and Techniques for Valuing Strategic Investments and Decisions* (Hoboken: Wiley Finance).

Murphy, J. (1998) *Technical Analysis of the Financial Markets: A Comprehensive Guide to Trading Methods and Applications* (New York: Institute of Finance).

Neftci, S. (2007) *Financial Engineering* (New Jersey: Academic Press).

Nelson, D. B. (1991) 'Conditional Heteroscedasticity in Asset Returns: A New Approach', *Econometrica*, Vol. 59, pp. 347–70.

Nomikos, N. and Alizadeh, A. (2002) 'Risk Management in the Shipping Industry: Theory and Practice', in *The Handbook of Maritime Economics and Business* (London: LLP Informa), pp. 693–730.

Nomikos, N. (1999) 'Price Discovery, Risk Management and Forecasting in the Freight Futures Market', unpublished PhD thesis, Cass Business School, London, UK.

Norman, Victor (1981) 'Market Strategies in Bulk Shipping', working paper, Norwegian School of Economics and Business Administration, Bergen.

Pantula, S. G. (1986) 'Modelling the Persistence of Conditional Variances: Comment', *Econometric Reviews*, Vol. 5, pp. 79–97.

Percy, R., J. Vincent, and M. Fingas (1996) 'Bunker "C" Fuel Iil and the Irving Whale', Environment Canada, Government of Canada.

Perrot, B. (2006) 'To ISDA or not to ISDA', *Baltic Magazine*, January.

Pilipovic, P. (2007) *Energy Risk: Valuing and Managing Energy Derivatives* (New York: McGraw Hill).

Politis, D. N. and J. P. Romano (1994) 'The Stationary Bootstrap', *Journal of the American Statistical Association*, Vol. 89, pp. 1303–13.

Reed Smith Richards Butler (2008) 'New FFABA – A Summary of the Key Differences between the FFABA 2005 and the FFABA 2007', Reed Smith Richards Butler Client Alert 08-039, available from www.reedsmith.com.

Shaw, N. and C. Weller (2006) 'FFA Risk and How to Deal with It', *Baltic Magazine*, January.

Shephard, N. (2005) *Stochastic Volatility: Selected Readings*, Advanced Texts in Econometrics (New York: Oxford University Press).

Sødal, S. (2006) 'Entry and Exit Decisions Based on a Discount Factor Approach', *Journal of Economic Dynamics and Control*, Vol. 30, No. 11, pp. 1963–86.

Sødal, S., S. Koekebakker and R. Adland (2008a) 'Market Switching in Shipping – a Real Option Model Applied to the Valuation of Combination Carriers', *Review of Financial Economics*, forthcoming.

Sødal, S., S. Koekebakker and R. Adland (2008b) 'Value-based Trading of Real Assets in Shipping under Stochastic Freight Rates', *Applied Economics*, forthcoming.

Stopford M. (1997) *Maritime Economics*, 2nd edition (London: Routledge).

Strandenes, S. P. (1984) 'Price Determination in the Time-charter and Second-hand Markets', Working paper No 06, Centre for Applied Research, Norwegian School of Economics and Business Administration, Bergen.

Taylor, S. (1986) *Modelling Financial Time Series* (Chichester: Wiley).

Tinbergen, J. (1934) 'Scheepsruimte en vrachten', *De Nederlandsche Conjunctuur*, March, pp. 23–35.

Trigeorgis, L. (ed.) (1995) *Real Options in Capital Investment. Models, Strategies and Applications* (London: Praeger).

Tsay, S. R. (2002) *Analysis of Financial Time Series*, Wiley Series in Probability and Statistics (Chichester: Wiley).

Tsolakis, S. D., C. Cridland and H. E. Haralambides (2003) 'Econometric Modelling of Second-hand Ship Prices', *Maritime Economics and Logistics*, Vol. 5, No. 4, pp. 347–77

Turnbull, S. M. and L. M. Wakeman (1991) 'A Quick Algorithm for Pricing European Average Options', *Journal of Financial and Quantitative Analysis*, Vol. 26, No. 3, pp. 377–89.

Tvedt, J. (1997) 'Valuation of VLCCs under Income Uncertainty', *Maritime Policy and Management*, Vol. 24, No. 2 , pp. 159–74.

Tvedt, J. (1998) 'Valuation of a European Futures Option in the BIFFEX Market', *Journal of Futures Markets*, Vol. 18, No. 2, pp. 167–75.

Vasicek, Oldrich A. (1984): 'Credit Valuation', unpublished paper (San Francisco: KMV Corp).

Veenstra, W. A. (1999) 'The Term Structure of Ocean Freight Rates', *Maritime Policy and Management*, Vol. 26, No. 3, pp. 279–93.

Vergottis, A. (1988) 'An Econometric Model of World Shipping', PhD thesis, City University Business School, London.

Visweswaran, R., (2000) 'Common Sense in Bunker Fuel Selection and Testing', at www.viswalabcorp.com/common_sense.html

Weiss, A.A. (1986) 'Asymptotic Theory for ARCH Models: Estimation and Testing', *Econometric Theory*, Vol. 2, pp. 107–31.

Wilmott, P., S. Howison and J. Dewynne (1997) *The Mathematics of Financial Derivatives: A Student Introduction* (Cambridge: Cambridge University Press).

Yor, M., (1993) 'From Planar Brownian Windings to Asian Options', *Insurance: Mathematics and Economics*, Vol. 13, pp. 23–34.

Zannetos, Z. S. (1966) *The Theory of Oil Tank Shipping Rates* (Boston: MIT Press)

Zhang, P. G. (1998) *Exotic Options: A Guide to Second-generation Options* (Singapore: World Scientific).

Index

Figures in **bold** refer to tables, Figures in *italic* refer to figures.

abandon/exit options   455–8
accidents   5
Adland, R.   181, **446**
Alizadeh, A. H.   48, 52, 94, 101, 102,
    105, 181, 209, 210, 211–15, 304,
    318, 425, 426
arbitrage   14–15, 19
arbitrageurs   14–15
ARCH models   85–6
arithmetic mean   67–8
Asian options   260–1, 265–6, 266–7,
    271–3, 276–81, 354–5;
    Delta hedging   290–2
asset risk   2
asset-price risk   4
autorepressive integrated moving
    average (ARIMA)   209

backwardation   16, *16*, 167n19
Baltic Capsize Index (BCI)   108–10, **109**
Baltic Clean Tanker Index (BCTI)
    113–15, **114**, *117*
Baltic Demolition Assessment   446–9,
    448, **450**
Baltic Dirty Tanker Index (BDTI)
    115–17, **116**, *117, 118*
Baltic Dry Index (BDI)   112–13, *114*
Baltic Exchange freight-market
    information   108–17
Baltic Forward Assessments (BFA)
    169–73, **172, 173**
Baltic Freight Index (BFI)   52–3
Baltic Handysize Index (BHSI)   111–2,
    113
Baltic indices, calculation of   118–21,
    121
Baltic International Freight Futures
    Exchange (BIFFEX)   122–3, *123*
Baltic International Tanker Routes
    (BITR)   **115**
Baltic Panamax Index (BPI)   **110**,
    110–11

Baltic Sale and Purchase Assessment
    439, **440**, *441*
Baltic Ship Value Assessment   439, *444*
Baltic Supramax Index (BSI)   111, **112**
bankruptcy costs   7
bare-boat contracts   41–2, 43, *44*
basis risk   16–18, 156, 160–4, *162*, **163**
BEKK model   101–2
Bendall, H. B.   451
Bera, A. K.   85
BIMCO 'Gencon' 38n7
Binomial Option Pricing Model   455,
    480–4, *483*
Bjerksund, P.   455
Black, F.   261
Blume, M. E.   192
Bollerslev, T.   81, 85, 86, 100
Bollinger Bands   194–7, **196**, *196*
Brealey, R. S. et al.   7
bulk carriers   27, *27*, 28, 29, **30**
bunker adjustment factor (BAF)   341–2
bunker costs   3–4
bunker market   339–40
bunker price risk   2, 22, 338–9, 341–2, 362
    bunker swap contracts   346–54;
    caps and floors   355–6, **357, 358**;
    collar options   356–62, **359**, *360, 361*;
    hedging using forward contracts
        343–6, **345, 346**;
    hedging using options   354–62;
    hedging using OTC instruments   343;
    spot prices   339–40, *340*, **340**
bunker swap contracts   346–7;
    differential swap   350–1
    double-up   354
    exotic   350
    extendable swap   351–2, **352**
    forward bunker swap   352–3, **353**
    participation   353
    plain vanilla   *347*, 347–50, *348*, **348**,
        349
    variable volume or swing   354

call options 12, 217–22, **218**, *220, 221*,
   222, 237–8, 241, **280**
   price boundary conditions 222–3,
   224
   put-call parity 224–5
capital, cost of 7–8
capital costs 42–3
capital structure 7–8
caplets and floorlets, interest-rate
   options 381–4, **383**, *385*, 386
cargo size 28–9
cargo-handling 44
cash flows, and hedging *17*, 17
Chance, D. 249
chart analysis 182–6, *183, 184*
chemical spillage 5
Chicago Board of Trade 8, 13
Christoffersen, P. 8, 333
clearing houses 138–40, **139**
Clewlow, L. 281, 290
coefficient of kurtosis 74–5, 80
coefficient of skewness 73, *74*
coefficient of variation 75–7, *76*
collars 356–62, *359, 360, 361*
   interest-rate options 388–91, *392*,
   393
collaterisation 415
collisions 5
commoditisation 1
commodity parcel size 28–9
conditional volatility 90–4
container shipping market 30–1
container ships 26, 27, *27, 27*, 28,
   30, *31*
contango 16, *16*, 167n19
contract options 460–1
contracts of affreightment 39–40, *44*
convenience yield 18–19
correlation 77–8
cost-of-carry model 18–20
costs 42
   allocations *44*
   capital 42–3
   cargo-handling 44
   operating 43
   voyage 43–4
counter-party risk 4
covariance 77–8
Cox, J. C. et al. 455, 480
credit default swaps 418–20, *419*, **420**

credit derivatives 417–18, *418*
   credit default swaps 418–20, *419*,
   420
   credit spread options 422–3, *424*
   total return swaps 420–2, *421*,
   422
credit rating agencies 402–3
credit risk 2, 4, 22, 399–400, 423–4
   credit ratings 402–4, **403**
   credit-spread risk 400
   default probability from trades bonds
   407–9, **409**
   default risk 400, 401
   downgrade risk 400
   estimating default probabilities
   using Merton's model 411–14, *413*
   estimating default probability 407
   forward freight agreements 137–47
   historical default probabilities **409**,
   409–11, **410**
   margining 141–5, *145*
   marking to market 142–5, *144*
   qualitative analysis 401–2, **402**
   quantitative analysis 402, 402
   shipping-high-yield bond issues
   404–7, *405*, **405**, *406, 407*
   sources of 400–1
credit risk management 414–15
   collaterisation 415
   contract design 416
   diversification 416–17
   downgrade triggers 415–16
   netting 416
credit spread options 422–3, *424*
Credit Value-at-Risk 417n4
Creditmetrics 417n4
credit-spread risk 400
crude oil **36**
Curran, M. 266
currency depreciation 364
currency risk 4
currency swaps 396–7, **397**, *397*
   pricing 397–8

data sources 65–7
data vendors 66
data-collection methods 65–7
debt, servicing 7–8
debt-to-equity ration 8

default probabilities, estimating 407
  estimating using Merton's model
    411–14, *413*
  historical **409**, 409–11, **410**
  from traded bonds 407, **409**
default risk 400, 401
delay (wait) options 462–3
demise-charter contracts 41–2
demurrage 39
derivative contracts 8–9
  exchange traded 8–9
  forward contracts 9–10, *10*, **11**, 11
  futures contracts 10–1, 13
  options 12–13
  over the counter 8, 9, 11, 12
  pricing 19–20
  swaps 12
derivatives, applications of 13
  arbitrageurs 14–15
  the cost-of-carry model 18–20
  hedging *16*, 16–18, *17*
  price discovery 15
  risk management 13
  on ship values 439
  speculators 14
descriptive statistics 67
  the arithmetic mean 67–8
  coefficient of kurtosis 74–5, 80
  coefficient of skewness 73, *74*
  coefficient of variation 75–7, *76*
  correlation 77–8
  covariance 77–8
  measures of central tendency
    67–8, *69*
  measures of dispersion 69
  median 68
  mode 68
  the range 69–70, *70*
  risk estimate comparisons 78–80, **79**
  standard deviation 70–3, *72*
  variance 70–3, *72*
discharging terms 38–9
dispatch 39
diversifiable risk 433
diversification 416–17, 432–8, *434*,
    434, *435*, **435, 437, 438**
Dixit, A. K. 455, 462
downgrade risk 400
downgrade triggers 415–16
draught factors *29*, 35

dry-bulk carriers 31, *32*
  forward freight agreement volume
    128–9, *130*
  newbuilding 58; prices *62*, *63*
  relative value trading rule 211
  risk estimate comparisons 78, **79**
  scrap *61*, 62
  seasonal behaviour of freight rates
    52–3, *53*, *54*, 55
  second-hand *59*
  ship-price risk 425, 427–8, **429**,
    430–1, *431*, 436–7, **437**, **445**, 445–6
  spread trading 203–7, *204*, **205**
dry-bulk commodities 33
dry-bulk market 31–4

Ederington, L. H. 23
Edwards, F. 15
efficient market hypothesis (EMH)
    207–9, 210, 426–7
Efron, B. 321
Engle, R. F. 81, 85, 101, 322
EURIBOR (Euro Interbank Offered Rate)
    365
Eurodollar futures contracts 374–5, **375**
  expand options 458–60
expenses 37, 41
exponentially weighted average variance
    83–4
exponentially weighted moving-average
    volatility 103, 104

Farna, E. 192
FFA market 21
FFABA 2007 Freight Options contract
    135–7, 174–80, 227, 250–7
filter rules 192–3
  Bollinger Bands 194–7, *196*,
    196
  moving average envelopes *193*,
    193–4, **194**
financial risk 363–4, 398. *see also*
    interest-rate risk; loans
flags 43
foreign exchange risk 2
forward contracts 2, 9–10, *10*, **11**, 11,
    449
forward curves: Baltic Forward
    Assessments (BFA) 169–73,
    172, 173

forward freight agreements 166–73, *168*, *169*
for ship prices *444*, 444–6, **445**, *447*
volatility models 97–9, *98*
Forward Freight Agreement Brokers Association (FFABA) 133
forward freight agreements 125–7, *127*, *128*, 142–5, 166–73, 173
Baltic Forward Assessments (BFA) 169–73, **172**, **173**
basis risk 160–4, *162*, **163**
clearing 137–47, *140*, 142, 146
clearing houses 138–40, **139**
contracts 134, 134–7, 138, 155–6, 174–80
credit risk 137–47
FFABA contract 135–7, 174–80
forward curves 166–73, *168*, *169*
hedging 147–64
hedging trip-charter freight-rate risk 148–9, **149**, *150*
hedging using voyage FFAs 150–2, **151**, **152**
ISDA® Master Agreement and Schedule 137
margining 141–5, *145*
marking-to-market 142–5, *144*
over the counter market 133–7
risk 156–7, 158–64, **159**, **162**, **163**
settlement risk 158–9, **159**; tanker hedging 157–8
®TC hedging 152–7, **154**, **156**
trade 130–47, *132*
trading via a 'hybrid' exchange 145–7, *146*
uses 164–6
volume 127–31, *129*, *130*, *131*
Forward Ship Value Agreements 439–43, **442**
forward-rate agreements 371–3
freight market information 107–8, *118*
Baltic Capsize Index (BCI) 108–10, **109**
Baltic Clean Tanker Index (BCTI) 113–15, **114**, *117*
Baltic Dirty Tanker Index (BDTI) 115–17, **116**, *117*, *118*
Baltic Dry Index (BDI) 112–13, *114*
Baltic Exchange freight-market information 108–17

Baltic Handysize Index (BHSI) 111–12, **113**
Baltic International Tanker Routes (BITR) **115**
Baltic Panamax Index (BPI) **110**, 110–11
Baltic Supramax Index (BSI) 111, **112**
calculation of the Baltic Indices 118–21, **121**
other indices 117–18
freight options 21
freight rate risk management 2
freight rates 1, 19, *53*
seasonal behaviour 52–5, *54*
spot freight-rate formation 44–7, *45*, *47*
time-charter equivalent of spot rates 51–2
time-charter rate formation *48–51*, *50*, *51*
freight-futures market 121–3, *123*
freight-rate risk 3
futures contracts 10–1, **11**, 13, 373–5, **375**

GARCH models 86–8, *88*, **96**, **97**, *100*
asymmetric 88–90, *89*
exponential 90–4, *92*, *93*, *94*
GJR threshold 90
Markov regime switching 94–7, **96**, *97*
multivariate 100–2
VaR estimation 313–14, 318
volatility forecasting 103–6, *105*
Geman, H. 276
Glen, D. et al. 48
Glosten, L. 90
Grammenos, C. T. et al. 406
Gray, S. F. 94
Greeks 282, 283–4
Delta 284–92, *286*, *288*, **289**, *290*, *291*, *292*, *294*, 300
dynamic hedging 300–1
Gamma 292–5, *293*, *294*, 299, 300
interpretation 300
relationship between theta, delta and gamma 297–8, *298*
Rho 299–300, 300

Greeks – *continued*
  Theta 295–7, *296*, *297*, 300
  and trading strategies 302
  Vega 298–9, *299*, 300

Hale, C. 48, 426
Hamilton, J. D. 94
Haug, E. G. et al. 265, 272
hedge ratio, the 18, 23
hedging 13, 14, *16*, 16–18, *17*, 21,
  122–3
  Baltic Demolition Assessment 449,
    450
  basis risk 160–4, *162*, **163**
  bunker price risk 343–6, **345**, **346**,
    354–62
  Delta 286–92, *288*, **289**, *290*
  dynamic 300–1
  error 155–7
  forward freight agreements 147–64
  interest-rate risk 371, **374**
  and option price curvature 293, *293*
  option risk management *282*, 282–3
  and options 227–9, *228*, 231–6, **233**,
    235
  settlement risk **159**
  tankers 157–8; TC 152–7, **154**, **156**
  trip-charter freight-rate risk 148–9,
    149, *150*
  using a collar 232–6, *235*
  using currency swaps 396–8, **397**,
    397
  voyage FFAs 150–2, **151**, **152**
Higgins, M. L. 85
historical volatility forecast 102–13,
  105
hull-to-debt ratio 470, *471*

Imarex 145–7
implied forward time-charter rates
  207–10, **209**
implied TC rates (IMTC) 209
insurance contracts 5
interest-rate collars 388–91, **390**, *392*,
  393
interest-rate futures 373–5
interest-rate options 381
  caplets and floorlets 381–4, **383**,
    385, 386
  caps and floors 384–8, **387**

collars 388–91, **390**, *392*, **393**
  currency swaps 396–8, **397**, *397*
  forward swaps 395–6
  pricing caps and floors 391–5, *394*,
    394–5
  swaptions 395–6
interest-rate risk 2, 4, 22, 363, *371. see
  also* financial risk; loans;
  forward-rate agreements 371–3
  futures 373–5, **375**
  hedging 371, **374**
  interest-rate swaps 375–81, *376*, **377**
  interest-rate swaps 375–8, *376*, **377**
  pricing and unwinding 378–81
international financial markets 364–6
International Maritime Exchange
  (Imarex) 145–7
interval estimates 474–5
investment, and technical trading rules
  211–15, **214**, *215*
investment strategies, shipping market
  214, *215*
ISDA® Master Agreement and Schedule
  137

Jagannathan, R. 90

Kavussanos, M. 34, 48, 52, 81, 101,
  122, 425, 426, 430
Kemna, A. 261
Klein, B. 81
Koekebakker, S. 181, 267, 273
Kolb, R. W. 249
Koutmos, G. 101
Kroner, K. 101

lay/can 38
laytime 39
lay-up options 461–2, *462*, *463*
Lévy, E. 265, 271
liability 5
LIBOR 365–6, *366*, 371, 372–3, **374**, 376
liners 29, 30
liquidity risk 156–7
liquified petroleum gas (LPG) 117,
  118
loading terms 38–9
loans: balloon payments 367
  floating-rate 367
  reference rates 364–6, *366*

term 366–71, **368, 370**
London Commodity Exchange 122
London Interbank Offered Rate (LIBOR)
365–6, *366*, 371, 372–3, **374**, 376
Lopez, J. A. 334

Ma, C. 15
Mandlebrot, B. 81
Manganelli, S. 322
manning costs 43
margining 141–5, *145*
market action 181–2
marking to market 142–5, *144*
Markov regime switching GARCH
models 94–7, **96**, *97*
Markowitz, H. M. 432
measures of central tendency 67–8, *69*
measures of dispersion 69
median 68
Merton, R. C. 261
mode 68
moments of a variable. *see* descriptive
statistics
momentum trading model 197–9, **198**,
199
moving average crossover trading rule
186–9, **188**, *190*
moving averages (MA) 186, *187*
envelopes *193*, 193–4, **194**
moving average crossover trading rule
186–9
multi-asset portfolios, value-at-risk
310–1, **311**
multivariate GARCH models 100–2
Murphy, J. 181–2

Neftci, S. 249
Nelson, D. B. 90
net present value 452–4, *453*, **454**, 458,
460, 462, 476, *477*, 480
netting 416
newbuilding orders options 467–70
Nguyen, V. N. 276
Nomikos, N. 94, 101, 105, 122, 181,
211–15, 425
Norman, V. 181
Notice of Readyness 38n6

oil spillage 5
Ollmar, F. 273

operating costs 3–4, 43
options 2, 12–13, 217, 249
see also call options; put options; real
options;
Asian 260–1, 265–6, 266–7, 271–3,
276–81, 290–2, 354–5
averaging 354–5
bunker caps and floors 355–6, **357**,
358
and bunker price risk 354–62
call-overwriting 231
collars 356–62, **359**, *360, 361*
contracts 226–7
credit spread 422–3, *424*
and hedging 227–9, *228*, 231–6, **233**,
235
interest-rate 381–91, **383**, *385*, 386
newbuilding orders 467–70
period TC extension 464–7
prices 222–6, *224*
purchase option on TC contract
470–2
put-call parity 224–5
risk management strategies using
227–36, *228*
trading 226–7
value-at-risk 322–8, *324*
writing off part of a debt 472–6, *474*
writing protective put 229–30, *230*
yield enhancement 231
options, pricing 258, 267–71, **269**,
280, 302
approaches 258–61
the Black model (1976) 263–4, 270
the Black-Scholes-Merton model
261–3, *284*, 411–14
closed form-solution 258–9
Curran's approximation 266–7, 281
the discrete Asian approximation
265–6
implied volatility 273–6, *274*
Monte Carlo simulation 259,
276–81, *279*
price trees 259
sensitivities *284*. *see also* Greeks; the
Turnbull and Wakeman
approximation 264–5, 270, 271
volatility 267–9, 271
volatility term structure 271–3

options, risk management   258, 281–2, 302. *see also* Greeks;
dynamic hedging   300–1
hedging   *282*, 282–3
options, trading strategies   236
bear spreads   *240*, 240–1
box spreads   *243*, 243–4
bull spreads   236–9, **237**, *238*, *239*
butterfly spreads   *248*, 248–9
ratio spreads   *241*, 241–3, *242*
straddle combinations   *244*, 244–5, *246*
strangle combinations   245–7, *246*
strips and straps   *247*, 247
switch   460–1
Overdahl, J. A.   249

period TC extension options   463–5
period-charter contracts   **38**
petroleum   28–9, 35
PIBOR (Paris Interbank Offered Rate)   365
Pindyck, R. S.   462
Politis, D. N.   321
port facilities   29
portfolio theory and diversification   432–8, *434*, **434**, *435*, **435**, **437**, **438**
price discovery   15, 166–73
price risk   3
principal component analysis (PCA)   **331**, *332*, 336–7
public listed companies, benefits of risk management   8
purchase option on TC contract   470–2
pure risk   5–6
put options   12, 217–22, **218**, *220*, *221*, **222**, 239, *239*, 240, *240*
price boundary conditions   224
put-call parity   224–5

range (statistical)   69–70, *70*
real option analysis   451, 452–4
real options   22, 451, *453*, 480. *see also* options
Binomial Option Pricing Model   455, 480–4, *483*
and financial options   451–2, **452**
and NPV   452–4, *453*, 458, 460, 462, 473, *474*
option to abandon/exit   455–8

option to contract   460–1
option to delay (wait)   462–3
option to expand   458–60
option to lay-up   461–2, *462*
option to switch   460–1
pricing   476–80, *478*, *479*
sensitivity analysis and interval estimates   477–80, *480*
valuation   451–5
realised volatility models   84
reference rates   364–6
regime-switching volatility models   94–7, **96**, *97*
relative value trading rule   211, *212*
relocation   156
risk   1–2;
pure   5–6
types of   3–6
risk estimates, comparisons   78–80, **79**
risk evaluation   6
risk identification   6
risk management   6–7, 303
application of derivatives and   13
motivation   7–8
options. *see* options, risk management
using options   227–36, *228*
risk monitoring   7
risk-and-return profiles   *77*
RiskMetrics   103, 104, 105, *105*, 304, 313
rolling-window variance   82
Romano, J. P.   321
root mean squared forecast error (RMSE)   209–10
route selection and changes   120
Runkle, E.   90

Scholes, M.   261
seaborne trade: classification   25–6;
volume   25, *25*
sensitivity analysis   477–80, *479*
settlement risk   158–9, **159**
share prices   8
ship market   55. *see also* ship-price risk
newbuilding   56–8, *57*
prices   4, 34, 55–6, *62*, 62–3, *63*
scrap   60–3, *61*, 429–30
second-hand   58–60, *59*, 211–15
shipping contracts   2
shipping fleet   *26*, 26–8, **27**, *27*

container 30–1, *31*
dry-bulk 31, *32*
tanker 34–5
shipping freight contracts 35, 37
bare-boat or demise-charter contracts 41–2, 43, *44*
contracts of affreightment 39–40, *44*
daily earnings 80
fixtures **38**, 38, 40
risk estimate comparisons **79**
time-charter contracts 38, 41, *44*
trip-charter contracts 38, 40–1
voyage charter contracts 37–9, **38**, *44*
shipping industry 24–8
market segmentation 28–9, 30
shipping investment, and trading strategies **214**, *215*
shipping market 24, 63–4
container 30–1
demand 45–6
dry-bulk 31–4
investment strategies 211–15, **214**, *215*
sector growth **27**
structure and organisation 19
supply 45–6
shipping-high-yield bond issues 404–7, **405**, **405**, *406*, *407*
ship-price risk 22, 425–6, 449–50
Baltic Demolition Assessment **450**
Baltic Demolition Index 446–9, *448*, **450**
comparison across sectors 427–30, **429**
derivatives on ship values 439
forward curves for ship prices *444*, 444–6, **445**, *447*
Forward Ship Value Agreements 439–43, **442**
management 432
portfolio theory and diversification 432–8, **434**, *434*, **435**, *435*, **437**, **438**
volatility 430–2, *431*
ship-prices 4, 34, 55–6, *62*, 62–3, *63*
formation 426–8
forward curves *444*, 444–6, **445**, *447*
newbuilding 56–8, 58
second-hand 58–60, *59*, 426
volatility 430–2
short positions 2

single-voyage charter 40
size mismatch 156
size optimisation 28–9
Sødal, S. et al. 455, 462
speculators 14
spot contracts 37
spot freight-rate formation 44–7, *45*, *47*
spread trading 199–200
dry-bulk 203–7, *204*, **205**
tanker *201*, 201–3, **203**
standard deviation 70–3, *72*
Standardised Portfolio Analysis of Risk (SPAN©) 141
Stent, F. 451
stochastic oscillators 188–92, *191*, **192**
stochastic volatility models 99–100, *100*, 318
Strickland, C. 281, 290
Suez Canal 35
support and resistance analysis 184–5, *185*
Susmel, R. 94
swaptions 395–6
switch options 461–2
systemic risk 433

tankers **27**, *27*, 28, 29, 30, *34*, **36**
forward curves 168–9, *169*
forward freight agreement volume 131, **131**
GARCH models **88**
hedging 157–8
market 34–5, **36**
prices *58*, 62, *62*
risk estimate comparisons **79**
scrap *61*
seasonal behaviour of freight rates 52, *53*, 55
second-hand *59*
ship-price risk 427, 429, **429**, 430–1, *431*, 434–6, **435**
spread trading *201*, 201–3, **203**
time-varying volatility *83*, 84
voyage rates 37n5
taxes 8
TC hedging 152–7, **154**, **156**
technical analysis 181–2, 215–16
chart analysis 182–6, *183*, *184*
filter rules 192–7, *193*, **194**, **196**, *196*

technical analysis – *continued*
  moving average crossover trading rule
    188, *190*
  moving averages (MA) 186, *187*
  stochastic oscillators 188–92
  support and resistance analysis
    184–5, *185*
  technical trading rules 186
  trend 182
technical trading rules 186
  and investment 211–15, **214**, *215*
term loans 366–7
  fixed-rate 367, 367–9, **368**
  floating-rate 369–71, **370**
Theil's U' statistics 210
time-charter contracts **38**, 41, *44*
  period extension options 463–6
  purchase options on 467–70
time-charter equivalent of spot rates
    51–2
time-charter rate formation 48–51,
    50, 51
time-varying volatility models 80–2, *83*
  exponentially weighted average
    variance 83–4
  realised volatility models 84
  rolling-window variance 82
total return swaps 420–2, *421, 422*
traded bonds, default probabilities from
    407–9, **409**
trading strategies 2
  and Greeks 302
  implied forward time-charter rates
    207–10, **209**
  momentum trading model 197–9,
    198, *199*
  performance **206**, 206–7, *207*
  profitability **213**
  relative value trading rule 211,
    212
  and shipping investment 211–15,
    214, *215*
  spread trading 199–207, *201*, **203**,
    203–7, *204*, **205**
  static buy **192**
  stochastic oscillators **192**
trend lines 183
trip-charter contracts 40–1
trip-charter freight-rate risk, hedging
    148–9, **149**, *150*

Tucker, M. 101
Tvedt, J. 267

value-at-risk 2, 21, 303–5, 335–6
  multi-asset portfolios 310–11, **311**
  non-linear instruments 322–8, *324*
  simple estimation 305–10, *306, 308*
value-at-risk, estimation methodologies
    312, *329*
  backtesting 333–4
  bootstrap method 321
  delta approximation 325
  delta-gamma approximation 325–8
  exponential weighted averages and
    RiskMetrics 313
  extreme value theory (EVT) 317
  GARCH models 313–14
  historical simulation 319–22, *320*;
    mapping 323–5
  Monte Carlo simulation 314–17,
    315, 316, **318**
  nonparametric methods 319–22
  parametric estimation 312–18
  principal component analysis (PCA)
    328–32, **331**, *332*, 336–7
  quantile regression 322
  regime switching GARCH models
    318
  sample variance and covariance
    312–18
  stochastic volatility models 318
  stresstesting 334–5
Vanags, A. 48, 426
variance 70–3, *72*
Vasicek, Oldrich A. 411
vector autoregressive rates (VAR) 209
vessels, size classifications 29, **30**
volatility. *see also* ARCH models,
    GARCH models
  clustering 81
  exponentially weighted average
    variance 83–4
  forward curve models 97–9, *98*
  implied 273–6, *274*
  realised volatility models 84
  regime switching 94–7, **96**, *97*
  rolling-window variance 82
  stochastic models 99–100, *100*
  term structure 271–3
  time-varying models 80–2

volatility forecasting   102, *105*
  exponentially weighted
    moving-average volatility   103, 104
  GARCH models   103–6
  historical   102–3
Vorst, A.   261
voyage charter contracts   37–9, **38**, *44*

voyage costs   43–4
voyage FFAs, hedging   150–2, **151**,
  152

writing protective put   229–30, *230*

Zannetos, Z. S.   48

Breinigsville, PA USA
26 January 2010
231387BV00002B/2/P